CENTURY 21® ACCOUNTING

INTRODUCTORY COURSE

SECOND CANADIAN EDITION

GARY E. PANSEGRAU

JAMES H. FOOTE

Based on
CENTURY 21 ACCOUNTING, Third Edition

   ROBERT M. SWANSON
   KENTON E. ROSS
   ROBERT D. HANSON
   LEWIS D. BOYNTON

 Introductory
Course

Contents

SECOND CANADIAN
EDITION

ACCOUNTING

gage EDUCATIONAL PUBLISHING COMPANY
A DIVISION OF CANADA PUBLISHING CORPORATION
TORONTO ONTARIO CANADA

Authorized adaptation of the original edition published by South-Western Publishing Co., Cincinnati, Ohio, United States of America. Copyright © 1982 in the United States of America by South-Western Publishing Co. All rights reserved.

Canadian Cataloguing in Publication Data

Pansegrau, Gary E.
   Century 21 accounting: introductory course

For use in high schools and community colleges.
Includes index.
ISBN 0-7715-0172-2

1. Accounting. I. Foote, James H. II. Swanson, Robert M. III. Title.

HF5635.P36 1986   657   C86-094297-X

ISBN: 0-7715-**0172-2**

1 2 3 4 5 6 BP 3 2 1 0 9 8 7 6

Printed and Bound in Canada

Preface

This textbook is the first in a two-volume series. CENTURY 21 ACCOUNTING, Introductory Course, is followed by CENTURY 21 ACCOUNTING, Advanced Course. The introductory text is for students who have a variety of career objectives. Some students desire beginning vocational preparation for careers in accounting. Other students look forward to careers in related business fields for which mastery of some accounting knowledge and skill is needed. Some students seek a foundation on which to continue studying business and accounting at a higher level.

The revisions made for this second Canadian edition of CENTURY 21 ACCOUNTING, Introductory Course, are based on suggestions received from classroom teachers, accounting students, and businesses surveyed, and on changes occurring in the accounting profession.

FROM SIMPLE TO COMPLEX

This edition of CENTURY 21 ACCOUNTING retains the spiral approach to learning. Greater emphasis is focussed on forms of business ownership. The study of accounting in Part 2 is based on a service business organized as a sole proprietorship. In Part 3 a merchandising business organized as a partnership is used. All learnings from Parts 2 and 3 are used in Part 4 for the study of accounting practices for a partnership using automated procedures. In Parts 5 and 6, the text is based on businesses organized as corporations. Partnership and corporation accounting had been described in two separate chapters in previous editions. The material from these two chapters is now distributed throughout the text. This new organization presents the complete accounting cycle for each form of business ownership. Study progresses from the complete accounting cycle for a sole proprietorship to the accounting cycle for a partnership to the accounting cycle for a corporation.

The spiral approach also is used to introduce accounting forms and records. Part 2 describes a business using a simple two-column general journal and a simple multi-column cash journal. The learnings from Part 2 are applied in Part 3 to the use of an expanded multi-column synoptic journal. In Part 5 special journals are introduced as an extension of the learnings about multi-column journals.

STUDENT-CENTRED LEARNING

This text is student-centred. The basic objective is helping students acquire accounting knowledges, understandings, and skills.

Competency-based organization and content

This edition has been revised according to predetermined general behavioral goals, terminal performance objectives, and enabling performance tasks. A complete section of the Teacher's Reference Guide is devoted to the specific types of behavior students are expected to demonstrate at the end of each learning experience. In addition, general behavioral goals are listed on each part opener of the text. Enabling performance tasks are listed at the beginning of each chapter.

Easy reading level

The reading level (as determined by *A Formula for Predicting Readability*, by Edgar Dale and Jeanne S. Chall, Bureau of Educational Research, Ohio State University) is appropriate for the typical accounting student. The authors have made a special effort to meet the criteria of this readability formula as applied to the exacting and specialized technical field of accounting.

Practice material for varying levels of students

The end-of-chapter practice materials provide various levels of difficulty. For example, chapters include drills and application problems for all students. Students with varying abilities are provided for through mastery and challenge problems. Also, recycling problems (formerly called review problems) are provided for those students who need additional practice. Reinforcement activities (formerly called projects) are provided to strengthen the basic learnings.

Visual and learning aids

Appropriate, realistic illustrations and the use of four-color photographs aid student motivation and learning.

Many supplemental learning aids are available to be used with this text. Materials such as working papers and study guides and business simulations provide the students an opportunity for individual learning activities. Supplemental learning packages are also available for use with microcomputers. These materials provide the students an opportunity to perform automated accounting tasks.

Testing program

The testing program has been expanded, reorganized, and completely revised. Each testing instrument measures student performance specified in the terminal performance objectives.

Objective tests are available in the Teacher's Reference Guide for use at convenient times each semester. In addition, two semester examinations are provided. The objective tests are a continuation of the very popular testing program available with previous editions.

Problem tests, also available in the Teacher's Reference Guide, have been expanded, and a problem test is now available for each chapter except Chapter 1. A single problem test can be administered as students finish each chapter or combined for use after several chapters have been completed.

Use of published objective and problem tests assures evaluation of important knowledges, understandings, and skills described in predetermined terminal performance objectives. The published tests combine easily with teacher-prepared quizzes and tests to provide for differences in course organization and objectives for individual schools.

Chapter content

Chapter 1 is a new chapter that contains information about accounting careers. This chapter is useful as a springboard for a more detailed study of accounting career possibilities in local communities. Chapter 1 also includes eleven commonly accepted accounting concepts that guide professional accountants. Throughout this text, reference is given each time an application of one of these accounting concepts occurs.

Part 6 of this text is new and contains information about accounting control systems. One chapter is provided for each control system — a voucher system, a petty cash system, and an inventory system.

ACKNOWLEDGMENTS

This second Canadian edition of CENTURY 21 ACCOUNTING follows the traditions established over the more than 75 years since its predecessor, 20TH CENTURY BOOKKEEPING AND ACCOUNTING was first published. However, this edition updates tradition and provides a more learnable, practical, and realistic tool for teachers and students. Combined with the supplementary materials, this text is a complete learning package. This revision is based on the efforts of a large number of persons including accounting teachers, professional accountants, students, and others who have offered suggestions, provided information, and worked with the authors in creating new materials. The authors express their sincere appreciation to all those persons who have contributed to this second Canadian edition of CENTURY 21 ACCOUNTING.

Robert M. Swanson
Kenton E. Ross
Robert D. Hanson
Lewis D. Boynton
Gary E. Pansegrau
James H. Foote

PART 4   AN AUTOMATED ACCOUNTING SYSTEM

PART 5   AN ACCOUNTING SYSTEM WITH SPECIAL JOURNALS

PART 6   ACCOUNTING CONTROL SYSTEMS

ACKNOWLEDGMENTS

For permission to reproduce the photographs on the pages indicated, acknowledgment is made to the following:

11	Courtesy of Armco, Inc.
112	Editorial Photocolor Archives, Inc.
120	Courtesy of A. E. Staley Mfg. Co.
136	Courtesy of Moore Business Systems
247	Monroe, The Calculator Company (A Division of Litton Industries)
295	Reprinted through the courtesy of New York Life Insurance Company
329	Photograph courtesy of Burroughs Corporation
330	Photo by Jim Ayers, American Business Products, Inc.
333	Courtesy of Prudential Insurance Company
347	Kidde, Inc., 1979 Annual Report
348	Photo Courtesy of IBM
349	Courtesy of Bell & Howell Company
350	Photos Courtesy of IBM
351	Photo Courtesy of Boise Cascade Corporation
354	Courtesy of National, a Division of Dennison Mfg. Co.
372	Courtesy of Cabot Corporation
456	Courtesy of Reynolds + Reynolds
510	Courtesy of Philip Morris Incorporated
521	Freelance Photographers Guild
528	Freelance Photographers Guild
535	Courtesy of Digital Equipment Corporation
542	Courtesy of Moore Business Systems
568	Photo by Tom Tracy, © The Image Bank
605	Photo Courtesy of Mohawk Data Sciences, Parsippany, New Jersey
607	Courtesy of Reynolds + Reynolds

1 ACCOUNTING AS A CAREER

GENERAL BEHAVIORAL GOALS

1. Know terminology related to accounting careers.
2. Understand entry-level positions, advancement-level positions, educational requirements, and career opportunities in accounting.
3. Understand basic accounting concepts.

Accounting Careers and Concepts

ENABLING PERFORMANCE TASKS

After studying Chapter 1, you will be able to:

a. Define terminology related to accounting careers.
b. Identify how accounting is a foundation for careers and personal financial life.
c. Identify the differences in the work of accountants, bookkeepers, accounting clerks, and general office clerks.
d. Identify applications of eleven basic accounting concepts.

One important decision a person makes in a lifetime is how to earn a living. Citizens must earn a living and successfully manage their personal finances. In Canada there are many careers for which people can prepare. The accounting field has many career opportunities for young persons.

WHAT IS ACCOUNTING?

Every business manager and owner needs *good* financial information to make *good* business decisions. Orderly records of businesses' financial activities are called accounting records. Planning, keeping, analysing, and interpreting financial records is called accounting.

Both large and small profit-making organizations use accounting information to make decisions. Managers and owners use accounting information to decide if the profits are sufficient. Should selling prices be increased or decreased? How many workers should be employed? Should different or additional products be sold? Should the size of a business be increased or decreased? Non-profit organizations, such as churches, social clubs, and city governments must keep expenditures within available income. Directors of non-profit organizations must decide on spending priorities to stay within the funds available. City governments must plan carefully to assure that tax rates are sufficient to provide adequate tax revenues. At the same time, city governments keep financial records to restrict expenditures to priority items. Thus, non-profit organizations also need accounting information as the basis for making decisions.

Inaccurate accounting records often contribute to business failure. Failure to *understand* accounting information can result in poor business decisions. Accounting training helps business owners and managers avoid business failure.

Business speaks an accounting language

Accounting is often referred to as the language of business. Everyone in business must be able to use this language. Word processing operators use accounting terms in keying financial statements and other accounting reports. Sales clerks or general office clerks prepare basic accounting papers. Secretaries use basic accounting language in taking dictation and preparing correspondence. These workers do their jobs better if they have some accounting knowledge and can use accounting terms. Many common accounting terms are used in all phases of business.

Accounting in everyday life

Wage earners must prepare and file an income tax return with Revenue Canada, Taxation. Everyone must plan ways to balance expenses with available income. Persons who know basic accounting principles and concepts are better able to plan and keep adequate personal records.

Some persons use a knowledge of accounting as a means of earning a living. Almost all persons use a knowledge of accounting in personal financial activities.

OCCUPATIONAL OPPORTUNITIES IN ACCOUNTING

The many available accounting jobs can be grouped into major categories. The four major accounting job categories are: accountants, bookkeepers, accounting clerks, and general office clerks.

Persons who plan, summarize, analyse, and interpret accounting information are called accountants. Persons who do general accounting work plus some summarizing and analysing are often called bookkeepers. Persons who record, sort, and file accounting information are often called accounting clerks. Persons doing general kinds of office tasks, including some accounting tasks, are called general office clerks.

According to the most recent Statistics Canada census figures (1981), there are approximately 150 000 persons employed as accountants. A further 440 000 persons classified as general office clerks do some accounting tasks. Many more persons are employed in areas where some accounting knowledge is needed. Some of these areas include banking, teaching, finance, automated processing, and management.

An increasing amount of future accounting work will be done using automated equipment. However, the estimated future personnel needs show that use of automated processing is not decreasing the need for accounting workers. The need for accountants and bookkeepers is expected to rise in spite of the expanded use of office machines. Business continues to need accountants, bookkeepers, and accounting clerks.

Accountants

Accountants plan accounting systems used by business. Accountants also interpret financial information and check the accuracy of that information. Accountants often supervise work of other accounting workers. In medium to large businesses, accountants help owners and managers make financial decisions.

Some accountants work as members of accounting firms that sell accounting services to other businesses. For example, a small grocery store may not need a full-time accountant. The owner or an employee normally does the day-to-day accounting tasks. These tasks include recording, summarizing, and reporting basic accounting information. To plan, summarize, analyse, and interpret accounting information, the owner hires an accounting firm. A business selling accounting services to the general public is called a public accounting firm. Public accounting firms provide a variety of accounting services to other businesses and individuals. Accounting services may include all accounting tasks as well as planning an accounting system. Accounting firms may periodically check the accuracy of a business' records and prepare annual statements and reports.

person in payro coordination of payroll activities. Salary depends on training and experience.

ACCOUNTANT. Local mfg. co. has opening for accountant to supervise gen'l and cost accounting.

ACCOUNTANT NEEDED. Seeking person with degree and 2-3 yrs. experience. Duties include credit and general accounting. Advancement to supervisory position possible.

ACCOUNTS PAYABLE CLERK

Immediate opening for an accounts payable clerk. Retail. Automated

The help-wanted advertisements shown in this chapter are typical of those found daily in newspapers throughout Canada.

Some accountants are employed by a single business. Private accountants' work is similar to that done by public accounting firms. However, a private accountant works for only one business.

Bookkeepers

A bookkeeper's tasks include recording, summarizing, and reporting basic accounting information. In a few businesses, bookkeepers may help owners and managers interpret accounting information. Many small or medium businesses employ a public accountant to plan an accounting system. However, a bookkeeper does all the remaining accounting tasks.

Bookkeepers in small firms also may do additional general office work. Many businesses want bookkeepers with keyboarding and filing skills. These two general office skills are closely related to the preparation of accounting reports.

FULL CHARGE BOOKKEEPER
Research company needs accurate bookkeeper. Work without supervsion. Experience must include ledger and payroll.

BOOKKEEPER/CLERICAL
Accts. receivable, ledger, and general office experience. Accurate keyboarding a must.

Accounting clerks

Some businesses have large quantities of day-to-day accounting tasks to be done. These businesses do not want their highly trained accountants doing the routine work. Instead, accounting clerks are responsible for day-to-day accounting tasks. Accountants are then free to plan and interpret financial information as well as supervise other accounting workers.

Accounting clerks' job titles often describe the accounting records on which they work. For example, an accounting clerk working with payroll records is sometimes known as a payroll clerk. Other common job titles include accounts receivable clerk, cash receipts clerk, inventory clerk, and vouchers clerk. These accounting clerks work with a small part of the total accounting activities. However, accounting clerks who know the total accounting system understand the importance of the work being done. Also, knowledge of a total accounting system helps an accounting clerk earn promotion to more responsible positions.

office experience. Accurate keyboarding a must.

ACCOUNTS PAYABLE CLERK

Immediate opening for an accounts payable clerk. Retail. Automated systems. Will train right person.

PAYROLL CLERK

Immediate opening for a responsible person in payroll dept. Duties include coordination of payroll activities.
Salary depends on training and experience.

General office clerks

Most office workers do some accounting work. A secretary may handle cash payments from a small cash fund. A W.P. operator may key accounting reports. A salesperson may prepare sales invoices.

Accounting tasks performed by general office clerks must be done according to basic accounting concepts and procedures. All persons performing some accounting tasks need to understand a business' basic accounting system. General office clerks with a knowledge of accounting better understand the importance of the accounting tasks they do.

SECRETARY. For our sales dept. 4 yrs secl expr., key 60 wpm, and at lease 1 yr bkkpg training or experience needed.

WANTED. W.P. operator with bookkeeping background for all phases of office work.

BUILDING CAREERS IN ACCOUNTING

An important reason for studying accounting is to prepare for a career in accounting. A career in accounting may begin immediately upon graduation from high school. Also, many students use their high school study as preparation for continued accounting study at the college level.

Accounting career ladder

The first jobs that individuals get are called entry-level jobs. Persons completing introductory accounting study may get entry-level jobs as bookkeepers, accounting clerks, or as general office clerks. Persons with accounting study beyond the introductory level may get entry-level jobs as bookkeepers or accountants.

The illustration below represents careers in accounting. The bottom step of the ladder represents those office jobs which are not primarily accounting. These jobs do however include some accounting tasks.

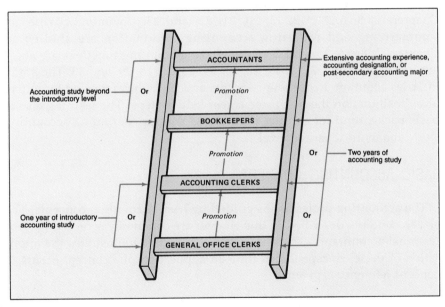

Accounting career ladder

The second career ladder step, accounting clerks, is where most persons with one year of introductory accounting study may find entry-level jobs. Some individuals with two years of accounting study can obtain entry-level jobs as bookkeepers, the third career ladder step. With experience, accounting clerks often can earn promotion to the next career ladder step. However, persons with both accounting study and experience are preferred when promotions are made.

Persons with post-secondary accounting education usually obtain entry-level jobs on the top career ladder step as accountants. Many professional accountants also earn a Chartered Accountant (CA), a Certified General Accountant (CGA), or a Certified Management Accountant (CMA) designation by passing rigorous examinations set by their respective professional accounting associations; namely, The Canadian Institute of Chartered Accountants, The Certified General Accountants Association, and The Society of Management Accountants. In some provinces any accredited member of a professional accounting association may offer services to the public; whereas, in other provinces, only CAs are eligible to obtain a licence to practise public accounting. CGAs and CMAs are often hired for top accounting positions within business organizations.

Starting a career in accounting

Introductory accounting study is an important step to an accounting career. Students completing study using this textbook will have a broad background in accounting principles, skills, and concepts. The study will include day-to-day accounting tasks such as analysing and recording financial information. Various typical accounting records are studied in Chapters 2, 5, 6, 11, 12, 13, 20, 21, 22, and 23. Common activities in summarizing and reporting accounting information are studied in Chapters 7, 8, 14, 15, and 27. Specialized accounting functions are studied in Chapters 10, 17, 18, 19, 22, 23, 24, 25, 26, 28, 29, and 30. The study includes common accounting concepts and procedures needed for entry-level positions on the first three career ladder steps. The learning also is basic background for earning promotions and for continuing accounting study at a more advanced level.

BASIC ACCOUNTING CONCEPTS

The accounting profession is guided by basic accounting concepts. The eleven concepts described in this chapter are commonly accepted by professional accountants. The material in this textbook illustrates the application of these concepts. Each time an application of a concept occurs, a concept reference is given.

CONCEPT: Accounting Period Cycle

Financial changes are reported for a specific period of time in the form of financial statements.

Accounting records are summarized periodically and reported to business owners or managers. The reports or statements are prepared for a specific period of time. The period of time may be once every month, every three months, every six months, or every year. Most individuals summarize personal financial information once every year in order to prepare tax returns.

CONCEPT: Adequate Disclosure

Financial statements should contain all information necessary for a reader to understand a business' financial condition.

Many persons need financial information about a business. These persons include owners, managers, bankers, and other executives. *All* financial information *must be* reported if good business decisions are to be made. A financial statement with incomplete information is similar to a book with some of the pages missing. The complete story is not told.

CONCEPT: Business Entity

A business' financial information is recorded and reported separately from the owner's personal financial information.

A person can own a business and also own a personal house and car. However, a business' financial records should *not* show information about personal houses and cars. Financial records for a business and for its owner's personal belongings should not be mixed. One bank account is used for the owner and another for the business. A business exists separately from its owner.

CONCEPT: Conservatism

When more than one accounting method is acceptable, the one used should result in the least amount of reported earnings or value of assets.

A business sells items to customers. What is the value of the items on hand for sale? Murray's Lumber Company paid 45¢ each for fence posts which are for sale to customers. The posts were bought a month ago. Today, Murray's would have to pay 50¢ each for the same posts. What is the value of the fence posts to Murray's? A common accounting practice is to use the lower of the price paid (cost) or what items now cost (market). In Murray's case, the cost is 45¢ and the current market price is 50¢. Therefore, Murray's will value the fence posts at 45¢, the more conservative value. At the same time, Murray's paid $11.00 each for wooden storm doors for sale to customers. The current market price is $10.00. Murray's would value the storm doors at the lower value, market, $10.00.

CONCEPT: Consistent Reporting

In the preparation of financial statements, the same accounting principles are applied in the same way in each accounting period.

Sally Holland walked to school this year. Last year Sally drove a car to school. Sally tells friends that getting to school cost less this year than last. Without knowing that a different method of getting to school was used, the friends cannot really understand Sally's report.

Owners and managers use information on financial statements when making business decisions. Financial information for one year is often compared to the previous year as a basis for making decisions. If accounting information is recorded differently from one year to the next, information reported on financial statements cannot be compared. Unless changes make information more easily understood, changes in accounting methods or statements are not made.

CONCEPT: Going Concern

Financial statements are prepared with the expectation that a business will remain in operation indefinitely.

Businesses are started with the expectation that they will be successful. Owners expect to continue operating their businesses well into the future. For example, Harry Landon starts a grocery store expecting to continue the business until he retires. Upon retirement, Mr. Landon expects to sell the business. He expects the new owner to continue the store's operation. All accounting records and statements are prepared as though the business will continue even after the present owner is gone. Even though the opposite eventually may be true, Mr. Landon expects his grocery store to continue in business indefinitely.

CONCEPT: Historical Cost

The actual amount paid or received is the amount recorded in accounting records.

A delivery truck is advertised at a sale price of $9 000.00. However, a business arranges to buy the truck for $8 500.00. The truck is recorded at a value of $8 500.00.

John Chan buys a used sports car for $5 000.00. He spends an additional $4 000.00 customizing the car. His total historical cost is $9 000.00. John believes he can sell the customized car four years later for $11 000.00. The car has become a collector's item. However, the only definite value John knows is the actual amount paid, $9 000.00. Accounting practice requires that all things be recorded at a historical value that is known. John's records should show the car's value as $9 000.00.

CONCEPT: Matching Expenses with Revenue

Revenue from business activities and expenses associated with earning that revenue are recorded in the same accounting period.

Jane Piedmont operates a home decorating service. In November, she spends $30.00 for gasoline driving back and forth to a customer's home. She also spends $270.00 for supplies. These amounts are expenses for her business. Ms. Piedmont receives $400.00 for her services to this customer. She should record the revenue ($400.00) and the expenses

($300.00) in the same accounting period. Ms. Piedmont's financial statements for November will show how much she earned ($400.00) and how much it cost her to earn it ($300.00).

CONCEPT: Objective Evidence

Each transaction is described by a business document that proves the transaction did occur.

Only business transactions that actually did occur should be recorded if accurate financial statements are to be prepared. The amounts recorded also must be accurate and true. Nearly all business transactions result in the preparation of a business form. One way to check the accuracy of accounting records is to look at the business papers giving details for transactions. For example, cheques are prepared for cash payments. Receipts are prepared for cash received. Sales slips are prepared for goods sold. Every accounting entry is supported by a business form or paper. When accounting information needs to be checked, accountants can look at the supporting business paper or form.

CONCEPT: Realization of Revenue

Revenue from business transactions is recorded when goods or services are sold.

Some businesses sell goods or services for cash only. Other businesses sell goods or services on one date but receive payment on a later date. For example, Marilyn Muldoon buys some personal items on credit. On October 25 she buys a dress from Junior Tops for $65.00. On November 15 she pays her account at the store. Junior Tops records the dress as sold for $65.00 on October 25. Revenue is recorded when the sale is made, not necessarily when the cash is received.

CONCEPT: Unit of Measurement

All business transactions are recorded in a common unit of measurement — the dollar.

Accounting records are used to prepare financial reports. Reports would not be clear if part of the information were in dollars and part in pesos. A hamburger shop could report the number of hamburgers sold. However, the owner would not know if the shop was earning a profit. Also, a financial report might show that 50 hamburgers and 30 ham sandwiches were sold. The owner would not know which kind of food was bringing in the most money. A record might be kept showing that the expenses were 50 dozen hamburger buns and 6 kg of meat. The revenue is shown as 45 hamburgers. The report still does not show if the shop is earning a profit. All values are reported in a common unit of measurement.

In Canada, accounting records are kept in dollar values. (Of course, in Mexico, the accounting records are kept in pesos.) When financial statements are prepared, the values are all reported in a common unit — the dollar. In this way the hamburger shop knows it sold $59.50 in hamburgers and $58.50 in ham sandwiches. The amount received from each kind of food sale can be compared.

ACCOUNTING TERMS

What is the meaning of each of the following?

1. accounting records
2. accounting
3. accountants
4. bookkeepers
5. accounting clerks
6. general office clerks
7. public accounting firm
8. entry-level jobs

QUESTIONS FOR INDIVIDUAL STUDY

1. What is one of the most important things that a person does in a lifetime as described in this chapter?
2. What must a business manager or owner have in order to make good business decisions?
3. What two things are stated in this chapter as reasons for business failures?
4. Why must wage earners know accounting concepts for personal reasons?
5. What are the four major categories of jobs in accounting?
6. What is happening in Canada to the need for persons with accounting education?
7. What effect will the expanded use of office machines have on the estimated need for accounting workers?
8. What three kinds of things do accountants do?
9. What do public accounting firms do?
10. What is the difference between a public accountant and a private accountant?
11. What kind of accounting work do bookkeepers do?
12. What is described by actual job titles for accounting clerks?
13. Why should general office clerks also study accounting?
14. What kinds of jobs may be obtained by persons with introductory accounting study?
15. What must a person do to earn the Chartered Accountant designation?
16. Which accounting concept states that financial reports should be prepared periodically?
17. Which accounting concept states that all financial information should be reported?
18. Which accounting concept states that a business and its owner are not the same?
19. Which accounting concept states that accounting information should be reported in the same way each year?
20. Which accounting concept is based on the expectation that a business will continue to operate indefinitely?
21. Which accounting concept is based on the idea that information recorded in accounting records comes from details on a business paper?
22. Which accounting concept is being followed when financial information in a Japanese business is recorded in yen?

CASES FOR MANAGEMENT DECISION

CASE 1 Michael and Vinney, two high school students, are discussing possible careers they might go into. Michael's brother graduated from high school last year. His brother obtained an entry-level job as an accounting clerk. Michael says that he is not going to study introductory accounting. His reason is that he does not want to spend the rest of his life as an accounting clerk, like his brother. Michael wants a job supervising other workers. Vinney has the same career objective as Michael. However, he is planning to study introductory accounting. Whose reasoning is better?

CASE 2 Arlene is planning her course selections. She would like to do accounting work as a career after she graduates. For this reason she plans to take two years of accounting study. However, she is not planning to take any other business courses. Arlene's parents suggest that she also plan to take a keyboarding course. Whose thinking is better in this matter? Explain.

CASE 3 Holder Company needs a new business machine. Business A offers to sell a new machine for $630.000. Business B's price for a new machine is $550.00. Business C offers a price of $690.00. After considering the cost and features of the three machines, Holder Company buys a machine from Business A for $630.00. What value should be recorded by Holder Company for this machine? Explain.

CASE 4 Linda Morrison starts a new business. During the first year, Mrs. Morrison sometimes uses the family car for business purposes. All expenses for operating the car are paid by and recorded as expenses of the business. These expenses include licence plates, gasoline, oil, tune-up, and new tires. Are Mrs. Morrison's procedures acceptable? Explain.

CASE 5 Charles Brown does the accounting work for his own business. When money is received from customers, Mr. Brown usually prepares a cash receipt form. Sometimes, when Mr. Brown is very busy with customers, he does not take time to prepare a receipt form for each amount of cash received. Instead, he writes the amounts received on a sheet of paper which he carries in his pocket. At the end of the day he records all the amounts written on the sheet of paper. Do you approve of Mr. Brown's procedures? Explain.

2 ACCOUNTING FOR A SERVICE BUSINESS

GENERAL BEHAVIORAL GOALS

1. Know accounting terminology related to a service business organized as a sole proprietorship.
2. Understand accounting principles and practices for a service business organized as a sole proprietorship.
3. Demonstrate accounting procedures for a service business organized as a sole proprietorship.

Putt Around, the business for Part 2, is a miniature golf facility.

PUTT AROUND
Chart of Accounts

(1) ASSETS	Account Number		(4) REVENUE	Account Number
Cash	11		Sales	41
Supplies	12			
Golf Equipment	13		**(5) EXPENSES**	
Maintenance Equipment	14		Advertising Expense	51
			Miscellaneous Expense	52
(2) LIABILITIES			Rent Expense	53
Melcor Equipment Company	21		Utilities Expense	54
Sasson Supply Company	22			
(3) CAPITAL				
Harry Rossi, Capital	31			
Harry Rossi, Drawing	32			
Income Summary	33			

The chart of accounts for Putt Around is illustrated above for
ready reference as you study Part 2 of this textbook.

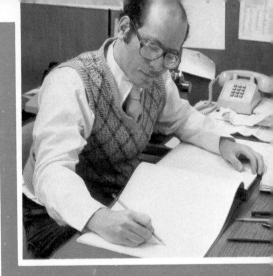

2

Starting an Accounting System

ENABLING PERFORMANCE TASKS

After studying Chapter 2, you will be able to:

a. Define accounting terms related to starting an accounting system.
b. Identify the accounting concepts and principles used in deciding on the procedures for starting an accounting system.
c. Classify financial items as assets, liabilities, or capital.
d. Prepare a beginning balance sheet for a small service business.
e. Record an opening entry in a two-column general journal.
f. Open accounts in a ledger guided by a chart of accounts.
g. Post an opening entry from a journal to a ledger.

Accounting records are needed to manage a business properly and to prepare financial reports. Accounting information may be recorded by hand, on accounting machines, or on automated equipment. The kind and size of a business determines how its accounting records are best kept. Regardless of the methods used, the accounting concepts and principles are the same.

THE ACCOUNTING EQUATION

The value of what a business owns equals the financial rights people have in the business. Anything of value that a business owns is called an asset. The financial rights to the assets of a business are called equities. The records and financial reports of a business are kept separate from the records of the persons supplying the assets. *(CONCEPT: Business Entity)*

A concept reference indicates an application of a specific accounting concept. For a complete statement and description of the concept, refer to pages 8–12 of Chapter 1.

In accounting, assets always equal equities. There are two kinds of equities. (1) *Equity of persons outside a business to whom amounts are owed.* An amount owed by a business is called a liability. (2) *Equity of the owner of a business.* The owner's equity is what remains when the value of liabilities is subtracted from the value of assets. The value of the owner's equity, or share of a business, is called capital.

An equation showing the relationship between the assets and equities of a business is called the accounting equation. The basic accounting equation is most often written as:

ASSETS = LIABILITIES + CAPITAL

STARTING AN ACCOUNTING SYSTEM

Harry Rossi operates a miniature golf business known as Putt Around. A business owned by one person is called a sole proprietorship. The property used by the business is rented. The business does furnish the equipment and supplies. Putt Around is expected to make money and to continue in business indefinitely. *(CONCEPT: Going Concern)*

Mr. Rossi decides to start a new accounting system for his business. To start a new system, he needs to list the assets and equities of the business. He lists these items on July 1, 1988.

What is owned (assets)		What is owed (liabilities)	
Cash on hand and in bank.	$1 100.00	Melcor Equipment	
Supplies.........................	500.00	Company	$ 650.00
Golf Equipment...............	2 200.00	Sasson Supply Company....	550.00
Maintenance Equipment....	900.00	Total owed	$1 200.00
Total owned....................	$4 700.00		

Mr. Rossi figures his equity (capital) as: Assets, $4 700.00, *minus* liabilities, $1 200.00, *equals* capital, $3 500.00. The information for the new accounting system in equation form is below.

ASSETS	=	LIABILITIES	+	CAPITAL
$4 700.00	=	$1 200.00	+	$3 500.00

Information in the records of a business is recorded in a common unit. In Canada the common unit of measurement is the dollar. *(CONCEPT: Unit of Measurement)*

A BALANCE SHEET

Details about the assets and equities, expressed as an accounting equation, are reported on a business form. A business form that reports the assets, liabilities, and capital on a specific date is called a balance sheet. A balance sheet presents a complete and accurate report of a business' assets and equities. *(CONCEPT: Adequate Disclosure)* The balance sheet for Putt Around prepared on July 1, 1988, is below.

Putt Around Balance Sheet July 1, 1988			
Assets		**Liabilities**	
Cash	1 100 00	Melcor Equipment Co.	650 00
Supplies	500 00	Sasson Supply Co.	550 00
Golf Equipment	2 200 00	Total Liabilities	1 200 00
Maintenance Equip.	900 00	**Capital**	
		Harry Rossi, Capital	3 500 00
Total Assets	4 700 00	Total Liab. and Capital	4 700 00

Heading of a balance sheet

The heading of a balance sheet includes three lines. (1) The name of the business. (2) The name of the report. (3) The date for which the report is prepared.

Body of a balance sheet

The body of the balance sheet prepared for Putt Around is in the shape of a capital T. The report has three major sections.

BALANCE SHEET	
Assets	Liabilities and Capital

1. Assets. Assets are listed on the left side of the report.

2. Liabilities. The liabilities are listed on the right side of the report.

3. Capital. The amount of the capital is listed beneath the liabilities on the right side of the report.

The right side of the balance sheet for Putt Around shows the equities of the business. The liabilities have first claim against the assets of a business. If the assets were to be sold and distributed, the liabilities owed would be paid first. Then the owners would be paid. For this reason the liabilities are listed on a balance sheet before the owner's capital.

On a completed balance sheet, the total of the left side must be the same as the total of the right side. A balance sheet shows the same relationship between assets and equities as does the accounting equation.

BALANCE SHEET		
Total Assets	=	Total Equities
		Liabilities 1 200.00
		+ Capital 3 500.00
4 700.00	=	4 700.00

STEPS IN PREPARING A BALANCE SHEET

Five steps are followed in preparing the balance sheet, page 19.

1 Write the heading on three lines. Centre each line.

2 Prepare the assets section on the left side.

- Write the word *Assets* in the centre of the first line of the left wide column. List the name and amount of each asset beginning on the next line.

3 Prepare the liabilities section on the right side.

- Write the word *Liabilities* in the centre on the first line of the right wide column. List the name and amount of each liability. Rule a single line across the amount column directly under the last amount. Write the total amount of the liabilities in the amount column. Write the words *Total Liabilities* in the wide column on the same line.

4 Prepare the capital section immediately below the liabilities section on the right side.

- Write the word *Capital* in the middle of the wide column on the next line. Write the name of the owner and the word *Capital* on the next line. Write the amount of the owner's equity on the same line in the same amount column.

5 Determine that the balance sheet is "in balance" and complete the form.

- Draw a single line across both the left and right amount columns under the last amount in the right amount column. Add both the left and right amount columns. The two column totals must be the same. Write the words *Total Assets* in the left wide column on the same line as the total. Write the words *Total Liabilities and Capital* in the right wide column. Rule double lines across both amount columns directly under each final amount. The double lines show that the work is completed and the balance sheet is "in balance."

  If necessary to fit the space available, the words written on any line of the balance sheet may be abbreviated. However, if space is available, words are not abbreviated in accounting records. Limited use of abbreviations makes reading easier by other persons.

RECORDING A BEGINNING BALANCE SHEET

Financial information about a business is first recorded in chronological order. This means that the information is recorded according to dates or in the order that it happens. A beginning balance sheet is the first information to be recorded in a new accounting system.

A journal

The record in which accounting information is recorded in chronological order is called a journal. Each item recorded in a journal is called an entry. An entry to record information from a beginning balance sheet is called an opening entry. There are different kinds of journals. The nature of a business and the number of entries to be made determine the kind of journal to be used.

A general journal. A journal with two amount columns in which all kinds of entries can be recorded is called a general journal. The two-column general journal used by Putt Around is below.

DATE	ACCOUNT TITLE	POST. REF.	DEBIT	CREDIT
GENERAL JOURNAL			PAGE	
1				1
2				2
3				3

Standard form of two-column general journal

Source document for an entry. When an entry is made in a journal, there should be some written business form to support the entry. The business paper from which information is obtained for a journal entry is called a source document.

The source document for the opening entry of Putt Around is the beginning balance sheet on page 19. (CONCEPT: *Objective Evidence*) The amounts on the left side of a balance sheet are recorded in the left or Debit column of a general journal. The amounts on the right side of a balance sheet are recorded in the right or Credit column of a general journal.

The meaning of the amount column headings, *Debit* and *Credit*, is explained later in this chapter.

Relationship of items on beginning balance sheet to general journal columns

A journal entry. Every journal entry has four parts. (1) The date of the entry. (2) The debit part of the entry. (3) The credit part of the entry. (4) An explanation or source document number.

Recording an opening entry

Each of the four parts of an opening entry is recorded as explained below.

1 *Date of entry.* Write the date of the opening entry in the Date column of the journal. The year and month are written only once on a general journal page in the Date column.

	DATE		ACCOUNT TITLE	POST. REF.	DEBIT	CREDIT	
	GENERAL JOURNAL					PAGE /	
1	1988 July	1	Cash		1 1 0 0 00		1
2			Supplies		5 0 0 00		2
3			Golf Equipment		2 2 0 0 00		3
4			Maintenance Equipment		9 0 0 00		4
5			Melcor Equipment Company			6 5 0 00	5
6			Sasson Supply Company			5 5 0 00	6
7			Harry Rossi, Capital			3 5 0 0 00	7
8			Balance sheet, July 1, 1988				8
9							9
10							10
11							11

Complete opening entry for Putt Around

2 *Debit part of entry.* Write the debit part of the opening entry. Write the name of each asset at the left edge of the Account Title column. Write the amount of each asset in the Debit column.

3 *Credit part of entry.* Write the credit part of the opening entry. Write the name of each liability and the name of the owner in the Account Title column. Write the word *Capital* after the owner's name. Indent the liability and capital account names about 1 cm from the left edge of the Account Title column. Write the amount of each credit item in the Credit column.

Indenting the names of the credit items helps to separate the debit and credit parts of the entry.

4 *Reason for entry.* Write the words *Balance Sheet, July 1, 1988.* For most entries, write the name or number of the source document as the fourth part of the entry. Persons who need more information can refer to the source document for details. The explanation is indented about 2 cm from the left of the Account Title column. This indentation helps separate the explanation from the credit part of the entry.

The use of the Post. Ref. column in the journal will be explained later in this chapter.

Checking an entry for accuracy

The total of the left side of a balance sheet is the same as the total of the right side. Also, the total debit amounts in a journal entry must be the same as the total credit amounts.

In the opening entry on page 22, the total of the debit amount column is $4 700.00. The total of the credit amount column is also $4 700.00. The debit part of the entry is equal to the credit part. The entry is in balance. As each entry is recorded in a journal, the equality of debits and credits must be checked.

POSTING TO A LEDGER

As a business conducts daily activities, changes occur in the value of balance sheet items. Goods and services are bought and sold. Cash is received. Cash is paid out. Supplies are bought. For example, Putt Around receives cash each time a customer plays a game of miniature golf. Accounting records should show any changes that occur.

A ledger

A separate record is kept of each asset, each liability, and the capital of a business. Changes in each of these items must be brought together in one place. This separate record will show how each item has changed. An accounting form used to sort and summarize changes in a specific item is called an account. A group of accounts is called a ledger. The separate accounts in a ledger may be on ledger cards, ledger sheets, or on sheets bound in book form.

Two-column account form. Account forms are printed in various ways. One form has two amount columns: a Debit amount column and a Credit amount column. The two-column account form is below.

ACCOUNT								ACCOUNT NO.	
DATE	ITEM	POST. REF.	DEBIT	DATE	ITEM	POST. REF.	CREDIT		
	Entries on the left side are debit entries				Entries on the right side are credit entries				

Two-column account form

The two-column account form has two sides, each with the same ruling. The left side of a two-column account form is called the debit side. The right side of a two-column account form is called the credit side.

When an entry is made on the left side of an account, it is referred to as a debit. An entry on the right side is referred to as a credit. The abbreviations *Dr.* for Debit and *Cr.* for Credit are commonly used in accounting.

Chart of accounts. Each account in a ledger is given a name and a number. A name given to a separate ledger account is called an account title. A number given to an account is called an account number. An account number usually shows the account's location in a ledger. The ledger contains an account for each item on the beginning balance sheet.

A list of account titles and numbers showing the location of the accounts in a ledger is called a chart of accounts. A partial chart of accounts for Putt Around is below.

Partial chart of accounts

Putt Around Chart of Accounts			
(1) Assets	Account Number	(2) Liabilities	Account Number
Cash...	11	Melcor Equipment Company.......	21
Supplies...	12	Sasson Supply Company............	22
Golf Equipment............................	13		
Maintenance Equipment..............	14	(3) Capital	
		Harry Rossi, Capital....................	31

The complete chart of accounts for Putt Around is on page 16.

The first digit of each account number shows in which division of the ledger the account is located. The chart of accounts above shows three divisions of the ledger. (1) Assets. (2) Liabilities. (3) Capital. All asset account numbers begin with *1* to show that the accounts are in the first division of the ledger. All liability account numbers begin with *2*. The capital account number begins with *3*.

The second digit of each account number shows the order in which an account is listed in each division. For example, in Putt Around's chart of accounts above Cash is numbered *11*. The second digit of this number shows that Cash is the first account in the asset division. The account number for Sasson Supply Company is *22*. The second digit of this number shows that Sasson Supply Company is the second account in the liabilities division.

Some businesses use more than two digits for account numbers. Charts of accounts with more than two digits are used and explained in later chapters.

Opening accounts in a ledger

Writing an account title and account number on the heading of an account form is called opening an account. An account is opened in the ledger for each item listed in a chart of accounts. Accounts are opened in the ledger in the same order that they appear on a chart of accounts.

Cash is the first account on the chart of accounts for Putt Around, page 24. The cash account is opened as explained below.

1 Write the name of the account, *Cash*, after the word Account in the heading of the account.

Opening the cash account

2 Write the account number, *11*, after the words Account No.

This procedure is used in opening all accounts on Putt Around's complete chart of accounts, page 16.

Posting an opening entry

Each amount in an opening entry is transferred to a ledger account. Transferring information from journal entries to ledger accounts is called posting. Posting sorts the information so that all activities affecting a single account are brought together in one place. For example, all information about changes in Cash are brought together in the cash account.

Posting the debit items of an opening entry. The steps in posting the debit items of an opening entry are below.

1 Write the *amount* of the cash debit, *$1 100.00*, in the Debit column of the cash account.

2 Write the *date* of the journal entry, *1988, July 1*, in the Date column. The year and the month are written only once on the same side of an account. The day is written once for each entry posted to an account.

3 Write the word *Balance* in the Item column of the account. The word Balance helps to separate the beginning balance in the account from other entries posted later.

First three steps in posting a debit entry to a ledger account

The final two steps in posting are to cross-reference the information. One part of the cross-reference tells where the entry in an account came from. The other part shows in the journal the account number to which the amount was posted. This cross-referencing is below.

Posting references in accounts and journals

4 Write *G1* in the Post. Ref. column of the cash account. The *G1* shows that the entry came from page 1 of the general journal.

> The *G* is used to show that this entry is posted from the *G*eneral journal.

5 Return to the journal and write the account number, *11*, in the Post. Ref. column of the journal. This notation shows to which account the item in the journal was posted.

> A person checking the records knows at a glance which items in a journal have not been posted. The items without account numbers in the Post. Ref. column have not been posted. For this reason, placing the account numbers in the journal Post. Ref. column *must* be the last step in posting.

The same five steps are used in posting all debit items in an opening entry.

Posting the credit items of an opening entry. The same five steps used to post debit items are used to post credit items of an opening entry. However, the items are posted to the *credit* side of the accounts involved.

Steps in posting a credit entry to a ledger account

A ledger after all items in an opening entry are posted. The ledger accounts on the next page are shown after all posting of the opening entry, page 22, is completed.

ACCOUNT *Cash*							ACCOUNT NO. *11*
DATE	ITEM	POST. REF.	DEBIT	DATE	ITEM	POST. REF.	CREDIT
1988 July 1	*Balance*	*G1*	*110000*				

ACCOUNT *Supplies*							ACCOUNT NO. *12*
DATE	ITEM	POST. REF.	DEBIT	DATE	ITEM	POST. REF.	CREDIT
1988 July 1	*Balance*	*G1*	*50000*				

ACCOUNT *Golf Equipment*							ACCOUNT NO. *13*
DATE	ITEM	POST. REF.	DEBIT	DATE	ITEM	POST. REF.	CREDIT
1988 July 1	*Balance*	*G1*	*220000*				

ACCOUNT *Maintenance Equipment*							ACCOUNT NO. *14*
DATE	ITEM	POST. REF.	DEBIT	DATE	ITEM	POST. REF.	CREDIT
1988 July 1	*Balance*	*G1*	*90000*				

ACCOUNT *Melcor Equipment Company*							ACCOUNT NO. *21*
DATE	ITEM	POST. REF.	DEBIT	DATE	ITEM	POST. REF.	CREDIT
				1988 July 1	*Balance*	*G1*	*65000*

ACCOUNT *Sasson Supply Company*							ACCOUNT NO. *22*
DATE	ITEM	POST. REF.	DEBIT	DATE	ITEM	POST. REF.	CREDIT
				1988 July 1	*Balance*	*G1*	*55000*

ACCOUNT *Harry Rossi, Capital*							ACCOUNT NO. *31*
DATE	ITEM	POST. REF.	DEBIT	DATE	ITEM	POST. REF.	CREDIT
				1988 July 1	*Balance*	*G1*	*350000*

Ledger accounts with all
items in the opening entry
posted

SUMMARY OF STARTING AN ACCOUNTING SYSTEM

A diagram showing the sequence of steps involved in a procedure is called a flowchart. The flowchart below summarizes the activities involved in starting an accounting system.

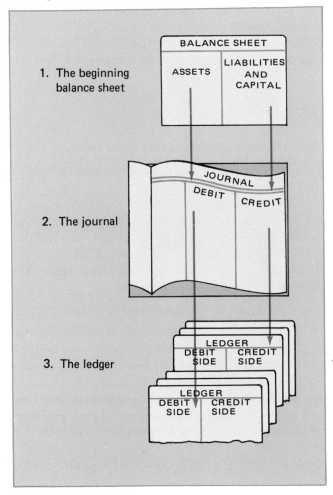

Flowchart for starting an accounting system

1. A beginning balance sheet is prepared listing the accounting equation as of the day the new accounting system is started.
2. The information on a beginning balance sheet is recorded as an opening entry. The opening entry is recorded in a journal. The assets are recorded as debits, and the equities (liabilities and capital) are recorded as credits.
3. The items recorded in the opening entry are posted to individual ledger accounts.

KEEPING BUSINESS AND PERSONAL RECORDS SEPARATE

The owner of a business has both personal and business assets. The owner also has both personal and business liabilities. The personal and business financial information must be kept separate. *(CONCEPT: Business Entity)* If the records are not kept separate, the owner will have difficulty determining how the business is doing. The owner's personal financial condition will also be difficult to determine. When a balance sheet is prepared for a business, only business assets and liabilities are listed.

COMMON ACCOUNTING PRACTICES

Some common accounting practices are given below.

1. Words are written in full when space permits. Words may be abbreviated when space is limited.
2. Dollar and cents signs and decimal points are not used when amounts are written on ruled accounting paper. Sometimes a color tint is used in amount columns to separate dollars and cents.
3. Two zeros are written in the cents column when an amount is in even dollars. If the cents column is left blank, there may be doubt later whether the cents had been omitted.

   Sometimes a dash (—) is used instead of two zeros to indicate "no cents."

4. When a single line is ruled under an amount, the single line means that a total or remainder will follow. The single line means that amounts have been added or subtracted.
5. A double line across an amount column indicates that work is complete and accurate. Double lines under the total assets amount on a balance sheet means that the information before the lines is completed.
6. For neatness, a ruler is used in drawing single and double lines.

Some common accounting practices

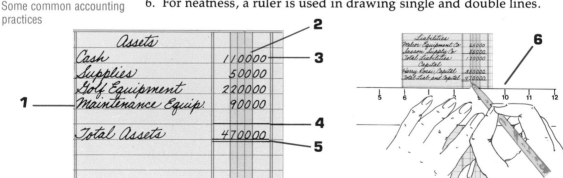

ACCOUNTING TERMS

What is the meaning of each of the following?

1. asset
2. equities
3. liability
4. capital
5. accounting equation
6. sole proprietorship
7. balance sheet
8. journal
9. entry
10. opening entry
11. general journal
12. source document
13. account
14. ledger
15. debit side
16. credit side
17. account title
18. account number
19. chart of accounts
20. opening an account
21. posting
22. flowchart

QUESTIONS FOR INDIVIDUAL STUDY

1. Why are liabilities and capital referred to as equities?
2. Why is the basic accounting equation written *Assets = Liabilities + Capital*?
3. What three items are included in the heading of a balance sheet?
4. What kind of information is placed on the left side of a balance sheet as described in this chapter? On the right side of a balance sheet?
5. Why are double lines ruled across both amount columns of the balance sheet, page 19?
6. Why are abbreviations usually *not* used in accounting?
7. What is meant by "recording information in chronological order"?
8. What are the column headings of the two-column general journal described in this chapter?
9. In which column of a general journal should the asset amounts of the beginning balance sheet be recorded?
10. In which column of a general journal are the liability amounts of the beginning balance sheet recorded?
11. In which column of a general journal is the amount of the capital from the beginning balance sheet recorded?
12. What are the four parts of a journal entry?
13. Why are account titles with credit amounts in the opening entry, page 22, indented in the Account Title column?
14. How can the accuracy of the opening entry, page 22, be checked?
15. Why are ledger accounts used?
16. What is the purpose of an account number?
17. The account numbers described in this chapter have two digits. What is shown by the first digit? By the second digit?
18. What does the account number 14 mean?
19. In what order are accounts opened in the ledger?
20. Why are journal entries posted?
21. Why is writing the account number in the journal Post. Ref. column the last step in posting?
22. What are the three basic activities in starting an accounting system?

CASES FOR MANAGEMENT DECISION

CASE 1 Michael Morgan started a summer lawn care business which is successful and he decides to continue it indefinitely. He realizes that he needs an accounting system to maintain necessary records. He asks your advice in starting the system. What would you do first? Where would you get the information needed to start Mr. Morgan's system for him?

CASE 2 Matilda Hormeyer is the owner of a plumbing business. Her balance for the year just ended shows her capital to be $26 000.00. The balance sheet for the end of the previous year showed her capital to be $27 500.00. What are some reasons for this decrease in capital?

CASE 3 Alice Martin started a new accounting system for her business. In the chart of accounts, she numbered all the accounts consecutively. The four asset accounts are numbered 1 to 4. The two liability accounts are numbered 5 and 6. The capital is numbered 7. Why is Miss Martin's system of numbering accounts not as satisfactory as the system described in this chapter?

DRILLS FOR UNDERSTANDING

DRILL 2-D 1 Classifying assets, liabilities, and capital

This drill gives you practice in classifying balance sheet items. The drill also gives you practice in deciding which general journal columns are used for an opening entry. Use a form similar to the one below to record your answers.

1	2	3	4	5
	Balance Sheet		General Journal	
Balance Sheet Items	Left-hand side	Right-hand side	Column in which amount in opening entry is recorded	
			Debit column	Credit column
1. Delivery Equipment............	Asset		√	

Instructions: 1. Classify each item listed below. Write *Asset*, *Liability*, or *Capital* in Columns 2 or 3 showing where on a balance sheet the item is listed.

(1) Delivery Equipment
(2) Mannies Supply Company
(3) Cash
(4) Office Equipment
(5) Office Supplies
(6) Zapata Equipment Company
(7) Dry Cleaning Equipment
(8) Supplies
(9) Golf Equipment
(10) Any amount owed
(11) Anything owned
(12) Bryan Dooley, Capital

Instructions: 2. Decide which general journal columns are used for an opening entry for each item listed in Instruction 1. If an amount goes in the debit amount column, place a check mark in Column 4. If an amount goes in the credit amount column, place a check mark in Column 5.

3. Cover your answers on the form. See how rapidly you can do this drill mentally without looking at your answers. Repeat this drill several times to increase your speed and accuracy.

DRILL 2-D 2 Preparing a chart of accounts

Fashion Barn has the items on page 33 listed on its beginning balance sheet.

Cash
Supplies
Store Equipment
Office Equipment
Delivery Equipment

A-1 Finance Company
Beulah's Garage and Repairs
Metro Office Equipment Company
Isaac Bloom, Capital

Instructions: Prepare a partial chart of accounts similar to the one on page 24.

APPLICATION PROBLEMS

PROBLEM 2-1   Preparing a beginning balance sheet

The following are assets and liabilities of Wilson's Self-Serve Laundry, owned and operated by Walter Wilson.

Assets		Liabilities	
Cash	$1 100.00	Miller's Repair Shop	$ 85.00
Supplies	320.00	Professional Appliances Company	2 900.00
Drying Equipment	3 000.00	O.K. Supply Company	150.00
Washing Equipment	5 000.00		

Instructions: 1. Prepare a beginning balance sheet for Wilson's Self-Serve Laundry. Use the date September 1 of the current year. Follow the steps in preparing a balance sheet given on page 20.
   2. Check the accuracy and completeness of your work with the questions given below.
     a. Is each of the items in the heading centred and on a separate line?
     b. Is each of the sectional headings in the body of the balance sheet centred?
     c. Are each of the assets, liabilities, and capital listed in the correct section of the balance sheet?
     d. Is the amount of total assets on the same line as the amount of total liabilities and capital?
     e. Are the totals at the bottom of the balance sheet the same?
     f. Are the single and double lines drawn across only the amount columns?
     g. Is the work neat? Is the handwriting legible?

PROBLEM 2-2   Recording an opening entry

Instructions: 1. Record an opening entry on page 1 of a general journal using the information on the balance sheet below. Use the date of August 1 of the current year.

Chu Realty Agency Balance Sheet August 1, 19--						
Assets			**Liabilities**			
Cash	700	00	Mabel Allison Company		170	00
Supplies	300	00	Michael Daniels Company		550	00
Automobile Equipment	6 000	00	Teri McIntyre Company	2	000	00
Office Equipment	1 000	00	Total Liabilities	2	720	00
			Capital			
			Yi Chu, Capital	5	280	00
Total Assets	8 000	00	Total Liabilities and Capital	8	000	00

Instructions: 2. Check the accuracy of your work by asking yourself the questions given below.

    a. Are the year, month, and day written at the top of the Date column in the journal?

    b. Is each debit item written at the extreme left edge of the Account Title column?

    c. Is each credit item in the Account Title column indented about 1 cm?

    d. Is the indication of the source document given at the end of the opening entry? Is it written in the Account Title column? Is it indented about 2 cm?

    e. Does the total of the debit amounts equal the total of the credit amounts?

The solution to Problem 2-2 is needed to complete Problem 2-3.

PROBLEM 2-3 Posting an opening entry

The solution to Problem 2-2 is needed to complete Problem 2-3.

Instructions: 1. Open the accounts as shown in the partial chart of accounts below.

Account Title	Account Number
Cash	11
Supplies	12
Automobile Equipment	13
Office Equipment	14
Mabel Allison Company	21
Michael Daniels Company	22
Teri McIntyre Company	23
Yi Chu, Capital	31

Instructions: 2. Post the opening entry recorded in Instruction 1 of Problem 2-2.

PROBLEM 2-4 Preparing a partial chart of accounts; preparing a beginning balance sheet; recording and posting an opening entry

Lester Sheng, a veterinarian, starts Westdell Animal Clinic. The information for the beginning balance sheet on September 1 of the current year is given below.

Assets: Cash $1 530.00; Medical Supplies, $1 350.00; Office Supplies, $810.00; Automobile, $4 860.00; Medical Equipment, $4 600.00; Kennel Equipment, $2 000.00.

Liabilities: Veterinary Supply Company, $3 000.00; Masson's Pet Store, $50.00; Medical Drug Company, $1 540.00.

Instructions: 1. Prepare a partial chart of accounts similar to the one on page 24.

2. Prepare a beginning balance sheet for Westdell Animal Clinic.

3. Record the opening entry for Westdell Animal Clinic. Use page 1 of a general journal.

4. Open ledger accounts for all items on the chart of accounts prepared in Instruction 1 above.

5. Post the opening entry.

ENRICHMENT PROBLEMS

MASTERY PROBLEM 2-M Preparing a beginning balance sheet; recording and posting an opening entry

Marilyn Lukens starts Lukens' Delivery Service. The information on page 35 is listed by Ms. Lukens for her beginning balance sheet.

Assets: Cash, $2 700.00; Truck Equipment, $5 300.00; Office Equipment, $2 900.00.

Liabilities: Russo's Supply Company, $2 000.00; Milton's Equipment Company, $1 200.00; Bullocks' Service Station, $96.00.

Instructions: 1. Prepare a beginning balance sheet for Lukens' Delivery Service. Use the date of September 1 of the current year. After you have prepared the beginning balance sheet, check it by asking the same questions listed in Instruction 2, Problem 2-1.

2. Record the opening entry for Lukens' Delivery Service. Use page 1 of a general journal. When you have completed the opening entry, check it by asking the same questions listed in Instruction 2, Problem 2-2.

3. Open ledger accounts for the partial chart of accounts below.

Account Title	Account Number
Cash	11
Truck Equipment	12
Office Equipment...	13
Russo's Supply Company	21
Milton's Equipment Company	22
Bullocks' Service Station	23
Marilyn Lukens, Capital...	31

Instructions: 4. Post the opening entry recorded in Instruction 2 above.

CHALLENGE PROBLEM 2-C   Preparing a balance sheet; recording an opening entry; keeping business and personal records separate

John Botsworth has operated a dry cleaning business, Welldone Dry Cleaning, for the past month. During this time he failed to keep any records of either his dry cleaning business or his personal affairs. The following information includes both his business and personal financial data.

Assets: Cash in Mr. Botsworth's personal chequing account, $625.00; cash in the business' current account, $1 248.00; delivery truck, $5 552.00; furniture in the family home, $5 540.00; dry cleaning equipment, $4 220.00; store equipment, $2 680.00; family automobile, $6 400.00; family home, $39 000.00; building in which business is located, $16 000.00; land on which business building is located, $12 000.00.

Liabilities: Auto Finance Company, owed on delivery truck, $3 200.00; Bank of Montreal, owed on family automobile, $1 600.00; Haskins Supply Company, owed on dry cleaning equipment, $2 000.00; Toronto-Dominion Bank, mortgage on home, $8 000.00; Royal Bank, mortgage on business building, $9 000.00.

Instructions: 1. Prepare a balance sheet for Welldone Dry Cleaning. Use July 1 of the current year.

2. Record an opening entry on page 1 of a general journal.

3

Changes Caused by Business Transactions

ENABLING PERFORMANCE TASKS

After studying Chapter 3, you will be able to:

a. Define accounting terms related to changes caused by business transactions.

b. Explain accounting principles and practices related to changes caused by business transactions.

c. Analyse business transactions to show how these transactions affect items on an expanded accounting equation.

d. Figure new balances after increases and decreases are shown in basic accounting equation items.

e. Determine that after each transaction's changes are shown on an expanded accounting equation, the basic equation is still "in balance."

f. Prepare a balance sheet from information on an expanded accounting equation after changes caused by a series of transactions are shown.

Each time a business conducts a business activity, the amounts in the accounting equation are changed. A normal business activity that changes assets, liabilities, or owner's equity is called a transaction. For example, a transaction may be a sale of services or goods. Also, a transaction may occur when a business buys supplies.

HOW TRANSACTIONS CHANGE THE BASIC ACCOUNTING EQUATION

As described in Chapter 2, the basic accounting equation for Putt Around is:

Assets	=	Liabilities	+	Capital
$4 700	=	$1 200	+	$3 500

Each time a transaction occurs two or more of the amounts in the basic equation will change. For example, Putt Around sells an old lawn mower for $50.00. The change in the equation is below.

	Assets	= Liabilities	+ Capital
Beg. Balances	$4 700	= $1 200	+ $3 500
Transaction	−50 (old equipment)		
	+50 (new received cash)		
New Balances	$4 700	= $1 200	+ $3 500

The net change in the basic accounting equation is made in two items on the same side of the equation. The net change to the left side is zero (−50, +50). The business has less equipment but more cash. Because the net change on the left side of the equation is zero, the same zero change affects the right side.

As another example, the business pays part of the liability owed, $200.00. The change in the basic equation is below.

	Assets	= Liabilities	+ Capital
Balances	$4 700	= $1 200	+ $3 500
Transaction	−200 (paid cash out)	−200 (paid liability)	
New Balances	$4 500	= $1 000	+ $3 500

As a result of this transaction to pay a liability, the basic accounting equation is changed. The total amount of assets is reduced, $200.00. The new amount of assets becomes $4 500.00. The total amount owed to other persons is reduced, $200.00. The new amount of liabilities becomes $1 000.00. The amount of the capital is not affected and remains the same, $3 500.00. After the effect of the transaction is shown, the basic accounting equation is still in balance. The total assets, $4 500.00, equal the total liabilities plus capital, $4 500.00 ($1 000.00 + 3 500.00).

As a third example, the business receives cash from customers. The cash register shows that a total of $250.00 has been received from customers during the day. Rather than record each individual daily transaction, the business treats all the day's sales as one transaction. Cash from sales increases a business' capital. An increase in capital resulting from the operation of a business is called revenue. The change in the equation is below.

	Assets	= Liabilities	+ Capital
Balances	$4 500	= $1 000	+ $3 500
Transaction	+250 (received cash)		+250 (revenue)
New Balances	$4 750	= $1 000	+ $3 750

In this transaction the total amount of assets is increased by $250.00, the amount of cash received from customers. This transaction does *not* affect liabilities. Therefore, the amount of liabilities is not changed. The owner's equity (capital) is increased by this transaction, $250.00. After the effect of this transaction is shown, the equation is still in balance. The total amount of assets, $4 750.00, equals the total liabilities plus capital, $4 750.00 ($1 000.00 + 3 750.00).

The following summarizes the effect of the three transactions on the basic accounting equation.

Transaction 1. The left side of the equation (assets) is both increased and decreased, $50.00. The net change in assets is zero. Therefore, the net change for the right side (liabilities, capital) is also zero.

Transaction 2. The left side of the equation (assets) is decreased, $200.00. The right side of the equation (liabilities) is also decreased, $200.00. Both sides of the equation are decreased by the same amount.

Transaction 3. The left side of the equation (assets) is increased, $250.00. The right side of the equation (capital) is increased, $250.00. The same net change to both sides is an increase of $250.00.

A summary of the changes caused by the three transactions is below.

	Assets =	**Liabilities** +	**Capital**
Beg. Balances	$4 700 =	$1 200	+ $3 500
Transaction 1	−50		
	+50		
	$4 700 =	$1 200	+ $3 500
Transaction 2	−200	−200	
	$4 500 =	$1 000	+ $3 500
Transaction 3	+250		+250
New Balances	$4 750 =	$1 000	+ $3 750

How transactions change the basic accounting equation

HOW TRANSACTIONS CHANGE THE DETAILS IN THE EXPANDED ACCOUNTING EQUATION

The basic equation for Putt Around can be expanded to show details of each of the elements.

	Assets			=	Liabilities		+	Capital
Cash	Supplies	Golf Equip.	Maint. Equip.		Melcor Equip. Co.	Sasson Supply Co.		
$1 100	$500	$2 200	$900 =		$650	$550	+	$3 500

The expanded accounting equation shows more details than does the basic accounting equation, page 36. The beginning balances are taken from the balance sheet, page 19. Each transaction will change at least two items in the expanded accounting equation.

Transaction 1: Received cash from sale of equipment

Received cash from sale of a lawn mower, $50.00.

The effect of Transaction 1 on the expanded accounting equation is below.

	Assets				=	Liabilities		+	Capital
	Cash	Supplies	Golf Equip.	Maint. Equip.	=	Melcor Equip. Co.	Sasson Supply Co.	+	
Beg. Balances	$1 100	$500	$2 200	$900	=	$650	$550	+	$3 500
Transaction 1	+50			−50					
New Balances	$1 150	$500	$2 200	$850	=	$650	$550	+	$3 500

After Transaction 1 is recorded in the expanded equation above, the accounting equation is still in balance. The total of the left side of the equation is $4 700.00 ($1 150 + 500 + 2 200 + 850). The total of the right side of the equation is also $4 700.00 ($650 + 550 + 3 500).

Transaction 2: Paid cash for an amount owed to liabilities

Paid cash to Sasson Supply Company, $200.00.

The effect of Transaction 2 on the expanded equation is below.

	Assets				=	Liabilities		+	Capital
	Cash	Supplies	Golf Equip.	Maint. Equip.	=	Melcor Equip. Co.	Sasson Supply Co.	+	
Balances	$1 150	$500	$2 200	$850	=	$650	$550	+	$3 500
Transaction 2	−200						−200		
New Balances	$ 950	$500	$2 200	$850	=	$650	$350	+	$3 500

The amount of cash is decreased on the left side, $200.00. The amount owed Sasson Supply Company is decreased on the right side, $200.00. The same amount of decrease is made on both sides of the equation. After Transaction 2 is recorded in the expanded equation, the equation is still in balance. The total of the left side is $4 500.00. The total of the right side is also $4 500.00.

Transaction 3: Received cash from sales

Received cash from the daily sales, $250.00.

The effect of Transaction 3 on the equation is below.

	Assets				=	Liabilities		+	Capital
	Cash	Supplies	Golf Equip.	Maint. Equip.	=	Melcor Equip. Co.	Sasson Supply Co.	+	
Balances	$ 950	$500	$2 200	$850	=	$650	$350	+	$3 500
Transaction 3	+250								+250
New Balances	$1 200	$500	$2 200	$850	=	$650	$350	+	$3 750

The amount of cash is increased on the left side, $250.00. The amount of the capital is increased on the right side for the same amount, $250.00. The same amount of increase is made on both sides of the equation. The equation is still in balance. The left-side total is $4 750.00. The right-side total is also $4 750.00.

Transaction 4: Paid cash for an expense

Paid cash for July rent, $600.00.

A decrease in capital resulting from the operation of a business is called an expense. Business expenses are the costs of items and services used to produce revenue.

The effect of Transaction 4 on the equation is below.

	Assets				=	Liabilities		+	Capital	
	Cash	Supplies	Golf Equip.	Maint. Equip.		Melcor Equip. Co.	Sasson Supply Co.			
Balances	$1 200	$500	$2 200	$850	=	$650	$350	+	$3 750	
Transaction 4	−600								−600	(expense)
New Balances	$ 600	$500	$2 200	$850	=	$650	$350	+	$3 150	

The amount of cash is decreased on the left side, $600.00. The amount of capital is decreased on the right side for the same amount, $600.00. The same amount of decrease is made on both sides of the equation. After Transaction 4, the equation is still in balance. The left side totals $4 150.00. The right side also totals $4 150.00.

Transaction 5: Received cash from the owner as an additional investment in the business

Received cash from the owner, Harry Rossi, as an additional investment in the business, $500.00.

The effect of Transaction 5 on the equation is below.

	Assets				=	Liabilities		+	Capital	
	Cash	Supplies	Golf Equip.	Maint. Equip.		Melcor Equip. Co.	Sasson Supply Co.			
Balances	$ 600	$500	$2 200	$850	=	$650	$350	+	$3 150	
Transaction 5	+500								+500	(invest.)
New Balances	$1 100	$500	$2 200	$850	=	$650	$350	+	$3 650	

Transaction 5 increases the left side of the equation (cash) by $500.00 and increases the right side (capital) by $500.00. Transaction 5 increases the *total* amount of assets. With each increase in total assets, there also must be a similar increase in total equity. The amount of liabilities is not changed by Transaction 5. Therefore, the change on the right side must be in the owner's equity (capital).

Transaction 6: Paid cash for supplies

Paid cash for supplies, $50.00.

The effect of Transaction 6 on the equation is below.

	Assets			=	Liabilities		+	Capital
			Golf Maint.		Melcor	Sasson		
	Cash	Supplies	Equip. Equip.		Equip. Co.	Supply Co.		
Balances	$1 100	$500	$2 200 $850	=	$650	$350	+	$3 650
Transaction 6	−50	+50						
New Balances	$1 050	$550	$2 200 $850	=	$650	$350	+	$3 650

The amount of cash is decreased and the amount of supplies is increased by $50.00. Both the increase and decrease are on the left side of the equation. Transaction 6 does not change the *total* amount of assets. Therefore, there is no change in the equity on the right side. No items are changed on the right side of the equation.

Transaction 7: Paid cash for an expense

Paid cash for telephone bill, $25.00.

The effect of Transaction 7 is below.

	Assets			=	Liabilities		+	Capital
			Golf Maint.		Melcor	Sasson		
	Cash	Supplies	Equip. Equip.		Equip. Co.	Supply Co.		
Balances	$1 050	$550	$2 200 $850	=	$650	$350	+	$3 650
Transaction 7	−25							−25
New Balances	$1 025	$550	$2 200 $850	=	$650	$350	+	$3 625

After Transaction 7, the equation is still in balance. The left side totals $4 625.00. The right side also totals $4 625.00.

Transaction 8: Paid cash to buy new equipment

Paid cash for a new lawn mower, $400.00.

The effect of Transaction 8 is below.

	Assets			=	Liabilities		+	Capital
			Golf Maint.		Melcor	Sasson		
	Cash	Supplies	Equip. Equip.		Equip. Co.	Supply Co.		
Balances	$1 025	$550	$2 200 $ 850	=	$650	$350	+	$3 625
Transaction 8	−400		+400					
New Balances	$ 625	$550	$2 200 $1 250	=	$650	$350	+	$3 625

Cash is decreased and maintenance equipment is increased on the left side, $400.00. The *total* amount of assets is not changed by Transaction 8. Therefore, no change is made in the equities on the right side of the equation.

Transaction 9: Paid cash to owner for personal use

Paid cash to the owner, Harry Rossi, for personal use, $100.00.

Assets taken out of a business for the personal use of the owner are called withdrawals. The owner might withdraw any kind of asset. For example, the owner might withdraw cash or supplies for personal use at home. In a few situations the owner might withdraw equipment for personal use. However, owners seldom withdraw equipment. The equipment is needed to operate the business and might be too expensive for the business to replace.

The effect of Transaction 9 is below.

	Assets				=	Liabilities		+	Capital
	Cash	Supplies	Golf Equip.	Maint. Equip.		Melcor Equip. Co.	Sasson Supply Co.		
Balances	$625	$550	$2 200	$1 250	=	$650	$350	+	$3 625
Transaction 9	−100								−100
New Balances	$525	$550	$2 200	$1 250	=	$650	$350	+	$3 525

Cash is decreased on the left side, $100.00. The owner's equity (capital) is decreased on the right side, $100.00. The *total* amount of assets is decreased. There must be a similar decrease in equity on the right side. The amount owed to liabilities is not affected by Transaction 9. Therefore, the decrease is in the owner's equity (capital).

Transaction 10: Paid cash for repairs

Paid cash for repair of a broken window, $10.00.

A business may have many kinds of expenses. As described on page 41, Putt Around paid a telephone bill. Cost of utilities is one kind of expense. Rent is another expense. Cost of repairs is also an expense. The repair transaction is the same as the telephone bill and rent transactions. All are expense transactions.

The effect of Transaction 10 on the accounting equation is below.

	Assets				=	Liabilities		+	Capital
	Cash	Supplies	Golf Equip.	Maint. Equip.		Melcor Equip. Co.	Sasson Supply Co.		
Balances	$525	$550	$2 200	$1 250	=	$650	$350	+	$3 525
Transaction 10	−10								−10
New Balances	$515	$550	$2 200	$1 250	=	$650	$350	+	$3 515

Cash is decreased on the left side, $10.00. The amount of the owner's equity is decreased on the right side, $10.00.

The effect of Transaction 10, above, is the same as the effect for Transaction 7, page 41. *Total* assets and the owner's equity are decreased.

SUMMARY OF HOW TRANSACTIONS CHANGE THE ACCOUNTING EQUATION

The illustration below summarizes the effect of Transactions 1 to 10 on the expanded accounting equation.

	Assets				=	Liabilities		+	Capital
	Cash	Supplies	Golf Equip.	Maint. Equip.		Melcor Equip. Co.	Sasson Supply Co.		
Beg. Balances	$1 100	$500	$2 200	$ 900	=	$650	$550	+	$3 500
Transaction 1	+50			−50					
	$1 150	$500	$2 200	$ 850	=	$650	$550	+	$3 500
Transaction 2	−200						−200		
	$ 950	$500	$2 200	$ 850	=	$650	$350	+	$3 500
Transaction 3	+250								+250
	$1 200	$500	$2 200	$ 850	=	$650	$350	+	$3 750
Transaction 4	−600								−600
	$ 600	$500	$2 200	$ 850	=	$650	$350	+	$3 150
Transaction 5	+500								+500
	$1 100	$500	$2 200	$ 850	=	$650	$350	+	$3 650
Transaction 6	−50	+50							
	$1 050	$550	$2 200	$ 850	=	$650	$350	+	$3 650
Transaction 7	−25								−25
	$1 025	$550	$2 200	$ 850	=	$650	$350	+	$3 625
Transaction 8	−400			+400					
	$ 625	$550	$2 200	$1 250	=	$650	$350	+	$3 625
Transaction 9	−100								−100
	$ 525	$550	$2 200	$1 250	=	$650	$350	+	$3 525
Transaction 10	−10								−10
New Balances	$ 515	$550	$2 200	$1 250	=	$650	$350	+	$3 515

On July 1 the expanded accounting equation above shows that Mr. Rossi's equity was $3 500.00. After Transaction 10, on July 2, the expanded equation shows the owner's equity to be $3 515.00. The amount of capital increased $15.00. The change in capital resulted from the transactions below.

How transactions change the expanded accounting equation

Transaction	Kind of Transaction	Amount of Change
3	Sales	+250
4	Rent expense	−600
5	Additional investment	+500
7	Telephone expense	− 25
9	Withdrawal of cash	−100
10	Repair expense	− 10
Net change		+ 15

An increase in capital resulting from the operation of a business is known as revenue. Most of the increases in capital are from revenue. Sometimes capital will be increased by additional investment. An increase because of investment is not due to the usual operations of the business. An investment is *not* revenue.

Most of the decreases in capital for a service business are because of expense transactions. Sometimes capital is decreased by withdrawals. A withdrawal occurs when an owner removes equity from the business. Withdrawals are *not* expenses of the business.

The following basic rules summarize how transactions affect the accounting equation.

1. Each transaction changes at least two items in the expanded accounting equation. For example, Transaction 1 changed Cash and Maintenance Equipment. Transaction 2 changed Cash and Sasson Supply Company. Transaction 3 changed Cash and Capital.

2. When a transaction changes two asset items, equity is not changed. For example, Transaction 1 changed two assets, Cash and Maintenance Equipment. Neither the liabilities nor the capital were changed.

3. When a transaction changes only one asset item, at least one equity item is changed. For example, Transaction 2 changed only one asset item, Cash. The *total* amount of assets is changed. Thus, an equity item on the right side of the equation must be changed. The equity item changed by this transaction is Sasson Supply Company. Because the liability is changed, no change is made in capital.

REPORTING A CHANGED ACCOUNTING EQUATION ON A BALANCE SHEET

The owner of a business can prepare a balance sheet on any date to report the accounting equation. (*CONCEPT: Accounting Period Cycle*) For example, Harry Rossi prepared a beginning balance sheet on July 1. This beginning balance sheet reports the accounting equation on July 1. This balance sheet is shown on page 19.

Mr. Rossi may want to know how his business stands after the ten transactions have occurred. A balance sheet could be prepared for Putt Around after ten transactions have been recorded. The information for the balance sheet is on the last line of the illustration, page 43. The balance sheet is prepared using the same steps described in Chapter 2, page 20.

The balance sheet prepared on July 2 is on page 45.

Putt Around
Balance Sheet
July 2, 1988

Assets		Liabilities	
Cash	515 00	Melcor Equipment Co.	650 00
Supplies	550 00	Sasson Supply Co.	350 00
Golf Equipment	2200 00	Total Liabilities	1000 00
Maintenance Equip.	1250 00	Capital	
		Harry Rossi, Capital	3515 00
Total Assets	4515 00	Total Liab. and Capital	4515 00

A comparison of the July 2 and the July 1 balance sheets on the basic accounting equation is below.

	Assets	=	Liabilities	+	Capital
July 1, 1988	$4 700	=	$1 200	+	$3 500
July 2, 1988	4 515	=	1 000	+	3 515
Net changes	−185	=	−200	+	+15

The same basic principles are followed in preparing each balance sheet for Putt Around. The principle used is that the assets always equal the liabilities plus the capital. *(CONCEPT: Consistent Reporting)* The two balance sheet equations show that the total assets decreased by $185.00. Also the total equity decreased by $185.00 (+15.00 capital, −200.00 liabilities).

A balance sheet can be prepared on any date. In practice, most owners and managers of businesses have balance sheets prepared infrequently. The periodic preparation of balance sheets is described in more detail in Chapter 8.

ACCOUNTING TERMS

What is the meaning of each of the following?

1. transaction   **2.** revenue   **3.** expense   **4.** withdrawals

QUESTIONS FOR INDIVIDUAL STUDY

1. What is the basic accounting equation?

2. In what way does the sale of an old piece of equipment for cash change the basic equation?

3. What must be the condition of amounts in the basic accounting equation after each transaction?

4. In Transaction 1, page 39, why is the amount of equity *not* changed?

5. What is the effect of Transaction 2, page 39, on the accounting equation?
6. Why was capital increased by Transaction 3, page 39, and Transaction 5, page 40?
7. Why is capital decreased by Transaction 7, page 41?
8. What kinds of things might be withdrawn from a business by the owner for personal use?
9. Why are Transaction 4, page 40, and Transaction 10, page 42, similar?
10. Why did Mr. Rossi's capital increase from $3 500.00 on July 1 to $3 515.00 on July 2 as shown on page 43?
11. What two kinds of increases in capital are described in this chapter?
12. What two kinds of decreases in capital are described in this chapter?
13. What are the three basic ways that transactions change the expanded accounting equation?
14. What net change is shown in the accounting equations reported on the balance sheets, pages 19 and 45?

CASES FOR MANAGEMENT DECISION

CASE 1 West End Car Wash and Downtown Car Emporium both have assets totaling $20 000.00. Maria Lugo's equity in West End Car Wash is $18 000.00. Peter Donoski's equity in Downtown Car Emporium is $9 000.00. Based on this information, which of the two businesses might find it easier to get a $5 000.00 loan at a bank? Why?

CASE 2 Marion Doyle owns Riverside Golf. The business pays part of the amount owed to Compton Supply Company, $350.00. Mrs. Doyle analyses the change caused by the transaction. What two accounting factors has Mrs. Doyle overlooked in making her analysis?

	Assets			=	Liabilities	+ Capital
	Cash	Supplies	Equipment		Compton Supply Co.	
Balances	$5 000	$300	$600	=	$500	+ $5 400
Transaction	−350					
New Balances	$4 650	$300	$600	=	$500	+ $5 400

DRILLS FOR UNDERSTANDING

DRILL 3-D 1 Determining how transactions change the basic accounting equation

For each transaction below, indicate how each element in the basic accounting equation is affected: increased or decreased. Use a form similar to the following. Place a check mark in the appropriate columns. Transaction 1 is shown as an example.

Trans. No.	Assets		=	Liabilities		+	Capital	
	Increased	Decreased		Increased	Decreased		Increased	Decreased
1.	√	√						

Transactions
1. Received cash from sale of an old piece of equipment.
2. Paid cash to Mizer Company (liability) for amount owed.

3. Received cash from week's sales.
4. Paid cash for month's rent.
5. Received cash from the owner as an additional investment in the business.
6. Paid cash for supplies.
7. Paid cash for the water bill.
8. Paid cash for a new piece of equipment.
9. Paid cash to the owner for personal use.
10. Paid cash for a miscellaneous expense.

DRILL 3-D 2 Determining how transactions change the expanded accounting equation

Use a form similar to the one below. Decide which items on the expanded accounting equation are affected by each transaction listed in Drill 3-D 1. Show your decisions for each transaction by checking the + column if the item is increased and the − column if the item is decreased. Transaction 1 is given as an example.

Trans. No.	Assets								= Liabilities				+ Capital	
	Cash		Supplies		Equipment		Mizer Co.		Seitz Co.					
	+	−	+	−	+	−	+	−	+	−	+	−		
1.	√					√								

APPLICATION PROBLEMS

PROBLEM 3-1 Determining how transactions change the expanded accounting equation

Speedy Delivery Service uses the items shown on the expanded accounting equation in the form below. The transactions below and on page 48 are a sample of those completed by the delivery service during one week. Use a form similar to the one below.

Trans. No.	Assets				=	Liabilities		+	Capital
	Cash	Supplies	Truck Equip.	Office Equip.		Sayles Equip. Co.	Truck Supply Co.		
Bal. 1.	1 200 +100	100	7 000	300 −100	=	200	50	+	8 350
Bal. 2.	1 300	100	7 000	200	=	200	50	+	8 350

Transactions
1. Received cash from the sale of an old desk, $100.00.
2. Received cash from the week's sales, $500.00.
3. Paid cash for month's rent, $100.00.
4. Paid cash to owner for personal use, $100.00.

5. Paid cash for repair of an office chair, $20.00.
6. Received cash from the week's sales, $400.00.
7. Paid cash to Sayles Equipment Company for part of amount owed, $100.00.
8. Paid cash for supplies, $75.00.
9. Paid cash for a new office desk, $300.00.
10. Paid cash for the heating bill, $55.00.
11. Paid cash for gasoline bill, $75.00.

Instructions: Complete steps a, b, and c for each transaction. (a) Analyse the transaction and show the amount increased (+) and the amount decreased (−) for the items affected on the equation. Transaction 1 is shown as an example. (b) Figure the new balance for each item and write it on the next line. (c) Check that *Assets* = *Liabilities* + *Capital* for each new balance line.

PROBLEM 3-2   Determining how transactions change the expanded accounting equation

Lucy Prince operates a small motel, Middletown Gardens. The transactions below are a sample of those completed by the motel during one week. Use a form similar to the one below.

Trans. No.	Assets				=	Liabilities		+	Capital
	Cash	Supplies	Motel Equip.	Maint. Equip.		Motel Supply Co.	Melmer Laundry		
Bal. 1.	4 200 −700	500	8 000	2 000	=	4 000	1 000	+	9 700 −700
Bal. 2.	3 500	500	8 000	2 000	=	4 000	1 000	+	9 000

Transactions
1. Paid cash for the month's rent, $700.00.
2. Received cash from day's sales, $1 500.00.
3. Paid cash for a supply of business forms, $150.00.
4. Received cash from the owner as an additional investment in the business, $2 000.00.
5. Paid cash for repair to an office door, $25.00.
6. Paid cash to Motel Supply Company for part of amount owed, $2 000.00.
7. Received cash from day's sales, $1 200.00.
8. Paid cash for the electric bill, $200.00.
9. Received cash from the sale of unused chairs, $250.00.
10. Paid cash for supply of towels used in guest rooms, $325.00.
11. Received cash from day's sales, $850.00.
12. Paid cash for new equipment to be used in guest rooms, $1 000.00.
13. Paid cash to the owner for personal use, $150.00.
14. Paid cash for the telephone bill, $200.00.
15. Paid cash for amount owed to Melmer Laundry, $1 000.00.
16. Paid cash for repainting office door, $35.00.
17. Received cash from day's sales, $1 100.00.
18. Paid cash for heating oil used to heat hot water, $300.00.

Instructions: Complete steps a, b, and c for each transaction. (a) Analyse the transaction and show the amount increased (+) and the amount decreased (−) for the items affected on the equation. Transaction 1 is shown as an example. (b) Figure the new balance for each item and write it on the next line. (c) Check that *Assets* = *Liabilities* + *Capital* for each new balance line.

The solution to Problem 3-2 is needed to complete Problem 3-3.

PROBLEM 3-3 Preparing a balance sheet based on a changed accounting equation

The solution to Problem 3-2 is needed to complete Problem 3-3.

Instructions: Prepare a balance sheet using the information on the last balance line of the solution to Problem 3-2. Use the date, September 4 of the current year. Review the steps in preparing a balance sheet, Chapter 2, page 20, before starting to work.

ENRICHMENT PROBLEMS

MASTERY PROBLEM 3-M Determining how transactions change the expanded accounting equation

Isabel Cardona operates a small service business known as The Conference Reporter. The transactions below are a sample of those completed during one week by the business. Use a form similar to the one below.

Trans. No.	Assets			=	Liabilities	+	Capital
	Cash	Supplies	Equipment		Gates Supply Co.		
Bal. 1.	3 000 −300	200	600	=	100	+	3 700 −300
Bal. 2.	2 700	200	600	=	100	+	3 400

Transactions
1. Paid cash for month's rent, $300.00.
2. Paid cash for repair and cleaning of a typewriter, $45.00.
3. Paid cash for supplies, $50.00.
4. Received cash from day's recording services at a local conference, $200.00.
5. Paid cash for electric bill, $50.00.
6. Paid cash for part of the amount owed to Gates Supply Company, $50.00.
7. Paid cash to printer for a supply of business letterheads, $25.00.
8. Received cash from day's services, $175.00.
9. Paid cash to Ms. Cardona, owner, for personal use, $100.00.
10. Paid cash for a new piece of equipment, $150.00.
11. Received cash from the sale of an old piece of equipment, $25.00.
12. Paid cash for the telephone bill, $45.00.
13. Received cash from day's services, $225.00.
14. Paid cash for a new piece of equipment, $200.00.
15. Received cash from day's services, $125.00.

Instructions: 1. Complete steps a, b, and c for each transaction. (a) Analyse the transaction and show the amount increased (+) and the amount decreased (−) for the items affected on the equation. Transaction 1 is shown as an example. (b) Figure the new balance for each item and write it on the next line. (c) Check that *Assets = Liabilities + Capital* for each new balance line.

2. Prepare a balance sheet using the information on the last balance line of the solution to Instruction 1. Use the date September 11 of the current year.

CHALLENGE PROBLEM 3-C   Figuring the missing amounts in the basic accounting equation

The information below shows two of the three amounts in a basic accounting equation.

> 1. Liabilities, $1 000.00; Capital, $4 500.00.
> 2. Assets, $5 000.00; Liabilities, $2 000.00.
> 3. Assets, $6 000.00; Capital, $5 500.00.
> 4. Assets, $7 500.00; Liabilities, $1 500.00.
> 5. Liabilities, $2 500.00; Capital, $6 500.00.
> 6. Assets, $10 000.00; Capital, $7 000.00.
> 7. Liabilities, $3 000.00; Capital, $6 200.00.
> 8. Assets, $1 000.00; Liabilities, $200.00.
> 9. Assets, $2 000.00; Capital, $800.00.
> 10. Assets, $1 900.00; Liabilities, $500.00.
> 11. Liabilities, $600.00; Capital, $1 200.00.
> 12. Assets, $7 500.00; Liabilities, $400.00.
> 13. Assets, $4 650.00; Capital, $2 925.00.
> 14. Liabilities, $1 800.00; Capital, $3 600.00.
> 15. Assets, $8 500.00; Liabilities, $1 700.00.

Instructions: 1. Use a form similar to the one below. Write the amounts shown above in the correct columns. The amounts for line 1 above are shown as an example.

Line	Assets	=	Liabilities	+	Capital
1.		=	1 000.00	+	4 500.00

Instructions: 2. For each line, figure the missing amount. Write the amount in the correct column on that line. For example, line 1 in the form above needs an amount for Assets to complete the equation. The amount for line 1 is found by adding the amounts of Liabilities and Capital: $1 000.00 + $4 500.00 = $5 500.00. The amount, $5 500.00, is written in the Assets column on the first line.

Line	Assets	=	Liabilities	+	Capital
1.	5 500.00	=	1 000.00	+	4 500.00

3. After all lines have been completed, check that the equality of the basic equation has been maintained on each line. Do *Assets = Liabilities + Capital*?

Analysing Transactions into Debit and Credit Parts

ENABLING PERFORMANCE TASKS

After studying Chapter 4, you will be able to:

a. Define accounting terms related to analysing transactions into debit and credit parts.
b. Explain accounting principles and practices related to analysing transactions into debit and credit parts.
c. Use T accounts to analyse transactions showing whether accounts are debited or credited for each transaction.
d. Recognize and check that debits equal credits for each transaction.

The analysis of transactions described in Chapter 3 shows how transactions affect items in an expanded accounting equation. Using the expanded accounting equation in an accounting system is not practical. The equation analysis does not show quickly in one place all the changes in any one specific item. To see how all the transactions have changed cash, for example, the entire equation record must be checked. For this reason, businesses use ledger accounts to show in one place all the changes to a single item.

The opening entry for Putt Around is described in Chapter 2. The items in the opening entry are posted to ledger accounts as described on pages 25–27. The changes in each of these items are recorded first in a journal and then posted to the ledger accounts. Before the transactions can be recorded in a journal, the transactions are analysed to determine how the accounts are changed.

ACCOUNT BALANCES

The difference between the totals of the amounts recorded on the two sides of an account is called the account balance. Each account has a balance after the opening entry is posted as shown in Chapter 2, page 28.

51

Each asset account has a beginning balance on its debit side. Each liability account has a beginning balance on its credit side. The capital account has a beginning balance on its credit side.

Balance side of an account

The balance side of an account may be determined by an account's location on the balance sheet as shown below.

ANY BALANCE SHEET	
ANY ASSET ACCOUNT	ANY LIABILITY ACCOUNT
Balance is a debit	Balance is a credit
	THE CAPITAL ACCOUNT
	Balance is a credit

The left side of an account is known as the debit side. The right side of an account is known as the credit side. An entry made on the left side of an account is called a debit. An entry made on the right side of an account is called a credit.

An account has two sides with amount columns headed *Debit* and *Credit*. The purpose of the debit and credit sides of an account is to show increases and decreases in account balances. If an account balance is increased, the amount is shown on the balance side. If an account balance is decreased, the amount is shown on the side opposite the balance side. The illustration below shows how changes are recorded to show increases or decreases in asset accounts.

ANY ASSET ACCOUNT	
Debit side	Credit side
a. Balance 1 800.00	c. Decreases −600.00
b. Increases +50.00	

a. Beginning balance is $1 800.00; shown on the debit or balance side.
b. The account is increased, $50.00; shown on the balance or debit side.
c. The account is decreased, $600.00; shown on the side opposite the balance side, or credit side.

A skeleton form of account showing the account title and the debit and credit sides is called a T account.

After the credit entry is recorded in the T account above, the new balance is figured by finding the difference between total debits and total credits.

Total debits ($1 800.00 + 50.00)	$1 850.00
Total credits	−600.00
New debit balance	$1 250.00

When an account has only one item recorded, this single amount is the account balance. This is shown in the illustration of Putt Around's ledger, page 28. Only one item has been recorded in each account and this single amount is each account's balance.

When the total debit amounts in an account are greater than the total credit amounts, the balance is a debit. This debit balance is shown in the illustration on page 52. When the total credit amounts in an account are greater than the total debit amounts, the balance is a credit. This credit balance is shown below.

ANY LIABILITY ACCOUNT	
Debit side	Credit side
Decrease −20.00	Balance 50.00
Decrease −70.00	Increase +100.00

Total credits ($50.00 + 100.00)...................	$150.00
Total debits ($20.00 + 70.00)....................	−90.00
New credit balance	$ 60.00

The account balance when the total debits exceed the total credits is called a debit balance. The account balance when the total credits exceed the total debits is called a credit balance.

Transactions change at least two account balances

Each transaction increases or decreases the balances of two or more accounts. For example, Putt Around receives cash for a piece of old maintenance equipment, $50.00. Two accounts are affected by this transaction: Cash and Maintenance Equipment. Cash is increased because the business has more cash than before. Maintenance Equipment is decreased because the business has less maintenance equipment. This change is shown in the two T accounts below.

Cash			Maintenance Equipment		
Beg. Bal. 1 100.00			Beg. Bal. 900.00	Decrease −50.00	
Increase +50.00					

After this transaction, the balance of Cash is $1 150.00. The balance of Maintenance Equipment is $850.00.

ANALYSING TRANSACTIONS

Every transaction is recorded in a journal before being recorded in a ledger account. The reason for this procedure is to first provide a record of transactions in chronological order. The information from the beginning balance sheet, page 19, is first recorded in a journal, page 22. Second, the information is posted to ledger accounts providing a record of all changes in each account in one place. The information from the opening entry, page 22, is posted to ledger accounts, page 28.

Before a transaction is recorded in a journal, the transaction is analysed into its debit and credit parts. The analysis shows which accounts are increased and which accounts are decreased. This analysis shows which accounts will be debited and which will be credited. When analysing the effect of a transaction on accounts, the following three questions are answered.

1 *What are the names of the accounts affected?*

2 *What is the classification of each of these accounts?* The answer to this question helps determine which is the balance side of the account. When the balance side of an account is known, the increase and decrease sides can be determined.

3 *How is the balance of each account affected?* If the account is increased, is this shown by a debit or a credit? If the account is decreased, is this shown by a debit or a credit?

ANALYSING TRANSACTIONS AFFECTING ASSETS, LIABILITIES, AND CAPITAL

Each business transaction must be analysed to determine the asset, liability, or capital accounts increased or decreased by the transaction.

Transaction: Two assets affected

July 1, 1988. Received cash from sale of an old lawn mower, $50.00.

1 *What are the names of the accounts affected?* Cash and Maintenance Equipment.

2 *What is the classification of each of these accounts?* Cash is an asset with a debit balance. Maintenance Equipment is an asset with a debit balance.

3 *How is the balance of each account affected?* Cash is increased by a debit, $50.00. Maintenance Equipment is decreased by a credit, $50.00.

Cash	
Beg. Bal.	1 100.00
Increase	+50.00

The T account at the left for Cash shows a debit balance of $1 100.00 before this transaction. The transaction increases the balance, $50.00. The new balance of Cash is $1 150.00.

The T account at the right for Maintenance Equipment shows a debit balance of $900.00 before this transaction. The transaction decreases the balance by a credit of $50.00. The new balance of Maintenance Equipment is $850.00.

Maintenance Equipment			
Beg. Bal.	900.00	Decrease	−50.00

> The basic meaning of *debit* and *credit* is related to the two sides of a two-column ledger account form. This is why a skeleton T account is used to analyse a transaction into debit and credit parts.

The debit and credit parts of a transaction are always equal. The debit amount, $50.00, in the transaction, page 54, equals the credit amount, $50.00. Also, for the accounting equation, the total of asset account balances always equals the total of liability and capital balances. These two guides provide a check on the accuracy of accounting records.

Transaction: One asset and one liability affected

> *July 1, 1988. Paid cash to Sasson Supply Company, $200.00.*

1 *What are the names of the accounts affected?* Sasson Supply Company and Cash.

2 *What is the classification of each of these accounts?* Sasson Supply Company is a liability with a credit balance. Cash is an asset with a debit balance.

3 *How is the balance of each account affected?* Sasson Supply Company is decreased by a debit, $200.00. Cash is decreased by a credit, $200.00.

The T account at the right for Sasson Supply Company shows that there is a credit balance before this transaction. The transaction decreases the balance on the opposite or debit side, $200.00.

Sasson Supply Company			
Decrease	200.00	Beg. Bal.	550.00

The T account for Cash shows a debit balance. Cash decreases on the opposite or credit side. Cash is credited, $200.00.

Cash			
Beg. Bal.	1 100.00	Decrease	200.00
Increase	50.00		

One account is debited and one account is credited for $200.00. The equality of debits and credits for this transaction is maintained.

Transaction: One asset and the capital affected

> *July 1, 1988. Received cash from the owner, Harry Rossi, as an additional investment in the business, $500.00.*

1 *What are the names of accounts affected?* Cash and Harry Rossi, Capital.

2 *What is the classification of each of these accounts?* Cash is an asset with a debit balance. Harry Rossi, Capital is a capital account with a credit balance.

3 *How is the balance of each account affected?* Cash is increased by a debit, $500.00. Harry Rossi, Capital is increased by a credit, $500.00.

Cash	
Balance side +500.00	

Harry Rossi, Capital	
	Balance side +500.00

The T accounts at the left show how this transaction affects the two accounts. Cash is increased on its balance or debit side. Harry Rossi, Capital is increased on its balance or credit side. Both accounts are increased $500.00. The equality of debits and credits is maintained for this transaction.

Transaction: Two assets affected

July 2, 1988. Paid cash for supplies, $50.00.

1 *Accounts affected?* Supplies and Cash.

2 *Account classifications?* Supplies is an asset with a debit balance. Cash is an asset with a debit balance.

Supplies	
Balance side +50.00	

Cash	
Balance side	−50.00

3 *How affected?* Supplies is increased by a debit, $50.00. Cash is decreased by a credit, $50.00.

The T accounts at the left show the effect of this transaction on ledger accounts. The equality of debits and credits is maintained for this transaction.

Transaction: Two assets affected

July 2, 1988. Paid cash for a new lawn mower, $400.00.

1 *Accounts affected?* Maintenance Equipment and Cash.

2 *Account classifications?* Maintenance Equipment is an asset with a debit balance. Cash is an asset with a debit balance.

Maintenance Equipment	
Balance side +400.00	

Cash	
Balance side	−400.00

3 *How affected?* Maintenance Equipment is increased by a debit, $400.00. Cash is decreased by a credit, $400.00.

The T accounts at the left show the effect of this transaction on ledger accounts. One asset, Maintenance Equipment, is increased and another asset, Cash, is decreased. The debit, $400.00, is the same as the credit, $400.00. The equality of debits and credits is maintained.

Transaction: One asset and the capital affected

> *July 2, 1988. Paid cash to the owner, Harry Rossi, for personal use, $100.00.*

Assets taken out of a business for an owner's personal use are known as withdrawals. The value of withdrawals could be recorded as debits directly in the owner's capital account. However, common accounting practice is to record withdrawals in a separate account titled Drawing. The balance of the drawing account easily shows the total amount of assets taken out of a business. Putt Around's ledger has an account titled Harry Rossi, Drawing for recording withdrawals.

A drawing account shows decreases in an owner's capital account. Thus, a drawing account has a debit balance. A drawing account is increased by debits and decreased by credits. The cash withdrawal transaction is analysed below.

1 *Accounts affected?* Harry Rossi, Drawing and Cash.

2 *Account classifications?* Harry Rossi, Drawing is a capital account with a debit balance. Cash is an asset with a debit balance.

3 *How affected?* Harry Rossi, Drawing is increased by a debit, $100.00. Cash is decreased by a credit, $100.00.

The T accounts at the right show the effect of this transaction on ledger accounts. The drawing account is debited and the cash account is credited for $100.00. The equality of debits and credits is maintained.

Harry Rossi, Drawing	
Balance side +100.00	

Cash	
Balance side	−100.00

ANALYSING TRANSACTIONS AFFECTING REVENUE AND EXPENSES

All revenue transactions increase capital. This is shown in the illustration, Chapter 3, page 37. When cash is received from sales, the amount of revenue is increased. The entry for this transaction on the expanded equation below shows that revenue increases capital.

Assets				=	Liabilities		+	Capital
Cash	Supplies	Golf Equip.	Maint. Equip.		Melcor Equip. Co.	Sasson Supply Co.		
+250								+250

Revenue increases the total amount of assets a business has. When the *total* assets increase, an equity is also increased. Revenue accounts show increases in an owner's equity or capital. As described in Chapter 3, increases in an owner's equity *could* be shown directly as increases in the capital account. When equity increases are shown in a capital account, the records do not show ·clearly what caused all the changes. Rather than record all increases and decreases in the capital account, separate revenue accounts are used.

Businesses use a variety of titles for revenue accounts. The account title should describe the kind of information recorded in the account. A bank receives revenue from interest on loans. A bank might use the account title Interest Income or Interest Revenue. A doctor has revenue from fees collected from patients and might use the account title Fees. The owner of an apartment building receives revenue from rent. The account title could be Rent or Rent Income or Rent Revenue. Putt Around has only one source of revenue and uses the account title Sales. At Putt Around, the title Sales is understood to mean "sales revenue."

Expenses decrease the total amount of assets a business has. For each decrease in *total* assets, there is also a decrease in equities. Expenses decrease the owner's equity or capital. Rather than record all the separate expense transactions in the capital account, separate expense accounts are used. In this way, the total amount of each kind of expense can be ·easily seen. *(CONCEPT: Adequate Disclosure)* Putt Around has several major kinds of expenses. The account titles for these expense accounts are shown on the chart of accounts, page 16.

The relationship of revenue and expense accounts to the owner's capital account is shown in the diagram below.

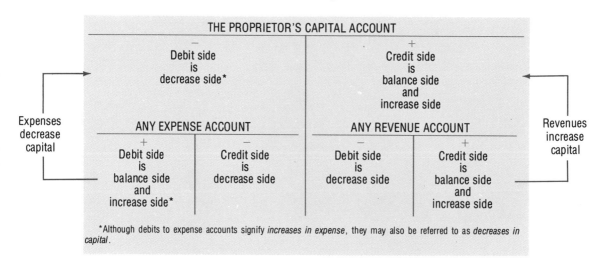

*Although debits to expense accounts signify *increases in expense*, they may also be referred to as *decreases in capital*.

The principles of debit and credit for revenue and expense accounts and their relationship to the capital account

An expense account shows decreases in the owner's capital. Decreases are shown on the debit side of a capital account. Therefore, expense accounts have debit balances. A revenue account shows increases in the owner's capital. Increases are shown on the credit side of a capital account. Therefore, revenue accounts have credit balances.

Transaction: Revenue — daily sales

July 1, 1988. Received cash from daily sales, $250.00.

The amount of revenue from *each* sale could be recorded as cash is received. The procedure would result in a large number of revenue transactions being recorded daily. To reduce the number of entries, Putt Around totals the sales revenue for each day. The *total* daily sales revenue is recorded as a single transaction at the end of each day. *(CONCEPT: Realization of Revenue)* The revenue transaction is analysed below.

1 *Accounts affected?* Cash and Sales.

2 *Account classifications?* Cash is an asset with a debit balance. Sales is a revenue account with a credit balance.

3 *How affected?* Cash is increased by a debit, $250.00. Sales is increased by a credit, $250.00.

The T accounts at the right show the effect of this transaction on ledger accounts. One account is debited, $250.00, and one account is credited, $250.00. The equality of debits and credits is maintained.

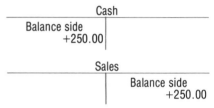

Transaction: Expense — rent

July 1, 1988. Paid cash for July rent, $600.00.

1 *Accounts affected?* Cash and Rent Expense.

2 *Account classifications?* Cash is an asset with a debit balance. Rent Expense is an expense account with a debit balance.

3 *How affected?* Cash is decreased by a credit, $600.00. Rent Expense is increased by a debit, $600.00.

The T accounts at the right show the effect of this transaction on ledger accounts. One account is debited and one account is credited for $600.00. The equality of debits and credits is maintained.

	Rent Expense	
Balance side		
+600.00		

	Cash	
Balance side		−600.00

Transaction: Expense — utility

July 2, 1988. Paid cash for telephone bill, $25.00.

Putt Around has transactions to pay for several kinds of utilities. The utilities are telephone, electricity, and water. Each of the utilities transactions is recorded as described on page 60 for the telephone bill.

1 *Accounts affected?* Cash and Utilities Expense.

2 *Account classifications?* Cash is an asset with a debit balance. Utilities Expense is an expense account with a debit balance.

Utilities Expense	
Balance side +25.00	

Cash	
Balance side	−25.00

3 *How affected?* Cash is decreased by a credit, $25.00. Utilities Expense is increased by a debit, $25.00.

The T accounts at the left show the effect of this transaction on ledger accounts. One account is debited and one account is credited for $25.00. The equality of debits and credits is maintained.

Transaction: Expense — miscellaneous

July 2, 1988. Paid cash for repair of a broken window, $10.00.

Some expense transactions occur so infrequently that a separate account is not kept in the ledger. One of these expenses is for the minor repairs to facilities and equipment. When a specific expense account is not kept for an expense, the amount is recorded in the miscellaneous expense account. The miscellaneous expense transaction is analysed below.

1 *Accounts affected?* Cash and Miscellaneous Expense.

2 *Account classifications?* Cash is an asset with a debit balance. Miscellaneous Expense is an expense account with a debit balance.

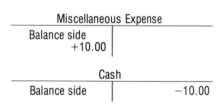

Miscellaneous Expense	
Balance side +10.00	

Cash	
Balance side	−10.00

3 *How affected?* Cash is decreased by a credit, $10.00. Miscellaneous Expense is increased by a debit, $10.00.

The T accounts at the left show the effect of this transaction on ledger accounts. One account is debited and one account is credited for $10.00. The equality of debits and credits is maintained.

SUMMARY OF HOW DEBITS AND CREDITS CHANGE LEDGER ACCOUNT BALANCES

Each ledger account kept by Putt Around has two sides, a debit side and a credit side. Each account has a balance side. An account's balance side is determined by an account's classification. Increases are recorded on an account's balance side. Decreases are recorded on the side opposite an account's balance side.

Changes in balances of asset accounts

The balance of any asset account is normally a debit. Increases in asset accounts are shown on the balance or debit side. Decreases in asset accounts are shown on the credit side opposite the balance side.

ANY ASSET ACCOUNT		ANY LIABILITY ACCOUNT	
+	−	−	+
Debit side is balance side and increase side	Credit side is decrease side	Debit side is decrease side	Credit side is balance side and increase side

The principles of debit and credit for asset and liability accounts

Changes in balances of liability accounts

The balance of any liability account is normally a credit. Increases in liability accounts are shown on the balance or credit side. Decreases in liability accounts are shown on the debit side opposite the balance side.

Changes in balances of capital accounts

The balance of a proprietor's capital account is normally a credit. Increases in the capital account are shown on the balance or credit side. Decreases are shown on the debit side opposite the balance side.

The drawing account shows decreases in the proprietor's capital account. Therefore, the owner's drawing account has a debit balance. Increases in the drawing account are shown on the balance or debit side. Decreases are shown on the credit side opposite the balance side.

THE PROPRIETOR'S CAPITAL ACCOUNT		THE PROPRIETOR'S DRAWING ACCOUNT	
−	+	+	−
Debit side is decrease side	Credit side is balance side and increase side	Debit side is balance side and increase side	Credit side is decrease side

The principles of debit and credit for the proprietor's capital and drawing accounts

Changes in balances of revenue accounts

All revenue transactions cause an increase in capital. Rather than crediting the proprietor's capital account directly, a revenue account is credited for revenue transactions.

The balance of a revenue account is normally a credit. Increases in revenue are shown on the balance or credit side. Decreases in revenue are shown on the debit side opposite the balance side.

ANY REVENUE ACCOUNT		ANY EXPENSE ACCOUNT	
−	+	+	−
Debit side is decrease side	Credit side is balance side and increase side	Debit side is balance side and increase side	Credit side is decrease side

The principles of debit and credit for revenue and expense accounts

Changes in balances of expense accounts

All expense transactions cause a decrease in capital. Rather than debiting the proprietor's capital account directly, expense accounts are debited for expense transactions. The balance of any expense account is normally a debit. Increases in expense accounts are shown on the balance or debit side. Decreases in expense accounts are shown on the credit side opposite the balance side.

Temporary capital accounts

The use of separate revenue and expense accounts provides detailed information needed for the best management of a business. The use of separate accounts keeps the proprietor's capital account from becoming cluttered with many debit and credit entries. Revenue and expense accounts used to store information until transferred to the capital account are called temporary capital accounts

How information is summarized and transferred to the capital account is described in Chapter 9.

Debits and credits in each transaction

Each transaction has a debit part and a credit part. The total debit amount equals the total credit amount in each transaction.

ACCOUNTING TERMS

What is the meaning of each of the following?

1. account balance
2. debit
3. credit
4. T account
5. debit balance
6. credit balance
7. temporary capital accounts

QUESTIONS FOR INDIVIDUAL STUDY

1. Why are ledger accounts used in accounting records?
2. What is done with information for a transaction before it is recorded in a ledger account?
3. In what way are the balances of asset accounts related to a balance sheet?
4. In what way are the balances of liability accounts related to a balance sheet?

5. In what way is the balance of the proprietor's capital account related to a balance sheet?

6. Why does a two-column ledger account have a debit and credit side?

7. On which side of an account is an increase recorded?

8. On which side of an account is a decrease recorded?

9. What kind of balance does an account have if the total debit amounts exceed the total credit amounts?

10. What kind of balance does an account have if the total credit amounts exceed the total debit amounts?

11. How many accounts are affected by each transaction?

12. What must be done with a transaction before it is recorded in a journal? Why?

13. What is the relationship of debit and credit parts for each transaction?

14. Why are increases in capital because of revenue recorded in separate revenue accounts instead of in the capital account?

15. Why do revenue accounts have credit balances?

16. Why do expense accounts have debit balances?

17. Why are revenue and expense accounts often known as temporary capital accounts?

CASES FOR MANAGEMENT DECISION

CASE 1 Wilbur Mooney owns a small business for which he bought a business machine for $520.00. He analyses this transaction as shown in the T accounts at the right. Did Mr. Mooney analyse the transaction correctly? Explain your answer.

Cash	
520.00	

Equipment	
520.00	

CASE 2 Vincente Delgado owns a beauty salon. The business receives revenue from services rendered to customers and from the sale of cosmetics. Revenue from both sources is recorded in an account titled *Sales*. Mr. Delgado would like to know how much revenue is being received from the services and how much from cosmetics. What changes in this accounting system would you suggest, and why?

CASE 3 Emi Iwasaki just bought a sports store. She finds that the former owner recorded all cash received as revenue. Miss Iwasaki believes that this is incorrect. Is the procedure correct or incorrect? Why?

DRILLS FOR UNDERSTANDING

DRILL 4-D 1   Determining the balance side, increase side, and decrease side of ledger accounts

Instructions: 1. Make a T account for each account title below. The T account for Cash is shown as an example.

Cash	

Account Titles

Cash
Office Furniture
Office Supplies
Garage Equipment

Bank of Montreal (liability)
Moser Equipment Company (liability)
Paul Richardson, Capital
Paul Richardson, Drawing

Sales
Advertising Expense
Delivery Expense
Miscellaneous Expense
Utilities Expense

Instructions: 2. Write *Debit side* and *Credit side* in each T account as in the example at the right.

Cash	
Debit side	Credit side

3. Write the words *Balance side* on the debit side of accounts that normally have debit balances. Write the words *Balance side* on the credit side of accounts that normally have credit balances. The T account at the right is an example.

Cash	
Debit side	Credit side
Balance side	

4. In each T account place a (+) on the increase side of the account. Place a (−) on the decrease side. The T account at the right is an example.

Cash	
Debit side	Credit side
Balance side	
+	−

DRILL 4-D 2   Analysing the effect of transactions on ledger accounts

The following transactions are typical of those described in Chapter 4.

1. Received cash from sale of an old piece of golf equipment.
2. Paid cash to Sasson Supply Company for amount owed.
3. Received cash from the owner as an additional investment in the business.
4. Paid cash for supplies.
5. Paid cash for a new piece of maintenance equipment.
6. Paid cash to the owner for personal use.
7. Received cash from day's sales.
8. Paid cash for month's rent.
9. Paid cash for the telephone bill.
10. Paid cash for a small repair bill.

Use a form similar to the one below.

1	2	3	4	5	6	7	8	9
Trans. No.	Account Title	Change In Account	Account Classifications					Debit or Credit
			Assets	Liabilities	Capital	Revenue	Expenses	
1.	Cash	+	√					Dr.
	Golf Equip.	−	√					Cr.

Instructions: 1. Use Putt Around's chart of accounts, page 16, for account titles. For each transaction, write in Column 2 the names of the two accounts affected. Transaction 1 is given as an example.
2. For each account title written in Column 2, place a (+) or a (−) in Column 3. The (+) or (−) shows whether the account is increased or decreased.
3. For each account title written in Column 2, place a check mark in one classification column 4-8. The check mark shows the classification of the account.
4. For each account title written in Column 2, write *Dr.* (for debit) or *Cr.* (for credit) in Column 9. The abbreviations show on which side of an account the amount is written.

PROBLEM 4-1 Analysing transactions into debit and credit parts

Ms. Sarah Plunkett operates an insurance agency. The business' ledger contains the accounts below.

Cash	Will's Garage (liability)	Sales
Office Supplies	Dolan's Stationery Store (liability)	Advertising Expense
Automobile	Jane's Equipment Company (liability)	Miscellaneous Expense
Office Furniture	Sarah Plunkett, Capital	Rent Expense
Office Machines	Sarah Plunkett, Drawing	Utilities Expense

The following are selected transactions completed by Ms. Plunkett's insurance agency:

1. Received cash from the sale of an old typewriter, $50.00.
2. Paid cash for a new business machine, $640.00.
3. Paid cash for the telephone bill, $36.00.
4. Received cash from day's sales, $780.00.
5. Paid cash for office supplies, $30.00.
6. Paid cash to Dolan's Stationery Store for part of amount owed, $100.00.
7. Received cash from the sale of an old desk, $45.00.
8. Received cash from day's sales, $275.00.
9. Paid cash for repairs to tiles on the office floor, $21.00.
10. Paid cash for the electric bill, $60.00.
11. Paid cash to the owner for personal use, $100.00.
12. Paid cash for newspaper advertising, $85.00.
13. Paid cash for a new office chair, $65.00.
14. Received cash from Ms. Plunkett as an additional investment, $1 000.00.
15. Paid cash to Jane's Equipment Company for part of amount owed, $250.00.

Instructions. Use a pair of T accounts for each transaction. Complete steps a, b, and c for each transaction. (a) Write the account titles affected on the T accounts. The T accounts at the right are examples. (b) Write the debit amount in the account to be debited. (c) Write the credit amount in the account to be credited.

1.

Cash	
50.00	

Office Machines	
	50.00

PROBLEM 4-2 Analysing transactions into debit and credit parts

Linda Russel operates a small quick-service repair shop. Some of the ledger accounts and their balances are below. When no amount is shown, the account has no beginning balance.

Cash, $1 800.00	Linda Russel, Capital, $3 980.00
Supplies, $700.00	Linda Russel, Drawing
Repair Equipment, $2 500.00	Sales
Office Equipment, $1 500.00	Advertising Expense
Bilmay Company (liability), $120.00	Miscellaneous Expense
Fell Equipment Company (liability), $2 000.00	Rent Expense
Reynolds Supply Company (liability), $400.00	Utilities Expense

Instructions: 1. Prepare T accounts for the accounts listed on page 65. Write the account balance in the T accounts for those accounts that have a balance.

2. Analyse each of the following transactions into debit and credit parts. Write the amounts in the correct T accounts for each transaction. The T accounts at the right show the accounts affected by Transaction 1 as an example.

Rent Expense	
(1) 450.00	

Cash	
Balance 1 800.00	(1) 450.00

Transactions

1. Paid cash for month's rent, $450.00.
2. Received cash from sale of an old piece of repair equipment, $30.00.
3. Received cash from sale of old broken chairs used in the office, $50.00.
4. Received cash from day's sales, $120.00.
5. Paid cash for part of amount owed to Reynolds Supply Company, $200.00.
6. Paid cash for new repair equipment, $245.00.
7. Received cash from day's sales, $235.00.
8. Paid cash for part of amount owed to Bilmay Company, $60.00.
9. Received cash from sale of an old adding machine, $20.00.
10. Paid cash for a new electronic calculator, $195.00.
11. Received cash from day's sales, $312.00.
12. Paid cash for the water bill, $48.00.
13. Paid cash for advertising placed in local newspapers, $45.00.
14. Received cash from day's sales, $275.00.
15. Paid cash for electric bill, $120.00.
16. Received cash from day's sales, $318.00.
17. Paid cash for telephone bill, $52.00.
18. Paid cash to the owner for personal use, $100.00.
19. Received cash from day's sales, $238.00.
20. Received cash from the owner as an additional investment in the business, $300.00.

ENRICHMENT PROBLEMS

MASTERY PROBLEM 4-M   Analysing transactions into debit and credit parts

William Alpine operates Makeway Delivery Service.

Instructions: 1. Prepare a T account for each of the ledger accounts used by the business. Cash; Delivery Equipment; Office Equipment; Creditable Motors (liability); William Alpine, Capital; William Alpine, Drawing; Delivery Revenue; Advertising Expense; Delivery Truck Expense; Miscellaneous Expense; and Telephone Expense.

2. For each of the following accounts, write the balance on the correct side of the T account. Cash, $1 350.00; Delivery Equipment, $8 640.00; Office Equipment, $1 520.00; Creditable Motors, $3 780.00; William Alpine, Capital, $7 730.00.

3. Analyse each of the transactions on page 67 into debit and credit parts. Write the amounts in the correct T accounts. The T accounts at the right are an example for Transaction 1.

Telephone Expense	
(1) 45.90	

Cash	
Balance 1 350.00	(1) 45.90

Transactions

1. Paid cash for telephone bill, $45.90.
2. Received cash from day's delivery revenue, $532.00.
3. Paid cash for gas and oil used in the delivery truck, $22.50.
4. Paid cash for a new office desk and chair, $297.00.
5. Received cash from the owner as an additional investment in the business, $1 000.00.
6. Paid cash for washing the delivery truck, $6.00.
7. Received cash from day's delivery revenue, $484.00.
8. Paid cash for leather gloves used by Mr. Alpine as part of his work, $10.00.
9. Paid cash for part of amount owed to Creditable Motors, $500.00.
10. Paid cash for new electronic calculator for use in the office, $225.00.
11. Paid cash for the electric bill, $75.00.
12. Received cash from day's delivery revenue, $560.00.
13. Paid cash for gas and oil used in the delivery truck, $117.00.
14. Paid cash to the owner for personal use, $100.00.
15. Paid cash for advertising in local newspaper, $60.00.
16. Paid cash for month's rent, $400.00.
17. Received cash from day's delivery revenue, $540.00.

CHALLENGE PROBLEM 4-C   Analyzing transactions already recorded in T accounts

Nancy Withers operates a car wash. The T accounts below show the beginning account balances and the debit and credit parts of transactions completed by the car wash.

Cash			
Balance	360.00	(1)	19.00
(3)	400.00	(2)	280.00
(6)	2 960.00	(4)	16.00
(8)	400.00	(5)	18.00
(11)	120.00	(7)	3 600.00
		(9)	36.00
		(10)	6.00
		(12)	160.00

Nancy Withers, Capital			
		Balance	3 680.00
		(3)	400.00

Car Wash Sales			
		(8)	400.00
		(11)	120.00

Truck			
Balance	2 960.00	(6)	2 960.00
(7)	3 600.00		

Advertising Expense			
(1)	19.00		
(5)	18.00		

Car Wash Equipment			
Balance	680.00		
(2)	280.00		

Car Wash Expense			
(9)	36.00		

Robert Mercer Equipment Co.			
(12)	160.00	Balance	320.00

Miscellaneous Expense			
(4)	16.00		
(10)	6.00		

Use a form similar to the one below.

1	2	3	4	5	6	7	8
Trans. No.	Account Debited			Account Credited			Description of the Transaction
	Title	Classification	Effect	Title	Classification	Effect	
1.	Advertising Expense	Expense	+	Cash	Asset	−	Paid cash for advertising expense

Instructions: 1. For each transaction, write the title of the account debited in Column 2. Write the title of the account credited in Column 5. Transaction 1 is recorded as an example. Transaction 1 can be identified with the (1) before the two amounts in the T accounts.

2. For each transaction, write the debited account's classification in Column 3. Write the credited account's classification in Column 6.

3. For each transaction, write in Column 4 whether the debited account is increased (+) or decreased (−). Write the same symbols in Column 7 to show whether the credited account is increased or decreased.

4. Write in Column 8 a brief description of each transaction.

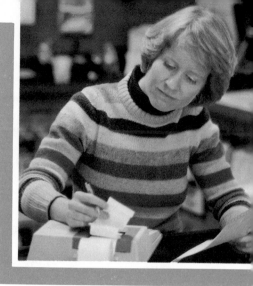

5

Journalizing Business Transactions

ENABLING PERFORMANCE TASKS

After studying Chapter 5, you will be able to:

a. Define accounting terms related to journalizing business transactions.
b. Explain accounting principles and practices related to journalizing business transactions.
c. Record transactions in a multi-column cash journal.
d. Prove cash.
e. Prove equality of debits and credits in a cash journal.
f. Total, rule, and forward totals from one page to another in a cash journal.
g. Rule a cash journal.

Before a transaction can be recorded, the transaction is analysed into its debit and credit parts. The procedure for analysing transactions is described in Chapter 4. After each transaction is analysed into its debit and credit parts, the transaction is recorded in a journal. Recording a business transaction in a journal is called journalizing .

Reasons for recording transactions in journals

As described in Chapter 4, information about each transaction could be recorded on a form showing an expanded accounting equation. However, generally accepted accounting practice requires a more permanent record of each transaction. A journal provides an orderly record from which information is posted to accounts in a ledger. The reasons why transactions are recorded first in a journal and not recorded directly in ledger accounts are below.

1. Accuracy. A journal entry shows the debit and credit parts of each transaction in one place. The equality of the debit and credit amounts is readily seen by looking at a journal entry. If only part of a transaction is recorded in one place, the omissions may not be easily seen. Errors in recording a transaction can be corrected in a journal before the information is posted to ledger accounts.

2. Chronological record of transactions. A journal contains the day-to-day transactions listed according to the date of the transactions. When facts about a transaction are needed some months or days afterwards, the journal is an easy source to use.

If transactions are recorded first in ledger accounts, the debit and credit parts will be on different pages. This procedure makes it difficult to find both the debit and credit parts of a single, specific transaction.

Double-entry accounting is complete accounting

The recording of the debit and credit parts of a transaction is called double-entry accounting. Double-entry accounting, used in most well-organized businesses, provides a complete record of each transaction. Complete accounting *is* double-entry accounting.

JOURNALIZING TRANSACTIONS IN A GENERAL JOURNAL

A two-column general journal is used by Putt Around for recording an opening entry. This procedure is described in Chapter 2, pages 22 and 23. A two-column general journal *could* be used to record all transactions of a business. For example, the five July 1 transactions described in Chapter 4 appear below.

	GENERAL JOURNAL			PAGE 1	
DATE	ACCOUNT TITLE	POST. REF.	DEBIT	CREDIT	
1	Cash		50 00		
	Maintenance Equipment			50 00	
	Receipt No. 10.				
1	Sasson Supply Company		200 00		
	Cash			200 00	
	Cheque No. 20.				
1	Cash		250 00		
	Sales			250 00	
	Cash Register Tape No. 1.				
1	Rent Expense		600 00		
	Cash			600 00	
	Cheque No. 21.				
1	Cash		500 00		
	Harry Rossi, Capital			500 00	
	Receipt No. 11.				

Entries recorded in a two-column general journal

Using *only* a two-column general journal has a disadvantage. Much space and time is required to record many transactions in a two-column general journal. To save time and space, Putt Around uses a cash journal described in this chapter.

A CASH JOURNAL

All but a few of the entries made in Putt Around's journals are cash transactions. Therefore, Putt Around uses one journal in which to record only cash transactions. Entries for other than cash transactions are recorded in a two-column general journal. The opening entry for Putt Around, described in Chapter 2, is not a cash transaction. For this reason the opening entry is recorded in a two-column general journal. A journal used to record only one kind of transaction is called a special journal. A special journal used only for cash transactions is called a cash journal.

Other kinds of special journals are described in Part 5.

Form of a cash journal

The cash journal used by Putt Around is shown below.

CASH		DATE	ACCOUNT TITLE	DOC. NO.	POST. REF.	GENERAL		SALES CREDIT	
DEBIT	CREDIT					DEBIT	CREDIT		
		1953 July 1	Balance on hand, $1,100.00		✓				1
5000		1	Maintenance Equipment	R10			5000		2
	20000	1	Sasson Supply Company	C20		20000			3
25000		1	✓	J1	✓			25000	4
	60000	1	Rent Expense	C21		60000			5
50000		1	Harry Rossi, Capital	R11			50000		6
									7

The five transactions recorded in the cash journal above are the same as those in the general journal, page 70.

Entries recorded in a cash journal

The entry on line 1 of the cash journal above is not for a business transaction. This entry is explained later in this chapter on page 73.

The form of a cash journal is different from that of a general journal. The cash journal has additional amount columns. The additional amount columns have account titles in the column headings. A journal amount column headed with an account title is called a special amount column. A special amount column is provided for each account for which many entries are made each month. For example, most of Putt Around's transactions result in either a debit or a credit to Cash. For this reason, the cash journal has both *Cash Debit* and *Cash Credit* special amount columns. Also, Putt Around has many entries for sales. Sales transactions result in a credit to Sales. For this reason, the cash journal has a *Sales Credit* amount column. The General Debit and General Credit amount columns are used for accounts that are affected infrequently by transactions.

The Cash Debit and Cash Credit columns are placed at the left of the Date column in the cash journal, page 71. These amount columns could have been placed at the right along with the other amount columns. However, with the Cash columns at the left, the amount of cash on hand can be easily checked.

Putt Around's first transaction in July is for cash received from the sale of equipment, $50.00. This entry is shown in the general journal, page 70, lines 9–11. The entry requires three lines in the general journal. The same entry is shown in the cash journal, page 71, line 2. The entry requires only one line in the cash journal. The account title, Cash, is written on line 9 of the general journal, page 70. On line 2 of the cash journal, page 71, only the amount is written in the Cash Debit column. The name of the account is not written because it is already in the column heading.

Advantages in using a cash journal

A cash journal with special amount columns has several advantages.

1. *Less space is required for recording* journal entries in a cash journal than in a two-column general journal. For example, the first transaction in both journals records $50.00 for the sale of an old piece of equipment. Each entry records the same information. The entry in the general journal requires three lines. The entry in the cash journal requires only one line. Thus, if used for all transactions, a two-column general journal is bulkier than a cash journal.

2. *Less time is required for recording* transactions in a cash journal than in a two-column general journal. A general journal entry requires that at least two account titles be written in the Account Title column. One account title is for the debit part and one is for the credit part of the entry. A cash journal entry requires that usually no more than one account title be written. The "cash" part of the transaction is recorded in one of the special Cash columns. For some transactions, both the debit and credit amounts are recorded in special amount columns. Using special amount columns eliminates the need to write an account title in the Account Title column. On line 4 of the cash journal, page 71, both the debit and credit amounts are recorded in special columns. A check mark ($\sqrt{}$) is placed in the Account Title column. The check mark shows that no account title needs to be written. The check mark also shows that the writing of an account title has not been overlooked.

3. *Less time is required for posting* from a cash journal than from a general journal. Every amount recorded in a two-column general journal is posted individually. The amounts entered in special columns

of the cash journal are not posted individually. Only the total of a special column is posted. Posting from a cash journal is described in Chapter 6.

Each business plans for amount columns in its cash journal to fit its needs. Examples of journals with various special columns are described in Chapters 11, 12, 20, and 21.

JOURNALIZING TRANSACTIONS IN A CASH JOURNAL

Before a transaction is recorded in any journal, the transaction is analysed into its debit and credit parts. The procedure for analysing transactions is described in Chapter 4.

Recording the cash on hand in a cash journal

A business sometimes needs to know the amount of cash that was on hand at the beginning of a month. The first line of a cash journal is used each month to record this information. This entry is not posted since this information is already in the cash account. This procedure avoids having to check the cash account in the general ledger to find the beginning cash balance.

On July 1, 1988, Putt Around's cash balance on hand, $1 100.00, is recorded on line 1 of the cash journal, page 71. The entry, including the amount, is written in the Account Title column. The year, month, and day are written in the Date column. A check mark is placed in the Post. Ref. column. The check mark shows that nothing is to be posted from this line. Nothing is written in the amount columns.

Source documents used for journalizing transactions

A business paper is prepared describing a transaction in detail. For example, a cheque stub is prepared for each cheque issued. Cheque stubs are the source documents for cash payments transactions. *(CONCEPT: Objective Evidence)*

When cash is received from sales, the amount is entered on a cash register. The cash register prints the amount on a paper tape inside the register. The paper tapes are the source documents for cash sales transactions. When cash is received from sources other than sales, a written receipt is prepared. This written receipt is the source document. A business paper from which information is obtained for any journal entry is known as a source document.

Journalizing a sale of an asset

July 1, 1988. Received cash from the sale of an old lawn mower, $50.00. Receipt No. 10.

Source document for a sale of an asset. A written acknowledgment given when cash is received is called a receipt. When Putt Around receives cash other than from sales, a receipt is prepared. Before preparing a receipt, a receipt stub is prepared. The receipt stub is the source document for a cash received transaction. *(CONCEPT: Objective Evidence)* Journal entries are made from information on the receipt stub. The receipt is given to the person from whom the cash is received. The receipt stub is kept by Putt Around.

The receipt stub and receipt issued by Putt Around for the $50.00 received for an old lawn mower are below.

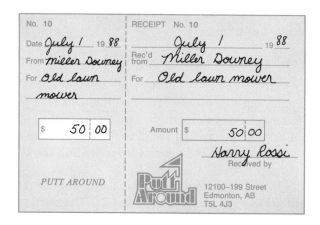

Receipt stub and receipt

Recording a sale of an asset. This transaction is analysed into debit and credit parts before it is recorded in a journal. The analysis of this transaction is described on pages 54 and 55. The results of the analysis are repeated in the T accounts at the left.

Cash	
50.00	

Maintenance Equipment	
	50.00

For this transaction, the balance of the asset Cash is increased by a debit, $50.00. The balance of the asset account Maintenance Equipment is decreased by a credit, $50.00. The entry to record this transaction is on line 2 of the cash journal, page 71.

This transaction is recorded in the cash journal as described below.

1 *Date of entry.* Write the date in the Date column. The year and month have already been written on this page. Therefore, only the day, *1*, needs to be written.

2 *Debit part of entry.* Debit the cash account by writing *$50.00* in the Cash Debit column on line 2. Writing *Cash* in the Account Title column is *not* necessary. The column heading, *Cash Debit*, shows that all amounts are debits to the cash account.

3 *Credit part of entry.* Credit the maintenance equipment account by writing $50.00 in the General Credit column. Also, write *Maintenance Equipment* in the Account Title column.

> The General Debit and Credit columns are used for accounts for which there are no special columns. The account title is written for each amount recorded in a General amount column.

4 *Indication of source document.* Write *R10* in the Doc. No. column to show that Receipt No. 10 is issued in this transaction. The letter *R* stands for *receipt*. The number *10* shows that this is Receipt No. 10. The number is obtained from the receipt stub.

> The journal entry does not show what item of maintenance equipment was sold. *R10* in the Doc. No. column of the cash journal shows where detailed information can be obtained. Therefore, such details are not repeated in the journal entry.

Journalizing a part payment of a liability

> July 1, 1988. Paid cash to Sasson Supply Company for part of the amount owed, $200.00. Cheque No. 20.

Source document for a part payment of a liability. A business form ordering a bank to pay cash from a depositor's bank account is called a cheque. Most businesses use cheques to make all major cash payments. Cheques are safer than money to send through the mail. After a cheque is cashed and processed, the bank returns it to the business that wrote it. The returned cheque shows that payment has been made.

The source document for recording a cash payment transaction is a cheque stub. *(CONCEPT: Objective Evidence)* Each cheque stub should be filled out completely. A cheque stub should contain all the information needed for journalizing a cash payments transaction.

The cheque stub and cheque prepared by Putt Around for the part payment to Sasson Supply Company are below.

Cheque stub and cheque

Recording a part payment of a liability. The analysis of this transaction into its debit and credit parts is explained on page 55. Line 3 of the illustration, page 71, shows how this transaction is recorded in a cash journal.

The steps in journalizing this transaction in a cash journal are below.

1 *Date of entry.* Write the day of the month, *1*, in the Date column.

2 *Debit part of entry.* Debit the Sasson Supply Company account by writing *$200.00* in the General Debit column. Also, write *Sasson Supply Company* in the Account Title column.

3 *Credit part of entry.* Credit Cash by writing *$200.00* in the Cash Credit column. The column heading, *Cash Credit*, shows the account to be credited. There is no need to write the account title.

4 *Indication of source document.* Write C20 in the Doc. No. column to show that Cheque No. 20 is issued for this transaction. C stands for *cheque.* The cheque number is obtained from the cheque stub. The cheque number in the Doc. No. column shows which cheque stub contains additional details about the transaction. Since this information can be located quickly, these details are not recorded in a journal.

Journalizing a revenue transaction

July 1, 1988. Received cash from daily sales, $250.00. Cash Register Tape No. T1.

Source document for a revenue transaction. All cash sales for each day are totalled at the end of the day. To save time, only one transaction is recorded for the total daily sales. *(CONCEPT: Realization of Revenue)* At the end of each day, Putt Around's cash register prints the total amount of the day's sales. A paper tape inside a cash register on which details of transactions are printed is called a detail tape. The tape for the day is removed from the cash register and numbered with an abbreviation, *T1.* The letter *T* is used by Putt Around as an abbreviation for *cash register tape.* The number *1* is the date on which the tape was printed by the cash register. The cash register tape is used as the source document for daily cash sales transactions. *(CONCEPT: Objective Evidence)*

Recording a revenue transaction. The July 1 daily cash sales transaction is analysed as described on page 59. The result of this analysis is recorded in Putt Around's cash journal, line 4, page 71.

The steps in journalizing this transaction in a cash journal are below.

1 *Date of entry.* Write the day of the month, *1*, in the Date column.

2 *Debit part of entry.* Debit the cash account by writing $250.00 in the Cash Debit column.

3 *Credit part of entry.* Credit the sales account by writing $250.00 in the Sales Credit column. Writing the account title *Sales* is not necessary. The heading of the special column shows clearly that the sales account is to be credited. Place a check mark in the Account Title column. A check mark shows that no account title needs to be written for this entry.

> Revenue from sales occurs almost daily at Putt Around. Thus, a special column for *Sales Credit* is provided in the cash journal. This special column saves time in journalizing.

4 *Indication of source document.* Write *T1* in the Doc. No. column. *T1* shows which cash register tape is the source document for this entry.

5 *For CASH sales only.* Place a check mark in the Post. Ref. column. This check mark shows that no separate amounts are to be posted from this line of the journal. Posting from special amount columns is described in Chapter 6.

Journalizing an expense transaction

July 1, 1988. Paid cash for July rent, $600.00. Cheque No. 21.

Source document for an expense transaction. The source document for this expense transaction is the cheque stub for Cheque No. 21. *(CONCEPT: Objective Evidence)*

Recording an expense transaction. This rent expense transaction is analysed into debit and credit parts as described on page 59. The entry is on line 5 of the cash journal below.

| | CASH | | DATE | ACCOUNT TITLE | DOC. NO. | POST. REF. | GENERAL | | SALES CREDIT | |
	DEBIT	CREDIT					DEBIT	CREDIT		
5		600 00		1 *Rent Expense*	C 21		600 00			5
6	500 00			1 *Harry Rossi, Capital*	R 11			500 00		6
7		50 00		2 *Supplies*	C 22		50 00			7
8		25 00		2 *Utilities Expense*	C 23		25 00			8
9		400 00		2 *Maintenance Equipment*	C 24		400 00			9
10		100 00		2 *Harry Rossi, Drawing*	C 25		100 00			10
11		10 00		2 *Miscellaneous Expense*	C 26		10 00			11
12										12
13										13

CASH JOURNAL   PAGE 1

Cash journal

The steps in recording this transaction in a cash journal are below.

1 *Date of entry.* Write the day of the month, *1*, in the Date column.

2 *Debit part of entry.* Debit the rent expense account by writing *$600.00* in the General Debit column. Also, write *Rent Expense* in the Account Title column.

3 *Credit part of entry.* Credit the cash account by writing *$600.00* in the Cash Credit column.

4 *Indication of source document.* Write *C21* in the Doc. No. column to show that Cheque No. 21 is issued for this transaction.

Journalizing an additional investment by an owner

July 1, 1988. Received cash from Harry Rossi, owner, as an additional investment in the business, $500.00. Receipt No. 11.

Source document for an additional investment by an owner. Cash received from a sales transaction is recorded on a cash register by Putt Around. Cash received from all other sources is recorded on printed receipt forms. The preparation of receipt forms is described on page 74. The source document for an additional investment transaction is the receipt stub prepared when the cash is received. *(CONCEPT: Objective Evidence)*

Recording an additional investment by an owner. This transaction is analysed into debit and credit parts as described on pages 55 and 56. The entry to record this transaction is on line 6 of the cash journal, page 77.

The steps in recording this transaction in a cash journal are below.

1 *Date of entry.* Write the day of the month, *1*, in the Date column.

2 *Debit part of entry.* Write the debit amount, *$500.00*, in the Cash Debit column. The name of an account need not be written in the Account Title column. The name of the account is already in the amount column heading.

3 *Credit part of entry.* Write the credit amount, *$500.00*, in the General Credit column. This amount is written in the General Credit column because there is no special amount column for Capital Credit. Write the name of the account, *Harry Rossi, Capital*, in the Account Title column. This account title is needed to show to which account the amount in the General Credit column will be posted.

4 *Source document.* Write the abbreviation for the source document, *R11*, in the Doc. No. column.

Journalizing a buying of supplies transaction

July 2, 1988. Paid cash for supplies, $50.00. Cheque No. 22.

Source document for a buying of supplies transaction. The cheque stub written for Cheque No. 22 is the source document for this transaction. *(CONCEPT: Objective Evidence)*

Recording a buying of supplies transaction. This transaction is analysed into debit and credit parts as described on page 56. The entry to record this transaction is on line 7 of the cash journal, page 77.

The steps in recording this transaction in a cash journal are below.

1 *Date of entry.* Write the date, *2*, in the Date column.

2 *Debit part of entry.* Write the debit amount, *$50.00*, in the General Debit column. Also, write *Supplies* in the Account Title column.

3 *Credit part of entry.* Write the credit amount, *$50.00*, in the Cash Credit column.

4 *Source document.* Write the abbreviation for the source document, *C22*, in the Doc. No. column.

Journalizing a utilities expense transaction

July 2, 1988. Paid cash for telephone bill, $25.00. Cheque No. 23.

Source document for a utilities expense transaction. The source document is the cheque stub for Cheque No. 23. *(CONCEPT: Objective Evidence)*

Recording a utilities expense transaction. This transaction is analysed into its debit and credit parts as described on pages 59 and 60. The entry to record this transaction is shown on line 8 of the cash journal, page 77.

The steps in recording this transaction in a cash journal are below.

1 *Date.* Write the day of the month, *2*, in the Date column.

2 *Debit part.* Write the debit amount, *$25.00*, in the General Debit column. Also, write *Utilities Expense* in the Account Title column.

3 *Credit part.* Write the credit amount, *$25.00*, in the Cash Credit column.

4 *Source document.* Write *C23* in the Doc. No. column.

Journalizing a buying of equipment transaction

> *July 2, 1988. Paid cash for a new lawn mower, $400.00. Cheque No. 24.*

Source document for a buying of equipment transaction. The source document for this transaction is the cheque stub for Cheque No. 24. *(CONCEPT: Objective Evidence)*

Recording a buying of equipment transaction. This transaction is analysed into debit and credit parts as described on page 56. The entry to record this transaction is on line 9 of the cash journal, page 77.

The steps in recording this transaction in a cash journal are below.

1 *Date.* Write the day of the month, 2, in the Date column.

2 *Debit part.* Write the debit amount, $400.00, in the General Debit column. Also, write *Maintenance Equipment* in the Account Title column.

3 *Credit part.* Write the credit amount, $400.00, in the Cash Credit column.

4 *Source document.* Write *C24* in the Doc. No. column.

Journalizing a cash withdrawal transaction

> *July 2, 1988. Paid cash to the owner, Harry Rossi, for personal use, $100.000. Cheque No. 25.*

Source document for a cash withdrawal transaction. The cheque stub for Cheque No. 25 is the source document for this transaction. *(CONCEPT: Objective Evidence)*

Recording a cash withdrawal transaction. This transaction is analysed into debit and credit parts as described on page 57. The entry to record this transaction is on line 10 of the cash journal, page 77.

The steps in recording this transaction in a cash journal are below.

1 *Date.* Write the date, 2, in the Date column.

2 *Debit part.* Write the debit amount, $100.00, in the General Debit column. Also, write *Harry Rossi, Drawing* in the Account Title column.

3 *Credit part.* Write the credit amount, $100.00, in the Cash Credit column.

4 *Source document.* Write the abbreviation, *C25*, in the Doc. No. column.

Journalizing a miscellaneous expense transaction

> *July 2, 1988. Paid cash for repair of broken window, $10.00. Cheque No. 26.*

Some expenses occur infrequently. Separate expense accounts are used only for the frequently occurring expenses. Those expenses occurring infrequently are recorded in an account titled Miscellaneous Expense.

Source document for a miscellaneous expense transaction. The source document for this transaction is the cheque stub for No. 26. *(CONCEPT: Objective Evidence)*

Recording a miscellaneous expense transaction. This transaction is analysed into debit and credit parts as described on page 60. The entry to record this transaction is shown on line 11 of the cash journal, page 77.

The steps in recording this transaction in a cash journal are below.

1 *Date.* Write the date, *2*, in the Date column.

2 *Debit part.* Write the debit amount, *$10.00*, in the General Debit column. Also, write *Miscellaneous Expense* in the Account Title column.

3 *Credit part.* Write the credit amount, *$10.00*, in the Cash Credit column.

4 *Source document.* Write *C26* in the Doc. No. column.

Journalizing other business transactions

Putt Around's transactions for the remainder of July are similar to those described in this chapter. The complete July cash journal for Putt Around is on pages 82 and 83.

Each transaction recorded by Putt Around during July requires a single line in the cash journal. Much time and space is saved by using a multi-column cash journal instead of a two-column general journal.

PROVING THE ACCURACY OF A CASH JOURNAL

The accuracy of recording in a cash journal must be checked. The procedures for verifying the accuracy of accounting work are known as proving.

	CASH		DATE	ACCOUNT TITLE	DOC. NO.	POST. REF.	GENERAL		SALES CREDIT	
	DEBIT	CREDIT					DEBIT	CREDIT		
				CASH JOURNAL					PAGE *1*	
1			1989 July 1	Balance on hand, $1 100.00		✓				1
2	5000		1	Maintenance Equipment	R10			5000		2
3		20000	1	Sasson Supply Company	C20		20000			3
4	25000		1	✓	J1	✓			25000	4
5		60000	1	Rent Expense	C21		60000			5
6	50000		1	Harry Rossi, Capital	R11			50000		6
7		5000	2	Supplies	C22		5000			7
8		2500	2	Utilities Expense	C23		2500			8
9		40000	2	Maintenance Equipment	C24		40000			9
10		10000	2	Harry Rossi, Drawing	C25		10000			10
11		1000	2	Miscellaneous Expense	C26		1000			11
12	10000		2	✓	J2	✓			10000	12
13	20000		3	✓	J3	✓			20000	13
14		6000	5	Utilities Expense	C27		6000			14
15	10000		5	✓	J5	✓			10000	15
16		2500	6	Advertising Expense	C28		2500			16
17	10000		6	✓	J6	✓			10000	17
18		1000	7	Miscellaneous Expense	C29		1000			18
19	8000		7	✓	J7	✓			8000	19
20	4500		8	✓	J8	✓			4500	20
21	5500		9	✓	J9	✓			5500	21
22	15000		10	✓	J10	✓			15000	22
23		7500	12	Supplies	C30		7500			23
24		10000	12	Golf Equipment	C31		10000			24
25	5200		12	✓	J12	✓			5200	25
26	168200	165500	12	Carried Forward		✓	165500	55000	113200	26
27										27

Completed cash journal

Proving the accuracy of each entry in a cash journal

Each transaction has an equal debit and credit part. After a transaction is recorded in any journal, the equality of debits and credits must be checked for that transaction. For example, the transaction on line 2 of the cash journal above has both a $50.00 debit and a $50.00 credit. Debits and credits are equal.

Proving the entire cash journal

The equality of all debits and credits for all entries in any journal must also be proved. Also, cash must be proved. These proofs are made before a cash journal is completed at the end of each month.

Proving cash. Determining that the amount of cash on hand agrees with the accounting records is called proving cash. Cash on hand includes the money in the bank plus all cash not deposited in the bank. Cash is proved daily in many businesses. Cash is always proved at the end of a month. Putt Around finds that proving cash once a month is sufficient. The amount of cash received is not great enough to require more frequent proof.

CASH JOURNAL   PAGE 2

CASH DEBIT	CASH CREDIT	DATE	ACCOUNT TITLE	DOC. NO.	POST. REF.	GENERAL DEBIT	GENERAL CREDIT	SALES CREDIT	
168200	165500	1988 July 12	Brought Forward		✓	165500	55000	113200	1
6000		13	✓	J13	✓			6000	2
8000		14	✓	J14	✓			8000	3
	1500	15	Miscellaneous Expense	C32		1500			4
5000		15	✓	J15	✓			5000	5
10000		16	✓	J16	✓			10000	6
15000		17	✓	J17	✓			15000	7
4000		19	✓	J19	✓			4000	8
	3200	20	Utilities Expense	C33		3200			9
4500		20	✓	J20	✓			4500	10
5100		21	✓	J21	✓			5100	11
	1800	22	Miscellaneous Expense	C34		1800			12
4300		22	✓	J22	✓			4300	13
	5000	23	Harry Rossi, Drawing	C35		5000			14
7500		23	✓	J23	✓			7500	15
	10000	24	Supplies	C36		10000			16
17500		24	✓	J24	✓			17500	17
3000		26	✓	J26	✓			3000	18
	500	27	Miscellaneous Expense	C37		500			19
4500		27	✓	J27	✓			4500	20
4000		28	✓	J28	✓			4000	21
5000		29	✓	J29	✓			5000	22
	1200	30	Miscellaneous Expense	C38		1200			23
8800		30	✓	J30	✓			8800	24
17500		31	✓	J31	✓			17500	25
297900	188700	31	Totals			188700	55000	242900	26

Completed cash journal

Putt Around proves cash at the end of July as explained below.

Beginning cash balance	$1 100.00
(This is the amount of cash on hand at the beginning of July. The amount is taken from line 1 of the cash journal, page 82.)	
Plus cash received during the month.............................	2 979.00
(This amount is the total of the Cash Debit column in the cash journal. The amount is found by adding the column.)	
Equals total	$4 079.00
Less cash paid out during the month.............................	1 887.00
(This amount is the total of the Cash Credit column in the cash journal.)	
Equals cash on hand at the end of the month..................	$2 192.00

The last amount in the cash proof, $2 192.00, should be the same as the amount of cash on hand. On July 31, 1988, all cash receipts have been deposited in the bank by Putt Around. Cheque Stub No. 39 in Putt Around's chequebook shows a balance of $2 192.00. The cash proof agrees with the chequebook balance. Cash is proved.

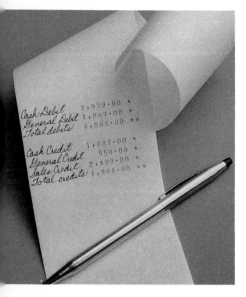

Totalling a cash journal. At the end of each month, a calculator is used by Putt Around to total all columns of the cash journal. Then, the totals of all debit columns are added. Also, the totals of all credit columns are added. The calculator tape at the left shows this work for the cash journal, page 83. The column headings from the cash journal are handwritten on the tape to help identify each amount.

As shown on the calculator tape, the total of the debit columns is $4 866.00. The total of the credit columns is also $4 866.00. The equality of the debits and credits in the complete journal has been maintained. Therefore, Putt Around assumes that the journal is accurate.

> If the total of all debits is not equal to the total of all credits, an error has been made. The error or errors must be found and corrected. No more work should be done until the errors are corrected.

Proving a journal

Three accuracy checks of the cash journal are made by Putt Around.
1. As each transaction is recorded, the equality of debits and credits is checked.
2. At the end of each month, cash is proved.
3. At the end of each month, the equality of debits and credits for the entire cash journal is checked.

RULING A CASH JOURNAL

When the three accuracy checks are made and proved, the cash journal is ruled.

Ruling a cash journal at the end of a month

At the end of each month, Putt Around's cash journal is ruled as shown below.

| CASH | | DATE | ACCOUNT TITLE | DOC. NO. | POST. REF. | GENERAL | | SALES CREDIT | |
DEBIT	CREDIT					DEBIT	CREDIT		
175000		31	✓	231	✓			175000	25
297900	188700	31	*Totals*			188700	55000	242900	26
									27

Cash journal totalled, proved, and ruled

The steps in ruling Putt Around's cash journal are below.

1 Draw a single line across all amount columns. The single line shows that the columns are being added.

2 Write the total of each column below the single line. The totals are taken from the calculator tape, page 84, prepared to prove the cash journal.

> If a calculator is not available, the columns may be added mentally. The totals are then written on a separate piece of paper.

3 Write the last day of the month in the date column.

4 Write the word *Totals* in the Account Title column.

5 Draw double lines across all amount columns below the column totals. The double lines show that the work of totalling and ruling is completed.

Forwarding totals to a new page

Sometimes a page in a cash journal is filled before the end of a month. If this happens, the page is totalled and the totals forwarded to a new page. The illustration below shows page 1 of Putt Around's cash journal with totals prepared for forwarding.

The steps in forwarding totals to a new journal page are below.

Column totals prepared for forwarding to a new page of a cash journal

1 Total all columns of the completed page.

2 Prove the equality of the debits and credits.

3 Draw a single line across all amount columns.

4 Write the total of each column below the single line.

5 Write the date in the Date column.

6 Write the words *Carried Forward* in the Account Title column.

7 Place a check mark in the Post. Ref. column to show that none of these totals is to be posted.

8 Draw double lines across all amount columns.

The illustration below shows page 2 of Putt Around's cash journal with totals carried forward.

				CASH JOURNAL						PAGE 2
CASH		DATE	ACCOUNT TITLE	DOC. NO.	POST. REF.	GENERAL		SALES CREDIT		
DEBIT	CREDIT					DEBIT	CREDIT			
168200	165500	1988 July 12	Brought Forward		✓	165500	55000	113200		

Column totals brought forward to a new page of a cash journal

The steps in entering totals brought forward to a new journal page are below.

1 Write the complete date in the Date column.

2 Write the words *Brought Forward* in the Account Title column.

3 Write the totals from the preceding page in each amount column.

> Prove that the debit totals equal the credit totals again to be sure the totals are forwarded correctly.

4 Place a check mark in the Post. Ref. column to show that none of these totals is to be posted.

MAKING CORRECTIONS

Sometimes the debit amounts will not equal the credit amounts in an entry. If an entry is not in balance, the errors must be found and corrected. If an error is made in writing an amount, cancel the error by drawing a line through the amount. The correct amount is then written immediately above the cancelled item. Also, if an error is made in any part of an entry, draw a line through the error. Then the correction is written immediately above the cancelled part of the entry. Corrections are shown in the illustration below.

				CASH JOURNAL						PAGE 5
CASH		DATE	ACCOUNT TITLE	DOC. NO.	POST. REF.	GENERAL		SALES CREDIT		
DEBIT	CREDIT					DEBIT	CREDIT			
25000		8	Supplies	J8	✓			~~25000~~ 25000		16
	1500	8	~~Miscellaneous Expense~~	C92		1500				17

Making corrections

On line 16 above, an error was made in writing an amount. On line 17 an error was made in writing an account title.

ACCOUNTING TERMS

What is the meaning of each of the following?

1. journalizing
2. double-entry accounting
3. special journal
4. cash journal
5. special amount column
6. receipt
7. cheque
8. detail tape
9. proving cash

QUESTIONS FOR INDIVIDUAL STUDY

1. Why is accounting information first recorded in a journal?
2. Why is double-entry accounting said to be complete accounting?
3. Why does Putt Around use a cash journal?
4. Why did Putt Around record the opening entry in a general journal instead of a cash journal?
5. For which accounts are special amount columns included in a multi-column journal? What are the special amount columns in Putt Around's cash journal?
6. What must be done with a transaction's information before it is recorded in a journal?
7. What are the two kinds of *source documents* used by Putt Around for receipt of cash transactions?
8. Why is the account title *Sales* not written in a cash journal's Account Title column for a cash sales transaction?
9. What is the source document for a cash payments transaction?
10. What kinds of transactions are recorded in a miscellaneous expense account?
11. What is the procedure for proving cash?
12. How is the accuracy of the cash journal proved?
13. How is a cash journal ruled?
14. Why might a cash journal be totalled and ruled before the end of a month?
15. If an error is made in writing an account title in a journal, how should a correction be made?

CASES FOR MANAGEMENT DECISION

CASE 1 Mrs. Malloy uses a two-column general journal to record all transactions for her business. She is thinking of changing to a multi-column cash journal similar to the one described in this chapter. Mr. Malloy recommends that she continue to use the two-column general journal for two reasons. (a) The equality of debits and credits can be checked more easily than in a cash journal. (b) The two-column general journal does not need to be totalled and ruled. Do you agree with Mr. or Mrs. Malloy? Why?

CASE 2 Nicole Weatherby owns a small bus service that carries young children to and from a nursery school. Ms. Weatherby refers to all cash payments of the business as "my expenses." Is Ms. Weatherby correct in referring to all cash payments as expenses? Why?

CASE 3 When Mr. Minot prepares a cheque, he fills in the cheque stub first and then writes the cheque. When Mr. Billingsly prepares a cheque, he writes the cheque first and then fills in the stub. Which is the preferred procedure? Why?

DRILLS FOR UNDERSTANDING

DRILL 5-D 1   Analysing transactions

Before transactions can be recorded in a journal, the transactions are analysed into debit and credit parts. This drill provides practice in analysing transactions. Use Putt Around's chart of accounts, page 16, for needed account titles.

Transactions

1. Received cash from week's sales, $100.00.
2. Paid cash for month's rent, $150.00.
3. Paid cash for telephone bill, $25.00.
4. Received cash from the owner as additional investment in the business, $500.00.
5. Paid cash for advertising, $40.00.
6. Paid cash for having store windows washed, $10.00.
7. Received cash from sale of worn out golf clubs, $30.00.
8. Paid cash to Melcor Equipment Company for amount owed, $100.00.
9. Paid cash for supplies, $20.00.
10. Paid cash for new maintenance equipment, $300.00.
11. Paid cash to the owner for personal use, $100.00.

Instructions: 1. Use two T accounts for each transaction. Write the name of the accounts affected on the T accounts. T accounts for Transaction 1 are at the right.

2. Use the T accounts prepared in Instruction 1. Write the debit amount on the debit side of the correct account. Write the credit amount on the credit side of the correct account. The T accounts for Transaction 1 are at the right.

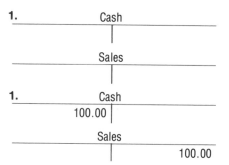

DRILL 5-D 2   Analysing transactions

A selected list of transactions is given below for a business.

Transactions

1. Received cash for fees from customers.
2. Paid cash for advertising in local newspaper.
3. Paid cash for month's rent.
4. Paid cash for telephone bill.
5. Received cash from sale of an old office chair.
6. Paid cash to owner for personal use.
7. Paid cash for gas and oil used in automobile.
8. Paid cash for postage stamps used in office.
9. Paid cash to Pfitzer Company for part of amount owed.
10. Paid cash for electric bill.
11. Paid cash for new electronic calculator to use in office.
12. Received cash from owner as additional investment in business.
13. Paid cash for supplies.

Some of the account titles on the business' chart of accounts are below.

Cash	Fees Revenue
Supplies	Advertising Expense
Office Equipment	Automobile Expense
Pfitzer Company (liability)	Miscellaneous Expense
Donna Major, Capital	Rent Expense
Donna Major, Drawing	Utilities Expense

Use a form similar to the one below. Transaction 1 is given on the form as an example.

	1	2	3	4	5	6
Trans. No.	Account Titles Affected	Account Classification	Account is		Balance of Account is	
			Debited	Credited	Increased	Decreased
1	Cash	Asset	√		√	
	Fees Revenue	Revenue		√	√	

Instructions: 1. In Column 1, write the names of the two accounts affected by each transaction.

2. In Column 2, write the account classification for each account title written in Column 1.

3. In either Column 3 or 4, place a check mark (√) to show if the account is debited or credited for this transaction.

4. In either Column 5 or 6, place a check mark (√) to show if the account balance is increased or decreased.

APPLICATION PROBLEMS

PROBLEM 5-1   Recording transactions in a cash journal

Ema Langhorn is a registered architect. She receives revenue from fees charged to clients. Mrs. Langhorn does not use a cash register. The receipt of all cash is first recorded on receipt forms. The receipt forms are the source documents for all cash received transactions.

The following accounts are used by Mrs. Langhorn's business. *Assets*: Cash, Automobile, Drafting Equipment, Office Equipment. *Liabilities*: Mixer Equipment Company. *Capital*: Ema Langhorn, Capital; Ema Langhorn, Drawing. *Revenue*: Fees. *Expenses*: Automobile Expense, Miscellaneous Expense, Rent Expense, Utilities Expense.

The following transactions were completed during May of the current year.

Transactions

May 1. Paid cash for office rent, $350.00. C201.
   1. Paid cash for minor repairs to business' automobile, $36.00. C202.
   2. Received cash from sale of an old office desk, $45.00. R110.
   2. Received cash from fees, $1 170.00. R111.
   2. Paid cash for gas and oil used in business' automobile, $11.50. C203.
   3. Paid cash for new office desk, $400.00. C204.
   4. Received cash from fees, $1 160.00. R112.

May 7. Received cash from fees, $810.00. R113.
9. Paid cash for new drafting equipment, $175.00. C205.
15. Received cash from fees, $360.00. R114.
18. Paid cash to Mixer Equipment Company for amount owed, $864.00. C206.
22. Paid cash for electric bill, $38.50. C207.
28. Received cash from fees, $810.00. R115.
28. Paid cash for telephone bill, $60.75. C208.
30. Received cash from fees, $270.00. R116.
31. Paid cash to owner for personal use, $2 000.00. C209.

Instructions: 1. Use a pair of T accounts for each transaction. Analyse each transaction into its debit and credit parts in the T accounts.

2. Use page 9 of a cash journal similar to the one on page 83. Record the beginning cash balance for May 1 of the current year, $720.00.

3. Record each transaction. Follow the T account analysis completed in Instruction 1.

4. Prove cash. The ending balance on Cheque Stub No. 209 is $1 409.25.

5. Prove the equality of debits and credits in the journal.

6. Rule the cash journal.

The solution to Problem 5-1 is needed to complete Problem 6-1 in the next chapter.

PROBLEM 5-2 Recording transactions in a cash journal

Richard Connelly operates a delivery service. The business uses a cash register to record revenue from the delivery services. All other cash received is recorded on receipt forms.

The following accounts are used by Connelly's Delivery Service. *Assets*: Cash, Supplies, Delivery Equipment, Office Equipment. *Liabilities*: Bank of Montreal, Gotman's Garage. *Capital*: Richard Connelly, Capital; Richard Connelly, Drawing. *Revenue*: Sales. *Expenses*: Advertising Expense, Automobile Expense, Miscellaneous Expense, Rent Expense, Utilities Expense.

Instructions: 1. Record the beginning cash balance for May 1 of the current year, $1 045.00. Use page 1 of a cash journal.

2. Record the transactions in the cash journal.

May 1. Received cash from sales, $375.00. T1.
1. Paid cash for month's rent, $600.00. C109.
3. Paid cash for telephone bill, $62.30. C110.
3. Received cash from sales, $250.00. T3.
4. Received cash from sales, $125.00. T4.
5. Paid cash for supplies, $60.00. C111.
5. Received cash from sales, $60.00. T5.
6. Received cash from sales, $75.00. T6.
7. Received cash from sale of old office chairs, $25.00. R4.
7. Received cash from sales, $210.00. T7.
10. Paid cash to local newspaper for classified advertising, $75.00. C112.
10. Received cash from sales, $100.00. T10.
11. Received cash from sales, $215.00. T11.
12. Received cash from sales, $95.00. T12.
13. Paid cash to Gotman's Garage for part of amount owed, $200.00. C113.
13. Received cash from sales, $80.00. T13.

May 14. Received cash from sales, $60.00. T14.
17. Paid cash for automobile gasoline and oil expense, $240.00. C114.
17. Received cash from sales, $325.00. T17.
18. Paid cash for expense of fixing lock on office door, $30.00. C115.
18. Received cash from sales, $115.00. T18.
19. Paid cash for new office chairs, $140.00. C116.
19. Received cash from sales, $50.00. T19.

Instructions: 3. Prepare page 1 of the cash journal for forwarding. Total the amount columns and prove the equality of debits and credits. Record the totals to be carried forward and rule the journal.

4. Record the totals brought forward on line 1 of page 2 of the cash journal. Prove the equality of debits and credits again.

5. Continue recording the transactions for May.

May 20. Received cash from sales, $70.00. T20.
21. Received cash from sales, $135.00. T21.
24. Received cash from sales, $115.00. T24.
25. Paid cash to the owner for personal use, $700.00. C117.
25. Received cash from sales, $50.00. T25.
26. Received cash from sales, $65.00. T26.
27. Paid cash for automobile gasoline and oil, $325.00. C118.
27. Paid cash for tune-up of automobile, $130.00. C119.
27. Received cash from sales, $55.00. T27.
28. Paid cash for supplies, $120.00. C120.
28. Received cash from sales, $70.00. T28.
31. Received cash from sales, $75.00. T31.
31. Paid cash for electric bill, $125.00. C121.
31. Paid cash for minor repairs to an office chair, $25.00. C122.

Instructions: 6. Prove cash. The balance on Cheque Stub No. 122 is $1 007.70.
7. Prove page 2 of the cash journal.
8. Rule page 2 of the cash journal.

ENRICHMENT PROBLEMS

MASTERY PROBLEM 5-M   Recording transactions in a cash journal

Neiman Townsend operates Blue Dart Taxi Service. The business' revenue account is titled *Fares Earned*. The business does not use a cash register. At the end of each day the fares are totalled and recorded on a receipt form. The receipt form is the source document for all cash received transactions.

The following are accounts used by the business. *Assets*: Cash, Supplies, Taxi Equipment. *Liabilities*: Jerry's Garage, TD Bank. *Capital*: Neiman Townsend, Capital; Neiman Townsend, Drawing. *Revenue*: Fares Earned. *Expenses*: Advertising Expense, Gas and Oil Expense, Rent Expense, Repairs and Maintenance Expense, Utilities Expense.

Instructions: 1. On page 3 of a cash journal, record the beginning cash balance on hand, $1 153.00. Use September 1 of the current year.

2. Record the transactions in the cash journal.

Sept. 1. Received cash from fares, $110.00. R1.
2. Paid cash for rent, $300.00. C21.

Sept. 2. Paid cash for gas and oil, $12.75. C22.
    3. Received cash from fares, $138.50. R2.
    4. Paid cash for telephone bill, $23.80. C23.
    6. Received cash from fares, $180.20. R3.
    6. Paid cash to Jerry's Garage for part of amount owed, $75.00. C24.
    7. Received cash from fares, $110.00. R4.
    8. Paid cash for repairs to taxi, $55.00. C25.
    9. Paid cash for gas and oil, $12.50. C26.
   11. Paid cash to TD Bank for amount owed, $170.00. C27.
   13. Paid cash for electric bill, $27.20. C28.
   15. Received cash from fares, $75.00. R5.
   16. Paid cash for gas and oil, $15.90. C29.
   18. Received cash from fares, $36.50. R6.
   20. Paid cash for supplies, $80.00. C30.
   21. Received cash from fares, $36.50. R7.
   23. Paid cash for gas and oil, $11.20. C31.
   25. Received cash from fares, $188.70. R8.
   27. Paid cash for newspaper advertising, $12.75. C32.
   29. Received cash from fares, $62.00. R9.
   30. Paid cash to owner for personal use, $50.00. C33.

Instructions: 3. Prove cash. The ending balance on Cheque Stub No. 33 is $1 244.30.
4. Prove the cash journal.
5. Rule the cash journal.

CHALLENGE PROBLEM 5-C   Recording transactions in a cash journal

Sue Lozier operates Pacific Travel Agency. The cash journal used by the business is similar to the one on page 83. However, the arrangement of the columns is not the same. The business' cash journal is below.

CASH JOURNAL								Page 2
		Doc. No.	Post. Ref.	General		Cash		Commissions Revenue
Date	Account Title			Debit	Credit	Debit	Credit	Credit

The following are some of the ledger accounts used by the business. Cash; Supplies; Office Equipment; Sue Lozier, Capital; Sue Lozier, Drawing; Commissions Revenue; Advertising Expense; Automobile Expense; Miscellaneous Expense; Rent Expense; Utilities Expense.

Instructions: 1. Record the beginning cash balance on hand, $2 475.00, on page 2 of the cash journal. Use October 1 of the current year.
2. Record the transactions in the cash journal.

Oct. 1. Received cash as commissions, $292.00. R10.
    1. Received cash from owner as additional investment in business, $1 000.00. R11.
    2. Paid cash for gas and oil for automobile, $78.65. C101.
    4. Paid cash for month's rent, $260.00. C102.
    5. Received cash as commissions, $455.00. R12.

Oct. 6. Received cash as commissions, $150.00. R13.
 8. Paid cash for supplies, $20.00. C103.
 11. Paid cash for advertising in local newspaper, $15.60. C104.
 13. Paid cash to have office cleaned, $25.00. C105.
 15. Paid cash for gas and oil, $23.70. C106.
 18. Received cash as commissions, $747.50. R14.
 20. Received cash as commissions, $625.00. R15.
 22. Received cash from sale of old piece of office furniture, $50.00. R16.
 25. Paid cash for telephone bill, $75.00. C107.
 28. Paid cash for advertising in local newspaper, $15.60. C108.
 29. Received cash as commissions, $1 040.00. R17.
 31. Paid cash to owner for personal use, $300.00. C109.

Instructions: 3. Prove cash. The ending balance on Cheque Stub No. 109 is $6 020.95.
4. Prove the cash journal.
5. Rule the cash journal.

Posting

ENABLING PERFORMANCE TASKS

After studying Chapter 6, you will be able to:

a. Explain accounting principles and practices related to posting.
b. Arrange accounts for a small service business in a chart of accounts.
c. Post amounts from General amount columns of a cash journal.
d. Post column totals of a cash journal.

The financial position of a business for a specific date is shown on a balance sheet. As transactions occur the balances of accounts listed on a balance sheet change. Therefore, each business transaction changes the financial position of a business.

The balance sheet in Chapter 2, page 19, shows the financial position of Putt Around on July 1, 1988. The transactions from July 1 to July 31 change the account balances for Putt Around. Thus, Putt Around's financial position is not the same on July 31 as it was on July 1. (CONCEPT: Accounting Period Cycle)

Putt Around records each transaction in a cash journal as described in Chapter 5. A cash journal does not show in one place the account balances on a specific date. To show how transactions change account balances, information is posted from journals to ledgers. The debits and credits in each account are used to determine a new account balance. The new account balances on a specific date provide the information for an up-to-date balance sheet. (CONCEPT: Adequate Disclosure)

Information on a source document → is recorded in a journal

Debit →
Credit →

then posted to accounts in a ledger

Debit →
Credit →

ARRANGING ACCOUNTS IN A LEDGER

Accounts in a ledger are arranged in the same order as they will appear on financial reports. Because the order is the same, information from the ledger accounts is easily transferred to financial statements. Putt Around's ledger accounts are listed in the order given at the right.

1   Assets
2   Liabilities
3   Capital
4   Revenue
5   Expenses

Each group of similar accounts is a division in the ledger. For example, asset accounts are in the first division of Putt Around's ledger. Expense accounts are in the last ledger division.

Balance-Column Form of Account

Accounting clerks prefer the *balance-column* form of account to summarize the changes caused by business transactions. This form has three *amount* columns (Debit, Credit, Balance) as shown below.

ACCOUNT							ACCOUNT NO.	
DATE	ITEM	POST. REF.	DEBIT	CREDIT	DR CR	BALANCE		

The Balance column is used to record the difference between the total debits and the total credits as each entry is made. If the debits are greater than the credits, then the difference is a *debit* balance; if the credits are greater than the debits, then the difference is a *credit* balance. The difference (the balance) is identified by writing *Dr* (debit) or *Cr* (credit) in the indicator column.

POSTING FROM A CASH JOURNAL

Line 1 of the cash journal, page 96, shows the cash balance on hand at the beginning of July. This entry is not for a transaction. A check mark is placed in the Post. Ref. column at the time the entry is recorded. The check mark shows that the entry for the July 1, 1988, beginning cash balance is not posted. The beginning cash balance is already recorded in the cash account.

Posting general amount columns

For each amount in a General Debit or General Credit column, an account title is written in the Account Title column. The amount is posted to the account written in the Account Title column.

Posting an amount from a General Credit column. The entry on line 2 of the cash journal, page 96, includes an amount in the General Credit column.

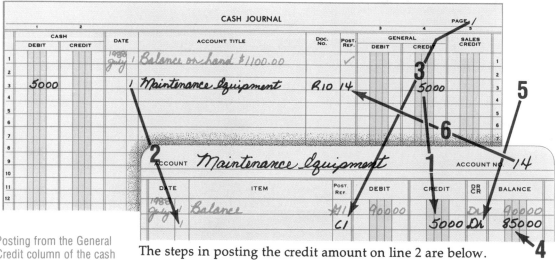

Posting from the General
Credit column of the cash
journal

The steps in posting the credit amount on line 2 are below.

1   Write the credit amount, *$50.00*, in the Credit column of the account
Maintenance Equipment.

2   Write the date of this journal entry in the Date column of the ledger
account.

>   Since this is the second entry in the account, only the day is written.

3   Write the journal page number, *C1*, in the Post. Ref. column of the
ledger account.

>   When written in a Post. Ref. column, *C* is the abbreviation for
>   the cash journal. When more than one journal is used, the page
>   number is coded with a journal abbreviation. Thus, *G1* means page
>   1 of a General journal. *C1* means page 1 of a Cash journal.

4   Subtract the $50.00 credit from the opening debit balance of $900.00.
Write the difference, *$850.00*, in the Balance column.

5   Identify the $850.00 balance as a *debit* balance by writing *Dr* (debit) in
the indicator column.

6   Return to the cash journal. Write the account number, *14*, in the cash
journal's Post. Ref. column.

>   The posting reference numbers serve three purposes. (1) An
>   entry in an account can be traced to its source in a journal. (2) An
>   entry in a journal can be traced to where it is posted in an account.
>   (3) If posting is interrupted, it is easy to see which entries still need
>   to be posted. The entries with no posting references in the journal
>   have not been posted. *The posting reference is always placed in the
>   journal as the last step in the posting procedure.*

Posting an amount from a General Debit column. The entry on line 3 of the
cash journal on page 97 includes an amount in a General Debit column.

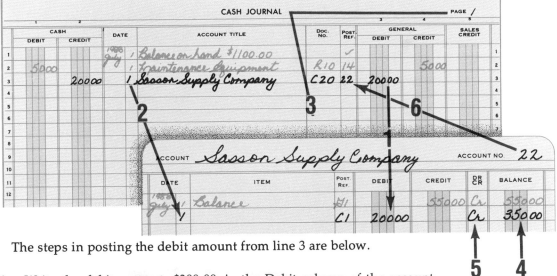

The steps in posting the debit amount from line 3 are below.

1   Write the debit amount, *$200.00*, in the Debit column of the account Sasson Supply Company.
2   Write the day of this entry, *1*, in the Date column of the ledger account.
3   Write the journal page, C1, in the Post. Ref. column of the ledger account.
4   Subtract the $200.00 debit from the opening credit balance of $550.00. Write the difference, *$350.00*, in the Balance column.
5   Identify the $350.00 balance as a *credit* balance by writing *Cr* (credit) in the indicator column.
6   Return to the cash journal. Write the account number, 22, in the cash journal's Post. Ref. column.

Posting from the General Debit column of a cash journal

Completing the posting of the two General columns of a cash journal. Each amount in the General Debit column is posted as described for line 3. Each amount in the General Credit column is posted as described for line 2. The amounts in the General Debit and General Credit columns are posted at frequent intervals. Frequent posting keeps accounts up to date and avoids doing all the posting at the end of a month. *(CONCEPT: Accounting Period Cycle)*

Each amount in a General Debit or a General Credit column is posted individually. Therefore, the totals of the General amount columns are *NOT* posted. The total of a journal column is posted only when an account title is listed in the column heading. A check mark (√) is placed in parentheses under each General amount column total. The check mark shows that the total of a column is not posted. The placing of the check marks below column totals is on page 98.

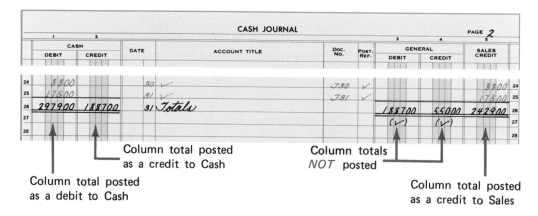

Column total posted
as a credit to Cash

Column total posted
as a debit to Cash

Column totals
NOT posted

Column total posted
as a credit to Sales

Posting special amount columns of a cash journal

Putt Around's cash journal has three special amount columns. The separate amounts written in these special amount columns are *NOT* posted individually. Only the total of a special amount column is posted. This procedure saves time in posting. For example, Putt Around's Cash Debit column for July has 29 entries recorded in it. Twenty-nine separate postings would be required to post these entries individually. Posting only the total means a savings of 28 postings.

The total of each special amount column *IS* posted to the account listed in the column heading. The total of the Cash Debit column is posted as a debit to Cash. The total of the Cash Credit column is posted as a credit to Cash. The total of the Sales Credit column is posted as a credit to Sales.

Posting the total of a Cash Debit column. Only the total of a Cash Debit column is posted. The separate amounts in this column are not posted individually.

Posting a Cash Debit
column total

The posting of a Cash Debit column total is below.

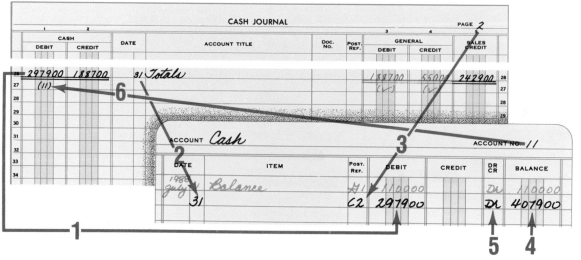

The steps in posting the Cash Debit column total are below.

1 Write the debit amount, *$2 979.00*, in the Debit column of the cash account.

2 Write the day, *31*, in the Date column of the cash account.

3 Write *C2* in the Post. Ref. column of the cash account.

4 Add the $2 979.00 debit to the opening debit balance of $1 100.00. Write the sum *$4 079.00*, in the Balance column.

5 Identify the $4 079.00 balance as a *debit* balance by writing *Dr* (debit) in the indicator column.

6 Return to the cash journal. Write the account number, *11*, in parentheses immediately below the Cash Debit column total.

Posting the total of a Cash Credit column. Only the total of a Cash Credit column is posted (see illustration below).

Posting a Cash Credit column total

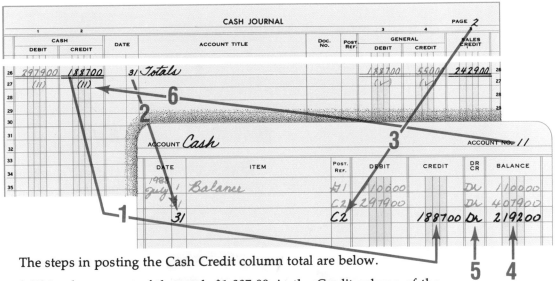

The steps in posting the Cash Credit column total are below.

1 Write the amount of the total, *$1 887.00*, in the Credit column of the cash account.

2 Write the day, *31*, in the Date column of the cash account.

3 Write *C2* in the Post. Ref. column of the cash account.

4 Subtract the $1 887.00 credit from the debit balance of $4 079.00. Write the difference, *$2 192.00*, in the Balance column.

5 Identify the $2 192.00 balance as a *debit* balance by writing *Dr* (debit) in the indicator column.

6 Return to the cash journal. Write the account number, *11*, in parentheses immediately below the Cash Credit column total.

Posting the total of a Sales Credit column. Only the total of a Sales Credit column is posted. The posting of a Sales Credit column total is below.

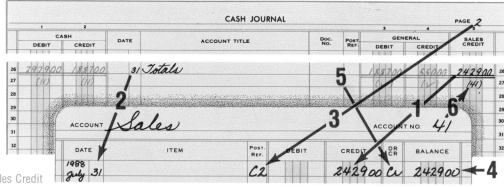

Posting a Sales Credit
column total

The steps in posting the Sales Credit column total are below.

1 Write the amount of the total, *$2 429.00*, in the Credit column of the sales account.

2 Write the date, *1988, July 31,* in the Date column of the sales account.
> This is the first entry in the sales account. For this reason, the complete date is written in the Date column.

3 Write *C2* in the Post. Ref. column of the sales account.

4 Write *$2 429.00* in the Balance column.

5 Identify the balance as a *credit* balance by writing *Cr* (credit) in the indicator column.

6 Return to the cash journal. Write the account number, *41,* in parentheses immediately below the Sales Credit column total.

A ledger after posting is completed

Putt Around's ledger is below and on pages 101 and 102. All posting for the month of July has been completed.

Ledger after posting is
completed

ACCOUNT	*Cash*					ACCOUNT NO	*11*	
DATE	ITEM	POST. REF.	DEBIT	CREDIT	DR CR	BALANCE		
1988 July 1	*Balance*	*✓1*	*110000*		*Dr*	*110000*		
31		*C2*	*297900*		*Dr*	*407900*		
31		*C2*		*188700*	*Dr*	*219200*		

ACCOUNT	*Supplies*					ACCOUNT NO	*12*	
DATE	ITEM	POST. REF.	DEBIT	CREDIT	DR CR	BALANCE		
1988 July 1	*Balance*	*✓1*	*50000*		*Dr*	*50000*		
2		*C1*	*5000*		*Dr*	*55000*		
12		*C1*	*7500*		*Dr*	*62500*		
24		*C2*	*10000*		*Dr*	*72500*		

Ledger after posting is completed (continued)

ACCOUNT: Golf Equipment — ACCOUNT NO. 13

DATE	ITEM	POST. REF.	DEBIT	CREDIT	DR/CR	BALANCE
1988 July 1	Balance	J1	220000		Dr	220000
12		C1	10000		Dr	230000

ACCOUNT: Maintenance Equipment — ACCOUNT NO. 14

DATE	ITEM	POST. REF.	DEBIT	CREDIT	DR/CR	BALANCE
1988 July 1	Balance	J1	90000		Dr	90000
1		C1		5000	Dr	85000
2		C1	40000		Dr	125000

ACCOUNT: Melcor Equipment Company — ACCOUNT NO. 21

DATE	ITEM	POST. REF.	DEBIT	CREDIT	DR/CR	BALANCE
1988 July 1	Balance	J1		65000	Cr	65000

ACCOUNT: Sasson Supply Company — ACCOUNT NO. 22

DATE	ITEM	POST. REF.	DEBIT	CREDIT	DR/CR	BALANCE
1988 July 1	Balance	J1		55000	Cr	55000
1		C1	20000		Cr	35000

ACCOUNT: Harry Rossi, Capital — ACCOUNT NO. 31

DATE	ITEM	POST. REF.	DEBIT	CREDIT	DR/CR	BALANCE
1988 July 1	Balance	J1		350000	Cr	350000
1		C1		50000	Cr	400000

ACCOUNT: Harry Rossi, Drawing — ACCOUNT NO. 32

DATE	ITEM	POST. REF.	DEBIT	CREDIT	DR/CR	BALANCE
1988 July 2		C1	10000		Dr	10000
23		C1	5000		Dr	15000

ACCOUNT: Sales — ACCOUNT NO. 41

DATE	ITEM	POST. REF.	DEBIT	CREDIT	DR/CR	BALANCE
1988 July 31		C2		242900	Cr	242900

ACCOUNT: Advertising Expense — ACCOUNT NO. 51

DATE	ITEM	POST. REF.	DEBIT	CREDIT	DR/CR	BALANCE
1988 July 6		C1	2500		Dr	2500

ACCOUNT	*Miscellaneous Expense*			ACCOUNT NO.			
DATE	ITEM	POST. REF.	DEBIT	CREDIT	DR CR	BALANCE	
1988 July 2		C1	10 00		Dr	10 00	
7		C1	10 00		Dr	20 00	
15		C2	15 00		Dr	35 00	
22		C2	18 00		Dr	53 00	
27		C2	5 00		Dr	58 00	
30		C2	12 00		Dr	70 00	

ACCOUNT	*Rent Expense*			ACCOUNT NO. 53			
DATE	ITEM	POST. REF.	DEBIT	CREDIT	DR CR	BALANCE	
1988 July 1		C1	600 00		Dr	600 00	

ACCOUNT	*Utilities Expense*			ACCOUNT NO 54			
DATE	ITEM	POST. REF.	DEBIT	CREDIT	DR CR	BALANCE	
1988 July 2		C1	25 00		Dr	25 00	
5		C1	60 00		Dr	85 00	
20		C2	32 00		Dr	117 00	

Ledger after posting is completed (concluded)

SUMMARY OF PROCEDURES FOR POSTING FROM A CASH JOURNAL TO A LEDGER

The procedures for posting from a cash journal are much the same as posting from any journal. A summary of the posting procedures is given below.

Posting from General amount columns

The procedures for posting from General amount columns of a cash journal are below. *Separate amounts in General Debit and General Credit*

Separate amounts are posted individually

Totals are NOT posted

Check marks show that totals are NOT posted

columns ARE posted individually to accounts listed in the Account Title column. The account number is written in the Post. Ref. column of a cash journal.

The totals of General Debit and General Credit columns ARE NOT posted to a ledger account. A check mark (√) is placed in parentheses under a General column total. This check mark shows that the column total is not posted.

Posting from special amount columns

The procedures for posting from special amount columns of a cash journal are below. *Separate amounts in special amount columns ARE NOT posted individually.* A check mark (√) is placed in the Post. Ref. column of a cash journal. The check mark shows that these individual amounts are not posted.

The totals of special amount columns ARE posted to the account listed in the column heading. An account number is written in parentheses immediately below a special amount column total. This account number shows to which account the total was posted.

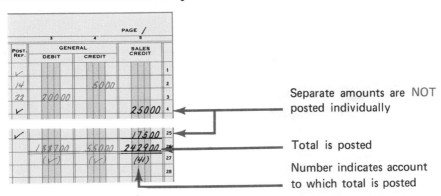

Separate amounts are NOT posted individually

Total is posted

Number indicates account to which total is posted

Writing account numbers in Post. Ref. column of a cash journal

The account number is written in a journal as the last step in posting each amount. These account numbers are written last to show that posting of the item is completed. Also, if work is interrupted, the item without a posting reference is the next item to be posted.

QUESTIONS FOR INDIVIDUAL STUDY

1. Why is Putt Around's balance sheet prepared on July 1, 1988, not the same as the balance sheet prepared on July 31, 1988?

2. What guide is used by Putt Around in arranging accounts in its ledger?

3. What are the major divisions of the ledger used by Putt Around?

4. What are the three amount columns used in the balance-column form of account? What is identified in the indicator column?

5. Why is the entry on line one of the cash journal, page 96, not posted?
6. What are the six steps in posting an amount from a cash journal's General Credit column?
7. What three purposes are served by the posting of reference numbers?
8. Why is posting of individual amounts in General Debit and General Credit columns done frequently during a month by Putt Around?
9. How does Putt Around determine if a column total in a cash journal needs to be posted?

10. Why are check marks placed under General Debit and General Credit amount column totals?
11. Why can it be determined by looking at the cash journal, page 98, that posting of the two General columns is completed?
12. What are the two rules for posting from General amount columns?
13. What are the two rules for posting from special amount columns?
14. Why are posting reference numbers placed in the journal as the last step in posting?

CASES FOR MANAGEMENT DECISION

CASE 1 Ken Wilovich does accounting work for a small business. When posting from a journal to a ledger, he records all the information in the ledger accounts first. Then, he goes back to the journal and writes all the account numbers in the Post. Ref. column at one time. Is this procedure satisfactory? Why?

CASE 2 Mildred Humphrey keeps records of her business much as is described in this chapter for Putt Around. Her husband recommends that she stop using a cash journal and record information directly in ledger accounts. Which procedure do you recommend? Why?

CASE 3 Winston Malby posts individually all separate amounts in all columns of a cash journal used in his business. He does not post any column totals. The cash journal is similar to the one described in this chapter for Putt Around. Do you agree with Mr. Malby's procedures? Why?

CASE 4 Jackie Bellinger keeps accounting records for a business. The ledger has dozens of accounts in it. Many pages of the journal are used each month. Ms. Bellinger needs to find information from a source document for one entry in the miscellaneous expense account. How would you suggest she go about finding the specific source document she needs?

DRILLS FOR UNDERSTANDING

DRILL 6-D 1 Assigning account numbers

Use the information on page 24, Chapter 2. Perform the drills below.

The list below refers to the location of accounts in a ledger.

1. The first asset account
2. The first liability account
3. The owner's capital account
4. The first revenue account
5. The first expense account

6. The third asset account
7. The second liability account
8. The owner's drawing account
9. The fourth expense account
10. The second asset account
11. The third expense account

Instructions: 1. Use a form such as the one below. Indicate the account number for each of the items listed. Item 1 is shown as an example.

Item	Account Number
1. *The first asset account*	*11*
2.	

Instructions: 2. Cover the Account Number column. See how rapidly you can recall the account numbers.

3. As a check, use Putt Around's chart of accounts, page 16. Check which account fits the description of each item above. Also, check if that account has the same account number you listed on the form. For example, on the chart of accounts, page 16, Putt Around's first asset account is *Cash*. The account number shown for Cash is 11.

DRILL 6-D 2 Analysing posting from a cash journal

Use the cash journal on pages 82 and 83, Chapter 5. Answer the questions below.

1. Which amounts on line 3 of the cash journal, page 83, are posted separately?
2. Which amounts on line 12 of the cash journal, page 83, are posted separately?
3. Which totals on line 26 of the cash journal, page 83, are posted?
4. Which totals on line 26 of the cash journal, page 83, are not posted?
5. What was the cash balance on hand, July 1, according to information in the cash journal, page 82?
6. How would you figure the amount of cash on hand, July 31, 1988?

Use the ledger accounts on pages 100–102. Answer the questions below.

7. What item or transaction is represented by each of the three amounts in the cash account, page 100?
8. Why is there only one amount recorded for all of July in the sales account, page 101?
9. Where will you find complete details for the transaction dated July 2, $400.00, in the maintenance equipment account, page 101? How did you decide where to find the details for this transaction?

APPLICATION PROBLEMS

PROBLEM 6-1 Posting from a cash journal ✓

The cash journal prepared in Problem 5-1 is needed to complete Problem 6-1.

Instructions: 1. Open ledger accounts for each of the following accounts. Write the account title and number at the top of the form. Record the account balance if the account has a balance. Write the word *Balance* in the Item column and place a check mark in the Post. Ref. column. Use May 1 of the current year.

Account Title	Acct. No.	Account Balance	Account Title	Acct. No.	Account Balance
Cash	11	$ 720.00	Fees	41	——
Automobile	12	5 350.00	Automobile Expense	51	——
Drafting Equipment	13	875.00	Miscellaneous Expense	52	——
Office Equipment	14	900.00	Rent Expense	53	——
Mixer Equipment Co.	21	864.00	Utilities Expense	54	——
Platt Company	22	600.00			
Ema Langhorn, Capital	31	6 381.00			
Ema Langhorn, Drawing	32	——			
Income Summary	33	——			

Instructions: 2. Post the individual amounts recorded in the General Debit and General Credit columns of the cash journal. Place check marks in parentheses under the General Debit and Credit columns. The check marks show that these column totals are not posted.

3. Post the special amount columns of the cash journal. Write an account number in parentheses under each special amount column total.

Solution to Problem 6-1 is needed to complete Problem 7-1 in Chapter 7.

PROBLEM 6-2   Posting from a cash journal ✓

A completed cash journal and ledger accounts for Robinson Repair Service are given in the working papers for this textbook.

Instructions: 1. Prove cash as of June 30 of the current year. The balance on Cheque Stub No. 114 is $2 153.90.

2. Total, prove, and rule the cash journal.

3. Post the amounts from the General Debit and Credit columns of the cash journal.

4. Post the special amount column totals of the cash journal.

ENRICHMENT PROBLEMS

MASTERY PROBLEM 6-M   Journalizing and posting using a cash journal

Dr. Milton Benson uses the ledger accounts below.

Account Title	Acct. No.	Account Balance	Account Title	Acct. No.	Account Balance
Cash	11	$ 8 841.00	Professional Fees	41	——
Automobile	12	8,820.00	Automobile Expense	51	——
Office Furniture	13	7,056.00	Miscellaneous Expense	52	——
Medical Equipment	14	9 450.00	Rent Expense	53	——
Grossman Furniture Co.	21	3 927.00	Utilities Expense	54	——
Health Supplies Co.	22	7 182.00			
Milton Benson, Capital	31	23 058.00			
Milton Benson, Drawing	32	——			

Instructions: 1. Open the accounts in a ledger. Record the balance for each account with a balance. Use July 1 of the current year.

2. Record the following transactions on page 7 of a cash journal similar to the one on page 100. The heading for the revenue column is *Professional Fees Credit* instead of *Sales Credit*. Source documents are abbreviated as: cheque, C; receipt, R.

July 1. Record cash balance on hand, $8 841.00.
1. Paid cash for July rent, $500.00. C230.
2. Received cash from professional fees, $283.50. R351.
5. Paid cash for new office furniture, $375.00. C231.
6. Paid cash for stamps, $15.00. C232.
9. Received cash from professional fees, $1 428.00. R352.
12. Paid cash to Grossman Furniture Company, $966.00 on account. C233.
15. Paid cash for electric bill, $200.00. C234.
16. Paid cash for automobile expense, $168.00. C235.
19. Received cash from professional fees, $1 302.00. R353.
20. Received cash from sale of old office furniture, $225.00. R354.
21. Paid cash to Health Supplies Company, $1 400.00 on account. C236.
23. Paid cash to Dr. Benson for personal use, $2 000.00. C237.
26. Paid cash for miscellaneous expense, $24.00. C238.
26. Received cash from professional fees, $1 400.00. R355.
27. Received cash from professional fees, $935.00. R356.
29. Paid telephone bill, $51.50. C239.
31. Received cash from professional fees, $374.00. R357.
31. Paid cash for automobile expense, $103.00. C240.

Instructions: 3. Prove cash. The balance on Cheque Stub No. 240 is $8 986.00
4. Total, prove, and rule the cash journal.
5. Post from the cash journal to the ledger.

CHALLENGE PROBLEM 6-C Journalizing and posting using a cash journal

Peter Roselle operates a business called Speedy Service Company. The cash journal used by the business is below.

CASH JOURNAL								
1	2					3	4	5
Cash Debit	General Debit	Date	Account Title	Doc. No.	Post. Ref.	General Credit	Sales Credit	Cash Credit

The following are ledger accounts used by the business. Cash, $4 631.00; Delivery Truck, $4 200.00; Office Furniture, $3 696.00; Delivery Equipment Company (liability), $3 762.00; Holliday Supply Company, (liability), $4 950.00; Peter Roselle, Capital, $3 815.00; Peter Roselle, Drawing; Sales; Delivery Expense; Miscellaneous Expense; Rent Expense; Utilities Expense.

Instructions: 1. Use page 8 of a cash journal similar to the one above. Record the beginning cash balance on hand, $4 631.00, on line 1 of the journal. Use August 1 of the current year.
2. Record the following selected transactions for August. Number all cheques beginning with C201. Number all receipts beginning with R370.

Aug. 1. Paid cash for August rent, $500.00.
2. Received cash from sales, $150.00.
3. Paid cash for new office furniture, $200.00.

Aug. 4. Paid cash for miscellaneous expense, $33.50.
      9. Received cash from sales, $750.00.
   10. Paid cash to Delivery Equipment Company for part of amount owed, $550.00.
   15. Paid cash for utilities expense, $200.00.
   16. Paid cash for delivery expense, $90.00.
   19. Received cash from sales, $700.00.
   20. Received cash from the sale of an old piece of office furniture, $88.50.
   21. Paid cash to Holliday Supply Company for part of amount owed, $800.00.
   23. Paid cash for miscellaneous expense, $16.00.
   24. Received cash from sales, $800.00.
   31. Received cash from sales, $675.00.
   31. Paid cash for delivery expense, $253.00.
   31. Paid cash for miscellaneous expense, $54.70.
   31. Paid cash to Mr. Roselle for personal use, $500.00.

Instructions: 3. Prove cash. The balance on Cheque Stub No. 211 is $4 597.30.
4. Total, prove, and rule the cash journal.
5. Post from the journal to the ledger accounts.

An Accounting Cycle for a Sole
Proprietorship Using a
Cash Journal

Reinforcement activities strengthen the learning of accounting concepts and procedures. Reinforcement Activity 1 is a single problem divided into four parts. Part A includes learnings from Chapters 2 to 6. Part B, page 129, includes learnings from Chapter 7. Part C, page 142, includes learnings from Chapter 8. Part D, page 160, includes learnings from Chapter 9. An accounting cycle is completed in Parts A to D for a single business: Wilson's Secretarial Service.

WILSON'S SECRETARIAL SERVICE

Anthony Wilson has been earning money part-time doing keyboarding work for various businesses and individuals. Mr. Wilson decides to start a full-time secretarial service offering the same services. The services include keying of letters, employment resumes, and reports. In addition, the business will provide bulk mailing and keying of some legal documents. Mr. Wilson rents a one-room office with a minimum of office furniture. Mr. Wilson also owns some of his own office equipment.

Chart of accounts

The chart of accounts for Wilson's Secretarial Service is below.

WILSON'S SECRETARIAL SERVICE Chart of Accounts			
(1) ASSETS	**Account Number**	**(4) REVENUE**	**Account Number**
Cash..	11	Secretarial Fees.......................................	41
Supplies..	12	**(5) EXPENSES**	
Office Equipment...............................	13	Advertising Expense...............................	51
(2) LIABILITIES		Cleaning Expense..................................	52
Evans Stationery................................	21	Electricity Expense................................	53
Mansoori Equipment Company............	22	Miscellaneous Expense	54
(3) CAPITAL		Rent Expense..	55
Anthony Wilson, Capital.......................	31	Telephone Expense...............................	56
Anthony Wilson, Drawing	32		
Income Summary.................................	33		

Beginning financial condition

On October 1 of the current year, Mr. Wilson prepares the beginning balance sheet below.

Wilson's Secretarial Service
Balance Sheet
October 1, 19--

Assets		Liabilities	
Cash	2 000 00	Evans Stationery	1 00 00
Supplies	1 70 00	Mansoori Equip. Co.	2 00 00
Office Equipment	7 00 00	Total Liabilities	3 00 00
		Capital	
		Anthony Wilson, Capital	2 57 0 00
Total Assets	2 87 0 00	Total Liabilities + Capital	2 87 0 00

Recording and posting an opening entry

On October 1, Mr. Wilson begins to record entries in the business' new records.

Instructions: 1. Record an opening entry on page 1 of a general journal. The source document is the balance sheet for October 1 of the current year.
    2. Open a ledger account for each account on the chart of accounts, page 109.
    3. Post the opening entry from the general journal to the accounts.

Recording transactions

Instructions: 4. Record each of the following transactions beginning on page 1 of a cash journal. Source documents are abbreviated as: cheques, C; receipts, R.

Oct. 1. Record the cash on hand, $2 000.00.
    1. Paid cash for October rent, $300.00. C100.
    1. Paid cash for a business licence (miscellaneous expense), $25.00. C101.
    1. Paid cash for a new business machine, $800.00. C102.
    4. Paid cash for advertising in local newspaper, $75.00. C103.
    4. Received cash for secretarial fees, $25.00. R10.
    5. Received cash for secretarial fees, $34.00. R11.
    6. Paid cash for notary seal (miscellaneous expense), $50.00. C104.
    6. Received cash for secretarial fees, $40.00. R12.
    7. Received cash for secretarial fees, $60.00. R13.
    8. Received cash for secretarial fees, $80.00. R14.
  11. Paid cash for direct mail advertising, $85.00. C105.
  11. Received cash for secretarial fees, $45.00. R15.
  12. Received cash for secretarial fees, $65.00. R16.
  13. Paid cash for sign painted on office door, $25.00. C106.
  13. Received cash for secretarial fees, $80.00. R17.
  14. Paid cash to Mansoori Equipment Company for part of amount owed, $100.00. C107.

Oct. 14. Received cash for secretarial fees, $45.00. R18.
    15. Paid cash for supplies, $200.00. C108.
    15. Received cash for secretarial fees, $95.00. R19.
    18. Paid cash for advertising in local newspaper, $80.00. C109.
    18. Received cash for secretarial fees, $30.00. R20.
    19. Received cash for secretarial fees, $100.00. R21.

Instructions: 5. Total, prove, and rule page 1 of the cash journal. Forward the totals to page 2 of a cash journal.
  6. Post individual items from the cash journal's General Debit and Credit columns.
  7. On page 2 of a cash journal record the transactions given below.

Oct. 20. Paid cash to Evans Stationery for part of amount owed, $50.00. C110.
    20. Received cash for secretarial fees, $50.00. R22.
    21. Received cash for secretarial fees, $10.00. R23.
    22. Received cash for secretarial fees, $90.00. R24.
    25. Paid cash for direct mail advertising, $100.00. C111.
    25. Received cash for secretarial fees, $60.00. R25.
    26. Paid cash for telephone bill, $90.00. C112.
    26. Received cash for secretarial fees, $80.00. R26.
    27. Received cash for secretarial fees, $75.00. R27.
    28. Paid cash for supplies, $100.00. C113.
    28. Received cash for secretarial fees, $55.00. R28.
    29. Paid cash for electric bill, $60.00. C114.
    29. Received cash for secretarial fees, $100.00. R29.
    31. Paid cash to owner for personal use, $500.00. C115.

Instructions: 8. Prove cash. The balance on unused Cheque Stub No. 116 is $579.00
  9. Total, prove, and rule page 2 of the cash journal.
  10. Post individual items from the cash journal's General Debit and Credit columns.
  11. Post the cash journal's special amount column totals.

  The ledger prepared in Reinforcement Activity 1, Part A, is needed to complete Parts B and D. The general journal used in Part A is needed to complete Part D.

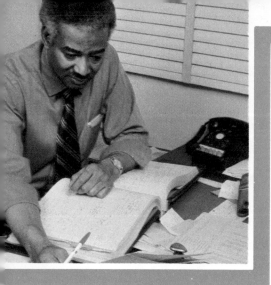

Six-Column Work Sheet

ENABLING PERFORMANCE TASKS

After studying Chapter 7, you will be able to:

a. Define accounting terms related to a six-column work sheet.
b. Explain accounting principles and practices related to a six-column work sheet.
c. Sort account balances on a six-column work sheet.
d. Prepare a trial balance on a six-column work sheet using information from ledger accounts.
e. Figure the net income or net loss on a six-column work sheet.
f. Complete a six-column work sheet.
g. Find and correct errors made in accounting records.

Managers and owners of businesses must know whether a profit or a loss is being made. Information needed to figure if a profit or loss is being made is contained in ledger accounts. Ledger accounts need to be analysed and information reported to the manager and owner of a business. Managers and owners need up-to-date information to make wise business decisions.

A business analyses its financial information at regular intervals. The length of time for which a business analyses business information is called a fiscal period . (CONCEPT: Accounting Period Cycle) A fiscal period is sometimes known as an accounting period. Each business chooses the fiscal period that meets its own needs. Some businesses, such as Putt Around, use a one-month fiscal period. Other businesses may use fiscal periods of three months, six months, or one year.

Putt Around's fiscal period begins on the first day of a calendar month and ends on the last day of the same month. For example, a fiscal period begins on July 1, 1988, and ends on July 31, 1988. Not all fiscal years begin and end with a calendar year. For example, a business might begin a fiscal year on July 1 of one year. The fiscal year would then end on June 30 of the following year.

> For tax purposes, most individuals begin a personal fiscal period on January 1 of a calendar year. The personal fiscal period ends on December 31 of the same year.

Before financial reports can be prepared, ledger accounts are summarized and reports planned. Accounting paper with a number of amount columns used in analysing ledger accounts is called analysis paper. Analysis paper on which the financial condition of a business is summarized is called a work sheet. A work sheet is used to plan the information to be put on financial reports. Putt Around's work sheet at the end of July, 1988, is on page 121.

> The preparation of financial statements for Putt Around is described in Chapters 8 and 9.

PREPARING A SIX-COLUMN WORK SHEET

Preparation of a six-column work sheet achieves three objectives. (1) Summarizing ledger account information on a trial balance. (2) Sorting ledger information according to financial reports to be prepared. (3) Figuring the amount of net income or net loss for a fiscal period.

Heading on a work sheet

The heading on a work sheet is similar to the heading of any accounting report. The illustration at the right shows the heading for Putt Around's work sheet prepared on July 31, 1988.

Line 1: Name of the business.
Line 2: Name of the report.
Line 3: Date of the report.

Putt Around
Work Sheet
For Month Ended July 31, 1988

The date shows that the work sheet covers the fiscal period from July 1 to July 31, 1988. Thus, the report is for the month ended July 31, 1988. (*CONCEPT: Accounting Period Cycle*)

Heading on a work sheet

Preparing a trial balance

Proof of the equality of debits and credits in a ledger is called a trial balance. To prepare a trial balance, all the debit balances are added and all the credit balances are added. The sum of all debit balances must equal the sum of all credit balances.

Figuring account balances. Balance-column account forms enable the accounting clerk to show an up-to-date account balance at the end of each posting. The balance is identified as a *debit* or a *credit* balance. A few rules must be followed when figuring account balances using balance-column account forms.

1. *Two debit amounts are* added *to produce a debit balance*. In the first part of the illustration below, the July 1 balance is a debit balance of $400.00. The July 15 entry is a debit posting of $300.00. Since both of the amounts are debits, they are *added* and the total, *$700.00*, is written in the Balance column. The new balance, $700.00, is identified as a *debit* balance by writing *Dr* (debit) in the indicator column.

2. *Two credit amounts are* added *to produce a credit balance*. In the second part of the illustration below, the July 1 balance is a credit balance of $200.00. The July 31 entry is a credit posting of $600.00. Since both of the amounts are credits, they are *added* and the total, *$800.00*, is written in the Balance column. The new balance, $800.00, is identified as a *credit* balance by writing *Cr* (credit) in the indicator column.

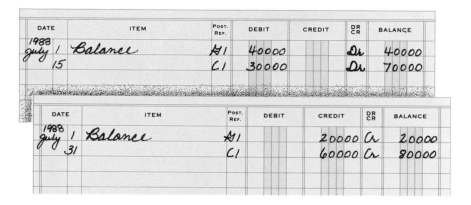

3. *When one amount is a debit and the other amount is a credit, the smaller amount is* subtracted *from the larger amount and the* difference *is written in the Balance column*.

The illustration at the top of page 115 shows three things. (1) If the debit amount is greater than the credit amount, then the difference is a *debit* balance. (2) If the credit amount is greater than the debit amount, then the difference is a *credit* balance. (3) If the debit amount is the same as the credit amount, then the difference is *zero*. A zero balance is shown by drawing a straight line through the entire Balance column. The indicator column is left blank because a zero balance is neither debit nor credit.

DATE	ITEM	POST. REF.	DEBIT	CREDIT	DR CR	BALANCE
1988 July 2		C1	90000		Dr	90000
15		C1		40000	Dr	50000

DATE	ITEM	POST. REF.	DEBIT	CREDIT	DR CR	BALANCE
1988 July 2		C1		100000	Cr	100000
31		C2	70000		Cr	30000

DATE	ITEM	POST. REF.	DEBIT	CREDIT	DR CR	BALANCE
1988 July 1	Balance	A1	50000		Dr	50000
20		C1		50000		

Putt Around's ledger with all account balances figured is below and on pages 116 and 117.

Ledger with all account balances figured

ACCOUNT *Cash*   ACCOUNT NO. 11

DATE	ITEM	POST. REF.	DEBIT	CREDIT	DR CR	BALANCE
1988 July 1	Balance	A1	110000		Dr	110000
31		C2	297900		Dr	407900
31		C2		188700	Dr	219200

ACCOUNT *Supplies*   ACCOUNT NO. 12

DATE	ITEM	POST. REF.	DEBIT	CREDIT	DR CR	BALANCE
1988 July 1	Balance	A1	50000		Dr	50000
2		C1	5000		Dr	55000
12		C1	7500		Dr	62500
24		C1	10000		Dr	72500

ACCOUNT *Golf Equipment*   ACCOUNT NO. 13

DATE	ITEM	POST. REF.	DEBIT	CREDIT	DR CR	BALANCE
1988 July 1	Balance	A1	220000		Dr	220000
12		C1	10000		Dr	230000

ACCOUNT *Maintenance Equipment*   ACCOUNT NO. *14*

DATE		ITEM	POST. REF.	DEBIT	CREDIT	DR CR	BALANCE
1988 July	1	Balance	G1	90000		Dr	90000
	1		C1		5000	Dr	85000
	2		C1	40000		Dr	125000

ACCOUNT *Melcor Equipment Company*   ACCOUNT NO. *21*

DATE		ITEM	POST. REF.	DEBIT	CREDIT	DR CR	BALANCE
1988 July	1	Balance	G1		65000	Cr	65000

ACCOUNT *Sasson Supply Company*   ACCOUNT NO. *22*

DATE		ITEM	POST. REF.	DEBIT	CREDIT	DR CR	BALANCE
1988 July	1	Balance	G1		55000	Cr	55000
	1		C1	20000			35000

ACCOUNT *Harry Rossi, Capital*   ACCOUNT NO. *31*

DATE		ITEM	POST. REF.	DEBIT	CREDIT	DR CR	BALANCE
1988 July	1	Balance	G1		350000	Cr	350000
	1		C1		50000	Cr	400000

ACCOUNT *Harry Rossi, Drawing*   ACCOUNT NO. *32*

DATE		ITEM	POST. REF.	DEBIT	CREDIT	DR CR	BALANCE
1988 July	2		C1	10000		Dr	10000
	23		C2	5000		Dr	15000

ACCOUNT *Income Summary*   ACCOUNT NO. *33*

DATE	ITEM	POST. REF.	DEBIT	CREDIT	DR CR	BALANCE

ACCOUNT *Sales*   ACCOUNT NO. *41*

DATE		ITEM	POST. REF.	DEBIT	CREDIT	DR CR	BALANCE
1988 July	31		C2		242900	Cr	242900

Ledger with all
account balances
figured
(continued)

ACCOUNT *Advertising Expense*				ACCOUNT NO. *51*		
DATE	ITEM	POST. REF.	DEBIT	CREDIT	DR CR	BALANCE
1988 July 6		C1	2500		Dr	2500

ACCOUNT *Miscellaneous Expense*				ACCOUNT NO. *52*		
DATE	ITEM	POST. REF.	DEBIT	CREDIT	DR CR	BALANCE
1988 July 2		C1	1000		Dr	1000
7		C1	1000		Dr	2000
15		C2	1500		Dr	3500
22		C2	1800		Dr	5300
27		C2	500		Dr	5800
30		C2	1200		Dr	7000

ACCOUNT *Rent Expense*				ACCOUNT NO. *53*		
DATE	ITEM	POST. REF.	DEBIT	CREDIT	DR CR	BALANCE
1988 July 1		C1	60000		Dr	60000

ACCOUNT *Utilities Expense*				ACCOUNT NO. *54*		
DATE	ITEM	POST. REF.	DEBIT	CREDIT	DR CR	BALANCE
1988 July 2		C1	2500		Dr	2500
5		C1	6000		Dr	8500
20		C2	3200		Dr	11700

The income summary account will be discussed in Chapter 9.

Recording account balances in a trial balance. Account titles and account balances are recorded on a work sheet form. All accounts in a ledger are listed even if some accounts have no balances. This procedure assures that no accounts with balances are omitted. *Debit* account balances are written in the Trial Balance Debit column; *credit* account balances are written in the Trial Balance Credit column. The column in which an amount is recorded shows the kind of balance an account has.

The steps in preparing and completing the work sheet Trial Balance columns are given below and on the next page.

1 Write the account titles in the Account Title column.

2 Write the account balances in either the Trial Balance Debit or Credit columns.

ACCOUNT TITLE	TRIAL BALANCE		INCOME STATEMENT		BALANCE SHEET	
	DEBIT	CREDIT	DEBIT	CREDIT	DEBIT	CREDIT
1 Cash	2 1 9 2 00					
2 Supplies	7 2 5 00					
3 Golf Equipment	2 3 0 0 00					
4 Maintenance Equipment	1 2 5 0 00					
5 Melcor Equipment Company		6 5 0 00				
6 Sasson Supply Company		3 5 0 00				
7 Harry Rossi, Capital		4 0 0 0 00				
8 Harry Rossi, Drawing	1 5 0 00					
9 Income Summary						
10 Sales		2 4 2 9 00				
11 Advertising Expense	2 5 00					
12 Miscellaneous Expense	7 0 00					
13 Rent Expense	6 0 0 00					
14 Utilities Expense	1 1 7 00					
15	7 4 2 9 00	7 4 2 9 00				

Putt Around
Work Sheet
For Month Ended July 31, 1988

Trial balance on work
sheet

3 Check the trial balance for accuracy.

- Rule a single line across the two Trial Balance columns below the last amount. This single line shows that the two columns are to be added.
- Add the Trial Balance Debit and Credit columns. Write the total of each column below the single line. (Use a calculator to do the arithmetic if one is available.)
- Compare the totals of the two columns. The totals must be the same if equality of debits and credits is maintained in the ledger. If the totals are not the same, an error has been made. If the totals are not the same, recheck the work to find the error or errors.
- Rule double lines across both columns immediately below the totals. The double lines are ruled only if the totals are the same. The double lines show that the two columns are in balance and assumed to be correct.

Other parts of a work sheet are not completed until the Trial Balance columns are in balance.

Extending account balances to Balance Sheet columns

Extend balance sheet account balances to the Balance Sheet columns.

1 Extend each asset account balance from the Trial Balance Debit column to the Balance Sheet Debit column.

2 Extend each liability account balance to the Balance Sheet Credit column.

3 Extend the owner's capital account balance to the Balance Sheet Credit column.

4 Extend the owner's drawing account balance to the Balance Sheet Debit column.

The extension of these account balances is below.

ACCOUNT TITLE	TRIAL BALANCE DEBIT	TRIAL BALANCE CREDIT	INCOME STATEMENT DEBIT	INCOME STATEMENT CREDIT	BALANCE SHEET DEBIT	BALANCE SHEET CREDIT	
Cash	219200				219200		1
Supplies	72500				72500		2
Golf Equipment	230000				230000		3
Maintenance Equipment	125000				125000		4
Melcor Equipment Company		65000				65000	5
Lasson Supply Company		35000				35000	6
Harry Rossi, Capital		400000				400000	7
Harry Rossi, Drawing	15000				15000		8

Putt Around / Work Sheet / For Month Ended July 31, 1988

Extending account balances to Income Statement columns

Extend the revenue and expense account balances to the Income Statement columns.

Asset, liability, and capital accounts extended to work sheet Balance Sheet columns

1 Extend each revenue account balance to the Income Statement Credit column.

> Putt Around has only one revenue account, Sales. Thus, only one revenue account balance is extended.

2 Extend each expense account balance to the Income Statement Debit column.

Revenue and expense accounts extended to work sheet Income Statement columns

The extension of these account balances is below.

ACCOUNT TITLE	TRIAL BALANCE DEBIT	TRIAL BALANCE CREDIT	INCOME STATEMENT DEBIT	INCOME STATEMENT CREDIT	BALANCE SHEET DEBIT	BALANCE SHEET CREDIT	
Sales		242900		242900			10
Advertising Expense	2500		2500				11
Miscellaneous Expense	7000		7000				12
Rent Expense	60000		60000				13
Utilities Expense	11700		11700				14

Putt Around / Work Sheet / For Month Ended July 31, 1988

Figuring net income or net loss on a work sheet

Figure the net income or net loss and complete a work sheet as described below.

1 Rule a single line across the Income Statement and Balance Sheet columns.

2 Add the amounts in the Income Statement and Balance Sheet Debit and Credit columns. Write each column total below the single line.

3 Figure the net income or net loss. Net income for Putt Around is figured below.

Total of Income Statement Credit column	$2 429.00
Minus Total of Income Statement Debit column	812.00
Equals Net Income	$1 617.00

When the amount of revenue is greater than the total expenses, the difference is called net income. When the total expenses are greater than the revenue, the difference is called net loss.

> The information shows a net income for Putt Around. The Income Statement Credit column total (revenue) is larger than the Income Statement Debit column total (expenses). If the Debit column is larger than the Credit column, there is a net loss.

4 Write the amount of net income below the Income Statement Debit column total. For Putt Around's work sheet, page 121, write *$1 617.00* below the column total, *$812.00*. Write *Net Income* on the same line in the Account Title column. The words Net Income identify the amount on this line as net income.

> If there is a net loss, write the amount in the Income Statement Credit column. Write *Net Loss* in the Account Title Column.

5 Write the amount of net income, *$1 617.00*, in the Balance Sheet Credit column. Write this amount on the same line as the words *Net Income*.

> A net loss amount is written in the Balance Sheet Debit column.

6 Rule a single line across the Balance Sheet and Income Statement columns.

7 Add the subtotal and the net income amount to get new column totals. Write each new column total below the single line.

	ACCOUNT TITLE	TRIAL BALANCE		INCOME STATEMENT		BALANCE SHEET		
		DEBIT	CREDIT	DEBIT	CREDIT	DEBIT	CREDIT	
1	Cash	2192 00				2192 00		1
2	Supplies	725 00				725 00		2
3	Golf Equipment	2300 00				2300 00		3
4	Maintenance Equipment	1250 00				1250 00		4
5	Melcor Equipment Company		650 00				650 00	5
6	Sasson Supply Company		350 00				350 00	6
7	Harry Rossi, Capital		4000 00				4000 00	7
8	Harry Rossi, Drawing	150 00				150 00		8
9	Income Summary							9
10	Sales		2429 00		2429 00			10
11	Advertising Expense	25 00		25 00				11
12	Miscellaneous Expense	70 00		70 00				12
13	Rent Expense	600 00		600 00				13
14	Utilities Expense	117 00		117 00				14
15		7429 00	7429 00	812 00	2429 00	6617 00	5000 00	15
16	Net Income			1617 00			1617 00	16
17				2429 00	2429 00	6617 00	6617 00	17
18								18
19								19
20								20
21								21
22								22

Putt Around
Work Sheet
For Month Ended July 31, 1988

8 Check that the totals of the two Income Statement columns are the same. Check that the totals of the two Balance Sheet columns are the same.

Completed six-column work sheet

> The totals of each pair of columns must be the same. If the column totals are not the same, an error has been made.

9 Rule double lines across all Income Statement and Balance Sheet columns as shown on the work sheet above. Double lines show that the columns are in balance and are assumed to be correct.

FINDING ERRORS ON A WORK SHEET

Each pair of columns on a work sheet must be in balance. If any pair of columns does not balance, add the columns again. Use a calculator, if available, to assure greater accuracy. If adding the columns again does not correct the error, use the procedures described below.

Check amounts recorded in Balance Sheet and Income Statement columns

1. Have amounts been copied correctly when extended from Trial Balance columns?

2. Has each amount in the Trial Balance *Debit* column been extended to the correct *Debit* column? Has each amount in the Trial Balance *Credit* column been extended to the correct *Credit* column?
3. Has the amount of net income or net loss been figured and recorded correctly?

Check account balances recorded in Trial Balance columns

1. Have *all* account balances been transferred from the ledger to the work sheet Trial Balance columns?
2. Have all *debit* account balances been recorded in the Trial Balance *Debit* column? Have all *credit* account balances been recorded in the Trial Balance *Credit* column?
3. Have the ledger account balances been figured correctly?

> If an error is found in an account balance, draw a line through the incorrect amount and write the correct balance above it. If an amount is incorrect on a work sheet, erase the error. Write the correct account balance on the work sheet. The work sheet is not a permanent part of the accounting records. Thus, the work sheet may be completed in pencil. Only permanent records, such as journals and ledgers, *must* be done in ink.

Check that posting to ledger accounts is correct

Have all amounts that need to be posted actually been posted? Have the amounts been posted to the correct amount column of an account?

> Each item is checked in the journal to assure that it has been posted. As the amount is checked, place a check mark next to the amount. This check mark shows that the posting has been checked.

For an amount posted to the wrong amount column of an account, draw a line through the incorrect posting and account balance. Record the posting and new balance correctly as shown below.

Corrected posting to wrong amount column of an account

For an amount posted to a wrong account, draw a line through all of the incorrect item. Record the posting in the correct account. Make the correction as shown on the next page.

Corrected posting to wrong account

For an amount that has not been posted, complete the posting to the correct account. In all cases where posting is corrected, refigure the account balance. When an omitted posting is recorded as described above, the dates in the account may be out of order. This procedure is better than not having the amount posted at all.

Errors in permanent records should *never* be erased. Erasures in permanent records raise questions about whether the information has been altered.

Check journals to assure that correct entries have been made

If errors discovered on a trial balance are not found by doing the procedures previously described, check the journal entries. For each journal entry, do debits equal credits? For each journal entry, are the amounts recorded in the correct journal columns? For each journal entry, is the information in the journal Account Title column correct?

For the completed journal, are the columns added correctly? Does the sum of debit column totals equal the sum of credit column totals? Have all the transactions been recorded?

Guides to finding typical arithmetic errors

When a pair of work sheet columns are not in balance, subtract the smaller total from the larger total. Check the difference between the column totals with the guides on the next page.

1. *The difference between column totals is an even 1.* (Such as $.01, $.10, $1.00, or $10.00). The error most often is in addition. Add the columns again.
2. *The difference between column totals can be divided evenly by 9.* (Such as $54.00 can be divided by 9 an even 6 times.) Look for a number involving a "slide" or a transposition. A "slide" is when numbers "slide" to the left or right in an amount column. (Such as $1.00 is recorded as $10.00, or $100.00 is recorded as $10.00.) A transposition is when two digits are reversed during recording. (Such as $45.00 is recorded as $54.00, or $236.00 is recorded as $326.00.)
3. *Look for an amount equal to the difference between column totals.* An amount may have been omitted from the trial balance. If the difference is $26.00, look for a $26.00 amount that has been omitted. The $26.00 amount may be an account balance not recorded on the trial balance. The $26.00 amount may be an amount not posted to a ledger account.
4. *Divide the difference between column totals by 2.* Look for the resulting number. (If the difference is $53.00, divide $53.00 by 2 which equals $26.50.) A debit amount may have been recorded or transferred as a credit. Look for a $26.50 *debit* amount recorded in a *credit* column. Also, look for a $26.50 *credit* amount recorded in a *debit* column.

The best way to prevent errors is to work carefully at all times. Check the work at each step in the accounting procedures. Most errors occur in doing the required arithmetic, especially in adding columns. Use a calculator if one is available. When an error is discovered, do no more work until the error is found and corrected.

ACCOUNTING TERMS

What is the meaning of each of the following?

1. fiscal period
2. analysis paper
3. work sheet
4. trial balance
5. net income
6. net loss

QUESTIONS FOR INDIVIDUAL STUDY

1. How long are typical fiscal periods of businesses?
2. What are the three lines in the heading of a work sheet?
3. Explain the rules for figuring account balances in Putt Around's ledger?
4. Why are *all* ledger accounts listed in the work sheet Trial Balance columns even if an account has no balance?
5. How are a work sheet's Trial Balance columns checked for accuracy?
6. To what columns are the asset, liability, and capital account balances extended on a work sheet?
7. To what columns are the revenue and expense account balances extended on a work sheet?
8. How is the net income figured for Putt Around's work sheet, page 121?
9. In the answer to question 8, how do you know there is a net income?
10. What is the relationship of the two

amounts written on line 16 of the work sheet, page 121?

11. Why are double lines ruled across all amount columns on a work sheet?

12. What is the first thing to do if the totals of any pair of work sheet columns do not balance?

13. What should be done if all the work on a work sheet appears correct, but columns are not in balance?

14. Why should errors in posting be corrected without erasing the incorrect items?

15. The totals of a work sheet's Trial Balance columns are: Debit, $4 321.00; Credit, $4 221.00. What kind of error probably has been made?

16. The totals of a work sheet's Trial Balance columns are: Debit, $4 345.00; Credit, $4 336.00. What kind of error probably has been made?

CASES FOR MANAGEMENT DECISION

CASE 1 Which of the following errors would *not* be indicated by Putt Around's work sheet trial balance? Why?

(a) A July 2 debit, $50.00, for supplies is posted as a debit to Miscellaneous Expense.

(b) A July 1 *credit* to Maintenance Equipment is posted as a *debit* to Maintenance Equipment.

(c) A July 31 balance of Utilities Expense, $117.00, is not recorded in the work sheet Trial Balance columns.

(d) A July 31 balance of Advertising Expense, $25.00, is written in the work sheet Trial Balance *Credit* column.

CASE 2 How would you correct each of the errors described in Case 1?

DRILLS FOR UNDERSTANDING

DRILL 7-D 1 Sorting account balances on a work sheet

The following accounts are used by Superior Lawncare Company. Advertising Expense; Brownstone Supply Company (liability); Cash; Entertainment Expense; Miscellaneous Expense; Office Equipment; Rent Expense; Roger Reynolds, Capital; Roger Reynolds, Drawing; Sales; Utilities Expense.

Use a form similar to the one below.

	1	2	3	4	5	6
	Trial Balance		Income Statement		Balance Sheet	
Account Title	Debit	Credit	Debit	Credit	Debit	Credit
1. *Advertising Expense*	✓		✓			

Instructions: 1. Write each account title on a separate line in the Account Title column of the form.

2. Place a check mark in either Column 1 or 2 to show what kind of balance each account normally has. Line 1 is shown in the form above as an example.

3. Place a check mark in Column 3, 4, 5, or 6 showing where the account balance is extended on a work sheet. The example above shows that the advertising expense account balance is extended to Column 3.

DRILL 7-D 2   Figuring net income or net loss on a work sheet

Totals from work sheet columns for four businesses are below.

	Income Statement		Balance Sheet	
	Debit	Credit	Debit	Credit
Company 1	$4 500.00	$5 300.00	$36 670.00	$35 870.00
Company 2	974.00	2 186.00	7 937.00	6 725.00
Company 3	4 050.00	3 994.00	25 669.00	25 725.00
Company 4	4 192.00	5 265.00	33 442.00	32 369.00

Instructions: 1. Use a form similar to the one below. Record the column totals for Company 2. The information for Company 1 is shown on line 1 as an example.

COMPANY 1

	Income Statement		Balance Sheet	
	Debit	Credit	Debit	Credit
1.	$4 500.00	$5 300.00	$36 670.00	$35 870.00
2. Net Income	800.00			800.00
3.	$5 300.00	$5 300.00	$36 670.00	$36 670.00

Instructions: 2. Figure the amount of net income or net loss for Company 2. Write the amount in the correct columns on line 2 of the form. Line 2 for Company 1 is shown above as an example. Label the amount on line 2 to show if it is a net income or a net loss.

3. Check the accuracy of your arithmetic by adding the four amount columns. Write the new column totals on line 3 of the form. Line 3 for Company 1 is shown above as an example. If each pair of columns does not balance, check your arithmetic.

4. Repeat Instructions 1, 2, and 3 for Company 3.

5. Repeat Instructions 1, 2, and 3 for Company 4.

APPLICATION PROBLEMS

PROBLEM 7-1   Preparing a trial balance on a work sheet

The ledger prepared for Problem 6-1 is needed to complete Problem 7-1.

Instructions: 1. Prepare the heading of a work sheet for Ema Langhorn, Architect. The business uses a one-month fiscal period.

2. Record a trial balance in the Trial Balance columns of the work sheet.

3. Total the Trial Balance columns. Check that the two columns are in balance. Rule the Trial Balance columns.

The solution to Problem 7-1 is needed to complete Problem 7-2.

PROBLEM 7-2 Completing a work sheet

The solution to Problem 7-1 is needed to complete Problem 7-2.

Instructions: 1. Use the work sheet with the trial balance completed in Problem 7-1. Extend the asset, liability, and capital account balances to the Balance Sheet columns.
2. Extend the revenue and expense account balances to the Income Statement columns.
3. Total the Income Statement and Balance Sheet columns.
4. Figure the amount of net income or net loss for the Income Statement columns. Record the net income or net loss in the correct Income Statement column. Identify the amount by writing *Net Income* or *Net Loss* in the Account Title column.
5. Write the amount of net income or net loss in the correct Balance Sheet column.
6. Total the Income Statement and Balance Sheet columns. Check that each pair of column totals is in balance. If the columns *are* in balance, rule double lines across the four columns. If the columns *are not* in balance, find and correct the errors.

The solution to Problem 7-2 is needed to complete Problem 8-1 in Chapter 8.

PROBLEM 7-3 Finding errors in accounting records

Robert Evans has completed a monthly work sheet for his business, Window Kleen. Window Kleen's ledger accounts and the work sheet are given in the working papers available with this textbook.
Mr. Evans asks you to check his work sheet to make sure he has not made any mistakes. He asks you to redo the work sheet and any other work that may be wrong.

Instructions: 1. Use the work sheet as a starting point. Check the work sheet for accuracy. Also check the ledger for errors that would affect amounts on the work sheet. Make a list of the errors you find.
2. Prepare a correct work sheet for Window Kleen.

PROBLEM 7-4 Completing a work sheet

Northwest Mall Cinema uses the following ledger accounts. Balances are shown for those accounts that have balances on October 31 of the current year.

Account Title	Balance	Account Title	Balance
Cash	$ 6 920.00	Admissions Revenue	$21 260.00
Seating Equipment	18 000.00	Vending Machine Revenue	3 260.00
Projection Equipment	59 000.00	Advertising Expense	3 862.00
Sound Equipment	28 840.00	Electricity Expense	2 928.00
Movies, Ltd. (liability)	7 788.00	Film Rental Expense	5 204.00
Theatre Sound Service (liability)	1 672.00	Maintenance Expense	540.00
National Studios (liability)	4 772.00	Miscellaneous Expense	444.00
Wilma Mercer, Capital	95 528.00	Rent Expense	7 000.00
Wilma Mercer, Drawing	700.00	Utilities Expense	842.00
Income Summary	——		

Instructions: 1. Prepare the heading for a work sheet. Northwest Mall Cinema uses a monthly fiscal period. Prepare a trial balance on the work sheet from the account information above.
2. Extend all account balances to the correct Income Statement and Balance Sheet columns.
3. Figure the net income or net loss and complete the work sheet.

ENRICHMENT PROBLEMS

MASTERY PROBLEM 7-M   Completing a work sheet

County Delivery Service's ledger accounts and balances on March 31 of the current year are shown below.

Account Title	Account Balance	Account Title	Account Balance
Cash	$ 3 432.00	Sales	$3 120.00
Delivery Truck	10 000.00	Advertising Expense	218.00
Office Equipment	1 644.00	Miscellaneous Expense	86.00
Boulder Supply Company (liability)	903.00	Rent Expense	540.00
Sisselman Motors (liability)	3 360.00	Truck Expense	300.00
Welman Company (liability)	1 712.00	Utilities Expense	362.00
Malcolm Vincent, Capital	7 727.00		
Malcolm Vincent, Drawing	240.00		
Income Summary	—		

Instructions: Prepare a work sheet for County Delivery Service. The business uses a one-month fiscal period.

CHALLENGE PROBLEM 7-C   Preparing a trial balance and a work sheet

On December 31 of the current year, Weller Service Company had a small fire in its office. Some of the business' accounting records were destroyed. The information below was reconstructed from the remaining records.

Reconstructed information from remains of the ledger

Account Title	Account Balance	Account Title	Account Balance
Supplies	$1 315.00	Advertising Expense	$ 414.00
Equipment	8 000.00	Rent Expense	378.00
James Weller, Drawing	192.00	Utilities Expense	289.00
Fees Revenue	2 496.00		

Reconstructed information from the business' chequebook

Cash balance on last unused cheque stub, $2 745.00.
Total payments made for miscellaneous expenses, $68.00.

Reconstructed information through inquiries to liabilities

Owed to Justin Supply Company, $2 688.00.
Owed to Richards Equipment Company, $1 551.00.

Instructions: 1. From the information above, prepare a trial balance on work sheet paper. Use the date December 31 of the current year. The business uses a one-month fiscal period.
2. Complete the work sheet.

An Accounting Cycle for a Sole Proprietorship Using a Cash Journal

The ledger used in Part A is needed to complete Part B.

Reinforcement Activity 1, Part B, includes the accounting activities needed to prepare a six-column work sheet for Wilson's Secretarial Service.

Preparing a work sheet

Instructions: 12. Prepare a trial balance on work sheet paper. Use a fiscal period of one month ended October 31 of the current year.

13. Complete a work sheet for Wilson's Secretarial Service.

The work sheet used in Reinforcement Activity 1, Part B, is needed to complete Parts C and D. The ledger used in Part B is needed to complete Part D.

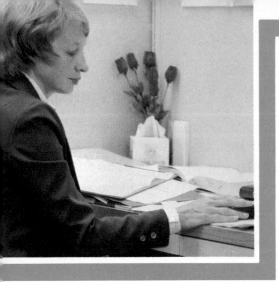

8

Financial Statements

ENABLING PERFORMANCE TASKS

After studying Chapter 8, you will be able to:

a. Define accounting terms related to financial statements.
b. Explain accounting principles and practices related to financial statements.
c. Prepare an income statement using information from a six-column work sheet.
d. Prepare a balance sheet using information from a six-column work sheet.

Business owners and managers need up-to-date financial information to make decisions about future operations. A business' financial information is recorded in ledger accounts. Transactions occurring during a fiscal period change the balances of ledger accounts. These changes should be reported periodically in the form of financial statements. (CONCEPT: Accounting Period Cycle)

Financial statements summarize the financial information contained in ledger accounts. (CONCEPT: Adequate Disclosure) A financial statement showing the assets and equities of a business on a specific date is known as a balance sheet. A financial statement showing the revenue, expenses, and net income or net loss of a business is called an income statement.

A balance sheet and an income statement can be prepared any time that the financial information is needed. Businesses always prepare these two statements at the end of a fiscal period. Financial statements prepared at the end of a fiscal period are called fiscal period statements. Financial statements prepared for periods shorter than a fiscal period are called interim statements. For example, Putt Around uses a one-month fiscal period. Putt Around prepares fiscal period statements at the end of each month. Financial statements that might be prepared on other dates during a month are interim statements for Putt Around.

An income statement shows financial information *over a specific period of time*. A balance sheet shows financial information *on a specific date*.

(CONCEPT: Accounting Period Cycle) Financial *progress* of a business in earning a net income or a net loss is shown by an income statement. Financial *condition* of a business on a specific date is shown by a balance sheet.

Information needed to prepare financial statements is contained in a business' ledger accounts. However, to assist in preparing financial statements, ledger information is summarized and sorted on a work sheet. Preparation of Putt Around's work sheet is described in Chapter 7.

AN INCOME STATEMENT

Revenue is a business' earnings from business activities. Expenses are what a business pays to run the business and earn the revenue. An income statement shows the total expenses of earning the revenue for a fiscal period. Thus, expenses are matched with revenue earned for a specific fiscal period. *(CONCEPT: Matching Expenses with Revenue)*

Source of information for an income statement

Information needed to prepare Putt Around's income statement is obtained from two places on the work sheet below.

Part of work sheet used in preparing income statement

First, account titles are taken from the Account Title column of the work sheet. Second, amounts are taken from the Income Statement columns of the work sheet.

Preparing an income statement

Based on the information obtained from the work sheet, Putt Around prepares the income statement below.

Income statement

Putt Around	
Income Statement	
For Month Ended July 31, 1988	
Revenue:	
Sales	2429 00
Expenses:	
Advertising Expense	25 00
Miscellaneous Expense	70 00
Rent Expense	600 00
Utilities Expense	117 00
Total Expenses	812 00
Net Income	1617 00

An income statement heading. All financial statements have three lines of information in the heading.

Income statement heading

1. *Name of the business.*
2. *Name of the statement.*
3. *Date of the statement.*

Putt Around
Income Statement
For Month Ended July 31, 1988

An income statement revenue section. Some businesses might have revenue from more than one source. Thus, gasoline stations might have revenue from sales of gas and oil as well as from repair services. Some businesses, such as Putt Around, receive revenue from only one source, sales of services.

Putt Around lists the heading for the revenue section of the income statement as shown below. The heading *Revenue* is written on the first line beginning at the left of the wide column.

Income statement revenue section

The title of the revenue account Sales is written on the next line. The account title is indented about 1 cm. This account title is taken from the Account Title column, line 10, of the work sheet, page 131. The account balance, *$2 429.00*, is written in the second amount column of the income statement. This amount is taken from the Income Statement Credit column, line 10, of the work sheet, page 131.

If there is more than one source of revenue, account balances are written in the first amount column. The amounts are added. The total revenue is written in the second amount column of the income statement.

An income statement expenses section. All expenses from operating the business are listed in the expenses section of the income statement. Putt Around lists the heading for the expenses section of the income statement as shown below. The heading *Expenses* is written on the next blank line at the left of the wide column.

Expenses:		
Advertising Expense	25 00	
Miscellaneous Expense	70 00	
Rent Expense	600 00	
Utilities Expense	117 00	
Total Expenses		812 00

Income statement expenses section

The title of each expense account is written in the wide column indented about 1 cm. Account titles are taken from the Account Title column, lines 11–14, of the work sheet, page 131. The account balance for each expense account is written in the first amount column. Amounts are taken from the work sheet's Income Statement Debit column, lines 11–14, page 131.

The words *Total Expenses* are written on the next blank line indented about 1 cm. The expense amounts are added. The total, *$812.00*, is written in the second amount column.

Figure the net income. A single line is ruled across the second amount column. Net income for Putt Around's income statement is figured as shown below.

Total revenue	$2 429.00
Less total expenses......................................	812.00
Equals net income.......................................	$1 617.00

If the expenses were greater than the revenue, a net loss would result. This is figured as shown below.

Total expenses..	$932.00
Less total revenue..	745.00
Equals net loss...	$187.00

The words *Net Income* are written at the left of the wide column on the income statement. The amount of net income, *$1 617.00*, is written in the second amount column as shown on the next page.

Total Expenses		81200
Net Income		161700

Completing an income statement

The amount of net income on an income statement must be the same
as that shown on a work sheet. The amount of net income figured for
Putt Around's income statement is $1 617.00. This amount is the same as
shown on line 16 of the work sheet, page 131.

When the amount of net income or net loss agrees with the work sheet,
the income statement is ruled. Double lines are ruled across both amount
columns of the income statement. Double lines show that amounts are
correct and the statement is completed. The completed income statement
for Putt Around is on page 132.

A BALANCE SHEET

The procedure for preparing Putt Around's balance sheet on July 1,
1988, is described in Chapter 2, page 20. The same procedure is used to
prepare all balance sheets for Putt Around.

Source of information for a balance sheet

Information needed by Putt Around to prepare a July 31 balance sheet
is contained in ledger accounts. However, to assist in preparing a balance sheet, Putt Around sorts the ledger information on a work sheet.
Information needed to prepare Putt Around's balance sheet is found in
two places on the work sheet below.

Putt Around
Work Sheet
For Month Ended July 31, 1988

	ACCOUNT TITLE	BALANCE SHEET	
		DEBIT	CREDIT
1	Cash	219200	
2	Supplies	72500	
3	Golf Equipment	230000	
4	Maintenance Equipment	125000	
5	Melcon Equipment Company		65000
6	Sasson Supply Company		35000
7	Harry Rossi, Capital		400000
8	Harry Rossi, Drawing	15000	
15		661700	500000
16	Net Income		161700
17		661700	661700

First, account titles are obtained from the Account Title column of the work sheet. Second, amounts are obtained from the Balance Sheet columns of the work sheet.

Preparing a balance sheet

Putt Around's July 31 balance sheet is below.

Balance sheet

A balance sheet heading. The three-line heading for the balance sheet is shown at the right.

1. *Name of the business.*
2. *Name of the statement.*
3. *Date of the statement.*

Balance sheet heading

A balance sheet reports financial information on a specific date. Thus, a balance sheet states the date on which it is prepared. A balance sheet *does not* report information covering a period of time as does an income statement.

A balance sheet assets section. Asset account titles are obtained from the Account Title column of the work sheet, page 134. Amounts are obtained from the Balance Sheet Debit column of the same work sheet.

Balance sheet assets section

The section heading, *Assets*, is written in the middle of the wide column as shown above. Immediately below this section title, the asset account titles are listed. The balance of each account is listed in the amount column.

The line for *Total Assets* is not prepared at this time. The total line is prepared later when the total liabilities and capital is determined.

A balance sheet liabilities section. Liability account titles are obtained from the Account Title column of the work sheet, page 134. Amounts are obtained from the Balance Sheet Credit column.

The section heading, *Liabilities*, is written in the middle of the wide column as shown below.

Balance sheet liabilities section

Liabilities
Melcor Equipment Co.	650 00
Sasson Supply Co.	350 00
Total Liabilities	1 000 00

Immediately below the section heading, each of the liability account titles is listed. The account balance for each liability account is listed in the amount column. A single line is drawn across the amount column. The words *Total Liabilities* are written on the next blank line. The liability amounts are added and the total written in the amount column.

A balance sheet capital section. Capital account titles are obtained from lines 7–8 of the work sheet's Account Title column, page 134. The amounts obtained are below.

Balance of capital account, line 7 .... $4 000.00
Balance of drawing account, line 8 .... 150.00
Amount of net income, line 16 .... 1 617.00

The amount of capital reported on the balance sheet is figured as shown below.

Capital account balance, line 7 of work sheet $4 000.00
Plus net income, line 16 of work sheet .... +1 617.00

Equals total $5 617.00
Less drawing account balance, line 8 .... − 150.00

Equals capital, July 31, 1988 .... $5 467.00

The section heading, *Capital*, is written in the middle of the wide column. The account title Harry Rossi, Capital is written on the next line. The amount of the capital, *$5 467.00*, is written in the amount column as shown below.

Balance sheet capital section

Capital
| Harry Rossi, Capital | 5 467 00 |

Completing a balance sheet

The balance sheet is completed by preparing the final lines for both the left and right sides of the statement. *On the same line* write the total lines as shown below.

Balance sheet total lines and final rulings

On the left side, write the words *Total Assets* in the wide column. On the right side write the words *Total Liabilities and Capital* in the wide column. In the amount columns write the total amounts.

The two final totals on the balance sheet must be the same. The two totals above are $6 467.00. Thus, the assets equal the equities.

If the two totals are the same, double lines are drawn across the amount columns. Double lines show that the statement is completed.

> If the two final totals on a balance sheet are not equal, errors must be found and corrected. Only when the two final totals are equal is the statement double ruled.

The completed balance sheet for Putt Around is on page 135.

Another method of reporting capital on a balance sheet

Putt Around's balance sheet, page 135, shows the ending capital on one line. How this amount is figured is not shown on the balance sheet. Some businesses prefer to show all the details on a balance sheet. When all the details are included, the capital section of a balance sheet appears as shown below.

Capital		
Harry Rossi, Capital,		
July 1, 1988	3 500.00	
Additional investment,		
July 1, 1988	500.00	
Total invested capital	4 000.00	
Net Income for		
July, 1988	1617.00	
Less Harry Rossi, Drawing	150.00	1467.00
Harry Rossi, Capital,		
July 31, 1988		5 467 00

Figuring amount of capital with a net loss

If a net loss results from business operations, the current capital would be figured as shown on the next page.

Capital, June 1, 1988...	$2 500.00
Less net loss shown on work sheet	900.00
Equals total...	$1 600.00
Less drawing account balance......................................	200.00
Equals capital, June 30, 1988.......................................	$1 400.00

The amount of ending capital to be shown on the balance sheet is $1 400.00.

ACCOUNTING TERMS

What is the meaning of each of the following?

1. income statement   **2.** fiscal period statements   **3.** interim statements

QUESTIONS FOR INDIVIDUAL STUDY

1. What is the major difference between the time covered by a balance sheet and an income statement?

2. What is the source of information needed to prepare Putt Around's income statement?

3. What are the three parts of a heading for an income statement?

4. For Putt Around's income statement, page 132, what is the information for each line of the statement heading?

5. What are the two main sections in the body of Putt Around's income statement?

6. If the total revenue is $3 500.00 and the total expenses are $1 950.00, what is the net income?

7. If the total revenue is $2 400.00 and the total expenses are $2 450.00, what is the net income or loss? How did you figure the amount?

8. How is the accuracy proved for the net income figured on an income statement?

9. What is the source of information needed to prepare a balance sheet?

10. What are the three main sections in the body of a balance sheet?

11. What can be done to check the accuracy of the balance sheet totals?

CASES FOR MANAGEMENT DECISION

CASE 1 Miss Melinda Boxer owns her own business. Net income reported on the income statement for the month ending October 31, 1988, was $2 950.00. Net income reported on the income statement for the next month ending November 30, 1988, is $2 800.00. What might have caused the change in the amount of net income from one month to the next?

CASE 2 Martha Wexler earns a salary for managing Family Miniature Golf. The business is owned by Maggie Malone. Mrs. Malone wants to sell the business and retire. What information should Miss Wexler obtain about the business before deciding if she will buy?

CASE 3 Roy Carlson owns and manages a business. The business has earned an average monthly net income of $1 500.00 for the past two years. Mr. Carlson has been offered a position as manager in a similar business at a monthly salary of $1 800.00. What information should Mr. Carlson consider before selling his current business and accepting a position with the new business?

DRILL 8-D 1   Classifying accounts

Use a form similar to the one below.

1	2	3	4	5	6	7	8
Account Title	Kind of Account					Financial Statement	
	Asset	Liab.	Capital	Revenue	Expense	Income Statement	Balance Sheet
1. *Cash*	√						√

Instructions: 1. In Column 1 copy the following list of account titles.

1. Cash
2. Alice Osborn, Capital
3. Advertising Expense
4. Central Supply Company (liability)
5. Miscellaneous Expense
6. Office Equipment
7. Page Company (liability)

8. Professional Fees
9. Rent Expense
10. Sales
11. Supplies
12. Thomas Tate, Drawing
13. Utilities Expense

Instructions: 2. Place a check mark in either Column 2, 3, 4, 5, or 6 to show each account's classification. The first account is given as an example.

3. Place a check mark in either Column 7 or 8 to show on which financial statement each account is reported. The first account is given as an example.

DRILL 8-D 2   Figuring net income or net loss

Information is given below for several companies.

Business	1 Total Assets	2 Total Liabilities	3 Balance of Capital	4 Balance of Drawing	5 Total Revenue	6 Total Expenses
A	$2 500.00	$ 900.00	$1 050.00	$ 50.00	$1 000.00	$ 400.00
B	3 250.00	1 170.00	1 265.00	65.00	1 400.00	520.00
C	4 750.00	1 440.00	2 430.00	80.00	1 600.00	640.00
D	4 250.00	1 260.00	2 220.00	70.00	1 400.00	560.00
E	4 750.00	1 710.00	1 795.00	95.00	2 100.00	760.00
F	7 125.00	2 565.00	2 567.00	142.00	3 275.00	1 140.00
G	6 056.00	2 180.00	2 185.00	120.00	2 780.00	969.00
H	9 690.00	3 500.00	6 432.00	190.00	4 448.00	4 500.00

Instructions: 1. Use the information in Columns 5 and 6. Figure the amount of net income or net loss for each company. As an example: Company A, Revenue, $1 000.00, *less* Expenses, $400.00, *equals* net income, $600.00.

2. Use the amount figured for Instruction 1 and the information in Columns 1 to 4. Figure the amount of ending capital for each business. As an example: Company A, Capital, $1 050.00, *plus* net income, $600.00, *less* drawing, $50.00, *equals* ending capital, $1.600.00.

APPLICATION PROBLEMS

PROBLEM 8-1 Preparing an income statement

The solution to Problem 7-2 is needed to complete Problem 8-1.

Instructions: Use the work sheet from Problem 7-2. Prepare an income statement. Use the illustration on page 132 as your guide.

PROBLEM 8-2 Preparing a balance sheet

The solution to Problem 7-2 is needed to complete Problem 8-2.

Instructions: Use the work sheet from Problem 7-2. Prepare a balance sheet. Use the illustration on page 135 as a guide.

PROBLEM 8-3 Preparing financial statements

A work sheet for the Westside Bowling Lanes is given in the working papers for this chapter.

Instructions: 1. Prepare an income statement.
2. Prepare a balance sheet.

ENRICHMENT PROBLEMS

MASTERY PROBLEM 8-M Preparing a work sheet and financial statements

The ledger accounts and balances for Masterson's Miniature Golf business on December 31 are below.

Cash	$ 2 252.00	Sales	$ 6 408.18
Supplies	3 009.00	Advertising Expense	149.76
Golf Equipment	45 900.00	Miscellaneous Expense	58.68
Maintenance Equipment	2 278.00	Rent Expense	1 530.00
Allison Company (liability)	2 040.00	Utilities Expense	242.78
Gentry Equipment Co. (liability)	4 622.98		
Uniform Supply Co. (liability)	521.82		
Sally Dorton, Capital	42 327.24		
Sally Dorton, Drawing	500.00		
Income Summary	———		

Instructions: 1. Prepare a work sheet for the three months ending December 31 of the current year.
2. Prepare an income statement.
3. Prepare a balance sheet.

CHALLENGE PROBLEM 8-C   Preparing a work sheet and financial statements

The ledger accounts and balances for Mensona Service Company on December 31 are below.

Cash	$2 400.30	Sales	$1 260.00
Supplies	88.48	Advertising Expense	58.80
Equipment	1 972.68	Miscellaneous Expense	242.90
Alsop Equipment Company (liability)	3 385.25	Rent Expense	840.00
Lawrence Company (liability)	224.28	Repairs Expense	131.04
Windfall Company (liability)	92.96	Utilities Expense	46.20
Jane Ruso, Capital	—		
Jane Ruso, Drawing	500.00		
Income Summary	—		

Instructions: 1. Figure the balance of the owner's capital account. ✔

2. Prepare a work sheet for the month ending December 31 of the current year.

3. Prepare an income statement.

4. Prepare a balance sheet. Show all details for figuring ending capital as described on page 137. (The owner made an additional investment of $500.00 on December 28.)

Reinforcement Activity 1

PART C

An Accounting Cycle for a Sole Proprietorship Using a Cash Journal

The work sheet prepared for Part B is needed to complete Part C.

Reinforcement Activity 1, Part C, includes the accounting activities needed to prepare the financial statements for Wilson's Secretarial Service.

Preparing financial statements

Instructions: 14. Use the work sheet to prepare an income statement.
15. Prepare a balance sheet.

The work sheet used in Reinforcement Activity 1, Part C, is needed to complete Part D.

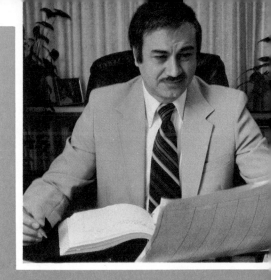

Closing the Ledger

After studying Chapter 9, you will be able to:

a. Define accounting terms related to closing a ledger.
b. Explain accounting principles and practices related to closing a ledger.
c. Analyse closing entries for a service business.
d. Record closing entries for a service business.
e. Post closing entries.
f. Prepare a post-closing trial balance.

A work sheet is prepared at the end of a fiscal period to sort and summarize a business' ledger accounts. From the completed work sheet, a business' financial progress and condition are reported in the form of financial statements. An income statement is prepared to report financial progress *over* a fiscal period. A balance sheet is prepared to report financial condition at the *end* of a fiscal period. *(CONCEPT: Accounting Period Cycle)*

Financial progress reported on an income statement is the amount of net income or loss resulting from business operations. The net income or loss affects a business' capital. Net income increases capital. Net loss decreases capital. After an income statement is prepared, the amount of net income or loss is transferred to a capital account. The new balance of the capital account is reported on a business' balance sheet. *(CONCEPT: Adequate Disclosure)*

NEED FOR CLOSING TEMPORARY CAPITAL ACCOUNTS

Separate revenue and expense accounts are used to record a business' financial progress. These revenue and expense accounts are known as temporary capital accounts. Balances of these temporary capital accounts provide the information needed to prepare an income statement. The difference between the balances of the revenue and expense accounts equals the net income or net loss.

Revenue and expenses are recorded separately for each fiscal period. *(CONCEPT: Matching Expenses with Revenue)* Therefore, each revenue and expense account must have a zero balance at the beginning of a new fiscal period. After an income statement is completed, the temporary accounts have served their purpose. The balance of each revenue and expense account is transferred to one ledger account. This single account summarizes the increases and decreases in capital. The journal entries transferring the revenue and expense account balances clear these accounts for the next fiscal period. An account that has had its balance transferred to another account is called a closed account. Journal entries used to prepare temporary capital accounts for a new fiscal period are called closing entries.

INCOME SUMMARY ACCOUNT

To close a temporary capital account, an amount equal to its balance is transferred out of the account. Temporary capital account balances are transferred to a summarizing account. The balances are not transferred directly to the owner's capital account. This procedure avoids having a capital account that is cluttered with many debit and credit entries.

The summarizing account used to close revenue and expense accounts is titled Income Summary. Accountants assume that a business will continue indefinitely and will earn a net income. *(CONCEPT: Going Concern)* For this reason, the title generally given the account is Income Summary. Income Summary is sometimes titled Income and Expense Summary.

After the temporary account balances are transferred, Income Summary shows the total revenue and total expenses for a fiscal period. The resulting balance of Income Summary is the net increase or decrease in capital from business operations. The balance of the income summary account is transferred to the owner's capital account. The chart below shows the flow of information in closing the revenue and expense accounts.

Chart showing the closing of temporary capital accounts

CLOSING ENTRIES

Putt Around's closing entries accomplish four things.
1. Close all revenue accounts.
2. Close all expense accounts.
3. Close income summary account and record net income in owner's capital account.
4. Close the owner's drawing account.

Account balances at the end of a fiscal period are summarized on a work sheet. The information needed to record closing entries is taken from a work sheet.

Closing revenue accounts

Information needed to close revenue accounts on July 31, 1988, is taken from line 10 of Putt Around's work sheet.

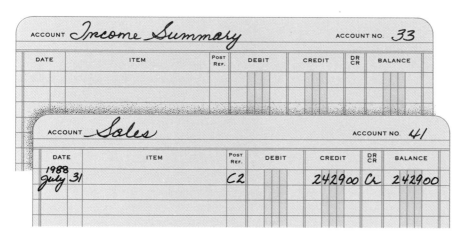

Before closing entries are posted, the accounts affected appear as shown below.

Sales has a *credit* balance of $2 429.00 before a closing entry is posted. The closing entry removes this credit balance and clears the sales account. Sales is debited for $2 429.00.

The entry is not complete without equal debits and credits. Thus, a credit of $2 429.00 is made to Income Summary.

The general journal entry to record the closing entry for Putt Around's revenue is on the next page.

Sales			
Closing	2 429.00	Balance	2 429.00

Income Summary			
		Closing	2 429.00

	GENERAL JOURNAL			PAGE /

	DATE	ACCOUNT TITLE	Post. Ref.	DEBIT	CREDIT	
9		*Closing Entries*				9
10	31	*Sales*		242900		10
11		*Income Summary*			242900	11

The words *Closing Entries* are written in the journal's Account Title column. Closing entries are not based on information from a source document. The heading in the Account Title column is the explanation for all closing entries. Thus, no source document number needs to be written for each of the entries.

The complete entry is written immediately following the heading for closing entries. In the journal above, the date, *31*, is written in the Date column. The account title, *Sales*, is written on the same line in the Account Title column. The amount, $2 429.00, is written in the Debit column. On the next line, indented about 1 cm, *Income Summary* is written in the Account Title column. The amount, $2 429.00, is written in the Credit column.

After Putt Around's closing entry for the revenue account is posted, the ledger accounts appear as shown below.

ACCOUNT *Income Summary*						ACCOUNT NO. 33	
DATE	ITEM	Post Ref.	DEBIT	CREDIT	DR CR	BALANCE	
1988 July 31		G1		242900	Cr	242900	

ACCOUNT *Sales*						ACCOUNT NO. 41	
DATE	ITEM	Post Ref.	DEBIT	CREDIT	DR CR	BALANCE	
1988 July 31		C2		242900	Cr	242900	
31		G1	242900			—	

The sales account has a zero balance. The original credit balance, $2 429.00, now appears as a credit in the income summary account.

If there were other revenue accounts, their balances also would be closed. The total of the balances would be recorded in the income summary account.

Closing expense accounts

Information needed to close expense accounts is taken from Putt Around's work sheet, lines 11–14.

ACCOUNT TITLE	TRIAL BALANCE		INCOME STATEMENT		BALANCE SHEET		
	DEBIT	CREDIT	DEBIT	CREDIT	DEBIT	CREDIT	
11 Advertising Expense	2500		2500				11
12 Miscellaneous Expense	7000		7000				12
13 Rent Expense	60000		60000				13
14 Utilities Expense	11700		11700				14

Expense accounts are all closed in a single entry. An entry that contains two or more debits or two or more credits is called a combined entry. A separate closing entry could be made for each expense account. This procedure would result in separate postings to Income Summary for each expense account balance. A combined entry results in only one posting to Income Summary. Thus, time is saved in recording and posting a combined entry.

> Putt Around's opening entry, Chapter 2, page 22, is another example of a combined entry.

The total of all expense account balances is figured. Putt Around's total expenses are $812.00. Income Summary is debited for this amount, $812.00.

Each expense account is credited for the amount of its balance. For example, Advertising Expense's balance is $25.00. This account is closed with a credit for $25.00.

The general journal entry to close the expense accounts is below.

Income Summary	
Closing 812.00	

Advertising Expense	
Balance 25.00	Closing 25.00

Miscellaneous Expense	
Balance 70.00	Closing 70.00

Rent Expense	
Balance 600.00	Closing 600.00

Utilities Expense	
Balance 117.00	Closing 117.00

GENERAL JOURNAL				PAGE 1	
DATE	ACCOUNT TITLE	POST. REF.	DEBIT	CREDIT	
12 31	Income Summary		81200		12
13	Advertising Expense			2500	13
14	Miscellaneous Expense			7000	14
15	Rent Expense			60000	15
16	Utilities Expense			11700	16

Closing entry for expense accounts

After Putt Around's closing entry for expenses is posted, the ledger accounts appear as shown below and on page 148.

ACCOUNT Income Summary						ACCOUNT NO. 33	
DATE	ITEM	POST. REF.	DEBIT	CREDIT	DR CR	BALANCE	
1988 July 31		41		242900	Cr	242900	
31		41	81200		Cr	161700	

ACCOUNT *Advertising Expense*						ACCOUNT NO. *51*	
DATE	ITEM	POST REF.	DEBIT	CREDIT	DR CR	BALANCE	
1988 July 6		C1	2500		Dr	2500	
31		J1		2500		————	

ACCOUNT *Miscellaneous Expense*						ACCOUNT NO. *52*	
DATE	ITEM	POST REF.	DEBIT	CREDIT	DR CR	BALANCE	
1988 July 2		C1	1000		Dr	1000	
7		C1	1000		Dr	2000	
15		C2	1500		Dr	3500	
22		C2	1800		Dr	5300	
27		C2	500		Dr	5800	
30		C2	1200		Dr	7000	
31		J1		7000		————	

ACCOUNT *Rent Expense*						ACCOUNT NO. *53*	
DATE	ITEM	POST REF.	DEBIT	CREDIT	DR CR	BALANCE	
1988 July 1		C1	60000		Dr	60000	
31		J1		60000		————	

ACCOUNT *Utilities Expense*						ACCOUNT NO. *54*	
DATE	ITEM	POST REF.	DEBIT	CREDIT	DR CR	BALANCE	
1988 July 2		C1	2500		Dr	2500	
5		C1	6000		Dr	8500	
20		C2	3200		Dr	11700	
31		J1		11700		————	

Each expense account now has a zero balance. The total amount of all expense account balances, *$812.00*, is a debit in Income Summary, page 147.

Closing income summary account and recording net income

After all revenue and expense accounts are closed, Putt Around's income summary account has a credit balance of $1 617.00. This balance is Putt Around's net income for the month ended July 31, 1988. The balance is checked with the amount of net income on the work sheet, page 121. The two amounts are the same. The first two closing entries are assumed to be correct.

The third closing entry closes Income Summary. The amount of net income is recorded as an increase in the owner's capital account. Income Summary has a credit balance, $1 617.00. Income Summary is debited, *$1 617.00*, to close the account. Harry Rossi, Capital is credited, *$1 617.00*, to record the net income. Putt Around's third closing entry is shown in the journal below.

	GENERAL JOURNAL			PAGE /	
DATE	ACCOUNT TITLE	POST. REF.	DEBIT	CREDIT	
17	31 *Income Summary*		1 617 00		17
18	*Harry Rossi, Capital*			1 617 00	18

Entry to close Income Summary and record net income in owner's capital account

If a business has a net loss, Income Summary would have a debit balance. Income Summary would be credited to close the account. The owner's capital account would be debited to record the net loss.

The effect of this closing entry to record net income is shown in the T accounts at the right. The income summary account has a zero balance. The income summary account is a temporary account used only to summarize other temporary capital accounts. *(CONCEPT: Matching Expenses with Revenue)* The account is used to make closing entries only at the end of a fiscal period. The use of Income Summary avoids the need to record all the information in the capital account. Only the net income or net loss is recorded in an owner's capital account each fiscal period.

Income Summary			
Expenses	812.00	Revenue	2 429.00
Closing	1 617.00		

Harry Rossi, Capital			
		Balance	4 000.00
		Closing	1 617.00

Closing an owner's drawing account

Withdrawals represent capital that an owner has taken out of a business. At the end of a fiscal period, the drawing account is closed. The drawing account balance is recorded as a decrease in the owner's capital account. The balance of the drawing account is obtained from the work sheet's Balance Sheet Debit column. Putt Around's fourth closing entry is shown in the journal below.

	GENERAL JOURNAL			PAGE /	
DATE	ACCOUNT TITLE	POST. REF.	DEBIT	CREDIT	
19	31 *Harry Rossi, Capital*		1 50 00		19
20	*Harry Rossi, Drawing*			1 50 00	20

Closing entry for owner's drawing account

On July 31, Putt Around's drawing account has a $150.00 debit balance. The account is closed with a $150.00 credit. Harry Rossi, Capital is debited for $150.00 to show the decrease in that account. The effect of this closing entry is shown in the T accounts at the right.

Harry Rossi, Capital			
Closing	150.00	Balance	4 000.00
		Closing	1 617.00

Harry Rossi, Drawing			
Balance	150.00	Closing	150.00

The drawing account has a zero balance. Information about withdrawals for the next fiscal period will be separated from information about previous fiscal periods.

The new balance of Harry Rossi, Capital is $5 467.00. This new balance is the amount of equity the owner has in Putt Around at the end of the fiscal period. This balance is the same as the amount of capital on the balance sheet, page 135.

Summary of closing entries

The following diagram summarizes the use of Income Summary to make closing entries.

Complete ledger after closing entries are posted

Putt Around's complete ledger after all closing entries are posted is below and on pages 151 and 152.

Ledger after closing entries are posted

Ledger after closing
entries are posted
(continued)

ACCOUNT: Golf Equipment — ACCOUNT NO. 13

DATE	ITEM	POST. REF.	DEBIT	CREDIT	DR CR	BALANCE
1988 July 1	Balance	#1	220000		Dr	220000
12		C1	10000		Dr	230000

ACCOUNT: Maintenance Equipment — ACCOUNT NO. 14

DATE	ITEM	POST. REF.	DEBIT	CREDIT	DR CR	BALANCE
1988 July 1	Balance	#1	90000		Dr	90000
1		C1		5000	Dr	85000
2		C1	40000		Dr	125000

ACCOUNT: Melcor Equipment Company — ACCOUNT NO. 21

DATE	ITEM	POST REF	DEBIT	CREDIT	DR CR	BALANCE
1988 July 1	Balance	#1		65000	Cr	65000

ACCOUNT: Sasson Supply Company — ACCOUNT NO. 22

DATE	ITEM	POST. REF.	DEBIT	CREDIT	DR CR	BALANCE
1988 July 1	Balance	#1		55000	Cr	55000
1		C1	20000		Cr	35000

ACCOUNT: Harry Rossi, Capital — ACCOUNT NO. 31

DATE	ITEM	POST. REF.	DEBIT	CREDIT	DR CR	BALANCE
1988 July 1	Balance	#1		350000	Cr	350000
1		C1		50000	Cr	400000
31		#1		161700	Cr	561700
31		#1	15000		Cr	546700

ACCOUNT: Harry Rossi, Drawing — ACCOUNT NO. 32

DATE	ITEM	POST. REF.	DEBIT	CREDIT	DR CR	BALANCE
1988 July 2		C1	10000		Dr	10000
23		C2	5000		Dr	15000
31		#1		15000		

ACCOUNT **Income Summary**   ACCOUNT NO. 33

DATE	ITEM	POST. REF.	DEBIT	CREDIT	DR CR	BALANCE
1988 July 31		J1		2429 00	Cr	2429 00
31		J1	812 00		Cr	1617 00
31		J1	1617 00			

ACCOUNT **Sales**   ACCOUNT NO. 41

DATE	ITEM	POST. REF.	DEBIT	CREDIT	DR CR	BALANCE
1988 July 31		C2		2429 00	Cr	2429 00
31		J1	2429 00			

ACCOUNT **Advertising Expense**   ACCOUNT NO. 51

DATE	ITEM	POST. REF.	DEBIT	CREDIT	DR CR	BALANCE
1988 July 6		C1	25 00			25 00
31		J1		25 00	Dr	

ACCOUNT **Miscellaneous Expense**   ACCOUNT NO. 52

DATE	ITEM	POST. REF.	DEBIT	CREDIT	DR CR	BALANCE
1988 July 2		C1	10 00			10 00
7		C1	10 00		Dr	20 00
15		C2	15 00		Dr	35 00
22		C2	18 00		Dr	53 00
27		C2	5 00		Dr	58 00
30		C2	12 00		Dr	70 00
31		J1		70 00	Dr	

ACCOUNT **Rent Expense**   ACCOUNT NO. 53

DATE	ITEM	POST. REF.	DEBIT	CREDIT	DR CR	BALANCE
1988 July 1		C1	600 00		Dr	600 00
31		J1		600 00		

ACCOUNT **Utilities Expense**   ACCOUNT NO. 54

DATE	ITEM	POST. REF.	DEBIT	CREDIT	DR CR	BALANCE
1988 July 2		C1	25 00		Dr	25 00
5		C1	60 00		Dr	85 00
20		C2	32 00		Dr	117 00
31		J1		117 00		

Ledger after closing entries are posted (concluded)

After all closing entries are posted, revenue accounts, expense accounts, Income Summary, and the drawing account all have zero balances.

POST-CLOSING TRIAL BALANCE

After closing entries are posted, a trial balance is prepared to test that debits still equal credits in the ledger. A trial balance prepared after the closing entries are posted is called a post-closing trial balance. Putt Around's post-closing trial balance, prepared on July 31, 1988, is below.

ACCOUNT TITLE	DEBIT	CREDIT
Putt Around		
Post-Closing Trial Balance		
July 31, 1988		
Cash	2 192 00	
Supplies	7 25 00	
Golf Equipment	2 300 00	
Maintenance Equipment	1 250 00	
Melcor Equipment Company		6 50 00
Sasson Supply Company		3 50 00
Harry Rossi, Capital		5 467 00
	6 467 00	6 467 00

Post-closing trial balance

Only accounts with balances at the end of a fiscal period are listed on a post-closing trial balance. For Putt Around, these accounts are assets, liabilities, and the owner's capital account. Accounts are listed in the same order that they appear in the ledger. Revenue and expense accounts are not listed because they have zero balances. Harry Rossi, Drawing and Income Summary are not listed because they also have zero balances.

The post-closing trial balance above has both debit and credit totals of $6 467.00. The equality of debits and credits in the ledger is proved. The ledger is in balance and ready for the next fiscal period.

SUMMARY OF THE ACCOUNTING CYCLE FOR A SERVICE BUSINESS

Chapters 3 to 9 include a description of Putt Around's accounting activities for a fiscal period. The fiscal period was one month in length. The fiscal period started on July 1 and ended on July 31, 1988. The complete series of accounting activities followed in recording financial information for a fiscal period is called an accounting cycle. *(CONCEPT: Accounting Period Cycle)* Putt Around's accounting cycle is summarized in the flowchart below.

Flowchart of the steps in the accounting cycle

Putt Around's accounting cycle starts with an analysis of source documents and ends with a post-closing trial balance. The parts of the accounting cycle are listed below.

1. Check source documents for accuracy and analyse transactions into debit and credit parts.
2. Record transactions in a journal.

3. Post entries from a journal to a ledger.
4. Prepare a work sheet.
5. Prepare financial statements.
6. Record closing entries in a journal.
7. Post closing entries to a ledger.
8. Prepare a post-closing trial balance.

Some accountants also balance and rule ledger accounts. This is done after the post-closing trial balance is prepared. An increasing number of accountants *do not* balance and rule accounts, however. Balancing and ruling procedures are described in the Appendix.

ACCOUNTING TERMS

What is the meaning of each of the following?

1. closed account
2. closing entries
3. combined entry
4. post-closing trial balance
5. accounting cycle

QUESTIONS FOR INDIVIDUAL STUDY

1. Why are closing entries recorded?
2. Why is an income summary account used in making closing entries?
3. What four things are achieved by Putt Around's closing entries?
4. What accounts are affected by Putt Around's closing entry for revenue? How are they affected?
5. Why is no source document recorded in Putt Around's general journal for closing entries?
6. What effect does Putt Around's closing entry for revenue have on the balance of the sales account?
7. Why does Putt Around make a combined entry to close expense accounts?
8. What accounts are affected by Putt Around's closing entry for expenses? How are they affected?
9. What effect does Putt Around's closing entry for expenses have on the expense account balances?
10. After Putt Around's closing entries for revenue and expenses are posted, what name can be given to the balance of Income Summary?
11. If the business has a net income, what accounts are affected by the entry to close Income Summary? How are they affected?
12. If Putt Around has a net loss, what accounts are affected by the entry to close Income Summary? How are they affected?
13. What accounts are affected by Putt Around's entry to close the drawing account? How are they affected?
14. Why is a post-closing trial balance prepared by Putt Around on July 31, 1988?
15. What ledger accounts are listed on a post-closing trial balance?
16. What are the parts of Putt Around's accounting cycle?

CASES FOR MANAGEMENT DECISION

CASE 1 Helen Moore records and posts closing entries for her business at the end of each fiscal period. She carefully checks the equality of debits and credits in each closing entry. Therefore, she does not prepare a post-closing trial balance. Frank Long does not prepare and post closing entries at the end of each fiscal period. He claims that his ledger has only 25 ac- counts and they do not need to be closed. Who is following the better accounting procedures, Ms. Moore or Mr. Long? Why?

CASE 2 When Roger McPierson records his closing entries, he does not close his drawing account. What effect will this have on his capital account?

CASE 3 The post-closing trial balance for Peckeral Company on September 30, 1988, shows the capital account balance to be $5 130.00. The post-closing trial bal- ance on August 31, 1988, shows the capi- tal account balance to be $4 330.00. What could cause the balance of this account to increase by $800.00?

DRILLS FOR UNDERSTANDING

DRILL 9-D 1   Identifying accounts affected by closing entries

The ledger accounts used by Mickleson Delivery Service are given below.

1. Advertising Expense
2. Baxter Company (liability)
3. Cash
4. Delivery Equipment
5. Delivery Expense
6. Delivery Revenue
7. Foxworthy Garage (liability)
8. Income Summary
9. Miscellaneous Expense
10. Office Equipment
11. Rent Expense
12. Sally Mickleson, Capital
13. Sally Mickleson, Drawing
14. Utilities Expense
15. Warehouse Equipment
16. Wilson Trucking Company (liability)

Use a form similar to the one below.

1	2	3	4
Account Title	Account is affected by a closing entry	After closing entries are posted, account has	
		a zero balance	a balance
1. *Advertising Expense*	√	√	

Instructions: 1. List the account titles in Column 1 of the form. The first account is given as an example.

2. For each account title, place a check mark in Column 2 if the account is affected by a closing entry. The first account is given as an example.

3. Determine if each account will have a balance or not after closing entries are posted. Place a check mark in either Column 3 or 4 to show your decision. The first account is given as an example.

DRILL 9-D 2   Analysing the effect of net income or net loss and withdrawals on capital

Information about 10 businesses is given on the next page.

1	2		3	4	5
Business	Account balances on trial balance			Net income or loss for fiscal period	Balance of capital account on post-closing trial balance
	Capital	Drawing			
1	$ 18 000.00	$ 500.00		$5 568.00	?
2	33 600.00	none		?	$ 31 740.00
3	54 720.00	2 000.00		7 740.00	?
4	24 960.00	800.00		4 056.00	?
5	67 800.00	2 500.00		?	63 800.00
6	46 620.00	none		?	51 840.00
7	44 256.00	?		3 168.00	43 824.00
8	111 000.00	5 000.00		?	106 144.00
9	?	500.00		2 844.00	31 696.00
10	5 600.00	250.00		750.00	?

Instructions: On a separate sheet of paper, figure the amount that is missing for each business. Businesses 1 and 2 are given as examples.

Business 1: Beginning capital (Column 2), $18 000.00, + net income (Column 4), $5 568.00 = total, $23 568.00. Total, $23 568.00 − drawing (Column 3), $500.00 = capital on post-closing trial balance (Column 5), $23 068.00.

Business 2: Capital on post-closing trial balance (Column 5), $31 740.00 − beginning capital (Column 2), $33 600.00 = −$1 860.00, net loss for Column 4. (A negative number indicates that there is a net loss. The amount should be written in Column 4 as *−$1 860.00* to show that it is a net loss.)

APPLICATION PROBLEMS

PROBLEM 9-1 Recording closing entries

The solution to Problem 7-2 is needed to complete Problem 9-1.

Instructions: Use the work sheet completed in Problem 7-2. Record the closing entries on page 1 of a general journal.

The solution to Problem 9-1 is needed to complete Problem 9-2.

PROBLEM 9-2 Posting closing entries

The solutions to Problem 7-1 and Problem 9-1 are needed to complete Problem 9-2.

Instructions: Use the ledger completed in Problem 7-1 and the solution to Problem 9-1. Post the closing entries.

The solution to Problem 9-2 is needed to complete Problem 9-3.

PROBLEM 9-3   Preparing a post-closing trial balance

The solution to Problem 9-2 is needed to complete Problem 9-3.

Instructions: 1. Use the ledger completed in Problem 9-2.
2. Prepare a post-closing trial balance.

PROBLEM 9-4   Recording closing entries

Parts of Miracle-Kleen's work sheet are given below.

Miracle-Kleen
Work Sheet
For Month Ended October 31, 19--

Account Title	Income Statement	
	Debit	Credit
Sales		1 820 00
Advertising Expense.....................................	86 80	
Electricity Expense.......................................	76 00	
Miscellaneous Expense................................	36 80	
Rent Expense	500 00	
Repairs Expense	37 00	
Water Expense	70 40	
	807 00	1 820 00
Net Income	1 013 00	
	1 820 00	1 820 00

The balance of the account Jerald Bessemer, Drawing on October 31 is $500.00.

Instructions: 1. Use page 1 of a general journal. Record the closing entry for revenue.
2. Record the closing entry for expenses.
3. Record the closing entry to close Income Summary and record net income in the capital account.
4. Record the closing entry to close the drawing account.

ENRICHMENT PROBLEMS

MASTERY PROBLEM 9-M   Recording closing entries

Parts of Continental Travel Agency's work sheet are given on the next page. The account Teresa Jason, Drawing has a balance of $1 000.00 on June 30 of the current year.

Instructions: Use page 1 of a general journal. Record the four closing entries.

Continental Travel Agency
Work Sheet
For Month Ended June 30, 19--

Account Title	Income Statement	
	Debit	Credit
Sales		5 293 65
Advertising Expense	335 25	
Automobile Expense	627 00	
Electricity Expense	486 00	
Miscellaneous Expense	160 20	
Rent Expense	2 025 00	
Utilities Expense	450 00	
	4 083 45	5 293 65
Net Income	1 210 20	
	5 293 65	5 293 65

CHALLENGE PROBLEM 9-C Preparing a work sheet; recording and posting closing entries; preparing a post-closing trial balance

Middletown Company's ledger accounts are given in the working papers accompanying this textbook.

Instructions: 1. Figure the account balances. Prepare a trial balance on a work sheet form.

2. Complete the work sheet.

3. Prepare the closing entries. Use page 1 of a general journal.

4. Post the closing entries.

5. Prepare a post-closing trial balance.

Reinforcement Activity 1

PART D

An Accounting Cycle for a Sole Proprietorship Using a Cash Journal

The work sheet prepared in Part B and used in Part C is needed to complete Part D. Also needed are the ledger used in Parts A and B and the general journal used in Part A.

Reinforcement Activity 1, Part D, includes the accounting activities needed to complete the end-of-fiscal-period work for Wilson's Secretarial Service.

Completing the end-of-fiscal-period work

Instructions: 16. Use the work sheet. Record closing entries on page 1 of the general journal.

17. Post the closing entries to the ledger.

18. Prepare a post-closing trial balance.

SUMMARY

The accounting cycle for Wilson's Secretarial Service is now complete. The activities listed below were included.

Part A • Recording an opening entry in a general journal.
 • Opening ledger accounts.
 • Posting an opening entry.
 • Recording transactions in a cash journal.
 • Proving cash.
 • Totalling, proving, ruling, and posting a cash journal.

Part B • Preparing a trial balance on work sheet paper.
 • Completing a work sheet.

Part C • Preparing financial statements (income statement; balance sheet).

Part D • Recording and posting closing entries.
 • Preparing a post-closing trial balance.

Current Account and Reconciling the Bank Statement

ENABLING PERFORMANCE TASKS

After studying Chapter 10, you will be able to:

a. Define accounting terms related to a current account and reconciling a bank statement.
b. Explain accounting principles and practices related to current accounts.
c. Prepare a bank deposit slip.
d. Endorse cheques to transfer ownership.
e. Prepare cheque stubs and write cheques.
f. Prepare a bank statement reconciliation.
g. Record a bank service charge in a cash journal.
h. Record a dishonored cheque in a cash journal.

All money kept at a place of business plus money in a bank is usually referred to as cash on hand. Money is less safe than most other assets for several reasons. (1) Money can be transferred from one person to another without ownership being questioned. Usually, cash is considered owned by the person possessing it. (2) Money can be lost because of mistakes in making change. (3) Errors can be made in recording cash receipts or cash payments.

Cash transactions occur in most businesses more frequently than other kinds of transactions. Thus, there are more chances to make recording errors affecting cash. Also, money can be lost or stolen. Therefore, most businesses deposit all cash receipts and make most cash payments by issuing cheques.

If all cash receipts are placed in a bank, a business has more evidence that accounting records for cash are accurate. The amount of cash received will equal the cash placed in a bank. Also, the amount of cash withdrawn from a bank equals the amount of cash payments. These procedures give some control over a business' cash.

OPENING A CURRENT ACCOUNT

Placing cash in a bank account is called making a deposit. The person or business in whose name cash is deposited is called a depositor. A bank account from which a business can order payments to others is called a current account. A business paper used to make payments from a current account is known as a cheque.

> Sometimes depositors wish to leave cash in a bank for a period of time to earn interest. A bank account on which a bank pays interest to a depositor is called a savings account. Some current accounts may also earn interest. These interest-bearing current accounts must have a minimum balance and are known as NOTICE accounts.

A signature card

Depositors must tell a bank which persons are authorized to sign cheques. A form signed by each person authorized to sign cheques is called a signature card. Putt Around's signature card signed by Harry Rossi is below.

THE TORONTO-DOMINION BANK

Authorized Signatures For:

PUTT AROUND   Date Opened: June 2, 1988
Address: 12100-199 Street   Current ☒   Savings ☐
Edmonton, AB T5L 4J3   Initial Deposit: $900.00
Telephone 470-3529   Account Number: 0874-0814211

Name and Title (please print)   Specimen Signature.
Harry Rossi, Manager   Harry Rossi

Signature card for a current account

When more than one person is authorized to sign cheques, each person's signature must appear on the signature card. Banks use signature cards to verify signatures on cheques presented for payment.

Cheques must always be signed with the same signatures shown on signature cards. Sometimes businesses need to change the persons authorized to sign cheques. When this occurs, a new signature card is prepared.

> Signature cards are also prepared for personal chequing accounts. A business owner should keep personal and business cash separate. *(CONCEPT: Business Entity)* For family joint chequing accounts, both partners sign a signature card.

A deposit slip

When making deposits, depositors prepare forms showing what is being deposited. A bank form on which a depositor lists all cash and cheques being deposited is called a deposit slip. A deposit slip prepared by Putt Around is below.

NAME OF ACCOUNT *Putt Around*			THE TORONTO-DOMINION BANK
ACCOUNT NUMBER 0 8 7 4 — 0 8 1 4 2 1 1			CURRENT ACCOUNT DEPOSIT
CHEQUES *August 1* 1988			CREDIT

NAME OR PLACE	AMOUNT				
1. *M. Dorons*	20	00			
2. *J. Sherman*	12	00			
3. *S. Pollis*	16	00			
4. *K. Mattle*	5	00			
5.					
6.					
7.					
8.					
9.					
10.					
11.					
12.					
13.					
14.					
15.					
16.					
17.					
TOTAL CHEQUES	53	00			

13220 (2-81)

Putt Around
12100 - 199 Strut
August 1 _____ 19 88
ACCOUNT NO.
0 8 7 4 — 0 8 1 4 2 1 1

15 x 1		15	00
x 2			
12 x 5		60	00
5 x 10		50	00
10 x 20		200	00
1 x 50		50	00
x 100			
COIN			
U.S. CURRENCY			
TOTAL CASH $		375	00
TOTAL CHEQUES		53	00
SUB-TOTAL $		428	00
ADD/DEDUCT ADJUSTMENT RE: U.S. ITEMS			
NET DEPOSIT $		428	00

A deposit slip is prepared in duplicate by the depositor and is then presented to the teller at the depositor's bank. The bank teller verifies the accuracy of the information, stamps the carbon copy to provide the depositor with a receipt, and enters the amount of the deposit in the bank's computer terminal to bring the depositor's balance up to date.

The cheques being deposited may be listed on the deposit slip by the person's name, the company name, or the name of the bank on which the cheque is drawn.

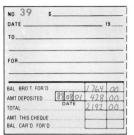

Deposit recorded on a
cheque stub

Recording deposits on cheque stubs

Putt Around records a deposit on the next unused cheque stub. Putt Around's August 1 deposit is on the cheque stub at the left.

Putt Around's cash receipts are recorded in a journal as cash is received. Thus, no journal entry is made to record a deposit. However, some journals have a special column for recording the amount of deposits. This deposit column information can be used to check that all cash received has been deposited.

CBA numbers

Identification numbers assigned to banks by the Canadian Bankers Association are called CBA numbers. CBA numbers are printed on cheques and may be printed on deposit slips. The CBA number for the Toronto-Dominion Bank, 004, is shown on the cheque below.

Cheque with CBA number
and magnetic ink
characters

The transit number, *83369*, is used by the banking system to route cheques to the area and bank on which the cheques are drawn. The first four digits identify the specific branch (Westmount) and the last digit identifies the province (Alberta) in which the bank is located.

Magnetic ink characters

Banks print special numbers along the bottom of cheques. These numbers are printed in special type and magnetic ink. The numbers are referred to as magnetic ink characters. Magnetic ink characters can be ''read'' by a bank's automated equipment. Using magnetic ink characters speeds a bank's sorting and recording of cheques. The numbers are pre-printed along the bottom of blank cheques received from a bank by a depositor.

When a bank receives a cheque, the amount is printed along the bottom in the same type and ink. The bank's automated equipment reads this bottom line and records the amount in the depositor's current account. Magnetic ink characters are printed along the bottom of the cheque, page 164.

TRANSFERRING CHEQUES

The name of the person to whom a cheque is issued is written on a cheque. The person to whom a cheque is issued becomes the owner of the cheque. Ownership of a cheque can be transferred. The cheque's owner transfers ownership by signing on the cheque's back. A signature or stamp on a cheque's back transferring ownership is called an endorsement.

Several endorsements are commonly used. Each endorsement has a specific use in transferring ownership.

Blank endorsement

An endorsement consisting only of the endorser's signature is called a blank endorsement. A lost or stolen cheque with a blank endorsement can be cashed by anyone who has the cheque. Ownership can be transferred without further endorsement. Blank endorsements should be used only when a depositor is at a bank ready to cash or deposit cheques.

Blank endorsement

Special endorsement

An endorsement stating to whom a cheque is to be paid is called a special endorsement. Special endorsements are sometimes known as endorsements in full. Only the person or business named in a special endorsement can cash or transfer a cheque.

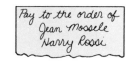

Special endorsement

Restrictive endorsement

An endorsement restricting transfer of a cheque is called a restrictive endorsement. Restrictive endorsements are often used when cheques are prepared for deposit. The endorsement can be either written or stamped on the cheque as shown at the right.

When using blank, special, or restrictive endorsements, endorsers guarantee payment of cheques. If a bank does not receive payment for a cheque, the endorser must pay the bank.

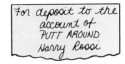

Restrictive endorsement

Putt Around stamps restrictive endorsements on cheques at the time they are received from customers. This procedure prevents unauthorized persons from cashing any cheques that might be lost or stolen.

WRITING CHEQUES

Most cheques used by businesses are prenumbered as part of the printing process. If cheque numbers are not printed, the numbers must be written on the cheques. Putt Around uses prenumbered cheques ordered from its bank. Consecutive numbers provide an easy way to identify each cheque. Also, the numbers help Putt Around assure that no blank cheques are lost or misplaced.

Preparing cheque stubs

A person or business issuing a cheque is called a drawer. A person or business to whom a cheque is issued is called a payee. A bank on which a cheque is drawn is called a drawee. Putt Around's Cheque No. 20 is below.

NO 20	$ 200.00			12100–199 Street Edmonton, AB T5L 4J3		NO 20
DATE _July 1_ 19 88				PAY TO THE		_July 1_ 19 88
TO _Sasson Supply Co._				ORDER OF _Sasson Supply Company_ — $ 200.00		
FOR _Payment on account_				_Two hundred and no/100_ ——— DOLLARS		
BAL. BRO'T. FOR'D	1100	00		**THE TORONTO-DOMINION BANK**		
AMT DEPOSITED				Westmount Shopping Centre, Edmonton, AB T5M 3L7		
TOTAL DATE	1100	00		FOR _Payment on account_ BY _Harry Rossi_		
AMT. THIS CHEQUE	200	00				
BAL. CAR'D. FOR'D	900	00		⑈020⑈ ⑊83369⑊004⑊ 0874⑊081421⑈		

Completed cheque stub and cheque

The following information is placed on Cheque Stub No. 20
1. Amount of the cheque, *$200.00*.
2. Date of the cheque, *July 1, 1988*.
3. Payee, *Sasson Supply Company*.
4. Purpose of the cheque, *Payment on account*.

The cheque's amount is subtracted from the cheque stub total to figure the new current account balance. (Total, *$1 100.00, less* amount of this cheque, *$200.00, equals* balance carried forward, *$900.00*.) The new balance, *$900.00*, is written on Cheque Stub No. 21.

Preparing a cheque

After a cheque stub is completed, a cheque is prepared. The procedure described below is for the cheque on page 166.

1 The date is written in the space for the date, *July 1, 1988*.

> The date written on a cheque should be the month, day, and year on which the cheque is issued. Banks will not accept cheques that have a future date. However, they will hold them until the due date and then deposit them in the customer's account. A cheque with a future date on it is known as a postdated cheque.

2 The name of the payee is written following the words "Pay to the Order of," *Sasson Supply Company*.

> If a payee is a business, use the business' name rather than the owner's name. If a payee is a person, use the person's name.

3 The amount is written following the dollar sign, *$200.00*.

> The figures are written close to the printed dollar sign. This procedure prevents anyone from writing another figure in front of the amount.

4 The amount is written in words on the line with the word "Dollars," *Two hundred and no/100*.

> This written amount verifies the amount written in figures. The words begin at the extreme left of the line provided. A line is drawn through the remaining space to the printed word *Dollars*. This line prevents anyone from inserting additional words to change the amount. If the amounts in figures and in words are not the same, a bank often will pay the amount in words. Sometimes, when the amounts do not agree, a bank will refuse to accept a cheque.
>
> Some businesses use a cheque-writing machine to prepare cheques. The amount is perforated into the cheque paper on the Dollar line. The amount perforated into the cheque cannot be changed without destroying the cheque.

5 The purpose of a cheque is written in the space provided, *Payment on account*.

> Some cheques have a small detachable slip on which to write the purpose. Many businesses use a cheque with a detachable slip so all details of the payment can be noted.

6 The cheque is signed by an authorized person, *Harry Rossi*.

> The last thing to do in preparing a cheque is to sign it. Before a cheque is signed, each item on the cheque and stub is verified. A cheque should *not* be signed until it has been verified for accuracy.

Voiding a cheque

Banks usually refuse to accept altered cheques. Banks often refuse to accept cheques when the amounts written in figures and words do not agree. Also, most banks refuse to accept postdated cheques. If any kind of error is made on a cheque, a new cheque is prepared. A cheque that is not issued should still be filed for the records. This procedure helps account for all prenumbered cheques and assures that no cheque is lost or misplaced.

If a cheque is not issued, the word *Void* is written across the face of the cheque. Marking a cheque so that it cannot be used is called voiding a cheque. A similar notation is placed on the cheque stub for a voided cheque.

Putt Around records all cheques in a cash journal. Inspection of the cash journal's Doc. No. column, pages 82 and 83, shows all cheque numbers in numerical order. If a cheque number is missing from the Doc. No. column, not all cheques are accounted for. Thus, Putt Around also records voided cheques in a cash journal. The words *Voided cheque* are written in the Account Title column. A dash is placed in the Cash Credit column. The cheque number is written in the Doc. No. column. A check mark is placed in the Post. Ref. column.

RECONCILING A BANK STATEMENT

Banks keep separate records for each depositor. Deposit slips and cheques are recorded in depositors' accounts on the day received by a bank. Many banks use automated machines to record items daily in depositors' accounts. This procedure keeps depositors' accounts up to date at all times. The up-to-date balance appearing on a depositor's bank records is called a bank balance

A bank statement

A copy of a depositor's bank records usually is sent to the depositor each month. A report of deposits, withdrawals, and bank balance sent to a depositor by a bank is called a bank statement.

Putt Around received the bank statement, page 169, on August 1, 1988. The last amount in the Balance column, $1 897.00, is the ending bank balance for this statement.

Some banks mail bank statements to all depositors at the end of each month. Many banks have a large number of depositors. Mailing all bank statements at the end of a month requires that all work be done at one time. Banks may use a system of preparing and mailing statements

Initials of last name of depositors	Day of month on which statements are mailed
A–H	10th
I–O	20th
P–Z	30th

		STATEMENT OF ACCOUNT FOR			ACCOUNT NUMBER
TD BANK Westmount Shopping Centre Edmonton, AB T5M 3L7		PUTT AROUND 12100-199 STREET EDMONTON, AB T5L 4J3			0874-0814211 STATEMENT DATE 1988 07 30

BALANCE FROM PREVIOUS STATEMENT	NO. OF CHEQUES	AMOUNT OF CHEQUES	NO. OF DEPOSITS	AMOUNT OF DEPOSITS	SERVICE CHARGES	STATEMENT BALANCE
1 190.00	18	1 842.00	5	2 551.00	2.00	1 897.00

DATE	CHEQUES			DEPOSITS	BALANCE
1988 06 30					1 190.00
1988 07 01	25.00			800.00	1 965.00
1988 07 02	60.00	5.00	600.00		1 300.00
1988 07 04	400.00	25.00	50.00	300.00	1 125.00
1988 07 05	10.00	100.00	200.00		815.00
1988 07 08	25.00	60.00			730.00
1988 07 09	10.00				720.00
1988 07 11				530.00	1 250.00
1988 07 16	75.00				1 175.00
1988 07 17	15.00	100.00		492.00	1 552.00
1988 07 25	50.00	32.00		429.00	1 899.00
1988 07 30	SC 2.00				1 897.00

PLEASE EXAMINE AT ONCE — IF NO ERROR IS REPORTED WITHIN 10 DAYS THE ACCOUNT WILL BE CONSIDERED CORRECT AND VOUCHERS GENUINE, REFER ANY DISCREPANCY TO OUR ACCOUNTING DEPARTMENT IMMEDIATELY

Bank statement

throughout the month. The schedule on page 168 is used by the Toronto-Dominion Bank. The bank prepares and mails Putt Around's bank statement on the 30th of each month. Putt Around receives the bank statement sometime around the first of the next month.

Checking the accuracy of a bank statement

Banks seldom make errors in depositors' bank records. However, a cheque might be charged to a wrong account. If errors are discovered on bank statements, depositors should notify the bank at once.

Errors may be made by depositors. The most common error is in arithmetic. However, businesses may make errors in entries for cheques issued or cash deposited. When depositors receive bank statements, the information should be verified with the business' accounting records.

All cheques charged to a depositor's account are returned by a bank with the bank statement. Cheques paid by a bank and returned to a depositor are called cancelled cheques. Cheques issued by a depositor but not yet received by a bank are called outstanding cheques. Not all deposits may be listed on the latest bank statement received by a depositor. Deposits made but not yet shown on a bank statement are called outstanding deposits.

Banks charge a fee for maintaining a depositor's chequing or current account. A charge made by a bank for maintaining a depositor's account is called a bank service charge. Banks deduct bank service charges from depositors' accounts. Bank service charges are listed on bank statements. Putt Around's bank statement, page 169, includes a service charge of $2.00.

> Some banks do not make a service charge if a depositor's current or chequing account balance is large enough. Each bank has its own regulations about service charges.

A bank's records and depositor's records may not agree for the reasons listed below.

1. A bank service charge is not recorded on a depositor's accounting records.
2. The bank statement does not show outstanding deposits.
3. A bank has not received outstanding cheques.
4. A depositor may have made errors in recording entries affecting cash.
5. The bank may have made an error.

In good accounting practice, a business' accounting records are verified to assure that they agree with the bank statement.

Reconciling a bank statement

Bringing bank statement and chequebook balances into agreement is called reconciling a bank statement. Putt Around reconciles its bank statement as soon as the statement is received from the bank. Before the reconciliation is prepared, Putt Around proves cash. A procedure for proving cash is described on page 83.

Cancelled cheques are arranged in numerical order. A check mark is placed on the cheque stub for each cancelled cheque. Cheque stubs with no check marks show that cheques were outstanding at the time the bank statement was prepared.

The reconciliation is prepared as shown on page 171. The procedure for reconciling Putt Around's bank statement is described below.

1 *Figure adjusted cheque stub balance.*

- List in the left amount column the balance shown on the next unused cheque stub. Cheque Stub No. 39 shows an ending balance of $2 192.00.

Putt Around Reconciliation of Bank Statement August 1, 1988					
Balance on Cheque Stub No. 39, August 1, 1988	2192 00		Balance on bank statement, July 30, 1988		1897 00
Deduct:			Add:		
Service charge for July	2 00		Outstanding deposit, July 31, 1988	428 00	
			Total	2325 00	
			Deduct:		
			Outstanding cheques		
			No. 34 18.00		
			No. 36 100.00		
			No. 37 5.00		
			No. 38 12.00	135 00	
Adjusted cheque stub balance, Aug. 1, 1988	2190 00		Adjusted bank balance August 1, 1988		2190 00

Reconciliation of a bank statement

- List the bank service charge, $2.00. Putt Around's bank service charge is obtained from the bank statement, page 169.

- Subtract the bank service charge from the cheque stub balance. List the difference, $2 190.00, on the reconciliation. Label this amount *Adjusted cheque stub balance, August 1, 1988*.

2 Figure adjusted bank balance.

- List in the right amount column the bank statement balance, $1 897.00. This is the last amount in the bank statement's Balance column, page 169.

- List any outstanding deposits not shown on the bank statement. Cheque Stub No. 39 shows a deposit of $428.00 that is not listed on the bank statement.

- Add the outstanding balance to the bank statement balance. Write the total, *$2 325.00*, in the right amount column.

- List the number and amount of each outstanding cheque. Four cheques are outstanding according to the verification of cancelled cheques.

- Add the amounts of all outstanding cheques. List the total, *$135.00*, in the right amount column.

- Subtract the total amount of outstanding cheques from the previous total. Write the difference, *$2 190.00*, in the amount column. Label this amount *Adjusted bank balance, August 1, 1988*.

3 *Compare adjusted balances*. Verify that the two adjusted amounts are the same. Putt Around's adjusted cheque stub balance is $2 190.00. The adjusted bank statement balance is the same amount. The two adjusted balances are the same. The bank statement is reconciled.

> If the two adjusted balances are not the same, an error has been made. The error must be found and corrected.

Printed form for reconciliation of bank statement

Sometimes banks print suggested reconciliation forms on the back of bank statements. A suggested printed reconciliation form is below.

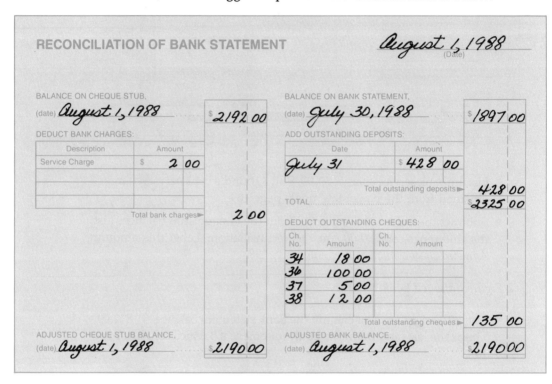

RECORDING A BANK SERVICE CHARGE

The bank service charge, *$2.00*, is deducted from Putt Around's current account by the bank. Putt Around must also record this payment on the appropriate cheque stub and in the cash journal.

Recording a bank service charge in a chequebook

Putt Around records the service charge on the next unused cheque stub, Cheque Stub No. 39. The words *July S/C* are written on the cheque stub to identify the amount. The amount is subtracted from the total on the cheque stub. The difference, *$2 190.00*, is written on the cheque stub at the left. The

Service charge recorded on a cheque stub

balance on the cheque stub, *$2 190.00*, is now correct. The balance is the same as the adjusted cheque stub balance on the bank reconciliation.

Recording a bank service charge in a cash journal

Putt Around's bank service charge is one cash payment for which no cheque is written. However, the bank service charge must still be recorded in the cash journal. A form is prepared describing the reason for the entry. A form on which a brief message is written is called a memorandum. Sometimes transactions occur for which there is no business paper. For the service charge entry, Putt Around prepares a memorandum as the source document. *(CONCEPT: Objective Evidence)* Putt Around's Memorandum No. 1 is below.

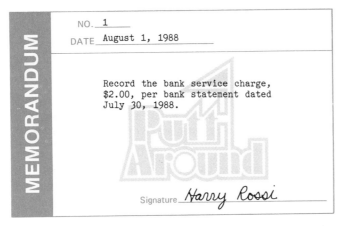

MEMORANDUM

NO. __1__

DATE __August 1, 1988__

Record the bank service charge, $2.00, per bank statement dated July 30, 1988.

Signature __Harry Rossi__

The effect of the bank service charge entry is shown in the T accounts at the right.

The entry increases Putt Around's expenses. Miscellaneous Expense is debited for $2.00. The entry also decreases the cash account. Cash is credited for $2.00.

Memorandum

Miscellaneous Expense	
2.00	

Cash	
	2.00

Putt Around's Memorandum No. 1 is the source document for the entry to record the bank service charge. *(CONCEPT: Objective Evidence)* Putt Around's cash journal entry for the August 1 bank service charge is below.

Entry to record a bank service charge

CASH		DATE	ACCOUNT TITLE	DOC. NO.	POST. REF.	GENERAL		SALES CREDIT	
DEBIT	CREDIT					DEBIT	CREDIT		
		1988 Aug. 1	*Balance on hand, $2 192.00*		✓				1
	200	1	*Miscellaneous Expense*	M1		200			2

CASH JOURNAL   PAGE *3*

The date, *1,* is written in the Date column. The debit to Miscellaneous Expense, *$2.00,* is written in the General Debit column. The credit to Cash, *$2.00,* is written in the Cash Credit column. The account title, *Miscellaneous*

Expense, is written in the Account Title column. The source document number, *M1*, is written in the Doc. No. column.

The abbreviation for memorandums is *M*. Thus, the abbreviation *M1* means that the source document is Memorandum No. 1.

RECORDING DISHONORED CHEQUES

Banks may not accept cheques for a number of reasons. (1) The amount on the cheque appears to have been altered. (2) The signature on a cheque may appear to be different than on the signature card. (3) The amount written in words may be different from the amount in figures. (4) The cheque may be postdated. (5) The depositor's account may have insufficient funds to pay the cheque. Any cheque that a bank refuses to cash is called a dishonored cheque.

Putt Around records cheques received as cash. The cheques are deposited in the bank. Putt Around records dishonored cheques as cash payments.

On August 5, the bank notifies Putt Around that a customer's cheque has been dishonored.

August 5, 1988. Notice received from bank of a dishonored cheque, $5.00, plus bank fee, $1.00. Memorandum No. 2.

A memorandum is prepared explaining the entry. The memorandum is the entry's source document. *(CONCEPT: Objective Evidence)* This entry is another cash payment not supported by a cheque stub as source document.

The entry affects Putt Around's accounts as shown in the T accounts at the left.

Miscellaneous Expense	
6.00	

Cash	
	6.00

Dishonored cheques are an expense. The total expense is the value of the dishonored cheque plus the bank fee. Miscellaneous Expense is debited for $6.00 to record the expense. The cash balance is decreased by this entry. Cash is credited for $6.00 to show this decrease.

The entry to record the dishonored cheque is below.

Entry to record a dishonored cheque

The date, *5*, is written in the Date column. The debit to Miscellaneous Expense, *$6.00*, is recorded in the General Debit column. The credit to Cash, *$6.00*, is recorded in the Cash Credit column. The account title, *Miscellaneous Expense*, is written in the Account Title column. The source document, *M2*, is written in the Doc. No. column.

The decrease in cash is also recorded on a cheque stub. The cheque stub entry for the dishonored cheque is at the right.

> If a dishonored cheque *is* collected later, Cash is debited and Miscellaneous Expense is credited.

Intentionally issuing a cheque with insufficient money to pay it, altering a cheque, or forging a cheque is illegal. When a cheque is dishonored, a question is raised about the maker's credit rating. A dishonored cheque is always a serious matter. Depositors must prepare cheques with care to assure that all cheques will be honored.

Dishonored cheque recorded on a cheque stub

ACCOUNTING TERMS

What is the meaning of each of the following?

1. making a deposit	9. blank endorsement	17. bank statement
2. depositor	10. special endorsement	18. cancelled cheques
3. chequing account	11. restrictive endorsement	19. outstanding cheques
4. savings account	12. drawer	20. outstanding deposits
5. signature card	13. payee	21. bank service charge
6. deposit slip	14. drawee	22. reconciling a bank statement
7. CBA numbers	15. voiding a cheque	23. memorandum
8. endorsement	16. bank balance	24. dishonored cheque

QUESTIONS FOR INDIVIDUAL STUDY

1. Why is cash less safe than most other assets?
2. Why is a depositor required to sign a signature card for a chequing account?
3. How may cheques be listed on a deposit slip?
4. What record does a depositor have that a deposit has been made in a chequing account?
5. Why is a deposit not recorded in Putt Around's cash journal?
6. What does each part of a transit number identify?
7. Why are magnetic ink characters printed along the bottom of a cheque?
8. What endorsements are often used by businesses to prepare cheques for deposit?
9. What might a bank do if the amounts in figures and in words on a cheque differ?
10. Why is signing a cheque the last thing to do in preparing a cheque?
11. What should be done if a cheque is prepared incorrectly?
12. What should be done with a bank statement when received by a depositor?
13. Why will a bank statement balance often *not* agree with a chequebook balance?
14. When should a bank statement reconciliation be prepared?
15. Why does Putt Around use a memorandum as the source document for an entry for bank service charges?
16. What two accounts are affected by Putt Around's entry to record a bank service charge? How are they affected?
17. Why might a bank dishonor a cheque?
18. What accounts are affected by Putt Around's entry, page 174, to record a dishonored cheque? How are they affected?

CASES FOR MANAGEMENT DECISION

CASE 1 Melody Hall recently opened a current account for her new business. She had all six of her employees sign the signature card. Is this a good practice? Explain your answer.

CASE 2 Michael O'Rielly owns a farm. He mails all deposits to the bank. In preparing cheques for deposit, Mr. O'Rielly uses a blank endorsement. Is this a good practice? Explain your answer.

CASE 3 Jeff Watson often writes cheques when he has insufficient money in his chequing account. He dates the cheques for the first of the next month. At the end of each month he deposits his paycheque to cover the cheques he has already written. What are the dangers in this practice?

CASE 4 Peter Fischer accumulates his monthly bank statements. Once every four months he reconciles his chequing account. Wanda Horowitz reconciles each monthly bank statement as it is received. Is Mr. Fischer or Ms. Horowitz using the better accounting practice? Explain your answer.

DRILLS FOR UNDERSTANDING

DRILL 10-D 1   Reconciling a bank statement

On June 30 of the current year, Wilma Phlong receives a bank statement dated June 25. The information below is obtained from the statement and her chequebook.

> Bank balance, $639.45.
> Service charge, $6.15.
> Outstanding cheques: No. 84, $32.40, and No. 102, $18.45.
> Balance on Cheque Stub No. 103, $594.75.

Instructions: Reconcile Miss Phlong's bank statement.

DRILL 10-D 2   Reconciling a bank statement

On November 1 of the current year, Theodore Anderson receives a bank statement dated October 27. The information below is obtained from the statement and his cheque book.

> Bank balance, $898.34.
> Service charge, $3.40.
> Outstanding deposit made on October 28, $128.94.
> Outstanding cheques: No. 1280, $12.99; No. 1296, $42.69; and No. 1299, $21.26.
> Balance on Cheque Stub No. 1304, $953.74.

Instructions: Reconcile Mr. Anderson's bank statement.

DRILL 10-D 3   Reconciling a bank statement

On May 25 of the current year, JoAnn Wilson receives a bank statement dated May 20. The information on the next page is obtained from the statement and her chequebook.

Instructions: Reconcile Mrs. Wilson's bank statement.

Bank balance, $473.92.
Service charge, $1.84.
Outstanding cheque No. 47, $41.04.
Two outstanding deposits: May 21, $32.00 and May 24, $125.00.
Balance on Cheque Stub No. 50, $591.72.

APPLICATION PROBLEMS

PROBLEM 10-1 Preparing a deposit slip

On October 14 of the current year, Business Services makes a deposit. The business' current account number is 74-34846-01. The items listed below are to be deposited.

Money on hand to be deposited
Currency $196.00
Coins 50.06

Cheques on hand to be deposited
Timothy Hedrick, drawn on the Canadian Imperial Bank of Commerce,
St. Albert, AB (CBA No. 010)... 65.00
Edna Falls, drawn on the Royal Bank of Canada, Sherwood Park, AB
(CBA No. 003)... 21.42
Rodger Milley, drawn on the Bank of Nova Scotia, Calgary, AB (CBA No. 002)........ 52.02

Instructions: 1. Prepare a deposit slip for this deposit. Identify the cheques by the name of the bank on which they are drawn.
2. Endorse the cheques being deposited. Use a restrictive endorsement similar to the one on page 165. Sign your own name as part of the endorsement.

PROBLEM 10-2 Preparing cheque stubs and writing cheques

You are authorized to sign cheques for Key Car Wash. The first cheque is numbered 21. The balance brought forward from Cheque Stub No. 20 is $389.16. Use the current date on all cheques.

Instructions: 1. Write the beginning balance on Cheque Stub No. 21.
2. Prepare cheque stubs and cheques Nos. 21 and 22.

Cheque No. 21: $25.00; payee, Waters Supply Company; payment on account.
Cheque No. 22: $75.50; payee, Nichols Equipment Company; keyboard repairs.

3. Record a deposit of $126.70 on Cheque Stub No. 23.
4. Prepare cheque stubs and cheques Nos. 23 and 24.

Cheque No. 23: $150.00; payee, Mercer Supply Company; for supplies.
Cheque No. 24: $100.00; payee, John Key (owner of Key Car Wash); for personal
use.

PROBLEM 10-3 Reconciling a bank statement and recording a bank service charge

On November 30 of the current year, Bonnie Scott receives a bank statement for her business, Scotty's Plumbing Service. The bank statement is dated November 26. A comparison of the bank statement and the business' chequebook shows the information given on the next page.

The chequebook balance on Cheque Stub No. 201 is $203.60.
The bank statement balance is $200.53.
An outstanding deposit was made on November 29, $52.25.
The outstanding cheques are: No. 196, $19.94.
                                No. 197, $8.91.
                                No. 201, $22.88.
The bank service charge is $2.55.

Instructions: 1. Prepare a bank reconciliation.
2. Record the bank service charge on page 8 of a cash journal. Memorandum No. 15.

ENRICHMENT PROBLEMS

MASTERY PROBLEM 10-M   Reconciling a bank statement and recording a bank service charge

In the working papers accompanying this textbook are business papers related to a current account for Lanes Service Company.

Instructions: 1. Check the cancelled cheques against the cheque stubs. Place a check mark next to the cheque stub number for each cheque returned by the bank.
2. Make a list of any cheques not returned showing cheque number and amount. These are the outstanding cheques.
3. Check the bank statement against the cheque stubs to determine if all the deposits are listed on the bank statement. List by date and amount any deposits shown on the cheque stubs and not shown on the bank statement. These are the outstanding deposits.
4. Prepare a bank reconciliation. Use the date October 4 of the current year.
5. Record the bank service charge on page 9 of a cash journal. Memorandum No. 22.
6. Record the bank service charge on Cheque Stub No. 805.

CHALLENGE PROBLEM 10-C   Writing cheques; reconciling a bank statement; recording a bank service charge and a dishonored cheque

You are authorized to sign cheques for Kraddock's Service Company. On October 31 of the current year, there are three cheques to be written. On November 1, the company receives a bank statement dated October 29.

Instructions: 1. Record the balance brought forward on Cheque Stub No. 53, $629.18.
2. Prepare cheque stubs and cheques Nos. 53, 54, and 55.

Cheque No. 53. $62.50; Dave's Garage; automobile repairs.
Cheque No. 54. $10.00; Hazelburg's Cleaning Service; washing windows.
Cheque No. 55. $25.00; Midtown Supply Company; supplies.

3. Prepare a bank reconciliation. Use November 1 of the current year.

Bank service charge, $5.60.
Outstanding deposit made on October 30, $178.50.
Outstanding cheques: Nos. 53, 54, and 55.
Bank statement balance, $445.08.

4. Record the bank service charge on page 10 of a cash journal. Memorandum No. 22.
5. Record a dishonored cheque on page 10 of a cash journal. Use November 5 of the current year. Amount of cheque, $5.00; bank fee, $1.00. Memorandum No. 23.

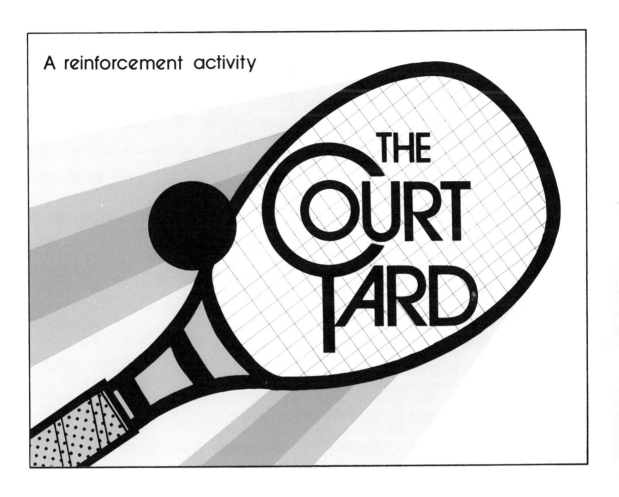

A reinforcement activity

THE COURT YARD

THE COURT YARD is a service business organized as a sole proprietorship. This reinforcement activity covers the transactions completed by a business that rents racquetball courts. A pictorial flowchart of the accounting cycle of THE COURT YARD is shown on the next two pages. This company uses a cash journal, general journal, and ledger. The books of account needed to complete this reinforcement activity are available from the publisher.

179

Flowchart of the Accounting Cycle of
THE COURT YARD

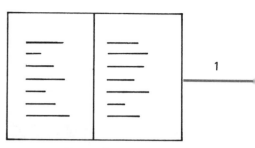

Transactions

1   Record transactions in the cash journal.
2   Post items to be posted individually from the cash journal to the ledger.
3   Post cash journal column totals to the ledger.
4   Prepare the trial balance on the work sheet.
5   Complete the work sheet.
6   Prepare financial statements.
7   Record closing entries in the general journal.
8   Post closing entries to the ledger.
9   Prepare a post-closing trial balance.

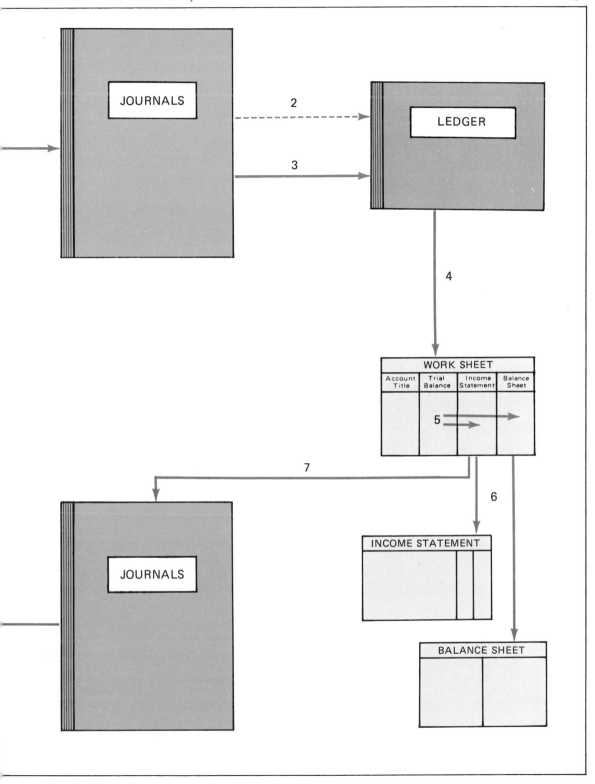

The Court Yard

THE COURT YARD

A racquetball facility is located near a local shopping centre. The building owner rents the facility to Judy Sauvé. Ms. Sauvé operates the business as a recreational centre open to the general public. The business name chosen by Ms. Sauvé is *The Court Yard*.

Individual racquetball courts are rented for half hour intervals. Thus, the business' revenue comes from court rentals.

The Court Yard is open seven days a week from 09:00 to 22:00. Racquets and balls are provided by the business if customers do not have their own personal equipment. The court rentals include use of a locker.

On November 1 of the current year, The Court Yard begins a new accounting system.

Flowchart of The Court Yard's accounting cycle

This reinforcement activity illustrates a complete accounting cycle. The Court Yard uses a one-month fiscal period. The flowchart of the accounting cycle is on pages 180 and 181.

Required materials

Transactions are recorded in a cash journal and a general journal. Ledger accounts are kept using balance-column ledger account forms. The business forms and records needed for the reinforcement activity may be obtained from the publisher of this textbook.

Model illustrations of the business forms and records are on the textbook pages listed below.

Business Forms and Records	Model Illustrations	Business Forms and Records	Model Illustrations
General journal	page 21	Income statement	page 132
Opening entry	page 22	Balance sheet	page 135
Cash journal.......................	pages 82 and 83	Bank reconciliation	page 171
Ledger accounts.................	pages 115–117	Closing entries...................	pages 145–149
Work sheet	page 121	Post-closing trial balance ..	page 153

The Court Yard's cash journal is the same as the one on page 82 except for the title of column 5. The revenue amount column is headed *Court Rentals Credit*.

Source documents

The Court Yard uses four different source documents.

Source Documents	Abbreviations	Transactions Used For
1. Cash register tapes	T	Cash received from racquetball court rentals
2. Receipts	R	Cash received from other than court rentals
3. Cheques/cheque stubs	C	Cash payments
4. Memorandums	M	Others not covered by items 1, 2, and 3 above

STARTING THE COURT YARD'S ACCOUNTING RECORDS

The Court Yard uses the chart of accounts below.

<table>
<tr><td colspan="4" align="center">The Court Yard
Chart of Accounts</td></tr>
<tr><td>(1) ASSETS</td><td>Account Number</td><td>(4) REVENUE</td><td>Account Number</td></tr>
<tr><td>Cash</td><td>11</td><td>Court Rentals</td><td>41</td></tr>
<tr><td>Supplies</td><td>12</td><td></td><td></td></tr>
<tr><td>Office Equipment</td><td>13</td><td>(5) EXPENSES</td><td></td></tr>
<tr><td>Racquetball Equipment</td><td>14</td><td></td><td></td></tr>
<tr><td></td><td></td><td>Advertising Expense</td><td>51</td></tr>
<tr><td>(2) LIABILITIES</td><td></td><td>Maintenance Expense</td><td>52</td></tr>
<tr><td>Meyers Supply Company</td><td>21</td><td>Miscellaneous Expense</td><td>53</td></tr>
<tr><td>Racquetball, Inc.</td><td>22</td><td>Rent Expense</td><td>54</td></tr>
<tr><td>Sports Store</td><td>23</td><td>Utilities Expense</td><td>55</td></tr>
<tr><td>(3) CAPITAL</td><td></td><td></td><td></td></tr>
<tr><td>Judy Sauvé, Capital</td><td>31</td><td></td><td></td></tr>
<tr><td>Judy Sauvé, Drawing</td><td>32</td><td></td><td></td></tr>
<tr><td>Income Summary</td><td>33</td><td></td><td></td></tr>
</table>

On November 1 of the current year, Ms. Sauvé prepares the beginning balance sheet below.

<table>
<tr><td colspan="4" align="center">The Court Yard
Balance Sheet
November 1, 19--</td></tr>
<tr><td align="center">Assets</td><td></td><td align="center">Liabilities</td><td></td></tr>
<tr><td>Cash</td><td>4 000 00</td><td>Meyers Supply Company</td><td>600 00</td></tr>
<tr><td>Supplies</td><td>600 00</td><td>Racquetball, Inc.</td><td>500 00</td></tr>
<tr><td>Office Equipment</td><td>1 000 00</td><td>Sports Store</td><td>1 000 00</td></tr>
<tr><td>Racquetball Equipment</td><td>3 500 00</td><td>Total Liabilities</td><td>2 100 00</td></tr>
<tr><td></td><td></td><td>Capital</td><td></td></tr>
<tr><td></td><td></td><td>Judy Sauvé, Capital</td><td>7 000 00</td></tr>
<tr><td>Total Assets</td><td>9 100 00</td><td>Total Liabilities and Capital</td><td>9 100 00</td></tr>
</table>

Instructions: 1. Record the opening entry on page 1 of the general journal. The source document is the November 1 balance sheet.

2. Open a ledger account for each account listed on the chart of accounts.

3. Post the opening entry to the ledger accounts.

RECORDING THE COURT YARD'S TRANSACTIONS

Instructions for recording transactions and doing other accounting tasks follow. Complete the tasks given in each instruction.

Instructions: 4. Analyse and record each of the following transactions. Begin on page 1 of the cash journal.

Trans.
No.

1	Nov. 1.	Record the cash on hand, $4 000.00.
2	1.	Paid cash for a new cash register, $500.00. C101.
3	1.	Paid cash for November rent, $1 500.00. C102.
4	1.	Paid cash for supplies, $25.00. C103.
5	1.	Received cash from court rentals, $250.00. T1.
6	2.	Paid cash for cleaning and maintenance, $100.00. C104.
7	2.	Paid cash for a new desk top calculator, $50.00. C105.
8	2.	Received cash from court rentals, $140.00. T2.
9	3.	Paid cash for new racquetball equipment, $500.00. C106.
10	3.	Paid cash for business licence, $50.00. C107.
11	3.	Received cash from court rentals, $310.00. T3.
12	3.	Paid cash for telephone bill, $90.00. C108.

Instructions: 5. Post individual items from the cash journal's General Debit and Credit columns.

6. Analyse and record the transactions below.

Trans.
No.

13	Nov. 4.	Paid cash for advertising in local newspaper, $100.00. C109.
14	4.	Received cash from court rentals, $225.00. T4.
15	5.	Paid cash for a new business machine, $500.00. C110.
16	5.	Paid cash for health department permit, $50.00. C111.
17	5.	Received cash from court rentals, $200.00. T5.
18	6.	Paid cash to owner for personal use, $200.00. C112.
19	6.	Received cash from court rentals, $480.00. T6.
20	7.	Received cash from court rentals, $120.00. T7.
21	8.	Paid cash for supplies, $25.00. C113.
22	8.	Paid cash for direct mail advertising, $150.00. C114.
23	8.	Paid cash for cleaning and maintenance, $100.00. C115.
24	8.	Received cash from court rentals, $335.00. T8.

Instructions: 7. Post individual items from the cash journal's General Debit and Credit columns.

8. Prove cash. The balance on the last used cheque stub is $2 120.00.

9. Total, prove, and rule page 1 of the cash journal.

10. Forward the column totals to page 2 of the cash journal.

11. Prepare a report of items as shown below. Give the report to your instructor.

Column totals for page ___ of the cash journal.	
Cash Debit... $_____	Cash Credit..................................... $_____
General Debit.................................. $_____	General Credit .... $_____
	Court Rentals Credit .... $_____
Total Debits..................................... $_____	Total Credits .... $_____

Instructions: 12. Analyse and record the transactions below.

Trans.
No.

25	Nov. 9.	Received cash from court rentals, $120.00. T9.
26	10.	Paid cash to Racquetball, Inc., for part of amount owed, $200.00. C116.
27	10.	Received cash from court rentals, $450.00. T10.
28	11.	Paid cash for new racquetball equipment, $500.00. C117.
29	11.	Received cash from court rentals, $276.00. T11.
30	12.	Paid cash to Sports Store for part of amount owed, $500.00. C118.
31	12.	Received cash from court rentals, $296.00. T12.
32	13.	Paid cash for new business sign to be used as advertising, $400.00. C119.
33	13.	Paid cash to owner for personal use, $200.00. C120.
34	13.	Received cash from court rentals, $438.00. T13.
35	14.	Received cash from court rentals, $204.00. T14.

Instructions: 13. Post individual items from the cash journal's General Debit and Credit columns.

14. Analyse and record the transactions below.

Trans.
No.

36	Nov. 15.	Paid cash for advertising in local newspaper, $100.00. C121.
37	15.	Paid cash for cleaning and maintenance, $100.00. C122.
38	15.	Received cash from court rentals, $252.00. T15.
39	16.	Received cash from court rentals, $300.00. T16.
40	17.	Paid cash to Meyers Supply Company for part of amount owed, $300.00. C123.
41	17.	Received cash from court rentals, $249.00. T17.
42	18.	Received cash from sale of an old cash register, $50.00. R1.
43	18.	Received cash from court rentals, $204.00. T18.
44	19.	Paid cash for new racquetball equipment, $300.00. C124.
45	19.	Received cash from court rentals, $190.00. T19.
46	20.	Paid cash to owner for personal use, $200.00. C125.
47	20.	Received cash from court rentals, $350.00. T20.

Instructions: 15. Post individual items from the cash journal's General Debit and Credit columns.

16. Prove cash. The balance on the last used cheque stub is $2 699.00.

17. Total, prove, and rule page 2 of the cash journal.

18. Forward the column totals to page 3 of the cash journal.

19. Prepare a report similar to the one in Instruction 11.

20. Analyse and record the transactions below.

Trans.
No.

48	Nov. 21.	Received cash from court rentals, $156.00. T21.
49	22.	Paid membership in local Chamber of Commerce, $50.00. C126.
50	22.	Paid cash for direct mail advertising, $150.00. C127.
51	22.	Paid cash for cleaning and maintenance, $100.00. C128.
52	22.	Received cash from court rentals, $252.00. T22.
53	23.	Received cash from court rentals, $444.00. T23.
54	24.	Paid cash to Sports Store for part of amount owed, $250.00. C129.
55	24.	Received cash from court rentals, $380.00. T24.
56	25.	Paid cash for supplies, $20.00. C130.
57	25.	Received cash from court rentals, $156.00. T25.
58	26.	Paid cash for water bill, $150.00. C131.
59	26.	Received cash from court rentals, $210.00. T26.

Instructions: 21. Post individual items from the cash journal's General Debit and Credit columns.

22. Analyse and record the transactions below.

Trans.
No.

60	Nov. 27.	Paid cash to owner for personal use, $200.00. C132.
61	27.	Received cash from court rentals, $240.00. T27.
62	28.	Received cash from court rentals, $192.00. T28.
63	29.	Paid cash for a miscellaneous expense, $35.00. C133.
64	29.	Paid cash for electric bill, $300.00. C134.
65	29.	Paid cash for cleaning and maintenance, $100.00. C135.
66	29.	Received cash from court rentals, $216.00. T29.
67	30.	Paid cash for a new file cabinet, $200.00. C136.
68	30.	Paid cash for supplies, $30.00. C137.
69	30.	Received cash from court rentals, $264.00. T30.

Instructions: 23. Prepare a reconciliation of The Court Yard's bank statement received on November 30. The bank statement is dated November 28. A comparison of the bank statement and The Court Yard's chequebook shows the information below.

Bank statement balance, $3 763.00.
Chequebook balance on Cheque Stub No. 137, $3 624.00.
Outstanding deposits: November 28, $192.00.
                                      November 29, $216.00.
                                      November 30, $264.00.
Outstanding cheques: Nos. 131, 133, 134, 135, 136, and 137.
Service charge listed on bank statement, $4.00.

24. Analyse and record the transaction given on the next page.

Trans.
No.

70   Nov. 30. Record the bank service charge, $4.00. M1.

Instructions: 25. Post the individual items from the cash journal's General Debit and Credit columns.

26. Prove cash. The balance on the last used cheque stub is $3 620.00.

27. Total, prove, and rule page 3 of the cash journal.

28. Post column totals from the cash journal to the ledger accounts.

29. Prepare a report similar to the one in Instruction 11.

COMPLETING THE END-OF-FISCAL-PERIOD WORK

The Court Yard uses a one-month fiscal period. Use the date November 30 of the current year.

Instructions: 30. Figure the ledger account balances.

31. Prepare a trial balance on work sheet paper.

32. Complete the work sheet.

33. Prepare an income statement.

34. Prepare a balance sheet.

35. Record the closing entries in the general journal.

36. Post the closing entries.

37. Prepare a post-closing trial balance.

38. Assemble all business forms and records in the order given below.

Journals	Income statement	Post-closing trial balance
Ledger	Balance sheet	Bank reconciliation
Work sheet		

Be sure your name is on each item. Present all of your completed reinforcement activity to your instructor.

3 ACCOUNTING FOR A MERCHANDISING BUSINESS

GENERAL BEHAVIORAL GOALS

1. Know accounting terminology related to a merchandising business organized as a partnership.
2. Understand accounting principles and practices for a merchandising business organized as a partnership.
3. Demonstrate accounting procedures for a merchandising business organized as a partnership.

Denim Threads, the business for Part 3, sells casual wearing apparel.

DENIM THREADS
Chart of Accounts

(1) ASSETS	Account Number		(4) REVENUE	Account Number
Cash	11		Sales	41
Accounts Receivable	12		**(5) COST OF MERCHANDISE**	
Merchandise Inventory	13			
Supplies	14		Purchases	51
Prepaid Insurance	15			
(2) LIABILITIES			**(6) EXPENSES**	
Accounts Payable	21		Credit Card Fee Expense	61
Sales Tax Payable	22		Insurance Expense	62
(3) CAPITAL			Miscellaneous Expense	63
			Rent Expense	64
Eva Burgos, Capital	31		Salary Expense	65
Eva Burgos, Drawing	32		Supplies Expense	66
Luis Perez, Capital	33			
Luis Perez, Drawing	34			
Income Summary	35			

The chart of accounts for Denim Threads is illustrated above for
ready reference as you study Part 3 of this textbook.

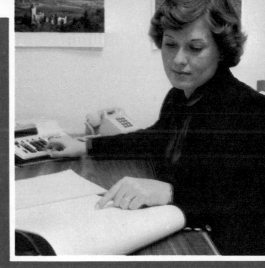

Journalizing Purchases
and Cash Payments

ENABLING PERFORMANCE TASKS

After studying Chapter 11, you will be able to:

a. Define accounting terms related to purchases and cash payments.
b. Explain accounting principles and practices related to purchases and cash payments.
c. Classify accounts related to purchases and cash payments.
d. Analyse transactions related to purchases and cash payments into debit and credit parts.
e. Journalize purchases and cash payments in a synoptic journal.

Putt Around, described in Part 2, is owned by one person. A business owned by one person is known as a sole proprietorship. Putt Around is a service business. The service is providing facilities for people to play miniature golf.

Two or more persons may own a single business. A business may need more capital than one owner can provide. The type of business may also require the skills of more than one person. A business in which two or more persons combine their assets and abilities is called a partnership. Each member of a partnership is called a partner. Partners agree to share in the profit or loss of a business. As in sole proprietorships, financial records and reports of partnerships are kept separate from those of persons supplying the assets. *(CONCEPT: Business Entity)*

Partnerships are common in small businesses that purchase and sell goods. A business that purchases and sells goods is called a merchandising business. Goods that a merchandising business purchases to sell are called merchandise.

Denim Threads, the business described in Part 3, is a partnership owned by Eva Burgos and Luis Perez. The business purchases and sells casual wearing apparel such as blue jeans, sweaters, shirts, and belts.

Denim Threads expects to make money and to continue in business indefinitely. *(CONCEPT: Going Concern)*

USING A SYNOPTIC JOURNAL

A service business generally has a large number of cash transactions and a limited number of noncash transactions to record. Noncash transactions are those that do not involve either the receipt or payment of cash. Putt Around uses a five-column cash journal, described in Chapter 5, to record all cash transactions. A two-column general journal is used to record the small number of noncash transactions.

Denim Threads, a merchandising business, has many noncash transactions. Noncash transactions would take much time to enter in a general journal. Therefore, Denim Threads uses only one journal in which all transactions are recorded.

A multi-column journal in which all transactions of a business are recorded is called a synoptic journal. A synoptic journal provides the additional special amount columns needed to record all cash and noncash transactions. The synoptic journal used by Denim Threads is below and on page 193.

Use of a synoptic journal is common in small merchandising businesses where only one person records transactions. Eva Burgos records all transactions for Denim Threads.

Form of synoptic journal

The synoptic journal for Denim Threads below has eleven amount columns. Special amount columns are provided for the recording of transactions related to the purchasing and selling of merchandise. The columns are arranged to make accurate recording and posting easier. Debit and credit columns for Cash, Accounts Receivable, and Accounts Payable are arranged in pairs. This arrangement helps avoid errors in recording amounts in the wrong columns. Since the Cash Debit and Credit columns are used often, they are placed at the left of the Account Title column. The remaining columns are placed at the right of the Account Title column. General Debit and Credit columns are placed first so that amounts in these columns will be close to the account titles.

Recording the beginning cash balance in a synoptic journal (left page)

PAGE 1			SYNOPTIC JOURNAL						
CASH		DATE	ACCOUNT TITLE	DOC. NO.	POST. REF.	**GENERAL**			
DEBIT	CREDIT					DEBIT	CREDIT		
		1988 Nov. 1	Balance on hand, $4 200.00		✓				

Recording the beginning cash balance

An entry for the beginning cash balance is recorded at the beginning of each month. The entry is recorded in the journal so that the beginning cash balance is readily available for proving cash. The cash balance entry for Denim Threads on November 1, 1988, is on line 1 of the synoptic journal on page 192. This entry is similar to the one in the cash journal, Chapter 5.

PURCHASES OF MERCHANDISE

The price of merchandise a business purchases to sell is called cost of merchandise. For a business to make a profit, the selling price of merchandise must be greater than the cost of merchandise. The amount added to the cost of merchandise to establish the selling price is called markup. Revenue earned from the sale of merchandise includes both the cost of merchandise and the markup. All costs of merchandise are deducted from revenue because only the markup increases capital. Accounts showing the costs of merchandise are kept in a separate division of the ledger. This division is shown in the chart of accounts, page 190.

A merchandising business purchases merchandise to sell and buys supplies and equipment for use in the business. An account that shows the cost of merchandise purchased to sell is titled Purchases. This account is used only to record the value of merchandise purchased. Therefore, only purchases of merchandise are recorded in the Purchases Debit column of the synoptic journal. All other items bought, such as supplies, are recorded in the General Debit column of a synoptic journal. Purchases and other items bought are recorded and reported at the price agreed upon at the time the transaction occurs. (CONCEPT: *Historical Cost*)

Purchases of merchandise on account

A transaction in which the merchandise purchased is to be paid for later is called a purchase on account. A business to which payment is owed is called a creditor. Some businesses purchasing on account from only a few companies keep a separate ledger account for each creditor.

FOR MONTH OF *November* 19 88 PAGE /							
ACCOUNTS RECEIVABLE		SALES CREDIT	SALES TAX PAYABLE CREDIT	ACCOUNTS PAYABLE		PURCHASES DEBIT	
DEBIT	CREDIT			DEBIT	CREDIT		
							1
							2
							3

Recording the beginning cash balance in a synoptic journal (right page)

Putt Around included separate accounts in its ledger, pages 150–152. However, a business that purchases on account from many firms will have many accounts with creditors. To avoid a bulky ledger, the total amount owed to all creditors can be summarized in a single ledger account. A liability account that summarizes the amounts owed to all creditors is titled Accounts Payable. Denim Threads uses the accounts payable account to summarize the amount owed to all creditors.

Source document for a purchase on account. When a seller sends merchandise to a buyer, the seller prepares a form showing what has been sent. A form describing the goods shipped, the quantity, and the price is called an invoice. An invoice used as a source document for recording a purchase on account transaction is called a purchase invoice. *(CONCEPT: Objective Evidence)* A purchase invoice received by Denim Threads is below.

Purchase invoice

A purchase invoice lists the quantity, the description, the price of each item, and the total amount of the invoice. A purchase invoice provides the information needed for recording a purchase on account.

When Denim Threads receives a purchase invoice, a date and a number are stamped in the upper right-hand corner. Numbers are assigned in sequence to identify all purchase invoices. The *37* stamped on the invoice above is the number assigned by Denim Threads to that purchase invoice. This number should not be confused with the seller's invoice number which is 4210.

A buyer needs to know that all of the items ordered have been received at the correct prices. The check marks on the invoice show that the items and amounts have been checked and are correct. The initials near the total are those of the person at Denim Threads who checked the invoice.

An agreement between a buyer and a seller about payment for merchandise is called the terms of sale. The terms of sale on the invoice, page 194, are 30 days. These terms mean that payment is due within 30 days from the date of the invoice. The invoice is dated October 26. Therefore, payment must be made by November 25.

Analysing a purchase on account. Denim Threads purchased merchandise on account.

> *November 2, 1988. Purchased merchandise on account from Denim Specialties, $822.00. Purchase Invoice No. 37.*

A purchases account has a debit balance. Therefore, a purchases account is increased on its debit side. A purchases account is decreased on its credit side.

This transaction increases the balance of the purchases account. The cost account Purchases is debited for $822.00.

This transaction also increases the amount owed to creditors. The liability account Accounts Payable has a credit balance and is increased on its credit side. Accounts Payable, therefore, is credited for $822.00.

Purchases	
Debit Side Balance Increase	Credit Side Decrease

Purchases	
822.00	

Accounts Payable	
	822.00

Recording a purchase on account. The entry to record this purchase on account is on line 3 of the partial synoptic journal below.

Recording a purchase on account in a synoptic journal

The date, 2, is written in the Date column. The debit amount, *$822.00*, is entered in the Purchases Debit column. The credit amount, *$822.00*, is written in the Accounts Payable Credit column. The name of the creditor, *Denim Specialties*, is entered in the Account Title column. The number of the purchase invoice, *P37*, is written in the Doc. No. column.

> Both debit and credit amounts are recorded in special amount columns. Therefore, the writing of the names of either ledger account in the Account Title column is not necessary. However, the name of the creditor is written in the Account Title column to show to whom the amount is owed. The way Denim Threads keeps records of the amount owed to each creditor is described in Chapter 13.

Purchases of merchandise for cash

Denim Threads pays cash for some purchases. All payments are made by cheque.

Source document for a cash purchase. The source document for a cash purchase transaction is the cheque stub of the cheque issued in payment. *(CONCEPT: Objective Evidence)* The source document for the transaction below is the cheque stub for Cheque No. 326.

Analysing a cash purchase. Denim Threads purchased merchandise for cash.

November 2, 1988. Purchased merchandise for cash, $425.00. Cheque No. 326.

This cash purchase transaction increases the balance of the purchases account. The cost account Purchases has a debit balance and is increased on its debit side. Thus, Purchases is debited for $425.00.

This transaction also decreases the balance of the cash account. The asset account Cash has a debit balance and is decreased on its credit side. Cash is therefore credited for $425.00.

Purchases	
425.00	

Cash	
	425.00

Recording a cash purchase. The entry to record this cash purchase is on line 4 of the partial synoptic journal below.

Recording a cash purchase in a synoptic journal

PAGE /		SYNOPTIC JOURNAL			PAGE /
1	2				11
CASH		DATE	ACCOUNT TITLE	Doc. No.	Post. Ref.	PURCHASES DEBIT
DEBIT	CREDIT					
4	42500	2 ✓		C326 ✓	42500	4
5						5
6						6

The date of the transaction, 2, is entered in the Date column. The debit amount, *$425.00*, is written in the Purchases Debit column. The credit amount, *$425.00*, is entered in the Cash Credit column. A check mark is placed in the Account Title column. The check mark shows that no account title needs to be written. The cheque number, *C326*, is entered in the Doc. No. column. A check mark is placed in the Post. Ref. column. The check mark in this column shows that amounts on this line are not to be posted individually.

BUYING SUPPLIES

Denim Threads buys supplies for use in the business. Supplies are not recorded in the purchases account because supplies are not intended for sale to customers. Wrapping paper, cash register tapes, and office supplies are examples of supplies.

Buying supplies on account

Denim Threads usually buys supplies for cash. Recording a transaction for buying supplies for cash is described in Chapter 4. Occasionally some supplies are bought on account.

Source document for buying supplies on account. When Denim Threads buys supplies on account, an invoice is received from the seller. This invoice is similar to the purchase invoice received when merchandise is purchased. To show that this invoice is for supplies, a brief note is attached to the invoice. The note indicates that the invoice is for supplies and not for purchases. A form on which a brief interoffice message is written is known as a memorandum. Memorandum No. 47 is below. A memorandum with its attached invoice is the source document for a buying supplies on account transaction. *(CONCEPT: Objective Evidence)* After entries have been made, the memorandums are filed numerically.

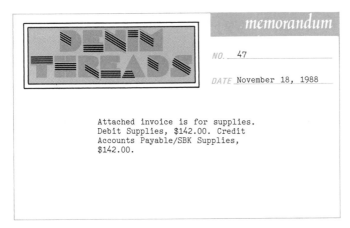

memorandum

NO. 47

DATE November 18, 1988

Attached invoice is for supplies.
Debit Supplies, $142.00. Credit
Accounts Payable/SBK Supplies,
$142.00.

Memorandum for buying supplies on account

Analysing buying supplies on account. Denim Threads bought supplies on account.

November 10, 1988. Bought supplies on account from SBK Supplies, $142.00. Memorandum No. 47.

Buying supplies on account increases the balance of the supplies account. The asset account Supplies has a debit balance and is increased on its debit side. Supplies therefore is debited for $142.00. This transaction also increases the amount owed to creditors. The liability Accounts Payable has a credit balance and is increased on its credit side. Therefore, Accounts Payable is credited for $142.00.

Supplies	
142.00	

Accounts Payable	
	142.00

Recording buying supplies on account. This transaction is recorded in the partial synoptic journal on the next page.

SYNOPTIC JOURNAL								19 **88**	
				3	**4**			**9**	**10**
DATE	ACCOUNT TITLE	Doc. No.	Post. Ref.	GENERAL				ACCOUNTS PAYABLE	
				DEBIT	CREDIT			DEBIT	CREDIT
{ 10	*Supplies*	M 47		14200					
	SBK Supplies								14200

Recording supplies bought
on account in a
synoptic journal

The date, *10*, is written in the Date column. No special amount column is provided for Supplies. Therefore, the debit amount for supplies, *$142.00*, is recorded in the General Debit column. The title, *Supplies*, is written in the Account Title column. Account titles are required for both the debit and the credit parts of the entry. Therefore, each amount and each account title is written on a separate line. The credit amount, *$142.00*, is entered in the Accounts Payable Credit column on the next line. The name of the creditor, *SBK Supplies*, is written in the Account Title column and is indented about 1 cm. A brace ({) is placed in the Date column to show that both entries on these two lines belong to the same transaction. The number of the memorandum, *M47*, is entered in the Doc. No. column.

Buying supplies for cash

Denim Threads buys most of its supplies for cash. Supplies are generally bought from local businesses.

Source document for buying supplies for cash. The source document for a supplies bought for cash transaction is the cheque stub issued in payment. *(CONCEPT: Objective Evidence)* The source document for the transaction below is the cheque stub for Cheque No. 328.

Analysing buying supplies for cash. Denim Threads bought supplies for cash.

*November 15, 1988. Bought supplies for cash, $86.00.
Cheque No. 328.*

This transaction increases the balance of the supplies account. The asset account Supplies has a debit balance and is increased on its debit side. Therefore, Supplies is debited for $86.00. The asset account Cash has a debit balance and is decreased on its credit side. Thus, Cash is credited for $86.00.

Recording buying supplies for cash. The entry to record this transaction is on line 19 of the partial synoptic journal on the next page.

PAGE /			SYNOPTIC JOURNAL						
1	2					3	4		
CASH		DATE	ACCOUNT TITLE	Doc. No.	Post. Ref.	GENERAL			
DEBIT	CREDIT					DEBIT	CREDIT		
19		8600	15 Supplies	C328		8600			19

Recording supplies bought for cash in a synoptic journal

A similar entry for Putt Around is described in Chapter 5.

The date, *15*, is written in the Date column. The debit amount for Supplies, *$86.00*, is recorded in the General Debit column. The title, *Supplies*, is entered in the Account Title column. The credit amount, *$86.00*, is written in the Cash Credit column. The cheque number, *C328*, is entered in the Doc. No. column.

CASH PAYMENTS

Payment to creditors is made according to the terms of sale on purchase invoices. Payment for an expense usually is made at the time the expense occurs.

Cash payment on account

Denim Threads pays by cheque for all cash purchases and for items bought on account.

Source document for a cash payment on account. The cheque stub for the cheque written to pay a creditor is the source document for a cash payment on account. *(CONCEPT: Objective Evidence)*

Analysing a payment on account. Denim Threads made a cash payment on account.

> *November 15, 1988. Paid on account to Westwood, Inc., $580.00. Cheque No. 329.*

This payment on account decreases the amount owed to creditors. The liability account Accounts Payable has a credit balance and is decreased on its debit side. Accounts Payable therefore is debited for $580.00. The balance of the asset account Cash is also decreased. Cash is credited for $580.00.

Accounts Payable	
580.00	

Cash	
	580.00

Recording a payment on account. The entry to record this payment on account is on line 20 of the partial synoptic journal on page 200.

The date, *15*, is written in the Date column. The amount debited to Accounts Payable, *$580.00*, is entered in the Accounts Payable Debit column. The amount credited to Cash, *$580.00*, is written in the Cash Credit col-

PAGE 1		SYNOPTIC JOURNAL				19 88	
CASH		DATE	ACCOUNT TITLE	Doc. No.	Post. Ref.	ACCOUNTS PAYABLE	
DEBIT	CREDIT					DEBIT	CREDIT
20	580 00	15	Westwood, Inc.	C329		580 00	20

Recording a payment on account in a synoptic journal

umn. The name of the creditor, *Westwood, Inc.*, is entered in the Account Title column. The number of the cheque, *C329*, is entered in the Doc. No. column.

Cash payment of an expense

Denim Threads pays for an expense at the time the transaction occurs or within a few days.

Source document for payment of an expense. The cheque stub for the cheque written to pay an expense is the source document for the entry. (CONCEPT: *Objective Evidence*)

Analysing a payment of an expense. Denim Threads made a payment of an expense.

November 15, 1988. Paid rent expense, $800.00. Cheque No. 330.

Rent Expense	
800.00	

Cash	
	800.00

Payment for the rent expense, *$800.00*, is due on the 15th day of each month. This payment increases the rent expense account. The expense account Rent Expense has a debit balance and is increased on its debit side. Rent Expense therefore is debited for $800.00. The balance of the asset account Cash is decreased. Cash therefore is credited for $800.00.

Recording a payment of an expense. This payment of an expense is on line 21 of the partial synoptic journal below.

PAGE 1		SYNOPTIC JOURNAL					
CASH		DATE	ACCOUNT TITLE	Doc. No.	Post. Ref.	GENERAL	
DEBIT	CREDIT					DEBIT	CREDIT
21	800 00	15	Rent Expense	C330		800 00	21

Recording a payment of an expense in a synoptic journal

A similar entry for Putt Around is in Chapter 5.

The date, *15*, is written in the Date column. The debit amount for rent expense, *$800.00*, is entered in the General Debit column. The name of the account, *Rent Expense*, is written in the Account Title column. The credit amount, *$800.00*, is entered in the Cash Credit column. The number of the cheque, *C330*, is written in the Doc. No. column.

OTHER TRANSACTIONS

Most transactions for a merchandising business relate to purchasing and selling merchandise. A merchandising business also has other transactions that must be recorded. A synoptic journal is also used to record these other transactions.

Changes in capital

The balances of capital accounts of a partnership are changed in three ways. (1) Partners may invest additional capital. (2) Partners may withdraw capital. (3) Net income or net loss is recorded.

An entry to record an additional cash investment for a sole proprietorship is described on page 78. The same procedure is followed to record additional investments by owners of a partnership. An entry to close net income or net loss into the capital account is described on pages 148 and 149. A similar closing entry in a synoptic journal is described in Chapter 16.

Assets taken out of a business for the personal use of the owner are known as withdrawals. Withdrawals reduce the amount of capital in the business. Since capital accounts have credit balances, decreases are recorded as debits. Withdrawals could be recorded as debits to the partners' capital accounts. However, withdrawals are normally recorded in separate accounts so that the total amounts are easily determined for each fiscal period. Denim Threads records withdrawals in accounts titled Eva Burgos, Drawing and Luis Perez, Drawing. Because drawing accounts show decreases in capital, drawing accounts have debit balances. An entry to record withdrawals for a sole proprietorship is described in Chapter 5.

Assets taken out of a business are generally of two types. (1) Owners withdraw cash. (2) Owners withdraw merchandise.

Source document for a cash withdrawal. When either Eva Burgos or Luis Perez withdraws cash from Denim Threads, a cheque is written for the payment. The cheque stub of the cheque is the source document for the transaction. *(CONCEPT: Objective Evidence)*

Analysing a cash withdrawal. Eva Burgos withdrew cash.

November 15, 1988. Eva Burgos, partner, withdrew cash, $300.00. Cheque No. 331.

This cash withdrawal increases the balance of the drawing account. The capital account, Eva Burgos, Drawing has a debit balance and is increased

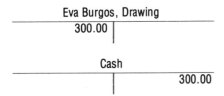

on its debit side. Eva Burgos, Drawing therefore is debited for $300.00. The transaction also decreases the asset account Cash. Therefore, Cash is credited for $300.00.

Recording a cash withdrawal. This cash withdrawal is on line 22 of the partial synoptic journal below.

Recording a cash withdrawal by a partner in a synoptic journal

The date, *15*, is written in the Date column. The amount debited to the drawing account, *$300.00*, is entered in the General Debit column. The name of the capital account, *Eva Burgos, Drawing*, is written in the Account Title column. The amount credited to the cash account, *$300.00*, is entered in the Cash Credit column. The number of the cheque, *C331*, is written in the Doc. No. Column.

Source document for a withdrawal of merchandise. A partner may take merchandise out of the business for personal use. The source document for this transaction is a memorandum prepared by the partner withdrawing the merchandise. *(CONCEPT: Objective Evidence)*

Analysing a withdrawal of merchandise. Luis Perez, partner, withdrew merchandise.

> *November 16, 1988. Luis Perez, partner, withdrew merchandise, $45.00. Memorandum No. 48.*

This transaction increases the balance of the drawing account. The capital account Luis Perez, Drawing has a debit balance and is increased on its debit side. Luis Perez, Drawing is therefore debited for $45.00.

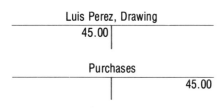

A withdrawal of merchandise decreases the amount of merchandise purchased for sale to customers. Therefore, the cost of merchandise withdrawn is deducted from the balance of the purchases account. The balance side of the purchases account is the debit side. This transaction decreases the balance of the purchases account. Purchases is therefore credited for $45.00.

Recording a withdrawal of merchandise. This withdrawal of merchandise is on lines 25 and 26 of the partial synoptic journal, page 203.

Recording a withdrawal of merchandise in a synoptic journal

The date, *16*, is entered in the date column. The debit amount, *$45.00*, is written in the General Debit column. The title of the account, *Luis Perez, Drawing*, is entered in the Account Title column. Merchandise withdrawals do not occur frequently. Therefore, neither a Drawing Debit nor a Purchases Credit column is provided in the synoptic journal. The amount credited to the purchases account, *$45.00*, is written in the General Credit column on the next line. The name of the account, *Purchases*, is entered in the Account Title column, indented about 1 cm. The source document number, *M48*, is written in the Doc. No. column. A brace is drawn in the Date column to show that both lines belong to the same transaction.

Correcting entry

Errors may be made even though care is taken in recording transactions. Simple errors may be corrected by ruling through the incorrect item as described on page 86. However, a transaction may have been improperly recorded in the journal and posted to the ledger. Errors of this type should be corrected with a journal entry. A journal entry made to correct an error in the ledger is called a correcting entry.

Source document for a correcting entry. If an accounting error is discovered, a memorandum is prepared showing the correction to be made. A memorandum for a correcting entry is on page 204. The memorandum is the source document for the correcting entry. (CONCEPT: *Objective Evidence*)

Analysing a correcting entry. Ms. Burgos discovered an accounting error that had been recorded in the journal and posted to the ledger.

> November 17, 1988. *Discovered that supplies bought on October 27 had been recorded and posted in error as a debit to Purchases instead of Supplies, $80.00. Memorandum No. 49.*

To correct the error, an entry is made to remove $80.00 from the purchases account. The entry must also add $80.00 to the supplies account.

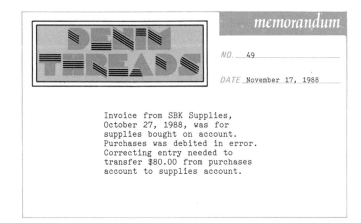

Supplies
_____
80.00

Purchases
_____
            80.00

The asset account Supplies is increased by this entry. Supplies therefore is debited for $80.00.

Purchases is decreased by this correcting entry. The cost account Purchases has a debit balance and is decreased on its credit side. Therefore, Purchases is credited for $80.00.

Recording a correcting entry. The correcting entry is on lines 27 and 28 of the partial synoptic journal below.

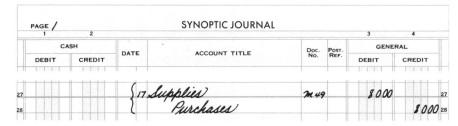

The date, *17*, is written in the Date column. The debit amount for supplies, *$80.00*, is entered in the General Debit column. The title of the account, *Supplies*, is written in the Account Title column. The amount credited to the purchases account, *$80.00*, is entered in the General Credit column on the next line. The name of the account, *Purchases*, is written in the Account Title column. The name is indented about 1 cm. The source document number, *M49*, is entered in the Doc. No. column. A brace is drawn in the Date column to show that both lines belong to the same transaction.

SUMMARY

The chart on page 205 summarizes the entries for purchases, cash payments, and other transactions recorded in a synoptic journal.

SYNOPTIC JOURNAL

| | CASH | | GENERAL | | ACCOUNTS RECEIVABLE | | SALES CREDIT | SALES TAX PAYABLE CREDIT | ACCOUNTS PAYABLE | | PURCHASES DEBIT |
| | DEBIT | CREDIT | DEBIT | CREDIT | DEBIT | CREDIT | | | DEBIT | CREDIT | |
	1	2	3	4	5	6	7	8	9	10	11
Purchase on account										X	X
Purchase for cash	X										X
Buying supplies on account			X							X	
Buying supplies for cash	X	X									
Cash payment on account		X							X		
Cash payment of an expense	X	X									
Cash withdrawal	X	X									
Merchandise withdrawal			X	X							

Summary of entries in a synoptic journal

ACCOUNTING TERMS

What is the meaning of each of the following?

1. partnership
2. partner
3. merchandising business
4. merchandise
5. synoptic journal

6. cost of merchandise
7. markup
8. purchase on account
9. creditor

10. invoice
11. purchase invoice
12. terms of sale
13. correcting entry

QUESTIONS FOR INDIVIDUAL STUDY

1. Why would two or more persons want to own a single business?
2. What are noncash transactions?
3. Why doesn't Denim Threads use a cash journal like the one used by Putt Around?
4. Why are costs of merchandise deducted from revenue?
5. What is the name of the account that shows the cost of merchandise purchased for sale?
6. Why would a business use a single ledger account to summarize the amount owed to all creditors?
7. What accounts are affected by a purchase on account transaction? How are the accounts affected?

8. Which amount columns in the synoptic journal are used to record a purchase on account transaction?
9. What is the source document for a purchase on account journal entry?
10. Why are the names Purchases and Accounts Payable for a purchase on account entry not written in the Account Title column?
11. What accounts are affected by a cash purchase of merchandise? How are the accounts affected?
12. Which amount columns in the synoptic journal are used to record a cash purchase of merchandise?
13. Why is a check mark placed in the Account Title column of a synoptic

journal for a cash purchase transaction?

14. What is the source document for buying supplies on account transactions?

15. What accounts are affected by a buying supplies on account transaction? How are the accounts affected?

16. Why is the debit amount for Supplies recorded in the General Debit column for supplies bought transactions?

17. What is the source document for a cash payment on account transaction?

18. What accounts are affected by a cash payment on account transaction?

How are the accounts affected?

19. Which amount columns in a synoptic journal are used to record a cash payment on account transaction?

20. What are the three kinds of entries that change the balances of capital accounts?

21. What accounts are affected by a withdrawal of merchandise transaction? How are the accounts affected?

22. What amount columns in a synoptic journal are used to record a withdrawal of merchandise?

23. When should a journal entry be made for errors in recording transactions?

CASES FOR MANAGEMENT DECISION

CASE 1 George Mason owns and operates the Sunnyside Gift Shop in a downtown shopping area. Business has been declining because of a shopping centre that was started in one of the suburbs. Mr. Mason has an opportunity to close the business downtown and move the business to the shopping centre. The future of the business is considered to be much better in the shopping centre. Additional capital however is required to move and operate the business in the new location. The local bank has agreed to loan the money needed. The business hours would be extended in the new location. The business would be open seven days a week. Therefore, the extended hours plus

the expected increase in business would require the hiring of one or two additional employees. Mr. Mason has been contacted by Mrs. Jan Perrigo, a person with similar experience who would like to become a partner. Mrs. Perrigo would provide the capital necessary to move the location of the business. For the capital provided, Mrs. Perrigo would share equally in the net income or loss of the business. Also, Mrs. Perrigo would share equally in the operation of the business. Which method of obtaining additional capital would be better? Should Mr. Mason (1) borrow the money from the bank, or (2) bring in a partner?

CASE 2 John Stewart, a high school student, works part-time in Rivera's Clothing Store. John observes several entries in the synoptic journal. He asks: "You use the purchase invoice as your source document

for recording purchases of merchandise. You use a memorandum as your source document for recording the entry when supplies are bought. Why don't you use the invoice for both entries?" How will you answer him?

DRILLS FOR UNDERSTANDING

DRILL 11-D 1   Analysing transactions into debit and credit parts

Instructions: Prepare two T accounts for each of the transactions on the next page. Show which account in the ledger is debited and which account is credited. The first transaction is given as an example.

Purchases	Accounts Payable
800.00	800.00

Transactions

1. Purchased merchandise on account from Smithfield Co., $800.00.
2. Bought supplies on account from Jack's Supply, $150.00.
3. Bought supplies for cash, $50.00.
4. Purchased merchandise for cash, $200.00.
5. Purchased merchandise on account from Komuro, Inc., $300.00.
6. Bought supplies for cash, $20.00.
7. Bought supplies on account from Watson Enterprises, $60.00.
8. Purchased merchandise for cash, $100.00.
9. Paid on account to Albert Grogan, $600.00.
10. Paid November rent, $500.00.
11. Paid for advertising, $50.00. (Miscellaneous Expense)
12. Mary McCormick, partner, withdrew cash, $400.00.
13. Jane Marsh, partner, withdrew cash, $400.00.
14. Paid on account to Southside Supply, $125.00.
15. Jane Marsh, partner, withdrew merchandise, $30.00.
16. Discovered that supplies bought last month had been recorded in error as a debit to Purchases instead of Supplies, $40.00.
17. Mary McCormick, partner, withdrew merchandise, $20.00.
18. Paid on account to Caldwell, Inc., $100.00.

The solution to Drill 11-D 1 is needed to complete Drill 11-D 2.

DRILL 11-D 2 Recording transactions using a synoptic journal

The solution to Drill 11-D 1 is needed to complete Drill 11-D 2.

Instructions: Use a form such as the one below. Based on the answers in Drill 11-D 1, show by a check mark which amount columns will be used to record the transactions. Transaction 1 is shown as an example.

Transaction	Cash		General		Accts. Pay.		Purch. Debit
	Debit	Credit	Debit	Credit	Debit	Credit	
1. Debit amount							✓
Credit amount						✓	

APPLICATION PROBLEM

PROBLEM 11-1 Journalizing transactions for purchases, supplies, and cash payments in a synoptic journal

Mary Boswell and Susan Turner, partners in a retail dress shop, completed the transactions, page 208, for November of the current year. The cash balance on November 1 was $4 750.00.

Instructions: 1. Record the cash balance on hand on page 12 of a synoptic journal like the one on pages 192 and 193.

2. Record the following transactions. Source documents are abbreviated as: purchase invoice, *P*; cheque, *C*; memorandum, *M*.

Nov. 1. Purchased merchandise on account from Baker Fashions, $900.00. P46.
2. Bought supplies for cash, $30.00. C220.
2. Bought supplies on account from Jansen Office Supply, $82.00. M23.
3. Purchased merchandise on account from Jason Co., $400.00. P47.
3. Purchased merchandise on account from Schmidt Co., $200.00. P48.
4. Bought supplies on account from Pacific Supply, $92.00. M24.
5. Purchased merchandise for cash, $120.00. C221.
5. Purchased merchandise for cash, $33.00. C222.
8. Bought supplies for cash, $25.00. C223.
9. Purchased merchandise for cash, $80.00. C224.
11. Bought supplies on account from Reese Supply, $42.00. M25.
13. Bought supplies for cash, $36.00. C225.
15. Mary Boswell, partner, withdrew cash, $500.00. C226.
15. Susan Turner, partner, withdrew cash, $500.00. C227.
16. Paid on account to Baker Fashions, $900.00. C228.
17. Paid on account to Jason Co., $400.00. C229.
19. Discovered that supplies bought last month had been recorded in error as a debit to Purchases instead of Supplies, $65.00. M26.
20. Paid telephone bill, $66.00. C230. (Miscellaneous Expense)
23. Paid on account to Jansen Office Supply, $82.00. C231.
24. Paid for advertising, $37.00. C232. (Miscellaneous Expense)
27. Susan Turner, partner, withdrew merchandise, $40.00. M27.
29. Paid on account to Schmidt Co., $400.00. C233.
30. Paid salaries, $1 200.00. C234.
30. Mary Boswell, partner, withdrew merchandise, $30.00. M28.

ENRICHMENT PROBLEMS

MASTERY PROBLEM 11-M   Journalizing transactions for purchases, supplies, and cash payments in a synoptic journal

Judy Fields and William Hurley, partners, own and operate a gift shop. The transactions below were completed during December of the current year. The cash balance on December 1 was $3 800.00.

Instructions: 1. Record the cash balance on hand on page 13 of a synoptic journal like the one on pages 192 and 193.

2. Record the following transactions. Source documents are abbreviated as: cheque, *C*; purchase invoice, *P*; memorandum, *M*.

Dec. 1. Paid December rent, $700.00. C310.
1. Paid salaries, $1 500.00. C311.
2. Judy Fields, partner, withdrew cash, $700.00. C312.
2. William Hurley, partner, withdrew cash, $700.00. C313.
3. Purchased merchandise on account from Thompson Novelties, $330.00. P82.
3. Paid on account to Lakeside Supply, $77.00. C314.
4. Purchased merchandise on account from Mason Giftware, $220.00. P83.

Dec. 7. William Hurley, partner, withdrew merchandise, $22.00. M32.
8. Paid telephone bill, $48.00. C315. (Miscellaneous Expense)
9. Bought supplies on account from Lakeside Supply, $49.00. M33.
9. Purchased merchandise for cash, $150.00. C316.
11. Paid on account to Thompson Novelties, $160.00. C317.
13. Purchased merchandise on account from Streetman, Inc., $440.00. P84.
14. Purchased merchandise for cash, $210.00. C318.
15. Bought supplies for cash, $40.00. C319.
15. Paid on account to Streetman, Inc., $360.00. C320.
16. Judy Fields, partner, withdrew merchandise, $18.00. M34.
17. Purchased merchandise for cash, $130.00. C321.
20. Bought supplies on account from Drake Supply, $52.00. M35.
21. Purchased merchandise on account from Niehaus Co., $750.00. P85.
23. Bought supplies for cash, $15.00. C322.
25. Discovered that supplies bought in November had been recorded in error as a debit to Purchases instead of Supplies, $83.00. M36.
27. Bought supplies on account from Macon Supply, $26.00. M37.
29. Paid on account to Thompson Novelties, $330.00. C323.
30. Purchased merchandise for cash, $215.00. C324.
30. Paid on account to Mason Giftware, $220.00. C325.

CHALLENGE PROBLEM 11-C   Journalizing correcting entries in a synoptic journal

The errors listed below were discovered in a synoptic journal.

Instructions: Record the needed correcting entries on page 8 of a synoptic journal like the one on pages 192 and 193. Use March 3 of the current year.

Mar. 3. Discovered that supplies bought had been recorded as a debit to Purchases, $225.00. M50.
3. Discovered that a payment for salaries had been recorded as a debit to Miscellaneous Expense, $500.00. M51.
3. Discovered that a withdrawal of merchandise by Christine Morgan, partner, had been recorded as a credit to Cash, $86.00. M52.
3. Discovered that a purchase of merchandise on account had been recorded as a debit to Supplies, $420.00. M53.
3. Discovered that a payment for rent had been recorded as a debit to Salary Expense, $650.00. M54.
3. Discovered that supplies bought on account had been recorded as a debit to Miscellaneous Expense, $46.00. M55.
3. Discovered that a withdrawal of cash for Cathy York, partner, had been recorded as a credit to Purchases, $300.00. M56.
3. Discovered that a payment for salaries had been recorded as a debit to Supplies, $500.00. M57.
3. Discovered that supplies bought had been recorded as a debit to Prepaid Insurance, $120.00. M58.

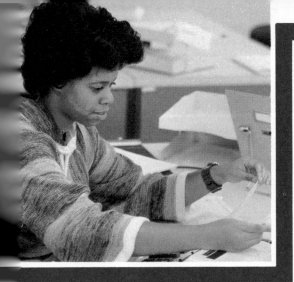

12

Journalizing Sales and Cash Receipts

ENABLING PERFORMANCE TASKS

After studying Chapter 12, you will be able to:

a. Define accounting terms related to sales and cash receipts.
b. Explain accounting principles and practices related to sales and cash receipts.
c. Classify accounts related to sales and cash receipts.
d. Analyse transactions related to sales and cash receipts into debit and credit parts.
e. Journalize sales and cash receipts in a synoptic journal.
f. Total, prove, and rule a synoptic journal.

A major activity of a merchandising business is the purchase of merchandise. Another major activity is the transfer of the merchandise to a person or firm. A person or firm to whom a business sells merchandise is called a customer. The transfer of merchandise to a customer in exchange for cash or a promise to pay is called a sale.

SALES TAX

A tax on a sale of goods is called a sales tax. Sales tax rates are set by each province and usually stated as a percentage of sales. Regardless of the rate used, the procedures are the same.

Every business collecting a sales tax needs accurate records of the amount of tax collected. Businesses must file reports with the government and pay the amount of sales tax collected. Records need to show (1) total sales and (2) total sales tax. For each sale made, a customer must pay for the price of the goods plus the sales tax. A sale of merchandise priced at $50.00 is on the next page.

In this book sales tax rates are arbitrary and are not intended to reflect the rates of the provinces to which they are applied.

Price of Goods	×	Sales Tax Rate	=	Sales Tax
$50.00	×	4%	=	$2.00
Price of Goods	+	Sales Tax	=	Total Amount of Sale
$50.00	+	$2.00	=	$52.00

A customer must pay $52.00 for the merchandise ($50.00 for the goods plus $2.00 for the sales tax). Denim Threads records the price of goods sold, the sales tax, and the total amount of a sale.

SALES AND CASH RECEIPTS FOR SALES

A sale of merchandise may be for (1) cash or (2) a promise to pay at a later date. A sale of merchandise increases the revenue of a business. Regardless of when payment is made, the increase in revenue should be recorded at the time of a sale. *(CONCEPT: Realization of Revenue)*

Cash sales

Denim Threads sells most of its merchandise for cash. A sale in which cash is received for the total amount of sale at the time of the transaction is called a cash sale.

Source document for cash sales. Denim Threads uses a cash register to list all cash sales. The cash register prints each transaction on a paper tape inside the machine. A printed receipt is also provided for each customer. Amounts on the cash register tape may be totalled daily or weekly.

Denim Threads records the total cash sales for each week. The cash register tape is used as the source document for the week's cash sales. *(CONCEPT: Objective Evidence)* The tape is marked with a symbol T and the day of the month it is removed from the cash register. Total sales for the week are then recorded as a single transaction.

Analysing a week's cash sales. Total cash sales for the week ending November 5, 1988, are below.

November 5, 1988. Cash sales for the week, $1 850.00, plus sales tax, $74.00. Total, $1 924.00. Cash Register Tape No. T6.

This transaction increases the balance of the asset account Cash by a debit for the total amount of cash received, $1 924.00.

Denim Threads has one revenue account Sales in the revenue division of the ledger. The total price of goods sold, $1 850.00, is recorded in this account. This transaction increases the balance of the revenue account Sales. Sales has a credit balance and is increased on its credit side by $1 850.00.

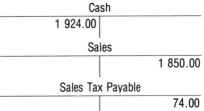

The amount of sales tax collected is a liability. Denim Threads owes this amount to the provincial government. The liability account Sales Tax Payable is credited for the amount of sales tax collected, $74.00.

Recording cash sales. The entry for the week's cash sales is on line 8 of the partial synoptic journal below.

Cash sales recorded in a synoptic journal

The date, 5, is written in the Date column. The amount debited to Cash, $1 924.00, is entered in the Cash Debit column. The amount credited to Sales, $1 850.00, is written in the Sales Credit column. The amount credited to Sales Tax Payable, $74.00, is entered in the Sales Tax Payable Credit column. A check mark is placed in the Account Title column. The check mark shows that no account title needs to be written for this transaction. The number of the cash register tape, T5, is entered in the Doc. No. column. A check mark is also placed in the Post. Ref. column. This check mark shows that amounts on this line do not need to be posted individually.

Sales on account

A sale for which payment will be made at a later date is called a sale on account. A sale on account is also known as a charge sale or a credit sale. A person or firm to whom a sale on account is made is called a charge customer.

Denim Threads summarizes in a ledger account, Accounts Receivable, the total amount due from all charge customers. Accounts Receivable is an asset account with a debit balance.

Source document for a sale on account. When a sale on account is made, the seller prepares a form showing what has been sold. A form issued to a charge customer describing the goods sold, the quantity, and the price is called a sales invoice. A sales invoice is also known as a sales ticket or a sales slip. The sales invoice used by Denim Threads is on page 213. Each sales invoice is prepared in duplicate. The original copy is used as the source document for recording the transaction. (CONCEPT: Objective Evidence) The carbon copy is given to the charge customer. Sales invoices are numbered in sequence. The number, 72, is the number of the sales invoice for Ada Miranda.

Sales invoice

The seller considers an invoice for a sale on account to be a sales invoice. The same invoice is considered by the buyer to be a purchase invoice.

Analysing a sale on account. The transaction for the Denim Threads' sales invoice is below.

November 4, 1988. Sold merchandise on account to Ada Miranda, $45.00, plus sales tax, $1.80. Total, $46.80. Sales Invoice No. 72.

This sale on account increases the amount to be collected from customers. The asset account Accounts Receivable has a debit balance and is increased on its debit side. Accounts Receivable is debited for the total sale of goods on account, $46.80.

Accounts Receivable	
46.80	

How Denim Threads keeps records of amounts to be collected from each charge customer is described in Chapter 13.

Sales is credited for the price of goods, $45.00. Sales Tax Payable is increased by a credit for the amount of sales tax on the sale, $1.80.

Sales	
	45.00

Sales Tax Payable	
	1.80

Recording a sale on account. The entry for this sale on account is re-corded in the partial synoptic journal below.

					5	6	7	8
		SYNOPTIC JOURNAL			ACCOUNTS RECEIVABLE		SALES CREDIT	SALES TAX PAYABLE CREDIT
	DATE	ACCOUNT TITLE	Doc. No.	Post. Ref.	DEBIT	CREDIT		
		4 Ada Miranda	S72		46 80		45 00	1 80

Sale on account recorded in a synoptic journal

The date, 4, is entered in the Date column. The amount debited to Accounts Receivable, $46.80, is written in the Accounts Receivable Debit col-umn. The amount credited to Sales, $45.00, is entered in the Sales Credit column. The amount of the sales tax, $1.80, is written in the Sales Tax Payable Credit column. The name of the charge customer, *Ada Miranda*, is entered in the Account Title column. The number of the sales invoice, *S72*, is written in the Doc. No. column.

Credit card sales

A special card is often used to identify approved charge customers. An embossed card used by a customer with an approved charge account is called a credit card. When a credit card is used, the card and a special sales invoice are placed in an imprinting device. This device records the customer's name and account number on all copies of the sales invoice.

Many gasoline companies and department store chains issue their own credit cards. When a business issues its own credit cards, the business bills each credit card holder for all credit card purchases. The card holder then pays the business. Because the business sends the bills and receives all payments, these credit card sales are recorded as regular charge sales.

Businesses may also subscribe to one or more of the major credit card systems. The major credit card system issues the credit card to a customer. The customer may then use the credit card at any business that has subscribed to the credit card system. In Canada, various banks are designated to handle the credit card systems.

When a major credit card system is used, each credit card holder is billed through the credit card system. The card holder then pays the credit card system rather than the business from which the purchase was made. Because the credit card system handles billing and collection, the business records credit card sales as regular cash sales.

A business that subscribes to a major credit card system periodically totals all credit card invoices. These invoices are then deposited at the bank designated to handle the credit card system. The bank credits the business' bank account for the total amount of the invoices. The bank charges the business a fee. The fee is based on a percentage of the credit card sales deposited by the business. At the end of the month, the bank includes the credit card fee on the bank statement.

Denim Threads subscribes to two major credit card systems. Both Visa and MasterCard credit cards are accepted in payment for merchandise sold. Credit card sales for each system are totalled and deposited separately with the designated bank at the end of each week.

Source documents for credit card sales. At the end of each week, Denim Threads totals all credit card sales on a calculator. Separate totals are figured for the price of goods sold, the sales tax charged, and the total amount of credit card sales. The symbol *CT* and the day of the month are written on the calculator tape. The calculator tape is used as the source document for the week's credit card sales. *(CONCEPT: Objective Evidence)*.

Analysing a week's credit card sales. Denim Threads gets credit for all credit card sales when the sales invoices are deposited at the bank. Therefore, the total weekly credit card sales are handled as cash sales rather than charge sales. Rather than recording each individual credit card sale, a weekly total of credit card sales is treated as one transaction. Total credit card sales for the week ending November 5, 1988, are below.

> *November 5, 1988. Credit card sales for the week, $1 300.00, plus sales tax, $52.00. Total, $1 352.00. Calculator Tape No. CT6.*

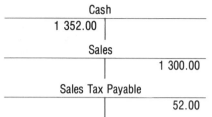

The balance of the asset account Cash is increased by a debit for the total credit card sales, $1 352.00.

The revenue account Sales is used for both cash sales and credit card sales. Sales is credited for the amount of credit card sales for the week, $1 300.00. Sales Tax Payable is credited for the amount of sales tax charged on the credit card sales, $52.00.

Recording credit card sales. The entry for the week's credit card sales is on line 9 of the partial synoptic journal below.

Recording credit card sales in a synoptic journal

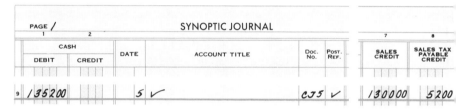

The date, 5, is entered in the Date column. The amount debited to Cash, *$1 352.00*, is written in the Cash Debit column. The amount credited to Sales, *$1 300.00*, is entered in the Sales Credit column. The amount credited to Sales Tax Payable, *$52.00*, is written in the Sales Tax Payable Credit column. A check mark is placed in the Account Title column. The check mark shows that no account title needs to be written for this transaction. The number, *CT5*, is written in the Doc. No. column. A check mark is placed in the Post Ref. column. This check mark shows that amounts on this line do not need to be posted individually.

The entry for credit card sales is the same as for regular cash sales. This is shown in the illustration on page 212.

Cash received on account

Denim Threads prepares a receipt when cash is received on account from a customer. The receipts are prenumbered so all receipts can be accounted for. The original copy of the receipt is given to the charge customer.

Source document for cash received on account. The carbon copy of the receipt is used as the source document for the cash received on account transaction. *(CONCEPT: Objective Evidence)*

Analysing cash received on account. Cash was received on account from a charge customer.

November 5, 1988. Received on account from Tien Yang, $78.00. Receipt No. 108.

The asset account Cash is increased by a debit for the amount of cash received, $78.00.

Cash	
78.00	

This transaction decreases the amount to be collected from charge customers. Therefore, the asset account Accounts Receivable is credited for $78.00.

Accounts Receivable	
	78.00

Recording cash received on account. The entry for this transaction is on line 7 of the partial synoptic journal below.

The date, *5*, is written in the Date column. The debit to Cash, *$78.00*, is entered in the Cash Debit column. The credit to Accounts Receivable, *$78.00*, is written in the Accounts Receivable Credit column. The name of the charge customer, *Tien Yang*, is entered in the Account Title column. The number of the receipt, *R108*, is written in the Doc. No. column.

Cash received on account recorded in a synoptic journal

SUMMARY OF SALES AND CASH RECEIPTS TRANSACTIONS

The chart below summarizes the entries in a synoptic journal for sales and cash receipts transactions.

	SYNOPTIC JOURNAL										
	1	2	3	4	5	6	7	8	9	10	11
	CASH		GENERAL		ACCOUNTS RECEIVABLE		SALES CREDIT	SALES TAX PAYABLE CREDIT	ACCOUNTS PAYABLE		PURCHASES DEBIT
	DEBIT	CREDIT	DEBIT	CREDIT	DEBIT	CREDIT			DEBIT	CREDIT	
Cash sales	X						X	X			
Sales on account					X		X	X			
Credit card sales	X						X	X			
Cash received on account	X					X					

Summary of sales and cash receipts transactions recorded in a synoptic journal

TOTALLING AND PROVING A SYNOPTIC JOURNAL

A synoptic journal is totalled and proved when a page is filled and when a fiscal period ends. The steps are similar to those described for Putt Around's cash journal in Chapter 5.

PAGE *1*

SYNOPTIC JOURNAL

	CASH		DATE	ACCOUNT TITLE	Doc. No.	Post. Ref.	GENERAL	
	DEBIT	CREDIT					DEBIT	CREDIT
1			1988 Nov. 1	Balance on hand, $4200.00		✓		
2		55000	1	Salary Expense	C325		55000	
3			2	Denim Specialties	P37			
4		42500	2	✓	C326	✓		
5		5300	3	Miscellaneous Expense	C327		5300	
6			4	Ada Miranda	S72			
7	7800		5	Tien Yang	R108			
8	192400		5	✓	J5	✓		
9	135200		5	✓	CJ5	✓		
10			8	Eastlake Clothiers	P38			
11			9	Lisa Anderson	S73			
12			10	Rick White	S74			
13			10	Supplies	M47		14200	
14				SBK Supplies				
15			12	George Landon	S75			
16			12	Gerando Manufacturing	P39			
17	172120		12	✓	J12	✓		
18	130000		12	✓	CJ12	✓		
19		8600	15	Supplies	C328		8600	
20		58000	15	Westwood, Inc.	C329			
21		80000	15	Rent Expense	C330		80000	
22		30000	15	Eva Burgos, Drawing	C331		30000	
23		30000	15	Luis Perez, Drawing	C332		30000	
24		55000	15	Salary Expense	C333		55000	
25			16	Luis Perez, Drawing	M48		4500	
26				Purchases				4500
27			17	Supplies	M49		8000	
28				Purchases				8000
29	6240		17	Ada Miranda	R109			
30	4160		18	Beth Ingram	R110			
31		82200	19	Denim Specialties	C334			
32	647920	446600	19	Carried Forward		✓	290600	12500

Synoptic journal totalled for forwarding (left page)

Forwarding the totals of a synoptic journal

Amount columns are totalled and proved when a synoptic journal page is filled. Line 32 of the illustration above and on page 219, shows the totals prepared for forwarding. The illustration, pages 220 and 221, shows how totals are brought forward to a new page. The procedures for forwarding totals are the same as those in Chapter 5.

FOR MONTH OF *November* 19 88 PAGE 1						
ACCOUNTS RECEIVABLE		SALES CREDIT	SALES TAX PAYABLE CREDIT	ACCOUNTS PAYABLE		PURCHASES DEBIT
DEBIT	CREDIT			DEBIT	CREDIT	
							(1)
							(2)
				82200	82200		(3)
						42500	(4)
							(5)
4680		4500	180				(6)
	7800						(7)
		185000	7400				(8)
		130000	5200				(9)
				68000	68000		(10)
10920		10500	420				(11)
5200		5000	200				(12)
							(13)
					14200		(14)
1560		1500	60				(15)
				41000	41000		(16)
		165500	6620				(17)
		125000	5000				(18)
							(19)
					58000		(20)
							(21)
							(22)
							(23)
							(24)
							(25)
							(26)
							(27)
							(28)
		6240					(29)
		4160					(30)
					82200		(31)
22360	18200	627000	25080	140200	205400	233700	(32)
							(33)

Synoptic journal totalled for forwarding (right page)

Proving a synoptic journal at the end of a month

Equality of debits and credits in a synoptic journal is proved at the end of each month. All columns are totalled on a calculator or on paper. A journal is proved when the sum of the debit totals is equal to the sum of the credit totals. The proof for the synoptic journal, pages 218 and 219, is on the next page.

PAGE 2			SYNOPTIC JOURNAL					
1	2						3	4
CASH		DATE	ACCOUNT TITLE	Doc. No.	Post. Ref.	GENERAL		
DEBIT	CREDIT					DEBIT	CREDIT	
1	6479 20	4466 00	*1988* Nov. 19	Brought Forward		✓	2906 00	125 00	1
27		300 00	30	Luis Perez, Drawing	C342		300 00		27
28	327 60		30	✓	J30	✓			28
29	67 60		30	✓	CJ30	✓			29
30	13551 20	6207 00	30	Totals			3705 00	125 00	30
31									31

Synoptic journal totalled and ruled (left page)

Col. No.	Column	Debit Totals	Credit Totals
1	Cash Debit	$13 551.20	
2	Cash Credit		$ 6 207.00
3	General Debit	3 705.00	
4	General Credit		125.00
5	Accounts Receivable Debit.......	639.60	
6	Accounts Receivable Credit......		353.60
7	Sales Credit		13 305.00
8	Sales Tax Payable Credit		532.20
9	Accounts Payable Debit...........	2 164.00	
10	Accounts Payable Credit..........		3 614.00
11	Purchases Debit	4 077.00	
	Totals	$24 136.80	$24 136.80

These two totals are equal. Equality of debits and credits in the synoptic journal of Denim Threads for November is proved.

Proving cash with a synoptic journal

Denim Threads figures the cash proof at the end of November as shown below.

Beginning cash balance	$ 4 200.00
(Line 1, page 1, synoptic journal, page 218)	
Plus total cash received	13 551.20
(Total of Cash Debit column, line 30, page 2, above)	
Total..	$17 751.20
Less total cash payments	6 207.00
(Total of Cash Credit column, line 30, page 2, above)	
Equals cash balance on hand at end of month	$11 544.20

The last cheque written in November, 1988, was Cheque No. 342. The chequebook balance after the last cheque had been written and after the last deposit was made is $11 544.20. Since the chequebook balance is the same as the balance on hand, cash is proved.

| | ACCOUNTS RECEIVABLE | | SALES CREDIT | SALES TAX PAYABLE CREDIT | ACCOUNTS PAYABLE | | PURCHASES DEBIT | |
	DEBIT	CREDIT			DEBIT	CREDIT		
1	22360	18200	627000	25080	140200	205400	233700	1
27								27
28			31500	1260				28
29			6500	260				29
30	63960	35360	1330500	53220	216400	361400	407700	30
31								31

FOR MONTH OF *November* 19 88   PAGE 2

Synoptic journal totalled and ruled (right page)

Ruling a synoptic journal at the end of each month

Denim Threads' synoptic journal is ruled at the end of each month. The illustration above and on page 220 shows the ruling of the synoptic journal for November. Ruling procedures are the same as those used by Putt Around in Chapter 5.

A complete illustration of page 2 of Denim Threads' synoptic journal is on pages 242 and 243, Chapter 13.

ACCOUNTING TERMS

What is the meaning of each of the following?

1. customer
2. sale
3. sales tax
4. cash sale
5. sale on account
6. charge customer
7. sales invoice
8. credit card

QUESTIONS FOR INDIVIDUAL STUDY

1. What are the two major activities of a merchandising business?
2. How are sales tax rates usually stated?
3. Why must every business that collects a sales tax keep accurate records of the amount of tax collected?
4. What two amounts must sales tax records show?
5. What is the source document for a cash sales transaction?
6. What effect does a cash sales transaction have on the revenue account Sales?
7. Why is sales tax collected considered to be a liability to a business?
8. What is the name of the ledger account used to summarize the total amount due from all charge customers?
9. What is the source document for a sale on account transaction?
10. What accounts are affected by a sale on account transaction? How are the accounts affected?
11. Which amount columns in a synoptic journal are used to record a sale on account transaction?
12. How are credit card sales recorded by a business that issues its own credit cards?
13. How are credit card sales recorded by a business that subscribes to a major credit card system?

14. What two accounts are affected when cash is received on account? How are the accounts affected?

15. At what two times is a synoptic journal totalled and proved?

CASES FOR MANAGEMENT DECISION

CASE 1 Judy Lawler operates an office supply store. A cash journal and a general journal similar to those described in Chapter 5 are used to record all transactions. The business sells merchandise for cash and also has a number of charge customers. The business also purchases most of its merchandise on account. Ms.

Lawler asked an accountant to check the accounting system and recommend changes. The accountant suggests that a synoptic journal similar to the one described in Chapter 12 be used. Which would be better: (a) the cash journal and general journal, or (b) the synoptic journal? Why?

CASE 2 Andres Rios, accountant for a hardware store, has noted a major increase in the amounts due from charge customers. All sales are due within 30 days. The amounts due from charge customers have reduced the amount of cash available for the normal operation of the business. The accountant recommends that (1) all regular sales on account be stopped and (2) the business subscribe to a major credit card system. The owner

is reluctant to accept the recommendations. One concern is that the business might lose some reliable customers who do not have a credit card. Another concern is the increased expenses because of the credit card fee the business must pay. How do you respond to the concerns of the owner? What alternatives to the accountant's recommendations would you suggest?

DRILLS FOR UNDERSTANDING

DRILL 12-D 1   Analysing transactions into debit and credit parts

Instructions: Prepare T accounts for each of the transactions below. Show which accounts in the ledger are debited and which accounts are credited. The first transaction is given as an example. Credit card sales are recorded as cash sales.

Cash		Sales		Sales Tax Payable	
1 680.00			1 600.00		80.00

Transactions

1. Cash sales for the week, $1 600.00, plus sales tax, $80.00. Total, $1 680.00.
2. Credit card sales for the week, $400.00, plus sales tax, $20.00. Total, $420.00.
3. Sold merchandise on account to Sally Sykes, $26.00, plus sales tax, $1.30. Total $27.30.
4. Received on account from Harold Johnson, $37.80.
5. Received on account from Elaine Mitchell, $16.80.
6. Sold merchandise on account to Jeff Walker, $55.00, plus sales tax, $2.75. Total $57.75.
7. Cash sales for the week, $1 800.00, plus sales tax, $90.00. Total, $1 890.00.
8. Credit card sales for the week, $600.00, plus sales tax, $30.00. Total, $630.00.

The solution to Drill 12-D 1 is needed to complete Drill 12-D 3.

DRILL 12-D 2 Analysing the effect of sales transactions on accounts

Instructions: 1. Prepare T accounts for the ledger accounts Cash, Accounts Receivable, Sales, Sales Tax Payable. Label the debit and credit parts of each transaction as shown in the T accounts at the right. Transaction 1 is given as an example.

2. Using the T accounts show which accounts are debited and credited for the following transactions. Add a 5% sales tax to each sale.

Transactions

1. Cash sales for the week, $2 000.00.
2. Sold merchandise on account to Steven Durand, $35.00.
3. Received on account from Sharon Jewel, $39.90.
4. Cash sales for the week, $2 200.00.
5. Received on account from Justin Lane, $18.90.
6. Sold on account to Jim McCoy, $15.00.

Cash	
(1) 2 100.00	

Accounts Receivable	

Sales	
	(1) 2 000.00

Sales Tax Payable	
	(1) 100.00

DRILL 12-D 3 Recording transactions using a synoptic journal

The solution to Drill 12-D 1 is needed to complete Drill 12-D 3.

Instructions: Use a form such as the one below. Based on the answers in Drill 12-D 1, show by a check mark which amount columns will be used to record the transactions. Transaction 1 is shown as an example.

Transaction	Cash		Accts. Rec.		Sales Credit	Sales Tax Pay. Credit
	Debit	Credit	Debit	Credit		
1. Debit amount	√					
Credit amount					√	
Credit amount						√

APPLICATION PROBLEM

PROBLEM 12-1 Journalizing sales and cash receipts in a synoptic journal

Mark Dalton and Don James, partners in an office supply store, completed the transactions, page 224, for November of the current year. The cash balance on November 1 was $4 300.00.

Instructions: 1. Record the cash balance on page 16 of a synoptic journal like the one on pages 218 and 219.

2. Record the following transactions. Credit card sales are recorded as cash sales. Source documents are abbreviated as: sales invoice, *S*; receipt, *R*; cash register tape, *T*; calculator tape, *CT*.

Nov. 1. Sold merchandise on account to Wallace Janes, $22.00, plus sales tax, $1.10. Total, $23.10. S62.
   2. Sold merchandise on account to Beverly Winters, $30.00, plus sales tax, $1.50. Total, $31.50. S63.
   3. Received on account from Timothy Jester, $29.40. R110.
   6. Cash sales for the week, $2 200.00, plus sales tax, $110.00. Total, $2 310.00. T6.
   6. Credit card sales for the week, $700.00, plus sales tax, $35.00. Total, $735.00. CT6.
   8. Sold merchandise on account to Carol Munson, $35.00, plus sales tax, $1.75. Total, $36.75. S64.
   9. Received on account from Cathy Curtis, $26.25. R111.
   9. Received on account from Dan Mendenhall, $42.00. R112.
  13. Cash sales for the week, $2 160.00, plus sales tax, $108.00. Total, $2 268.00. T13.
  13. Credit card sales for the week, $555.00, plus sales tax, $27.75. Total, $582.75. CT13.
  15. Sold merchandise on account to Bradley Mondale, $60.00, plus sales tax, $3.00. Total, $63.00. S65.
  16. Sold merchandise on account to Carol Munson, $45.00, plus sales tax, $2.25. Total, $47.25. S66.
  17. Received on account from Baker Co., $126.00. R113.
  20. Cash sales for the week, $2 240.00, plus sales tax, $112.00. Total, $2 352.00. T20.
  20. Credit card sales for the week, $560.00, plus sales tax, $28.00. Total, $588.00. CT20.
  22. Received on account from Wallace Janes, $23.10. R114.
  23. Received on account from Westside Grocery, $47.25. R115.
  24. Sold merchandise on account to Carol Munson, $15.00, plus sales tax, $.75. Total, $15.75. S67.
  27. Cash sales for the week, $1 950.00, plus sales tax, $97.50. Total, $2 047.50. T27.
  27. Credit card sales for the week, $345.00, plus sales tax, $17.25. Total, $362.25. CT27.
  27. Received on account from Beverly Winters, $31.50. R116.
  29. Sold merchandise on account to Cathy Curtis, $60.00, plus sales tax, $3.00. Total, $63.00. S68.
  30. Cash sales for the week, $720.00, plus sales tax, $36.00. Total, $756.00. T30.
  30. Credit card sales for the week, $105.00, plus sales tax, $5.25. Total, $110.25. CT30.

Instructions: 3. Total the amount columns on the synoptic journal. Prove the equality of debits and credits.
   4. Rule the synoptic journal. Use the illustration on pages 220 and 221 as a guide.

ENRICHMENT PROBLEMS

MASTERY PROBLEM 12-M Journalizing transactions in a synoptic journal

Gloria Jackson and John Lyons, partners, operate a hardware store. The transactions on the next page were completed during December of the current year. The cash balance on December 1 was $5 300.00.

Instructions: 1. Record the cash balance on page 14 of a synoptic journal like the one on pages 218 and 219.

2. Record the following transactions. Credit card sales are recorded as cash sales. A 5% sales tax is to be added to all sales. Source documents are abbreviated as: cheque, *C*; memorandum, *M*; purchase invoice, *P*; receipt, *R*; sales invoice, *S*; cash register tape, *T*; calculator tape, *CT*.

Dec. 1. Paid salaries, $3 800.00. C218.
1. Paid December rent, $850.00. C219.
1. Paid telephone bill, $64.00. C220. (Miscellaneous Expense)
2. Purchased merchandise on account from Dannon, Inc., $670.00. P62.
3. Paid on account to Silva Co., $980.00. C221.
4. Cash sales for the week, $1 600.00. T4.
4. Credit card sales for the week, $230.00. CT4.
6. Sold merchandise on account to Donald Pearson, $84.00. S85.
6. Paid on account to Jefferson Hardware, $835.00. C222.
7. Received on account from Lois Arnold, $26.25. R240.
8. Discovered that a purchase of merchandise on account had been recorded as a debit to Supplies instead of Purchases, $142.00. M52.
9. Purchased merchandise for cash, $980.00. C223.
10. Bought supplies on account from Navarro Supply, $86.00. M53.
10. Sold merchandise on account to Benjamin Preston, $125.00. S86.
11. Received on account from Marsha Rankin, $86.10. R241.
11. Cash sales for the week, $2,450.00. T11.
11. Credit card sales for the week, $530.00. CT11.
13. Purchased merchandise on account from Higgins Hardware, $920.00. P63.
13. Bought supplies for cash, $22.00. C224.
15. Gloria Jackson, partner, withdrew cash, $650.00. C225.
15. John Lyons, partner, withdrew cash, $650.00. C226.
16. Paid on account to Dannon, Inc., $930.00. C227.
18. Cash sales for the week, $2 260.00. T18.
18. Credit card sales for the week, $486.00. CT18.
20. Purchased merchandise for cash, $710.00. C228.
20. Bought supplies on account from Navarro Supply, $45.00. M54.
21. Gloria Jackson, partner, withdrew merchandise, $56.00. M55.

Instructions: 3. Prepare page 14 of the synoptic journal for forwarding. Total the amount columns. Prove the equality of debits and credits and record on line 32 the totals to be carried forward.

4. Record the totals brought forward on line 1 of page 15 of the synoptic journal. Prove the equality of debits and credits again.

5. Record on page 15 the transactions listed below.

Dec. 22. Received on account from Donald Pearson, $57.80. R242.
24. Sold merchandise on account to Charles Tyler, $16.00. S87.
24. Discovered that a withdrawal of supplies for John Lyons, partner, had been recorded as a credit to Purchases instead of Supplies, $12.00. M56.
24. Cash sales for the week, $2 540.00. T24.
24. Credit card sales for the week, $720.00. CT24.
27. John Lyons, partner, withdrew merchandise, $42.00. M57.
29. Purchased merchandise on account from Mason, Inc., $330.00. P64.
30. Purchased merchandise for cash, $920.00. C229.
31. Cash sales for the week, $1 820.00. T31.
31. Credit card sales for the week, $280.00. CT31.

Instructions: 6. Total all amount columns of page 15 of the synoptic journal. Prove the equality of debits and credits.

7. Prove cash. The balance on Cheque Stub No. 230 is $7 640.95.

8. Rule page 15 of the synoptic journal.

The synoptic journal prepared in Mastery Problem 12-M is needed to complete Mastery Problem 13-M in Chapter 13.

CHALLENGE PROBLEM 12-C   Journalizing transactions in a synoptic journal

A synoptic journal may be ruled in different ways. For example, the synoptic journal on pages 218 and 219 is referred to as a divided-column form. The amount columns are divided by the Account Title column. Some of the amount columns are to the left and some are to the right of the Account Title column. Another common arrangement is to have all amount columns to the right of the Account Title column.

Instructions: 1. Use a synoptic journal ruled as shown below.

Date	Account Title	Doc. No.	Post. Ref.	General		Cash		Accounts Payable		Accounts Receivable		Purchases	Sales	Sales Tax Pay.
				Dr.	Cr.	Dr.	Cr.	Dr.	Cr.	Dr.	Cr.	Dr.	Cr.	Cr.

2. Use the transactions and instructions for Mastery Problem 12-M. Complete all of the instructions using the synoptic journal above.

The synoptic journal prepared in Challenge Problem 12-C is needed to complete Challenge Problem 13-C in Chapter 13.

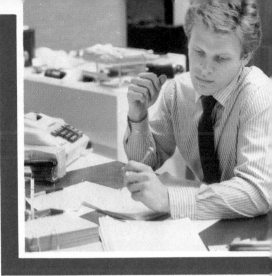

13

Posting to Ledgers

ENABLING PERFORMANCE TASKS

After studying Chapter 13, you will be able to:

a. Define accounting terms related to posting to ledgers.
b. Explain accounting principles and practices related to posting to ledgers.
c. Open accounts in subsidiary ledgers.
d. Post to ledgers from a synoptic journal.
e. Prepare subsidiary schedules.
f. Prove equality of debits and credits in the general ledger.

Business activities entered in a journal are sorted and summarized in ledger accounts. Transferring information from journals to ledger accounts is known as posting. Posting information from a journal to ledger accounts brings together in one place all activities affecting each single account.

LEDGERS AND CONTROLLING ACCOUNTS

The type and size of a business determine the number of ledgers used in the accounting system.

General ledger

A business with transactions involving mostly the receipt and payment of cash will generally use a single ledger. In Part 2, Putt Around uses only a single ledger. This single ledger sorts and summarizes all of the information affecting income statement and balance sheet accounts. A ledger that contains all accounts needed to prepare an income statement and a balance sheet is called a general ledger. Denim Threads uses a general ledger. The chart of accounts is on page 190. Because of the nature of the business, Denim Threads also uses additional ledgers in its accounting system.

Subsidiary ledgers

Accounts that are similar in nature are placed in a separate ledger. Besides the receipt and payment of cash, Denim Threads purchases merchandise on account and sells merchandise on account. A business must keep an individual account for each creditor and charge customer. A business needs to know the amount owed each creditor as well as the amount due from each charge customer.

A general ledger could contain an account for each creditor and for each charge customer. However, a business with many creditors and charge customers would have a bulky general ledger and a long trial balance. Denim Threads eliminates these problems by keeping separate ledgers for individual accounts of creditors and charge customers.

The total amount owed to all creditors is summarized in a single general ledger account, Accounts Payable. Likewise, the total amount due from all charge customers is summarized in a single general ledger account, Accounts Receivable. A ledger that is summarized in a single account in a general ledger is called a subsidiary ledger.

Controlling accounts

An account in a general ledger that summarizes all the accounts in a subsidiary ledger is called a controlling account. The separate ledger kept by Denim Threads for creditors is a subsidiary ledger. The general ledger account Accounts Payable is the controlling account. Denim Threads also keeps a subsidiary ledger for charge customers. The general ledger account Accounts Receivable is the controlling account. The balance of a controlling account equals the total of all the account balances in its related subsidiary ledger.

POSTING TO AN ACCOUNTS PAYABLE LEDGER

When the balance of a creditor's account is changed, the balance of the controlling account Accounts Payable is also changed. A subsidiary ledger that contains only accounts with creditors is called an accounts payable ledger. The relationship between the accounts payable ledger and the general ledger account Accounts Payable is on page 229.

Accounts payable ledger form

Denim Threads uses a three-column account form in the accounts payable ledger. The ledger form is on page 229.

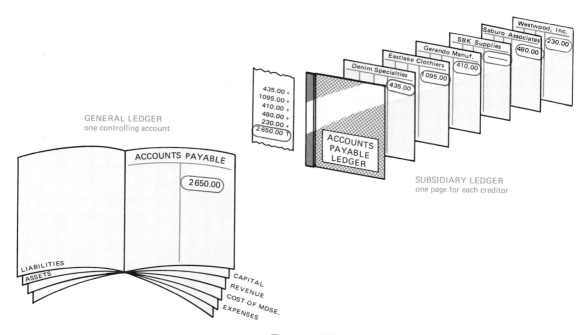

The sum of the balances of the creditor's accounts in the accounts payable ledger is summarized in Accounts Payable.

Each creditor's account has three amount columns. One column is for debit amounts, one column is for credit amounts, and one column is for the balance. Since accounts payable are liabilities and liabilities have credit balances, the last column is titled Credit Balance. With this third column, the balance of the account can be updated after each posting. After posting is completed, an accounts payable ledger shows how much is owed to each creditor.

NAME					
ADDRESS					
DATE	ITEM	POST. REF.	DEBIT	CREDIT	CREDIT BALANCE

Three-column account form used in an accounts payable ledger

Opening creditor accounts

Each new account is opened by writing the creditor's name and address on the first two lines of the ledger form. The account opened for

Denim Specialties is below. The name and address are obtained from the first purchase invoice received from a creditor.

NAME *Denim Specialties*					
ADDRESS *156 Church Street, Amherst, NS B4H 3C4*					
DATE	ITEM	Post. Ref.	DEBIT	CREDIT	CREDIT BALANCE

Opening a creditor's account in the accounts payable ledger

Individual accounts for the creditors of Denim Threads are arranged alphabetically in a loose-leaf binder. Periodically accounts for new creditors are added and old accounts not used any more are removed from the subsidiary ledger. Therefore, to avoid the difficulty of keeping the accounts in order, the ledger pages are not numbered.

> If a business has many accounts in the accounts payable ledger, each account may be given a number. The accounts then may be arranged in numerical order. A separate alphabetic card file is used to help locate a creditor's account number.

Posting from a synoptic journal to an accounts payable ledger

Each entry in the accounts payable columns of a synoptic journal affects the creditor named in the Account Title column. Each amount listed in these two columns is posted daily to a creditor's account in the accounts payable ledger. Posting daily keeps each creditor's account balance up to date. Totals of these special amount columns are posted at the end of the month.

Posting a credit to an accounts payable ledger. Posting a purchase on account from a synoptic journal to an accounts payable ledger is on page 231.

Steps to post the entry on line 3 are below.

1 Write the amount, *$822.00*, in the Credit column of the account.

2 Add the amount in the Credit column to the previous balance in the Credit Balance column. (Denim Specialties has no previous balance; therefore, 0 + $822.00 = $822.00.) Write the new balance, *$822.00*, in the Credit Balance column.

3 Write the date, *1988, Nov. 2*, in the Date column.

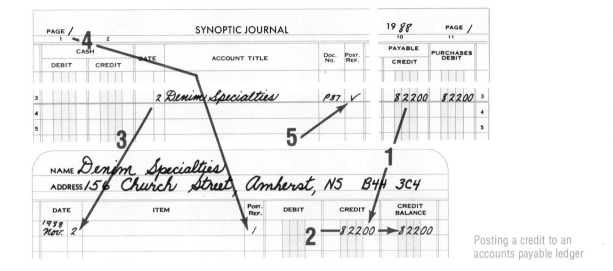

Posting a credit to an accounts payable ledger

4 Write the page number of the synoptic journal, *1*, in the Post Ref. column of the account.

>In Part 2 Putt Around used two journals. The posting reference was written as *C1* to show posting from the cash journal. G1 showed posting from the general journal. Denim Threads uses only one journal. Therefore, there is no need to put a letter code on the page number of the journal.

5 Place a check mark in the Post. Ref. column of the synoptic journal. The check mark shows that the posting for this entry is completed.

>Individual accounts in the accounts payable ledger do not have page numbers. Therefore, a check mark is used to show that posting is completed. If individual accounts were numbered, the account number would be written in the Post. Ref. column of the synoptic journal.

Accounts Payable, the controlling account in the general ledger, is also increased because of this entry. At the end of a month, the Accounts Payable Credit column total is posted to the controlling account Accounts Payable. Posting of column totals is described on page 241.

Posting a debit to an accounts payable ledger. The same steps are followed to post a debit to a creditor's account as are used to post a credit. The difference is that the amount is entered in the Debit column of the account. The debit amount is then subtracted from the previous credit balance. Posting a payment on account, line 17 of the synoptic journal, to the subsidiary ledger is on the next page.

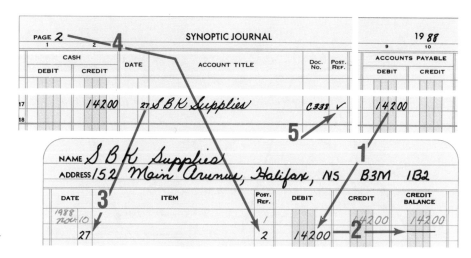

Posting a debit to an accounts payable ledger

Opening a new page for a creditor in an accounts payable ledger

The number of entries that may be recorded on each ledger form depends on the number of lines provided. When all lines have been used, a new page is prepared. The name and address plus the account balance are recorded on the new page.

On November 1, 1988, Denim Threads prepared a new page for Gerando Manufacturing in the accounts payable ledger. On that day, the account balance was $360.00. The account is below.

NAME *Gerando Manufacturing*
ADDRESS *257 Brookside Street, Glace Bay, NS B1A1M1*

DATE	ITEM	POST. REF.	DEBIT	CREDIT	CREDIT BALANCE
1988 nov. 1	Balance	✓			360 00

Opening a new page for a creditor in the accounts payable ledger

The name and address of the creditor are written at the top of the account page. The account balance, *$360.00*, is written in the Credit Balance column. The date, *1988, Nov. 1*, is entered in the Date column. The word *Balance* is written in the Item column. A check mark is placed in the Post. Ref. column. The check mark shows that the entry was not posted from the synoptic journal.

Completed accounts payable ledger

The accounts payable ledger for Denim Threads after all posting has been completed is on pages 233 and 234. Denim Threads posts daily each line from the Accounts Payable columns of the synoptic journal. This procedure keeps all accounts with creditors up to date. Accounts Payable column total in the synoptic journal are posted at the end of each month.

NAME *Denim Specialties*
ADDRESS *156 Church Street, Amherst, NS B4H 3C4*

DATE		ITEM	POST. REF.	DEBIT	CREDIT	CREDIT BALANCE
1988 Nov.	2		1		82200	82200
	19		1	82200		
	24		2		43500	43500

NAME *Eastlake Clothiers*
ADDRESS *61 High Street, Bedford, NS B4A 1M7*

DATE		ITEM	POST. REF.	DEBIT	CREDIT	CREDIT BALANCE
1988 Nov.	8		1		68000	68000
	28		2		41500	109500

NAME *Gerando Manufacturing*
ADDRESS *257 Brookside Street, Glace Bay, NS B1A 1M1*

DATE		ITEM	POST. REF.	DEBIT	CREDIT	CREDIT BALANCE
1988 Nov.	1	Balance	✓			36000
	12		1		41000	77000
	28		2	36000		41000

NAME *SBK Supplies*
ADDRESS *152 Main Avenue, Halifax, NS B3M 1B2*

DATE		ITEM	POST. REF.	DEBIT	CREDIT	CREDIT BALANCE
1988 Nov.	10		1		14200	14200
	26		2	14200		

NAME *Saburo Associates*
ADDRESS *644 King Street, Bridgewater, NS B4V 1B4*

DATE		ITEM	POST. REF.	DEBIT	CREDIT	CREDIT BALANCE
1988 Nov.	1	Balance	✓			26000
	22		2	26000		
	24		2		48000	48000

DATE		ITEM	POST. REF.	DEBIT	CREDIT	CREDIT BALANCE
1988 Nov.	1	Balance	✓			580 00
	15		1	580 00		
	25		2		230 00	230 00

NAME *Westwood, Inc.*
ADDRESS *169 Hawthorne Street, Antigonish, NS B2G 1B3*

Accounts payable ledger
(concluded)

POSTING TO AN ACCOUNTS RECEIVABLE LEDGER

When a charge customer's account is changed, the controlling account Accounts Receivable is also changed. A subsidiary ledger that contains only accounts with charge customers is called an accounts receivable ledger. The relationship between the accounts receivable ledger and the general ledger account Accounts Receivable is below.

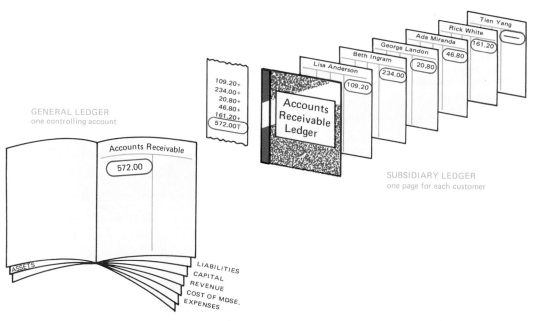

The sum of the balances of the customers' accounts in the accounts receivable ledger is summarized in Accounts Receivable.

Accounts receivable ledger form

Denim Threads uses a three-column account form in the accounts receivable ledger.

NAME *Lisa Anderson*
ADDRESS *39 Rupert Street, Amherst, NS B4H 3R7*

DATE	ITEM	POST. REF.	DEBIT	CREDIT	DEBIT BALANCE

Three-column account form used in an accounts receivable ledger

The form for the accounts receivable ledger is similar to the one used for the accounts payable ledger. Accounts receivable are assets and assets have debit balances. Therefore, the form used in the accounts receivable ledger has a Debit Balance column instead of a Credit Balance column.

Opening customers' accounts

Procedures for opening customers' accounts are similar to those used for opening creditors' accounts. The account opened for Lisa Anderson is above. For each customer's account the name and address are taken from the first sales invoice issued. Accounts are arranged in alphabetical order.

Posting from a synoptic journal to an accounts receivable ledger

Each entry in the accounts receivable columns of a synoptic journal affects the customer named in the Account Title column. Each amount listed in these two columns is posted daily to a customer's account in an accounts receivable ledger. Posting daily keeps each customer's account balance up to date. Totals of accounts receivable special amount columns are posted at the end of the month.

Posting a debit to an accounts receivable ledger. Posting a charge sale from a synoptic journal to an accounts receivable ledger is below.

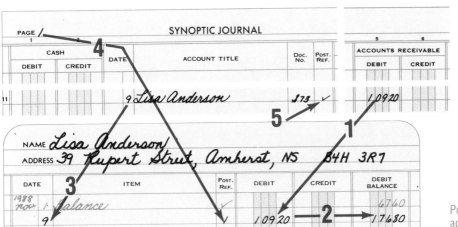

Posting a debit to an accounts receivable ledger

Steps to post this entry to the accounts receivable ledger are below.

1 Write the amount of the sale, *$109.20*, in the Debit column of the account for Lisa Anderson.

2 Add the amount in the Debit column to the previous balance in the Debit Balance column ($67.60 + $109.20 = $176.80). Write the new balance, *$176.80*, in the Debit Balance column.

3 Write the date, *9*, in the Date column.

4 Write the page number of the synoptic journal, *1*, in the Post Ref. column of the account.

5 Place a check mark in the Post Ref. column of the synoptic journal. The check mark shows that the item on line 11 is posted.

Accounts Receivable, the controlling account in the general ledger, is also increased by this entry. The total of the Accounts Receivable Debit column is posted to the controlling account Accounts Receivable. Posting column totals is described on page 241.

Posting a credit to an accounts receivable ledger. The same steps are followed to post a credit to a customer's account as are used to post a debit. However, the credit amount is written in the Credit column of the customer's account. The credit amount is then subtracted from the previous debit balance. Posting cash received on account, line 7 of the synoptic journal, to the subsidiary ledger is below.

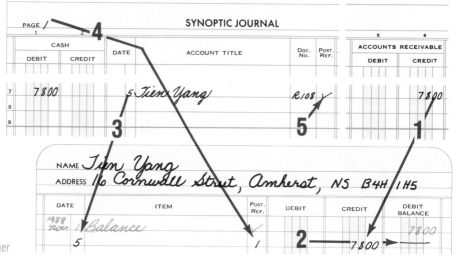

Posting a credit to an accounts receivable ledger

Accounts Receivable, the controlling account in the general ledger, is decreased by this entry. The Accounts Receivable Credit column total is posted to the controlling account Accounts Receivable at the end of the month.

Opening a new page for a customer in an accounts receivable ledger

Procedures for opening a new page in an accounts receivable ledger are similar to those for an accounts payable ledger. When all lines on a page have been used, a new page is prepared. The name and address of the customer are written at the top of the account page. The account balance however is recorded in the Debit Balance column rather than the Credit Balance column.

Completed accounts receivable ledger

The accounts receivable ledger for Denim Threads after all posting has been completed is below and on the next page. Denim Threads posts daily each line from the Accounts Receivable columns of the synoptic journal. This procedure keeps all customers' accounts up to date. The Accounts Receivable column totals in the synoptic journal are posted at the end of the month.

Accounts receivable ledger

NAME **Lisa Anderson**
ADDRESS **39 Rupert Street, Amherst, NS   B4H 3R7**

DATE		ITEM	POST. REF.	DEBIT	CREDIT	DEBIT BALANCE
1988 nov.	1	Balance	✓			67 60
	9		1	109 20		176 80
	26		2		67 60	109 20

NAME **Beth Ingram**
ADDRESS **62 Park Street, Amherst, NS   B4H 2R7**

DATE		ITEM	POST. REF.	DEBIT	CREDIT	DEBIT BALANCE
1988 nov.	1	Balance	✓			78 00
	18		1		41 60	36 40
	25		2		36 40	—
	28		2	62 40		62 40
	30		2	171 60		234 00

NAME George Landon
ADDRESS 18 Minto Street, Amherst, NS B4H 1H2

DATE	ITEM	POST. REF.	DEBIT	CREDIT	DEBIT BALANCE
1988 Nov. 12		1	1560		1560
23		2	2080		3640
26		2		1560	2080

NAME Ada Miranda
ADDRESS 340 King Street, Bridgewater, NS B4V 1A9

DATE	ITEM	POST. REF.	DEBIT	CREDIT	DEBIT BALANCE
1988 Nov. 1	Balance	✓			6240
4		1	4680		10920
17		1		6240	4680

NAME Rick White
ADDRESS 99 Hickman Street, Amherst, NS B4H 2M7

DATE	ITEM	POST. REF.	DEBIT	CREDIT	DEBIT BALANCE
1988 Nov. 10		1	5200		5200
23		2	16120		21320
29		2		5200	16120

NAME Tien Yang
ADDRESS 16 Cornwall Street, Amherst, NS B4H 1H5

DATE	ITEM	POST. REF.	DEBIT	CREDIT	DEBIT BALANCE
1988 Nov. 1	Balance	✓			7800
5		1		7800	—

Accounts receivable ledger
(concluded)

POSTING TO A GENERAL LEDGER

Daily account balances are usually not necessary for general ledger
accounts. Balances of general ledger accounts are needed only when finan-

cial statements are prepared. Therefore, posting from a synoptic journal to a general ledger is done periodically throughout a month. The number of transactions determines how often to post to a general ledger. A business with many transactions would normally post more often than a business with few transactions. Posting must be done at least once a month.

General ledger account form

All businesses, including Putt Around described in Part 2, use ledger account forms that show an up-to-date account balance after each entry is posted. An example is the account forms used by Denim Threads for subsidiary ledgers. Denim Threads also uses a balance-ruled form of account for its general ledger. The form is similar to the balance-column ledger account used by Putt Around but has four amount columns: Debit, Credit, Debit Balance, and Credit Balance. The form is below.

ACCOUNT						ACCOUNT NO.	
						BALANCE	
DATE	ITEM	Post. Ref.	DEBIT	CREDIT		DEBIT	CREDIT

Four-column account form used in a general ledger

The four-column account form shows the amount of each debit and each credit posted to the account. The amount of the new balance after an entry is posted is recorded in the appropriate Balance column. Asset, cost, and expense accounts normally have debit balances. Whereas, liability, capital, and revenue accounts normally have credit balances. Therefore, both Debit Balance and Credit Balance columns are needed for general ledger accounts.

> Some businesses using the four-column ledger form determine account balances only after all monthly postings have been completed. Then only the end-of-month balance is recorded in the proper balance column.

Posting from the General columns in a synoptic journal

Each amount in the General Debit and General Credit columns of a synoptic journal is posted individually. The amount is posted to the account shown in the Account Title column.

Posting a debit to a general ledger account. Posting a salary expense transaction from a synoptic journal to a general ledger is below.

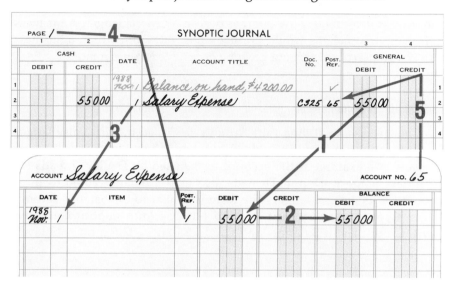

Posting a debit to a
general ledger

Steps to post the General Debit amount on line 2 of the synoptic journal to the general ledger are below.

1 Write the amount, *$550.00*, in the Debit column of the general ledger account Salary Expense.

2 Add the amount in the Debit column to the amount of the previous balance in the Debit Balance column. (There is no previous balance; therefore, 0 + $550.00 = $550.00.) Write the new balance, *$550.00*, in the Debit Balance column.

3 Write the date, *1988, Nov. 1*, in the Date column.

4 Write the page number of the synoptic journal, *1*, in the Post. Ref. column of the account.

5 Write the number of the salary expense account, *65*, in the Post. Ref. column of the synoptic journal. Writing the account number in the Post Ref. column shows that posting this line in the journal is completed.

Posting a credit to a general ledger account. A credit is posted by entering the amount in the Credit column of the general ledger account shown in the Account Title column. The new balance is figured by deducting the credit from the previous debit balance. If the previous balance is a credit, add the credit to the balance. The purchases account is shown below after the entry on line 28 of the synoptic journal is posted.

Posting a credit to a general ledger

Posting totals of the special columns in a synoptic journal

The total of each special column of a synoptic journal is posted to the account named in the column heading. After each column total is posted, the number of the account is written in parentheses below the column total. Totals of the General columns are not posted because each amount in these columns is posted individually. When totals are not to be posted, a check mark is placed in parentheses below the column total.

Illustrations on pages 242 and 243 show page 2 of the synoptic journal for November 1988. All individual items in the General, the Accounts Receivable, and the Accounts Payable columns have been posted. Totals of all special columns also have been posted.

The cash account in the general ledger is shown below. Totals of the Cash Debit and Cash Credit columns of the synoptic journal for November have been posted.

ACCOUNT *Cash*						BALANCE	ACCOUNT NO. *11*
DATE	ITEM	POST. REF.	DEBIT	CREDIT		DEBIT	CREDIT
1988 *Nov.* 1	*Balance*	✓				4 2 0 0 00	
30		2	1 3 5 5 1 20			1 7 7 5 1 20	
30		2		6 2 0 7 00		1 1 5 4 4 20	

Cash account after totals have been posted from a synoptic journal

	CASH		DATE	ACCOUNT TITLE	Doc. No.	Post. Ref.	GENERAL		
	DEBIT	**CREDIT**					**DEBIT**	**CREDIT**	
				PAGE 2 — SYNOPTIC JOURNAL					
1	647920	446600	Nov. 19	Brought Forward		✓	290600	12500	1
2	197600		19	✓	J19	✓			2
3	138840		19	✓	CJ19	✓			3
4		2900	22	Miscellaneous Expense	C335	63	2900		4
5		26000	22	Saburo Associates	C336	✓			5
6			23	Rick White	S76	✓			6
7			23	George Landon	S77	✓			7
8			24	Saburo Associates	P40	✓			8
9			24	Denim Specialties	P41	✓			9
10		18000	25	✓	C337	✓			10
11			25	Westwood, Inc.	P42	✓			11
12	3640		25	Beth Ingram	R111	✓			12
13	1560		26	George Landon	R112	✓			13
14	182520		26	✓	J26	✓			14
15	131560		26	✓	CJ26	✓			15
16	6760		26	Lisa Anderson	R113	✓			16
17		14200	26	S B K Supplies	C338	✓			17
18			28	Beth Ingram	S78	✓			18
19			28	Eastlake Clothiers	P43	✓			19
20		36000	28	Gerardo Manufacturing	C339	✓			20
21		200	28	Miscellaneous Expense	M49	63	200		21
22		13500	28	Credit Card Fee Expense	M50	61	13500		22
23		3300	28	Supplies	C340	14	3300		23
24	5200		29	Rick White	R114	✓			24
25			30	Beth Ingram	S79	✓			25
26		30000	30	Eva Burgos, Drawing	C341	32	30000		26
27		30000	30	Luis Perez, Drawing	C342	34	30000		27
28	32760		30	✓	J30	✓			28
29	6760		30	✓	CJ30	✓			29
30	1355120	620700	30	Totals			370500	12500	30
31	(11)	(11)					(✓)	(✓)	31
32									32
33									33
34									34

Synoptic journal after posting has been completed (left page)

Completed general ledger

The general ledger for Denim Threads is on pages 244–246. All entries in the synoptic journal for the month of November have been posted.

FOR MONTH OF *November* 19 88 PAGE 2

	ACCOUNTS RECEIVABLE		SALES CREDIT	SALES TAX PAYABLE CREDIT	ACCOUNTS PAYABLE		PURCHASES DEBIT	
	DEBIT	CREDIT			DEBIT	CREDIT		
1	22360	18200	627000	25080	140200	205400	233700	1
2			190000	7600				2
3			133500	5340				3
4								4
5					26000			5
6	16120		15500	620				6
7	2080		2000	80				7
8						48000	48000	8
9						43500	43500	9
10							18000	10
11						23000	23000	11
12		3640						12
13		1560						13
14			175500	7020				14
15			126500	5060				15
16		6760						16
17					14200			17
18	6240		6000	240				18
19						41500	41500	19
20					36000			20
21								21
22								22
23								23
24		5200						24
25	17160		16500	660				25
26								26
27								27
28			31500	1260				28
29			6500	260				29
30	63960	35360	1330500	53220	216400	361400	407700	30
31	(12)	(12)	(4)	(22)	(21)	(21)	(51)	31
32								32
33								33
34								34

Synoptic journal after posting has been completed (right page)

No postings appear in the following accounts: Income Summary, Insurance Expense, and Supplies Expense. Transactions for November did not affect these accounts. The use of these three accounts is described in Chapters 14 and 16.

ACCOUNT *Cash*   ACCOUNT NO. *11*

DATE		ITEM	POST. REF.	DEBIT	CREDIT	BALANCE DEBIT	BALANCE CREDIT
1988 nov.	1	Balance	✓			420000	
	30		2	1355120		1775120	
	30		2		620700	1154420	

ACCOUNT *Accounts Receivable*   ACCOUNT NO. *12*

DATE		ITEM	POST. REF.	DEBIT	CREDIT	BALANCE DEBIT	BALANCE CREDIT
1988 nov.	1	Balance	✓			28600	
	30		2	63960		92560	
	30		2		35360	57200	

ACCOUNT *Merchandise Inventory*   ACCOUNT NO. *13*

DATE		ITEM	POST. REF.	DEBIT	CREDIT	BALANCE DEBIT	BALANCE CREDIT
1988 nov.	1	Balance	✓			6800000	

ACCOUNT *Supplies*   ACCOUNT NO. *14*

DATE		ITEM	POST. REF.	DEBIT	CREDIT	BALANCE DEBIT	BALANCE CREDIT
1988 nov.	1	Balance	✓			16000	
	10		1	14200		30200	
	15		1	8600		38800	
	17		1	8000		46800	
	29		2	3300		50100	

ACCOUNT *Prepaid Insurance*   ACCOUNT NO. *15*

DATE		ITEM	POST. REF.	DEBIT	CREDIT	BALANCE DEBIT	BALANCE CREDIT
1988 nov.	1	Balance	✓			43000	

ACCOUNT *Accounts Payable*   ACCOUNT NO. *21*

DATE		ITEM	POST. REF.	DEBIT	CREDIT	BALANCE DEBIT	BALANCE CREDIT
1988 nov.	1	Balance	✓				120000
	30		2	216400			96400
	30		2		361400		265000

General ledger after
synoptic journal is
posted

ACCOUNT *Sales Tax Payable*   ACCOUNT NO. 22

DATE		ITEM	POST. REF.	DEBIT	CREDIT	BALANCE DEBIT	BALANCE CREDIT
1988 Nov.	1	Balance	✓				35680
	30		2		53220		88900

ACCOUNT *Eva Burgos, Capital*   ACCOUNT NO. 31

DATE		ITEM	POST. REF.	DEBIT	CREDIT	BALANCE DEBIT	BALANCE CREDIT
1988 Nov.	1	Balance	✓				3575960

ACCOUNT *Eva Burgos, Drawing*   ACCOUNT NO. 32

DATE		ITEM	POST. REF.	DEBIT	CREDIT	BALANCE DEBIT	BALANCE CREDIT
1988 Nov.	15		1	30000		30000	
	30		2	30000		60000	

ACCOUNT *Luis Perez, Capital*   ACCOUNT NO. 33

DATE		ITEM	POST. REF.	DEBIT	CREDIT	BALANCE DEBIT	BALANCE CREDIT
1988 Nov.	1	Balance	✓				3575960

ACCOUNT *Luis Perez, Drawing*   ACCOUNT NO. 34

DATE		ITEM	POST. REF.	DEBIT	CREDIT	BALANCE DEBIT	BALANCE CREDIT
1988 Nov.	15		1	30000		30000	
	16		1	4500		34500	
	30		2	30000		64500	

ACCOUNT *Income Summary*   ACCOUNT NO. 35

DATE	ITEM	POST. REF.	DEBIT	CREDIT	BALANCE DEBIT	BALANCE CREDIT

ACCOUNT *Sales*   ACCOUNT NO. 41

DATE		ITEM	POST. REF.	DEBIT	CREDIT	BALANCE DEBIT	BALANCE CREDIT
1988 Nov.	30		2		1330500		1330500

General ledger after
synoptic journal is
posted (continued)

ACCOUNT *Purchases*   ACCOUNT NO. *51*

DATE	ITEM	POST. REF.	DEBIT	CREDIT	BALANCE DEBIT	BALANCE CREDIT
1988 Nov. 16		1		4500		4500
17		1		8000		12500
30		2	407700		395200	

ACCOUNT *Credit Card Fee Expense*   ACCOUNT NO. *61*

DATE	ITEM	POST. REF.	DEBIT	CREDIT	BALANCE DEBIT	BALANCE CREDIT
1988 Nov. 28		2	13500		13500	

ACCOUNT *Insurance Expense*   ACCOUNT NO. *62*

DATE	ITEM	POST. REF.	DEBIT	CREDIT	BALANCE DEBIT	BALANCE CREDIT

ACCOUNT *Miscellaneous Expense*   ACCOUNT NO. *63*

DATE	ITEM	POST. REF.	DEBIT	CREDIT	BALANCE DEBIT	BALANCE CREDIT
1988 Nov. 3		1	5300		5300	
22		2	2900		8200	
28		2	200		8400	

ACCOUNT *Rent Expense*   ACCOUNT NO. *64*

DATE	ITEM	POST. REF.	DEBIT	CREDIT	BALANCE DEBIT	BALANCE CREDIT
1988 Nov. 15		1	80000		80000	

ACCOUNT *Salary Expense*   ACCOUNT NO. *65*

DATE	ITEM	POST. REF.	DEBIT	CREDIT	BALANCE DEBIT	BALANCE CREDIT
1988 Nov. 1		1	55000		55000	
15		1	55000		110000	

ACCOUNT *Supplies Expense*   ACCOUNT NO. *66*

DATE	ITEM	POST. REF.	DEBIT	CREDIT	BALANCE DEBIT	BALANCE CREDIT

General ledger after
synoptic journal is
posted (concluded)

ELECTRONIC POSTING TO A GENERAL LEDGER

Machines can be used to help process accounts receivable and accounts payable transactions. These machines print needed information on business forms. The machines also are able to add, subtract, multiply, or divide. A general-purpose accounting machine is at the right.

The principles of accounting used with an accounting machine are the same as those used when recording the information manually. The business forms may differ slightly because of the method used to record the information. For example, in manual accounting the accounts receivable account for Denim Threads appears as below.

General-purpose accounting machine

ACCOUNT *Accounts Receivable*					ACCOUNT NO. *12*	
DATE	ITEM	Post. Ref.	DEBIT	CREDIT	BALANCE DEBIT	BALANCE CREDIT
1988 *nov.* 1	*Balance*	✓			28600	
30		2	63960		92560	
30		2		35360	57200	

General ledger account used for processing information manually

The same information recorded by using a general-purpose accounting machine would appear as shown below.

LEDGER

ACCOUNT TITLE ACCOUNTS RECEIVABLE   ACCOUNT NO. 12

DATE	REFERENCE	DEBITS	CREDITS	BALANCE
1988 11 01			BALANCE FWD. →	286.00
1988 11 30	2	639.60		925.60
1988 11 30	2		353.60	572.00

General ledger card used for processing information on a general-purpose accounting machine

Using a general-purpose accounting machine has several advantages over recording information manually.

1. The machine figures the new balance for each customer's account.
2. The machine prints more readable copy than when information is written manually.
3. The machine does the arithmetic more accurately than when done manually.
4. The machine makes more legible copies than can be done manually.

SUMMARY OF POSTING STEPS FROM A SYNOPTIC JOURNAL

A summary of the posting steps from a cash journal is on pages 102 and 103. The steps described for Putt Around, Part 2, also apply to posting from a synoptic journal. Special amount columns and controlling accounts, however, require an additional set of posting steps.

Posting from general columns

As shown below, individual amounts in General columns *are* posted separately. Totals of General columns are *not* posted.

Posting from special columns

As shown below, totals of special columns *are* posted to the account named in the column heading. The total of the column shown is posted as a credit to the sales account. Individual amounts in special columns are *not* posted separately unless the columns are for a controlling account.

Posting from special columns for controlling accounts

As shown on page 249, individual amounts *and* total amounts are posted from special columns for controlling accounts. Individual amounts in the Accounts Receivable Debit and Credit columns *are* posted separately to charge customers' accounts. These accounts are found in an accounts receivable ledger. A check mark is placed in the

Post. Ref. column of the journal. The check mark shows that an individual amount has been posted to a customer's account.

Totals of special columns *are* posted to the controlling accounts named in the column heading. The total of an Accounts Receivable Debit column is posted as a debit to Accounts Receivable in a general ledger. The total of an Accounts Receivable Credit column is posted as a credit to Accounts Receivable in a general ledger. An account number is placed in parentheses under the total of a special column. The number shows the general ledger account to which the total was posted.

The same principles used for Accounts Receivable columns also apply to Accounts Payable columns in a synoptic journal.

PROVING THE ACCURACY OF POSTING

A single error in posting to a ledger account may cause the balance sheet to be out of balance. An error in posting may also cause the profit to be understated or overstated on the income statement. An error in posting may also cause a business to overpay or underpay its creditors. Consequently, posting must be accurate to assure correct account balances in the ledgers.

Proving cash

The way to prove cash is described in Chapter 12. After posting is completed the balance of the general ledger cash account is compared with the cash proof. The cash proof total is also compared with the balance on the last completed cheque stub in the chequebook. The balance of the cash account on November 30, page 244, is $11 544.20. The same amount was found when cash was proved following the procedures on page 220. The chequebook balance also showed the same amount.

The cash proof is important. Because so many transactions affect the cash account, there are many chances to make an error in *Cash*.

Proving the subsidiary ledgers

A controlling account balance in a general ledger must equal the sum of all account balances in a subsidiary ledger.

Proving accounts payable. A listing of creditors' accounts, account balances, and total amount due all creditors is called a schedule of accounts payable. A schedule of accounts payable is prepared after all current entries in a journal are posted. The schedule prepared on November 30, 1988, for Denim Threads is below.

Denim Threads	
Schedule of Accounts Payable	
November 30, 1988	
Denim Specialties	43500
Eastlake Clothiers	109500
Gerando Manufacturing	41000
Saburo Associates	48000
Westwood, Inc.	23000
Total Accounts Payable	265000

Schedule of accounts payable

The balance of the accounts payable account in the general ledger, page 244, is $2 650.00. The total of the schedule of accounts payable is the same, $2 650.00. The accounts payable ledger has been proved.

Proving accounts receivable. A listing of customers' accounts, account balances, and total amount due from all customers is called a schedule of accounts receivable. A schedule of accounts receivable is prepared after all current entries in a journal are posted. The schedule prepared on November 30, 1988, for Denim Threads is below.

Denim Threads	
Schedule of Accounts Receivable	
November 30, 1988	
Lisa Anderson	10920
Beth Ingram	23400
George Landon	2080
Ada Miranda	4680
Rick White	16120
Total Accounts Receivable	57200

Schedule of accounts receivable

The balance of the accounts receivable account in the general ledger, page 244, is $572.00. The total of the schedule of accounts receivable is the same, $572.00. The accounts receivable ledger has been proved.

Proving equality of debits and credits in a general ledger

Debits and credits recorded in a journal must be equal. Debits and credits in the general ledger must also be equal. Therefore, balances of all accounts with debit balances are added. Then balances of all accounts with credit balances are added. The total of debit balances must equal the total of credit balances. The illustration at the right shows that both debit and credit balances in Denim Threads' general ledger total $88 363.20. Therefore, equality of debits and credits in the general ledger is proved. If the totals do not agree, one or more errors have been made. These errors must be found and corrected before work is continued.

DEBIT BALANCES	CREDIT BALANCES
11 544.20	
572.00	
68 000.00	
501.00	
430.00	
600.00	
645.00	
3 952.00	2 650.00
135.00	889.00
84.00	35 759.60
800.00	35 759.60
1 100.00	13 305.00
88 363.20T	13 305.00
	88 363.20T

Calculator tapes used to prove equality of debits and credits in the general ledger after posting is completed

What is the meaning of each of the following?

1. general ledger
2. subsidiary ledger
3. controlling account
4. accounts payable ledger
5. accounts receivable ledger
6. schedule of accounts payable
7. schedule of accounts receivable

1. What determines the number and kinds of ledgers used in an accounting system?
2. What ledger contains all the accounts needed to prepare an income statement and a balance sheet?
3. Why must a business keep an individual account for each creditor and charge customer?
4. What kind of ledger is summarized in a single account in a general ledger?
5. What is the name of the general ledger controlling account for creditors?
6. Why does the three-column account form used in an accounts payable ledger have a Credit Balance column?
7. How are the name and address obtained for opening a new creditor's account in an accounts payable subsidiary ledger?
8. Why is a check mark placed in the Post. Ref. column when a new page for a creditor is opened?
9. Why is each amount listed in the accounts payable columns of a synoptic journal posted daily?
10. Why is a credit entry to an accounts payable account added to the previous balance?
11. Why does the three-column account form used in an accounts receivable ledger have a Debit Balance column?
12. How are the name and address obtained for opening a new customer's account in an accounts receivable subsidiary ledger?

13. Why is each amount listed in the accounts receivable columns of a synoptic journal posted daily?
14. Why is posting to a general ledger done only periodically throughout the month?
15. Why does the general ledger account form have both a Debit balance column and Credit balance column?

16. Why are the totals of the General Debit and Credit columns not posted at the end of the month?
17. Why is the cash proof important?
18. How are subsidiary ledgers proved at the end of the month?
19. How is a general ledger proved at the end of the month?

CASES FOR MANAGEMENT DECISION

CASE 1 Melinda Stevens is asked to evaluate the accounting system of Jefferson Supply Company. The general ledger of Jefferson Supply Company includes individual accounts for each creditor and charge customer. When checking the records and accounting procedures, Mrs. Stevens notes the bulky general ledger and long trial balance. Jefferson Supply Company uses a synoptic journal to record all transactions. A general ledger is used to maintain all income statement, balance sheet, creditor, and charge customer accounts. Transactions affecting creditor or charge customer accounts are recorded in the General Debit or General Credit columns of the synoptic journal. Creditor and charge customer entries are then posted individually to accounts in the general ledger. What recommendations should Mrs. Stevens make concerning the handling of creditor and charge customer accounts?

CASE 2 Jose Ramos observes his accountant at work and says, "You post each individual accounts receivable entry in the synoptic journal. Then you post the totals of the accounts receivable columns. You are posting these entries twice, which will make the records wrong." The accountant disagrees that the posting procedure is incorrect. Is Mr. Ramos or his accountant correct? Why?

CASE 3 Ruben's Gift Shop received a call from a customer, Beth Evans. Miss Evans stated she had purchased $50.00 worth of merchandise on account five weeks ago. She sent a cheque for $50.00 two weeks ago in payment of the account. Although no additional purchases had been made, she recently received a bill that listed her balance due as $100.00. What probably caused this error? When would the error probably be discovered?

DRILLS FOR UNDERSTANDING

DRILL 13-D 1   Analysing transactions of a merchandising business

Instructions: Prepare T accounts for each of the transactions below. Show which general ledger accounts are to be debited and credited. A 5% sales tax is to be added to all sales transactions. The first transaction is shown as an example.

Accounts Receivable		Sales		Sales Tax Payable	
84.00			80.00		4.00

1. Sold merchandise on account to Lois Sailer, $80.00.
2. Cash sales for the week, $2 000.00.
3. Purchased merchandise on account from Marcourt Enterprises, $350.00.
4. Purchased merchandise for cash, $250.00.
5. Paid December rent, $750.00.
6. Bought supplies for cash, $40.00.
7. Received on account from Ed Gilbert, $62.25.
8. Ralph Manson, partner, withdrew merchandise, $38.00.
9. Paid on account to Bennington Supply, $200.00.
10. Discovered that a payment for rent had been recorded as a debit to Salary Expense instead of Rent Expense, $900.00.
11. Bought supplies on account from Northland Supply, $85.00.
12. Carol Benson, partner, withdrew cash, $300.00.

The solution to Drill 13-D 1 is needed to complete Drill 13-D 2.

DRILL 13-D 2 Recording and posting transactions of a merchandising business

The solution to Drill 13-D 1 is needed to complete Drill 13-D 2.

Instructions: 1. Use a form like the one below. Use the answers to Drill 13-D 1. Show by a check mark which amount columns in the synoptic journal will be used to record the transactions. Transaction 1 is shown as an example.

Transaction	Amount columns in the synoptic journal										
	Cash		General		Accts. Rec.		Sales Credit	Sales Tax Pay. Credit	Accts. Pay.		Purch. Debit
	Debit	Credit	Debit	Credit	Debit	Credit			Debit	Credit	
1. Debit amount					✓						
Credit amount							✓				
Credit amount								✓			

Instructions: 2. Use a form such as the one below. Use the answers to Instruction 1. Show by a check mark whether the amount will or will not be posted separately to the ledgers. Transaction 1 is shown as an example.

Transaction	Posted separately to			Not posted separately to any ledger
	General Ledger	Accts. Rec. Ledger	Accts. Pay. Ledger	
1. Debit amount		✓		
Credit amount				✓
Credit amount				✓

APPLICATION PROBLEM

PROBLEM 13-1   Posting to ledgers from a synoptic journal

The synoptic journal for Webster's Variety Store is given in the working papers.

Instructions: 1. Open the following creditors' accounts in the accounts payable ledger. Record the balances as of November 1 of the current year.

Creditor	Address	Account Balance
Harrison Supplies	725 Murray Avenue, Bathurst, NB E2A 1V3	——
Miranda Specialties	112 Dover Street, Campbellton, NB E3N 1P8	$670.00
Mission Supply	157 Burlington Avenue, Moncton, NB E1E 2A4	——
Smith Supply	620 George Street, Fredericton, NB E3B 1K3	430.00

2. Open the following customers' accounts in the accounts receivable ledger. Record the balances as of November 1 of the current year.

Customer	Address	Account Balance
Helen Fields	387 Water Street, Summerside, PE C1N 1C7	$157.50
Marsha Harris	226 University Avenue, Charlottetown, PE C1A 4L7	——
Adrian Leon	77 Hilsboro Street, Charlottetown, PE C1A 4W3	262.50
Carlos Mendez	182 Duke Street, Summerside, PE C1N 3S4	210.00

3. Open the following accounts in the general ledger of Webster's Variety Store. Record the balances as of November 1 of the current year.

Account Title	Acct. No.	Account Balance
Cash	11	$ 4 600.00
Accounts Receivable	12	630.00
Merchandise Inventory	13	83 211.00
Supplies	14	360.00
Prepaid Insurance	15	900.00
Accounts Payable	21	1 100.00
Sales Tax Payable	22	526.40
Sherry Marshall, Capital	31	44 037.30
Sherry Marshall, Drawing	32	——
Harold Stark, Capital	33	44 037.30
Harold Stark, Drawing	34	——
Income Summary	35	——
Sales	41	——
Purchases	51	——
Credit Card Fee Expense	61	——
Insurance Expense	62	——
Miscellaneous Expense	63	——
Rent Expense	64	——
Salary Expense	65	——
Supplies Expense	66	——

Instructions: 4. Post the individual items recorded in the following columns of the synoptic journal. (a) General Debit and Credit. (b) Accounts Receivable Debit and Credit. (c) Accounts Payable Debit and Credit.

5. Post the totals of the special columns of the synoptic journal.

6. Prove cash. The balance on Cheque Stub No. 126 is $13 170.00.

7. Prepare a schedule of accounts payable similar to the one on page 250. Compare the total of the schedule with the balance of the controlling account Accounts Payable in the general ledger. If the totals are not the same, find and correct the errors.

8. Prepare a schedule of accounts receivable similar to the one on page 250. Compare the total of the schedule with the balance of the controlling account Accounts Receivable in the general ledger. If the totals are not the same, find and correct the errors.

9. Prove the equality of debits and credits in the general ledger. On a calculator or on a sheet of paper, add the balances of all accounts with debit balances. Then add the balances of all the accounts with credit balances. If the two totals are not the same, find and correct the errors.

ENRICHMENT PROBLEMS

MASTERY PROBLEM 13-M   Posting to ledgers from a synoptic journal

The synoptic journal prepared in Mastery Problem 12-M is needed to complete Mastery Problem 13-M.

The ledgers of J & L Hardware are given in the working papers.

Instructions: 1. Post the individual items recorded in the following columns of the synoptic journal prepared in Mastery Problem 12-M. (a) General Debit and Credit. (b) Accounts Receivable Debit and Credit. (c) Accounts Payable Debit and Credit.

2. Post the totals of the special columns of the synoptic journal.

3. Prove cash. The balance on Cheque Stub No. 230 is $7 640.95.

4. Prepare a schedule of accounts payable and a schedule of accounts receivable. Prove the accuracy of the subsidiary ledgers. Compare the schedule totals with the balances of the controlling accounts in the general ledger. If the totals are not the same, find and correct the errors.

5. Prove the equality of debits and credits in the general ledger. On a calculator or sheet of paper, add the balances of all accounts with debit balances. Then add the balances of all accounts with credit balances. If the two totals are not the same, find and correct the errors.

CHALLENGE PROBLEM 13-C   Posting to Ledgers from a synoptic journal

The synoptic journal prepared in Challenge Problem 12-C is needed to complete Challenge Problem 13-C.

Instructions: Follow the instructions for Mastery Problem 13-M above. However, use the synoptic journal prepared for Challenge Problem 12-C in Chapter 12.

Reinforcement Activity 2

PART A

An Accounting Cycle for a Partnership Using a Synoptic Journal

Source documents

↓

Journalize transactions in synoptic journal

↓

Post items to be posted individually to general ledger and subsidiary ledgers

↓

Post column totals to general ledger

↓

Prepare subsidiary schedules

Reinforcement Activity 2 is designed to strengthen learnings from Part 3, Chapters 11–16. The activity covers a complete accounting cycle for a merchandising business organized as a partnership. Reinforcement Activity 2 is divided into two parts. Part A includes learnings from Chapters 11–13. Part B, page 322, includes learnings from Chapters 14–16.

Accounting work for a one-month fiscal period is included for a single merchandising business. However, the records kept and reports prepared illustrate the application of accounting concepts for all merchandising businesses. The business uses a credit card service in addition to its own company charge for sales transactions. The flowchart at the left shows that part of the accounting cycle covered in Reinforcement Activity 2, Part A.

INFOCUS

Ruth Dunn and Frank Gallagher, partners, own and operate a merchandising business called Infocus. The business sells cameras and related supplies and equipment. The business is located in a downtown shopping area and is open for business Monday through Saturday. A monthly rent is paid for the building, equipment, and furniture.

Infocus' chart of accounts

Infocus uses the chart of accounts shown on the next page.

Infocus' journal and ledgers

The journal and ledgers used by Infocus are listed below. Pages of this textbook on which the journal and ledgers are illustrated are also given.

INFOCUS Chart of Accounts			
	Account Number		Account Number
(1) ASSETS		**(4) REVENUE**	
Cash................................	11	Sales	41
Accounts Receivable...........................	12	**(5) COST OF MERCHANDISE**	
Merchandise Inventory........................	13		
Supplies..................................	14	Purchases..............................	51
Prepaid Insurance	15	**(6) EXPENSES**	
(2) LIABILITIES		Credit Card Fee Expense	61
Accounts Payable..............................	21	Insurance Expense.............................	62
Sales Tax Payable...............................	22	Miscellaneous Expense	63
(3) CAPITAL		Rent Expense...	64
		Salary Expense	65
Ruth Dunn, Capital.............................	31	Supplies Expense	66
Ruth Dunn, Drawing.............................	32		
Frank Gallagher, Capital......................	33		
Frank Gallagher, Drawing....................	34		
Income Summary.................................	35		

Opening Infocus' set of books

The required forms for the journal and ledgers are given in the working papers.

Instructions: 1. Begin numbering the synoptic journal with page 22.

2. Open all general ledger accounts that appear in the chart of accounts for Infocus, above. Open the accounts in the order in which they are listed. Record the beginning account balances given below as of December 1 of the current year.

	Account Balances	
Balance Sheet Accounts	Debit	Credit
Cash	$ 8 340.00	——
Accounts Receivable...	932.00	——
Merchandise Inventory..	74 500.00	——
Supplies..	430.00	——
Prepaid Insurance...	640.00	——
Accounts Payable	——	$ 4 160.00
Sales Tax Payable...	——	1 235.00
Ruth Dunn, Capital	——	40 790.00
Frank Gallagher, Capital	——	38 657.00

3. Open an account in the accounts receivable ledger for each customer listed below. Record each customer's beginning balance as of December 1 of the current year.

Customers' Names and Addresses	Account Balances
Iris Adams, 719 Yale Avenue, Moncton, NB E1B 2C3......................................	$260.50
Olivia Espino, 242 Crown Street, Saint John, NB E2L 2X8................................	——
James Fitzgerald, 325 Pleasant Street, Newcastle, NB E1V 1Z1.....................	136.25
Eva Lawson, 168 West Lane, Moncton, NB E1C 6V2.....................................	345.15
Ralph Moya, 623 High Street, Moncton, NB E1C 6G3.....................................	190.10
Steven Reynolds, 159 Burlington Avenue, Moncton, NB E1E 2A4	

4. Open an account in the accounts payable ledger for each creditor listed below. Record the balances as of December 1 of the current year.

Creditors' Names and Addresses	Account Balances
A & M Photo, 94 Elizabeth Drive, Gander, NF A1V 1G7...	$1 860.00
Beach Camera Company, 359 Curling Street, Corner Brook, NF A2H 3K4....................	830.50
Fisher Office Supply, 92 Prince Street, Saint John, NB E2M 1P1.............................	——
Garland Photo Products, 363 Water Street, St. John's, NF A1C 1C2...........................	——
Mori Photo Equipment, 350 Carolina Avenue, Stephenville, NF A2N 2S8....................	1 469.50
Newberry Office Supply, 89 Park Avenue, Mount Pearl, NF A1N 1J6..........................	——

5. Record the cash on hand, *$8 340.00*, on line 1 of the synoptic journal.

Recording Infocus' transactions

Instructions: 6. Record the following transactions. Credit card sales are recorded as cash sales. Source documents are abbreviated as: cheque, *C*; memorandum, *M*; purchase invoice, *P*; receipt, *R*; sales invoice, *S*; cash register tape, *T*; calculator tape, *CT*

Dec. 1. Paid December rent, $850.00. C320.
   1. Paid salaries, $800.00. C321.
   1. Ruth Dunn, partner, withdrew cash, $800.00. C322.
   1. Frank Gallagher, partner, withdrew cash, $800.00. C323.
   2. Sold merchandise on account to Olivia Espino, $125.00, plus sales tax, $5.94. Total, $130.94. S83.
   2. Paid on account to Beach Camera Company, $830.50. C324.
   3. Paid on account to Mori Photo Equipment, $1 469.50. C325.
   4. Cash sales for the week, $1 570.00, plus sales tax, $74.58. Total, $1 644.58. T4.
   4. Credit card sales for the week, $625.00, plus sales tax, $29.69. Total, $654.69. CT4.
      Posting: Post the items that are to be posted individually.
   6. Bought supplies on account from Newberry Office Supply, $135.00. M42.
   6. Purchased merchandise on account from A & M Photo, $960.00. P74.
   6. Paid telephone bill, $62.00. C326. (Miscellaneous Expense)
   7. Frank Gallagher, partner, withdrew merchandise, $38.00. M43.
   8. Sold merchandise on account to Steven Reynolds, $350.00, plus sales tax, $16.63. Total, $366.63. S84.
   8. Sold merchandise on account to Iris Adams, $83.25, plus sales tax, $3.95. Total, $87.20. S85.
   9. Received on account from James Fitzgerald, $136.25. R90.
   9. Received on account from Ralph Moya, $190.10. R91.
   10. Discovered that supplies bought in November had been recorded in error as a debit to Prepaid Insurance, $65.00. M44.
   11. Cash sales for the week, $2 430.00, plus sales tax, $115.43. Total, $2 545.43. T11.
   11. Credit card sales for the week, $910.00, plus sales tax, $43.23. Total, $953.23. CT11.
   11. Ruth Dunn, partner, withdrew merchandise, $28.00. M45.
      Posting: Post the items that are to be posted individually.
   13. Bought supplies for cash, $46.00. C327.
   13. Paid utility bill, $83.00. C328. (Miscellaneous Expense)
   14. Paid on account to A & M Photo, $1 860.00. C329.
   15. Sold merchandise on account to James Fitzgerald, $48.50, plus sales tax, $2.30. Total, $50.80. S86.

Dec. 15. Paid salaries, $800.00. C330.

     Posting: Post the items that are to be posted individually.

     Forwarding: Total the amount columns. Prove the equality of debits and credits and record on line 32 the totals to be carried forward. Record the totals brought forward on line 1 of page 23 of the synoptic journal.

  16. Purchased merchandise on account from Garland Photo Products, $645.00. P75.

  16. Purchased merchandise for cash, $430.00. C331.

  17. Received on account from Eva Lawson, $238.62. R92.

  18. Cash sales for the week, $2 560.00, plus sales tax, $121.60. Total, $2 681.60. T18.

  18. Credit card sales for the week, $820.00, plus sales tax, $38.95. Total, $858.95. CT18.

  18. Purchased merchandise on account from Mori Photo Equipment, $950.00. P76.

     Posting: Post the items that are to be posted individually.

  20. Paid for advertising, $65.00. C332. (Miscellaneous Expense)

  20. Purchased merchandise on account from Beach Camera Company, $348.00. P77.

  21. Received on account from Iris Adams, $260.50. R93.

  22. Sold merchandise on account to Steven Reynolds, $34.95, plus sales tax, $1.66. Total, $36.61. S87.

  22. Sold merchandise on account to Ralph Moya, $73.50, plus sales tax, $3.49. Total, $76.99. S88.

  23. Purchased merchandise for cash, $220.00. C333.

  23. Bought supplies on account from Newberry Office Supply, $74.00. M46.

  24. Cash sales for the week, $2 310.00, plus sales tax, $109.73. Total, $2 419.73. T24.

  24. Credit card sales for the week, $420.00, plus sales tax, $19.95. Total, $439.95. CT24.

  24. Received on account from Eva Lawson, $106.53. R94.

     Posting: Post the items that are to be posted individually.

  27. Purchased merchandise on account from Garland Photo Products, $720.00. P78.

  27. Bought supplies on account from Fisher Office Supply, $93.00. M47.

  28. Purchased merchandise for cash, $247.00. C334.

  28. Ruth Dunn, partner, withdrew merchandise, $65.00. M48.

     Reconciling a bank statement: Prepare a reconciliation of Infocus' bank statement. Use illustration, page 171, as a guide. Information from the bank statement dated December 27 is below.

       Balance shown on bank statement, $9 551.05.

       Balance shown on Cheque Stub No. 334, $12 107.16.

       Outstanding deposit made on December 24, $2 966.21.

       Outstanding cheques are Nos. C332, C333, C334.

       Service charge shown on bank statement, $4.10.

       Credit Card Fee Expense shown on bank statement, $117.80.

     Infocus' bank charges a fee for handling the collection of credit card sales. The fee is based on a percentage of the credit card sales deposited during the month. The credit card fee is deducted from Infocus' bank account. The amount is then shown on the bank statement. The credit card fee is recorded in the synoptic journal as a reduction in cash. The entry is similar to the one for a current account bank service charge, page 173.

  28. Record the bank service charge, $4.10. M49. (Miscellaneous Expense)

  28. Record the credit card fee, $117.80. M50. (Debit Credit Card Fee Expense; credit Cash.)

  29. Purchased merchandise on account from Mori Photo Equipment, $840.00. P79.

  30. Bought supplies for cash, $22.50. C335.

Dec. 30. Paid on account to A & M Photo, $960.00. C336.
 31. Cash sales for the week, $2 240.00, plus sales tax, $106.40. Total, $2 346.40. T31.
 31. Credit card sales for the week, $440.00, plus sales tax, $20.90. Total, $460.90. CT31.

  Posting: Post the items that are to be posted individually.

Proving Infocus' synoptic journal at the end of the month

Instructions: 7. Total all amount columns of page 23 of the synoptic journal. Prove the equality of debits and credits.

8. Prove cash. Cheque Stub No.337 shows a balance on hand of $13 810.06.

9. Rule page 23 of the synoptic journal.

Posting totals of the special columns of Infocus' synoptic journal

Instructions: 10. Post the totals of the special columns of the synoptic journal.

Proving Infocus' general ledger

Instructions: 11. On a piece of paper or calculator, total all general ledger accounts with debit balances. Then total all general ledger accounts with credit balances. If the two totals are not the same, find and correct the errors.

Proving Infocus' subsidiary ledgers

Instructions: 12. Prepare a schedule of accounts payable and a schedule of accounts receivable. Compare the schedule totals with the balances of the controlling accounts in the general ledger. If the two totals are not the same, find and correct the errors.

The ledgers used in Reinforcement Activity 2, Part A, will be needed to complete Part B.

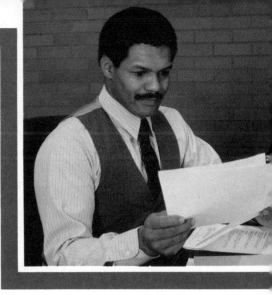

Eight-Column Work Sheet

ENABLING PERFORMANCE TASKS

After studying Chapter 14, you will be able to:

a. Define accounting terms related to an eight-column work sheet.
b. Explain accounting principles and practices related to the use of an eight-column work sheet.
c. Record a trial balance on an eight-column work sheet.
d. Plan adjustments on an eight-column work sheet.
e. Complete an eight-column work sheet.

Information about how well a business is doing is needed to make management decisions about future plans of operation. An owner or manager of a business must know if a profit is being made or if money is being lost. This profit or loss information helps an owner or manager make decisions that may increase profits. Profit and loss information is also needed to prepare required tax reports.

To figure profit or loss of a business, a work sheet is prepared at the end of each fiscal period. A work sheet may be prepared at the end of each month, each three months, each six months, or each year. (CONCEPT: Accounting Period Cycle) Denim Threads prepares a work sheet monthly.

Putt Around uses a six-column work sheet as described in Chapter 7. Denim Threads uses an eight-column work sheet. An eight-column work sheet is used because some accounts must be brought up to date before the profit or loss is figured. Two additional columns headed Adjustments Debit and Credit provide the space to plan how to bring accounts up to date. The completed eight-column work sheet used by Denim Threads is on page 274.

RECORDING A TRIAL BALANCE ON A WORK SHEET

At the end of a fiscal period, accuracy of posting is proved as described in Chapter 13. A trial balance is then entered in the Trial Balance columns of a work sheet. General ledger accounts are listed in the same order in which they appear in a general ledger. All accounts are listed regardless of whether there is a balance or not. Listing all accounts reduces the possibility of overlooking an account needing to be brought up to date.

Denim Threads' trial balance on November 30, 1988, is on the partial work sheet below. The following accounts do not show a balance in the Trial Balance columns: Income Summary, Insurance Expense, and Supplies Expense.

Denim Threads
Work Sheet
For Month Ended November 30, 1988

	ACCOUNT TITLE	TRIAL BALANCE DEBIT	TRIAL BALANCE CREDIT
1	Cash	1154420	
2	Accounts Receivable	57200	
3	Merchandise Inventory	6800000	
4	Supplies	50100	
5	Prepaid Insurance	43000	
6	Accounts Payable		265000
7	Sales Tax Payable		88900
8	Eva Burgos, Capital		3575960
9	Eva Burgos, Drawing	60000	
10	Luis Perez, Capital		3575960
11	Luis Perez, Drawing	64500	
12	Income Summary		
13	Sales		1330500
14	Purchases	395200	
15	Credit Card Fee Expense	13500	
16	Insurance Expense		
17	Miscellaneous Expense	8400	
18	Rent Expense	80000	
19	Salary Expense	110000	
20	Supplies Expense		
21		8836320	8836320
22			
23			
24			
25			
26			
27			

Recording a trial balance on a work sheet

GENERAL LEDGER ACCOUNTS NEEDING TO BE BROUGHT UP TO DATE

Some general ledger accounts do not show a true, up-to-date balance at the end of a fiscal period. These general ledger accounts do not have an up-to-date balance though all transactions have been journalized and posted. For example, Denim Threads debits the asset account Supplies each time supplies are bought. To credit Supplies each time an item of supplies is used however would not be practical. The balance of the supplies account therefore needs to be brought up to date at the end of a fiscal period.

Changes recorded to update ledger account balances at the end of a fiscal period are called adjustments. Denim Threads' general ledger accounts needing adjustments are Merchandise Inventory, Supplies, and Prepaid Insurance.

Adjustments for the general ledger accounts are first planned in the Adjustments columns of a work sheet. Every adjustment has a debit and a credit. Therefore, at least two accounts must be used in each adjustment. An adjustment transfers part or all of the balance of one account to another account. This transfer is planned by writing the debit part in the Adjustments Debit column. The credit part is entered in the Adjustments Credit column.

Adjustments recorded on a work sheet are for planning purposes only. All changes in general ledger accounts result only from posting journal entries. Journal entries made to bring general ledger accounts up to date are called adjusting entries. The accuracy of the adjusting entries can be checked on a work sheet before they are actually recorded in a journal.

> Recording adjusting entries in a synoptic journal is described in Chapter 16.

ADJUSTMENTS FOR MERCHANDISE INVENTORY

An itemized list showing the value of goods on hand is called an inventory. An itemized list showing the value of goods on hand for sale to customers is called merchandise inventory. The general ledger account in which merchandise inventory is recorded is Merchandise Inventory.

> Procedures for taking an inventory are described in Chapter 30.

Adjusting a merchandise inventory account affects two financial statements. The correct value of merchandise inventory will be shown on a balance sheet. The cost of merchandise sold will be shown on an income statement. Denim Threads prepares financial statements at the end of each month. The merchandise inventory account therefore is adjusted at the end of each month.

Some businesses prepare financial statements only at the end of a year. For these businesses an inventory adjustment is needed only at the end of a year.

Need for adjusting a merchandise inventory account

Denim Threads' merchandise inventory account on November 1, 1988, has a debit balance of $68 000.00. The balance of the merchandise inventory account on the November 30, 1988, trial balance is the same amount,

Merchandise Inventory
Nov. 1 Bal. 68,000.00

$68 000.00. The account has the same beginning and ending balance because no entries have been made during the fiscal period. The changes in inventory resulting from purchases and sales transactions have not been recorded.

Each purchase transaction increases the amount of merchandise on hand. All purchases however are recorded in the purchases account. Each sale transaction decreases the amount of merchandise on hand. However, all sales are recorded in the sales account. This procedure makes it easier to determine quickly the total purchases and sales during a fiscal period. The merchandise inventory account balance is adjusted to reflect the changes resulting from purchases and sales during a fiscal period.

Merchandise inventory and cost of merchandise sold

The total original purchase price of all merchandise sold during a fiscal period is called the cost of merchandise sold. *(CONCEPT: Historical Cost)* Cost of merchandise sold is sometimes known as cost of goods sold or cost of sales. Cost of merchandise sold is figured as shown below.

	Beginning Merchandise Inventory
Plus	Purchases
Equals	Total Merchandise Available for Sale
Minus	Ending Merchandise Inventory
Equals	Cost of Merchandise Sold

The cost of merchandise sold makes up a large part of the total costs of operating most merchandising businesses.

Analysing an adjustment for a beginning merchandise inventory. The two accounts used to adjust the beginning merchandise inventory are Merchandise Inventory and Income Summary. The T accounts at the left and on page 265 show the merchandise inventory account and the income summary account. The accounts are shown before and after the adjustment for a beginning merchandise inventory is made.

BEFORE ADJUSTMENT

Merchandise Inventory
Nov. 1 Bal. 68 000.00

Income Summary

The beginning merchandise inventory, as shown in the merchandise inventory account, is *$68 000.00*. The merchandise inventory account however is not up to date. The actual count of merchandise on November 30 shows that the inventory is valued at *$64 000.00*.

The first step in updating the inventory account is to transfer the beginning inventory to the income summary account. The beginning merchandise inventory, *$68 000.00*, is credited to Merchandise Inventory and debited to Income Summary.

After the beginning merchandise inventory adjustment is journalized and posted, Merchandise Inventory has a zero balance. The value of the beginning inventory appears as a debit in the income summary account.

AFTER ADJUSTMENT

Merchandise Inventory

Nov. 1 Bal. 68 000.00	Nov. 30 (a) 68 000.00

Income Summary

Nov. 30 (a) 68 000.00	

Recording a beginning merchandise inventory adjustment on a work sheet. The adjustment for the beginning merchandise inventory is shown in the Adjustments columns of the partial work sheet below.

Recording an adjustment for a beginning merchandise inventory on a work sheet

Steps in recording Denim Threads' adjustment for beginning merchandise inventory on a work sheet are given below.

1 Write the amount, *$68 000.00*, in the Adjustments Debit column on the line with the account title Income Summary. (Line 12)

2 Write the amount, *$68 000.00*, in the Adjustments Credit column on the line with the account title Merchandise Inventory. (Line 3)

3 Write the small letter "a" in parentheses, *(a)*, before the amounts in the Adjustments columns.

> A small letter is assigned according to the order in which adjustments are entered on a work sheet. This labelling helps locate the two parts of an adjustment when the adjusting entries are journalized.

Analysing an adjustment for an ending merchandise inventory. The T accounts on the next page show the merchandise inventory and income

BEFORE ADJUSTMENT

Merchandise Inventory

Nov. 1 Bal. 68 000.00	Nov. 30 (a) 68 000.00

Income Summary

Nov. 30 (a) 68 000.00	

AFTER ADJUSTMENT

Merchandise Inventory

Nov. 1 Bal. 68 000.00	Nov. 30 (a) 68 000.00
Nov. 30 (b) 64 000.00	

Income Summary

Nov. 30 (a) 68 000.00	**Nov. 30 (b) 64 000.00**

summary accounts. The accounts are shown before and after the adjustment for an ending merchandise inventory is made.

The merchandise inventory account is debited for *$64 000.00*, the value of the ending inventory. The same amount, *$64 000.00*, is credited to the income summary account.

The merchandise inventory account is brought up to date. The balance of the merchandise inventory account after the adjustment is the value of the ending inventory, *$64 000.00*.

Recording an ending merchandise inventory adjustment on a work sheet. The adjustment for the ending merchandise inventory is shown in the Adjustments columns of the partial work sheet below.

Recording an adjustment for an ending merchandise inventory on a work sheet

Steps in recording Denim Threads' adjustment for ending merchandise inventory on a work sheet are given below.

1 Write the amount, *$64 000.00*, in the Adjustments Debit column on the line with the account title Merchandise Inventory. (Line 3)

2 Write the amount, *$64 000.00*, in the Adjustments Credit column on the line with the account title Income Summary. (Line 12)

3 Write the small letter "b" in parentheses, *(b)*, before the amounts in the Adjustments columns.

ADJUSTMENTS FOR SUPPLIES AND PREPAID INSURANCE

Amounts paid in advance for assets to be used later and for services to be received are called prepaid expenses. For example, supplies are recorded in an asset account when bought. However, a portion of the supplies becomes an expense when used. Recording the expense each time supplies are used is not practical.

Need for adjusting a supplies account

The balance of a supplies account may be partly an asset and an expense. All expenses must be recorded for the fiscal period in which they occur. (*CONCEPT: Matching Expenses with Revenue*) Therefore, an adjustment is made at the end of the fiscal period to update the supplies account.

Analysing an adjustment for supplies. The asset account Supplies needs to be brought up to date at the end of a fiscal period. The supplies account balance will then be the same as the ending inventory of supplies on hand at that time.

Supplies	
Nov. 1 Bal. 160.00	
10 142.00	
15 86.00	
17 80.00	
29 33.00	
501.00	

The T account at the right shows Denim Threads' supplies account on November 30, 1988. Denim Threads had a beginning supplies balance of $160.00. Supplies valued at $341.00 were bought during the month. Supplies has a debit balance of $501.00 at the end of the fiscal period.

Supplies used during the fiscal period are an expense of a business. The two accounts used in the adjustment for supplies are Supplies and Supplies Expense.

Denim Threads' supplies and supplies expense accounts are shown in T accounts at the right. Accounts are shown before and after the adjustment for supplies.

Four questions are asked in analysing the adjustment for supplies.

1. What is the balance of the supplies account?........ $501.00
2. What should the balance be for this account?....... $241.00
3. What must be done to correct the account balance? ....Subtract $260.00
4. What adjusting entry is made?
   ....Debit Supplies Expense $260.00
   Credit Supplies $260.00

BEFORE ADJUSTMENT

Supplies	
Nov. 1 Bal. 160.00	
10 142.00	
15 86.00	
17 80.00	
29 33.00	
501.00	

Supplies Expense	

AFTER ADJUSTMENT

Supplies	
Nov. 1 Bal. 160.00	Nov. 30 (c) 260.00
10 142.00	
15 86.00	
17 80.00	
29 33.00	
501.00	

Supplies Expense	
Nov. 30 (c) 260.00	

The cost of supplies used is recorded as a credit to Supplies to show a decrease in this asset account. The total of the debit side, *$501.00*, less the credit side, *$260.00*, equals the ending inventory of supplies, *$241.00*.

The balance of the supplies expense account, *$260.00*, is the cost of supplies used during the fiscal period. The supplies account balance, *$241.00*, is the value of supplies on hand at the end of the fiscal period.

Recording a supplies adjustment on a work sheet. The supplies adjustment is shown in the Adjustments columns of the partial work sheet below.

Recording an adjustment for supplies on a work sheet

Steps in recording Denim Threads' adjustment for supplies on a work sheet are given below.

1 Write the amount, *$260.00*, in the Adjustments Debit column on the line with the account title Supplies Expense. (Line 20)

2 Write the amount, *$260.00*, in the Adjustments Credit column on the line with the account title Supplies. (Line 4)

3 Label the two parts of this adjustment with the small letter "c" in parentheses, *(c)*.

Need for adjusting a prepaid insurance account

Insurance premiums paid in advance are a prepaid expense. The portion of the prepaid insurance premiums not used up during the fiscal period is an asset. The portion of the insurance premiums that has been used up (expired) during the fiscal period is an expense.

Analysing an adjustment for prepaid insurance. Denim Threads' prepaid insurance account has a debit balance of $430.00 on November 1, 1988. For every day that passed since that date, the business is entitled to insurance coverage for one less day. Thus, the value of this asset is being reduced constantly. Keeping this account up to date by making daily entries to record the value of insurance used is not practical. Instead, the prepaid insurance account is brought up to date at the end of a fiscal period.

Prepaid Insurance
Nov. 1 Bal. 430.00

The two accounts used in an adjustment for prepaid insurance are Prepaid Insurance and Insurance Expense.

Denim Threads' prepaid insurance and insurance expense accounts are shown in T accounts at the right. The accounts are shown before and after the adjustment for prepaid insurance.

Before the adjustment, the prepaid insurance account has a debit balance of $430.00. A review of the insurance policies showed that as of November 30, $75.00 of the prepaid insurance had expired. Thus, the value of the prepaid insurance at the end of the fiscal period is $355.00. The prepaid insurance account therefore must be adjusted to show its true value. At the same time, the insurance expense must be recorded for the fiscal period.

Four questions are asked in analysing the adjustment for prepaid insurance.

BEFORE ADJUSTMENT

Prepaid Insurance

Nov. 1 Bal. 430.00

Insurance Expense

AFTER ADJUSTMENT

Prepaid Insurance

Nov. 1 Bal. 430.00 | Nov. 30 (d) 75.00

Insurance Expense

Nov. 30 (d) 75.00

1. What is the balance of the prepaid insurance account? $430.00
2. What should the balance be for this account? $355.00
3. What must be done to correct the account balance? ....Subtract $ 75.00
4. What adjusting entry is made? ....Debit Insurance Expense $ 75.00
                                        Credit Prepaid Insurance $ 75.00

The prepaid insurance account balance, $355.00, is the value of Prepaid Insurance at the end of the fiscal period. The insurance expense account balance, $75.00, is the value of the insurance premiums expired during the fiscal period.

Recording a prepaid insurance adjustment on a work sheet. Denim Threads' prepaid insurance adjustment is shown in the Adjustments columns of the partial work sheet below.

Recording an adjustment for prepaid insurance on a work sheet

Steps in recording Denim Threads' adjustment for prepaid insurance on a work sheet are given below.

1 Write the amount, $75.00, in the Adjustments Debit column on the line with the account title Insurance Expense. (Line 16)

2 Write the amount, $75.00, in the Adjustments Credit column on the line with the account title Prepaid Insurance. (Line 5)

3 Label the two parts of this adjustment with the small letter "d" in parentheses, *(d)*.

PROVING THE EQUALITY OF DEBITS AND CREDITS IN THE ADJUSTMENTS COLUMNS OF A WORK SHEET

After all adjustments have been recorded on a work sheet, a single line is ruled across the Adjustments columns. The two columns are totalled. Columns are totalled to prove the equality of debits and credits. The first four columns of Denim Threads' work sheet below are totalled, proved, and ruled.

Denim Threads
Work Sheet
For Month Ended November 30, 1988

	ACCOUNT TITLE	TRIAL BALANCE DEBIT	TRIAL BALANCE CREDIT	ADJUSTMENTS DEBIT	ADJUSTMENTS CREDIT
1	Cash	1154420			
2	Accounts Receivable	57200			
3	Merchandise Inventory	6800000		(b) 6400000	(a) 6800000
4	Supplies	50100			(c) 26000
5	Prepaid Insurance	43000			(d) 7500
6	Accounts Payable		265000		
7	Sales Tax Payable		88900		
8	Eva Burgos, Capital		3575960		
9	Eva Burgos, Drawing	60000			
10	Luis Perez, Capital		3575960		
11	Luis Perez, Drawing	64500			
12	Income Summary			(a) 6800000	(b) 6400000
13	Sales		1330500		
14	Purchases	395200			
15	Credit Card Fee Expense	13500			
16	Insurance Expense			(d) 7500	
17	Miscellaneous Expense	8400			
18	Rent Expense	80000			
19	Salary Expense	110000			
20	Supplies Expense			(c) 26000	
21		8836320	8836320	13233500	13233500

Adjustments columns on a work sheet totalled and ruled

The total of the Adjustments Debit column, *$132 335.00*, is the same as the total of the Adjustments Credit column, *$132 335.00*. Debits and Credits in the Adjustments columns are proved because the column totals are the same. Double lines are ruled across the Adjustments columns.

COMPLETING AN EIGHT-COLUMN WORK SHEET

Denim Threads' eight-column work sheet, page 274, is completed as described below.

1 Extend the balance sheet items to the Balance Sheet columns.

- Extend balance sheet items *not* affected by adjustments. Extend balances from Trial Balance columns (Columns 1 or 2) to appropriate Balance Sheet columns (Columns 7 or 8).

- Extend balance sheet items affected by adjustments. Extend *adjusted* balances to appropriate Balance Sheet columns.

Adjusted balance sheet items on Denim Threads' work sheet are given below.

Line 3, Merchandise Inventory.

Trial Balance Debit column	$ 68 000.00
Plus Adjustments Debit column	64 000.00
	$132 000.00
Less Adjustments Credit column	68 000.00
Balance Sheet Debit column	$ 64 000.00

Line 4, Supplies.

Trial Balance Debit column	$501.00
Less Adjustments Credit column	260.00
Balance Sheet Debit column	$241.00

Line 5, Prepaid Insurance.

Trial Balance Debit column	$430.00
Less Adjustments Credit column	75.00
Balance Sheet Debit column	$355.00

2 Extend the revenue, cost, and expense items to the Income Statement columns.

- Extend income statement items *not* affected by adjustments. Extend balances from Trial Balance columns (Columns 1 or 2) to appropriate Income Statement columns (Columns 5 or 6).

- Extend income statement items *affected* by adjustments. Extend *adjusted* balances to appropriate Income Statement columns.

Extension of Income Summary is an exception to this procedure. Income Summary, line 12, has no balance in the Trial Balance columns. The Adjustments Debit column amount, *$68 000.00*, the beginning inventory, is extended to the Income Statement Debit column. The Adjustments Credit column amount, *$64 000.00*, the ending inventory, is extended to the Income Statement Credit column. Both these amounts are extended because they will be used in preparing the income statement.

Adjusted income statement items on Denim Threads' work sheet are given below.

Line 16, Insurance Expense.

Trial Balance Debit column..	–0–
Plus Adjustments Debit column	$ 75.00
Income Statement Debit column......................................	$ 75.00

Line 20, Supplies Expense.

Trial Balance Debit column..	–0–
Plus Adjustments Debit column	$260.00
Income Statement Debit column......................................	$260.00

3 Figure the net income on the work sheet.

- Rule a single line across the Income Statement columns and the Balance Sheet columns to indicate addition.
- Add each column and write the totals on the same line as the Trial Balance totals. (Line 21)
- Subtract the smaller total from the larger total in the Income Statement columns.

Total of Income Statement Credit column	$77 305.00
Less Total of Income Statement Debit column	74 406.00
Equals Net Income	$ 2 899.00

4 Balance the Income Statement columns.

- Write the amount of the net income, *$2 899.00*, immediately below the smaller total in the Income Statement columns. (Line 22)
- Write the words *Net Income* in the Account Title column on the same line as the amount of the net income.

- Total the Income Statement columns. (Line 23)

5 Balance the Balance Sheet columns.

- Extend the net income, *$2 899.00*, to the Balance Sheet Credit column on the same line with the words *Net Income*.

- Total the Balance Sheet columns. (Line 23) Figures on the work sheet are considered to be correct since the Balance Sheet Debit and Credit columns are equal.

6 Rule double lines below the proving totals of the Income Statement and Balance Sheet columns.

FIGURING A NET LOSS ON A WORK SHEET

When the Income Statement Debit column total exceeds the Credit column total, there is a net loss. An example of a net loss is shown on the partial work sheet below.

		5	6	7	8	
	ACCOUNT TITLE	INCOME STATEMENT		BALANCE SHEET		
		DEBIT	CREDIT	DEBIT	CREDIT	
19		8254000	8132000	8614000	8736000	19
20	*Net Loss*		122000	122000		20
21		8254000	8254000	8736000	8736000	21
22						22
23						23
24						24
25						25
26						26
27						27
28						28

Showing a net loss on a work sheet

The total of the Income Statement Debit column is larger than the total of the Income Statement Credit column. (Line 19) The costs and expenses are greater than the revenues. Therefore, the net loss amount, *$1 220.00*, is written in the Income Statement Credit column. (Line 20) The net loss amount, *$1 220.00*, is then extended to the Balance Sheet Debit column. The words *Net Loss* are written on the same line.

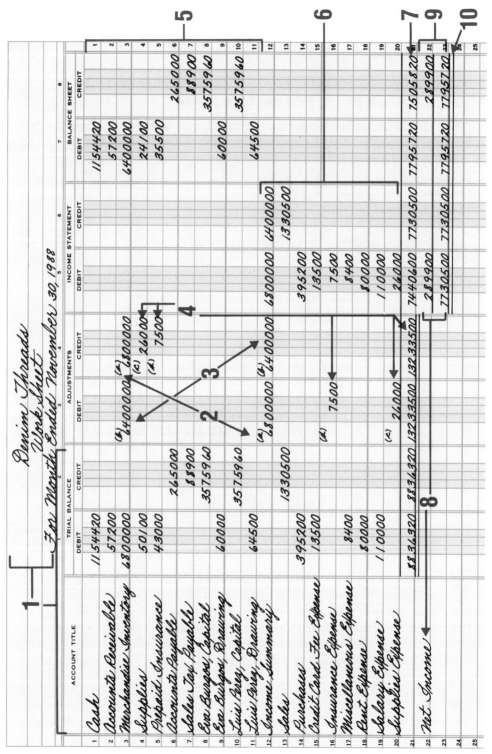

Completed eight-column work sheet

PREPARING AN EIGHT-COLUMN WORK SHEET

1 Write the heading and record the trial balance.

2 Record the beginning merchandise inventory in the Adjustments columns — adjustment (a).
- Write the amount in the Adjustments Debit column on the line with the account title Income Summary.
- Write the amount in the Adjustments Credit column on the line with the account title Merchandise Inventory.

3 Record the ending merchandise inventory in the Adjustments columns — adjustment (b).
- Write the amount in the Adjustments Debit column on the line with the account title Merchandise Inventory.
- Write the amount in the Adjustments Credit column on the line with the account title Income Summary.

4 Record the remaining adjustments in the Adjustments columns — adjustments (c) and (d).
- Write the amount of the supplies adjustment debiting Supplies Expense and crediting Supplies.
- Write the amount of the insurance adjustment debiting Insurance Expense and crediting Prepaid Insurance.
- Rule a single line across both Adjustments columns under the last amount listed.
- Add each Adjustments column and compare the totals.
- Rule double lines below the proving totals of the Adjustments columns.

5 Extend all of the balance sheet items after adjustments into the Balance Sheet columns.
- Extend the amount of each asset after adjustments into the Balance Sheet Debit column (Column 7).
- Extend the amount of each liability, capital, and drawing account into the appropriate Balance Sheet column (Column 7 or 8).

6 Extend all of the income statement items after adjustments into the Income Statement columns.
- Extend both adjustments to Income Summary for merchandise inventory to the respective Income Statement columns (Columns 5 and 6).
- Extend the amount of revenue into the Income Statement Credit column (Column 6).
- Extend the amount of purchases and each expense after adjustments into the Income Statement Debit column (Column 5).

7 Total the Income Statement columns and the Balance Sheet columns.
- Rule a single line across the Income Statement columns and the Balance Sheet columns.
- Add each column and write the totals on the same line as the Trial Balance totals.

8 Figure and record the net income (or the net loss).
- Subtract the smaller total in the Income Statement columns from the larger total.
- Write the amount of the net income (or the net loss) immediately below the smaller of the two totals.
- Write the words Net Income (or Net Loss) in the Account Title column.
- Rule a single line across the Income Statement columns. Add and write the proving totals on the next line.

9 Extend the net income (or the net loss) to the Balance Sheet columns.
- Extend the net income into the Balance Sheet Credit column (or net loss into the Balance Sheet Debit column).
- Rule a single line across the Balance Sheet columns. Add and write the proving totals on the next line.

10 Rule double lines below the proving totals of the Income Statement columns and the Balance Sheet columns.

ACCOUNTING TERMS

What is the meaning of each of the following?

1. adjustments
2. adjusting entries
3. inventory
4. merchandise inventory
5. cost of merchandise sold
6. prepaid expenses

QUESTIONS FOR INDIVIDUAL STUDY

1. Why does the owner of a business need to know the amount of profit or loss made by the business?
2. How often does Denim Threads prepare a work sheet?
3. Why does Denim Threads use an eight-column work sheet?
4. What are the headings for the columns used to provide the space necessary for planning the adjustments?
5. Why are all general ledger accounts listed on the Trial Balance columns of a work sheet?
6. Which Denim Threads' general ledger accounts need to be adjusted?
7. Why are the adjustments planned on a work sheet before they are recorded in a journal?
8. What two financial statements are affected by the merchandise inventory adjustment?

9. What are the two accounts used to adjust the beginning merchandise inventory? How are the accounts adjusted?
10. What are the two accounts used to adjust the ending merchandise inventory? How are the accounts adjusted?
11. Why are the two parts of an adjustment labelled on a work sheet?
12. Why is the supplies account adjusted at the end of a fiscal period?
13. What are the two accounts used in the adjustment for supplies?
14. Why is it necessary to adjust the prepaid insurance account at the end of a fiscal period?
15. What are the two accounts used in the adjustment for prepaid insurance?
16. Why are the Adjustments columns on a work sheet totalled?

CASES FOR MANAGEMENT DECISION

CASE 1 Mary Dextor prepared her business' work sheet at the end of the fiscal period. The proper adjustment for the beginning merchandise inventory was made. However, Ms. Dextor forgot to make the adjustment for the ending inventory. What effect will this omission have on the net income shown on the work sheet?

CASE 2 After completing a work sheet, Marsha Delfield finds an error was made in preparing the supplies inventory. Three large boxes of office supplies were counted twice. The value of the supplies counted twice was $100.00. How does this error affect the amount of net income as figured on the work sheet for the fiscal period?

CASE 3 Crandon Company paid $648.00 for a one-year fire insurance policy. The company prepares income statements and balance sheets every three months. However, the accountant prepares an adjusting entry only at the end of the year. Mr. Crandon, the owner, thinks the prepaid insurance should be adjusted every three months. Who is correct. Why?

DRILL 14-D 1   Adjusting the merchandise inventory, supplies, and prepaid insurance accounts

The chart below contains adjustment information related to the preparation of work sheets for three businesses.

Business	Trial Balance Debit Column	End-of-Period Information
A	Merchandise Inventory... $48 500.00 Supplies.......................... 520.00 Prepaid Insurance........... 560.00	Inventory on hand.......... $45 000.00 Supplies on hand............ 380.00 Insurance remaining....... 480.00
B	Merchandise Inventory... $52 600.00 Supplies.......................... 450.00 Prepaid Insurance........... 720.00	Inventory on hand.......... $54 200.00 Supplies on hand............ 380.00 Insurance remaining....... 610.00
C	Merchandise Inventory... $62 000.00 Supplies.......................... 640.00 Prepaid Insurance........... 180.00	Inventory on hand.......... $59 000.00 Supplies on hand............ 520.00 Insurance remaining....... None

Use a form similar to the one below.

1	2	3	4	5
Business	Adjustment Number	Accounts Affected	Adjustment Column	
			Debit	Credit
A	1.	*Income Summary* *Merchandise Inventory*	$48 500.00	$48 500.00

Instructions: For each business list the accounts affected and the amounts for each adjustment given below. List the names of the accounts in Column 3 and the amounts in either Column 4 or 5. Adjustment Number 1 for Business A is given as an example.

1. Adjustment for beginning merchandise inventory.
2. Adjustment for ending merchandise inventory.
3. Adjustment for supplies.
4. Adjustment for prepaid insurance.

DRILL 14-D 2   Extending balance sheet and income statement items

Jacobs and Nelson Company's partial work sheet showing the completed Trial Balance and Adjustments columns is on the next page.

Instructions: 1. Extend the balance sheet items to the Balance Sheet columns of the work sheet.

2. Extend the income statement items to the Income Statement columns of the work sheet.

Jacobs and Nelson Company
Work Sheet
For Month Ended November 30, 19--

	Account Title	Trial Balance		Adjustments	
		1	2	3	4
		Debit	Credit	Debit	Credit
1	Cash	9 640 00			
2	Accounts Receivable	820 00			
3	Merchandise Inventory	82 000 00		(b) 80 000 00	(a) 82 000 00
4	Supplies	610 00			(c) 180 00
5	Prepaid Insurance	980 00			(d) 85 00
6	Accounts Payable		3 120 00		
7	Sales Tax Payable		720 00		
8	J. B. Jacobs, Capital		41 690 00		
9	J. B. Jacobs, Drawing	500 00			
10	S. K. Nelson, Capital		41 690 00		
11	S. K. Nelson, Drawing	500 00			
12	Income Summary			(a) 82 000 00	(b) 80 000 00
13	Sales		14 200 00		
14	Purchases	4 100 00			
15	Credit Card Fee Expense	160 00			
16	Insurance Expense			(d) 85 00	
17	Miscellaneous Expense	110 00			
18	Rent Expense	700 00			
19	Salary Expense	1 300 00			
20	Supplies Expense			(c) 180 00	
21		101 420 00	101 420 00	162 265 00	162 265 00

3. Complete the work sheet.
 a. Add the Income Statement columns and the Balance Sheet columns.
 b. Figure and record the net income or net loss.
 c. Total and rule the Income Statement and Balance Sheet columns.

APPLICATION PROBLEMS

PROBLEM 14-1 Preparing a work sheet

The accounts and their balances in Downtown Sporting Goods' general ledger appear on page 279. Ending inventories and the value of insurance policies are also given.

Instructions: 1. Prepare a trial balance on a work sheet for the monthly fiscal period ending December 31 of the current year. Use as a guide the partial work sheet, page 262.
 2. Enter the adjustment for beginning merchandise inventory on the work sheet. Use as a guide the partial work sheet, page 265.
 3. Enter the adjustment for ending merchandise inventory on the work sheet. Use as a guide the partial work sheet, page 266.

Account Title	Balance
Cash	$ 8 820.00
Accounts Receivable	740.00
Merchandise Inventory	92 600.00
Supplies	530.00
Prepaid Insurance	760.00
Accounts Payable	4 610.00
Sales Tax Payable	622.00
Eileen Brandon, Capital	45 600.00
Eileen Brandon, Drawing	700.00
Diane Baxter, Capital	44 800.00
Diane Baxter, Drawing	650.00
Income Summary	——
Sales	15 560.00
Purchases	3 820.00
Credit Card Fee Expense	280.00
Insurance Expense	——
Miscellaneous Expense	92.00
Rent Expense	950.00
Salary Expense	1 250.00
Supplies Expense	——

Adjustment Information, December 31

Merchandise inventory	$87 500.00
Supplies inventory	250.00
Value of insurance policies	670.00

4. Enter the adjustment for supplies on the work sheet. Use as a guide the partial work sheet, page 268.

5. Enter the adjustment for prepaid insurance on the work sheet. Use as a guide the partial work sheet, page 269.

6. Figure and record net income or loss. Use as a guide the work sheets, pages 274 and 273.

7. Complete the work sheet for the monthly fiscal period ending December 31 of the current year. Use as a guide the completed work sheet, page 274.

The solution to Problem 14-1 is needed to complete Problem 15-1 and Problem 16-1 in Chapters 15 and 16.

PROBLEM 14-2 Preparing a work sheet

The accounts and their balances in Quality Office Supply's general ledger appear below and on the next page. Ending inventories and the value of insurance policies are also given.

Account Title	Balance
Cash	$ 9 350.00
Accounts Receivable	960.00
Merchandise Inventory	86 300.00
Supplies	670.00
Prepaid Insurance	840.00
Accounts Payable	6 400.00
Sales Tax Payable	865.00
Alice Brown, Capital	43 025.00
Alice Brown, Drawing	750.00
Harold Brown, Capital	39 600.00
Harold Brown, Drawing	700.00
Income Summary	——

Account Title	Balance
Sales	$17 300.00
Purchases	4 320.00
Credit Card Fee Expense	380.00
Insurance Expense	
Miscellaneous Expense	130.00
Rent Expense	1 250.00
Salary Expense	1 540.00
Supplies Expense	——

Adjustment Information, December 31

Merchandise inventory	$84 600.00
Supplies inventory	420.00
Value of insurance policies	560.00

Instructions: Prepare Quality Office Supply's eight-column work sheet for the monthly fiscal period ending December 31 of the current year. Use as a guide the eight-column work sheet, page 274.

ENRICHMENT PROBLEMS

MASTERY PROBLEM 14-M   Preparing a work sheet

The accounts and their balances in Value Appliances' general ledger appear below. Ending inventories and the value of insurance policies are also given.

Instructions: Prepare Value Appliances' eight-column work sheet for the monthly fiscal period ending October 31 of the current year. Use as a guide the eight-column work sheet, page 274.

Account Title	Account Balance
Cash	$ 10 400.00
Accounts Receivable	1 920.00
Merchandise Inventory	120 000.00
Supplies	860.00
Prepaid Insurance	520.00
Accounts Payable	6 230.00
Sales Tax Payable	915.00
C. K. Fields, Capital	63 800.00
C. K. Fields, Drawing	1 000.00
John Miller, Capital	65 650.00
John Miller, Drawing	900.00
Income Summary	——
Sales	18 300.00
Purchases	16 200.00
Credit Card Fee Expense	340.00
Delivery Expense	190.00
Insurance Expense	——
Miscellaneous Expense	65.00
Rent Expense	1 000.00
Salary Expense	1 500.00
Supplies Expense	——

Adjustment Information, October 31

Merchandise inventory	$126 000.00
Supplies inventory	685.00
Value of insurance policies	410.00

CHALLENGE PROBLEM 14-C   Preparing a work sheet

The accounts and their balances in C & B Hardware's general ledger appear below. Ending inventories and the value of insurance policies are also given.

Instructions: Prepare C & B Hardware's eight-column work sheet for the monthly fiscal period ending January 31 of the current year. Use as a guide the eight-column work sheet, page 274.

Account Title	Account Balance
Cash	$ 8 830.00
Accounts Receivable	960.00
Merchandise Inventory	93 500.00
Supplies	480.00
Prepaid Insurance	930.00
Accounts Payable	4 120.00
Sales Tax Payable	560.00
Carmen Lopez, Capital	49 700.00
Carmen Lopez, Drawing	800.00
Janet Carter, Capital	48 610.00
Janet Carter, Drawing	850.00
Income Summary	——
Sales	10 200.00
Purchases	2 800.00
Credit Card Fee Expense	230.00
Insurance Expense	——
Miscellaneous Expense	60.00
Rent Expense	950.00
Salary Expense	2 800.00
Supplies Expense	——

Adjustment Information, January 31

Merchandise inventory	$89 800.00
Supplies inventory	360.00
Value of insurance policies	850.00

Financial Statements of a Partnership

ENABLING PERFORMANCE TASKS

After studying Chapter 15, you will be able to:

a. Define accounting terms related to financial statements.
b. Explain accounting principles and practices related to financial statements.
c. Prepare an income statement with a cost of merchandise sold section.
d. Prepare a distribution of net income statement.
e. Prepare a capital statement.
f. Prepare a balance sheet.

Journals and ledgers are used during a fiscal period to classify and record information about a business' financial activities. A work sheet is used at the end of a fiscal period to organize and summarize this financial information. All of these activities are done so that the financial progress and condition of a business can be reported. The financial progress and condition of a business are reported on financial statements. Financial statements should contain all information necessary to understand a business' financial progress and condition. *(CONCEPT: Adequate Disclosure)* In the preparation of financial statements, accounting principles are applied the same way from one fiscal period to the next. *(CONCEPT: Consistent Reporting)*

FINANCIAL STATEMENTS OF A PARTNERSHIP

Businesses organized as partnerships report their financial progress and condition by preparing four financial statements. (1) Income statement. (2) Distribution of net income statement. (3) Capital statement. (4) Balance sheet. Financial statements of a partnership are similar to those prepared by a sole proprietorship. However, for a partnership, the distribution of net income or net loss is reported separately for each partner.

Also, the equity of each partner is reported separately on the financial statements.

INCOME STATEMENT

An income statement reports the financial progress of a business. Revenue, cost of merchandise sold, gross profit on sales, expenses, and net income or loss are reported for merchandising businesses. Current and previous income statements can be compared to determine the reasons for increases or decreases in net income.

Preparing an income statement

The Account Title and Income Statement columns of a completed work sheet are used to prepare the income statement. Denim Threads' partial work sheet for the month ended November 30, 1988, is on the next page.

The complete work sheet for Denim Threads is on page 274.

Denim Threads' income statement, page 285, has three main sections. (1) Revenue section. (2) Cost of merchandise sold section. (3) Expenses section.

Steps in preparing Denim Threads' income statement are given below.

1 Write the heading of the income statement on three lines.

2 Prepare the revenue section. Use the information from the Income Statement Credit column of the work sheet.

- Write the name of this section, *Revenue*, at the extreme left of the wide column on the first line.

- Write the title of the revenue account, *Sales*, on the next line, indented about 1 cm.

- Write the balance of the sales account, *$13 305.00*, in the second amount column. This amount is also the total of the revenue section for Denim Threads.

> If there is more than one source of revenue, each revenue account title is listed in the wide column. The balance of each account is written in the first amount column. The words *Total Revenue* are written in the wide column on the next line below the last revenue account title. The total amount of revenue is written in the second amount column.

3 Prepare the cost of merchandise sold section. Use the information from the Income Statement columns of the work sheet.

| | ACCOUNT TITLE | | INCOME STATEMENT | |
			DEBIT	CREDIT
12	*Income Summary*		6800000	6400000
13	*Sales*			1330500
14	*Purchases*		395200	
15	*Credit Card Fee Expense*		13500	
16	*Insurance Expense*		7500	
17	*Miscellaneous Expense*		8400	
18	*Rent Expense*		80000	
19	*Salary Expense*		110000	
20	*Supplies Expense*		26000	
21			7440600	7730500
22	*Net Income*		289900	
23			7730500	7730500
24				
25				
26				
27				
28				
29				
30				

Partial work sheet showing income statement columns

The cost of merchandise sold is determined as described below.

Beginning merchandise inventory, November 1, 1988......	$68 000.00
(This amount is shown as a debit to Income Summary in the Income Statement Debit column of the work sheet.)	
Plus purchases made during the fiscal period.................	3 952.00
(This amount is shown as a debit to Purchases in the Income Statement Debit column of the work sheet.)	
Equals total cost of merchandise available for sale during the fiscal period	$71 952.00
Less ending merchandise inventory, November 30, 1988...	64 000.00
(This amount is shown as a credit to Income Summary in the Income Statement Credit column of the work sheet.)	
Equals cost of merchandise sold during the fiscal period ...	$ 7 952.00

The cost of merchandise sold section is entered on the income statement.

• Write the name of this section, *Cost of Merchandise Sold*, at the extreme left of the wide column.

Denim Threads				
Income Statement				
For Month Ended November 30, 1988				
Revenue:				
Sales				1330500
Cost of Merchandise Sold:				
Merchandise Inventory, Nov. 1, 1988		6800000		
Purchases		395200		
Total Cost of Mdse. Available for Sale		7195200		
Less Mdse. Inventory, Nov. 30, 1988		6400000		
Cost of Merchandise Sold				795200
Gross Profit on Sales				535300
Expenses:				
Credit Card Fee Expense		13500		
Insurance Expense		7500		
Miscellaneous Expense		8400		
Rent Expense		80000		
Salary Expense		110000		
Supplies Expense		26000		
Total Expenses				245400
Net Income				289900

Income statement for a merchandising business

- Indent 1 cm and write in the wide column items needed to figure cost of merchandise sold. Write the amount of each item in the first amount column.

- Write the amount of the cost of merchandise sold, $7 952.00, in the second amount column.

4 Figure the gross profit on sales. The revenue remaining after cost of merchandise sold has been deducted is called gross profit on sales.

- Write the words *Gross Profit on Sales* on the next line at the extreme left of the wide column.

- Subtract cost of merchandise sold, $7 952.00, from total revenue, $13 305.00, to find gross profit on sales, $5 353.00. Write the amount of the gross profit on sales, $5 353.00, in the second amount column.

5 Prepare the expenses section. Use the information from the Income Statement Debit column on the work sheet.

- Write the name of this section, *Expenses*, at the extreme left of the wide column.

- Indent 1 cm and list the expense account titles in the order in which they appear on the work sheet. Write the amount of each expense account balance in the first amount column.

- Write the words *Total Expenses* in the wide column on the next line below the last expense account title. Total the individual expenses and write the total, *$2 454.00*, in the second amount column on the total line.

6 Figure the net income.

- Write the words *Net Income* on the next line at the extreme left of the wide column.

- Subtract total expenses, *$2 454.00*, from gross profit on sales, *$5 353.00*, to find net income, *$2 899.00*. Write this amount in the second amount column on the net income line.

    Compare the amount of net income figured on the income statement, *$2 899.00*, with the amount on the work sheet, *$2 899.00*. The two amounts must be the same.

- Rule double lines across both amount columns on the income statement to show that the statement has been completed.

Income statement showing a net loss

When the expenses of a business are greater than the gross profit on sales, the difference is known as a net loss. For example, the partial income statement below shows a loss of $1 220.00 for the fiscal period.

Gross Profit on Sales		2 983 00
Expenses:		
Delivery Expense	49 3 00	
Miscellaneous Expense	20 5 00	
Rent Expense	1 250 00	
Salary Expense	1 750 00	
Supplies Expense	50 5 00	
Total Expenses		4 203 00
Net Loss		1 220 00

Partial income statement
showing a net loss

The net loss is found by subtracting the gross profit on sales, *$2 983.00*, from the total expenses, *$4 203.00*. The difference, *$1 220.00*, is written in the second amount column on the line with the words *Net Loss*.

DISTRIBUTION OF NET INCOME STATEMENT

The net income or net loss of a partnership may be divided in any way agreed upon by the partners. For example, partners may agree to share the net income or net loss (1) equally or (2) unequally. Eva Burgos and Luis Perez, partners in Denim Threads, agreed to share net income or net loss equally.

The distribution of net income or net loss of a partnership is usually shown in a separate financial statement. A partnership financial statement showing net income or loss distribution to partners is called a distribution of net income statement

Preparing a distribution of net income statement

The net income, $2 899.00, from the income statement, page 285, is used to prepare the distribution of net income statement. The distribution of net income statement for Denim Threads is below.

Distribution of net income statement of a partnership

Steps in preparing Denim Threads' distribution of net income statement are described below.

1 Write the heading of the distribution of net income statement on three lines.

2 Write the name *Eva Burgos* on the first line at the extreme left of the wide column.

3 Indent 1 cm and write on the next line Eva Burgos' share of net income, *50% of Net Income*. Write Ms. Burgos' share of net income, *$1 449.50* (50% × $2 899.00) in the amount column on the same line.

4 Write the name *Luis Perez* on the next line at the extreme left of the wide column.

5 Indent 1 cm and write on the next line Luis Perez's share of net income, *50% of Net Income*. Write Mr. Perez' share of net income, *$1 449.50* (50% × $2 899.00), in the amount column on the same line.

6 Write the words *Net Income* on the next line at the extreme left of the wide column. Add the distribution of net income for Eva Burgos, *$1 449.50*, and for Luis Perez, *$1 449.50*. Write the total amount, *$2 899.00*, in the amount column.

> Compare the total amount, *$2 899.00*, with the net income reported on the income statement, *$2 899.00*. The two amounts must be the same.

7 Rule double lines across the amount column on the distribution of net income statement. The ruling shows that the statement has been completed.

Distribution of net income statement with unequal distribution of earnings

The steps in preparing a distribution of net income statement are the same regardless of how earnings are shared. The only difference is the description of how the earnings are to be shared by the partners. A partial distribution of net income statement with unequal shares of earnings is below.

Harriett Crandon	
60 % of Net Income	2400 00
Susan Fulton	
40 % of Net Income	1600 00
Net Income	4000 00

Distribution of net income statement with unequal distribution of earnings

Harriett Crandon and Susan Fulton, partners, agree to share net income or loss unequally. Harriett Crandon gets 60% of net income or loss. Susan Fulton gets 40% of net income or loss. With a net income of $4 000.00, Harriett Crandon receives 60% or $2 400.00. Susan Fulton receives 40% or $1 600.00.

CAPITAL STATEMENT

The amount of net income earned by a business is important to the owners. Owners are also interested in changes that occur in the capital during a fiscal period. A financial statement that summarizes the changes in capital during a fiscal period is called a capital statement . Owners of a business can review a capital statement to determine if and why the capital is increasing or decreasing. There are three reasons why changes in the amount of capital occur.

1. Additional investments are made.
2. Cash, merchandise, or other assets are withdrawn.
3. Net income or net loss occurs from business operations.

Preparing a capital statement

Information about changes in the capital of each partner during a fiscal period is shown in a partnership capital statement. Information needed to prepare a capital statement is obtained from the capital accounts in the general ledger. Information is also obtained from the Balance Sheet columns of the work sheet and the distribution of net income statement. Information from the general ledger includes the beginning balance of each capital account and any additional investments. Information from the work sheet includes the withdrawals for the fiscal period. The distribution of net income statement provides the amount of each partner's share of net income.

The general ledger capital accounts for Eva Burgos and Luis Perez, partners, are below.

ACCOUNT *Eva Burgos, Capital*					ACCOUNT NO. *31*		
DATE	ITEM	POST. REF.	DEBIT	CREDIT	BALANCE		
					DEBIT	CREDIT	
1988 *Nov.* 1	*Balance*	✓				3575960	

ACCOUNT *Luis Perez, Capital*					ACCOUNT NO. *33*		
DATE	ITEM	POST. REF.	DEBIT	CREDIT	BALANCE		
					DEBIT	CREDIT	
1988 *Nov.* 1	*Balance*	✓				3575960	

Partners' capital accounts

Neither Eva Burgos nor Luis Perez invested any additional capital during November, 1988. Therefore, the beginning and ending capital balances are the same as recorded in the trial balance on the work sheet. If additional investments had been made, the ending balance on November 30 would be greater than the beginning balance.

The portions of the work sheet needed to prepare the capital statement are on the next page. The distribution of net income statement is on page 287.

Denim Threads
Work Sheet
For Month Ended November 30, 1988

ACCOUNT TITLE	BALANCE SHEET	
	DEBIT	CREDIT
8	Eva Burgos, Capital		35 759 60	8
9	Eva Burgos, Drawing	600 00		9
10	Luis Perez, Capital		35 759 60	10
11	Luis Perez, Drawing	645 00		11

Partial work sheet
showing balance sheet
columns

Denim Threads' capital statement prepared on November 30, 1988, is below.

Denim Threads
Capital Statement
For Month Ended November 30, 1988

Eva Burgos
  Capital, November 1, 1988 .... 35 759 60
  Share of Net Income 1 449 50
  Less Withdrawals 600 00
  Net Increase in Capital 849 50
  Capital, November 30, 1988 .... 36 609 10
Luis Perez
  Capital, November 1, 1988 .... 35 759 60
  Share of Net Income 1 449 50
  Less Withdrawals 645 00
  Net Increase in Capital 804 50
  Capital, November 30, 1988 .... 36 564 10
Total Capital, November 30, 1988 .... 73 173 20

Capital statement

Steps in preparing Denim Threads' capital statement are described below.

1 Write the heading of the capital statement on three lines.

2 Write the name *Eva Burgos* on the first line at the extreme left of the wide column.

3 Figure the net increase in capital for Eva Burgos.

- Indent 1 cm and write on the next line the words *Capital, November 1, 1988*. Write the beginning capital amount, $35 759.60, in the second amount column on the same line. (This amount is obtained from Ms. Burgos' capital account.)

- Indent 1 cm and write on the next line the words *Share of Net Income*. On the same line write the share of net income amount, *$1 449.50*, in the first amount column. (This amount is obtained from the Distribution of Net Income Statement.)

- Indent 1 cm and write on the next line the words *Less Withdrawals*. On the same line write the withdrawals amount, *$600.00*, in the first amount column. (This amount is obtained from the work sheet.)

- Indent 1 cm and write on the next line the words *Net Increase in Capital*. Subtract the withdrawals, *$600.00*, from the share of net income, *$1 449.50*. On the same line write the difference, *$849.50*, in the second amount column.

- Indent 1 cm and write on the next line the words *Capital, November 30, 1988*. Add the November 1 capital, *$35 759.60*, and the net increase in capital, *$849.50*, to obtain the November 30 capital, *$36 609.10*. On the same line write the November 30 capital amount, *$36 609.10*, in the third amount column.

4 Write the name *Luis Perez* on the next line at the extreme left of the wide column.

5 Figure the net increase in capital for Luis Perez.

- Indent 1 cm and write on the next line the words *Capital, November 1, 1988*. On the same line write the beginning capital amount, *$35 759.60*, in the second amount column.

- Indent 1 cm and write on the next line the words *Share of Net Income*. On the same line write the share of net income amount, *$1 449.50*, in the first amount column.

- Indent 1 cm and write on the next line the words *Less Withdrawals*. On the same line write the withdrawals amount, *$645.00*, in the first amount column.

- Indent 1 cm and write on the next line the words *Net Increase in Capital*. On the same line write the difference, *$804.50*, in the second amount column.

- Indent 1 cm and write on the next line the words *Capital, November 30, 1988*. On the same line write the November 30 capital amount, *$36 564.10*, in the third amount column.

6 Write the words *Total Capital, November 30, 1988*, on the next line at the extreme left of the wide column. On the same line write the total capital amount, $73 173.20, in the third amount column.

7 Rule double lines across the three amount columns on the capital statement. The ruling shows that the statement has been completed.

> In some businesses the information on the capital statement may be included as part of the balance sheet. An example of this method of reporting changes in capital is on page 137.

Preparing a capital statement with an additional investment and with a net loss

On December 31, 1988, the capital accounts of Alice Jefferson and William Richards showed additional investments of $3 000.00 each. Also, the work sheet, page 273, showed a net loss of $1 220.00. The net loss of $1 220.00 was also shown on the income statement, page 286. The partners agreed to share net income or net loss equally. The capital statement for J & R Clothiers is below.

J & R Clothiers Capital Statement For Month Ended December 31, 1988			
Alice Jefferson			
Capital, December 1, 1988	42 500 00		
Plus Additional Investment	3 000 00		
Total		45 500 00	
Share of Net Loss	6 100 0		
Plus Withdrawals	8 000 0		
Net Decrease in Capital		1 410 00	
Capital, December 31, 1988			44 090 00
William Richards			
Capital, December 1, 1988	43 200 00		
Plus Additional Investment	3 000 00		
Total		46 200 00	
Share of Net Loss	6 100 0		
Plus Withdrawals	6 500 0		
Net Decrease in Capital		1 260 00	
Capital, December 31, 1988			44 940 00
Total Capital, December 31, 1988			89 030 00

Capital statement showing an additional investment and a net loss

BALANCE SHEET

Owners make many management decisions about the business. Some of these decisions can best be made after owners have determined the amount of assets, liabilities, and capital. Owners obtain some of the information needed by inspecting general ledger accounts. The information needed may also be found on a work sheet. However, the information is easier to use when organized and reported on financial statements. A balance sheet reports the financial condition of a business: assets and equities.

Two forms of balance sheet

A balance sheet may be prepared in one of two forms: (1) account form or (2) report form. A balance sheet listing assets on the left and equities on the right is called an account form of balance sheet. The account form of balance sheet, used by Putt Around, is described in Chapter 8.

A balance sheet listing the assets, liabilities, and capital vertically is called a report form of balance sheet. Denim Threads uses the report form of balance sheet.

Report form of balance sheet

The portion of the work sheet used in preparing Denim Threads' balance sheet is below.

ACCOUNT TITLE	BALANCE SHEET DEBIT	BALANCE SHEET CREDIT	
1 Cash	11 544 20		1
2 Accounts Receivable	572 00		2
3 Merchandise Inventory	6400 00		3
4 Supplies	241 00		4
5 Prepaid Insurance	355 00		5
6 Accounts Payable		2650 00	6
7 Sales Tax Payable		889 00	7

Denim Threads Work Sheet For Month Ended November 30, 1988

Partial work sheet showing balance sheet columns

Denim Threads' report form of balance sheet prepared on November 30, 1988, is on the next page.

Steps in preparing Denim Threads' balance sheet are described below.

1 Write the heading of the balance sheet on three lines.

2 Prepare the assets section of the balance sheet. Use the information in the Balance Sheet Debit column of the work sheet above.

- Write the section title, *Assets*, in the middle of the wide column.

- Write the titles of asset accounts on separate lines at the extreme left of the wide column. Write the balance of each asset account in the first amount column.

Denim Threads
Balance Sheet
November 30, 1988

Assets		
Cash	11 544 20	
Accounts Receivable	572 00	
Merchandise Inventory	64 000 00	
Supplies	241 00	
Prepaid Insurance	355 00	
Total Assets		76 712 20
Liabilities		
Accounts Payable	2 650 00	
Sales Tax Payable	889 00	
Total Liabilities		3 539 00
Capital		
Eva Burgos, Capital	36 609 10	
Luis Perez, Capital	36 564 10	
Total Capital		73 173 20
Total Liabilities and Capital		76 712 20

Balance sheet

- Write the words *Total Assets* below the last asset account title at the extreme left of the wide column. Total the individual assets and write the total, $76 712.20, in the second amount column on the total line.

- Rule double lines across both amount columns.

3 Prepare the liabilities section of the balance sheet. Use the information in the Balance Sheet Credit column of the work sheet, page 293.

- Write the title of the section, *Liabilities*, in the middle of the wide column.

- Write the titles of liability accounts on separate lines at the extreme left of the wide column. Write the balance of each liability account in the first amount column.

- Write the words *Total Liabilities* below the last liability account title. Write the words on the next line at the extreme left of the wide column. Add the individual liabilities and write the total, $3 539.00, in the second amount column on the total line.

4 Prepare the capital section of the balance sheet. Use the information in the capital statement, page 290.

- Write the title of the section, *Capital*, in the middle of the wide column.

- On the next line write the account title, *Eva Burgos, Capital*, at the extreme left of the wide column. On the same line write the amount of current capital for Eva Burgos, *$36 609.10*, in the first amount column.

- On the next line write the account title, *Luis Perez, Capital*, at the extreme left of the wide column. On the same line write the amount of current capital for Luis Perez, *$36 564.10*, in the first amount column.

- Write the words *Total Capital* on the next line at the extreme left of the wide column. Total the two capital accounts and write the total, *$73 173.20*, in the second amount column on the total line.

5 Total the liabilities and capital section of the balance sheet.

- Write the words *Total Liabilities and Capital* on the next line at the extreme left of the wide column. Add the amounts in the second amount column. Write the total, *$76 712.20*, in the second amount column on the total line.

> Compare the total amount of assets and the total amount of liabilities and capital. These two amounts must be the same. The two amounts, *$76 712.20*, are the same. The balance sheet is assumed to be correct.

- Rule double lines across both amount columns to show that the balance sheet has been completed.

Supporting schedules for a balance sheet

A report prepared to give details about an item on a principal financial statement is called a supporting schedule. A supporting schedule is sometimes known as a supplementary report or an exhibit.

Two supporting schedules are prepared by Denim Threads to accompany the balance sheet. The supporting schedules are a schedule of accounts payable and a schedule of accounts receivable. A balance sheet shows only the total amount of accounts payable. An account balance of each creditor is not shown. When this detailed information is needed, a supporting schedule of accounts payable is usually prepared. When information about the account balance of each charge customer is needed, a supporting schedule of accounts receivable is prepared. These supporting schedules for Denim Threads on November 30, 1988, are in Chapter 13, page 250.

STATEMENT OF ACCOUNT

A business usually sends to each charge customer a monthly statement showing the amount owed by the customer. The statement may include only the total balance owed. Most businesses, however, include all information about sales to and cash received from the customer. A business form showing the charges, receipts, and balance of a customer's account is called a statement of account.

Denim Threads sends statements of account to charge customers at the end of each month. An example of the statement of account used by Denim Threads is below.

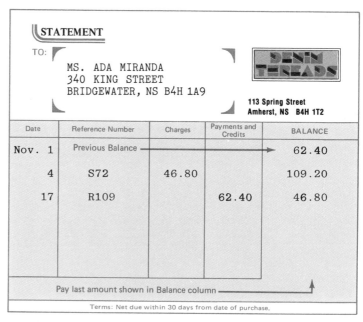

Statement of account

Customers should compare statements of account with their records. If an error is found on the statement, the business from whom the statement is received should be notified.

Many businesses mail statements of account to a portion of their charge customers on different days of a month. This procedure spreads out the work of preparing the statements over the month. Preparing and mailing statements of account to customers on different days of each month is called cycle billing. A cycle billing schedule is at the left. For example, on the 4th of each month, statements are mailed to customers whose names begin with A to D.

Initial of customers' last names	Date on which statement of account is prepared and mailed
A to D	4th
E to K	10th
L to P	16th
Q to S	22d
T to Z	28th

Cycle billing schedule

When mailing dates fall on weekends or holidays, statements are mailed on the next regular business day.

> Businesses with a small number of accounts receivable seldom use cycle billing. All statements of account are prepared and mailed once each month. Denim Threads, with few accounts receivable, mails statements once a month.

ACCOUNTING TERMS

What is the meaning of each of the following?

1. gross profit on sales
2. distribution of net income statement
3. capital statement
4. account form of balance sheet
5. report form of balance sheet
6. supporting schedule
7. statement of account
8. cycle billing

QUESTIONS FOR INDIVIDUAL STUDY

1. Why does a business prepare financial statements at the end of a fiscal period?
2. What four financial statements are prepared by a partnership?
3. What are the major differences in reporting owners' equity for a partnership and for a sole proprietorship?
4. Which financial statement reports the financial progress of a business?
5. Where does a business find the information needed to prepare an income statement?
6. What are the three main sections of Denim Threads' income statement?
7. How is the cost of merchandise sold figured?
8. How is the gross profit on sales figured?
9. How is the net income figured?
10. What are two ways that partners may agree to share the net income or net loss of a partnership?
11. Why does a partnership prepare a distribution of net income statement?
12. Why does a partnership prepare a capital statement?
13. What three factors change the amount of capital during a fiscal period?
14. Where is information obtained to use in preparing a capital statement?
15. Which financial statement reports the financial condition of the business?
16. What are the two forms in which a balance sheet may be prepared? Which form is used by Denim Threads?
17. What are the two supporting schedules prepared by Denim Threads?
18. Why do some businesses use cycle billing?

CASES FOR MANAGEMENT DECISION

CASE 1 Jack Gruber and Andy Sweeney, partners, compared their current income statement with their income statement of a year ago. They noted that sales this year are 15% higher than a year ago. They also have noted that expenses have increased nearly 20%. What points should be considered in deciding whether the increase in expenses is justified?

CASE 2 Curtis Danfield and Bradley Marshall own a sporting goods store. The store is on a yearly fiscal period. At the end of each year, a public accountant is employed to prepare financial statements. At the end of each month during the year, Mr. Marshall prepares a work sheet. The work sheet is prepared to determine if the business is making or losing money for that month. The public accountant suggests that monthly financial statements also be prepared. Mr. Marshall believes, however, that the monthly work sheet is sufficient to determine how the business is doing. Do you agree with Mr. Marshall or with the public accountant? Why?

CASE 3 Alice Abernathy and Steven Clemmons differ as to which financial statement is most important to them. Miss Abernathy believes the income statement is most important; Mr. Clemmons believes the balance sheet is most important. Who is correct? Explain.

DRILLS FOR UNDERSTANDING

DRILL 15-D 1   Figuring the cost of merchandise sold

Information from the work sheets of three businesses appears below.

Business	Account Title	Income Statement Debit	Income Statement Credit
1	Purchases	$ 4 600.00	
	Income Summary	62 000.00	$64 000.00
2	Purchases	$ 3 980.00	
	Income Summary	74 000.00	$72 000.00
3	Purchases	$ 4 350.00	
	Income Summary	68 000.00	$66 350.00

Instructions: Figure the cost of merchandise sold for each business.

DRILL 15-D 2   Figuring the net income or loss

Information from the work sheets of three businesses appears below.

Business	Account Title	Income Statement Debit	Income Statement Credit
1	Income Summary	$54 000.00	$52 500.00
	Sales		14 100.00
	Purchases	3 600.00	
	Total Expenses	1 800.00	
2	Income Summary	$36 200.00	$33 900.00
	Sales		10 200.00
	Purchases	9 850.00	
	Total Expenses	4 730.00	
3	Income Summary	$44 200.00	$46 400.00
	Sales		12 400.00
	Purchases	3 200.00	
	Total Expenses	1 400.00	

Instructions: Figure the net income or loss for each business.

DRILL 15-D 3 Figuring the distribution of net income or loss

Instructions: 1. Assume that each business shown at the right earned a net income of $15 000.00. What is the amount of income to be distributed to each partner in each business?

2. Assume that each business shown at the right had a loss of $8 000.00. What is the amount of loss to be distributed to each partner in each business?

Business	Partner	Agreement on sharing of income or loss
1	A	50% of income or loss
	B	50% of income or loss
2	A	60% of income or loss
	B	40% of income or loss
3	A	40% of income or loss
	B	30% of income or loss
	C	30% of income or loss

APPLICATION PROBLEMS

PROBLEM 15-1 Preparing financial statements

The work sheet completed in Problem 14-1 is needed to complete Problem 15-1.

Instructions: 1. Prepare an income statement similar to the one on page 285.
2. Prepare a distribution of net income statement similar to the one on page 287. The net income is to be shared equally.
3. Prepare a capital statement similar to the one on page 290. No additional investments were made.
4. Prepare a balance sheet in report form similar to the one on page 294.

The solution to Problem 15-1 is needed to complete Problem 16-1 in Chapter 16.

PROBLEM 15-2 Preparing a distribution of net income statement and capital statement

Mary Clancy and Karen Jordon are partners in a merchandising business. The following information was taken from the records on December 31 of the current year, the end of a monthly fiscal period.

Partner	Balance of capital account	Balance of drawing account	Distribution of net income
Clancy	$63 000.00	$840.00	70%
Jordon	$27 000.00	$620.00	30%

Instructions: 1. Assume that on December 31 the partnership had a net income of $9 400.00 as shown on the income statement. Prepare a distribution of net income statement for the partnership of Clancy & Jordon Sales.
2. Prepare a capital statement. No additional investments were made.
3. Assume that on December 31 the partnership had a loss of $5 600.00 instead of a net income. Prepare a distribution of net income statement showing the loss.
4. Prepare a capital statement showing the loss.

ENRICHMENT PROBLEMS

MASTERY PROBLEM 15-M   Preparing a work sheet and financial statements

The accounts and their balances in Household Furniture's general ledger appear below. Ending inventories and the value of insurance policies are also given.

Account Title	Account Balance
Cash	$ 9 800.00
Accounts Receivable	1 100.00
Merchandise Inventory	115 000.00
Supplies	460.00
Prepaid Insurance	730.00
Accounts Payable	6 120.00
Sales Tax Payable	748.00
Frank Garcia, Capital	56 800.00
Frank Garcia, Drawing	950.00
James Allen, Capital	57 403.00
James Allen, Drawing	875.00
Income Summary	——
Sales	18 700.00
Purchases	7 200.00
Credit Card Fee Expense	420.00
Delivery Expense	250.00
Insurance Expense	——
Miscellaneous Expense	86.00
Rent Expense	1 100.00
Salary Expense	1 800.00
Supplies Expense	——

Adjustment Information, December 31	
Merchandise inventory	$113 000.00
Supplies inventory	280.00
Value of insurance policies	635.00

Instructions: 1. Prepare Household Furniture's eight-column work sheet for the monthly fiscal period ending December 31 of the current year.

2. Prepare an income statement.

3. Prepare a distribution of net income statement. Net income is to be shared equally.

4. Prepare a capital statement. No additional investments were made.

5. Prepare a balance sheet in report form.

The work sheet prepared for Mastery Problem 15-M is needed to complete Challenge Problem 15-C.

CHALLENGE PROBLEM 15-C   Preparing financial statements (unequal distribution of net income; additional investment)

The work sheet completed for Mastery Problem 15-M is needed to complete Challenge Problem 15-C.

Instructions: 1. Prepare a distribution of net income statement. The net income is to be shared as follows: Frank Garcia, 60%; James Allen, 40%. Use the net income from the work sheet completed in Mastery Problem 15-M.

2. Prepare a capital statement. Mr. Allen made an additional investment of $5 000.00 during the month.

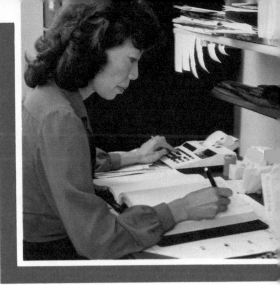

16

Adjusting and Closing Entries

ENABLING PERFORMANCE TASKS

After studying Chapter 16, you will be able to:

a. Explain accounting principles and practices related to adjusting and closing entries.
b. Journalize adjusting entries.
c. Journalize closing entries.
d. Post adjusting and closing entries.
e. Prepare a post-closing trial balance.

A merchandising business uses an eight-column work sheet at the end of a fiscal period for three reasons. (1) To plan adjustments of general ledger accounts. (2) To assemble information needed for preparing financial statements. (3) To assemble information needed for making closing entries.

Accounts in a general ledger are changed only by posting journal entries. Information needed for journalizing adjusting entries is taken from the work sheet's Adjustments columns. Information needed for journalizing closing entries is taken from two places. (1) Work sheet Income Statement and Balance Sheet columns. (2) Distribution of net income statement.

ADJUSTING ENTRIES

Each adjustment in a work sheet's Adjustments columns is journalized and posted to general ledger accounts. Four adjustments are shown in Denim Threads' work sheet, page 274.

Adjusting entry for beginning merchandise inventory

Denim Threads' adjustment for beginning merchandise inventory on November 30, 1988, is shown in the partial work sheet on the next page.

The debit and. credit parts of this adjustment are identified by the letter
(*a*). ·

Partial work sheet
showing adjustment for
beginning merchandise
inventory

ACCOUNT TITLE	TRIAL BALANCE		ADJUSTMENTS	
	DEBIT	CREDIT	DEBIT	CREDIT
3 *Merchandise Inventory*	6800000			(a)6800000
12 *Income Summary*			(a)6800000	

Denim Threads' adjusting entry for beginning merchandise inventory is
shown in the synoptic journal below. The general ledger accounts affected
by this entry are also shown.

*Journal entry to adjust
beginning merchandise
inventory*

PAGE *3*   SYNOPTIC JOURNAL

CASH		DATE	ACCOUNT TITLE	Doc. No.	Post. Ref.	GENERAL	
DEBIT	CREDIT					DEBIT	CREDIT
			Adjusting Entries				
		1988 Nov. 30	*Income Summary*		35	6800000	
			Mdse. Inventory		13		6800000

ACCOUNT *Income Summary*   ACCOUNT NO. *35*

DATE	ITEM	Post. Ref.	DEBIT	CREDIT	BALANCE	
					DEBIT	CREDIT
1988 Nov. 30		3	6800000		6800000	

ACCOUNT *Merchandise Inventory*   ACCOUNT NO. *13*

DATE	ITEM	Post. Ref.	DEBIT	CREDIT	BALANCE	
					DEBIT	CREDIT
1988 nov. 1	*Balance*	✓			6800000	
30		3		6800000		

General ledger accounts
after posting adjusting
entry for beginning
merchandise inventory

The words *Adjusting Entries* are written in the middle of the journal's
Account Title column. This heading explains all of the adjusting entries
that follow. Therefore, indicating a source document is unnecessary.

The first adjusting entry is recorded on the next line below the heading. The adjusting entry for beginning merchandise inventory debits Income Summary and credits Merchandise Inventory for $68 000.00. The debit
transfers the beginning balance of the merchandise inventory account to
the income summary account. The credit cancels the debit balance in the
merchandise inventory account. The merchandise inventory account has
a zero balance after the adjusting entry for beginning merchandise inventory is posted.

Adjusting entry for ending merchandise inventory

Denim Threads' adjustment for ending merchandise inventory is shown in the partial work sheet below. The debit and credit parts of this adjustment are identified by the letter (b).

ACCOUNT TITLE	TRIAL BALANCE		ADJUSTMENTS	
	DEBIT	CREDIT	DEBIT	CREDIT
3 Merchandise Inventory	6800000		(b) 6400000	(b) 6800000
12 Income Summary			(b) 6800000	(b) 6400000

Partial work sheet showing adjustment for ending merchandise inventory

Denim Threads' adjusting entry for the ending merchandise inventory is shown in the partial synoptic journal below. The general ledger accounts affected by this entry are also shown.

PAGE *3*

SYNOPTIC JOURNAL

CASH		DATE	ACCOUNT TITLE	Doc. No.	Post. Ref.	GENERAL	
DEBIT	CREDIT					DEBIT	CREDIT
		30	Merchandise Inventory		13	6400000	
			Income Summary		35		6400000

Journal entry to adjust ending merchandise inventory

ACCOUNT *Merchandise Inventory*   ACCOUNT NO. *13*

DATE	ITEM	POST. REF.	DEBIT	CREDIT	BALANCE	
					DEBIT	CREDIT
1988 Nov. 1	Balance	✓			6800000	
30		3		6800000		
30		3	6400000		6400000	

General ledger accounts after posting adjusting entry for ending merchandise inventory

ACCOUNT *Income Summary*   ACCOUNT NO. *35*

DATE	ITEM	POST. REF.	DEBIT	CREDIT	BALANCE	
					DEBIT	CREDIT
1988 Nov. 30		3	6800000		6800000	
30		3		6400000	400000	

The adjusting entry for ending merchandise inventory debits Merchandise Inventory and credits Income Summary for $64 000.00. This adjusting entry brings the asset account Merchandise Inventory up to date. The ending merchandise inventory, $64 000.00, is now recorded as a debit to the merchandise inventory account. This adjusting entry also records the ending merchandise inventory as a credit to the income summary account.

Adjusting entry for supplies

Denim Threads' adjustment for supplies on November 30, 1988, is shown on the partial work sheet below. The debit and credit parts of the adjustment are identified by the letter (c).

Partial work sheet showing adjustment for supplies

	ACCOUNT TITLE	TRIAL BALANCE		ADJUSTMENTS	
		DEBIT	CREDIT	DEBIT	CREDIT
4	*Supplies*	50100			(c) 26000
20	*Supplies Expense*			(c) 26000	

Denim Threads' entry to record the supplies adjustment is below. The general ledger accounts affected by this entry are also shown.

Journal entry to adjust supplies

PAGE **3**   SYNOPTIC JOURNAL

CASH		DATE	ACCOUNT TITLE	Doc. No.	Post. Ref.	GENERAL	
DEBIT	CREDIT					DEBIT	CREDIT
			Adjusting Entries				
		30	*Supplies Expense*		66	26000	
			Supplies		14		26000

General ledger accounts after posting adjusting entry for supplies

ACCOUNT *Supplies Expense*   ACCOUNT NO. **66**

DATE	ITEM	Post. Ref.	DEBIT	CREDIT	BALANCE DEBIT	BALANCE CREDIT
1988 Nov. 30		3	26000		26000	

ACCOUNT *Supplies*   ACCOUNT NO. **14**

DATE	ITEM	Post. Ref.	DEBIT	CREDIT	BALANCE DEBIT	BALANCE CREDIT
1988 Nov. 1	Balance	✓			16000	
10		1	14200		30200	
15		1	8600		38800	
17		1	8000		46800	
29		2	3300		50100	
30		3		26000	24100	

After the adjusting entry for supplies is posted, the supplies expense account has a debit balance of $260.00. The $260.00 debit to Supplies Expense is the expense resulting from the use of supplies during the fiscal period. The supplies account has a debit balance of $241.00. The $260.00 credit to Supplies is the decrease in the balance of this asset account.

Adjusting entry for prepaid insurance

Denim Threads' adjustment for prepaid insurance on November 30, 1988, is shown on the partial work sheet below. The debit and credit parts of the adjustment are identified by the letter (d).

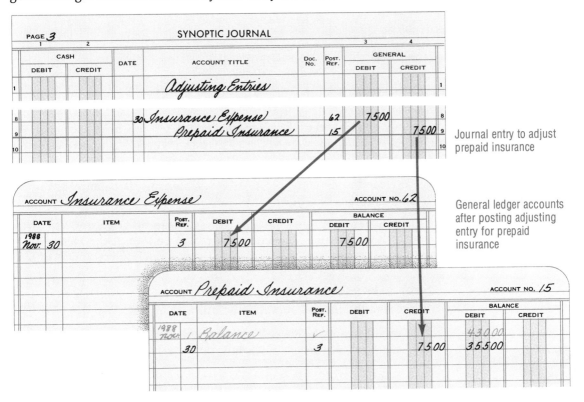

Partial work sheet showing adjustment for prepaid insurance

The entry to record the prepaid insurance adjustment is below. The general ledger accounts affected by this entry are also shown.

Journal entry to adjust prepaid insurance

General ledger accounts after posting adjusting entry for prepaid insurance

When the adjusting entry for prepaid insurance is posted, the insurance expense account has a debit balance of $75.00. The $75.00 debit to Insurance Expense is the expense resulting from the insurance expired during the fiscal period. The prepaid insurance account has a debit balance of $355.00. The $75.00 credit to Prepaid Insurance is the decrease in the balance of this asset account.

Summary of adjusting entries

Denim Threads' four adjusting entries recorded on November 30, 1988, are below.

CASH		DATE	ACCOUNT TITLE	Doc. No.	Post. Ref.	GENERAL		
DEBIT	CREDIT					DEBIT	CREDIT	
		1988	*Adjusting Entries*					1
		Nov. 30	*Income Summary*	35		6800000		2
			Mdse. Inventory	13			6800000	3
		30	*Merchandise Inventory*	13		6400000		4
			Income Summary	35			6400000	5
		30	*Supplies Expense*	66		26000		6
			Supplies	14			26000	7
		30	*Insurance Expense*	62		7500		8
			Prepaid Insurance	15			7500	9

PAGE *3* · SYNOPTIC JOURNAL

Adjusting entries

CLOSING ENTRIES

Closing entries prepare a general ledger for the next fiscal period. (*CONCEPT: Accounting Period Cycle*) Denim Threads has four reasons for recording closing entries.

1. To close the revenue account by transferring its balance to the income summary account.

    Amounts in the revenue account for the next fiscal period are separated from amounts of past fiscal periods. Each revenue account begins a new fiscal period with a zero balance. (*CONCEPT: Matching Expenses with Revenue*)

2. To close the cost and expense accounts by transferring their balances to the income summary account.

    Amounts in the cost and expense accounts for the next fiscal period are separated from amounts of past fiscal periods. Each cost and expense account begins a new fiscal period with a zero balance. (*CONCEPT: Matching Expenses with Revenue*)

3. To close Income Summary and record the net income or net loss.

    A closing entry is made to record the net income (or net loss) in the partners' capital accounts. The balance of the income summary account is equal to the net income (or net loss) for a fiscal period. (*CONCEPT: Accounting Period Cycle*)

4. To close the partners' drawing accounts by transferring their balances to the partners' capital accounts.

A closing entry is made to transfer the balances of the partners' drawing accounts to the capital accounts. After these drawing accounts are closed, amounts for the next fiscal period are separated from amounts of past fiscal periods. Each drawing account begins a new fiscal period with a zero balance.

Information needed for the closing entries is obtained from two places. (1) Work sheet Income Statement and Balance Sheet columns. (2) Distribution of net income statement.

Closing entry for revenue account

The part of Denim Threads' work sheet needed to close the revenue, cost, and expense accounts is below.

ACCOUNT TITLE	INCOME STATEMENT	
	DEBIT	CREDIT
13 Sales		1330500
14 Purchases	395200	
15 Credit Card Fee Expense	13500	
16 Insurance Expense	7500	
17 Miscellaneous Expense	8400	
18 Rent Expense	80000	
19 Salary Expense	110000	
20 Supplies Expense	26000	
21	7440600	7730500
22 Net Income	289900	
23	7730500	7730500
24		

Partial work sheet showing revenue, cost, and expense accounts balances

Information needed for closing the revenue account is taken from line 13 of the Income Statement Credit column. Sales is Denim Threads' only revenue account. Denim Threads' entry to close the revenue account Sales is below.

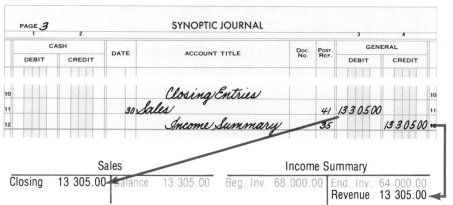

Journal entry to close the revenue account

The words *Closing Entries* are written in the middle of the journal's Account Title column. This heading is the explanation for all closing entries that follow. A source document is not indicated when journalizing closing entries.

The first closing entry is recorded on the next line below the heading. After Denim Threads' closing entry for revenue is posted, the sales account has a zero balance. The balance of the sales account, *$13 305.00*, is transferred as a credit to the income summary account.

Closing entry for cost and expense accounts

Information needed for closing the cost and expense accounts is taken from Denim Threads' work sheet, page 307. The information is in the Income Statement Debit column, lines 14–20. All account balances in the Income Statement Debit column of the work sheet are closed with one combined journal entry. Cost and expense accounts are closed with credit entries. One combined journal entry eliminates separate debit entries in Income Summary for each cost and expense account. The journal entry to close the cost and expense accounts is below.

Journal entry to close the cost and expense accounts

	CASH		DATE	ACCOUNT TITLE	Doc. No.	Post. Ref.	GENERAL	
	DEBIT	CREDIT					DEBIT	CREDIT
10				Closing Entries				
13			30	Income Summary	35		6 406 00	
14				Purchases		51		3 952 00
15				Credit Card Fee Exp.		61		135 00
16				Insurance Expense		62		75 00
17				Miscellaneous Exp.		63		84 00
18				Rent Expense		64		800 00
19				Salary Expense		65		1 100 00
20				Supplies Expense		66		260 00

PAGE 3 — SYNOPTIC JOURNAL

Income Summary		Miscellaneous Expense	
Beg. Inv. 68 000.00 End. Inv. 64 000.00		Balance 84.00 Closing 84.00	
Cost & Exp. 6 406.00 Revenue 13 305.00			

Purchases		Rent Expense	
Balance 3 952.00 Closing 3 952.00		Balance 800.00 Closing 800.00	

Credit Card Fee Expense		Salary Expense	
Balance 135.00 Closing 135.00		Balance 1 100.00 Closing 1 100.00	

Insurance Expense		Supplies Expense	
Balance 75.00 Closing 75.00		Balance 260.00 Closing 260.00	

The income summary account is debited for the total of these account balances, $6 406.00. Each account in the Income Statement Debit column is credited for the amount of its balance. After the closing entry for cost and expense accounts is posted, the accounts have zero balances.

When closing entries for revenue, cost, and expenses are posted, the income summary account has a credit balance of $2 899.00. This credit balance, *$2 899.00*, is the amount of net income. This amount is the same as on line 22 of the work sheet, page 307. When net income (or net loss) is the same in both places, closing entries are assumed to be correct.

Closing entry for recording net income (or net loss) in the partners' capital accounts

The net income is recorded in the partners' capital accounts. Information needed for this entry is obtained from the distribution of net income statement, page 287. This entry is recorded as shown below.

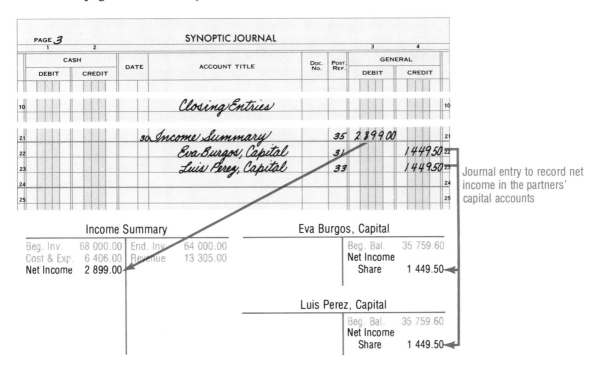

Journal entry to record net income in the partners' capital accounts

When the entry to record the net income is posted, Income Summary has a zero balance. An equal amount, *$1 449.50*, is recorded as a credit in each partner's capital account. The two amounts recorded in the partners' capital accounts total the net income, *$2 899.00*.

> If a business has a net loss, the income summary account has a debit balance. The partners' capital accounts would then be debited and the income summary account credited for the net loss.

Closing entries for partners' drawing accounts

Withdrawals by partners decrease capital. The drawing accounts are closed into the partners' respective capital accounts at the end of a fiscal period. *(CONCEPT: Accounting Period Cycle)* Information needed for closing partners' drawing accounts is obtained from the work sheet's Balance Sheet Debit column. The portion of Denim Threads' work sheet showing partners' drawing account balances is below.

| | ACCOUNT TITLE | | BALANCE SHEET | |
			DEBIT	CREDIT
8	Eva Burgos, Capital			35759 60
9	Eva Burgos, Drawing		600 00	
10	Luis Perez, Capital			35759 60
11	Luis Perez, Drawing		645 00	
12				

Partial work sheet showing partners' drawing accounts

Line 9 of the partial work sheet above shows the balance of Eva Burgos' drawing account, $600.00. Line 11 shows the balance of Luis Perez' drawing account, $645.00. The closing entries to close each drawing account are below.

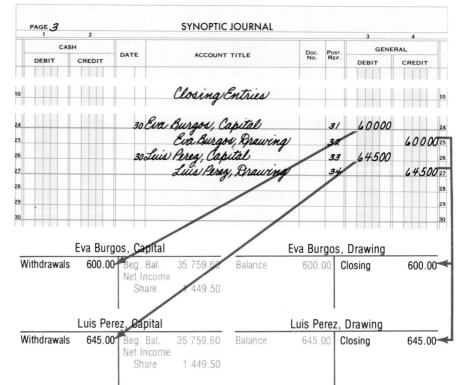

Journal entries to close the drawing accounts

When the closing entries for the partners' drawing accounts are posted, these accounts have zero balances. Also, the capital accounts of Eva Burgos and Luis Perez show the decrease in capital because of withdrawals.

Summary of closing entries

Denim Threads' closing entries on November 30, 1988, are below.

CASH DEBIT	CASH CREDIT	DATE	ACCOUNT TITLE	Doc. No.	Post. Ref.	GENERAL DEBIT	GENERAL CREDIT	
			Closing Entries					10
		30	*Sales*	41		1330500		11
			Income Summary		35		1330500	12
		30	*Income Summary*		35	640600		13
			Purchases		51		395200	14
			Credit Card Fee Exp.		61		13500	15
			Insurance Expense		62		7500	16
			Miscellaneous Exp.		63		8400	17
			Rent Expense		64		80000	18
			Salary Expense		65		110000	19
			Supplies Expense		66		26000	20
		30	*Income Summary*		35	289900		21
			Eva Burgos, Capital		31		144950	22
			Luis Perez, Capital		33		144950	23
		30	*Eva Burgos, Capital*		31	60000		24
			Eva Burgos, Drawing		32		60000	25
		30	*Luis Perez, Capital*		33	64500		26
			Luis Perez, Drawing		34		64500	27

PAGE *3*

SYNOPTIC JOURNAL

Closing entries

CHECKING THE ACCURACY OF A GENERAL LEDGER AFTER ADJUSTING AND CLOSING ENTRIES HAVE BEEN POSTED

Denim Threads uses a four-column general ledger account form. The form has separate columns for Debit Balance and Credit Balance. Each time an entry is posted to a general ledger account, the account balance is figured. The balance is then recorded in the appropriate balance column. When an account is closed, a short line is drawn in both the Debit and Credit Balance columns. Each general ledger account shows its current balance at all times. The ending balance for one fiscal period is the beginning balance for the next fiscal period.

Completed general ledger

Denim Threads' general ledger appears as shown below and on pages 313 to 315 after adjusting and closing entries are posted.

ACCOUNT *Cash*   ACCOUNT NO. *11*

DATE	ITEM	POST. REF.	DEBIT	CREDIT	BALANCE DEBIT	BALANCE CREDIT
1988 Nov. 1	Balance	✓			4 200 00	
30		2	13 551 20		17 751 20	
30		2		6 207 00	11 544 20	

ACCOUNT *Accounts Receivable*   ACCOUNT NO. *12*

DATE	ITEM	POST. REF.	DEBIT	CREDIT	BALANCE DEBIT	BALANCE CREDIT
1988 Nov. 1	Balance	✓			286 00	
30		2	639 60		925 60	
30		2		353 60	572 00	

ACCOUNT *Merchandise Inventory*   ACCOUNT NO. *13*

DATE	ITEM	POST. REF.	DEBIT	CREDIT	BALANCE DEBIT	BALANCE CREDIT
1988 Nov. 1	Balance	✓			68 000 00	—
30		3		68 000 00		
30		3	64 000 00		64 000 00	

ACCOUNT *Supplies*   ACCOUNT NO. *14*

DATE	ITEM	POST. REF.	DEBIT	CREDIT	BALANCE DEBIT	BALANCE CREDIT
1988 Nov. 1	Balance	✓			160 00	
10		1	142 00		302 00	
15		1	86 00		388 00	
17		1	80 00		468 00	
29		2	33 00		501 00	
30		3		260 00	241 00	

ACCOUNT *Prepaid Insurance*   ACCOUNT NO. *15*

DATE	ITEM	POST. REF.	DEBIT	CREDIT	BALANCE DEBIT	BALANCE CREDIT
1988 Nov. 1	Balance	✓			430 00	
30		3		75 00	355 00	

General ledger after adjusting and closing entries are posted

General ledger after adjusting and closing entries are posted (continued)

ACCOUNT *Accounts Payable* ACCOUNT NO. 21

DATE		ITEM	POST. REF.	DEBIT	CREDIT	BALANCE DEBIT	BALANCE CREDIT
1988 Nov.	1	Balance	✓				120000
	30		2		361400		265000
	30		2	216400			96400

ACCOUNT *Sales Tax Payable* ACCOUNT NO. 22

DATE		ITEM	POST. REF.	DEBIT	CREDIT	BALANCE DEBIT	BALANCE CREDIT
1988 Nov.	1	Balance	✓				35680
	30		2		53220		88900

ACCOUNT *Eva Burgos, Capital* ACCOUNT NO. 31

DATE		ITEM	POST. REF.	DEBIT	CREDIT	BALANCE DEBIT	BALANCE CREDIT
1988 Nov.	1	Balance	✓				3575960
	30		3		144950		3720910
	30		3	60000			3660910

ACCOUNT *Eva Burgos, Drawing* ACCOUNT NO. 32

DATE		ITEM	POST. REF.	DEBIT	CREDIT	BALANCE DEBIT	BALANCE CREDIT
1988 Nov.	15		1	30000		30000	
	30		2	30000		60000	
	30		3		60000	—	—

ACCOUNT *Luis Perez, Capital* ACCOUNT NO. 33

DATE		ITEM	POST. REF.	DEBIT	CREDIT	BALANCE DEBIT	BALANCE CREDIT
1988 Nov.	1	Balance	✓				3575960
	30		3		144950		3720910
	30		3	64500			3656410

ACCOUNT *Luis Perez, Drawing* ACCOUNT NO. 34

DATE		ITEM	POST. REF.	DEBIT	CREDIT	BALANCE DEBIT	BALANCE CREDIT
1988 Nov.	15		1	30000		30000	
	16		1	4500		34500	
	30		2	30000		64500	
	30		3		64500	—	—

ACCOUNT *Income Summary*   ACCOUNT NO. *35*

DATE	ITEM	POST. REF.	DEBIT	CREDIT	BALANCE DEBIT	BALANCE CREDIT
1988 Nov. 30		3	6800000		6800000	
30		3		6400000	400000	
30		3		1330500		930500
30		3	640600			289900
30		3	289900		—	—

ACCOUNT *Sales*   ACCOUNT NO. *41*

DATE	ITEM	POST. REF.	DEBIT	CREDIT	BALANCE DEBIT	BALANCE CREDIT
1988 Nov. 30		2		1330500		1330500
30		3	1330500		—	—

ACCOUNT *Purchases*   ACCOUNT NO. *51*

DATE	ITEM	POST. REF.	DEBIT	CREDIT	BALANCE DEBIT	BALANCE CREDIT
1988 Nov. 16		1		4500		4500
17		1		8000		12500
30		2	407700		395200	
30		3		395200	—	—

ACCOUNT *Credit Card Fee Expense*   ACCOUNT NO. *61*

DATE	ITEM	POST. REF.	DEBIT	CREDIT	BALANCE DEBIT	BALANCE CREDIT
1988 Nov. 28		2	13500		13500	
30		3		13500	—	—

ACCOUNT *Insurance Expense*   ACCOUNT NO. *62*

DATE	ITEM	POST. REF.	DEBIT	CREDIT	BALANCE DEBIT	BALANCE CREDIT
1988 Nov. 30		3	7500		7500	
30		3		7500	—	—

ACCOUNT *Miscellaneous Expense*   ACCOUNT NO. *63*

DATE	ITEM	POST. REF.	DEBIT	CREDIT	BALANCE DEBIT	BALANCE CREDIT
1988 Nov. 3		1	5300		5300	
22		2	2900		8200	
28		2	200		8400	
30		3		8400	—	—

General ledger after adjusting and closing entries are posted (continued)

General ledger after
adjusting and closing
entries are posted
(concluded)

ACCOUNT *Rent Expense* ACCOUNT NO. 64

DATE	ITEM	POST. REF.	DEBIT	CREDIT	BALANCE DEBIT	BALANCE CREDIT
1988 Nov. 15		1	80000		80000	
30		3		80000		

ACCOUNT *Salary Expense* ACCOUNT NO. 65

DATE	ITEM	POST. REF.	DEBIT	CREDIT	BALANCE DEBIT	BALANCE CREDIT
1988 Nov. 1		1	55000		55000	
15		1	55000		110000	
30		3		110000		

ACCOUNT *Supplies Expense* ACCOUNT NO. 66

DATE	ITEM	POST. REF.	DEBIT	CREDIT	BALANCE DEBIT	BALANCE CREDIT
1988 Nov. 30		3	26000		26000	
30		3		26000		

Balance sheet accounts (assets, liability, and capital accounts) all have up-to-date balances on November 30, 1988. Balances in the balance sheet accounts agree with the amounts on the balance sheet, page 294. General ledger account balances on November 30, 1988, are the beginning balances for December 1, 1988.

Income statement accounts (revenue, cost, and expense accounts) all have zero balances to begin the new fiscal period.

Post-closing trial balance

A post-closing trial balance is prepared after adjusting and closing entries have been posted. The post-closing trial balance is prepared to prove the equality of debits and credits in the general ledger. Denim Threads' post-closing trial balance, prepared on November 30, 1988, is on the next page.

General ledger accounts that have balances are listed on a post-closing trial balance. Accounts are listed in the same order as they appear in the general ledger. Accounts with zero balances are not listed on a post-closing trial balance.

ACCOUNT TITLE	DEBIT	CREDIT
Denim Threads		
Post-Closing Trial Balance		
November 30, 1988		
Cash	11 544 20	
Accounts Receivable	572 00	
Merchandise Inventory	64 000 00	
Supplies	241 00	
Prepaid Insurance	355 00	
Accounts Payable		2 650 00
Sales Tax Payable		889 00
Eva Burgos, Capital		36 609 10
Luis Perez, Capital		36 564 10
	76 712 20	76 712 20

Post-closing trial balance

Account balances on the post-closing trial balance above agree with the balances on the balance sheet, page 294. Also, on the post-closing trial balance, the debit and credit balance totals are the same, $76 712.20. The equality of debits and credits in the general ledger is proved. The general ledger is ready for the next fiscal period. (CONCEPT: *Accounting Period Cycle*)

SUMMARIZING AN ACCOUNTING CYCLE FOR A MERCHANDISING BUSINESS

An accounting cycle contains the same basic steps for a merchandising business as for a service business. Also, the accounting cycle is similar for a sole proprietorship and a partnership. Minor variations occur when subsidiary ledgers are used. Variations also occur in preparing financial statements. The steps in Putt Around's accounting cycle are shown in the flowchart on page 154. The flowchart, page 317, shows the steps in Denim Threads' accounting cycle.

QUESTIONS FOR INDIVIDUAL STUDY

1. Why are the adjustments, as planned on a work sheet, recorded as entries in a journal?
2. Where is the information obtained for journalizing the adjusting entries?
3. Where is the information obtained for journalizing closing entries?
4. Where is the explanation for the adjusting entries written in a synoptic journal?
5. Why does the merchandise inventory account have a zero balance after posting the adjusting entry for beginning merchandise inventory?

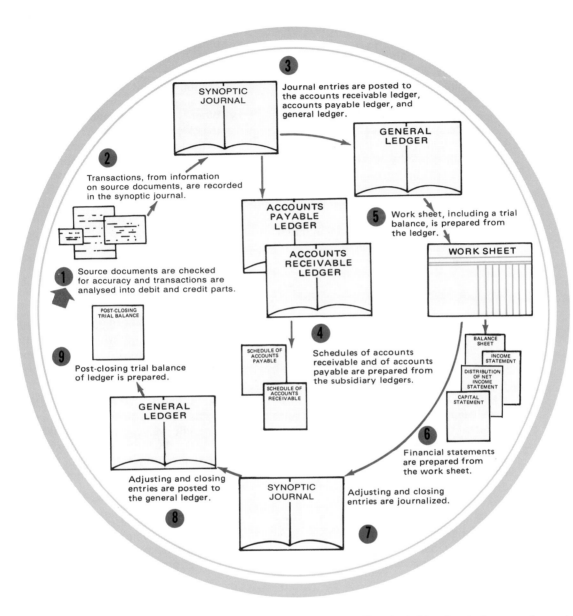

Flowchart of the steps in the accounting cycle

6. Why does the adjustment for ending inventory bring the asset account Merchandise Inventory up to date?

7. Why does the adjustment for supplies debit Supplies Expense and credit Supplies?

8. Why does the adjustment for prepaid insurance debit Insurance Expense and credit Prepaid Insurance?

9. Why are closing entries needed at the end of a fiscal period?

10. Why is the revenue account closed at the end of a fiscal period?

11. Why do cost and expense accounts

begin a new fiscal period with a zero balance?

12. Why is the balance of the income summary account transferred to the partners' capital accounts?

13. Why are the partners' drawing accounts transferred to the capital accounts by a closing entry?

14. Where is the information obtained for making the entry to close a revenue account?

15. Where is the explanation for the closing entries written in a synoptic journal?

16. Why is a source document number not written for closing entries?

17. Where is the information obtained for making the entry to close cost and expense accounts?

18. Why are the account balances in the work sheet's Income Statement Debit column closed with one combined journal entry?

19. Where is the information obtained for the closing entry to record net income or net loss in the capital accounts?

20. Where is the information obtained for the entry to close the drawing accounts?

21. What is the reason for preparing a post-closing trial balance?

22. What accounts are listed on a post-closing trial balance?

CASES FOR MANAGEMENT DECISION

CASE 1 Crestline Furniture had a debit balance of $580.00 in the prepaid insurance account on January 1. On January 31, an adjusting entry was made. Debit Prepaid Insurance $40.00; credit Insurance Expense $40.00. What effect will this adjusting entry have on the net income? On Capital?

CASE 2 Donley's, a merchandising business, prepares a work sheet and financial statements at the end of each month. However, the business uses a yearly fiscal period ending December 31. No adjusting or closing journal entries are made at the end of each month. Steven Donley, partner, suggests that adjusting and closing entries should be made at the end of each month. Marie Donley, partner, suggests that adjusting and closing entries need be made only at the end of the fiscal year. Do you agree with Marie Donley or Steven Donley?

CASE 3 Two businesses have been using different accounting practices. One business first closes the drawing accounts and then records the net income in the capital accounts. The other business records the net income first and then closes the drawing accounts. Which practice is correct? Explain.

DRILLS FOR UNDERSTANDING

DRILL 16-D 1   Recording adjusting entries

A partial work sheet of Anderson Supply is on the next page.

Instructions: 1. Prepare T accounts for each account on the partial work sheet. For those accounts that have a balance, record the balance on the proper side of the T account.

2. Record the adjustments for merchandise inventory, supplies, and prepaid insurance in the appropriate T accounts.

Account Title	Trial Balance		Adjustments	
	Debit	Credit	Debit	Credit
Merchandise Inventory..	42 900 00		(b) 44 600 00	(a) 42 900 00
Supplies........................	390 00			(c) 60 00
Prepaid Insurance.........	260 00			(d) 110 00
Income Summary..........			(a) 42 900 00	(b) 44 600 00
Insurance Expense			(d) 110 00	
Supplies Expense			(c) 60 00	

DRILL 16-D 2 Recording adjusting entries

Information for three businesses is below. This information is related to adjustments needed at the end of a fiscal period.

Business	Account Title	Account Balance in General Ledger	Adjustment Information Ending Inventories	Ending Value
1	Merchandise Inventory	$39 500.00	$41 000.00	
	Supplies	430.00	320.00	
	Prepaid Insurance	720.00		$580.00
2	Merchandise Inventory	$62 300.00	$58 800.00	
	Supplies	530.00	460.00	
	Prepaid Insurance	480.00		$320.00
3	Merchandise Inventory	$47 600.00	$45 800.00	
	Supplies	490.00	370.00	
	Prepaid Insurance	650.00		$560.00

Instructions: 1. Prepare six T accounts for each of the three businesses. (1) Merchandise Inventory. (2) Supplies. (3) Prepaid Insurance. (4) Income Summary. (5) Insurance Expense. (6) Supplies Expense. Record the account balance on the proper side of each T account.

2. Record the adjustments for merchandise inventory, supplies, and prepaid insurance in the appropriate T accounts for each business.

DRILL 16-D 3 Recording closing entries

A partial work sheet for Smithfield Plumbing is below.

Account Title	Income Statement	
	Debit	Credit
Income Summary..................	42 650 00	45 300 00
Sales		12 510 00
Purchases........................	3 180 00	
Credit Card Fee Expense	270 00	
Insurance Expense	120 00	
Miscellaneous Expense.........	60 00	
Rent Expense.......................	900 00	
Salary Expense	1 300 00	
Supplies Expense	160 00	

Instructions: 1. Prepare a T account for each account on the partial work sheet. In each T account, record the amount that is shown in the Income Statement columns.
2. Record the debit and credit amounts to close the revenue, cost, and expense accounts.

APPLICATION PROBLEMS

PROBLEM 16-1   Completing the work at the end of a fiscal period

The solutions to Problems 14-1 and 15-1 are needed to complete Problem 16-1.

Instructions: 1. On page 3 of a synoptic journal record the adjusting entries shown in the Adjustments columns of the work sheet. Use the adjusting entries, page 306, as a guide.
2. Record in the synoptic journal the closing entries from information on the work sheet and distribution of net income statement. Use the closing entries, page 311, as a guide.
3. Post the adjusting and closing entries to the general ledger.
4. Prepare a post-closing trial balance. Use the post-closing trial balance, page 316, as a guide.

PROBLEM 16-2   Completing a work sheet; recording adjusting and closing entries

The ledger accounts of Melbourne Supply as of November 30 are given in the working papers.

Instructions: 1. Prepare a trial balance in the Trial Balance columns of a work sheet.
2. Complete the work sheet. The information about inventories and value of insurance policies on November 30 is below.

Merchandise inventory, November 30.................................	$47 600.00
Supplies inventory, November 30.......................................	392.00
Value of insurance policies, November 30	530.00

3. Prepare an income statement from the information on the work sheet.
4. Prepare a distribution of net income statement. Net income or loss is to be distributed equally.
5. Prepare a capital statement.
6. Prepare a balance sheet.
7. On page 6 of a synoptic journal record the adjusting entries shown in the Adjustments columns of the work sheet.
8. Record in the synoptic journal the closing entries from information on the work sheet and distribution of net income statement.
9. Post the adjusting and closing entries to the general ledger.
10. Prepare a post-closing trial balance.

ENRICHMENT PROBLEMS

MASTERY PROBLEM 16-M   Completing the work at the end of a fiscal period

The ledger accounts of Dubolt Associates as of October 31 are given in the working papers.

Instructions: 1. Prepare a trial balance in the Trial Balance columns of a work sheet.

2. Complete the work sheet. The information about inventories and value of insurance policies on October 31 is below.

Merchandise inventory, October 31	$53 250.00
Supplies inventory, October 31	435.00
Value of insurance policies, October 31	620.00

3. Prepare an income statement from the information on the work sheet.

4. Prepare a distribution of net income statement. Net income or loss is to be distributed equally.

5. Prepare a capital statement.

6. Prepare a balance sheet.

7. On page 4 of a synoptic journal record the adjusting entries shown in the Adjustments columns of the work sheet.

8. Record in the synoptic journal the closing entries from information on the work sheet and distribution of net income statement.

9. Post the adjusting and closing entries to the general ledger.

10. Prepare a post-closing trial balance.

CHALLENGE PROBLEM 16-C Locating and correcting errors on a completed work sheet

Mayberry Electronics' work sheet for the month ended January 31, 1989, is given in the working papers. The information about inventories and value of insurance policies is below.

Ending merchandise inventory, January 31	$35 200.00
Supplies used during January	120.00
Insurance expired during January..	90.00

The totals of the Balance Sheet Debit and Credit columns do not balance after net income is added.

Instructions: Locate the errors made in preparing the work sheet and prepare a new work sheet. The trial balance on the work sheet has been checked and is correct.

Reinforcement Activity 2

PART B

An Accounting Cycle for a Partnership Using a Synoptic Journal

The ledgers used in Part A are needed to complete Part B.

Reinforcement Activity 2, Part B, covers those accounting activities needed to complete Infocus' accounting cycle. The flowchart at the left shows that part of the accounting cycle covered in Reinforcement Activity 2, Part B.

Completing Infocus' end-of-fiscal-period work

Instructions: 1. Prepare a trial balance on an eight-column work sheet. Use December 31 of the current year as the date.

2. Complete the work sheet using the adjustment information below.

Adjustment Information, December 31

Merchandise inventory	$72 300.00
Supplies inventory	520.50
Value of insurance policies	506.00

3. Prepare an income statement from the information on the work sheet.

4. Prepare a distribution of net income statement. Net income or loss is to be distributed equally.

5. Prepare a capital statement.

6. Prepare a balance sheet.

7. On page 24 of a synoptic journal record the adjusting entries shown in the Adjustments columns of the work sheet.

8. Record in the synoptic journal the closing entries from the information on the work sheet and distribution of net income statement.

9. Post the adjusting and closing entries to the general ledger.

10. Prepare a post-closing trial balance.

Complete trial balance on work sheet

Enter adjustments and complete work sheet

Prepare financial statements

Journalize adjusting and closing entries

Post adjusting and closing entries to general ledger

Prepare post-closing trial balance

322

A BUSINESS SIMULATION

QUADRASONICS

ELECTRONIC SOUND EQUIPMENT

QUADRASONICS is a wholesaler dealer in quadraphonic and stereotronic equipment. Though it is a sole proprietorship, owned and operated by Janice Ray, its records illustrate the application of general accounting principles that apply to all businesses, including partnerships. This company uses a synoptic journal, general ledger, accounts receivable and accounts payable ledgers, and a chequebook. A pictorial flowchart of the accounting cycle of QUADRASONICS is shown on the next two pages. This business simulation is available from the publisher.

Flowchart of the
Accounting Cycle of

QUADRASONICS

Source Documents

1   Record transactions in the synoptic journal from source documents.
1a File source documents.
2   Post items to be posted individually to the general ledger and
    subsidiary ledgers.
3   Post column totals to the general ledger.
4   Prepare schedules of accounts receivable and accounts payable
    from subsidiary ledgers.
5   Prepare the trial balance on the work sheet.
6   Plan adjustments and complete the work sheet.
7   Prepare financial statements.
8   Record adjusting and closing entries from the work sheet.
9   Post adjusting and closing entries to the general ledger.
10 Prepare a post-closing trial balance from the general ledger.

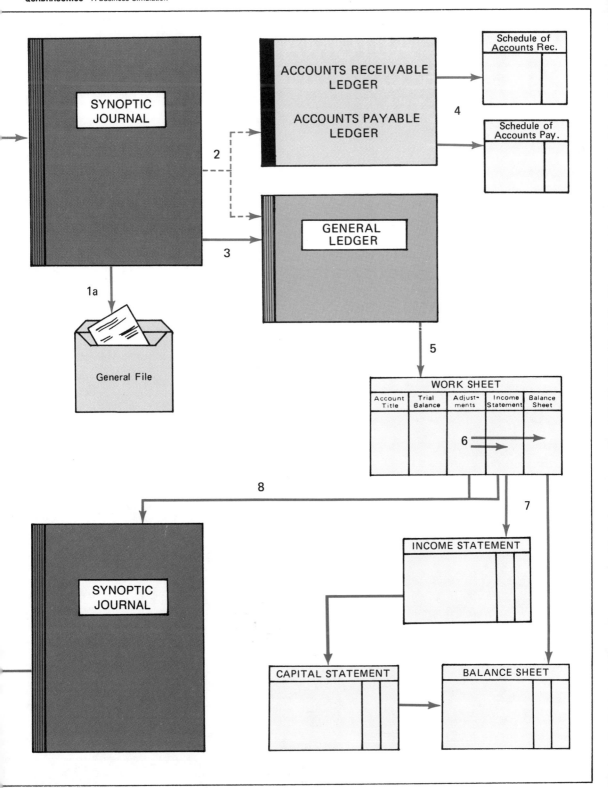

4 AN AUTOMATED ACCOUNTING SYSTEM

GENERAL BEHAVIORAL GOALS

1. Know terminology related to automated accounting for a merchandising business organized as a partnership.
2. Understand automated accounting principles and practices for a merchandising business organized as a partnership.
3. Demonstrate automated accounting procedures for a merchandising business organized as a partnership.

Allsports, the business for Part 4, sells sporting goods.

ALLSPORTS
Chart of Accounts

Account Number	(1) ASSETS	Account Number	(4) REVENUE
11000	Cash	41000	Sales
11500	Accounts Receivable		
12000	Merchandise Inventory		**(5) COST OF MERCHANDISE**
12500	Office Supplies	51000	Purchases
13000	Store Supplies		
13500	Prepaid Insurance		**(6) EXPENSES**
14000	Delivery Equipment		
14500	Office Equipment	61000	Advertising Expense
15000	Store Equipment	61500	Credit Card Fee Expense
		62000	Delivery Expense
	(2) LIABILITIES	62500	Insurance Expense
		63000	Miscellaneous Expense
21000	Accounts Payable	63500	Office Supplies Expense
		64000	Rent Expense
	(3) CAPITAL	64500	Salary Expense
		65000	Store Supplies Expense
31000	Helen Lewis, Capital		
31500	Helen Lewis, Drawing		
32000	Samuel Sullivan, Capital		
32500	Samuel Sullivan, Drawing		
33000	Income Summary		

The chart of accounts for Allsports is illustrated above for
ready reference as you study Part 4 of this textbook.

Data Processing Systems

ENABLING PERFORMANCE TASKS

After studying Chapter 17, you will be able to:

a. Define terminology related to automated general ledger accounting for a merchandising business.
b. Explain automated general ledger accounting principles and practices.
c. Assign account numbers to accounts in a general ledger.
d. Prepare a chart of accounts setup form.
e. Prepare financial statement setup forms.

Procedures for recording and reporting a business' financial activities are described in earlier chapters. Recording and reporting procedures vary according to business size and type. The accounting cycle for Putt Around, a small service business, is described in Part 2. The accounting cycle for Denim Threads, a small merchandising business, is described in Part 3. Effective business decisions can be made only when the information is current, accurate, and complete. As a business becomes larger, the volume of information to be recorded and reported also increases. When the volume of information increases, a business generally needs faster recording and reporting procedures. The use of machines is one way to speed the recording and reporting processes.

DATA PROCESSING

Detailed or factual information is called data. Many different kinds of data are used in business. One important kind of data in any business is financial data. To be useful data must be recorded, organized, and reported. A series of operations performed upon data is called data processing. A combination of procedures, forms, and machines converting data into useful information is called a data processing system.

329

Helen Lewis and Samuel Sullivan, partners, operate a retail store known as Allsports. *(CONCEPT: Business Entity)* The store sells a complete sporting goods line. Sales are made to individuals as well as to school systems. A monthly rent is paid for the use of building and fixtures. Helen and Samuel want to improve their data processing system. They want the work done faster and less expensively.

Types of data processing systems

Data processing systems are classified in many ways. One way to classify these systems is according to the procedures and equipment used. Two common types of data processing systems are used. (1) Manual data processing. (2) Automated data processing.

A system in which data are processed mostly by hand is called manual data processing. The financial data in previous chapters was processed through manual data processing procedures. A manual system may not be adequate to complete all the accounting work. The total amount of data in the system may be too large or efficiency may need improvement. Ms. Lewis found both to be true for Allsports. The amount of data had increased. More efficient procedures were needed.

A process by which work is done mostly by machines is called automation. A system using automated machines to process data is called automated data processing (ADP). Even in automated data processing some procedures are done manually.

Planning for automated data processing

Planning for automated data processing is similar to planning for manual data processing. Planning any data processing system consists of two steps. (1) Setting goals — deciding what is to be processed and reported. (2) Establishing procedures and determining the equipment needed to process the data. Allsports had such goals when the current manual data processing system was planned.

Accuracy in every detail is equally important in both automated and manual data processing. Results in any data processing system can only be as accurate as the information put into the system. For example, if an accountant records an amount as $15.80 rather than $18.50, information on financial statements will be incorrect.

Phases of a data processing system

A data processing system consists of four phases. (1) Input. (2) Processing. (3) Storage. (4) Output. These four phases are illustrated on page 329.

Data put into a system are called input. Input may be data on sales invoices, purchase invoices, and other business forms. Working with data according to precise instructions is called processing. Filing or hold-

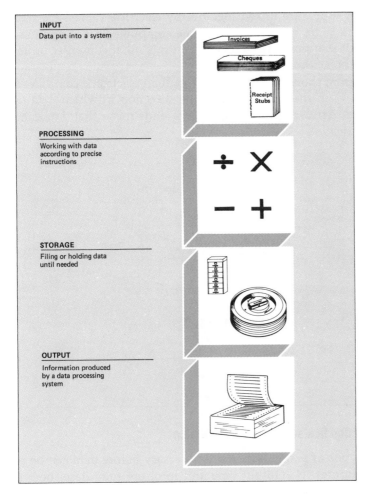

INPUT
Data put into a system

PROCESSING
Working with data
according to precise
instructions

STORAGE
Filing or holding data
until needed

OUTPUT
Information produced
by a data processing
system

Phases of a data
processing system

ing data until needed is called storage. Storage may involve using filing
cabinets or other devices. Information produced by a data processing
system is called output. Examples of output are facts about assets, liabilities, capital, revenue, and expenses reported on financial statements.
Output can also be printed on forms such as cheques and invoices. Output
may be facts that will be further processed.

ELECTRONIC DATA PROCESSING

A group of interconnected machines that process data according to
stored instructions is called a computer. Automated data processing
using a computer is called electronic data processing (EDP). Electronic
data processing is the most common automated data processing system.

A computer handles data in all four data processing phases: input,
processing, storage, and output. Separate machines, often referred to as

computer units, are linked together by electrical cables. Electrical cables allow data to be transferred from one computer unit to another. A computer unit that processes data and controls other computer units is called a central processing unit (CPU).

A diagram showing data flow through an electronic computer is below. The arrows in the diagram show the direction in which data move in a computer. Arrows with points at both ends mean that data can move in either direction.

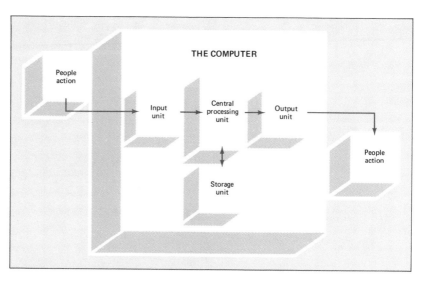

Data flow in a computer

People action in electronic data processing

Five types of people action are necessary before data can be processed by a computer. (1) Output type and form are fully described. (2) Flowcharts are prepared showing the sequence for each job to be processed. (3) Instructions are written for the computer. (4) Data (input) to be processed are arranged according to set procedures and checked for accuracy. (5) Input is entered into the computer.

Two types of people action are necessary after data have been processed by a computer. (1) Output is inspected. (2) Output is given to people who can interpret and use it.

Planning instructions for a computer

Step-by-step instructions for doing each job must be prepared before data can be processed by a computer. A set of instructions followed by a computer to process data is called a computer program. The term "program" may also describe a set of step-by-step instructions for processing data by manual means. For example, on page 20 is a program for manually preparing a balance sheet. A person who prepares a computer program is called a computer programmer.

Computer programmers need special training in electronic data processing. Understanding accounting principles is helpful to a computer programmer. However, such understanding is not essential to program a computer. Understanding the basic concepts of a computer system is important to an accountant using computer services. Steps of the accounting cycle that are computer processed and steps that require manual processing must be understood. Using a computer does not change basic accounting principles. Only the equipment changes.

COMPUTER SERVICE CENTRE

For many years automated data processing was used only by larger businesses. The high cost of computers made it impossible for smaller businesses to go beyond manual systems. Today, however, small businesses use automated data processing. The cost of computer services is based on the amount and type of data processed. A business established to sell computer services is called a computer service centre. A computer service centre is also known as a computer service bureau or a business service bureau.

After gathering facts about data processing systems, Ms. Lewis decides that Allsports will benefit by using automated data processing (ADP). More complete accounting information can be obtained by using an automated system. Allsports does not have the amount of data needed to justify owning the automated equipment. Therefore, Ms. Lewis decides that Allsports will use the services of a computer service centre.

Services provided for small businesses

Processing accounting data for small businesses is one of the most important services provided by a computer service centre. Accounting services are also provided for professional people such as doctors, dentists, and lawyers. Five major services are provided. (1) Assist in training personnel who will prepare data to be processed by a computer. (2) Assist in designing procedures for a business' data processing system. (3) Assist in designing a business' output reports. (4) Enter input data into a computer. (5) Process data to produce output reports.

Services provided for large businesses

Businesses that own computers often use a computer service centre. Most businesses have peak periods of business activity. Using a computer service centre during these peak periods avoids installing additional costly, new and larger automated machines.

Using a computer service centre does not eliminate an accountant's need to master basic accounting principles. A computer performs routine and repetitive operations based on accounting principles and concepts.

AUTOMATED GENERAL LEDGER ACCOUNTING

Many computer service centres provide training sessions for clients. The training sessions help acquaint clients with the automated services available. Various approaches can be taken in designing an automated accounting system. Two major items need to be considered when deciding on the automated accounting procedures to use. (1) Immediate and future data processing needs of a business. (2) Cost.

Based on immediate and future needs plus cost, Ms. Lewis decides that an automated general ledger accounting system will be used. Allsports operates primarily on a cash basis with credit card privileges available to customers. Regular charge privileges are available only to area school systems. Allsports has a small number of suppliers from whom to buy merchandise and supplies. Ms. Lewis determines that the cost of automating the subsidiary ledgers is not justified when compared with benefits received. Therefore, the decision is made to continue to maintain manually the subsidiary ledgers. Only entries to the general ledger controlling accounts will be entered into the computer system.

Coding the chart of accounts

A computer service centre first asks a client to submit a list of ledger accounts. Each account title has meaning for a client. However, automated machines work more efficiently with numbers. Account titles therefore are assigned numbers with which machines can work.

A chart of accounts coding system for an automated accounting system provides for three items. (1) A numeric sequence within each division. (2) A proper order within each division. (3) Enough digits to provide for addition of new accounts. Businesses using EDP will normally need at least a five-digit account number. Less than five digits will not allow enough digits to sequentially add new accounts within each division. Each business numbers its accounts according to its particular needs. A partial chart of accounts with five-digit account numbers is below.

CHART OF ACCOUNTS GENERAL LEDGER		
Account Number (1) ASSETS		**Account Number** (2) LIABILITIES
11000 Cash		21000 Accounts Payable
11500 Accounts Receivable		
12000 Merchandise Inventory		
12500 Supplies		
13000 Prepaid Insurance		

Partial chart of accounts for a general ledger

A breakdown of the five-digit coding system is on the next page.

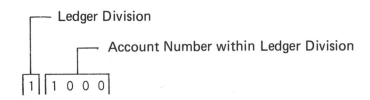

The first digit of the chart of accounts coding system identifies the ledger division. The second through the fifth digits provide identification of accounts within each division. For the account Cash, the *1* indicates the account is an asset. The number *1000* indicates that the asset account Cash is the first account in the asset division. For Accounts Payable, page 334, the 2 indicates the account is a liability. The number *1000* indicates that Accounts Payable is the first account in the liability division. Remaining accounts within each division are assigned numbers by five hundreds. For example, Accounts Receivable, page 334, is assigned the asset number 11500.

New accounts added at the end of a division are assigned the next five-hundred number. For example, a new account *Store Equipment* is added to the assets division on page 334 following Prepaid Insurance. The Prepaid Insurance number is 13000. Therefore, the Store Equipment number is 13500.

New accounts added between two existing accounts are assigned the unused middle number. For example, a new account Office Equipment is inserted between Prepaid Insurance (13000) and Store Equipment (13500). The Office Equipment number is 13250. Assigning new numbers between two existing accounts is below.

Existing Account Numbers	Assignment of One New Account Number	Additional Account Numbers Available
13000		13001–13249
	◄————— 13250	
13500		13251–13499

Coding procedures for new accounts, described above, keep the chart of accounts in numeric sequence. The unused middle number is always assigned to new accounts inserted between two existing accounts. Also, the illustration above shows that the numbers 13001–13249 and 13251–13499 are still available. If Delivery Equipment is added between Prepaid Insurance and Office Equipment, the number 13125 is assigned.

Prepaid Insurance	13000
DELIVERY EQUIPMENT	13125
Office Equipment	13250

If no exact middle number is available, either of the two numbers closest to the middle is used. For example, the middle number between

13000 and 13125 is 13062.5. The
number 13062.5 contains six digits and
cannot be assigned in a five-digit coding system. Therefore, either 13062 or
13063 is used.

Prepaid Insurance	13000
NEW ACCOUNT	13062
Delivery Equipment	13125

Allsports uses a five-digit coding system for its chart of accounts as
described above. Allsports' chart of accounts is on page 328.

Chart of accounts setup

The chart of accounts, page 328, shows all balance sheet and income
statement sections. The chart further lists all accounts within each section. The accounts are listed in the same order as they will appear on the
balance sheet and income statement.

Before data from a chart of accounts are entered into a computer, a
special form is prepared. The form shows the account numbers, account
classifications, account titles, and normal balances. An EDP form used to
describe chart of accounts data is called a chart of accounts setup form.

Setup for Allsports' general ledger chart of accounts. General ledger
chart of accounts data are recorded by Ms. Lewis on the chart of accounts
setup form, page 337. This printed form is supplied by the computer
service centre.

Steps in preparing the chart of accounts setup form. Allsports' chart of
accounts setup form is prepared as described below.

1 Enter the business' name in the space provided.

2 Enter the client number, *320*, in the space provided. The client
   number is assigned by the computer service centre and is used for
   all data transmitted to the centre.

3 Enter the account number obtained from the chart of accounts, page
   328. All account titles are identified by numbers in numeric sequence.

4 Enter the account classification code. Code *AS* is used for an asset
   account. Code *LI* is used for a liability account. Code *CA* is used for
   a capital account. Code *RE* is used for a revenue account. Code *CO* is
   used for a cost account. Code *EX* is used for an expense account.

5 Enter the account title just as it will appear on the output.

6 Enter the account normal balance code. Code *Dr* is used for debit.
   Code *Cr* is used for credit.

CHART OF ACCOUNTS SETUP

CLIENT NO. _320_   NAME OF BUSINESS _Allsports_

	ACCOUNT NUMBER	ACCT. CLASS.	ACCOUNT TITLE	NORM. BAL.	
1	1 1 0 0 0	AS	CASH	DR	1
2	1 1 5 0 0	AS	ACCOUNTS RECEIVABLE	DR	2
3	1 2 0 0 0	AS	MERCHANDISE INVENTORY	DR	3
4	1 2 5 0 0	AS	OFFICE SUPPLIES	DR	4
5	1 3 0 0 0	AS	STORE SUPPLIES	DR	5
6	1 3 5 0 0	AS	PREPAID INSURANCE	DR	6
7	1 4 0 0 0	AS	DELIVERY EQUIPMENT	DR	7
8	1 4 5 0 0	AS	OFFICE EQUIPMENT	DR	8
9	1 5 0 0 0	AS	STORE EQUIPMENT	DR	9
10	2 1 0 0 0	LI	ACCOUNTS PAYABLE	CR	10
11	3 1 0 0 0	CA	HELEN LEWIS, CAPITAL	CR	11
12	3 1 5 0 0	CA	HELEN LEWIS, DRAWING	DR	12
13	3 2 0 0 0	CA	SAMUEL SULLIVAN, CAPITAL	CR	13
14	3 2 5 0 0	CA	SAMUEL SULLIVAN, DRAWING	DR	14
15	3 3 0 0 0	CA	INCOME SUMMARY	CR	15
16	4 1 0 0 0	RE	SALES	CR	16
17	5 1 0 0 0	CO	PURCHASES	DR	17
18	6 1 0 0 0	EX	ADVERTISING EXPENSE	DR	18
19	6 1 5 0 0	EX	CREDIT CARD FEE EXPENSE	DR	19
20	6 2 0 0 0	EX	DELIVERY EXPENSE	DR	20
21	6 2 5 0 0	EX	INSURANCE EXPENSE	DR	21
22	6 3 0 0 0	EX	MISCELLANEOUS EXPENSE	DR	22
23	6 3 5 0 0	EX	OFFICE SUPPLIES EXPENSE	DR	23
24	6 4 0 0 0	EX	RENT EXPENSE	DR	24
25	6 4 5 0 0	EX	SALARY EXPENSE	DR	25
26	6 5 0 0 0	EX	STORE SUPPLIES EXPENSE	DR	26

ACCOUNT CLASSIFICATION:
AS = ASSET   CA = CAPITAL   CO = COST
LI = LIABILITY   EX = EXPENSE   RE = REVENUE

PREPARED BY _Helen Lewis_

DATE _1989 02 10_

Chart of accounts setup form for general ledger chart of accounts

Adding new general ledger accounts. A chart of accounts setup form is also used to describe new accounts that are added to a general ledger. For example, a new account Utilities Expense would be included on a chart of accounts setup form as shown below.

CHART OF ACCOUNTS SETUP

CLIENT NO. _320_   NAME OF BUSINESS _Allsports_

	ACCOUNT NUMBER	ACCT. CLASS.	ACCOUNT TITLE	NORM. BAL.	
1	6 5 5 0 0	EX	UTILITIES EXPENSE	DR	1

Chart of accounts setup form adding a new general ledger account

The account number is determined using procedures described on page 335.

Financial statements setup

Formats for financial statements to be prepared by a computer service centre are described on setup forms. An EDP form used to describe output format of financial statements is called a financial statement setup form.

Setup forms for Allsports' financial statements. Allsports' four financial statements are prepared by the computer service centre at the end of each month. *(CONCEPT: Accounting Period Cycle)* Allsports' financial statements are similar to those used by Denim Threads in Chapter 15. (1) Income statement — similar to form on page 285. (2) Distribution of net income statement — similar to form on page 287. (3) Capital statement — similar to form on page 290. (4) Balance sheet — similar to form on page 294. Each statement is described on a financial statement setup form. The printed setup form is supplied by the computer service centre. Completed financial statement setup forms are on page 339–341. Each statement heading (business name, statement name, and date) prints as a result of computer program instructions.

Steps in preparing the setup form. Each of Allsports' financial statement setup forms is prepared as described below.

1 Enter client number, *320*, in space provided.

2 Enter account number from chart of accounts, page 328. The Account Number column is left blank for all headings that appear on the forms. For example, the heading Revenue appears on line 1 of the setup form for the income statement, page 329. Therefore, the Account Number column is left blank.

3 Enter financial statement code. Code *1* is used for Income Statement. Code *2* is used for Distribution of Net Income Statement. Code *3* is used for Capital Statement. Code *4* is used for Balance Sheet.

4 Enter column code. Code *0* is used when only the description is to print. Code *1* is used when both description and amount are to print. Code *2* is used when both description and total amount are to print.

> For codes *1* and *2* a line will print only when an account or heading has a balance. For example, line 22, income statement setup form, page 339, would not print when there is a net income. Likewise, line 21 would not print when there is a net loss.

FINANCIAL STATEMENT SETUP

CLIENT NO. _320_

	ACCOUNT NUMBER	STMT. CODE	COL. CODE	DESCRIPTION	
1		/	0	REVENUE:	1
2	41000	/	1	SALES	2
3		/	0	COST OF MERCHANDISE SOLD:	3
4	12000	/	1	BEGINNING MDSE. INVENTORY	4
5	51000	/	1	PURCHASES	5
6		/	2	TOTAL COST OF MDSE. AVAILABLE	6
7	12000	/	1	ENDING MERCHANDISE INVENTORY	7
8		/	2	COST OF MERCHANDISE SOLD	8
9		/	2	GROSS PROFIT ON SALES	9
10		/	0	EXPENSES:	10
11	61000	/	1	ADVERTISING EXPENSE	11
12	61500	/	1	CREDIT CARD FEE EXPENSE	12
13	62000	/	1	DELIVERY EXPENSE	13
14	62500	/	1	INSURANCE EXPENSE	14
15	63000	/	1	MISCELLANEOUS EXPENSE	15
16	63500	/	1	OFFICE SUPPLIES EXPENSE	16
17	64000	/	1	RENT EXPENSE	17
18	64500	/	1	SALARY EXPENSE	18
19	65000	/	1	STORE SUPPLIES EXPENSE	19
20		/	2	TOTAL EXPENSES	20
21		/	2	NET INCOME	21
22		/	2	NET LOSS	22

STATEMENT CODE:
1 = INCOME STATEMENT
2 = DISTRIBUTION OF NET INCOME STATEMENT
3 = CAPITAL STATEMENT
4 = BALANCE SHEET

COLUMN CODE:
0 = ONLY DESCRIPTION PRINTS
1 = DESCRIPTION AND AMOUNT PRINT
2 = DESCRIPTION AND TOTAL AMOUNT PRINT

PREPARED BY *Helen Lewis*

DATE *1989 02 16*

Setup form for income statement

5 Enter headings and account titles for the body of each financial statement as they will appear on output. An account title or heading must be entered for all possible lines of required output. For example, lines 3 and 4, capital statement setup form, page 340, may not print each time. These lines would print only when an additional investment is made. Likewise, lines 5 or 6, not both, will print. Line 5 will print if there is a net income. Line 6 will print if there is a net loss.

On all financial statements other than the balance sheet, the description is either aligned at the left or indented. When the description is indented, the first letter of the description starts in space 3. On the setup form for the income statement above, line 1, the heading Revenue is left aligned. The account title Sales, line 2, is indented starting in space 3.

FINANCIAL STATEMENT SETUP

CLIENT NO. *320*

	ACCOUNT NUMBER	STMT. CODE	COL. CODE	DESCRIPTION	
1		2	0	HELEN LEWIS	1
2		2	1	60% OF NET INCOME	2
3		2	1	60% OF NET LOSS	3
4		2	0	SAMUEL SULLIVAN	4
5		2	1	40% OF NET INCOME	5
6		2	1	40% OF NET LOSS	6
7		2	2	NET INCOME	7
8		2	2	NET LOSS	8

Setup form for distribution of net income statement

FINANCIAL STATEMENT SETUP

CLIENT NO. *320*

	ACCOUNT NUMBER	STMT. CODE	COL. CODE	DESCRIPTION	
1		3	0	HELEN LEWIS	1
2	31000	3	1	BEGINNING CAPITAL	2
3	31000	3	1	PLUS ADDITIONAL INVESTMENT	3
4		3	2	TOTAL	4
5		3	1	SHARE OF NET INCOME	5
6		3	1	SHARE OF NET LOSS	6
7	31500	3	1	LESS WITHDRAWALS	7
8	31500	3	1	PLUS WITHDRAWALS	8
9		3	2	NET INCREASE IN CAPITAL	9
10		3	2	NET DECREASE IN CAPITAL	10
11		3	2	ENDING CAPITAL	11
12		3	0	SAMUEL SULLIVAN	12
13	32000	3	1	BEGINNING CAPITAL	13
14	32000	3	1	PLUS ADDITIONAL INVESTMENT	14
15		3	2	TOTAL	15
16		3	1	SHARE OF NET INCOME	16
17		3	1	SHARE OF NET LOSS	17
18	32500	3	1	LESS WITHDRAWALS	18
19	32500	3	1	PLUS WITHDRAWALS	19
20		3	2	NET INCREASE IN CAPITAL	20
21		3	2	NET DECREASE IN CAPITAL	21
22		3	2	ENDING CAPITAL	22
23		3	2	TOTAL ENDING CAPITAL	23

STATEMENT CODE:
1 = INCOME STATEMENT
2 = DISTRIBUTION OF NET INCOME STATEMENT
3 = CAPITAL STATEMENT
4 = BALANCE SHEET

COLUMN CODE:
0 = ONLY DESCRIPTION PRINTS
1 = DESCRIPTION AND AMOUNT PRINT
2 = DESCRIPTION AND TOTAL AMOUNT PRINT

PREPARED BY *Helen Lewis*

DATE *1989 02 16*

Setup form for capital statement

FINANCIAL STATEMENT SETUP

CLIENT NO. _320_

	ACCOUNT NUMBER	STMT. CODE	COL. CODE	DESCRIPTION	
1		4	0	ASSETS	1
2	1 1 0 0 0	4	1	CASH	2
3	1 1 5 0 0	4	1	ACCOUNTS RECEIVABLE	3
4	1 2 0 0 0	4	1	MERCHANDISE INVENTORY	4
5	1 2 5 0 0	4	1	OFFICE SUPPLIES	5
6	1 3 0 0 0	4	1	STORE SUPPLIES	6
7	1 3 5 0 0	4	1	PREPAID INSURANCE	7
8	1 4 0 0 0	4	1	DELIVERY EQUIPMENT	8
9	1 4 5 0 0	4	1	OFFICE EQUIPMENT	9
10	1 5 0 0 0	4	1	STORE EQUIPMENT	10
11		4	2	TOTAL ASSETS	11
12		4	0	LIABILITIES	12
13	2 1 0 0 0	4	1	ACCOUNTS PAYABLE	13
14		4	0	CAPITAL	14
15	3 1 0 0 0	4	1	HELEN LEWIS, CAPITAL	15
16	3 2 0 0 0	4	1	SAMUEL SULLIVAN, CAPITAL	16
17		4	2	TOTAL CAPITAL	17
18		4	2	TOTAL LIABILITIES AND CAPITAL	18
19					19
20					20
21					21

STATEMENT CODE:
1 = INCOME STATEMENT
2 = DISTRIBUTION OF NET INCOME STATEMENT
3 = CAPITAL STATEMENT
4 = BALANCE SHEET

COLUMN CODE:
0 = ONLY DESCRIPTION PRINTS
1 = DESCRIPTION AND AMOUNT PRINT
2 = DESCRIPTION AND TOTAL AMOUNT PRINT

PREPARED BY _Helen Lewis_

DATE _1989 02 16_

Setup form for balance sheet

Allsports' report form of balance sheet has section names centred over the account titles. The computer program provides for a maximum of 32 spaces (characters and spaces) per line. The location of the section name ASSETS is figured below.

a. Number of positions available on line 32
b. *Less* number of letters in the section name (Assets) 6

   Remainder 26
c. *Divide* remainder by 2 13
d. This position is the space on the line for writing the first letter of the name 13

On line 1 of the setup form above the word *Assets* is centred starting in space 13. If division by 2 (c. above) results in a fraction, round answer to next nearest whole number. For example, the location of the section name LIABILITIES is figured on the next page.

a. Number of positions available on line.................................. 32
b. *Less* number of letters in section name (Liabilities)................. 11

  Remainder.. 21
c. *Divide* remainder by 2 .... 10.5
d. *Round* to the next nearest whole number. This number is the
   position on the line for writing the first letter of the name 11

On line 12 of the setup form, page 341, the word *Liabilities* is centred starting in space 11.

Processing the chart of accounts and financial statement setup forms

Allsports' completed chart of accounts and financial statement setup forms are sent to the computer service centre. At the computer service centre the data from the forms are entered into the computer. This procedure is described in Chapter 18.

ACCOUNTING TERMS

What is the meaning of each of the following?

1. data
2. data processing
3. data processing system
4. manual data processing
5. automation
6. automated data processing (ADP)
7. input
8. processing
9. storage
10. output
11. computer
12. electronic data processing (EDP)
13. central processing unit (CPU)
14. computer program
15. computer programmer
16. computer service centre
17. chart of accounts setup form
18. financial statement setup form

QUESTIONS FOR INDIVIDUAL STUDY

1. Why is current, accurate, and complete information important to a business?
2. When would a business find a need for faster recording and reporting procedures?
3. What is one way to speed up the recording and reporting procedures?
4. What is one of the most important kinds of data in any business?
5. What must be done to make data useful?
6. What are the two most common types of data processing systems?
7. What are the two steps involved in planning for any data processing system?
8. What are the four data processing phases?
9. Give one example of input.
10. What is the most common type of automated data processing system?
11. What five types of people action are necessary before a computer can process data?
12. What two types of people action are necessary after data have been processed by a computer?
13. Does using a computer change basic accounting principles? Why?
14. Why did Allsports decide to use a computer service centre?

15. What is one of the most important services provided by a computer service centre?

16. What are the five services provided by a computer service centre?

17. What are the two major items a business must consider when deciding on the automated accounting procedures to use?

18. Why did Allsports decide not to automate the subsidiary ledger?

19. What three items must the chart of accounts coding system provide?

20. What is normally the least number of digits used for a business' account number when using EDP?

21. Assume that a new account is to be added following account number 17000. What account number would be assigned to the new account?

22. Assume that a new account is to be added between two existing accounts — 14000 and 14500. What account number would be assigned to the new account?

23. What four types of data are entered on the chart of accounts setup form?

24. What are the four financial statements that Allsports will have the computer service centre prepare?

25. When is column code *0* used on a financial statement setup form?

26. Why must all possible lines of output be entered on a financial statement setup form?

CASES FOR MANAGEMENT DECISION

CASE 1 James King and Ellen Frazer, partners, own and operate a home improvement business called J and E Supply. The business uses a manual accounting system. Ms. Frazer does all the accounting herself. Other business activities have been taking more and more of her time. Consequently, she has been having difficulty finding time to run an efficient accounting system. Ms. Frazer has also considered hiring an accountant. What factors should be considered in making the decision to either automate the accounting system or hire an accountant?

CASE 2 Jason Imports uses a manual accounting system with two-digit, general ledger account numbers. Plans are being made to change to an automated accounting system. The business plans to continue using a two-digit account number. What problems, if any, will a two-digit account number create in an automated accounting system?

DRILLS FOR UNDERSTANDING

DRILL 17-D 1 Adding new general ledger accounts

This drill provides practice in assigning account numbers to new accounts being added to general ledger chart of accounts.

Instructions: A partial chart of accounts is on the next page. New accounts to be added to this chart of accounts are also given. Use the form given in your working papers and assign account numbers to the new accounts. Use the "unused middle number" method of assigning new accounts as explained on page 335

Account Number	Account Title	New Accounts to be Added
12000	Merchandise Inventory	Office Supplies
12500	Store Supplies	Office Equipment
13000	Delivery Equipment	Credit Card Fee Expense
13250	Store Equipment	Insurance Expense
61000	Advertising Expense	Office Supplies Expense
61250	Delivery Expense	Store Supplies Expense
61500	Miscellaneous Expense	
62000	Rent Expense	
62500	Salary Expense	

DRILL 17-D 2   Analysing a chart of accounts setup form

Instructions: Refer to the completed chart of accounts setup form, page 337, and answer the following questions.

1. Who assigns the client number?
2. What is Allsports' client number?
3. What is the maximum number of digits that may be recorded in the Account Number column?
4. How many account classification codes may be entered?
5. What account classification code is entered in the Acct. Class. column for an asset account?
6. What account classification code is entered in the Acct. Class. column for a liability account?
7. What account classification code is entered in the Acct. Class. column for a capital account?
8. What normal balance code is entered in the Norm. Bal. column for an asset account?
9. What normal balance code is entered in the Norm. Bal. column for a liability account?
10. What normal balance code is entered in the Norm. Bal. column for an owner's capital account?

DRILL 17-D 3   Analysing a financial statement setup form

Instructions: Refer to the completed financial statement setup forms, pages 339–341, and answer the following questions.

1. When is the Account Number column left blank?
2. What financial statement code is entered in the Stmt. Code column for an income statement?
3. What financial statement code is entered in the Stmt. Code column for a capital statement?
4. What financial statement code is entered in the Stmt. Code column for a distribution of net income statement?
5. What financial statement code is entered in the Stmt. Code column for a balance sheet?
6. What column code is entered in the Col. Code column when both description and

amount are to print?

7. What column code is entered in the Col. Code column when only the description is to print?

8. What column code is entered in the Col. Code column when both description and total amount are to print?

9. When a description is to be indented, in which space of the Description column is the first letter entered?

10. For Allsports' financial statements, which statement is to have section names centred over account titles?

APPLICATION PROBLEMS

PROBLEM 17-1   Preparing a general ledger chart of accounts setup form

The general ledger chart of accounts for Soto Auto Supply is below.

Account Number	ASSETS	Account Number	REVENUE
11000	Cash	41000	Sales
11500	Accounts Receivable		
12000	Merchandise Inventory		COST OF MERCHANDISE SOLD
12500	Office Supplies	51000	Purchases
13000	Store Supplies		
13500	Prepaid Insurance		EXPENSES
14000	Office Equipment		
14500	Store Equipment	61000	Advertising Expense
		61500	Credit Card Fee Expense
	LIABILITIES	62000	Insurance Expense
		62500	Miscellaneous Expense
21000	Accounts Payable	63000	Office Supplies Expense
		63500	Rent Expense
	CAPITAL	64000	Salary Expense
31000	Alice Soto, Capital	64500	Store Supplies Expense
31500	Alice Soto, Drawing		
32000	Frank Soto, Capital		
32500	Frank Soto, Drawing		
33000	Income Summary		

Instructions: Prepare a general ledger chart of accounts setup form dated February 22 of the current year. Soto Auto Supply's client number is 183. Use chart of accounts setup form, page 337, as a guide.

The chart of accounts prepared in Problem 17-1 is needed to complete Problems 18-1, 19-1, and 19-2, Chapters 18 and 19.

PROBLEM 17-2   Preparing financial statement setup forms

Instructions: Prepare the following financial statement setup forms dated February 23 of the current year for Soto Auto Supply. (1) Income statement. (2) Distribution of net income statement. (3) Capital statement. (4) Balance sheet. Use financial statement setup forms, pages 339–341, as a guide. Use the chart of accounts given in Problem 17-1. The client number is 183. Net income is to be shared equally.

ENRICHMENT PROBLEMS

MASTERY PROBLEM 17-M Adding new accounts to general ledger chart of accounts

The general ledger chart of accounts for the Appliance Centre is given in the working papers. New accounts that are being added appear in their proper order within each division.

Instructions: 1. Assign account numbers to the new accounts. Use the "unused middle number" method described on page 335.

2. Prepare a chart of accounts setup form dated March 16 of the current year for the new accounts. Appliance Centre's client number is 274. Follow procedures given on page 336.

> *The chart of accounts prepared in Mastery Problem 17-M is needed to complete Mastery Problems 18-M and 19-M, Chapters 18 and 19.*

CHALLENGE PROBLEM 17-C Adding new accounts to general ledger chart of accounts

The general ledger chart of accounts for Adkins Leather Goods is given in the working papers. New accounts that are being added appear in their proper order within each division.

Instructions: 1. Assign account numbers to the new accounts. Use the "unused middle number" method described on page 334.

2. Prepare a chart of accounts setup form dated April 19 of the current year for the new accounts. Adkins Leather Goods' client number is 422. Follow procedures given on page 336.

3. Prepare a distribution of net income statement setup form dated April 20 of the current year. Net income is to be distributed as follows: Susan Adkins, 40%; Marsha Gilbert, 25%; Patricia Mason, 35%. Use distribution of net income statement setup form, page 340, as a guide.

> *The chart of accounts prepared in Challenge Problem 17-C is needed to complete Challenge Problems 18-C and 19-C, Chapters 18 and 19.*

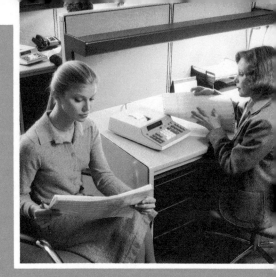

18

Automated General Ledger Accounting: Processing the Chart of Accounts, Setup Forms, and Opening Entry

ENABLING PERFORMANCE TASKS

After studying Chapter 18, you will be able to:

a. Define terminology related to automated general ledger accounting for a merchandising business.
b. Explain automated general ledger accounting principles and practices for processing chart of accounts and financial statement setup data and an opening entry.
c. Analyse a systems flowchart.
d. Prepare a journal entry transmittal for an opening entry.

A business must consider all possible approaches before deciding to change accounting procedures. Immediate and future needs plus the cost of a change must be considered. Chapter 17 described methods followed by Allsports to decide whether or not to change accounting procedures. First, Ms. Lewis learned about the two data processing systems. Based on her study of data processing systems, a number of decisions and preparations were made. Allsports decided to automate the accounting procedures and to use a computer service centre. Also, Allsports decided to automate only the general ledger accounting procedures. New general ledger account numbers were assigned and a general ledger chart of accounts setup form was prepared. Lastly, a financial statement setup form for each financial statement was prepared. The data on the setup forms are processed by computer at the computer service centre.

ELECTRONIC DATA PROCESSING (EDP)

Data moves through a data processing system following a set of procedures. A system using a computer to process data is known as electronic data processing (EDP). In EDP, data are processed with a minimum of human effort. The computer service centre processing accounting data for Allsports uses EDP.

COMPUTER UNITS

Each EDP phase uses a different computer unit. Computer units are machines linked together by electrical cables. Data move from unit to unit through the electrical cables. A computer is divided into four separate units. (1) Central processing unit (CPU). (2) Input unit. (3) Output unit. (4) External storage unit. Each unit serves a special function. The four computer units are shown in the block diagram, below.

The four EDP units are combined to form a computer. However, the central processing unit (CPU) is often referred to as the "computer."

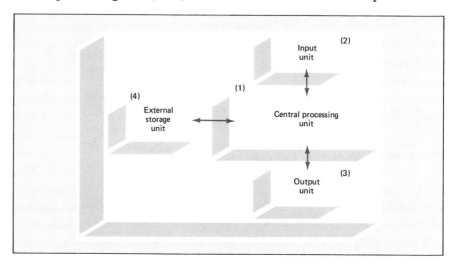

Computer units

Central processing unit (CPU)

A central processing unit (CPU) performs three distinct functions. (1) Controls (directs) all units of a computer. (2) Stores (files) computer instructions and data to be processed. (3) Processes data that have been stored.

Central processing unit

Input unit

Before data are processed by a computer, data must be converted to machine-readable form. A computer unit that converts data from human-readable to machine-readable form is called an input unit. Input units are linked to and controlled by a CPU. A CPU uses program instructions to direct an input unit. Many different kinds of input units may be used by modern day computers.

Direct-entry terminal. A common input unit is a direct-entry terminal. A direct-entry terminal converts data into machine-readable form. A direct-entry terminal looks much like a small television set equipped with a keyboard. Operation of a direct-entry terminal is similar to operation of a regular keyboard. Copy however is displayed on the screen of a terminal. Data entered on a direct-entry terminal are sent to a CPU based on instructions in a computer program. The computer service centre processing Allsports' accounting data uses direct-entry terminals as input units.

Direct-entry terminal

Card punch machine. Some input units read punched cards. Holes are punched in a card in special places. Placement of holes forms a code. The complete code for punching numbers, the alphabet, and special characters in a card is below.

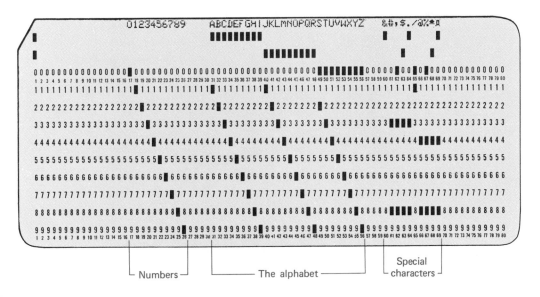

Numbers — The alphabet — Special characters

A machine used to make holes in a card representing data is known as a card punch machine. This machine is also known as a keypunch machine. A card punch machine is not linked to a computer and is not

Punched card

considered an input unit. A card punch machine is used only for preparing punched cards.

Card punch

Card reader

Card reader. Punched cards are read by an input unit known as a card reader. A card reader is linked to a CPU. Data on punched cards are read and sent to a CPU by a card reader. Data on punched cards are sent to a CPU as a result of instructions in a computer program.

Output unit

The end result of processing data by a computer is the computer output. A computer unit that converts data from machine-readable to human-readable form is called an output unit. An output unit is linked to and controlled by a CPU. Many different kinds of output units may be used by computers.

Direct-entry terminal. A direct-entry terminal used as an input unit, page 347, may also function as an output unit. Processing results not requiring a printed copy may be displayed as output on a direct-entry terminal screen.

Printer. An output unit producing a printed, human-readable copy of processed data is known as a printer. A printer is the most common computer output unit. Computer output in printed, human-readable form is called a printout.

Printer

A printer, linked to a CPU, can produce a wide variety of forms and paper sizes. Printers produce output data at high speeds because an entire line is printed at one time.

External storage unit

A CPU has limited space for the internal storage of data. A computer's capacity can be expanded by linking external storage units to a CPU. External storage units attached to and under control of a CPU are sometimes known as auxiliary or secondary storage. Data are transferred from external storage to a CPU as needed during processing. A CPU uses a computer program to direct an external storage unit. Computers may use many different kinds of external storage units.

The computer service centre processing Allsports' accounting data uses a magnetic disk drive as external storage. Data are recorded on removable magnetic disk packs. Disk packs come in different sizes. Each of the disks in a pack looks something like a record for a stereo system. Amount of data that can be stored on a disk pack depends on the size of a pack. Most packs will store several million characters. Disk packs can be removed from a disk drive. Therefore, amount of data that can be stored on magnetic disk packs is unlimited. More external storage can be made available simply by adding new packs.

A magnetic disk drive is the storage unit used for placing data on or reading data from disk packs. A magnetic disk drive is linked to and directed by a CPU.

Disk pack and disk drive

AUTOMATED GENERAL LEDGER ACCOUNTING

Allsports' automated general ledger accounting system requires the same basic accounting principles as a manual system. Only equipment and procedures are different.

Flowcharting procedures

A chart made of symbols showing steps required in EDP is called a systems flowchart. A systems flowchart shows a plan for computer processing of data. After consulting with Ms. Lewis, the computer service centre prepared a systems flowchart for each general ledger accounting job. Common, standard flowchart symbols are on the next page.

A computer program provides instructions to a CPU. Several computer programs may be needed for different parts of an EDP general ledger accounting cycle. Allsports' computer programs are stored on external magnetic disk storage.

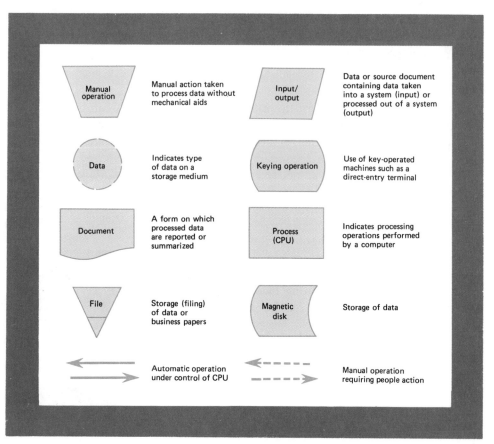

Flowchart symbols

The computer service centre uses computer programs to complete each of the following accounting activities. (1) Recording general ledger chart of accounts on magnetic disk. (2) Recording each financial statement setup form on magnetic disk. (3) Posting an opening entry to general ledger stored on magnetic disk. (4) Posting daily transactions to general ledger stored on magnetic disk. (5) Printing each set of transactions processed. A computer printout of transaction data entered into a computer is called an entry register. An entry register is also known as a transaction register. (6) Preparing work sheet printout with trial balance. (7) Posting adjusting entries to general ledger stored on magnetic disk. (8) Preparing financial statements. (9) Posting closing entries to general ledger stored on magnetic disk. (10) Preparing post-closing trial balance. Processing the chart of accounts setup, financial statement setups, and opening entry is described later in this chapter. The processing of daily transactions and end-of-fiscal-period work is described in Chapter 19.

The systems flowchart, page 353, shows Allsports' complete EDP general ledger accounting cycle. Eight steps are required to process each

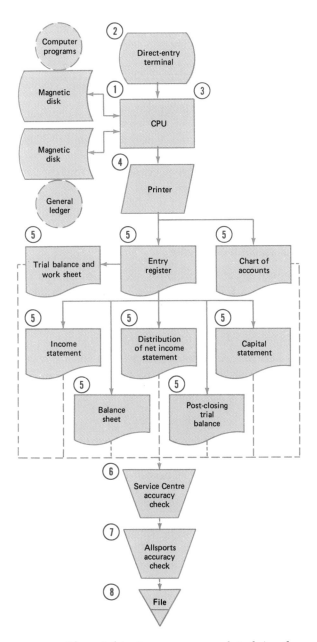

Systems flowchart of EDP general ledger accounting cycle

computer program. The eight steps are completed in the order given below.

1 CPU reads computer program instructions and directs terminal input unit to accept data from terminal keyboard.

2 Data are entered on terminal keyboard and transmitted to CPU.

3 CPU directs data processing based on computer program instructions.

4 CPU transfers processed data to printer output unit.

5 Printer prepares processed data printout.

6 Printout is inspected for accuracy and forwarded to Allsports.

7 Allsports checks printout for accuracy and makes decisions about business progress and condition.

8 Allsports files printout for future reference.

Processing chart of accounts setup data

In manual accounting an account for each account title is opened on a separate ledger page. A ledger is usually a loose-leaf book or sheets in a file. A ledger is a storage phase of manual data processing. In Allsports' EDP general ledger accounting cycle, each account title is stored on magnetic disk. The magnetic disk represents the EDP storage phase.

The computer service centre uses the chart of accounts setup form prepared by Ms. Lewis. The chart of accounts data are entered on the direct-entry terminal keyboard and transferred to the CPU. The CPU, based on computer program instructions, transmits the data to magnetic disk storage. A computer printout of the chart of accounts is prepared and forwarded to Allsports. Ms. Lewis checks the printout for accuracy and then files the chart of accounts printout for future reference. The computer printout of Allsports' chart of accounts is on page 355.

Processing financial statement setup data

The computer service centre uses the financial statement setup forms prepared by Ms. Lewis. Data for each financial statement setup are entered on the direct-entry terminal and sent to the CPU. The CPU, based on computer program instructions, stores the financial statement setup data on magnetic disk. Data are stored on magnetic disk in the same format as described on financial statement setup forms. At the end of a fiscal period, the amounts needed to complete each financial statement are figured by the CPU. These amounts plus the financial statement setup data on magnetic disk provide the information needed to prepare a financial statement.

Setup form data are used by the computer service centre to prepare Allsports' end-of-fiscal-period reports. Computer printouts of the financial statements described on the setup forms are prepared at the end of the fiscal period. (CONCEPT: Accounting Period Cycle) Any future

```
ALLSPORTS
CHART OF ACCOUNTS
GENERAL LEDGER
FEBRUARY 10, 1989
CLIENT NO. 320
```

ACCOUNT NUMBER	ACCOUNT CLASSIFICATION	ACCOUNT TITLE	NORMAL BALANCE
11000	AS	CASH	DR
11500	AS	ACCOUNTS RECEIVABLE	DR
12000	AS	MERCHANDISE INVENTORY	DR
12500	AS	OFFICE SUPPLIES	DR
13000	AS	STORE SUPPLIES	DR
13500	AS	PREPAID INSURANCE	DR
14000	AS	DELIVERY EQUIPMENT	DR
14500	AS	OFFICE EQUIPMENT	DR
15000	AS	STORE EQUIPMENT	DR
21000	LI	ACCOUNTS PAYABLE	CR
31000	CA	HELEN LEWIS, CAPITAL	CR
31500	CA	HELEN LEWIS, DRAWING	DR
32000	CA	SAMUEL SULLIVAN, CAPITAL	CR
32500	CA	SAMUEL SULLIVAN, DRAWING	DR
33000	CA	INCOME SUMMARY	CR
41000	RE	SALES	CR
51000	CO	PURCHASES	DR
61000	EX	ADVERTISING EXPENSE	DR
61500	EX	CREDIT CARD FEE EXPENSE	DR
62000	EX	DELIVERY EXPENSE	DR
62500	EX	INSURANCE EXPENSE	DR
63000	EX	MISCELLANEOUS EXPENSE	DR
63500	EX	OFFICE SUPPLIES EXPENSE	DR
64000	EX	RENT EXPENSE	DR
64500	EX	SALARY EXPENSE	DR
65000	EX	STORE SUPPLIES EXPENSE	DR

changes in a financial statement format require that a new financial statement setup form be prepared.

Computer printout of general ledger chart of accounts

Processing opening entry

Ms. Lewis closes the books for Allsports' manual accounting system on February 28, 1989. She changes to EDP general ledger accounting on March 1, 1989.

Source document for the opening entry. Allsports' February 28, 1989, balance sheet, page 356, is the source document for the opening entry. *(CONCEPT: Objective Evidence)*

Recording the opening entry. When Ms. Lewis started Allsports' manual accounting system, the opening entry was recorded in a general journal. The computer service centre could process the opening entry data directly from a balance sheet. However, the centre prefers that all original documents be retained in a client's accounting office. Ms. Lewis is

Allsports
Balance Sheet
February 28, 1989

Assets		
Cash	940000	
Accounts Receivable	38500	
Merchandise Inventory	2374600	
Office Supplies	18000	
Store Supplies	11500	
Prepaid Insurance	27000	
Delivery Equipment	720000	
Office Equipment	94000	
Store Equipment	340000	
Total Assets		25935000
Liabilities		
Accounts Payable		463000
Capital		
Helen Lewis, Capital	1335600 0	
Samuel Sullivan, Capital	1211600 0	
Total Capital		25472000
Total Liabilities and Capital		25935000

Balance sheet

instructed to write the opening entry data on a special form supplied by the computer service centre. All future entries and transactions will be written on this special form. A special EDP form used for recording accounting transactions is called a journal entry transmittal (JET). A journal entry transmittal (JET) is also known as a transaction transmittal.

A JET form resembles the general journal presently used by Allsports. The arrangement of columns on a JET form has special meaning. Data are recorded on a JET form in the same order as data are entered on direct-entry terminals. The advantages of using a JET form are below.

1. All source documents are kept in the client's accounting department. This method reduces the possibility of documents being lost.
2. Entering data on direct-entry terminal keyboards is faster. Terminal operators read from single sheets the data arranged in the same order as data are entered into a terminal.

Allsports' completed JET form for the opening entry is on page 357. Steps followed by Ms. Lewis in recording Allsports' opening entry on the JET form are below.

1 Enter client number, *320.*

2 Enter date, *1989 03 01.*

	BCH. NO.	REF. NUMBER	ACCOUNT NUMBER	EXPLANATION	DEBIT	CREDIT	
	1	2	3	4	5	6	

JOURNAL ENTRY TRANSMITTAL

CLIENT NO. *320*   DATE *1989 03 01*   PAGE *1* OF *1* PAGES

	BCH. NO.	REF. NUMBER	ACCOUNT NUMBER	EXPLANATION	DEBIT	CREDIT	
1			11000	*Opening Entry*	9400.00		1
2			11500		385.00		2
3			12000		23746.00		3
4			12500		180.00		4
5			13000		115.00		5
6			13500		270.00		6
7			14000		7200.00		7
8			14500		940.00		8
9			15000		3400.00		9
10			21000			4630.00	10
11			31000			13356.00	11
12			32000			12116.00	12

PREPARED BY *Helen Lewis*   PAGE TOTALS 25935.00 25935.00

Journal entry transmittal
for opening entry

3 Enter page number, *1*. (Delay filling in number of pages until total number of pages needed for opening entry has been determined.)

4 Leave Bch. No. column, *Column 1*, blank for opening entry. The opening entry does not require the use of this column. (Use of the Bch. No. column is described in Chapter 19.)

5 Leave Ref. Number column, *Column 2*, blank for opening entry. The opening entry does not require the use of this column. (Use of the Ref. Number column is described in Chapter 19.)

6 Enter account number in Account Number column, *Column 3*, for each general ledger account with a balance. These accounts are listed on the balance sheet, page 356. The account numbers are listed on the chart of accounts, page 328.

7 Enter explanation for entries in Explanation column, *Column 4*. The explanation written for the completed JET form above is *Opening Entry*. Account titles were stored on magnetic disk during the processing of the chart of accounts. Therefore, account titles need not be entered again. Accounts are identified and processed by account number.

8 Enter Debit or Credit amount in appropriate column, *Column 5 or 6*.

9 Add debit entries, *Column 5*, and record sum in space provided for Page Totals.

10 Add credit entries, *Column 6*, and record sum in space provided for Page Totals.

11 Compare the two totals to be sure that debits and credits are equal.

12 Enter number of pages being submitted, *1*, in space provided at top of form.

> If two pages are required for an opening entry, the first page is numbered page 1 of 2 pages. The second page is numbered page 2 of 2 pages. This numbering system helps keep all pages together and assures that all pages have been accounted for.

The complete opening entry JET form is sent to the computer service centre. Opening entry data on the JET form are entered on the direct-entry terminal and sent to the CPU. The CPU, based on computer program instructions, transmits the data to the general ledger stored on magnetic disk. An entry register of the opening entry is then prepared by the printer output unit. Allsports' entry register for the opening entry is below.

```
                              ALLSPORTS
                            ENTRY REGISTER
                            OPENING ENTRY
                            MARCH 1, 1989
CLIENT NO. 320                                        PAGE 1 OF 1 PAGES

ACCOUNT
NUMBER            EXPLANATION             DEBIT            CREDIT

 11000     CASH                      $   9 400.00
 11500     ACCOUNTS RECEIVABLE             385.00
 12000     MERCHANDISE INVENTORY       237 460.00
 12500     OFFICE SUPPLIES                 180.00
 13000     STORE SUPPLIES                  115.00
 13500     PREPAID INSURANCE               270.00
 14000     DELIVERY EQUIPMENT            7 200.00
 14500     OFFICE EQUIPMENT                940.00
 15000     STORE EQUIPMENT              3 400.00
 21000     ACCOUNTS PAYABLE                           $   4 630.00
 31000     HELEN LEWIS, CAPITAL                         133 560.00
 32000     SAMUEL SULLIVAN, CAPITAL                     121 160.00


           TOTALS                    $259 350.00*      $259 350.00*
```

Entry register for opening entry

The entry register is sent to Allsports. Ms. Lewis checks the accuracy of the entry register. The JET form and entry register are then filed for future reference.

In EDP where a card reader is used as an input unit, punched cards are first prepared on a card punch machine. A similar chart of accounts setup form, financial statement setup form, and JET form are used. Completed punched cards are placed in a card reader and data are read into the CPU. CPU processing of data is the same regardless of input unit used.

ACCOUNTING TERMS

What is the meaning of each of the following?

1. input unit
2. output unit

3. printout
4. systems flowchart

5. entry register
6. journal entry transmittal (JET)

QUESTIONS FOR INDIVIDUAL STUDY

1. What are the four computer units?
2. What computer unit is often referred to as the "computer"?
3. What are the three distinct functions of a CPU?
4. What is the major difference between a direct-entry terminal and a regular keyboard?
5. What machine makes holes in a card to represent data?
6. What input unit reads punched cards?
7. What is the end result of processing data by a computer?
8. What is the most common computer output unit?

9. What external storage unit is used by the computer service centre that processes Allsports' data?
10. Why is there no limit to the amount of data stored on magnetic disk packs?
11. What type of chart shows the data flow among EDP machines?
12. What is Allsports' opening entry source document for the general ledger accounts?
13. What form commonly used in manual accounting resembles the JET form used in EDP?
14. What are the advantages of using a JET form?

CASES FOR MANAGEMENT DECISION

CASE 1 Oakwood Gift Centre's accounting data are processed by a computer service centre. Source documents for transactions are sent directly to the computer service centre for processing. Recently, one set of source documents got lost in the mail and was never recovered. The loss of these source documents created serious problems in accounting for the data that were lost. How could the method of sending transactions to the computer service centre be improved?

CASE 2 Ferguson Supply uses a computer service centre to process its accounting data. Ferguson Supply prepares a JET form for data to be processed by the computer service centre. A direct-entry terminal is used at the computer service centre to key in the transaction data for computer processing. Ferguson Supply is considering installing a card punch machine to prepare data for computer processing. Ferguson Supply feels time could be saved because data could be keyed directly from source documents. Also, they would not have to pay the computer service centre for preparing the input data. The punched cards could be mailed to the computer service centre for processing directly on the computer. What factors should Ferguson Supply consider before deciding whether or not to install a card punch machine?

DRILL FOR UNDERSTANDING

DRILL 18-D 1   Analysing a systems flowchart

Instructions: Refer to Allsports' systems flowchart, page 353, and answer the following questions.

1. How many total steps are required to complete Allsports' EDP general ledger accounting system?
2. In which step does the processing take place?
3. How many output reports are prepared?
4. Which steps indicate manual operations?
5. What external storage is used for computer program storage?
6. What external storage is used for general ledger storage?
7. In which step are output reports prepared?
8. In which step does Allsports receive processed data output?
9. Why is the line broken between steps 6 and 7?
10. In which step are data entered into the computer?

APPLICATION PROBLEM

PROBLEM 18-1   Recording an opening entry in an EDP general ledger accounting system

The chart of accounts prepared in Problem 17-1, Chapter 17, is needed to complete Problem 18-1.

Soto Auto Supply's balance sheet for February 28 of the current year is below.

<table>
<tr><td colspan="4" align="center">Soto Auto Supply
Balance Sheet
February 28, 19—</td></tr>
<tr><td align="center">Assets</td><td></td><td></td><td></td></tr>
<tr><td>Cash...</td><td align="right">9 850 00</td><td></td><td></td></tr>
<tr><td>Accounts Receivable...........................</td><td align="right">840 00</td><td></td><td></td></tr>
<tr><td>Merchandise Inventory........................</td><td align="right">225 420 00</td><td></td><td></td></tr>
<tr><td>Office Supplies ....</td><td align="right">670 00</td><td></td><td></td></tr>
<tr><td>Store Supplies ....</td><td align="right">410 00</td><td></td><td></td></tr>
<tr><td>Prepaid Insurance ....</td><td align="right">930 00</td><td></td><td></td></tr>
<tr><td>Office Equipment...............................</td><td align="right">1 100 00</td><td></td><td></td></tr>
<tr><td>Store Equipment...............................</td><td align="right">1 840 00</td><td></td><td></td></tr>
<tr><td>Total Assets...................................</td><td></td><td align="right">241 060 00</td><td></td></tr>
<tr><td align="center">Liabilities</td><td></td><td></td><td></td></tr>
<tr><td>Accounts Payable..............................</td><td></td><td align="right">4 680 00</td><td></td></tr>
<tr><td align="center">Capital</td><td></td><td></td><td></td></tr>
<tr><td>Alice Soto, Capital.............................</td><td align="right">119 840 00</td><td></td><td></td></tr>
<tr><td>Frank Soto, Capital............................</td><td align="right">116 540 00</td><td></td><td></td></tr>
<tr><td>Total Capital...................................</td><td></td><td align="right">236 380 00</td><td></td></tr>
<tr><td>Total Liabilities and Capital ....</td><td></td><td align="right">241 060 00</td><td></td></tr>
</table>

Instructions: Record the opening entry for Soto Auto Supply, Client No. 183, on a journal entry transmittal. Use March 1 of the current year as the date of the opening entry. Use account numbers from the chart of accounts prepared in Problem 17-1. Use the journal entry transmittal, page 357, as a model.

ENRICHMENT PROBLEMS

MASTERY PROBLEM 18-M   Recording an opening entry in an EDP general ledger accounting system

The chart of accounts prepared in Mastery Problem 17-M, Chapter 17, is needed to complete Mastery Problem 18-M.

Appliance Centre's balance sheet for March 31 of the current year is below.

Appliance Centre Balance Sheet March 31, 19--				
Assets				
Cash..	8 760 00			
Accounts Receivable...........................	690 00			
Merchandise Inventory........................	190 520 00			
Office Supplies	530 00			
Store Supplies	315 00			
Prepaid Insurance	640 00			
Delivery Equipment	7 620 00			
Office Equipment................................	955 00			
Store Equipment................................	730 00			
Total Assets.....................................		210 760 00		
Liabilities				
Accounts Payable...............................		3 480 00		
Capital				
Carol Bennett, Capital.........................	104 510 00			
Steve Franklin, Capital	102 770 00			
Total Capital.....................................		207 280 00		
Total Liabilities and Capital		210 760 00		

Instructions: Record the opening entry for the Appliance Centre, Client No. 274, on a journal entry transmittal. Use April 1, of the current year as the date of the opening entry. Use account numbers from the chart of accounts prepared in Mastery Problem 17-M.

CHALLENGE PROBLEM 18-C   Recording an opening entry in an EDP general ledger accounting system

The chart of accounts prepared in Challenge Problem 17-C, Chapter 17, is needed to complete Challenge Problem 18-C.

Adkins Leather Goods' balance sheet for April 30 of the current year is on the next page.

Adkins Leather Goods Balance Sheet April 30, 19--							
Assets							
Cash...	9	100	00				
Accounts Receivable.........................		735	00				
Merchandise Inventory......................	205	200	00				
Office Supplies		675	00				
Store Supplies		460	00				
Prepaid Insurance		740	00				
Office Equipment.............................	1	240	00				
Store Equipment..............................		830	00				
Total Assets...................................				218	980	00	
Liabilities							
Accounts Payable............................				3	860	00	
Capital							
Susan Adkins, Capital.......................	90	120	00				
Marsha Gilbert, Capital.....................	50	000	00				
Patricia Mason, Capital.....................	75	000	00				
Total Capital..................................				215	120	00	
Total Liabilities and Capital..............				218	980	00	

Instructions: Record the opening entry for Adkins Leather Goods, Client No. 422, on a journal entry transmittal. Use May 1 of the current year as the date of the opening entry. Use account numbers from the chart of accounts prepared in Challenge Problem 17-C.

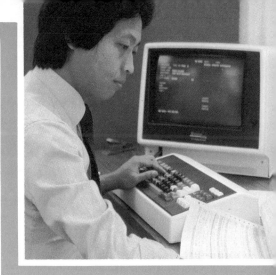

19

Automated General Ledger Accounting: Processing Transactions and End-of-Fiscal-Period Reports

ENABLING PERFORMANCE TASKS

After studying Chapter 19, you will be able to:

a. Define terminology related to automated general ledger accounting for a merchandising business.
b. Explain automated general ledger accounting principles and practices for processing transactions and end-of-fiscal-period reports.
c. Analyse a completed journal entry transmittal.
d. Prepare a journal entry transmittal with batched transactions.
e. Plan adjusting entries on a work sheet printout and complete the work sheet printout.
f. Record adjusting and closing entries on a journal entry transmittal.

Chapter 18 described electronic data processing (EDP) procedures used by a computer service centre to process Allsports' data. Allsports prepared and submitted three types of forms. (1) Chart of accounts setup form. (2) Financial statement setup forms. (3) Journal entry transmittal (JET) form for opening entry. Data submitted on these forms was processed by the computer service centre. Allsports verified the printouts received from the computer centre. Now, Ms. Lewis submits JET forms describing accounting transactions to the computer service centre. Also, Ms. Lewis submits data needed by the computer centre to prepare Allsports' end-of-fiscal-period financial statements.

PROCESSING TRANSACTIONS

All accounting transactions are submitted on JET forms weekly to the computer service centre for processing.

Arranging transaction data for EDP processing

Source documents are required as objective evidence for each transaction processed through EDP procedures. *(CONCEPT: Objective Evidence)* Manual and automated accounting transactions use the same types of source documents. Methods of arranging transactions for EDP vary depending on the business involved. Allsports uses the following methods.

Batching transactions. Ms. Lewis records all transactions on a JET form. Transactions are manually arranged by groups before the entries are made. For example, accounts payable transactions are in one group and cash payments transactions are in another group. Arranging similar transaction documents in one group is called batching. Batching reduces the number of journal entries to be made. For example, five accounts payable transactions would require five accounts payable credit entries. By batching, the five accounts payable transactions are combined into one entry with only one accounts payable credit entry.

Allsports arranges daily transactions into five batches. (1) Accounts payable. (2) Cash payments. (3) Accounts receivable. (4) Cash receipts. (5) General.

Assigning reference numbers to batched transactions. Allsports combines all daily transactions on a weekly JET form. As transactions are completed during a week, Ms. Lewis files each transaction source document according to one of the five batches. On the next business day following the close of a week's business, Ms. Lewis prepares a weekly JET form. Transactions are entered on the weekly JET forms in batches according to the order given on page 365. Some source documents may affect the same general ledger account. For example, on March 6, 1989, Ms. Lewis has six source documents in the accounts payable batch. (a) Three source documents for office supplies bought on account. (b) One source document for store supplies bought on account. (c) Two source documents for merchandise purchased on account. Data from the six source documents are combined and recorded as one entry. When data are combined into one entry, some reference must be made to individual source documents. Using individual source document numbers becomes cumbersome when many source documents affect a single general ledger account in a single week.

Allsports uses a number to identify a single or a group of source documents for a week's batched transactions. A number used to identify a single or a group of source documents is called a reference number. The reference number is written on the source documents and on the JET form. For example, the following are the total data for the accounts payable batch on March 6, 1989.

Bought office supplies on account....	$140.00.	M14.	
Bought office supplies on account....	$ 40.00.	M15.	Ref. No. 1000
Bought office supplies on account....	$ 60.00.	M16.	
Bought store supplies on account	$130.00.	M17.	Ref. No. 1001
Purchased merchandise on account .	$460.00.	P21.	Ref. No. 1002
Purchased merchandise on account .	$165.00.	P22.	
Total accounts payable...............	$995.00.		

Thus, all like kinds of source documents in the same batch have the same reference number written on them. Three memorandums for office supplies bought on account (M14, M15, and M16) have reference number 1000 written on them. The single memorandum for store supplies bought on account (M17) has reference number 1001 written on it. The two purchase invoices (P21 and P22) have reference number 1002 written on them. The accounts payable batch entry is entered on the JET form, page 367, lines 1–4. Source documents may be traced by locating the source documents with reference numbers 1000, 1001, and 1002 written on them.

Allsports assigns reference numbers sequentially in the order given below.

Batches	Reference Numbers
Accounts Payable	1000–1999
Cash Payments...................................	2000–2999
Accounts Receivable	3000–3999
Cash Receipts	4000–4999
General..	5000–5999

Reference numbers 1000, 1001, 1002 were used for the accounts payable batch on March 6, 1989, JET form. On the JET form for the next week, the accounts payable reference numbers will start with 1003.

Recording accounts payable transactions

All supplies and equipment bought on account and all purchases of merchandise on account are included in the accounts payable batch. Total accounts payable transactions are recorded in general ledger accounts. Allsports' accounts payable transactions for week ended March 6, 1989, are above. The accounts payable transactions showing only total amounts affecting general ledger accounts are below.

Bought office supplies on account..................	*$240.00.*	*Ref. No. 1000.*
Bought store supplies on account..................	*$130.00.*	*Ref. No. 1001.*
Purchased merchandise on account................	*$625.00.*	*Ref. No. 1002.*
Total accounts payable..................................	*$995.00.*	

ACCOUNTS PAYABLE BATCH

Office Supplies
240.00

Store Supplies
130.00

Purchases
625.00

Accounts Payable
995.00

Analysing batched accounts payable transactions. Office Supplies is debited for the total office supplies bought on account, *$240.00*. Store Supplies is debited for the total store supplies bought on account, *$130.00*. Purchases is debited for the total purchases of merchandise on account, *$625.00*. Accounts Payable is credited for the total supplies bought and merchandise purchased on account, *$995.00*.

Recording batched accounts payable transactions on a JET form. The accounts payable batch for week ended March 6, 1989, is on lines 1–4, JET form, page 367.

Steps in recording the accounts payable batch on a JET form are below.

1 Enter client number, *320*.

2 Enter date, *1989 03 06*. Enter the date of the last business day for the week's transactions.

3 Enter page number, *1*.

4 Enter batch number, *1*, in Bch. No. column, *Column 1*. The batch number is entered just once for each batch. Lines 1–4 contain data for the first batch.

5 Enter reference numbers in Ref. Number column, *Column 2*. Each reference number refers to a single or a group of source documents. The source documents for batch 1 are memorandums and purchase invoices. On line 4, since there is no related source document, no reference number is entered in the Ref. Number column. Reference numbers are entered on the same line as the general ledger account to which the reference number applies. For example, *1000* is entered on line 1 for Office Supplies.

6 Enter account number in *Column 3*. Use account numbers from the chart of accounts, page 326. For example, on line 1, enter *12500*, the account number for Office Supplies. As data are recorded on remaining lines, enter the numbers of the accounts affected.

7 Enter explanation of transactions included in batch in *Column 4* on first line of batch. For example, the batch 1 explanation written in Column 4, line 1, is Accounts Payable. Account titles were stored on magnetic disk during the processing of the chart of accounts. There-

fore, the account titles need not be entered again. Accounts are identified and processed by account number.

8 Enter Debit or Credit amounts in appropriate column, *Column 5 or 6.*

JOURNAL ENTRY TRANSMITTAL

CLIENT NO. 320   DATE 1989 03 06   PAGE 1 OF 1 PAGES

	BCH. NO.	REF. NUMBER	ACCOUNT NUMBER	EXPLANATION	DEBIT	CREDIT	
1	1	1000	12500	Accounts Payable	24000		1
2		1001	13000		13000		2
3		1002	51000		62500		3
4			21000			99500	4
5	2	2000	12500	Cash Payments	16000		5
6		2001	13000		10500		6
7		2002	13500		68000		7
8		2003	21000		54000		8
9		2004	31500		60000		9
10		2005	32500		60000		10
11		2006	51000		43000		11
12		2007	63000		1800		12
13		2008	64000		80000		13
14		2009	64500		100000		14
15			11000			49330	15
16	3	3000	11500	Accounts Receivable	9200		16
17			41000			9200	17
18	4		11000	Cash Receipts	38050		18
19		4000	11500			3850	19
20		4001	41000			34200	20
21	5	5000	31500	General	4200		21
22		5001	32500		7800		22
23			51000			12000	23
24							24
25							25
26							26

PREPARED BY Helen Lewis   PAGE TOTALS   99450 0   99450 0

Journal entry transmittal for batched transactions

Recording cash payments transactions

The cash payments batch includes payments for expenses, withdrawals, and payments on account. Allsports had the following cash payments transactions for week ended March 6, 1989.

Bought office supplies for cash	$ 160.00.	Ref. No. 2000.
Bought store supplies for cash	$ 105.00.	Ref. No. 2001.
Paid for insurance policy	$ 680.00.	Ref. No. 2002.
Paid on account	$ 540.00.	Ref. No. 2003.
Helen Lewis, partner, withdrew cash	$ 600.00.	Ref. No. 2004.
Samuel Sullivan, partner, withdrew cash	$ 600.00.	Ref. No. 2005.
Purchased merchandise for cash	$ 430.00.	Ref. No. 2006.
Paid miscellaneous expense	$ 18.00.	Ref. No. 2007.
Paid March rent	$ 800.00.	Ref. No. 2008.
Paid salaries	$1 000.00.	Ref. No. 2009.
Total cash payments	$4 933.00.	

CASH PAYMENTS BATCH

Office Supplies

160.00

Store Supplies

105.00

Prepaid Insurance

680.00

Accounts Payable

540.00

Helen Lewis, Drawing

600.00

Samuel Sullivan, Drawing

600.00

Purchases

430.00

Miscellaneous Expense

18.00

Rent Expense

800.00

Salary Expense

1 000.00

Cash

· 4 933.00

Analysing batched cash payments transactions. Office Supplies is debited for total office supplies bought for cash, *$160.00*. Store Supplies is debited for total store supplies bought for cash, *$105.00*. Prepaid Insurance is debited for total cash paid for insurance policy, *$680.00*. Accounts Payable is debited for total cash paid on account, *$540.00*. Helen Lewis, Drawing, and Samuel Sullivan, Drawing, are debited for cash withdrawals, *$600.00* each. Purchases is debited for total merchandise purchased for cash, *$430.00*. Miscellaneous Expense is debited for total cash paid for miscellaneous items, *$18.00*. Rent Expense is debited, *$800.00*. Salary Expense is debited, *$1 000.00*. Cash is credited, *$4 933.00*, for total cash payments for week ended March 6, 1989.

Recording batched cash payments on a JET form. The batched cash payments for week ended March 6, 1989, are on lines 5–15, JET form, page 367. Data are recorded in each column in the same way as data recorded for batch 1. The cash payments batch is the second one recorded. Therefore, the number 2 is entered in the Bch. No. column, *Column 1*, line 5. The words *Cash Payments* are written in the Explanation column, *Column 4*, line 5, to explain the transactions included in batch 2. The single credit to Cash, *$4 933.00*, line 15, has no related source document. Therefore, the Ref. Number column, *Column 2*, line 15, is left blank.

Recording accounts receivable transactions

All sales of merchandise on account transactions are included in the accounts receivable batch. Allsports had the following accounts receivable transactions for week ended March 6, 1989.

Sold merchandise on account .	$92.00.	Ref. No. 3000.
Total accounts receivable	$92.00.	

Analysing batched accounts receivable transactions. Accounts Receivable is debited and Sales is credited for the total sales of merchandise on account, *$92.00*.

ACCOUNTS RECEIVABLE
BATCH

Accounts Receivable	
92.00	

Sales	
	92.00

Recording batched accounts receivable on a JET form. The accounts receivable batch for week ended March 6, 1989, is on lines 16–17, JET form, page 367. The accounts receivable batch is the third one recorded. Therefore, the number 3 is entered in the Bch. No. column, *Column 1*, line 16. The words *Accounts Receivable* are written in the Explanation column, *Column 4*, line 16, to explain the transactions included in batch 3. The single credit to Sales, *$92.00*, has no related source document. Therefore, the Ref. Number column, *Column 2*, line 17, is left blank.

Recording cash receipts transactions

The cash receipts batch includes total cash received on account and total cash received from sales. Allsports had the following cash receipts transactions for week ended March 6, 1989.

Cash received on account..................................	*$ 385.00. Ref. No. 4000.*
Cash received from sales	*$3 420.00. Ref. No. 4001.*
Total cash receipts	*$3 805.00.*

Analysing batched cash receipts transactions. Cash is debited for total cash received, *$3 805.00*. Accounts Receivable is credited for total cash received on account, *$385.00*. Sales is credited for total cash received from sales, *$3 420.00*.

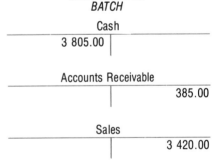

CASH RECEIPTS
BATCH

Cash	
3 805.00	

Accounts Receivable	
	385.00

Sales	
	3 420.00

Recording batched cash receipts on a JET form. The cash receipts batch for week ended March 6, 1989, is on lines 18–20, JET form, page 367. The cash receipts batch is the fourth one recorded. Therefore, the number 4 is entered in the Bch. No. column, *Column 1*, line 18. The single debit to Cash, *$3 805.00*, has no related source document. Therefore, the Ref. Number column, *Column 2*, line 18, is left blank. The words *Cash Receipts* are written in the Explanation column, *Column 4*, line 18, to explain the transactions included in batch 4.

Recording general transactions

The general batch includes all transactions that cannot be included in any of the other four batches. One example is the withdrawal of merchandise. Allsports had the following general transactions for week ended March 6, 1989.

Helen Lewis, partner, withdrew merchandise... $ 42.00. *Ref. No. 5000.*
Samuel Sullivan, partner, withdrew merchan-
dise... $ 78.00. *Ref. No. 5001.*
Total withdrawals of merchandise.................. $120.00.

*GENERAL TRANSACTIONS
BATCH*

Helen Lewis, Drawing

| 42.00 | |

Samuel Sullivan, Drawing

| 78.00 | |

Purchases

| | 120.00 |

Analysing batched general transactions. Helen Lewis, Drawing, is debited for her withdrawal of merchandise, *$42.00.* Samuel Sullivan, Drawing, is debited for his withdrawal of merchandise, *$78.00.* Purchases is credited for the total withdrawal of merchandise by the partners, *$120.00.*

Recording batched general transactions on a JET form. The general batch for week ended March 6, 1989, is on lines 21–23, JET form, page 367. The general transactions batch is the fifth one recorded. Therefore, the number *5* is entered in the Bch. No. column, *Column 1*, line 21. The word *General* is written in the Explanation column, *Column 4*, line 21, to explain the transactions included in batch 5. The single credit to Purchases, *$120.00*, has no related source document. Therefore, the Ref. Number column, *Column 2*, line 23, is left blank.

When a JET form page is full, Ms. Lewis does the following to complete the page.

1 Add debit entries and record sum in space provided for Page Totals, *Column 5.*

2 Add credit entries and record sum in space provided for Page Totals, *Column 6.*

3 Compare the two totals to be sure debits equal credits.

4 Enter number of pages being submitted, *1*, in the space provided at top of form.

> If two pages had been required for these five batches, the first page is numbered page 1 of 2 pages. The second page is numbered page 2 of 2 pages. This numbering system helps keep all pages together and assures that all pages have been accounted for.

Allsports' completed JET form is sent to the computer service centre. Data on the JET form are entered on a direct-entry terminal and sent to the CPU. The CPU, based on computer program, posts transaction data to general ledger accounts stored on magnetic disk.

After posting general ledger transaction data, the computer prints an entry register. Total debits and total credits are figured by the computer and printed on the entry register. Totals on an entry register are identified with an asterisk (*) next to each total. The computer operator compares entry register totals with totals on the JET form prepared by Ms. Lewis. This comparison is made to prove accuracy of data entered and processed by the computer. A copy of Allsports' entry register based on the JET form, page 367, is below. Total debits and total credits on the entry register below and JET form, page 367, are the same. Therefore, the entry register data are assumed to be correct.

Entry register for batched transactions

```
                                ALLSPORTS
                             ENTRY REGISTER
                      FOR WEEK ENDED MARCH 6, 1989
  CLIENT NO. 320                                    PAGE 1 OF 1 PAGES

  LINE   BATCH   REFERENCE   ACCOUNT
   NO.    NO.      NO.        NO.      EXPLANATION           DEBIT      CREDIT

    1      1      1000       12500   OFFICE SUPPLIES      $   240.00
    2             1001       13000   STORE SUPPLIES           130.00
    3             1002       51000   PURCHASES                625.00
    4                        21000      ACCOUNTS PAYABLE                 $  995.00

    5      2      2000       12500   OFFICE SUPPLIES          160.00
    6             2001       13000   STORE SUPPLIES           105.00
    7             2002       13500   PREPAID INSURANCE        680.00
    8             2003       21000   ACCOUNTS PAYABLE         540.00
    9             2004       31500   HELEN LEWIS, DRAWING     600.00
   10             2005       32500   SAMUEL SULLIVAN, DRAWING 600.00
   11             2006       51000   PURCHASES               430.00
   12             2007       63000   MISCELLANEOUS EXPENSE    18.00
   13             2008       64000   RENT EXPENSE            800.00
   14             2009       64500   SALARY EXPENSE        1 000.00
   15                        11000      CASH                              4 933.00

   16      3      3000       11500   ACCOUNTS RECEIVABLE      92.00
   17                        41000      SALES                               92.00

   18      4                 11000   CASH                   3 805.00
   19             4000       11500      ACCOUNTS RECEIVABLE               385.00
   20             4001       41000      SALES                           3 420.00

   21      5      5000       31500   HELEN LEWIS, DRAWING     42.00
   22             5001       32500   SAMUEL SULLIVAN, DRAWING 78.00
   23                        51000      PURCHASES                         120.00

                                    TOTALS           $9 945.00*   $9 945.00*
```

PROCESSING END-OF-FISCAL-PERIOD WORK

Financial statements are prepared by the computer service centre at the end of each monthly fiscal period. *(CONCEPT: Accounting Period Cycle)*

Four financial statements are prepared. (1) Income statement. (2) Distribution of net income statement. (3) Capital statement. (4) Balance sheet. Financial statement printouts follow the format indicated on financial statement setup forms prepared by Ms. Lewis, pages 339–341. All possible headings and account titles for the body of each financial statement are stored on magnetic disk. *(CONCEPT: Adequate Disclosure)* These data were stored when setup forms were processed as described in Chapter 17. The computer determines the amount for each printout line. Before preparing financial statement printouts, two things are done. (1) The computer service centre prepares a trial balance and work sheet printout. The trial balance is printed on the work sheet to prove equality of general ledger debits and credits. (2) Ms. Lewis plans adjustments to general ledger accounts on the trial balance and work sheet printout.

Preparing a work sheet

The computer service centre prepares a trial balance and a work sheet printout at the end of each fiscal period. The computer, based on a computer program, figures and arranges the general ledger data for the trial balance. The work sheet printout with completed trial balance is sent to Allsports. The work sheet printout provides spaces for planning adjusting entries and extending amounts to income statement and balance sheet columns.

Planning adjusting entries

At the end of a fiscal period, certain general ledger accounts need to be brought up to date. Adjustments to these general ledger accounts are planned and entered in the Adjustments columns of the work sheet printout. The data needed for Allsports' adjustments are below.

Ending merchandise inventory	$232 500.00
Ending office supplies inventory	455.00
Ending store supplies inventory	235.00
Ending value of insurance policies	804.00

Allsports follows the same procedures as Denim Threads, Chapter 14, for completing the work sheet. Allsports' completed work sheet is on page 371.

Recording adjusting entries

Each adjustment must be processed by computer and posted to general ledger accounts stored on magnetic disk. Allsports' five adjusting entries are shown in the completed work sheet printout, page 373. Ms. Lewis records the adjusting entries on a JET form. The completed JET form for the adjusting entries is on page 374.

ALLSPORTS
WORK SHEET
FOR MONTH ENDED MARCH 31, 1989

	TRIAL BALANCE DEBIT	TRIAL BALANCE CREDIT	ADJUSTMENTS DEBIT	ADJUSTMENTS CREDIT	INCOME STATEMENT DEBIT	INCOME STATEMENT CREDIT	BALANCE SHEET DEBIT	BALANCE SHEET CREDIT
CASH	$ 16 420.00						16 420.00	
ACCOUNTS RECEIVABLE	580.00						580.00	
MERCHANDISE INVENTORY	237 460.00		(a) 232 500.00	(b) 237 460.00			232 500.00	
OFFICE SUPPLIES	580.00			(c) 125.00			455.00	
STORE SUPPLIES	350.00			(d) 115.00			235.00	
PREPAID INSURANCE	950.00			(e) 146.00			804.00	
DELIVERY EQUIPMENT	7 200.00						7 200.00	
OFFICE EQUIPMENT	940.00						940.00	
STORE EQUIPMENT	3 400.00						3 400.00	
ACCOUNTS PAYABLE		$ 4 256.00						4 256.00
HELEN LEWIS, CAPITAL		133 560.00						133 560.00
HELEN LEWIS, DRAWING	672.00						672.00	
SAMUEL SULLIVAN, CAPITAL		121 160.00						121 160.00
SAMUEL SULLIVAN, DRAWING	690.00						690.00	
INCOME SUMMARY			(b) 237 460.00	(a) 232 500.00	237 460.00	232 500.00		
SALES		16 840.00				16 840.00		
PURCHASES	3 240.00				3 240.00			
ADVERTISING EXPENSE	66.00				66.00			
CREDIT CARD FEE EXPENSE	252.00				252.00			
DELIVERY EXPENSE	86.00				86.00			
INSURANCE EXPENSE			(e) 146.00		146.00			
MISCELLANEOUS EXPENSE	130.00				130.00			
OFFICE SUPPLIES EXPENSE			(c) 125.00		125.00			
RENT EXPENSE	800.00				800.00			
SALARY EXPENSE	2 000.00				2 000.00			
STORE SUPPLIES EXPENSE			(d) 115.00		115.00			
	$275 816.00	$275 816.00	470 346.00	470 346.00	244 420.00	249 340.00	263 896.00	258 976.00
Net Income					4 920.00			4 920.00
					249 340.00	249 340.00	263 896.00	263 896.00

Completed work sheet printout

JOURNAL ENTRY TRANSMITTAL

CLIENT NO. *320*   DATE *1989 03 31*   PAGE *1* OF *1* PAGES

	BCH. NO.	REF. NUMBER	ACCOUNT NUMBER	EXPLANATION	DEBIT	CREDIT	
1	1		33000	*Adjusting Entries*	2374600.0		1
2			12000			2374600.0	2
3			12000		2325000.0		3
4			33000			2325000.0	4
5			63500		12500		5
6			12500			12500	6
7			65000		11500		7
8			13000			11500	8
9			62500		14600		9
10			13500			14600	10

PREPARED BY *Helen Lewis*   PAGE TOTALS 4703460.0 4703460.0

Journal entry transmittal
for adjusting entries

The completed JET form is sent to the computer service centre. Data are entered on a direct-entry terminal. The computer posts the adjusting entries to general ledger accounts stored on magnetic disk. The computer also prepares an entry register for adjustments. Allsports' entry register for adjustments is below. Total debits and total credits on the entry register below and JET form above are the same. Therefore, the entry register data for adjustments are assumed to be correct.

ALLSPORTS
ENTRY REGISTER
ADJUSTING ENTRIES
MARCH 31, 1989

CLIENT NO. 320   PAGE 1 OF 1 PAGES

LINE NO.	BATCH NO.	REFERENCE NO.	ACCOUNT NO.	EXPLANATION	DEBIT	CREDIT
1	1		33000	INCOME SUMMARY	$237 460.00	
2			12000	MERCHANDISE INVENTORY		$237 460.00
3			12000	MERCHANDISE INVENTORY	232 500.00	
4			33000	INCOME SUMMARY		232 500.00
5			63500	OFFICE SUPPLIES EXPENSE	125.00	
6			12500	OFFICE SUPPLIES		125.00
7			65000	STORE SUPPLIES EXPENSE	115.00	
8			13000	STORE SUPPLIES		115.00
9			62500	INSURANCE EXPENSE	146.00	
10			13500	PREPAID INSURANCE		146.00
				TOTALS	$470 346.00*	$470 346.00*

Entry register for
adjustments

Preparing financial statements

In manual accounting the financial statements are prepared from a completed work sheet. In automated accounting the financial statements are prepared by a computer from data stored on magnetic disk. Allsports' financial statements are below and on page 376.

The entry register and financial statements prepared by the computer are forwarded to Allsports. Ms. Lewis inspects the financial statements to make business decisions. These decisions are based on the financial progress and condition at the end of the fiscal period. The entry register and financial statements are filed for future reference.

Income statement printout

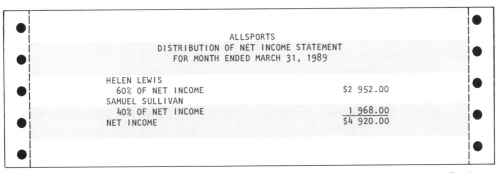

Distribution of net income statement printout

```
ALLSPORTS
CAPITAL STATEMENT
FOR MONTH ENDED MARCH 31, 1989

HELEN LEWIS
  BEGINNING CAPITAL                              $133 560.00
  SHARE OF NET INCOME            $2 952.00
  LESS WITHDRAWALS                  672.00
  NET INCREASE IN CAPITAL                          2 280.00
  ENDING CAPITAL                                               $135 840.00
SAMUEL SULLIVAN
  BEGINNING CAPITAL                               121 160.00
  SHARE OF NET INCOME            $1 968.00
  LESS WITHDRAWALS                  690.00
  NET INCREASE IN CAPITAL                          1 278.00
  ENDING CAPITAL                                                122 438.00
TOTAL ENDING CAPITAL                                          $258 278.00
```

Capital statement printout

```
ALLSPORTS
BALANCE SHEET
MARCH 31, 1989

              ASSETS
CASH                                   $ 16 420.00
ACCOUNTS RECEIVABLE                         580.00
MERCHANDISE INVENTORY                   232 500.00
OFFICE SUPPLIES                             455.00
STORE SUPPLIES                              235.00
PREPAID INSURANCE                           804.00
DELIVERY EQUIPMENT                        7 200.00
OFFICE EQUIPMENT                            940.00
STORE EQUIPMENT                           3 400.00
TOTAL ASSETS                                          $262 534.00
            LIABILITIES
ACCOUNTS PAYABLE                                      $   4 256.00
            CAPITAL
HELEN LEWIS, CAPITAL                   $135 840.00
SAMUEL SULLIVAN, CAPITAL                122 438.00
TOTAL CAPITAL                                          258 278.00
TOTAL LIABILITIES AND CAPITAL                         $262 534.00
```

Balance sheet printout

Recording closing entries

Closing entries are needed to prepare Allsports' general ledger for the next fiscal period. *(CONCEPT: Accounting Period Cycle)* Information needed for the closing entries is obtained from two places. (1) Work sheet Income Statement and Balance Sheet columns. (2) Distribution of net income statement. Ms. Lewis records Allsports' closing entries on a JET form, page 377.

JOURNAL ENTRY TRANSMITTAL					

CLIENT NO. 320   DATE 1989 03 31   PAGE 1 OF 1 PAGES

	BCH. NO.	REF. NUMBER	ACCOUNT NUMBER	EXPLANATION	DEBIT	CREDIT	
1	1		41000	Closing Entries	168400 0		1
2			33000			168400 0	2
3			33000		69600 0		3
4			51000			32400 0	4
5			61000			660 0	5
6			61500			252 0 0	6
7			62000			860 0	7
8			62500			1460 0	8
9			63000			1300 0	9
10			63500			1250 0	10
11			64000			800 0 0	11
12			64500			20000 0	12
13			65000			115 0 0	13
14			33000		49200 0		14
15			31000			29520 0	15
16			32000			19680 0	16
17			31000		672 0 0		17
18			31500			672 0 0	18
19			32000		690 0 0		19
20			32500			690 0 0	20

PREPARED BY Helen Lewis   PAGE TOTALS | 3008200 | 3008200 |

Journal entry transmittal
for closing entries

Allsports' JET form for closing entries is sent to the computer service centre. Data are entered on a direct-entry terminal. The computer posts the closing entries to general ledger accounts stored on magnetic disk. The computer also prepares an entry register for the closing entries. Allsports' entry register for closing entries is on page 378.

The totals on the entry register, page 378, and JET form above are the same. Therefore, the entry register for closing entries is assumed to be correct. The entry register for closing entries is sent to Allsports. At Allsports, Ms. Lewis files the entry register for future reference.

Preparing a post-closing trial balance

In Allsports' previous manual accounting system, the post-closing trial balance was prepared from general ledger accounts. In Allsports' new EDP accounting system, the post-closing trial balance is prepared by the computer from data stored on magnetic disk. Allsports' EDP post-closing trial balance is on page 378.

```
                              ALLSPORTS
                           ENTRY REGISTER
                           CLOSING ENTRIES
   CLIENT NO. 320              MARCH 31, 1989              PAGE 1 OF 1 PAGES

   LINE  BATCH  REFERENCE  ACCOUNT
   NO.   NO.    NO.        NO.      EXPLANATION          DEBIT        CREDIT

    1      1               41000  SALES              $16 840.00
    2                      33000    INCOME SUMMARY                $16 840.00
    3                      33000  INCOME SUMMARY        6 960.00
    4                      51000    PURCHASES                       3 240.00
    5                      61000    ADVERTISING EXPENSE                66.00
    6                      61500    CREDIT CARD FEE EXPENSE           252.00
    7                      62000    DELIVERY EXPENSE                   86.00
    8                      62500    INSURANCE EXPENSE                 146.00
    9                      63000    MISCELLANEOUS EXPENSE            130.00
   10                      63500    OFFICE SUPPLIES EXPENSE          125.00
   11                      64000    RENT EXPENSE                     800.00
   12                      64500    SALARY EXPENSE                 2 000.00
   13                      65000    STORE SUPPLIES EXPENSE           115.00
   14                      33000  INCOME SUMMARY        4 920.00
   15                      31000    HELEN LEWIS, CAPITAL           2 952.00
   16                      32000    SAMUEL SULLIVAN, CAPITAL       1 968.00
   17                      31000  HELEN LEWIS, CAPITAL    672.00
   18                      31500    HELEN LEWIS, DRAWING             672.00
   19                      32000  SAMUEL SULLIVAN, CAPITAL  690.00
   20                      32500    SAMUEL SULLIVAN, DRAWING         690.00

                                   TOTALS            $30 082.00*   $30 082.00*
```

Entry register for closing
entries

```
                              ALLSPORTS
                       POST-CLOSING TRIAL BALANCE
                           MARCH 31, 1989

        CASH                          $ 16 420.00
        ACCOUNTS RECEIVABLE                580.00
        MERCHANDISE INVENTORY         232 500.00
        OFFICE SUPPLIES                   455.00
        STORE SUPPLIES                    235.00
        PREPAID INSURANCE                 804.00
        DELIVERY EQUIPMENT              7 200.00
        OFFICE EQUIPMENT                  940.00
        STORE EQUIPMENT                 3 400.00
        ACCOUNTS PAYABLE                            $   4 256.00
        HELEN LEWIS, CAPITAL                          135 840.00
        SAMUEL SULLIVAN, CAPITAL                      122 438.00

        TOTALS                        $262 534.00    $262 534.00
```

Post-closing trial balance
printout

SUMMARY OF AUTOMATED GENERAL LEDGER
ACCOUNTING SYSTEM

The flowchart, page 379, outlines Allsports' automated general ledger
accounting system. Steps 1 and 2 are described in Chapter 17. Steps 3–6

are presented in Chapter 18. Steps 7–15 are described in Chapter 19 to complete the accounting cycle.

Flowchart of steps for automated general ledger accounting

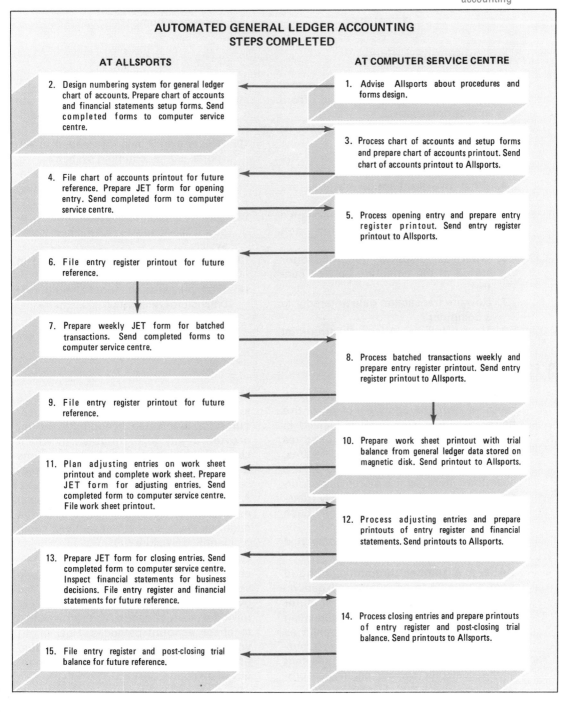

AUTOMATED GENERAL LEDGER ACCOUNTING
STEPS COMPLETED

AT ALLSPORTS

2. Design numbering system for general ledger chart of accounts. Prepare chart of accounts and financial statements setup forms. Send completed forms to computer service centre.

4. File chart of accounts printout for future reference. Prepare JET form for opening entry. Send completed form to computer service centre.

6. File entry register printout for future reference.

7. Prepare weekly JET form for batched transactions. Send completed forms to computer service centre.

9. File entry register printout for future reference.

11. Plan adjusting entries on work sheet printout and complete work sheet. Prepare JET form for adjusting entries. Send completed form to computer service centre. File work sheet printout.

13. Prepare JET form for closing entries. Send completed form to computer service centre. Inspect financial statements for business decisions. File entry register and financial statements for future reference.

15. File entry register and post-closing trial balance for future reference.

AT COMPUTER SERVICE CENTRE

1. Advise Allsports about procedures and forms design.

3. Process chart of accounts and setup forms and prepare chart of accounts printout. Send chart of accounts printout to Allsports.

5. Process opening entry and prepare entry register printout. Send entry register printout to Allsports.

8. Process batched transactions weekly and prepare entry register printout. Send entry register printout to Allsports.

10. Prepare work sheet printout with trial balance from general ledger data stored on magnetic disk. Send printout to Allsports.

12. Process adjusting entries and prepare printouts of entry register and financial statements. Send printouts to Allsports.

14. Process closing entries and prepare printouts of entry register and post-closing trial balance. Send printouts to Allsports.

ACCOUNTING TERMS

What is the meaning of each of the following?

1. batching

2. reference number

QUESTIONS FOR INDIVIDUAL STUDY

1. What EDP form is used to record transaction data obtained from source documents?
2. How often does Allsports submit its daily transactions?
3. Why does batching reduce the number of journal entries?
4. What five transaction batches are used by Allsports?
5. Why are reference numbers assigned to source documents within each batch?
6. Where is Allsports' general ledger stored at the computer service centre?
7. How are transaction data entered into a computer?
8. How often are Allsports' financial statements prepared?
9. What four financial statements are prepared for Allsports by the computer service centre?
10. Why is a trial balance needed in Allsports' EDP accounting system?
11. How are adjustments planned and recorded in Allsports' EDP accounting system?
12. How are financial statements prepared in Allsports' EDP accounting system?
13. How are closing entries recorded in Allsports' EDP accounting system?
14. Who prepares the post-closing trial balance for Allsports?

CASES FOR MANAGEMENT DECISION

CASE 1 Steven Parker and Todd Brent, partners, own and operate a chain of five hardware stores. One store is located in the downtown shopping area. Four stores are located in suburban shopping centres. A computer system is installed in the downtown store. All five stores use a journal entry transmittal to record daily transactions for computer processing. Each morning a JET form is prepared for the previous day's business. The completed forms are delivered to the downtown store to be processed by computer. The procedures for automated accounting do not provide a way to distinguish in which store transactions occur. All transactions are batched together. The data are processed as if only one store were involved. A need exists to be able to analyse business activity by store. What changes might be made so that transactions could be identified by store?

CASE 2 A lumber company changed from a manual to an automated general ledger accounting system. A computer service centre processes the accounting data. Source documents are batched as they occur and recorded weekly on a journal entry transmittal. The JET form is sent to the computer service centre for processing. A filing system is used for storing source documents in five batches. The owner has expressed a concern over not having a manual general ledger available to check account balances. How might you provide the owner with individual general ledger account balances when requested?

DRILL 19-D 1   Batching transactions

This drill provides practice in arranging transactions in groups. Use a form similar to the one below.

Trans. No.	Accounts Payable Batch	Cash Payments Batch	Accounts Receivable Batch	Cash Receipts Batch	General Batch
1.	√				

Instructions: For each transaction below, indicate the batch in which the transaction would be entered by checking the appropriate column. Transaction No. 1 is given as an example.

Transactions

1. Bought office supplies on account.
2. Received cash on account.
3. Purchased merchandise for cash.
4. Paid salaries.
5. Purchased merchandise on account.
6. Partner withdrew cash.
7. Sold merchandise on account.
8. Bought store supplies on account.
9. Partner withdrew merchandise.
10. Paid on account.

DRILL 19-D 2   Analysing a journal entry transmittal

Instructions: Refer to the completed journal entry transmittal, page 367, and answer the following questions.

1. How many batches are recorded?
2. In batch 1, line 1, which account is affected? How?
3. How many reference numbers were assigned to batch 1?
4. In batch 1, line 4, why is the Ref. Number column left blank?
5. Why are account titles not recorded on a journal entry transmittal?
6. Why is there only one entry to Cash for batch 2 on lines 5–15?
7. Did the accounts payable account increase or decrease as a result of the transactions? How much?
8. Did the accounts receivable account increase or decrease as a result of the transactions? How much?
9. Did the purchases account increase or decrease as a result of the transactions? How much?
10. Did the cash account increase or decrease as a result of the transactions? How much?

APPLICATION PROBLEMS

PROBLEM 19-1   Recording weekly batched transactions for EDP using a journal entry transmittal

The chart of accounts prepared in Problem 17-1, Chapter 17, is needed to complete Problem 19-1.

Soto Auto Supply arranges transaction source documents into five batches. (1) Accounts payable. (2) Cash payments. (3) Accounts receivable. (4) Cash receipts. (5) General. Reference numbers are assigned to transaction source documents within each batch. The batched transactions are recorded as combined entries weekly. Batched transactions for week ended March 5 of current year are below.

Accounts payable

Bought office supplies on account	$ 141.00.	Ref. No. 1000.
Bought store supplies on account	$ 74.00.	Ref. No. 1001.
Purchased merchandise on account	$2 100.00.	Ref. No. 1002.
Total accounts payable	$2 315.00.	

Cash payments

Bought store supplies for cash	$ 36.00.	Ref. No. 2000.
Paid for insurance policy	$ 320.00.	Ref. No. 2001.
Paid on account	$2 160.00.	Ref. No. 2002.
Alice Soto, partner, withdrew cash	$ 750.00.	Ref. No. 2003.
Frank Soto, partner, withdrew cash	$ 750.00.	Ref. No. 2004.
Purchased merchandise for cash	$ 380.00.	Ref. No. 2005.
Paid March rent	$ 850.00.	Ref. No. 2006.
Paid salaries	$1 200.00.	Ref. No. 2007.
Total cash payments	$6 446.00.	

Accounts receivable

Sold merchandise on account	$ 370.00.	Ref. No. 3000.
Total accounts receivable	$ 370.00.	

Cash receipts

Cash received on account	$ 344.00.	Ref. No. 4000.
Cash received from sales	$3 680.00.	Ref. No. 4001.
Total cash receipts	$4 024.00.	

General

Alice Soto, partner, withdrew merchandise	$ 42.00.	Ref. No. 5000.
Frank Soto, partner, withdrew merchandise	$ 28.00.	Ref. No. 5001.
Total withdrawals of merchandise by partners	$ 70.00.	

Instructions: Record the batched transactions for Soto Auto Supply, Client No. 183, on a journal entry transmittal. Use March 5 of the current year as the date of the last business day for the week's business. Use account numbers from the chart of accounts prepared in Problem 17-1. Use the journal entry transmittal, page 367, as your model.

PROBLEM 19-2   Recording adjusting and closing entries for EDP using a journal entry transmittal

The chart of accounts prepared in Problem 17-1, Chapter 17, is needed to complete Problem 19-2.

Soto Auto Supply's trial balance is shown in the partial work sheet printout on the next page. Ending inventories and the value of insurance policies are also given.

```
SOTO AUTO SUPPLY
WORK SHEET
FOR MONTH ENDED MARCH 31, 19--
                              TRIAL BALANCE
                            DEBIT        CREDIT
CASH...................   $ 14 086.00   _____
ACCOUNTS RECEIVABLE.....      760.00    _____
MERCHANDISE INVENTORY...  225 420.00    _____
OFFICE SUPPLIES.........      811.00    _____
STORE SUPPLIES..........      520.00    _____
PREPAID INSURANCE.......    1 250.00    _____
OFFICE EQUIPMENT........    1 100.00    _____
STORE EQUIPMENT.........    1 840.00    _____
ACCOUNTS PAYABLE........                $  4 330.00
ALICE SOTO, CAPITAL.....                 119 840.00
ALICE SOTO, DRAWING.....    1 542.00
FRANK SOTO, CAPITAL.....                 116 540.00
FRANK SOTO, DRAWING.....    1 528.00    _____
INCOME SUMMARY..........  _____    _____
SALES...................                  15 580.00
PURCHASES...............    3 820.00    _____
ADVERTISING EXPENSE.....       68.00    _____
CREDIT CARD FEE EXPENSE.      215.00    _____
INSURANCE EXPENSE.......  _____    _____
MISCELLANEOUS EXPENSE...       80.00    _____
OFFICE SUPPLIES EXPENSE.  _____    _____
RENT EXPENSE............      850.00    _____
SALARY EXPENSE..........    2 400.00    _____
STORE SUPPLIES EXPENSE..  _____    _____
                         $256 290.00   $256 290.00
```

Adjustment Information, March 31

Merchandise inventory	$221 860.00
Office supplies inventory	671.00
Store supplies inventory	410.00
Value of insurance policies	1 125.00

Instructions: 1. Enter adjustments and complete work sheet printout for month ended March 31 of the current year. Use as a guide the work sheet printout, page 373.

2. Record adjusting entries for Soto Auto Supply, Client No. 183, on a journal entry transmittal. Use account numbers from the chart of accounts prepared in Problem 17-1. Use the journal entry transmittal, page 374, as your model.

3. Record closing entries for Soto Auto Supply on a journal entry transmittal. Distribution of net income statement printout shows net income shared equally: Alice Soto, $2 106.00; Frank Soto, $2 106.00.

ENRICHMENT PROBLEMS

MASTERY PROBLEM 19-M Recording weekly batched transactions for EDP using a journal entry transmittal

The chart of accounts prepared in Mastery Problem 17-M, Chapter 17, is needed to complete Mastery Problem 19-M.

The Appliance Centre arranges source documents into five batches. (1) Accounts payable. (2) Cash payments. (3) Accounts receivable. (4) Cash receipts. (5) General. Reference numbers are assigned to transaction source documents within each batch. The batched transactions are recorded as combined entries weekly. Batched transactions for week ended April 16 of the current year are below.

Accounts payable

Bought office supplies on account	$ 110.00.	Ref. No. 1016.
Bought store supplies on account	$ 120.00.	Ref. No. 1017.
Purchased merchandise on account	$ 640.00.	Ref. No. 1018.
Total accounts payable	$ 870.00.	

Cash payments

Paid on account	$ 520.00.	Ref. No. 2021.
Carol Bennett, partner, withdrew cash	$ 600.00.	Ref. No. 2022.
Steve Franklin, partner, withdrew cash	$ 600.00.	Ref. No. 2023.
Purchased merchandise for cash	$ 320.00.	Ref. No. 2024.
Paid salaries	$1 350.00.	Ref. No. 2025.
Total cash payments	$3 390.00.	

Accounts receivable

Sold merchandise on account	$ 500.00.	Ref. No. 3011.
Total accounts receivable	$ 500.00.	

Cash receipts

Cash received on account	$ 120.00.	Ref. No. 4013.
Cash received from sales	$2 850.00.	Ref. No. 4014.
Total cash receipts	$2 970.00.	

Instructions: Record the batched transactions for the Appliance Centre, Client No. 274, on a journal entry transmittal. Use April 16 of the current year as the date of the last business day for the week's transactions. Use account numbers from the chart of accounts prepared in Mastery Problem 17-M. Use the journal entry transmittal, page 367, as your model.

CHALLENGE PROBLEM 19-C Recording weekly batched transactions for EDP using a journal entry transmittal

The chart of accounts prepared in Challenge Problem 17-C, Chapter 17, is needed to complete Challenge Problem 19-C.

Adkins Leather Goods arranges source documents into four batches. (1) Accounts payable. (2) Cash payments. (3) Cash receipts. (4) General. On May 15 the business stopped issuing credit other than on credit card purchases. Therefore, Adkins Leather Goods no longer has any accounts receivable. Reference numbers are assigned to transaction source documents within each batch. The batched transactions are recorded as combined entries weekly. Batched transactions for week ended May 21 of the current year are on the next page.

Accounts payable

Purchased merchandise on account .... $1 010.00.   Ref. No. 1123.
   Total accounts payable .... $1 010.00.

Cash payments

Paid advertising expense .... $ 75.00.   Ref. No. 2330.
Paid on account .... $ 900.00.   Ref. No. 2331.
Purchased merchandise for cash .... $ 180.00.   Ref. No. 2332.
Paid miscellaneous expense .... $ 25.00.   Ref. No. 2333.
   Total cash payments .... $1 180.00.

Cash receipts

Cash received from sales .... $2 450.00.   Ref. No. 4021.
   Total cash receipts .... $2 450.00.

General

Susan Adkins, partner, withdrew merchandise .... $ 30.00.   Ref. No. 5008.
   Total withdrawals of merchandise by partners .... $ 30.00.

Instructions: Record the batched transactions for Adkins Leather Goods, Client No. 422, on a journal entry transmittal. Use May 21 of the current year as the date of the last business day for the week's transactions. Use account numbers from the chart of accounts prepared in Challenge Problem 17-C. Use the journal entry transmittal, page 367, as your model.

Reinforcement Activity 3

An Accounting Cycle for a Partnership Using Automated Data Processing

Code chart of accounts

↓

Prepare chart of accounts setup form

↓

Prepare financial statement setup forms

↓

Prepare JET form for opening entry

↓

Prepare JET forms for batched transactions

↓

Plan adjustments on work sheet printout

↓

Complete work sheet

↓

Prepare JET form for adjusting entries

↓

Prepare JET form for closing entries

Reinforcement Activity 3 is designed to strengthen learnings from Part 4, Chapters 17–19. Accounting activities necessary to convert from a manual to an automated general ledger accounting system are covered. Accounting work is then included for a one-month fiscal period for a merchandising business organized as a partnership. The business uses a credit card service in addition to its own limited company charge accounts. The activities illustrate the application of automated general ledger accounting concepts to merchandising businesses. The flowchart at the left shows the activities covered in Reinforcement Activity 3.

BACKPACKERS

Anne and Martha Palmer, partners, own and operate a merchandising business called Backpackers. The business sells backpacks, camping supplies, hiking footwear, outdoor clothing, and sleeping bags. A monthly rent is paid for the store space.

A decision is made to convert from a manual to an automated general ledger accounting system beginning June 1 of the current year. Backpackers will use a computer service centre for automated processing of general ledger accounting data. Transactions will be batched and submitted weekly to the computer service centre on journal entry transmittal (JET) forms for processing. Backpackers will arrange daily transactions into five batches. (1) Accounts payable. (2) Cash payments. (3) Accounts receivable. (4) Cash receipts. (5) General.

Backpackers' setup and JET forms

Pages on which setup and JET forms are illustrated are below.

Blank forms needed to complete Reinforcement Activity 3 are given in the working papers.

Backpackers' chart of accounts coding system

Backpackers will use a five-digit coding system for its chart of accounts. The general ledger chart of accounts with five-digit account numbers assigned is below.

BACKPACKERS Chart of Accounts			
Account Number	**(1) ASSETS**	**Account Number**	**(4) REVENUE**
11000	Cash	41000	Sales
11500	Accounts Receivable		
12000	Merchandise Inventory		**(5) COST OF MERCHANDISE SOLD**
12500	Office Supplies	51000	Purchases
13000	Store Supplies		
13500	Prepaid Insurance		**(6) EXPENSES**
14000	Office Equipment	61000	Advertising Expense
14500	Store Equipment	61500	Credit Card Fee Expense
		62000	Insurance Expense
	(2) LIABILITIES	62500	Miscellaneous Expense
21000	Accounts Payable	63000	Office Supplies Expense
		63500	Rent Expense
	(3) CAPITAL	64000	Salary Expense
		64500	Store Supplies Expense
31000	Anne Palmer, Capital		
31500	Anne Palmer, Drawing		
32000	Martha Palmer, Capital		
32500	Martha Palmer, Drawing		
33000	Income Summary		

Preparing Backpackers' chart of accounts setup

Instructions: 1. Prepare a general ledger chart of accounts setup form, Client Number 286, dated May 19 of the current year. Use Backpackers' general ledger chart of accounts given above.

Preparing Backpackers' financial statement setups

Instructions: 2. Prepare the following financial statement setup forms, Client Number 286, dated May 23 of the current year. (1) Income statement. (2) Distribution of net income statement. Net income is to be shared equally. (3) Capital statement. (4) Balance sheet. Computer printouts of the financial statements are prepared by the computer service centre at the end of the monthly fiscal period.

Recording Backpackers' opening entry

Backpackers' balance sheet for May 31 of the current year is on the next page.

Instructions: 3. Record Backpackers' opening entry, Client Number 286, on a JET form. Use June 1 of the current year as the date of the opening entry. Use the account numbers from the chart of accounts above.

<table>
<tr><td colspan="3" align="center">*Backpackers*
Balance Sheet
May 31, 19--</td></tr>
<tr><td colspan="3" align="center">*Assets*</td></tr>
<tr><td>*Cash*</td><td align="right">9 200 00</td><td></td></tr>
<tr><td>*Accounts Receivable*</td><td align="right">740 00</td><td></td></tr>
<tr><td>*Merchandise Inventory*</td><td align="right">123 500 00</td><td></td></tr>
<tr><td>*Office Supplies*</td><td align="right">280 00</td><td></td></tr>
<tr><td>*Store Supplies*</td><td align="right">160 00</td><td></td></tr>
<tr><td>*Prepaid Insurance*</td><td align="right">720 00</td><td></td></tr>
<tr><td>*Office Equipment*</td><td align="right">1 160 00</td><td></td></tr>
<tr><td>*Store Equipment*</td><td align="right">2 820 00</td><td></td></tr>
<tr><td>*Total Assets*</td><td></td><td align="right">138 580 00</td></tr>
<tr><td colspan="3" align="center">*Liabilities*</td></tr>
<tr><td>*Accounts Payable*</td><td></td><td align="right">3 180 00</td></tr>
<tr><td colspan="3" align="center">*Capital*</td></tr>
<tr><td>*Anne Palmer, Capital*</td><td align="right">68 600 00</td><td></td></tr>
<tr><td>*Martha Palmer, Capital*</td><td align="right">66 800 00</td><td></td></tr>
<tr><td>*Total Capital*</td><td></td><td align="right">135 400 00</td></tr>
<tr><td>*Total Liabilities and Capital*</td><td></td><td align="right">138 580 00</td></tr>
</table>

Recording Backpackers' batched transactions

Instructions: 4. Record the following batched transactions, Client Number 286, on a JET form. Reference numbers are assigned to single and groups of transactions. Use June 5 of the current year as the date of the last business day for the week's business. Use the account numbers from the chart of accounts, page 387.

Accounts Payable

Bought office supplies on account	$ 112.00.	Ref. No. 1000.
Bought store supplies on account	$ 93.00.	Ref. No. 1001.
Purchased merchandise on account	$1 840.00.	Ref. No. 1002.
Total accounts payable	$2 045.00.	

Cash Payments

Bought store supplies for cash	$ 62.00.	Ref. No. 2000.
Paid on account	$1 840.00.	Ref. No. 2001.
Anne Palmer, partner, withdrew cash	$ 800.00.	Ref. No. 2002.
Martha Palmer, partner, withdrew cash	$ 800.00.	Ref. No. 2003.
Paid June rent	$1 200.00.	Ref. No. 2004.
Paid salaries	$ 900.00.	Ref. No. 2005.
Total cash payments	$5 602.00.	

Accounts Receivable

Sold merchandise on account	$ 84.00.	Ref. No. 3000.
Total accounts receivable	$ 84.00.	

Cash Receipts

Cash received on account	$ 340.00.	Ref. No. 4000.
Cash received from sales	$2 620.00.	Ref. No. 4001.
Total cash receipts	$2 960.00.	

General

Anne Palmer, partner, withdrew merchandise	$ 103.00.	Ref. No. 5000.
Total withdrawal of merchandise by partners	$ 103.00.	

Instructions: 5. Record the following batched transactions, Client Number 286, on a JET form. Use June 12 of the current year as the date of the last business day for the week's business. Use the account numbers from the chart of accounts, page 387.

Accounts Payable

Bought store supplies on account	$ 48.00.	Ref. No. 1003.
Purchased merchandise on account	$1 350.00.	Ref. No. 1004.
Total accounts payable	$1 398.00.	

Cash Payments

Paid on account	$ 675.00.	Ref. No. 2006.
Purchased merchandise for cash	$ 380.00.	Ref. No. 2007.
Paid advertising expense	$ 83.00.	Ref. No. 2008.
Paid miscellaneous expense	$ 48.00.	Ref. No. 2009.
Total cash payments	$1 186.00.	

Accounts Receivable

Sold merchandise on account	$ 116.00.	Ref. No. 3001.
Total accounts receivable	$ 116.00.	

Cash Receipts

Cash received on account	$ 88.00.	Ref. No. 4002.
Cash received from sales	$3 610.00.	Ref. No. 4003.
Total cash receipts	$3 698.00.	

Instructions: 6. Record the following batched transactions, Client Number 286, on a JET form. Use June 19 of the current year as the date of the last business day for the week's business. Use the account numbers from the chart of accounts, page 387.

Accounts Payable

Bought office supplies on account	$ 38.00.	Ref. No. 1005.
Purchased merchandise on account	$1 960.00.	Ref. No. 1006.
Total accounts payable	$1 998.00.	

Cash Payments

Paid on account	$ 230.00.	Ref. No. 2010.
Purchased merchandise for cash	$ 161.00.	Ref. No. 2011.
Paid miscellaneous expense	$ 36.00.	Ref. No. 2012.
Paid salaries	$ 900.00.	Ref. No. 2013.
Total cash payments	$1 327.00.	

Accounts Receivable

Sold merchandise on account	$ 320.00.	Ref. No. 3002.
Total accounts receivable	$ 320.00.	

Cash Receipts

Cash received on account	$ 260.00.	Ref. No. 4004.
Cash received from sales	$3 730.00.	Ref. No. 4005.
Total cash receipts	$3 990.00.	

General

Martha Palmer, partner, withdrew merchandise	$	96.00.	Ref. No. 5001.
Total withdrawal of merchandise by partners	$	96.00.	

Instructions: 7. Record the following batched transactions, Client Number 286, on a JET form. Use June 26 of the current year as the date of the last business day for the week's business. Use the account numbers from the chart of accounts, page 387.

Accounts Payable

Bought office supplies on account	$	41.00.	Ref. No. 1007.
Bought store supplies on account	$	62.00.	Ref. No. 1008.
Purchased merchandise on account	$	240.00.	Ref. No. 1009.
Total accounts payable	$	343.00.	

Cash Payments

Paid on account	$	435.00.	Ref. No. 2014.
Paid advertising expense	$	96.00.	Ref. No. 2015.
Paid credit card fee expense	$	240.00.	Ref. No. 2016.
Paid miscellaneous expense	$	41.00.	Ref. No. 2017.
Total cash payments	$	812.00.	

Accounts Receivable

Sold merchandise on account	$	162.00.	Ref. No. 3003.
Total accounts receivable	$	162.00.	

Cash Receipts

Cash received from sales	$3	460.00.	Ref. No. 4006.
Total cash receipts	$3	460.00.	

Instructions: 8. Record the following batched transactions, Client Number 286, on a JET form. Use June 30 of the current year as the date of the last business day for the monthly fiscal period. Use the account numbers from the chart of accounts, page 387.

Accounts Payable

Bought store supplies on account	$	32.00.	Ref. No. 1010.
Purchased merchandise on account	$	470.00.	Ref. No. 1011.
Total accounts payable	$	502.00.	

Cash Payments

Bought office supplies for cash	$	16.00.	Ref. No. 2018.
Bought store supplies for cash	$	34.00.	Ref. No. 2019.
Purchased merchandise for cash	$	160.00.	Ref. No. 2020.
Paid advertising expense	$	46.00.	Ref. No. 2021.
Total cash payments	$	256.00.	

Cash Receipts

Cash received on account	$	24.00.	Ref. No. 4007.
Cash received from sales	$2	180.00.	Ref. No. 4008.
Total cash receipts	$2	204.00.	

General

Anne Palmer, partner, withdrew merchandise	$	26.00.	Ref. No. 5002.
Martha Palmer, partner, withdrew merchandise	$	96.00.	Ref. No. 5003.
Total withdrawal of merchandise by partners	$	122.00.	

Recording Backpackers' adjusting and closing entries

Backpackers' trial balance is in the partial work sheet printout on page 391. Ending inventories and the value of insurance policies are also given.

```
   BACKPACKERS
   WORK SHEET
FOR MONTH ENDED JUNE 30, 19--

                                    TRIAL BALANCE
                                 DEBIT        CREDIT
CASH.....................    $ 16 329.00    _____
ACCOUNTS RECEIVABLE......       710.00      _____
MERCHANDISE INVENTORY....    123 500.00     _____
OFFICE SUPPLIES..........       487.00      _____
STORE SUPPLIES...........       491.00      _____
PREPAID INSURANCE........       720.00      _____
OFFICE EQUIPMENT.........     1 160.00      _____
STORE EQUIPMENT..........     2 820.00      _____
ACCOUNTS PAYABLE.........      _____     $  6 286.00
ANNE PALMER, CAPITAL.....      _____      68 600.00
ANNE PALMER, DRAWING.....       929.00      _____
MARTHA PALMER, CAPITAL...      _____      66 800.00
MARTHA PALMER, DRAWING...       992.00      _____
INCOME SUMMARY...........      _____     _____
SALES....................      _____      16 282.00
PURCHASES................     6 240.00      _____
ADVERTISING EXPENSE......       225.00      _____
CREDIT CARD FEE EXPENSE..       240.00      _____
INSURANCE EXPENSE........      _____     _____
MISCELLANEOUS EXPENSE....       125.00      _____
OFFICE SUPPLIES EXPENSE..      _____     _____
RENT EXPENSE.............     1 200.00      _____
SALARY EXPENSE...........     1 800.00      _____
STORE SUPPLIES EXPENSE...      _____     _____
                            $157 968.00    $157 968.00
```

Adjustment Information, June 30

Merchandise inventory...	$121 790.00
Office supplies inventory...	427.00
Store supplies inventory...	401.00
Value of insurance policies..	660.00

Instructions: 9. Enter adjustments and complete work sheet printout for month ended June 30 of the current year.

10. Record Backpackers' adjusting entries, Client Number 286, on a JET form. Use the account numbers from the chart of accounts, page 387.

11. Record Backpackers' closing entries, Client Number 286, on a JET form. Use the account numbers from the chart of accounts, page 387. Net income is shared equally by the two partners.

5 AN ACCOUNTING SYSTEM WITH SPECIAL JOURNALS

GENERAL BEHAVIORAL GOALS

1. Know accounting terminology related to a merchandising business organized as a corporation.
2. Understand accounting principles and practices for a merchandising business organized as a corporation.
3. Demonstrate accounting procedures for a merchandising business organized as a corporation.

Lin's Music Center, the business for Part 5, sells musical instruments, records, and tapes.

LIN'S MUSIC CENTRE
Chart of Accounts

Balance Sheet Accounts

(1) ASSETS	Account Number

11 Current Assets

Cash	1101
Notes Receivable	1102
Accounts Receivable	1103
Allowance for Uncollectible Accounts	1103.1
Merchandise Inventory	1104
Supplies	1105
Prepaid Insurance	1106

12 Fixed Assets

Delivery Equipment	1201
Accumulated Depreciation — Delivery Equipment	1201.1
Office Equipment	1202
Accumulated Depreciation — Office Equipment	1202.1
Store Equipment	1203
Accumulated Depreciation — Store Equipment	1203.1

(2) LIABILITIES

21 Current Liabilities

Notes Payable	2101
Accounts Payable	2102
Employees' Income Tax Payable	2103
Federal Income Tax Payable	2105
CPP Payable	2105
Sales Tax Payable	2106
UI Payable	2107
Health Care Premiums Payable	2108
Hospital Insurance Premiums Payable	2109
Canada Savings Bonds Payable	2110
United Way Donations Payable	2111
Dividends Payable	2112
Salaries Payable	2113

(3) SHAREHOLDERS' EQUITY

Capital Stock	3101
Retained Earnings	3201
Income Summary	3301

Income Statement Accounts

(4) OPERATING REVENUE	Account Number
Sales	4101
Sales Returns and Allowances	4101.1

(5) COST OF MERCHANDISE

Purchases	5101
Purchases Returns and Allowances	5101.1
Purchases Discount	5101.2

(6) OPERATING EXPENSES

Advertising Expense	6101
Bad Debts Expense	6102
Credit Card Fee Expense	6103
Delivery Expense	6104
Depreciation Expense — Delivery Equipment	6105
Depreciation Expense — Office Equipment	6106
Depreciation Expense — Store Equipment	6107
Insurance Expense	6108
Miscellaneous Expense	6109
CPP Expense	6110
UI Expense	6111
Rent Expense	6112
Salary Expense	6113
Supplies Expense	6114

(7) OTHER REVENUE

Interest Income	7101

(8) OTHER EXPENSES

Interest Expense	8101

(9) INCOME TAX

Federal Income Tax	9101

The chart of accounts for Lin's Music Centre is illustrated above for ready reference as you study Part 5 of this textbook.

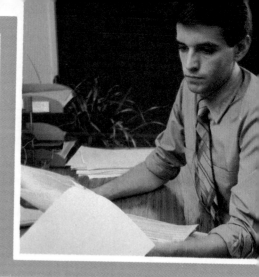

20

Recording Transactions with Special Journals: Purchases and Cash Payments

ENABLING PERFORMANCE TASKS

After studying Chapter 20, you will be able to:

a. Define accounting terms related to purchases and cash payments.
b. Explain accounting principles and practices related to purchases and cash payments.
c. Analyse transactions affecting purchases and cash payments.
d. Journalize purchases on account transactions in a purchases journal.
e. Post from a purchases journal.
f. Journalize cash payments transactions in a cash payments journal.
g. Post from a cash payments journal.
h. Journalize purchases returns and allowances and buying of supplies on account transactions in a general journal.
i. Post from a general journal.

A business should use an accounting system that provides the desired financial information with the least amount of effort. Most businesses expect to remain in business for an indefinite time. Therefore, accounting records should be kept with the assumption that the business will continue indefinitely. (CONCEPT: Going Concern)

The preferred type of accounting system may vary with the size and kind of business. A business with few transactions may need only one bookkeeper or accounting clerk to record all the transactions. When one person records all the transactions, a business may prefer the convenience of recording all entries in one journal. In Part 3, Denim Threads uses a synoptic journal to record all transactions. However, a business with many daily transactions may need several accounting clerks to record the transactions. Normally these larger businesses use several journals. Using several journals permits the accounting clerks to specialize in the kind of transactions recorded. This specialization generally helps improve the efficiency of recording transactions. A journal in which only one kind of business transaction is recorded is known as a special journal.

Lin's Music Centre is a corporation that sells musical instruments, stereo equipment, records, tapes, and music. Lin's uses five journals to record its transactions.

1. Purchases journal — for all purchases on account
2. Cash payments journal — for all cash payments
3. Sales journal — for all sales on account
4. Cash receipts journal — for all cash receipts
5. General journal — for all other transactions

Many businesses are organized as corporations. An organization with the legal rights of a "person" and which may be owned by many persons is called a corporation. A corporation is formed by receiving approval from a provincial or federal agency. A corporation can own property, incur liabilities, and enter into contracts in its own name. A corporation may sell ownership in itself in the form of capital stock.

Lin's was formed as a corporation because several owners can provide larger amounts of capital than one owner. The principal difference between the accounting records of sole proprietorships, partnerships, and corporations is in the capital accounts. A corporation has a separate capital account for the stock issued and for the earnings kept in the business. The different capital accounts will be explained in Chapter 27. As in sole proprietorships and partnerships, information in a corporation accounting system relates to a specific business entity. *(CONCEPT: Business Entity)*

RECORDING PURCHASES ON ACCOUNT IN A PURCHASES JOURNAL

A special journal used to record only purchases on account is called a purchases journal.

The purchases journal used by Lin's Music Centre is on page 397. A purchase on account can be recorded on one line in the purchases journal. Each entry in the single amount column is both a debit to Purchases and a credit to Accounts Payable. Since the debit and credit entries are always to the same accounts, recording time is shortened by using one column. The names of both general ledger accounts are listed in the column heading.

Journalizing purchases on account in a purchases journal

The source document for recording a purchase on account is a purchase invoice received from a creditor. *(CONCEPT: Objective Evidence)*

Lin's dates, numbers, and checks its purchase invoices as shown on page 194 for Denim Threads. Lin's purchased merchandise on account.

February 1, 1989. Purchased merchandise on account from Slater Company, $2 648.00. Purchase Invoice No. 33.

In this entry, Purchases is debited for $2 648.00 and Accounts Payable is credited for $2 648.00. Purchases are recorded at their cost. *(CONCEPT: Historical Cost)* The entry to record this transaction in a purchases journal is below.

	DATE	ACCOUNT CREDITED	PURCH. NO.	POST. REF.	PURCHASES, DR. ACCTS. PAY. CR.	
1	1989 Feb. 1	Slater Company	33		2 648 00	1
2						2
3						3

PURCHASES JOURNAL   PAGE 2

Purchases on account recorded in a purchases journal

The date, *1989, Feb. 1*, is written in the Date column. The amount of the invoice, *$2 648.00*, is written in the amount column. The name of the creditor, *Slater Company*, is written in the Account Credited column. The number stamped on the invoice, *33*, is written in the Purch. No. column.

Each purchase on account is recorded in the purchases journal in the same way.

Posting a purchases journal to an accounts payable ledger

Each amount in a purchases journal is posted as a credit to the named creditor's account in the accounts payable ledger.

Lin's posts daily to the accounts payable ledger. In this way, each creditor's account always shows an up-to-date daily balance. The illustration on the next page shows the posting of the entry on line 1 of the purchases journal.

Write the amount, *$2 648.00*, in the Credit column of the creditor's account. Add the amount in the Credit column to the previous balance in the Credit Balance column ($963.00 + $2 648.00 = $3 611.00). Write the new balance, *$3 611.00*, in the Credit Balance column. Write the date, *1*, in the Date column. Write the abbreviation for the purchases journal, *P2*, in the Post. Ref. column of the account. Place a check mark in the Post. Ref. column of the purchases journal to show completion of the posting of this line.

> When several journals are used, an abbreviation is used to show the journal from which the posting is made. *P* is the abbreviation used for the purchases journal. The abbreviation *P2* means page 2 of the purchases journal.

This procedure is the same as posting from an Accounts Payable Credit column of a synoptic journal. Posting from a synoptic journal is described in Chapter 13.

Posting the totals of a purchases journal to a general ledger

At the end of each month, a purchases journal is totalled and ruled. A single line is drawn across the amount column under the last amount recorded, and the column is added. The total is written directly below the single line as illustrated on page 399. The date of the last day of the month, *28*, is written in the Date column. The word *Total* is written in the Account Credited column. Double lines are ruled across the amount column under the total amount.

The purchases journal total is posted to two general ledger accounts. The total is posted once to Purchases as a debit. The total is also posted once to Accounts Payable as a credit. The same total amount is posted as both a debit and a credit. This maintains the equality of debits and credits in the general ledger. The illustration, page 399, shows the posting of the purchases journal to the general ledger accounts.

The total amount of the purchases journal is posted to two general ledger accounts. The total amount, *$42 870.00*, is posted to Purchases as a debit and to Accounts Payable as a credit. After the total is posted to Purchases, the account number, *5101*, is written under the total in the purchases journal. After this same total is posted to Accounts Payable, the account number, *2102*, is written under the purchases journal total. Both account numbers are written within parentheses.

Summary of journalizing and posting from a purchases journal

(1) Lin's Music Centre records all purchases on account in a one-column purchases journal. (2) Items in the amount column are posted daily to creditors' accounts in the accounts payable ledger. (3) At the end of the

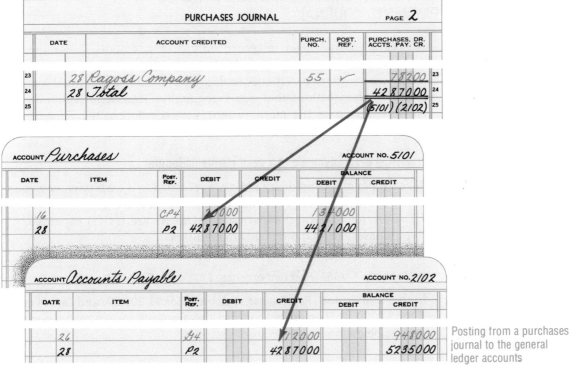

Posting from a purchases journal to the general ledger accounts

month, the purchases journal total is posted to two general ledger accounts. Purchases is debited; Accounts Payable is credited. The flowchart below shows this procedure.

Flowchart showing journalizing and posting purchases on account using a purchases journal

RECORDING CASH PAYMENTS IN A CASH PAYMENTS JOURNAL

A special journal used to record only cash payments transactions is called a cash payments journal. Lin's Music Centre uses a five-column cash payments journal. This journal, shown below, has special amount columns for transactions that occur frequently. Transactions that do not occur often, such as the monthly rent, are recorded in the General columns.

Journalizing cash payments in a cash payments journal

All cash payments made by Lin's are recorded in a cash payments journal. The source document for each cash payment is a cheque stub. *(CONCEPT: Objective Evidence)* Most cash payments are for (1) expenses, (2) cash purchases, and (3) payments to creditors.

Lin's paid an expense.

> *February 1, 1989. Paid rent expense, $1 200.00. Cheque No. 98.*

In this transaction, Rent Expense is debited for $1 200.00, and Cash is credited for $1 200.00. The entry to record this transaction in a cash payments journal is below on line 1.

CASH PAYMENTS JOURNAL   PAGE 4

	DATE	ACCOUNT TITLE	CHEQUE No.	POST. REF.	GENERAL DEBIT	GENERAL CREDIT	ACCOUNTS PAYABLE DEBIT	PURCHASES DISCOUNT CREDIT	CASH CREDIT	
1	1989 Feb. 1	Rent Expense	98		120000				120000	1
2	1	Purchases	99		18000				18000	2
3	2	Kuhns Paint Company	100				64400		64400	3

Cash payments recorded in a cash payments journal

The date, *1989, Feb. 1*, is written in the Date column. The amount debited to Rent Expense, *$1 200.00*, is written in the General Debit column. The name of the account debited, Rent Expense, is written in the Account Title column. The amount credited to Cash, *$1 200.00*, is written in the Cash Credit column. The number of the cheque, *98*, is written in the Cheque No. column.

Line 2 of the illustration above shows an entry for a cash purchase. Line 3 shows a payment on account to a creditor.

Figuring discounts

The total amount shown on an invoice is not always the amount that the buyer will pay. Discounts may affect the amount to be paid.

Trade discount. Many manufacturers and wholesalers print price lists and catalogues to describe their products. Generally prices listed in catalogues are the manufacturers' suggested retail prices. A business' printed or catalogue price is called a list price. When a merchandising business purchases a number of products from a manufacturer, the price frequently is quoted as "list price less a trade discount." A reduction in the list price granted to customers is called a trade discount. Trade discounts are used to quote different prices for different quantities purchased without changing catalogue or list prices.

When a trade discount is granted, the seller's invoice shows the actual amount charged. This is the net amount after the trade discount has been deducted from the list price. Only the net amount of the invoice is used in a journal entry. The invoice is recorded by both the seller and buyer at the same amount. No journal entry is made to show the amount of a trade discount.

On February 1, 1989, Lin's purchased six tape storage cabinets for cash. The list price quoted to Lin's was $50.00 per cabinet less 40% trade discount. The total purchase price is figured in three steps.

Step 1:	List price	times	Trade discount rate	equals	Trade discount
	$50.00	×	40%	=	$20.00
Step 2:	List price	less	Trade discount	equals	Net amount
	$50.00	−	$20.00	=	$30.00
Step 3:	Net amount	times	Number of cabinets	equals	Total purchase price
	$30.00	×	6	=	$180.00

The journal entry for this purchase is a debit to Purchases, $180.00, and a credit to Cash, $180.00. This journal entry is on line 2 of the cash payments journal, page 400.

Cash discount. A buyer is expected to pay the seller for a credit sale within the credit period agreed upon. To encourage earlier payment, a seller may allow a deduction from the amount of the invoice. A deduction that a seller allows on the amount of an invoice to encourage prompt payment is called a cash discount.

A cash discount is usually stated as a percentage that can be deducted from the amount of the invoice. For example, the terms of sale on an invoice may be written as 2/10, n/30. These terms are commonly read *two ten, net thirty*. The term *two ten* means 2% of the invoice amount may be deducted if paid within 10 days from invoice date. The term *net thirty* means that the total amount of the invoice *must* be paid within 30 days. A business also may indicate the date for full payment of an invoice as *EOM*. This means that full payment is expected not later than the *end of the month*.

Purchases discount. A cash discount on purchases taken by a buyer is called a purchases discount. When a purchases discount is taken, the buyer pays less cash than the purchase price recorded on the books. Therefore, purchases discounts are deducted from purchases when net purchases are figured. Purchases discounts are recorded in a general ledger account titled Purchases Discount.

In Lin's general ledger, the account Purchases Discount is numbered 5101.2. The purchases discount account is in the cost of merchandise division of the general ledger, as shown on page 394. An account that reduces a related account on financial statements is called a contra account.

> The decimal in the account number of Purchases Discount, *5101.2*, indicates the account is a contra or minus account. Thus on the income statement, this account is deducted from the balance of the account with the number 5101, *Purchases*. The balance of any account with a decimal account number is deducted from the balance of the account having the same whole number.

Journalizing cash payments on account with purchases discounts

Lin's tries to pay all creditors on or before the last date to take the purchases discount. This policy reduces the cost of merchandise purchased by Lin's.

Lin's paid on account.

February 9, 1989. Paid on account to Slater Company, $2 621.52, for Purchase Invoice No. 33, for $2 648.00 less 1% discount of $26.48. Cheque No. 115.

Accounts Payable is debited for the amount of the purchase invoice, $2 648.00. This debit decreases the amount owed to creditors. This same amount, $2 648.00, also is debited to the account of Slater Company in the accounts payable ledger.

Cash is credited for the amount of the cheque, $2 621.52.

Purchases Discount is credited for the amount of the purchases discount, $26.48. The discount is figured by multiplying the amount of the purchase invoice, $2 648.00, by the discount rate, 1% ($2 648.00 × .01 = $26.48). On an income statement, the balance of a purchases discount account is deducted from the balance of a purchases account. A purchases account has a debit balance. Therefore, to show a deduction from Purchases a purchases discount account has a credit balance.

The entry for this payment on account with a purchases discount is shown in the cash payments journal on the next page.

The amount of the purchase invoice, *$2 648.00*, is written in the Accounts Payable Debit column. The amount of the purchases discount, *$26.48*, is written in the Purchases Discount Credit column. The amount of cash paid, *$2 621.52*, is written in the Cash Credit column. The name

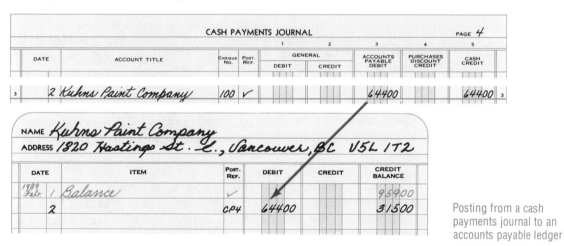

	DATE	ACCOUNT TITLE	CHEQUE No.	POST. REF.	GENERAL DEBIT	GENERAL CREDIT	ACCOUNTS PAYABLE DEBIT	PURCHASES DISCOUNT CREDIT	CASH CREDIT	
18	9	Slater Company	115				264800	2648	262152	18
19										19
20										20

CASH PAYMENTS JOURNAL   PAGE 4

of the creditor, *Slater Company*, is written in the Account Title column.
The total of the two credits ($26.48 + $2 621.52) is $2 648.00 and is equal
to the one debit of $2 648.00.

Payment on account with purchases discount recorded in cash payments journal

Purchases discounts are recorded frequently by Lin's. Therefore, a
special amount column for Purchases Discount Credit is provided in the
cash payments journal.

Posting a cash payments journal to an accounts payable ledger

Each entry in the accounts payable column of a cash payments journal
affects the creditor named in the Account Title column. Each amount
listed in this column is posted daily to the proper creditor's account in
the accounts payable ledger. In this way, each creditor's account always
shows an up-to-date balance. The illustration below shows the posting of
a cash payments journal entry to a creditor's account.

CASH PAYMENTS JOURNAL   PAGE 4

	DATE	ACCOUNT TITLE	CHEQUE No.	POST. REF.	GENERAL DEBIT	GENERAL CREDIT	ACCOUNTS PAYABLE DEBIT	PURCHASES DISCOUNT CREDIT	CASH CREDIT	
3	2	Kuhns Paint Company	100	✓			64400		64400	3

NAME *Kuhns Paint Company*
ADDRESS *1820 Hastings St. E., Vancouver, BC   V5L 1T2*

DATE	ITEM	POST. REF.	DEBIT	CREDIT	CREDIT BALANCE
1989 Feb. 1	Balance	✓			95900
2		CP4	64400		31500

Posting from a cash payments journal to an accounts payable ledger

The amount in the Accounts Payable Debit column, *$644.00*, is posted
to the Debit column of the creditor's account. After the amount is posted,
CP4 is written in the Post. Ref. column of the creditor's account. The
abbreviation CP4 means page 4 of the cash payments journal. As a last
step, place a check mark in the Post. Ref. column of the cash payments
journal. This check mark shows that the posting for this entry is complete.

Posting a cash payments journal to a general ledger

Each amount in the General columns of a cash payments journal is posted to a general ledger account. However, only the monthly total of each special column is posted to a general ledger account.

Posting from the General columns of a cash payments journal. Each amount in the General columns is posted individually to the general ledger account named in the Account Title column. The illustration below shows the posting from a General column of a cash payments journal to a general ledger account.

Posting from the general columns of a cash payments journal to a general ledger

The amount in the General Debit column, $1 200.00, is posted to the Debit column of the general ledger account Rent Expense. After the amount is posted, *CP4* is written in the Post. Ref. column of the account Rent Expense. The abbreviation *CP4* means page 4 of the cash payments journal. Last, the number of the rent expense account, *6112*, is written in the Post. Ref. column of the cash payments journal. This account number shows that posting of the General amount on this line in the journal is complete.

Posting totals of the special columns in a cash payments journal. At the end of each month, equality of debits and credits is proved for a cash payments journal. The cash payments journal is then ruled as shown on the next page. Next the total for each special column is posted to the account named in the cash payments journal column headings. The illustration on the next page shows the posting of cash payments journal special column totals to the general ledger accounts.

After a special column total is posted, *CP6* is written in the Post. Ref. column of the posted account. Last, the account number of the posted account is written under the related cash payments journal special column total. The account number is written within parentheses.

The totals of the General columns are not posted. Each amount in these columns was posted individually to a general ledger account. To indicate that these totals are not to be posted, a check mark is placed in parentheses below each column total.

				GENERAL		ACCOUNTS PAYABLE DEBIT	PURCHASES DISCOUNT CREDIT	CASH CREDIT	
				1	2	3	4	5	
	DATE	ACCOUNT TITLE	CHEQUE No.	POST. REF.	DEBIT	CREDIT			
1	1989 Feb. 21	Brought Forward		✓	1371800	152700	3026500	35400	4210200	1
26	28	Delivery Expense	183 6104	8400				8400	26
27	28	Totals			1959700	218200	4323600	50500	6014600	27
28					(✓)	(✓)	(2102)	(5101.2)	(1101)	28

CASH PAYMENTS JOURNAL   PAGE 6

ACCOUNT Accounts Payable   ACCOUNT NO. 2102

DATE	ITEM	POST. REF.	DEBIT	CREDIT	BALANCE DEBIT	BALANCE CREDIT
28		P2		4287000		5235000
28		CP6	4323600			911400

ACCOUNT Purchases Discount   ACCOUNT NO. 5101.2

DATE	ITEM	POST. REF.	DEBIT	CREDIT	BALANCE DEBIT	BALANCE CREDIT
1989 Feb. 28		CP6		50500		50500

ACCOUNT Cash   ACCOUNT NO. 1101

DATE	ITEM	POST. REF.	DEBIT	CREDIT	BALANCE DEBIT	BALANCE CREDIT
1989 Feb. 1	Balance	✓			6826800	
28		CR10	7041530		13868330	—
28		CP6		6014600	7853730	

Posting from a cash receipts journal to the cash account, shown on line 2, is described in Chapter 21.

Posting totals of the special columns in a cash payments journal to a general ledger

Summary of journalizing and posting cash payments using a cash payments journal

(1) Lin's Music Centre records all cash payments in a five-column cash payments journal. (2) Amounts in the Accounts Payable Debit column are posted daily to the named creditor's account in the accounts payable ledger. (3) Individual items in the General Debit and Credit columns are posted often during the month to the general ledger. (4) At the end of the month, the totals of the special columns are posted to the general ledger.

The flowchart below shows the procedure for journalizing and posting cash payments using a cash payments journal.

Flowchart showing journalizing and posting of cash payments using a cash payments journal

RECORDING TRANSACTIONS IN A GENERAL JOURNAL

Lin's Music Centre uses a general journal, page 408, to record transactions that cannot be recorded in the special journals. Two merchandise and supplies transactions that are not recorded in a special journal are described below.

Purchases returns and allowances

A buyer may not want to keep merchandise that is inferior in quality or is damaged when received. A buyer may be allowed to return part or all of the merchandise purchased. Merchandise returned by a buyer for credit is called a purchases return. Sometimes the seller lets the buyer keep the merchandise at a reduced price. Credit allowed for part of the price of merchandise that is not returned is called a purchases allowance.

A purchases return or allowance should be confirmed in writing. The details may be stated in a letter or on a form. A form prepared by the buyer showing the price deduction taken by the buyer for returns and allowances is called a debit memorandum. The form is called a debit memorandum because the amount is a deduction (debit) from the liability account Accounts Payable.

The buyer may use a copy of the debit memorandum as the source document for journalizing purchases returns and allowances. However, the buyer may wait for written confirmation from the seller and use that confirmation as the source document. Lin's issues a debit memorandum for each purchases return or allowance. This debit memorandum is used as the source document for purchases returns and allowances transactions. (CONCEPT: Objective Evidence) The transaction then can be recorded immediately without waiting for written confirmation from the seller. The original of the debit memorandum is sent to the creditor. The carbon copy is kept by Lin's. The debit memorandum form used by Lin's is below.

DEBIT MEMORANDUM NO. 15				
Lin's Music Centre		DATE		
		February 7, 1989		
2404 Granville Street		TO		
Vancouver, BC V6H 3G6		DESPAIN MUSIC COMPANY		
		401 MAIN STREET		
We have this day debited your account as follows.		PENTICTON, BC V2A 5C4		
Quantity	Description		Price	Total
5	#621 speaker wire rolls, your Invoice No. 88613, are being returned by motor freight. Our order specified #721 wire.		6.00	30.00
If the above is incorrect please return stating difference.				

Debit memorandum for purchases returns and allowances

Purchases returns and allowances decrease the amount of purchases. Some businesses credit the purchases account for the amount of the purchases return or allowance. However, better information is provided if these amounts are credited to a separate account Purchases Returns and Allowances. A business then can see how large its purchases returns and allowances are. Also, the business can see if purchases returns and allowances are increasing or decreasing from year to year. If the amounts are large, one account may be kept for purchases returns and another account for purchases allowances. Usually a single, combined account is satisfactory.

Lin's uses a single account Purchases Returns and Allowances. The account is in the cost of merchandise division of the general ledger as shown on page 394. The account number, 5101.1, shows that this contra purchases account is a deduction from the balance of account number 5101, Purchases.

Journalizing purchases returns and allowances

Lin's recorded a purchases returns and allowances transaction.

February 7, 1989. Returned merchandise to DeSpain Music Company, $30.00. Debit Memorandum No. 15.

GENERAL LEDGER

Accounts Payable

30.00	Bal. 8 730.00

Purchases Returns and Allowances

	30.00

ACCOUNTS PAYABLE LEDGER

DeSpain Music Company

30.00	Bal. 420.00
	290.00

The source document for this purchases return is a debit memorandum. (*CONCEPT: Objective Evidence*)

The amount owed to a creditor is decreased by this transaction. Accounts Payable is debited for the amount of the return, $30.00. The same amount is also debited to the account of DeSpain Music Company in the accounts payable ledger. Because Purchases has a debit balance, the contra purchases account, Purchases Returns and Allowances, has a credit balance. Therefore, the purchases returns and allowances account is increased on the credit side. Since this transaction increases the purchases returns and allowances account, Purchases Returns and Allowances is credited for $30.00.

The entry to record this purchases returns and allowances transaction in a general journal is below.

Purchases returns and allowances recorded in a general journal

The date, *1989, Feb. 7,* is written in the Date column. The amount of the debit, *$30.00,* is written in the Debit column. The accounts to be debited, *Accounts Payable/DeSpain Music Company,* are written in the Account Title column. The amount of the credit, *$30.00,* is written on the next line in the Credit column. The account to be credited, *Purchases Returns and Allowances,* is written in the Account Title column. This account title is indented about 1 cm. The source document for the entry, *Debit Memo. No. 15,* is written on the next line and is indented another centimetre.

Both the controlling account, Accounts Payable, and the creditor's name, DeSpain Music Company, are written in the Account Title column. The single debit amount is posted both to the general ledger account and the accounts payable ledger account. A diagonal line is placed between the two account titles to separate them clearly. A diagonal line also is placed in the Post. Ref. column to show that the debit is posted to two accounts.

Journalizing buying of supplies on account

Lin's generally buys supplies on account. Supplies are not merchandise. Only merchandise purchased on account is recorded in the purchases journal. Therefore, buying on account any item that is not merchandise is recorded in the general journal.

Lin's received an invoice for supplies bought on account.

> *February 8, 1989. Bought supplies on account from Ruhl Office Supplies, $146.00. Memorandum No. 31.*

The source document for this transaction is a memorandum. *(CONCEPT: Objective Evidence)* A memorandum is used as the source document so the supplies will not accidentally be recorded as merchandise. The invoice received from Ruhl Office Supplies is attached to the memorandum to confirm the price paid.

This transaction increases the balance of the supplies account. Supplies is debited for $146.00.

The amount owed to a creditor is increased by this transaction. Therefore, Accounts Payable is credited for $146.00. The same amount also is credited to the account of Ruhl Office Supplies in the accounts payable ledger.

The entry to record this transaction in a general journal is below.

GENERAL LEDGER

Supplies	
Bal. 480.00	
146.00	

Accounts Payable	
	Bal. 8 700.00
	146.00

ACCOUNTS PAYABLE LEDGER

Ruhl Office Supplies	
	146.00

		GENERAL JOURNAL			PAGE 2	
	DATE	ACCOUNT TITLE	POST. REF.	DEBIT	CREDIT	
4	8	Supplies		14600		4
5		Accts. Pay. / Ruhl Office Supplies			14600	5
6		Memorandum No. 31.				6
7						7
8						8
9						9

Buying of supplies on account recorded in a general journal

The date, *8*, is written in the Date column. The amount of the debit, *$146.00*, is written in the Debit column. The account to be debited, *Supplies*, is written in the Account Title column. The amount of the credit, *$146.00*, is written on the next line in the Credit column. The accounts to be credited, *Accounts Payable/Ruhl Office Supplies*, are written in the Account Title column. These accounts are indented about 1 cm. The source document, *Memorandum No. 31*, is written on the next line and is indented another centimetre.

Posting from a general journal

Each amount in the general journal Debit and Credit columns is posted to a general ledger account. The posting of an entry for supplies bought on account from a general journal is below.

Posting a buying supplies on account entry from a general journal

The amount in the Debit column, *$146.00*, is posted to the Debit column of the general ledger account Supplies. After the amount is posted, *G2* is written in the Post. Ref. column of the account Supplies. Then the supplies account number, *1105*, is written in the Post. Ref. column of the general journal.

The amount in the Credit column, *$146.00*, is posted twice. The amount is posted as a credit to the general ledger account Accounts Payable. The amount also is posted as a credit to the Ruhl Office Supplies account in the accounts payable ledger. After the amount is posted, *G2* is written in the Post. Ref. column of both Accounts Payable and Ruhl Office Supplies.

Last, the account number of Accounts Payable, *2102*, is written in the Post. Ref. column of the general journal. The number is written at the left of the diagonal line. A check mark, placed at the right of the diagonal line, shows the completion of posting to the subsidiary ledger.

ACCOUNTING TERMS

What is the meaning of each of the following?

1. corporation
2. purchases journal
3. cash payments journal
4. list price

5. trade discount
6. cash discount
7. purchases discount
8. contra account

9. purchases return
10. purchases allowance
11. debit memorandum

QUESTIONS FOR INDIVIDUAL STUDY

1. What kind of accounting system should a business use?
2. How can an equality of debits and credits be maintained when only one amount is recorded in a purchases journal?
3. What is a common source document for recording a purchase on account?
4. Purchases journal entries are posted to what two ledgers?
5. What should be the last step in posting a purchases journal to a general ledger that shows the posting is complete?
6. Which cash payments made by Lin's Music Centre are recorded in a cash payments journal?
7. How is a trade discount recorded on a purchaser's books?
8. What is meant by terms of sale 2/10, n/30?
9. Why is the purchases discount account given an account number with a decimal, as 5101.2?
10. When Lin's Music Centre issues a cheque on account for a purchase with a purchases discount, what accounts are debited and credited?
11. Why are the column totals from the General Debit and Credit columns of a cash payments journal *not* posted?
12. If purchases returns and allowances are a decrease in purchases, why are returns and allowances credited to a separate account?
13. What accounts are debited and credited by a buyer to record a purchases returns and allowances transaction?
14. When supplies are bought on account, why is the entry made in a general journal instead of a purchases journal?
15. What is meant by the posting reference P2? CP6? G2?

CASES FOR MANAGEMENT DECISION

CASE 1 Alice Simpson manages a sports equipment store. The store has been using a synoptic journal. The company's accountant has suggested that because the store is increasing its total amount of sales, special journals be used. What should Mrs. Simpson consider in making a decision either to stay with the synoptic journal or to change to special journals?

CASE 2 O'Brien Lumber Company has employed an accounting firm to install a new accounting system using special journals. You and two others are design-ing the special journals. John, one of the accountants, recommends a cash payments journal with one special column, Cash Credit. Mary, another accountant, recommends a cash payments journal with three special columns, Purchases Debit, Purchases Discount Credit, and Cash Credit. You have been asked to make the decision as to the cash payments journal to be used. Give your decision and the reason for that decision.

CASE 3 Fred Arvin, accounting clerk for Zaloudek Company, has been recording supplies bought on account in a purchases journal. When the manager questioned him, Fred said, "It won't affect the net income, and recording in a purchases journal is much quicker than recording in a general journal." Is Fred right or wrong? Explain.

DRILLS FOR UNDERSTANDING

DRILL 20-D 1   Analysing transactions affecting purchases and cash payments

Use a form similar to the one below.

Trans. No.	(a) Account Debited	(b) Account Credited	(c) Journal in Which Recorded	(d) (e) Name of Amount Column Used in Journal	
				For Amount Debited	For Amount Credited
1.	Purchases	Cash	Cash Payments	General Debit	Cash Credit

Instructions: Do each of the following for the transactions listed below. Write in Column a the name of the account(s) debited. Write in Column b the name of the account(s) credited. Write in Column c the name of the journal in which the transaction is recorded. Write in Columns d and e the names of the journal amount column(s) in which debit and credit amounts are recorded. Transaction 1 is given as an example in the form above.

1. Paid cash for purchases of merchandise.
2. Purchased merchandise on account from Cannon Music Company.
3. Paid cash on account to Cannon Music Company; no discount.
4. Paid cash for supplies.
5. Issued a debit memorandum and returned merchandise to Cannon Music Company.
6. Paid cash on account to Nichols Company for a purchase invoice less the amount of purchases discount.
7. Bought supplies on account from Plouff Company.
8. Purchased merchandise on account from Winston Music Shop.
9. Paid cash for February rent.
10. Issued a debit memorandum to Winston Music Shop for faulty merchandise returned.

DRILL 20-D 2   Posting transactions from special journals

Use a form similar to the one on the next page.

Instructions: 1. Write in Column a the account titles affected by each transaction in Drill 20-D 1. These account titles are taken from Columns a and b of the completed Drill 20-D 1.

	(a)	(b) (c) Amounts posted separately to		(d) Amounts not posted
Trans. No.	Accounts affected	General Ledger	Accounts Payable Ledger	separately to any ledger
1.	*Purchases*	✓		
	Cash			✓

2. Place a check mark in Column b if the amount is posted separately to the general ledger. Place a check mark in Column c if the amount is posted separately to the accounts payable ledger. Place a check mark in Column d if the amount is not posted separately to any ledger. Transaction 1 is given above as an example.

APPLICATION PROBLEMS

PROBLEM 20-1 Journalizing and posting transactions affecting purchases

The accounts payable ledger and general ledger accounts of Karl's Florist are given in the working papers. The balances are recorded as of February 1 of the current year.

ACCOUNTS PAYABLE LEDGER

Creditor	Account Balance
Brozek Company, 203 Argyle Street, Regina, SK S4R 4C5	$ 245.00
Eagle Company, 604 College Avenue, Regina, SK S4N 0X5	896.00
Franz Supplies, 1925 7th Avenue, Regina, SK S4R 1C1	——
Kinlaw Company, 1422 Victoria Avenue, Regina, SK S4P 0P3	1 215.00
Ortiz Company, 6007 1st Avenue N., Regina, SK S4T 6Z6	87.00

PARTIAL GENERAL LEDGER

Account Title	Account No.	Account Balance
Accounts Payable	2102	$2 443.00
Purchases	5101	——

Instructions: 1. The following purchases on account were made by Karl's Florist during February of the current year. Record these transactions on page 4 of a purchases journal similar to the one illustrated in this chapter. The abbreviation for purchase invoice is *P*.

Feb. 1. Purchased merchandise on account from Kinlaw Company, $135.00. P37.
  · 2. Purchased merchandise on account from Ortiz Company, $74.00. P38.
   7. Purchased merchandise on account from Franz Supplies, $489.00. P39.
   9. Purchased merchandise on account from Brozek Company, $932.00. P40.
  11. Purchased merchandise on account from Kinlaw Company, $1 578.00. P41.
  14. Purchased merchandise on account from Eagle Company, $2 403.00. P42.
  15. Purchased merchandise on account from Brozek Company, $386.00. P43.
  22. Purchased merchandise on account from Ortiz Company, $198.00. P44.
  24. Purchased merchandise on account from Eagle Company, $898.00. P45.
  28. Purchased merchandise on account from Kinlaw Company, $579.00. P46.

Instructions: 2. Post each amount in the purchases journal to the accounts payable ledger.

3. Total and rule the purchases journal. Post the total.

4. Prepare a schedule of accounts payable similar to the one on page 250. Compare the schedule total with the balance of the accounts payable account in the general ledger. The total and the balance should be the same.

PROBLEM 20-2 Journalizing and posting transactions affecting cash payments

The accounts payable ledger and general ledger accounts of Superior Company are given in the working papers. The balances are recorded as of February 1 of the current year.

ACCOUNTS PAYABLE LEDGER

Creditor	Account Balance
Ayala Company, 826 Robie Street, Halifax, NS B3H 3C1	$1 258.00
Clark's Furnishings, 3433 Windsor Street, Halifax, NS B3K 5G5	2 903.00
Irvine Company, 107 Main Street, Dartmouth, NS B2X 1R6	830.00
Ragland Company, 163 King Street, Bridgewater, NS B4V 1A51	1 793.00

PARTIAL GENERAL LEDGER

Account Title	Account No.	Account Balance
Cash	1101	$22 375.00
Supplies	1105	745.00
Accounts Payable	2102	6 784.00
Purchases	5101	——
Purchases Discount	5101.2	——
Delivery Expense	6103	——
Rent Expense	6110	——

Instructions: 1. The following cash payments were made by Superior Company during February of the current year. Record these cash payments in a cash payments journal similar to the one illustrated in this chapter. Use page 6 for the cash payments journal. The abbreviation for cheque is *C*.

Feb. 1. Paid February rent, $600.00. C102.
   2. Paid on account to Clark's Furnishings, $1 440.60, covering invoice for $1 470.00 less a 2% cash discount of $29.40. C103.
   4. Bought supplies for cash, $126.00. C104.
   7. Paid on account to Ragland Company, $1 267.20, covering invoice for $1 280.00 less a 1% cash discount of $12.80. C105.
   9. Paid delivery expense, $48.00. C106.
   10. Purchased merchandise for cash, $385.00. C107.
   15. Paid on account to Ayala Company, $1 258.00. No discount. C108.
   22. Bought supplies for cash, $93.00. C109.
   25. Paid on account to Irvine Company, $830.00. No discount. C110.
   28. Paid delivery expense, $26.00. C111.

Instructions: 2. Post accounts payable amounts to the appropriate accounts in the accounts payable ledger.

3. Post the amounts in the General columns to the appropriate general ledger accounts.

4. Total, prove, and rule the cash payments journal. Post the special column totals to the appropriate general ledger accounts.

PROBLEM 20-3   Journalizing and posting transactions affecting purchases and cash payments

The accounts payable ledger and general ledger accounts of Jacob's Cycle Shop are given in the working papers. The balances are recorded as of February 1 of the current year.

ACCOUNTS PAYABLE LEDGER

Creditor	Account Balance
Barton Company, 423 Yonge Street, Toronto, ON M5B 1T2	$ 348.00
Cycle Enterprises, 280 Adelaide Street W., Toronto, ON M5V 1P6	——
Gear Shop Supplies, 33 Grove Street E., Barrie, ON L4M 2N8	3 312.00
Jessup Company, 694 College Avenue W., Guelph, ON N1G 1V1	1 290.00
Symiyo Motorcycles, 1546 Main Street W., Hamilton, ON L8S 1E5	——

PARTIAL GENERAL LEDGER

Account Title	Acct. No.	Account Balance
Cash	1101	$26 880.00
Supplies	1105	1 061.30
Accounts Payable	2102	4 950.00
Purchases	5101	——
Purchases Returns and Allowances.......	5101.1	——
Purchases Discount................................	5101.2	——
Delivery Expense....................................	6103	——
Miscellaneous Expense..........................	6108	——
Rent Expense	6110	——

Instructions: 1. The following transactions affecting purchases and cash payments were completed by Jacob's Cycle Shop during February of the current year. Record these transactions in a purchases journal, a general journal, and a cash payments journal similar to those in this chapter. Use page 4 for each journal. Source documents are abbreviated as: cheque, C; memorandum, M; purchase invoice, P; debit memorandum, DM.

Feb. 1. Purchased merchandise on account from Gear Shop Supplies, $2 304.00. P43.
   1. Paid February rent, $900.00. C92.
   3. Returned merchandise to Gear Shop Supplies, $144.00. DM8.
   4. Purchased merchandise on account from Cycle Enterprises, $2 246.00. P44.
      Posting. Post the items that are to be posted individually. Post from the journals in this order: purchases journal, general journal, and cash payments journal.
   7. Bought supplies on account from Barton Company, $302.00. M10.
   9. Paid on account to Jessup Company, $1 277.10, covering P39 for $1 290.00 less a 1% cash discount of $12.90. C93.
      Posting. Post the items that are to be posted individually.
   14. Purchased merchandise for cash, $504.00. C94.
   15. Paid on account to Cycle Enterprises, $2 223.54, covering P44 for $2 246.00 less a 1% discount of $22.46. C95.
   16. Purchased merchandise on account from Sumiyo Motorcycles, $3 916.00. P45.
   19. Purchased merchandise on account from Cycle Enterprises, $2 720.00. P46.
      Posting. Post the items that are to be posted individually.

Feb. 21. Paid on account to Gear Shop Supplies for February 1 beginning balance of $3 312.00; no discount. C96.
22. Paid miscellaneous expense, $43.00. C97.
22. Paid on account to Barton Company, $348.00; no discount. C98.
22. Paid delivery expense, $86.00. C99.
23. Purchased merchandise on account from Jessup Company, $1 440.00. P47.
25. Paid on account to Sumiyo Motorcycles, $3 837.68, covering P45 for $3 916.00 less a 2% discount of $78.32. C100.
25. Purchased merchandise on account from Gear Shop Supplies, $948.00. P48.
    Posting. Post the items that are to be posted individually.
28. Paid on account to Barton Company, $302.00; no discount. C101.
28. Purchased merchandise on account from Sumiyo Motorcycles, $1 132.00. P49.
28. Paid on account to Cycle Enterprises, $2 692.80, covering P46 for $2 720.00 less a 1% discount of $27.20. C102.
28. Purchased merchandise on account from Cycle Enterprises, $1 036.00. P50.
28. Paid on account to Gear Shop Supplies, $2 160.00, covering P43 for $2 304.00 less DM8 for $144.00; no discount. C103.
28. Paid miscellaneous expense, $118.00. C104.
28. Returned merchandise to Cycle Enterprises, $346.00. DM9.
    Posting. Post the items that are to be posted individually.

Instructions: 2. Total and rule the purchases journal. Post the total.
3. Total, prove, and rule the cash payments journal. Post the totals of the special columns.
4. Prepare a schedule of accounts payable similar to the one shown on page 250. Compare the schedule total with the balance of the accounts payable account in the general ledger. The total and the balance should be the same.

ENRICHMENT PROBLEMS

MASTERY PROBLEM 20-M Journalizing and posting transactions affecting purchases and cash payments

The accounts payable ledger and general ledger accounts of Travis Paint Centre are given in the working papers. The balances are recorded as of May 1 of the current year.

ACCOUNTS PAYABLE LEDGER

Creditor	Account Balance
Ajax Paint Company, 2047 Ste-Foy Chemin, Quebec, PQ G1V 1R3	$ 317.00
Drake Supply Company, 1771 4E Avenue, Quebec, PQ G1J 3C6	——
Keminiski Company, 4182 Chambly Chemin, St-Hubert, PQ J3Y 3M6	616.00
Leidy Paint Supply, 410 Du Havre Boulevard, Valleyfield, PQ J6S 1T2	——
Patterson Company, 2325 5E Avenue, Shawinigan, PQ G9P 1P4	1 294.00

PARTIAL GENERAL LEDGER

Account Title	Account No.	Account Balance
Cash	1101	$16 170.00
Supplies	1105	326.30
Accounts Payable	2102	2 227.00
Purchases	5101	——
Purchases Returns and Allowances	5101.1	——
Purchases Discount	5101.2	——

Account Title	Account No.	Account Balance
Delivery Expense......................................	6103	——
Miscellaneous Expense...........................	6108	——
Rent Expense	6110	——

Instructions: 1. The following transactions affecting purchases and cash payments were completed by Travis Paint Centre during May of the current year. Record these transactions in a purchases journal, general journal, and cash payments journal similar to those in this chapter. Use page 10 for the purchases and cash payments journals. Use page 6 for the general journal.

Source documents are abbreviated as: cheque, C; memorandum, M; purchase invoice, P; debit memorandum, DM.

May   2. Paid May rent, $950.00. C121.
    2. Returned merchandise to Keminiski Company, $132.00. DM16.
    3. Paid on account to Ajax Paint Company, $313.83, covering P110 for $317.00 less a 1% cash discount of $3.17. C122.
    4. Purchased merchandise on account from Patterson Company, $554.00. P112.
    5. Purchased merchandise on account from Ajax Paint Company, $436.00. P113.
    6. Paid on account to Patterson Company, $1 268.12, covering P111 for $1 294.00 less a 2% discount of $25.88. C123.
       Posting. Post the items that are to be posted individually. Post from the journals in this order: purchases journal, general journal, and cash payments journal.
    9. Paid on account to Keminiski Company, $484.00, covering P109 for $616.00 less DM16 for $132.00; no discount. C124.
    9. Paid cash for delivery expense, $40.00. C125.
  10. Bought supplies on account from Leidy Paint Supply, $198.00. M30.
  12. Purchased merchandise on account from Keminiski Company, $653.00. P114.
  13. Paid on account to Patterson Company, $542.92, covering P112 for $554.00 less a 2% discount of $11.08. C126.
  13. Paid on account to Ajax Paint Company, $431.64, covering P113 for $436.00 less a 1% discount of $4.36. C127.
       Posting. Post the items that are to be posted individually.
  16. Returned merchandise to Keminiski Company, $84.00. DM17.
  16. Discovered that supplies bought for cash in April had been recorded in error as a debit to Purchases, $150.00. M31.
  17. Purchased merchandise on account from Patterson Company, $625.00. P115.
  18. Purchased merchandise on account from Ajax Paint Company, $578.00. P116.
  20. Paid on account to Leidy Paint Supply, $198.00; no discount. C128.
  20. Paid on account to Keminiski Company, $569.00, covering P114 for $653.00 less DM17 for $84.00; no discount. C129.
       Posting. Post the items that are to be posted individually.
  23. Bought supplies on account from Leidy Paint Supply, $308.00. M32.
  24. Paid miscellaneous expenses, $125.00. C130.
  24. Discovered that supplies bought on account from Drake Supply Co. in April had been recorded as a credit to Cash instead of Accounts Payable, $225.00. M33.
  25. Purchased merchandise on account from Keminiski Company, $250.00. P117.
  27. Paid on account to Ajax Paint Company, $572.22, covering P116 for $578.00 less a 1% discount of $5.78. C131.
       Posting. Post the items that are to be posted individually.

Instructions: 2. Total and rule the purchases journal. Post the total.

3. Total, prove, and rule the cash payments journal. Post the totals of the special columns.

4. Prepare a schedule of accounts payable similar to the one on page 250. Compare the schedule total with the balance of the accounts payable account in the general ledger. The total and the balance should be the same.

CHALLENGE PROBLEM 20-C Journalizing transactions in a combined purchases-cash payments journal

The accountant for Travis Paint Centre has suggested that time could be saved if the purchases journal and the cash payments journal were combined into one journal. She suggests using a journal such as the one below.

PURCHASES — CASH PAYMENTS JOURNAL

				1	2	3	4	5	6	7
Date	Account Title	Doc. No.	Post. Ref.	General		Purchases Debit	Accounts Payable		Purchases Discount Credit	Cash Credit
				Debit	Credit		Debit	Credit		

Carlos Valdez, manager, has asked the accountant to show him how the journal would appear after transactions have been recorded.

Instructions: 1. Use page 10 of a journal like the one above. Use page 6 of a general journal like the one on page 408. Journalize the transactions given in Mastery Problem 20-M, page 416.

2. Total, prove, and rule the combined purchases-cash payments journal.

3. Do you agree with the accountant that the combined purchases-cash payments journal used in this problem saves time in journalizing and posting? Why?

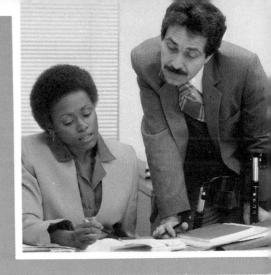

21

Recording Transactions with Special Journals: Sales and Cash Receipts

ENABLING PERFORMANCE TASKS

After studying Chapter 21, you will be able to:

a. Define accounting terms related to sales and cash receipts.
b. Explain accounting principles and practices related to sales and cash receipts.
c. Analyse transactions affecting sales and cash receipts.
d. Journalize sales on account transactions in a sales journal.
e. Post from a sales journal.
f. Journalize cash receipts transactions in a cash receipts journal.
g. Post from a cash receipts journal.
h. Journalize sales returns and allowances and correcting entries in a general journal.
i. Post from a general journal.

Lin's Music Centre uses a system of special journals to record accounting transactions. Five journals are used. A sales journal, cash receipts journal, and general journal are described in this chapter. A purchases journal and cash payments journal were described in Chapter 20.

RECORDING SALES ON ACCOUNT IN A SALES JOURNAL

A special journal used to record only sales on account is called a sales journal. Regardless of when cash is received, revenue should be recorded when merchandise is sold. *(CONCEPT: Realization of Revenue)* Lin's Music Centre uses a sales journal, page 420, to record only sales on account transactions. A sale on account can be recorded on one line in a sales journal. Lin's uses a sales journal with three amount columns: Accounts Receivable Debit, Sales Credit, and Sales Tax Payable Credit. The province where Lin's is located has a sales tax on many items sold at retail. A retail business must collect the sales tax from customers and periodically

419

send the sales tax collected to the province. Customers must pay a sales tax on items sold by Lin's. Therefore, Lin's uses a sales journal that includes a special column for Sales Tax Payable Credit. This column permits the company to keep a record of sales tax separate from sales.

Journalizing sales on account in a sales journal

Lin's prepares a sales invoice in duplicate for each sale on account. The original copy is given to the charge customer. The carbon copy is the source document for recording sales on account transactions. (CONCEPT: *Objective Evidence*) The sales invoice used by Lin's is similar to the one on page 213.

Lin's sold merchandise on account.

GENERAL LEDGER

Accounts Receivable

| 472.50 | |

Sales

| | 450.00 |

Sales Tax Payable

| | 22.50 |

*ACCOUNTS RECEIVABLE
LEDGER*

Yolanda Bergdahl

| 472.50 | |

February 1, 1989. Sold merchandise on account to Yolanda Bergdahl, $450.00, plus sales tax, $22.50. Sales Invoice No. 86.

In this entry, Accounts Receivable is debited for $472.50, the amount of the sale plus the sales tax. Sales is credited for $450.00, the amount of the sale. Sales Tax Payable is credited for $22.50, the amount of the tax on this sale. Lin's owes the tax to the provincial government. Therefore, the amount of sales tax charged each customer is a liability.

Yolanda Bergdahl's account in the accounts receivable ledger is also debited for $472.50.

The entry to record this transaction in a sales journal is below.

					1	2	3	
SALES JOURNAL							PAGE 6	
	DATE	ACCOUNT DEBITED	SALE NO.	POST. REF.	ACCOUNTS RECEIVABLE DEBIT	SALES CREDIT	SALES TAX PAYABLE CREDIT	
1	1989 Feb. 1	Yolanda Bergdahl	86		47250	45000	2250	1
2								2

Sale on account recorded
in a sales journal

The date, *1989, Feb. 1*, is written in the Date column. The amount of the sale plus the sales tax, *$472.50*, is written in the Accounts Receivable Debit column. The amount of the sale, *$450.00*, is written in the Sales Credit column. The amount of sales tax, *$22.50*, is written in the Sales Tax Payable Credit column. The name of the charge customer, *Yolanda Bergdahl*, is written in the Account Debited column. The sales invoice number, *86*, is written in the Sale No. column. Each sale on account is recorded in the sales journal in this same way.

Posting a sales journal to an accounts receivable ledger

Each amount in the Accounts Receivable Debit column of a sales journal is posted to an accounts receivable ledger. Each amount is posted as a debit to the charge customer's account listed in the account title column. Lin's posts daily to the accounts receivable ledger. With daily posting, each customer's account always shows an up-to-date daily balance. The illustration below shows the posting of the entry on line 1 of the sales journal.

Posting from a sales journal to an accounts receivable ledger

Write the amount, $472.50, in the Debit column of the customer's account. Add the amount in the Debit column to the previous balance in the Debit Balance column ($127.00 + $472.50 = $599.50). Write the new balance, $599.50, in the Debit Balance column. Write the date, 1, in the Date column. Write the abbreviation for the sales journal, S6, in the Post. Ref. column of the account. Place a check mark in the Post. Ref. column of the sales journal to show completion of posting of this line.

This procedure is the same as posting from an Accounts Receivable Debit column of a synoptic journal. Posting from a synoptic journal is described in Chapter 13.

Posting the totals of a sales journal to a general ledger

At the end of each month, equality of debits and credits is proved for a sales journal. The sales journal then is ruled as shown on page 422. A single line is drawn across the amount columns under the last amounts. The column totals are written below the single line as shown on page 422. The last day of the month, 28, is placed in the Date column. The word *Totals* is written in the Account Debited column. Double lines are ruled across the amount columns under the totals. Next, each amount column total is posted to the general ledger account named in the sales journal column headings.

The illustration on the next page shows the posting of sales journal amount column totals.

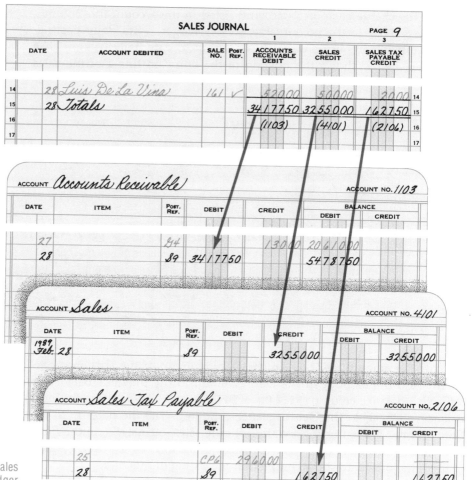

Posting totals of the special columns in a sales journal to a general ledger

When each sales journal amount column total is posted, *S9* is written in the Post. Ref. column of the accounts. The accounts receivable account number, *1103*, is written under the column total in the sales journal. The sales account number, *4101*, is written under the total of the Sales Credit column. The sales tax payable account number, *2106*, is written under the total of the Sales Tax Payable Credit column. All three account numbers are written within parentheses.

Summary of journalizing and posting from a sales journal

(1) Lin's Music Centre records all sales on account in a three-column sales journal. (2) Individual items in the sales journal are posted daily. The items are posted to the individual accounts for charge customers in the accounts receivable ledger. (3) At the end of each month, each amount column total is posted. The Accounts Receivable Debit column

total is posted to Accounts Receivable as a debit. The Sales Credit column total is posted to Sales as a credit. The Sales Tax Payable Credit column total is posted to Sales Tax Payable as a credit. The flowchart below shows this procedure.

Flowchart showing journalizing and posting of sales on account using a sales journal

RECORDING CASH RECEIPTS IN A CASH RECEIPTS JOURNAL

A special journal in which only cash receipts transactions are recorded is called a cash receipts journal. The cash receipts journal used by Lin's Music Centre is on page 424. The cash receipts journal has special amount columns for those kinds of cash receipts transactions that occur most often. For example, Lin's has many cash sales transactions. *(CONCEPT: Realization of Revenue)* Special amount columns are provided for Cash Debit, Sales Credit, and Sales Tax Payable Credit entries.

Journalizing cash receipts in a cash receipts journal

All cash receipts are recorded in a cash receipts journal. Most cash receipts are for (1) cash received from customers on account, (2) cash sales, and (3) credit card sales. The source document for cash sales is a cash register tape. The source document for credit card sales is a calculator tape for the day's credit card sales. A common source document for other cash receipts is the stub of a receipt. *(CONCEPT: Objective Evidence)*

At the beginning of each month, an entry is made to record the cash balance on hand in the cash receipts journal. This entry makes the beginning cash balance readily available for proving cash. This entry in a cash receipts journal is below on line 1.

Lin's received cash on account.

> *February 1, 1989. Received cash on account from Luis Garcez, $504.00. Receipt No. 202.*

In this transaction, Cash is debited for $504.00 and Accounts Receivable is credited for $504.00. The entry to record this transaction in a cash receipts journal is below on line 2.

	DATE	ACCOUNT TITLE	Doc. No.	Post. Ref.	GENERAL DEBIT	GENERAL CREDIT	ACCOUNTS RECEIVABLE CREDIT	SALES CREDIT	SALES TAX PAYABLE CREDIT	CASH DEBIT	
					1	2	3	4	5	6	
1	1989 Feb. 1	Balance on hand, $68 268.00		✓							1
2	1	Luis Garcez	R202				50400			50400	2
3	1	✓	J1	✓				45560	2278	47838	3
4	1	✓	CJ1	✓				68340	3417	71757	4

CASH RECEIPTS JOURNAL   PAGE 6

Cash receipts transactions recorded in a cash receipts journal

The date, *1*, is written in the Date column. The amount credited to Accounts Receivable, *$504.00*, is written in the Accounts Receivable Credit column. The amount of cash received, *$504.00*, is written in the Cash Debit column. The name of the charge customer, *Luis Garcez*, is written in the Account Title column. The number of the receipt, *R202*, is written in the Doc. No. column.

Line 3 above shows cash sales for the day. Line 4 above shows credit card sales for the day.

Posting a cash receipts journal to an accounts receivable ledger

Each entry in the Accounts Receivable Credit column affects the charge customer named in the Account Title column. Each amount listed in this column is posted daily to the proper customer's account in the accounts receivable ledger. Posting of a cash receipts journal entry to a customer's account is on the next page.

The amount in the Accounts Receivable Credit column, *$504.00*, is posted to the Credit column of the customer's account. After the amount is posted, *CR6* is written in the Post. Ref. column of the customer's account. The abbreviation CR6 means page 6 of the cash receipts journal. As a last step, place a check mark in the Post. Ref. column of the cash receipts journal.

CASH RECEIPTS JOURNAL — PAGE 6

	DATE	ACCOUNT TITLE	Doc. No.	Post. Ref.	GENERAL DEBIT	GENERAL CREDIT	ACCOUNTS RECEIVABLE CREDIT	SALES CREDIT	SALES TAX PAYABLE CREDIT	CASH DEBIT	
1	1989 Feb. 1	Balance on hand, $68 268.00		✓							1
2	1	Luis Garcez	R202	✓			504 00			504 00	2

NAME *Luis Garcez*
ADDRESS *816 Howe Street, Vancouver, BC   V6Z 1N4*

DATE	ITEM	Post. Ref.	DEBIT	CREDIT	DEBIT BALANCE
1989 Feb. 1	Balance	✓			504 00
1		CR6		504 00	———

Posting from a cash receipts journal to an accounts receivable ledger

Posting a cash receipts journal to a general ledger

Each amount in the General columns of a cash receipts journal is posted to a general ledger account. However, only the monthly total of each special column is posted to a general ledger account.

Posting from the General columns of a cash receipts journal. Each amount in the General columns is posted individually to the general ledger account named in the Account Title column. Transactions involving entries in the General Debit and Credit columns are described in Chapter 26.

Posting totals of the special columns in a cash receipts journal. At the end of each month, equality of debits and credits is proved for a cash receipts journal. Cash is then proved. The cash proof for Lin's at the end of February is below.

Beginning cash balance, February 1, 1989	$ 68 268.00
(Line 1 of cash receipts journal, page **424**)	
Plus total cash received	70 415.30
(Total of Cash Debit column, cash receipts journal, page **426**)	
Total...	$138 683.30
Less total cash payments	60 146.00
(Total of Cash Credit column, cash payments journal, page **405**)	
Equals cash balance, February 28, 1989	$ 78 537.30

The balance after the last cheque (Cheque Stub No. 183) was written is $78 537.30. The balance on the cheque stub agrees with the balance figured above. Therefore, cash is proved.

After cash is proved, the cash receipts journal is ruled as shown on page **426**. Next the total for each special column is posted to the account named in the cash receipts journal column headings. Posting of cash receipts journal special column totals to the general ledger accounts is below.

Posting totals of the special columns in a cash receipts journal to a general ledger

Posting from a cash payments journal to the cash account was described in Chapter 20.

When each special column total is posted, *CR10* is written in the Post. Ref. column of the accounts. The general ledger account number is written under the related cash receipts journal special column total. The account numbers, written within parentheses, show that posting of a column total is complete.

The totals of the General columns are not posted. Each amount in these columns was posted individually to a general ledger account. To indicate that these totals are not to be posted, a check mark is placed in parentheses below each column total.

Summary of journalizing and posting cash receipts using a cash receipts journal

(1) Lin's Music Centre records all cash receipts in a six-column cash receipts journal. (2) Amounts in the Accounts Receivable Credit column are posted daily to the customer's account in the accounts receivable ledger. (3) At the end of the month, the totals of the special columns are posted to the general ledger. This procedure is shown in the flowchart below.

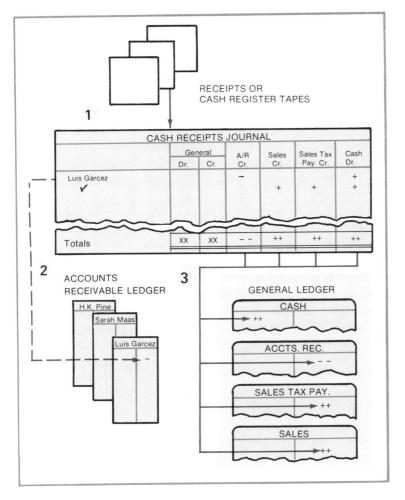

Flowchart showing journalizing and posting of cash receipts using a cash receipts journal

RECORDING OTHER TRANSACTIONS IN A GENERAL JOURNAL

Some purchases-related transactions recorded in a general journal were described in Chapter 20. Lin's Music Centre also records two sales-related transactions in a general journal.

1. Sales returns and allowances.
2. Correcting entries affecting charge customers' accounts but not the controlling account.

Sales returns and allowances

Most merchandising businesses expect to have some merchandise returned because a customer may decide not to keep the merchandise. A customer may have received the wrong style, the wrong size, or damaged goods. A customer may return merchandise to the seller and ask for a credit on account or a cash refund. Merchandise returned from a customer for a credit on account or a cash refund is called a sales return.

A seller may grant credit to a customer without asking for the return of damaged or imperfect merchandise. Credit allowed a customer for part of the sales price of merchandise not returned is called a sales allowance. An allowance also may be given because of a shortage in a shipment.

A seller usually informs a buyer in writing when a sales return or a sales allowance is granted. A form prepared by the seller showing the amount deducted for returns and allowances is called a credit memorandum. The form is called a *credit* memorandum because the asset account Accounts Receivable is decreased by the transaction. Decreases in asset accounts are recorded as credits.

Lin's issues a credit memorandum in duplicate for each sales return or sales allowance. The original copy is given to the customer. The carbon copy is used as the source document for sales returns and allowances. *(CONCEPT: Objective Evidence)* The credit memorandum form used by Lin's is on the next page.

Sales returns and sales allowances decrease the amount of sales. Some businesses debit the sales account for the amount of a return or allowance. However, better information is provided if these amounts are debited to a separate account *Sales Returns and Allowances*. A separate account shows how large the sales returns and allowances are. Also, a business can see if returns and allowances are increasing or decreasing from year to year. If the amounts are large, one account may be kept for sales returns and another account for sales allowances. Usually a single, combined account is used.

Lin's uses a single account Sales Returns and Allowances. The account is in the revenue division of the general ledger, page 394. The account number, 4101.1, shows that this contra sales account is a deduction from

CREDIT MEMORANDUM NO. 36

Lin's Music Centre

2404 Granville Street
Vancouver, BC V6H 3G6

We have this day credited
your account as follows:

	DATE
	February 11, 1989

	TO
	CALVIN RONEY 406 5th Avenue Kimberley, BC V1A 2S7

Quantity	Description	Price	Total
1	Speaker, Model SR1032	200.00	
	Sales Tax	10.00	210.00

If the above is incorrect please return stating difference.

Credit memorandum

the balance of account 4101, Sales. A customer is entitled to credit for the amount of a sales return or allowance. The credit must include the sales tax on the return or allowance.

Journalizing sales returns and allowances

On February 7, Lin's sold merchandise on account to Calvin Roney for $400.00. Mr. Roney's account was debited for $420.00, $400.00 sales and $20.00 sales tax. On February 11, Mr. Roney returned part of the merchandise.

> *February 11, 1989. Granted credit to Calvin Roney for merchandise returned, $200.00, plus sales tax, $10.00. Credit Memorandum No. 36.*

The source document for this sales return is a credit memorandum. *(CONCEPT: Objective Evidence)* Because Sales has a credit balance, the contra sales account, Sales Returns and Allowances, has a debit balance. Therefore, the sales returns and allowances account is increased on the debit side. Since this transaction increases the balance of the account, Sales Returns and Allowances is debited for $200.00.

The sales tax payable account, a liability account, has a credit balance. Therefore, the sales tax payable account is increased on the credit side. Since this transaction decreases the balance of the account, Sales Tax Payable is debited for $10.00. The debit to Sales Tax Payable is for the amount of tax on the returned merchandise.

The amount to be collected from the charge customer is decreased. Mr. Roney is entitled to a $200.00 credit for the

GENERAL LEDGER

Sales Returns and Allowances

200.00	

Sales Tax Payable

10.00	

Accounts Receivable

	210.00

ACCOUNTS RECEIVABLE LEDGER

Calvin Roney

Bal. 420.00	210.00

merchandise returned and a $10.00 credit for sales tax. Therefore, Accounts Receivable is credited for the total amount, $210.00. The same amount also is credited to Calvin Roney's account in the accounts receivable ledger.

The entry to record this sales returns and allowances transaction in a general journal is below.

<table>
<tr><td colspan="6" align="center">GENERAL JOURNAL</td><td align="right">PAGE 2</td></tr>
<tr><td colspan="2">DATE</td><td>ACCOUNT TITLE</td><td>POST. REF.</td><td>DEBIT</td><td>CREDIT</td><td></td></tr>
<tr><td>13</td><td>11</td><td>Sales Returns and Allowances</td><td></td><td>200 00</td><td></td><td>13</td></tr>
<tr><td>14</td><td></td><td>Sales Tax Payable</td><td></td><td>10 00</td><td></td><td>14</td></tr>
<tr><td>15</td><td></td><td>Accts. Rec./Calvin Roney</td><td>/</td><td></td><td>210 00</td><td>15</td></tr>
<tr><td>16</td><td></td><td>Credit Memo. No. 36.</td><td></td><td></td><td></td><td>16</td></tr>
<tr><td>17</td><td></td><td></td><td></td><td></td><td></td><td>17</td></tr>
</table>

Sales returns and allowances recorded in a general journal

The date, *11*, is written in the Date column. The amount of the debit, *$200.00*, is written in the Debit column. *Sales Returns and Allowances* is written in the Account Title column. The amount of the debit, *$10.00*, is written on the next line in the Debit column. *Sales Tax Payable* is written in the Account Title column. The amount of the credit, *$210.00*, is written on the next line in the Credit column. The accounts credited, *Accounts Receivable/Calvin Roney*, are written in the Account Title column. These account titles are indented about 1 cm. The source document, *Credit Memo. No. 36*, is written on the next line indented about 2 cm.

Both the controlling account, *Accounts Receivable*, and the customer's name, Calvin Roney, are written in the Account Title column. The single credit amount is posted both to the general ledger account and the accounts receivable ledger account. A diagonal line is placed between the two account titles to separate them. A diagonal line is placed in the Post. Ref. column to show that the credit is posted to two accounts.

Journalizing a correcting entry affecting charge customers' accounts

Errors may be made in recording amounts in subsidiary ledgers that do not affect the general ledger controlling account. For example, a sale on account may be recorded for the wrong charge customer in the sales journal. The column total posted from the sales journal to the general ledger is correct. The accounts receivable account shows the correct balance. However, two of the charge customers' accounts in the accounts receivable ledger show incorrect balances. To correct this error, only the subsidiary ledger accounts need to be corrected.

Lin's discovered and corrected an error.

February 12, 1989. Discovered that a sale on account to Ann Bryan on January 26 was incorrectly charged to Anna Bryant, $126.00. Memorandum No. 35.

The source document for this correcting entry is a memorandum. (*CONCEPT: Objective Evidence*)

The total of the Accounts Receivable Credit column in the sales journal, posted January 31, is correct. Accounts Receivable was debited $126.00; Sales was credited $120.00; Sales Tax Payable was credited $6.00. No correction is needed for these amounts. The correcting entry involves only subsidiary ledger accounts. The account of Anna Bryant was debited for $126.00 when the account of Ann Bryan should have been debited. The Ann Bryan account is debited for $126.00 to record the charge sale in the correct account. The Anna Bryant account is credited for $126.00 to cancel the incorrect entry. No entry is made for the sales tax of $6.00. The sales tax was correctly recorded and posted at the time of sale.

The entry to record this correcting entry in a general journal is below.

ACCOUNTS RECEIVABLE
LEDGER

Ann Bryan

Feb. 12	126.00

Anna Bryant

Jan. 26	126.00	Feb. 12	126.00

	GENERAL JOURNAL			PAGE 2
DATE	ACCOUNT TITLE	POST. REF.	DEBIT	CREDIT
17	12 Ann Bryan		12600	
18	Anna Bryant			12600
19	Memorandum No. 35.			
20				

Correcting entry recorded in a general journal

The date, *12*, is written in the Date column. The amount of the debit, *$126.00*, is written in the Debit column. The name of the correct charge customer, *Ann Bryan*, is written in the Account Title column. On the next line, the amount of the credit, *$126.00*, is written in the Credit column. The name of the incorrectly charged customer, *Anna Bryant*, is written in the Account Title column. This account name is indented about 1 cm. The source document, *Memorandum No. 35*, is written on the next line indented about 2 cm.

Posting from a general journal

Each amount in the Debit and Credit columns is posted to the account or accounts named in the Account Title column. The posting of a general journal is described in Chapter 20, pages 410–411. The two general journal entries described in this chapter are posted in the same way.

ORDER OF POSTING FROM SPECIAL JOURNALS

Items affecting customers' or creditors' accounts are posted often during the month. Some businesses post daily so that the balances of the subsidiary ledger accounts will be up to date daily. Items affecting general ledger accounts are posted less often during the month because daily balances are not needed. All items, including the totals of special columns, must be posted before a trial balance is prepared.

The best order in which to post the journals is listed below.

1. Sales journal.
2. Purchases journal.
3. General journal.
4. Cash receipts journal.
5. Cash payments journal.

This order of posting usually puts the debits and credits in the accounts in the order the transactions occurred.

ACCOUNTING TERMS

What is the meaning of each of the following?

1. sales journal
2. cash receipts journal
3. sales return
4. sales allowance
5. credit memorandum

QUESTIONS FOR INDIVIDUAL STUDY

1. Why does Lin's Music Centre use a three-column sales journal?
2. What source document does Lin's use for a sale on account?
3. How can a journal entry be found that supports an amount posted to a general ledger account?
4. What should determine whether a special column, such as Accounts Receivable Credit, is needed in a cash receipts journal?
5. What source document does Lin's use for a cash received on account transaction?
6. What source document does Lin's use for a cash sales transaction?
7. Why does Lin's enter the cash balance on hand on the first line of the cash receipts journal?
8. What general ledger accounts are affected by a cash receipt from a customer on account transaction? In what way?
9. Which amounts in a cash receipts journal are posted individually to general ledger accounts?
10. What source document does Lin's use for a sales returns and allowances transaction?
11. Why does the account number for Sales Returns and Allowances, 4101.1, have a decimal number?
12. What accounts in the general ledger are affected by a sales returns and allowances transaction? How are the accounts affected?
13. In what order should special journals be posted? Why?

CASES FOR MANAGEMENT DECISION

CASE 1 Crowell Appliances uses a three-column sales journal with special columns similar to the one on page 420. The company records sales tax payable at the time a sale on account is made. David Suarez, the office manager, questions this practice. He suggests that sales tax payable not be recorded until cash is actually collected for this sale. Which procedure is preferable? Why?

CASE 2 Crosby Restaurant Supply Company uses a six-column cash receipts journal similar to the one on page 424. The company records only cash receipts transactions in this journal. Vanessa Evers, an accounting clerk, suggested that since the cash receipts journal has General Debit and Credit columns, non-cash receipt transactions could be recorded also. This change would eliminate the necessity for a general journal. Who is correct? Why?

CASE 3 Oaks Musical Instruments uses a general journal similar to the one on page 430. Fred Scales, the company accountant, suggested a special column titled Sales Returns and Allowances Debit be added to the general journal. Under what circumstances would this special column be acceptable in a general journal?

DRILLS FOR UNDERSTANDING

DRILL 21-D 1   Analysing transactions affecting sales and cash receipts

Use a form similar to the one below.

Trans. No.	(a) Account Debited	(b) Account Credited	(c) Journal in Which Recorded	(d) (e) Name of Amount Column Used in Journal	
				For Amount Debited	For Amount Credited
1.	Cash	Sales Sales Tax Pay.	Cash Receipts	Cash Debit	Sales Credit Sales Tax Pay. Credit

Instructions: Do each of the following for the transactions listed below. Write in Column a the name of the account(s) debited. Write in Column b the name of the account(s) credited. Write in Column c the name of the journal in which the transaction is recorded. Write in Columns d and e the names of the journal amount column(s) in which debit and credit amounts are recorded. Transaction 1 is given as an example in the form above.

1. Recorded cash sales plus sales tax for the day.
2. Sold merchandise on account with sales tax to Mary Olcott.
3. Recorded credit card sales plus sales tax.
4. Received cash on account from Dale Haley.
5. Granted credit to Betty Cleland for merchandise she returned plus sales tax on merchandise.
6. Discovered that a sale on account to Ralph Brock was incorrectly charged to Ralf Brook.
7. Granted credit to Darold Cole as an allowance for damaged merchandise delivered to him plus sales tax on merchandise.

DRILL 21-D 2   Posting transactions from special journals

Use a form similar to the one on the next page.

Instructions: 1. Write in Column a the account titles affected by each transaction in Drill 21-D 1. Use account titles from Columns a and b of the completed Drill 21-D 1.

2. Place a check mark in Column b if the amount is posted separately to the general ledger. Place a check mark in Column c if the amount is posted separately to the accounts

Trans. No.	(a) Accounts affected	(b) (c) Amounts posted separately to		(d) Amounts not posted separately to any ledger
		General Ledger	Accounts Receivable Ledger	
1.	Cash			√
	Sales			√
	Sales Tax Pay.			√

receivable ledger. Place a check mark in Column d if the amount is not posted separately to any ledger. Transaction 1 is given above as an example.

APPLICATION PROBLEMS

PROBLEM 21-1　Journalizing and posting sales on account transactions

The accounts receivable ledger and general ledger accounts of Simpson Company are given in the working papers. The balances are recorded as of March 1 of the current year.

ACCOUNTS RECEIVABLE LEDGER

Charge Customer	Account Balance
Cara Adamson, 1775 Portage Avenue, Winnipeg, MB　R3J 0E8	$421.00
Sara Adkinson, 686 Main Street, Winnipeg, MB　R3B 1E6	144.00
Martha James, 1419 Rosser Avenue, Brandon, MB　R7A 0M5	360.00
Sherman Kook, 229 Green Street, Flin Flon, MB　R8A 0G8	334.50
Samual Sammons, 168 Main Street, Selkirk, MB　R1A 1R3	248.00
Roger Watkins, 3105 Assiniboine Avenue, Winnipeg, MB　R3K 0A2	255.00

PARTIAL GENERAL LEDGER

Account Title	Acct. No.	Account Balance
Accounts Receivable.......	1103	$1 762.50
Sales Tax Payable............	2106	——
Sales	4101	——

Instructions 1. The following sales on account were made by Simpson Company during March of the current year. Record these transactions on page 10 of a sales journal similar to the one illustrated in this chapter. The abbreviation for sales invoice is *S*.

Mar.　1. Sold merchandise on account to Sara Adkinson, $150.00, plus sales tax, $7.50. S76.

　　　2. Sold merchandise on account to Sherman Kook, $123.00, plus sales tax, $6.15. S77.

　　　7. Sold merchandise on account to Samual Sammons, $75.00, plus sales tax, $3.75. S78.

　　11. Sold merchandise on account to Cara Adamson, $89.00, plus sales tax, $4.45. S79.

　　14. Sold merchandise on account to Martha James, $145.00, plus sales tax, $7.25. S80.

Mar. 17. Sold merchandise on account to Roger Watkins, $133.00, plus sales tax, $6.65. S81.

22. Sold merchandise on account to Sara Adkinson, $85.00, plus sales tax, $4.25. S82.

25. Sold merchandise on account to Samual Sammons, $113.00, plus sales tax, $5.65. S83.

28. Sold merchandise on account to Martha James, $83.50, plus sales tax, $4.18. S84.

31. Sold merchandise on account to Sherman Kook, $160.00, plus sales tax, $8.00. S85.

Instructions: 2. Post each amount in the Accounts Receivable Debit column of the sales journal to the accounts receivable ledger.

3. Total, prove, and rule the sales journal. Post the totals of the special columns.

4. Prepare a schedule of accounts receivable similar to the one on page 250. Compare the schedule total with the balance of the accounts receivable account in the general ledger. The total and the balance should be the same.

PROBLEM 21-2   Journalizing and posting cash receipts transactions

The accounts receivable ledger and general ledger accounts of Annie Claire Toys are given in the working papers. The balances are recorded as of March 1 of the current year.

ACCOUNTS RECEIVABLE LEDGER

Charge Customer	Account Balance
Martin Chambers, 625 Union Street, Fredericton, NB E3A 3N6	$150.00
Nancy Fitzgerald, 1526 King Avenue, Bathurst, NB E2A 1T1	450.00
Paul Gionet, 430 Water Street, Chatham, NB E1N 1B8	189.00
Terri Johnston, 2017 Main Street, Moncton, NB E1E 1J2	115.00
Carrie Sciotto, 3610 Loch Lomond Road, Saint John, NB E2N 1C2	253.00

PARTIAL GENERAL LEDGER

Account Title	Acct. No.	Account Balance
Cash..................................	1101	$7 752.50
Accounts Receivable.......	1103	1 157.00
Sales Tax Payable............	2106	——
Sales	4101	——

Instructions: 1. The following cash receipts were received by Annie Claire Toys during March of the current year. Record these cash receipts in a cash receipts journal similar to the one illustrated in this chapter. Use page 12 for the cash receipts journal. Source documents are abbreviated as: receipt, R; cash register tape, T; credit card sales calculator tape, CT.

Mar. 1. Recorded the cash balance on hand in the cash receipts journal, $7 752.50.

2. Received cash on account from Paul Gionet, $189.00. R39.

5. Received cash on account from Nancy Fitzgerald, $175.00. R40.

10. Received cash on account from Terri Johnston, $115.00. R41.

12. Recorded cash sales, $2 979.00, plus sales tax, $148.95. T12.

12. Recorded credit card sales, $2 588.00, plus sales tax, $129.40. CT12.

14. Received cash on account from Martin Chambers, $150.00. R42.

Mar. 18. Received cash on account from Carrie Sciotto, $190.00. R43.
    25. Received cash on account from Nancy Fitzgerald, $160.00. R44.
    31. Recorded cash sales, $2 686.00, plus sales tax, $134.30. T31.
    31. Recorded credit card sales, $2 534.00, plus sales tax, $126.70. CT31.

Instructions: 2. Post each amount in the Accounts Receivable Credit column of the cash receipts journal to the accounts receivable ledger.

3. Prove the equality of debits and credits for the cash receipts journal.

4. Prove cash. The total of the Cash Credit column of the cash payments journal for Annie Claire Toys is $10 890.40. The balance on the last cheque stub on March 31 is $9 167.45.

5. Rule the cash receipts journal. Post the special column totals.

PROBLEM 21-3 Journalizing and posting sales and cash receipts transactions

The accounts receivable ledger and general ledger accounts of Kahler Ceramics are given in the working papers. The balances are recorded as of February 1 of the current year.

ACCOUNTS RECEIVABLE LEDGER

Charge Customer	Account Balance
Kevin Hoffman, 5006 109 Avenue, Edmonton, AB T6A 1S1	$179.00
Stephen Norstrand, 3703 50 Avenue, Red Deer, AB T4N 3Y7	495.00
Sara Norwood, 513 North Railway Street, Medicine Hat, AB T1A 2Z4	435.00
Doris Schultz, 2408 6 Street N. E., Calgary, AB T2E 3Z1	335.00
Lucy Stacy, 20 Grenfell Avenue, St. Albert, AB T8N 0Z1	580.00
Samuel Wilton, 1911 7 Avenue S., Lethbridge, AB T1J 1M4	549.00
Karl Zimmerman, 24 Moose Street, Banff, AB T0L 0C0	267.00

PARTIAL GENERAL LEDGER

Account Title	Acct. No.	Account Balance
Cash..................................	1101	$5 593.40
Accounts Receivable......................	1103	2 840.00
Sales Tax Payable	2106	——
Sales..............................	4101	——
Sales Returns and Allowances.......	4101.1	——

Instructions: 1. The following transactions affecting sales and cash receipts were completed by Kahler Ceramics during February of the current year. Record these transactions in a sales journal, general journal, and cash receipts journal similar to those illustrated in this chapter. Use page 6 of each journal. Source documents are abbreviated: sales invoice, S; receipt, R; cash register tape, T; credit card sales calculator tape, CT; credit memorandum, CM; memorandum, M.

Feb. 1. Recorded the cash balance on hand in the cash receipts journal, $5 593.40.
    1. Sold merchandise on account to Sara Norwood, $175.00, plus sales tax, $8.75. S78.
    2. Received cash on account from Kevin Hoffman, $179.00. R26.
    3. Received cash on account from Stephen Norstrand, $225.00. R27.
    3. Sold merchandise on account to Karl Zimmerman, $135.00, plus sales tax, $6.75. S79.
    3. Received cash on account from Lucy Stacy, $189.00. R28.

Feb. 4. Found that on January 19 a sale on account to Sara Norwood (S64) was incorrectly charged to Stephen Norstrand, $135.00. M57.

5. Recorded cash sales for the week, $889.00, plus sales tax, $44.45. T5.

5. Recorded credit card sales for the week, $572.00, plus sales tax, $28.60. CT5.

Posting. Post the items that are to be posted individually. Post from the journals in this order: sales journal, general journal, and cash receipts journal.

7. Credited Samuel Wilton's account for merchandise returned, $35.00, plus sales tax, $1.75. CM22.

7. Received cash on account from Karl Zimmerman, $235.00. R29.

7. Received cash on account from Doris Schultz, $135.00. R30.

8. Sold merchandise on account to Kevin Hoffman, $256.00, plus sales tax, $12.80. S80.

9. Sold merchandise on account to Stephen Norstrand, $117.00, plus sales tax, $5.85. S81.

10. Received cash on account from Samuel Wilton, $195.00. R31.

11. Sold merchandise on account to Doris Schultz, $182.00, plus sales tax, $9.10. S82.

12. Recorded cash sales for the week, $1 702.00, plus sales tax, $85.10. T12.

12. Recorded credit card sales for the week, $888.00, plus sales tax, $44.40. CT12.

Posting. Post the items that are to be posted individually.

14. Received cash on account from Sara Norwood, $435.00. R32.

15. Received cash on account from Lucy Stacy, $391.00. R33.

17. Received cash on account from Sara Norwood, $183.75. R34.

18. Received cash on account from Samuel Wilton, $317.25. R35.

19. Recorded cash sales for the week, $1 127.00, plus sales tax, $56.35. T19.

19. Recorded credit card sales for the week, $709.00, plus sales tax, $35.45. CT19.

Posting. Post the items that are to be posted individually.

22. Sold merchandise on account to Stephen Norstrand, $225.00, plus sales tax, $11.25. S83.

24. Sold merchandise on account to Lucy Stacy, $167.00, plus sales tax, $8.35. S84.

25. Received cash on account from Karl Zimmerman, $32.00. R36.

26. Recorded cash sales for the week, $978.00, plus sales tax, $48.90. T26.

26. Recorded credit card sales for the week, $610.00, plus sales tax, $30.50. CT26.

Posting. Post the items that are to be posted individually.

28. Received cash on account from Doris Schultz, $200.00. R37.

28. Sold merchandise on account to Samuel Wilton, $245.00, plus sales tax, $12.25. S85.

28. Recorded cash sales for the week, $304.00, plus sales tax, $15.20. T28.

28. Recorded credit card sales for the week, $189.00, plus sales tax, $9.45. CT28.

Posting. Post the items that are to be posted individually.

Instructions: 2. Total, prove, and rule the sales journal. Post the totals of the special columns.

3. Prove the equality of debits and credits for the cash receipts journal.

4. Prove cash. The total of the Cash Credit column of the cash payments journal for Kahler Ceramics is $10 729.50. The balance on the last cheque stub on February 28 is $5 947.30.

5. Rule the cash receipts journal. Post the special column totals.

6. Prepare a schedule of accounts receivable similar to the one on page 250. Compare the schedule total with the balance of the accounts receivable account in the general ledger. The total and the balance should be the same.

ENRICHMENT PROBLEMS

MASTERY PROBLEM 21-M Journalizing and posting sales and cash receipts transactions

The accounts receivable ledger and general ledger accounts of Klondike Company are given in the working papers. The balances are recorded as of April 1 of the current year.

ACCOUNTS RECEIVABLE LEDGER

Charge Customer	Account Balance
Grady Graham,533 Rebecca Street, Oakville, ON L6K 1L2	$275.00
Melinda Grant, 472 Drew Street, Oshawa, ON L1H 5B5	187.00
David Hill, 5467 Victoria Avenue, Niagara Falls, ON L2G 3L3	435.00
Preston Miles, 187 Bank Street, Ottawa, ON K2P 1W7	198.00
Ralph Needham, 479 Carlton Street, St. Catharines, ON L2M 4Y6	342.00
Titus Newton, 291 Richmond Street, London, ON N6B 2H8	245.00
Melvin Peterson, 1528 Dundas Street W., Mississauga, ON L5C 1E4	525.00

PARTIAL GENERAL LEDGER

Account Title	Acct. No.	Account Balance
Cash.................................	1101	$5 872.51
Accounts Receivable......................	1103	2 207.00
Sales Tax Payable	2106	——
Sales...............................	4101	——
Sales Returns and Allowances.......	4101.1	——

Instructions: 1. The following transactions affecting sales and cash receipts were completed by Klondike Company during April of the current year. Record these transactions in a sales journal, general journal, and cash receipts journal similar to those illustrated in this chapter. Use page 9 of each journal. Source documents are abbreviated: sales invoice, S; receipt, R; cash register tape, T; credit card sales calculator tape, CT; credit memorandum, CM; memorandum, M.

Apr. 1. Recorded the cash balance on hand in the cash receipts journal, $5 872.51.
　　2. Recorded cash sales for the week, $256.00, plus sales tax, $12.80. T2.
　　2. Recorded credit card sales for the week, $176.00, plus sales tax, $8.80. CT2.
　　5. Credited Ralph Needham's account for merchandise returned $40.00, plus sales tax, $2.00. CM31.
　　5. Received cash on account from Ralph Needham, $100.00. R92.
　　6. Sold merchandise on account to Melinda Grant, $226.00, plus sales tax, $11.30. S69.
　　8. Received cash on account from Titus Newton, $245.00. R93.
　　9. Recorded cash sales for the week, $782.50, plus sales tax, $39.13. T9.
　　9. Recorded credit card sales for the week, $345.00, plus sales tax, $17.25. CT9.
　　　　Posting. Post the items that are to be posted individually. Post from the journals in this order: sales journal, general journal, and cash receipts journal.
　　11. Received cash on account from Melvin Peterson, $300.00. R94.
　　12. Sold merchandise on account to Ralph Needham, $125.00, plus sales tax, $6.25. S70.
　　12. Received cash on account from Melinda Grant, $187.00. R95.
　　13. Credited David Hill's account for merchandise returned $125.00, plus sales tax, $6.25. CM32.
　　15. Received cash on account from Preston Miles, $198.00. R96.

Apr. 16. Recorded cash sales for the week, $992.00, plus sales tax, $49.60. T16.
   16. Recorded credit card sales for the week, $567.00, plus sales tax, $28.35. CT16.
      Posting. Post the items that are to be posted individually.
   18. Received cash on account from Grady Graham, $275.00. R97.
   19. Received cash on account from Melinda Grant, $237.30. R98.
   21. Sold merchandise on account to Titus Newton $139.00, plus sales tax, $6.95. S71.
   22. Found that on March 12 a sale on account to Titus Newton (S55) was incorrectly charged to the account of Ralph Needham, $200.00. M66.
   22. Received cash on account from Melvin Peterson, $225.00. R99.
   22. Sold merchandise on account to Preston Miles, $336.00, plus sales tax, $16.80. S72.
   23. Received cash on account from David Hill, $303.75. R100.
   23. Recorded cash sales for the week, $1 253.00, plus sales tax, $62.65. T23.
   23. Recorded credit card sales for the week, $567.00, plus sales tax, $28.35. CT23.
      Posting. Post the items that are to be posted individually.
   25. Sold merchandise on account to Grady Graham, $337.00, plus sales tax, $16.85. S73.
   26. Received cash on account from Titus Newton, $145.95. R101.
   26. Received cash on account from Ralph Needham, $131.25. R102.
   27. Sold merchandise on account to David Hill, $289.00, plus sales tax, $14.45. S74.
   28. Received cash on account from Titus Newton, $200.00. R103.
   29. Received cash on account from Preston Miles, $352.80. R104.
   30. Recorded cash sales for the week, $1 575.00, plus sales tax, $78.75. T30.
   30. Recorded credit card sales for the week, $753.00, plus sales tax, $37.65. CT30.
      Posting. Post the items that are to be posted individually.

Instructions: 2. Total, prove, and rule the sales journal. Post the totals of the special columns.

3. Prove the equality of debits and credits for the cash receipts journal.

4. Prove cash. The total of the Cash Credit column of the cash payments journal for Klondike Equipment Company is $11 846.20. The balance on the last cheque stub on April 30 is $4 557.19.

5. Rule the cash receipts journal. Post the special column totals.

6. Prepare a schedule of accounts receivable similar to the one on page 250. Compare the schedule total with the balance of the accounts receivable account in the general ledger. The total and the balance should be the same.

CHALLENGE PROBLEM 21-C Journalizing and posting sales, purchases, cash receipts, and cash payments transactions

The accounts receivable, accounts payable, and general ledger accounts of Kohnke Company are given in the working papers. The balances are recorded as of March 1 of the current year.

ACCOUNTS RECEIVABLE LEDGER

Charge Customer	Account Balance
Earl Butler, 326 Elizabeth Drive, Gander, NF A1V 1J9	$367.00
Chelsea Eastman, 103 Broadway, Corner Brook, NF A3H 4E3	178.00
Franklin Fox, 4032 Bartlett Drive, Labrador City, NF A2V 2P9	299.00
Loretta Linwood, 85 Empire Avenue, St. John's, NF A1C 3E8	115.00
Jennifer Wellman, 291 Water Street, St. John's, NF A1C 1B9	456.00

ACCOUNTS PAYABLE LEDGER

Creditor	Account Balance
Foster Company, 111 Queen Street, Charlottetown, PE C1A 4B3	$1 298.00
Newton Paint Company, 394 University Avenue, Charlottetown, PE C1A 4N6	1 500.00
Shell Supply Company, 76 Summer Street, Summerside, PE C1N 3H9	153.00
Tomah Company, 207 Granville Street, Summerside, PE C1N 3A7	2 345.00

PARTIAL GENERAL LEDGER

Account Title	Acct. No.	Account Balance
Cash	1101	$5 700.00
Accounts Receivable	1103	1 415.00
Supplies	1105	267.00
Accounts Payable	2102	5 296.00
Sales Tax Payable	2106	——
Sales	4101	——
Sales Returns and Allowances	4101.1	——
Purchases	5101	——
Purchases Returns and Allowances	5101.1	——
Purchases Discount	5101.2	——
Delivery Expense	6103	——
Miscellaneous Expense	6108	——
Rent Expense	6110	——

Instructions: 1. The following transactions affecting sales, purchases, cash receipts, and cash payments were completed during March of the current year. Kohnke Company must collect a 5% sales tax on all sales. Figure and record Sales Tax Payable on all sales as described on page 418. Record the transactions in a sales journal, purchases journal, general journal, cash receipts journal, and cash payments journal. Use page 11 of each journal. Source documents are abbreviated: cheque, C; sales invoice, S; receipt, R; cash register tape, T; credit card sales calculator tape, CT; credit memorandum, CM; memorandum, M; purchase invoice, P; debit memorandum, DM.

Mar. 1. Recorded the cash balance on hand in the cash receipts journal, $5 700.00.
   2. Paid March rent, $585.00. C89.
   2. Received cash on account from Loretta Linwood, $115.00. R35.
   3. Returned merchandise to Tomah Company, $205.00. DM16.
   3. Paid on account to Shell Supply Company, $151.47, covering P83 for $153.00 less a 1% cash discount of $1.53. C90.
   5. Recorded cash sales for the week, $680.00, plus sales tax. T5.
   5. Recorded credit card sales for the week, $578.00, plus sales tax. CT5.
      Posting. Post the items that are to be posted individually. Post from the journals in this order: sales journal, purchases journal, general journal, cash receipts journal, and cash payments journal.
   7. Paid on account to Newton Paint Company, $1 500.00, no discount. C91.
   7. Received cash on account from Jennifer Wellman, $206.00. R36.
   8. Sold merchandise on account to Chelsea Eastman, $145.00, plus sales tax. S72.
   8. Purchased merchandise on account from Newton Paint Company, $1 354.00. P101.
   9. Paid on account to Tomah Company, $2 097.20, covering P78 for $2 345.00 less DM16 for $205.00, and less a 2% discount of $42.80. C92.

Mar. 10. Received cash on account from Earl Butler, $367.00. R37.
  10. Sold merchandise on account to Jennifer Wellman, $376.00, plus sales tax. S73.
  11. Bought supplies on account from Foster Company, $368.00. M27.
  12. Recorded cash sales for the week, $720.00, plus sales tax. T12.
  12. Recorded credit card sales for the week, $677.00, plus sales tax. CT12.
    Posting. Post the items that are to be posted individually.
  14. Paid on account to Foster Company, $1 298.00, no discount. C93.
  14. Paid cash for delivery expense, $35.00. C94.
  14. Purchased merchandise on account from Newton Paint Company, $1 678.00. P102.
  14. Sold merchandise on account to Loretta Linwood, $545.00, plus sales tax. S74.
  15. Credited Chelsea Eastman's account for merchandise returned, $78.00, plus sales tax. CM56.
  15. Sold merchandise on account to Earl Butler, $490.00, plus sales tax. S75.
  16. Sold merchandise on account to Chelsea Eastman, $682.00, plus sales tax. S76.
  17. Received cash on account from Franklin Fox, $299.00. R38.
  18. Bought supplies on account from Shell Supply Company, $135.00. M28.
  19. Recorded cash sales for the week, $648.00, plus sales tax. T19.
  19. Recorded credit card sales for the week, $669.00, plus sales tax. CT19.
    Posting. Post the items that are to be posted individually.
  21. Paid on account to Newton Paint Company, $1 354.00, no discount. C95.
  22. Paid miscellaneous expenses, $125.00. C96.
  23. Received cash on account from Jennifer Wellman, $250.00. R39.
  24. Purchased merchandise on account from Tomah Company, $750.00. P103.
  26. Recorded cash sales for the week, $650.00, plus sales tax. T26.
  26. Recorded credit card sales for the week, $690.00, plus sales tax. CT26.
    Posting. Post the items that are to be posted individually.
  28. Paid on account to Shell Supply Company, $133.65, covering M28 for $135.00 less 1% discount of $1.35. C97.
  31. Recorded cash sales for the week, $680.00, plus sales tax. T31.
  31. Recorded credit card sales for the week, $643.00, plus sales tax. CT31.
    Posting. Post the items that are to be posted individually.

Instructions: 2. Total, prove, and rule the sales journal. Post the totals of the special columns.

3. Total and rule the purchases journal. Post the total.

4. Prove the equality of debits and credits for the cash receipts and cash payments journals.

5. Prove cash. The balance on the last cheque stub on March 31 is $6 624.43.

6. Rule the cash receipts journal. Post the special column totals.

7. Rule the cash payments journal. Post the totals of the special columns.

8. Prepare a schedule of accounts receivable similar to the one on page 250. Prepare a schedule of accounts payable similar to the one on page 250. Compare the schedules' totals with the balances of the accounts in the general ledger. The total and the balance of accounts receivable should be the same. The total and the balance of accounts payable should be the same.

Payroll Records

ENABLING PERFORMANCE TASKS

After studying Chapter 22, you will be able to:

a. Define accounting terms related to payroll records.
b. Explain accounting principles and practices related to payroll records.
c. Figure an employee's earnings from a time card.
d. Determine payroll income tax deductions
e. Apply for a social insurance number.
f. Complete payroll time cards.
g. Prepare a semimonthly payroll.
h. Prepare a payroll register.
i. Prepare an employee's earnings record.
j. Write a payroll cheque.

A business periodically pays employees for their services. The money paid for an employee's services is known as a salary. The period covered by a salary payment is called a pay period. Not all businesses base their salary payments on the same length of time. A pay period may be weekly, biweekly, semimonthly, or monthly. The same procedure is used for figuring a salary regardless of the length of the pay period.

A list of employees that shows the payments due them for a pay period is called a payroll. Various methods of recording payroll are used by different companies. The method used depends on the number of employees and the type of office equipment available. To speed the preparation of payroll, many businesses use automated data processing equipment. The basic accounting principles are the same regardless of whether manual or automated methods are used.

PAYROLL TAXES

Taxes based on the payroll of a business are called payroll taxes. A business is required by law to withhold certain payroll taxes from salaries earned by employees. A business also is required to pay certain payroll taxes. All payroll taxes are based on employees' earnings. Accurate and detailed payroll records therefore are important. Errors in payroll records could cause incorrect payroll tax payments. A business may have to pay a penalty for failure to pay taxes on time.

Employees' income tax

A business is required by law to withhold federal and provincial income taxes levied upon its employees' salaries. The business must also forward the taxes withheld to the government. Each qualified person supported by the employee, including the employee, entitles the worker to a reduction in the amount of income tax to be paid. For example, a married individual supporting a spouse and two children pays less income tax than a single person with the same weekly earnings. A deduction for each qualified person supported by a taxpayer is called an exemption. One exemption is allowed for the employee, one exemption for a spouse, and one exemption for each additional person who qualifies as a dependant. An additional personal exemption is allowed for those persons 65 years of age and over.

The number of exemptions a worker declares and the maritial status of the worker affect the amount that is deducted each pay period for income tax. Whenever a business employs a new worker, that person must report the number of exemptions and the marital status to the employer. The worker does this by filling out and signing Form TD1, Tax Exemption Return. A completed Form TD1 is shown on page 444 and indicates that the employee was single and claimed a basic personal exemption of $4 180 for 1986.

The law requires that each employer have on file a properly filled out Form TD1 for each employee. A revised form should be filed with the employer if the number of exemptions or the marital status changes. Failure to do so may cause the employee to be liable to a penalty of $10 per day for each day of default, up to a total penalty of $2 500. The payroll clerk uses the information from the completed Form TD1 to determine the amount of income tax to be withheld each pay period.

Payroll taxes withheld represent a liability to the employer until payment to the government is made. Each employer is required to remit all taxes withheld to the Receiver General of Canada. The remittance must be made by the 15th day of the month following the month in which taxes were withheld. The only province for which the federal government does not collect the provincial income tax is Quebec.

Unemployment Insurance (UI)

The Unemployment Insurance Act of 1971 requires that all persons (with a few exceptions outlined in the Act) employed under a contract of service pay unemployment insurance premiums based on insurable earnings.

◼ ✦ Revenue Canada   **Revenu Canada**   **TAX EXEMPTION RETURN**   **TD1**
       Taxation   Impôt   **DÉCLARATION D'EXEMPTION D'IMPÔT**   Rev. 1986

1. You must complete this form and give it to your employer when you start work, if

   (a) you earn salary, wages, commissions or other remuneration

  or given to the payer, if

   (b) you receive a superannuation or pension (including an annuity payment) under a superannuation or pension fund or plan, or

   (c) you receive a payment under the Unemployment Insurance Act, 1971, or

   (d) you receive a training allowance under the National Training Act unless it was paid as an allowance for personal or living expenses while you are living away from home,

  but in every case,

   (e) **within seven** days of a change in your exemptions.

2. This form need not be completed if you are resident in Canada and claim only the "Basic Personal Exemption". Income tax will be deducted by using Net Claim Code "1".

3. You should ask your District Taxation Office to authorize an increase in exemptions if

   (a) you believe you are entitled to more deductions (e.g. alimony payments), or

   (b) as a non-resident you can establish that all or substantially all (at least 90%) of your world income for the year will be included in taxable income EARNED in Canada.

4. Net income of your spouse or dependants includes any pension or supplement under the Old Age Security Act or similar Act of a province, benefits under the Canada or Quebec Pension Plan and the Unemployment Insurance Act, 1971.

1. Vous êtes tenu de remplir la présente formule et de la remettre à votre employeur au début de votre emploi,

   a) si vous gagnez un traitement, un salaire, des commissions ou toute autre rémunération;

  ou de la remettre au payeur,

   b) si vous recevez des prestations de retraite ou de pension (y compris des paiements de rentes) en vertu d'un fond ou d'un régime de pensions ou de retraite;

   c) si vous recevez des paiements en vertu de la Loi de 1971 sur l'assurance-chômage; ou

   d) si vous recevez une allocation de formation en vertu de la Loi nationale sur la formation, sauf si elle est versée comme frais de subsistance ou frais personnels engagés pendant que vous vivez loin de chez vous;

  dans les deux cas, vous devez remettre cette formule

   e) dans les **sept** jours qui suivent tout changement dans vos exemptions.

2. Vous n'avez pas à remplir cette formule si vous êtes résident du Canada et si vous ne demandez que l'«exemption personnelle de base»; vos retenues d'impôt seront alors faites selon le code de demande nette «1».

3. Vous devez demander à votre bureau de district d'impôt l'autorisation d'augmenter votre exemption de retenue,

   a) si vous croyez avoir droit à des déductions plus élevées (p. ex. si vous versez une pension alimentaire), ou

   b) si, en qualité de non-résident, vous pouvez établir que la totalité ou la presque totalité (au moins 90%) de votre revenu de toutes provenances pour l'année sera inclus dans votre revenu imposable GAGNÉ au Canada.

4. Le revenu net de votre conjoint ou des personnes à votre charge comprend toute pension ou tout supplément en vertu de la Loi sur la sécurité de la vieillesse ou de toute loi provinciale semblable, et les prestations du Régime de pensions du Canada, du Régime de rentes du Québec ou de la Loi de 1971 sur l'assurance-chômage.

FAMILY NAME (Print) - *NOM DE FAMILLE (en majuscules)*	USUAL FIRST NAME AND INITIALS - *PRÉNOM USUEL ET INITIALES*	EMPLOYEE NO. - *NUMÉRO DE L'EMPLOYÉ*
MORREY	JEAN E.	109

ADDRESS - *ADRESSE*	FOR NON-RESIDENT ONLY - *RÉSERVÉ AUX NON-RÉSIDENTS* COUNTRY OF PERMANENT RESIDENCE *PAYS DE LA RÉSIDENCE PERMANENTE*	SOCIAL INSURANCE NUMBER *NUMÉRO D'ASSURANCE SOCIALE*
4195 W16 Avenue	–	7 0 6 1 9 7 9 7
Vancouver BC V6R 3E4		DATE OF BIRTH - *DATE DE NAISSANCE* Day/*Jour* 11 Month-*Mois* May Year-*Année* 1967

Complete the "Claim for Exemptions" on verso and enter your "Net Claim", if

   (i) you are resident in Canada, or

   (ii) you satisfy item 3 (b) above.

Refer to the "Table" below and enter the applicable "Net Claim Code". Enter "0" if not resident in Canada unless claim established under 3 (b).

Net Claim - *Demande nette*   ▶ **$4 180** ◀

Net Claim Code - *Code de demande nette*   ▶ **1** ◀

Remplissez la section «Exemptions demandées» au verso et inscrivez votre «Demande nette»,

   (i) si vous êtes résident du Canada, ou

   (ii) si vous remplissez la condition en 3b) ci-dessus.

Consultez la «Table» ci-dessous et inscrivez le Code de demande nette» approprié. Inscrivez «0» si vous êtes non-résident du Canada, sauf si votre demande est établie en vertu de 3b) ci-dessus.

Table of Net Claim Codes 1986 *Table des codes de demande nette*

Net Claim - *Demande nette* Exceeding - Not exceeding *Excédant - N'excédant pas*	Net Claim Code *Code de demande nette*	Net Claim - *Demande nette* Exceeding - Not exceeding *Excédant - N'excédant pas*	Net Claim Code *Code de demande nette*
For use re: Tables 11 and 12 *Utilisation: Tables 11 et 12*	0	$ 7,800 — 8,570	8
$4,179 — 4,230	1	8,570 — 9,370	9
4,230 — 4,890	2	9,370 — 10,250	10
4,890 — 5,610	3	10,250 — 11,110	11
5,610 — 6,240	4	11,110 — 11,930	12
6,240 — 7,060	5	11,930 — 12,570	13
7,060 — 7,430	6	12,570 and up — *et plus*	X
7,430 — 7,800	7	No tax withholding required *Aucune retenue d'impôt requise*	E

- Your "Net Claim Code" is used by the employer or the payer to decide what tax deduction is to be made from the payments listed in 1 (a) to (d) above.

- *L'employeur ou le payeur utilise votre «Code de demande nette» pour savoir quel montant d'impôt il doit retenir sur les paiements énumérés en 1a) à d) ci-dessus.*

Claim for Exemption from Tax Deduction — *Valid for 1986 only.*

My estimated income for 1986 from all sources (excluding Family Allowance payments) is $_____ . This does not exceed the amount of my Net Claim.

If you qualify for this exemption your net claim code is "E".

Note: Subject to 3(b) above, no exemptions may be claimed here by a person not resident in Canada during the year.

Demande d'exemption de retenues d'impôt — *Valable seulement pour 1986.*

Mon revenu estimatif de toutes provenances pour 1986 (à l'exclusion des allocations familiales) est de _____ $ Ce montant ne dépasse pas celui de ma «Demande nette».

Si vous avez droit à cette exemption, votre code de demande nette est «E».

Note: Sous réserve de la condition en 3b) ci-dessus, cette demande d'exemption ne peut être faite ici par une personne ne résidant pas au Canada pendant l'année.

Certification

I HEREBY CERTIFY that the information given in this return is correct and complete.

Signature   *Jean E. Morrey*   Date ___September 14___ 19 86

It is an offence to make a false return — *Faire une fausse déclaration constitue une infraction*

Attestation

J'ATTESTE PAR LES PRÉSENTES que les renseignements donnés dans cette formule sont exacts et complets.

Warning: An employer or payer should refer a form TD1 containing doubtful statements to the District Taxation Office. Any person who knowingly accepts a form TD1 containing false or deceptive statements commits a serious offence. Employers and payers must retain completed forms TD1 for inspection by officers of the Department of National Revenue, Taxation.

Avertissement: L'employeur ou le payeur doit soumettre au bureau de district d'impôt toute formule TD1 renfermant une déclaration douteuse. Quiconque accepte sciemment une formule TD1 renfermant une déclaration fausse ou trompeuse commet une infraction grave. Les employeurs et les payeurs doivent conserver les formules TD1 dûment remplies pour inspection par les agents de Revenu Canada, Impôt.

Form authorized and prescribed by order of the Minister of National Revenue.

Formule autorisée et prescrite en vertu d'un ordre du Ministre du Revenu national.

Form TD1, Tax Exemption Return

The range of insurable earnings and the employee and employer premium rates are set annually by Revenue Canada, Taxation, which is the federal government department responsible for administering the collection of unemployment insurance premiums and the insurance coverage.

In 1985 the range of insurable earnings in Canada was from a minimum of $92 per week to a maximum of $460 per week. This means that no premiums were paid on earnings under $92. A person earning more than $460 per week paid the same premium of $10.81 as someone earning exactly $460 per week.

The 1985 employee premium rate was 2.35%, or $2.35 on every $100 of insurable earnings. The employer premium rate for 1985 was 1.4 times the employees' premiums, unless the employer qualified for a reduced rate. Therefore, if the employees' premium contributions totalled $90.72 for a given month, the employer's premium would be $127.01 (1.4 × $90.72).

Officers of Revenue Canada, Taxation may visit employers from time to time to audit records and to ensure that the required premiums are being withheld and remitted.

Canada Pension Plan (CPP)

The Canada Pension Plan was established under federal law in 1965 to provide a basic pension at retirement for all employed Canadians or Canadian residents except those living in the province of Quebec. Quebec residents receive similar coverage under the Quebec Pension Plan.

All working persons between the ages of 18 and 70 have had to make contributions to the Canada Pension Plan since January 1966 at the rate of 1.8% of ''pensionable earnings.'' Since 1966 the amount of pensionable earnings has changed each year. The maximum amount of pensionable earnings for 1985 was $23 400 with a basic exemption of $2 300. Thus, a person earning more than $23 400 during 1985 made the same contribution to the Canada Pension Plan ($379.80) as someone who earned exactly $23 400.

Every employer is required to make a contribution of an amount equal to the contributions deducted from their employees.

Retention of records

Employers are required to keep all payroll records showing payments and deductions for six years. Permission to destroy records must be obtained from Revenue Canada, Taxation whose auditors may grant the request after reviewing the records.

Employers are responsible under the provisions of the Canada Pension Plan and the Unemployment Insurance Acts to ensure that all employees who do not have a social insurance number (SIN) comply with the requirements necessary to obtain this number. A SIN card can be obtained by completing Form EMP 2120 and forwarding it along with the required

Social insurance card, or SIN card

documents and fee to the Social Insurance Registration Central Index, Bathurst, NB E2A 4L8.

Replacement of or amendment to a SIN card can be accomplished by completing Form EMP 2120 or EMP 2121 respectively.

Need for a social insurance number

It is important that each employee have a permanent social insurance number. Canada Pension Plan records are maintained under an account

Form EMP 2120, Application for a Social Insurance Number

identified by the social insurance number of the employee. Similarly, an employee's unemployment insurance premiums and benefit payments are recorded under this number. Anyone who does not obtain a social insurance number is still required to make contributions. However, these amounts will not count toward future benefits.

PAYROLL TIME CARDS

A payroll system must include an accurate record of the time each employee has worked. Several means are available for keeping time records. Employee time records most frequently are kept on time cards. Time cards provide the information required by law about the hours worked by each employee. Time cards are used as the basic source of data to prepare a payroll. The time worked by each employee may be recorded on a time card by hand or by a time clock.

A time card showing hours worked may be recorded by a supervisor who knows when employees arrive and leave work. Some businesses record only the total hours worked each day. Other firms record the exact time employees arrive and leave.

Time clock

Many companies have a time clock which their employees use to record times of arrival and departure. These times are imprinted by the time clock on a time card. Each employee has a time card in a rack beside the time clock. The employee uses the time clock to register arrival and departure times. Executives usually are not required to use a time clock. Their pay is not affected by brief absences from the office.

Lin's Music Centre uses a time clock to record arrival and departure times of each employee each day. The time card for Joann D. Boyd, stock clerk, for the semimonthly period ending February 15 is below.

Analysing a payroll time card

At the top of the card is Mrs. Boyd's employee number. Below the employee number are her name, her social insurance number, and the date of the payroll period.

Lin's time cards have three sections, Morning, Afternoon, and Overtime, with In and Out columns under each section. When Ms. Boyd reported for work on February 1, she inserted the card in the time clock. The clock recorded her time of arrival as 07:50. The other entries on this line indicate that she left for lunch at 12:00. She returned at 12:55 and left for the day at 17:02. On February 2 she worked 2½ hours overtime, as shown on the line for February 2.

Lin's figures overtime pay for each employee who works over 8 hours in any one day.

EMPLOYEE NO. __5__

NAME __Joann D. Boyd__

SIN __143 050 832__   *Lin's*

PERIOD ENDING __1989 02 15__

MORNING		AFTERNOON		OVERTIME		HOURS	
IN	OUT	IN	OUT	IN	OUT	REG	OT
-07:50	-12:00	-12:55	-17:02			8	
~07:50	~12:00	~12:59	~17:01	~18:00	~20:31	8	2½

≃07:51	≃12:01	≃12:50	≃17:04			8	
≃08:00	≃12:05	≃13:01	≃17:03			8	

	HOURS	RATE	AMOUNT
REGULAR	88	5.50	484.00
OVERTIME	2½	8.25	20.63
TOTAL HOURS	90½	TOTAL EARNINGS	504.63

Payroll time card

Figuring each employee's total earnings from a time card

Each employee's hours of work and earnings are figured.

1 Examine the time card for tardiness and early departure.

> Ms. Boyd's working day is from 08:00 to 17:00 with a one-hour lunch period from 12:00 until 13:00. She reportd to work one minute late on the afternoon of February 15. Lin's does not deduct for tardiness periods of ten or fewer minutes.

2 Extend the regular hours into the Hours Reg. column.

> The regular hours for Ms. Boyd are 8 hours each day.

3 Figure the number of hours of overtime for each day and enter the amount in the Hours OT column.

> Mrs. Boyd worked from 18:00 to 20:31 on February 2. Therefore, 2½ hours are recorded in the OT column (18:00 to 20:31 equals 2½ hours).

4 Add the Regular Hours column and enter the total in the space provided at the bottom of the card.

> Ms. Boyd worked 88 regular hours (8 hours × 11 days). Therefore, 88 is recorded in the Regular Hours space at the bottom of the card.

5 Enter the rate for regular time. Figure the regular earnings by multiplying hours times rate.

> Ms. Boyd's regular rate is $5.50 per hour. Enter $5.50 in the Regular Rate space. Regular earnings are $484.00 (88 hours × $5.50 rate). Regular earnings, $484.00, are entered in the appropriate amount space.

6 Add the Overtime Hours column and enter the total in the space provided at the bottom of the card.

> Ms. Boyd worked 2½ overtime hours during the semimonthly pay period. Therefore, 2½ is recorded in the Overtime Hours space at the bottom of the card.

7 Enter the rate for overtime. Figure the overtime earnings by multiplying hours times rate.

> Ms. Boyd is paid one and one-half times her regular rate for overtime work. Thus her overtime rate is $8.25 per hour ($5.50 × 1½). Enter $8.25 in the Overtime Rate space. Overtime earnings are $20.63 (2½ hours × $8.25 rate). Overtime earnings, $20.63, are entered in the appropriate amount space.

8 Add the Hours column to find the total hours. Add the Amount column to find the total earnings.

> Ms. Boyd earned $504.63 for the semimonthly period. Total hours, 90½, (88 regular plus 2½ overtime hours) are entered in the Total Hours space. Total earnings, $504.63, ($484.00 regular plus $20.63 overtime earnings) are entered in the Total Earnings space.
> The total pay due for a pay period before deductions is called total earnings. Total earnings are sometimes known as gross pay or gross earnings.

PAYROLL REGISTER

A payroll register contains information concerning all employees for each pay period. This form is the source document from which payroll accounting entries will be prepared. In completing this form it is necessary to use Income Tax, Unemployment Insurance, and Canada Pension Plan tables to determine each employee's payroll deductions. Lin's payroll register for the semimonthly period ended February 15 is shown below. The employee's number, name, marital status, and net claim code are listed for each employee who has performed work during the pay period. The amounts of total earnings obtained from the time cards or other sources are entered in the Total Earnings column opposite the employees' names. Listed under the Deductions columns are amounts deducted for income tax, Canada Pension Plan, unemployment insurance, health care, hospital insurance, donations and other deductions, and the total of these deductions. The net pay and payroll cheque numbers are shown in the last two columns.

PAYROLL REGISTER

SEMIMONTHLY PERIOD ENDED *1989 02 15*   DATE OF PAYMENT *1989 02 15*

EMPL. NO.	EMPLOYEE'S NAME	MARITAL STATUS	NET CLAIM CODE	TOTAL EARNINGS	INCOME TAX	CPP	UI	MEDICAL	HOSPITAL	OTHER		TOTAL	NET PAY	CH. NO.
6	Allen, Don J.	m	3	484 00	34 30	6 99	11 37	28 00	8 78 uw		3 00	92 44	391 56	323
9	Boyd, Joann D.	S	1	504 63	53 55	7 36	11 86	14 00	2 61 B		5 00	94 38	410 25	324
4	Danner, Thomas J.	m	2	386 75	16 20	5 24	9 09	28 00	8 78			67 31	319 44	325
10	De Lozier, Irene H.	S	1	182 50	—	1 56	4 29	14 00	2 61			22 46	160 04	326
2	Flores, Charles A.	m	5	506 00	23 60	7 38	11 89	28 00	8 78 B		5 00	84 65	421 35	327
8	Kurtz, Richard L.	S	1	276 00	1 60	3 24	6 49	14 00	2 61			27 94	248 06	328
9	Lyason, Debi M.	S	1	416 00	27 60	5 76	9 78	14 00	2 61			59 75	356 25	329
1	Roark, Carl J.	m	3	850 00	136 35	13 58	19 98	28 00	8 78 B		10 00	216 69	633 31	330
7	Sabourin, Louise M.	m	2	462 00	35 75	6 59	10 86	—	— uw		2 00	55 20	406 80	331
5	Spears, Phyllis R.	m	1	528 00	59 45	7 78	12 41	28 00	8 78 uw		3 00	119 42	408 58	332
11	Wong, Peter L.	S	1	218 50	—	2 21	5 13	14 00	2 61 B	20 00		23 95	194 55	333
	Totals			4814 38	388 40	67 69	113 15	210 00	569 5 uw B		8 00	864 19	3950 19	

OTHER DEDUCTIONS: B—BONDS; GI—GROUP INSURANCE; UW—UNITED WAY

ALBERTA — SEMI-MONTHLY TAX DEDUCTIONS / RETENUES D'IMPÔT SEMI-MENSUELLES

Basis — 24 Pay Periods per Year / Basis — 24 Pay Periods per Year
Base — 24 périodes de paie par année

TABLE 4

IF THE EMPLOYEE'S "NET CLAIM CODE" ON FORM TD1 IS — SI LE "CODE DE DEMANDE NETTE" DE L'EMPLOYÉ SELON LA FORMULE TD1 EST DE

DEDUCT FROM EACH PAY — *RETENEZ SUR CHAQUE PAIE*

SEMI-MONTHLY PAY — Use appropriate bracket / PAIE SEMI-MENSUELLE — Utilisez le palier approprié	1	2	3	4	5	6	7	8	9	10	11	12	13	Column A / Colonne A (See note on page 26 / Voir remarque p. 26)
$ 413.00 - 416.99	32.10	27.65	19.55	14.05	8.95	4.95	2.50							
417.00 - 420.99	33.30	28.75	20.70	14.70	9.65	5.60	3.15							
421.00 - 424.99	34.50	29.90	21.80	15.40	10.30	6.25	3.75							
425.00 - 428.99	35.70	31.00	22.95	16.05	11.00	6.90	4.40	.65						
429.00 - 432.99	36.85	32.15	24.05	16.75	11.70	7.50	5.05	1.30						
433.00 - 436.99	38.05	33.35	25.20	17.45	12.35	8.20	5.70	1.95						
437.00 - 440.99	39.25	34.55	26.30	18.45	13.05	8.85	6.35	2.55						
441.00 - 444.99	40.45	35.75	27.45	19.60	13.70	9.55	6.95	3.20						
445.00 - 448.99	41.65	36.90	28.55	20.70	14.40	10.20	7.60	3.85						
449.00 - 452.99	42.80	38.10	29.70	21.85	15.10	10.90	8.30	4.50						
453.00 - 456.99	44.00	39.30	30.80	22.95	15.75	11.60	8.95	5.15						
457.00 - 460.99	45.20	40.50	31.95	24.10	16.45	12.25	9.65	5.75	.55					
461.00 - 464.99	46.40	41.70	33.15	25.20	17.10	12.95	10.30	6.40	1.20					
465.00 - 468.99	47.60	42.85	34.30	26.35	17.95	13.60	11.00	7.05	1.85					
469.00 - 472.99	48.75	44.05	35.50	27.45	19.10	14.30	11.70	7.70	2.50					
473.00 - 476.99	49.95	45.25	36.70	28.60	20.20	15.00	12.35	8.35	3.15					
477.00 - 480.99	51.15	46.45	37.90	29.70	21.35	15.65	13.05	9.05	3.75					
481.00 - 484.99	52.35	47.65	39.05	30.85	22.45	16.35	13.70	9.70	4.40					
485.00 - 488.99	53.55	48.80	40.25	31.95	23.60	17.00	14.40	10.40	5.05					
489.00 - 492.99	54.70	50.00	41.45	33.15	24.70	17.80	15.10	11.10	5.70	.10				
493.00 - 496.99	55.90	51.20	42.65	34.35	25.85	18.95	15.75	11.75	6.35	.75				
497.00 - 500.99	57.10	52.40	43.85	35.55	26.95	20.05	16.45	12.45	6.95	1.40				
501.00 - 504.99	58.30	53.60	45.00	36.70	28.10	21.15	17.10	13.10	7.60	2.05				
505.00 - 508.99	59.45	54.75	46.20	37.90	29.20	22.30	17.95	13.80	8.25	2.70				
509.00 - 512.99	60.65	55.95	47.40	39.10	30.35	23.40	19.10	14.50	8.95	3.30				
513.00 - 522.99	62.75	58.05	49.50	41.20	32.30	25.40	21.05	15.65	10.15	4.45				
523.00 - 532.99	65.80	61.00	52.45	44.15	35.30	28.20	23.85	17.35	11.85	6.05	.30			
533.00 - 542.99	68.95	64.00	55.40	47.15	38.25	31.00	26.50	20.05	13.55	7.65	1.90			
543.00 - 552.99	72.10	67.10	58.40	50.10	41.25	33.95	29.50	22.85	15.25	9.35	3.50			
553.00 - 562.99	75.25	70.25	61.40	53.10	44.20	36.90	32.30	25.70	16.95	11.05	5.10			
563.00 - 572.99	78.35	73.40	64.35	56.05	47.20	39.90	35.30	28.50	19.35	12.75	6.70	1.15		
573.00 - 582.99	81.50	76.55	67.50	59.05	50.15	42.85	38.25	31.30	22.15	14.45	8.35	2.75		
583.00 - 592.99	84.65	79.70	70.65	62.00	53.15	45.85	41.25	34.25	25.00	16.15	10.05	4.35		
593.00 - 602.99	87.80	82.80	73.80	65.05	56.10	48.80	44.20	37.20	27.80	18.00	11.75	5.95	1.10	1.10
603.00 - 612.99	90.70	85.95	76.95	68.15	59.10	51.80	47.20	40.20	30.60	20.80	13.45	7.55	2.70	2.70
613.00 - 622.99	93.45	89.10	80.05	71.30	62.05	54.75	50.15	43.15	33.50	23.65	15.15	9.20	4.30	4.30
623.00 - 632.99	96.15	91.85	83.20	74.45	65.10	57.75	53.15	46.15	36.45	26.45	16.85	10.90	5.90	5.00
633.00 - 642.99	98.90	94.60	86.35	77.60	68.25	60.70	56.10	49.10	39.45	29.25	19.20	12.60	7.50	5.10
643.00 - 652.99	101.60	97.30	89.45	80.75	71.35	63.70	59.10	52.10	42.40	32.05	22.00	14.30	9.20	5.10
653.00 - 662.99	104.35	100.05	92.20	83.85	74.50	66.80	62.05	55.05	45.40	35.05	24.80	16.00	10.90	5.10

Section of income tax deduction table for semimonthly pay period

Figuring the deductions sections of a payroll register

> Tables for Alberta income tax, CPP, and UI deductions have been provided in this text for illustrative purposes only. It is recommended to cover all examples and problems that accounting students use current local tables which may be obtained from District Taxation Offices.

The Deductions section of a payroll register is used to record the various amounts deducted from employees' earnings. Certain payroll taxes must be deducted to comply with government regulations. Also, some companies deduct amounts for hospitalization and group insurance premiums, retirement plans, union dues, Canada Savings Bonds, or donations to the United Way or other charities. These deductions will vary from one company to another depending on policies established by the management or by employment contracts.

1 The Income Tax column is used to record the amount of income tax withheld from each employee's earnings. This amount is determined from tables furnished by the government that take into account the amount of earnings and the exemptions that are claimed. A section of a table showing the tax to be withheld based on semimonthly earnings is shown on page 450.

   Contributions to the Canada Pension Plan and Unemployment Insurance are exempt from income tax to avoid double taxation. To determine the income tax for Joann Boyd on the $504.63 she earned, the payroll clerk must first subtract $7.36 (CPP) and $11.86 (UI) from $504.63 to arrive at her taxable earnings of $485.41. The Semi-Monthly Tax Deductions table on page 450 shows that for a wage bracket of $485.00-488.99 the income tax to be withheld for Net Claim Code 1 is $53.55.

   > Income tax tables are also available for daily, weekly, semimonthly, monthly, 10-month, and yearly periods.

2 The CPP column is used to record the amount withheld for Canada Pension Plan contributions. Refer to the page in the table corresponding to the pay period, then look in the "Remuneration" column for the bracket which includes the employee's earnings. The amount in the adjoining "CPP" column is the amount of the contribution to be withheld from the employee's pay. For Joann Boyd's earnings of $504.63 (wage bracket $504.45-504.99) the CPP contribution is $7.36. The sample table on page 469 is used for this calculation.

3 The UI column is used to record the amount withheld for Unemployment Insurance premiums. To determine the amount to be withheld refer to the page in the table corresponding to the pay period, then look in the "Remuneration" column for the bracket which includes the employee's earnings. The amount in the adjoining "UI Premium" column is the amount to be withheld from the employee's pay.

For Joann Boyd's earnings of $504.63 (wage bracket $504.47-504.89) the UI contribution is $11.86. The sample table on page 470 is used for this calculation.

4 The Medical column is used to record health care premiums. At the time of writing, the Alberta premiums were $14.00 for single and $28.00 for family coverage. These amounts are deducted from the first payment of each month only.

5 The Hospital column is used to record hospital and group insurance premiums. At the time of writing, the Alberta premiums were $2.61 for single and $8.78 for family coverage. Premium rates may vary since they are determined by insurance companies. Amounts for hospital insurance are deducted from the first pay period of each month only.

6 The Other column is used to list amounts withheld for which no special column is provided. These withholdings are voluntary deductions requested by an employee. The entries in this column are identified by code letters. Lin's uses the letter *B* to identify amounts withheld for buying Canada Savings Bonds, *UW* is used to identify amounts withheld for contributions to the United Way. A separate total is shown for each different type of deduction.

> Ms. Boyd has authorized Lin's to withhold $5.00 each pay period to buy Canada Savings Bonds for her.

7 The Total column is used to record total deductions. All deductions on a line for each employee are added. The total deductions are recorded in the Total column.

> Total deductions for Ms. Boyd are $94.38 ($53.55, $7.36, $11.86, $14.00, $2.61, and $5.00).

Figuring the net pay column of a payroll register

The Net Pay column is used to record the amount due each employee. Net pay is figured by subtracting the amount of each employee's total deductions from the employee's total earnings.

> Ms. Boyd's net pay is $410.25 (total earnings, $504.63, less total deductions, $94.38). Payroll cheque number 324 was issued to Ms. Boyd.

Completing a payroll register

After the net pay has been recorded for each employee, each amount column is totalled. The accuracy of these additions is verified by subtracting the Total Deductions column total from the Total Earnings column total. The result should equal the total of the Net Pay column. If the totals do not agree, the errors must be found and corrected. After the totals are proved, a double rule is drawn below the totals across all amount columns.

Total earnings on line 12 of Lin's payroll register, page 449, are $4 814.38. Total deductions, on line 12, are $864.19. Total net pay for February 15, 1989, is $3 950.19 (total earnings, $4 814.38, less total deductions, $864.19.

Before a cheque is written for each employee's net pay, the payroll computations are checked for accuracy. The manager approves the payroll after the accuracy is verified. After each cheque is written, the cheque number is recorded in the Ch. No. column.

PAYROLL CHEQUES

Lin's pays its employees by cheque. A special payroll cheque form is used that has a detachable stub on which are recorded earnings and amounts deducted. Employees detach the stubs for a record of deductions and cash received.

The information used to prepare payroll cheques is taken from a payroll register. A payroll cheque for the pay period ending February 15 is below.

Lin's Music Centre

STATEMENT OF EMPLOYEE EARNINGS AND PAYROLL DEDUCTIONS

PERIOD ENDING	HOURS	EARNINGS		TOTAL EARNINGS	INCOME TAX	CPP	UI	MEDICAL	HOSPITAL	OTHER	TOTAL	NET PAY
		REGULAR	OVERTIME									
1989 02 15	90½	484.00	20.63	504.63	53.55	7.36	11.86	14.00	2.61	B5.00	94.38	410.25
YEAR-TO-DATE TOTALS		1 408.00	20.63	1 428.63	135.65	20.55	33.57	28.00	5.22	15.00	237.99	1190.64

Payroll cheque with detachable stub

A cheque for the total amount of the payroll is written on Lin's regular current account. This cheque is deposited in a separate bank account for payroll cheques only. A separate bank account for payroll cheques provides additional protection and control. Amounts on cheques could be increased or unauthorized payroll cheques could be prepared. The payroll account would then have insufficient funds to pay the cheques. Also, the payroll account equals the payroll register total net amount and can be reconciled easily against the payroll records. Only the cheque drawn for the total payroll is recorded in the cash payments journal. Detailed data about employees' payroll cheques are obtained from a payroll register.

Some businesses will deposit pay directly to an employee's bank account. The payroll must still be figured. But individual cheques are not written and do not have to be distributed. Under this system the payroll department prepares the payroll register and a statement of earnings and deductions for each employee. The employees' statements are given to them on payday to compare with the amount of the payroll deposit.

EMPLOYEES' EARNINGS RECORDS

A business form showing details of all items affecting payments made to an employee is called an employee's earnings record. This information is recorded each pay period. The record includes earnings, deductions, net pay, and accumulated earnings for the calendar year.

Recording information on an employee's earnings record

Lin's keeps all employee's earnings records on cards. One card is used for each calendar quarter of the year. Quarterly totals are used in the preparation of reports required by the government. Each quarter the last amount in the Accumulated Earnings column is carried forward to the Accumulated Earnings section for the following quarter. Therefore, the Accumulated Earnings column always reflects total earnings of an employee from the beginning of the year.

After a payroll register has been prepared, the payroll data for each employee are recorded on the employee's earnings record. The February 15 payroll register data for Joann D. Boyd, page 449, is recorded on her first quarter earnings record below.

EARNINGS RECORD FOR QUARTER ENDING   **1989 03 31**

Boyd / Joann / D.   EMPLOYEE NO. **3**   MARITAL STATUS **S**   NET CLAIM CODE **1**
LAST NAME / FIRST / MIDDLE INITIAL   SOCIAL INSURANCE NO. **143 050 832**
POSITION **Stock Clerk**

PAY PERIOD		TOTAL EARNINGS	DEDUCTIONS								NET PAY	ACCUMULATED EARNINGS
WEEK NO.	WEEK ENDED		INCOME TAX	CPP	CPP TO DATE	UI	MEDICAL	HOSP. INS.	OTHER	TOTAL		
1	01/15	44000	3450	620	620	1034	1400	261 B	500	7265	36735	44000
2	01/31	48400	4760	699	1319	1157		B	500	7096	41304	92400
3	02/15	50463	5355	736	2055	1186	1400	261 B	500	9438	41025	142863
4	02/28	39600	2310	368	2423	931		B	500	4109	35491	182463
5	03/15	51700	5710	586	3009	1215	1400	261 B	500	9672	42028	234163
6	03/31	52800	6065	605	3614	1241		B	500	8411	44389	286963
QUARTERLY TOTALS		286963	27650	3614	———	6744	4200	783 B	3000	45991	240972	

Employee's earnings record

Analysing an employee's earnings record

Ms. Boyd's earnings record for the first quarter is on page 454. Her name, employee number, social insurance number, and other payroll data are entered at the top of her earnings record.

Amount columns of an employee's earnings record are the same as amount columns of a payroll register. In addition the earnings record has an Accumulated Earnings column. Amounts opposite an employee's name on a payroll register are recorded in the corresponding columns of the employee's earnings record. The pay period ending February 15 is the third pay period in the first quarter. Ms. Boyd's earnings and deductions for that week are therefore entered on line 3 of her earnings record. Total earnings are added to the accumulated earnings on line 2 to get the new total earnings to date. Accumulated earnings are sometimes known as year-to-date earnings.

The Accumulated Earnings column shows the earnings for Ms. Boyd since the first of the year. The first entry in this column is zero since this is the beginning of the fiscal year. The last entry in this column, $2 869.63, will be carried forward to Ms. Boyd's earnings record for the second quarter. The amounts in the Accumulated Earnings column supply an up-to-date reference for an employee's year-to-date earnings. The CPP to Date column provides the payroll clerk with the current total of contributions to the Canada Pension Plan accumulated for the year. When the annual maximum contribution of $379.80 is reached (based on tables at the time of writing), no further deductions are made.

The Quarterly Totals line provides space for the totals for the quarter. These totals are needed to prepare required government reports.

OTHER METHODS OF PROCESSING A PAYROLL

Preparing a payroll requires computing, recording, and reporting payroll information. Each business selects a system of preparing the payroll resulting in adequate control for the least amount of cost.

Pegboard processing of a payroll

A special device used to write the same information at one time on several forms is called a pegboard. The pegboard is also known as an account board. One form of a pegboard is on the next page.

The name, pegboard, comes from pegs along one side of the board. The forms used with this device have holes punched along one side. Each of the forms is placed on the pegs. Thus, the line on each form on which data are to be written is aligned one below the other.

When a payroll is recorded, a page of the payroll register is attached to the pegboard. Next, the employee's earnings record is properly posi-

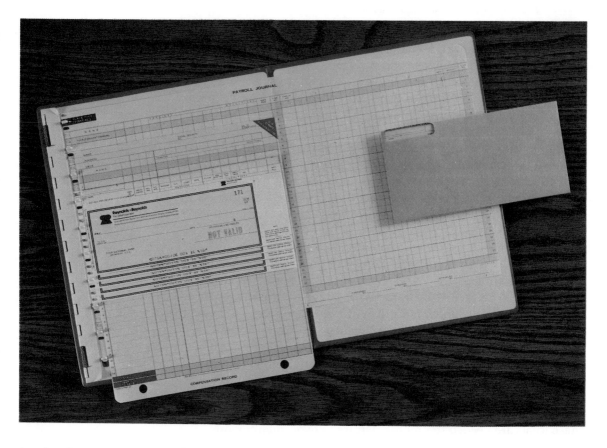

A pegboard

tioned on top of the payroll register page. Then, the cheque is positioned on top of both of these sheets. As the cheque stub is written, the same data are recorded on the employee's earnings record and the payroll register. The data are written only once. However, the data are recorded on three different records at the same time. Recording data on several forms with one writing is called the write-it-once principle.

The pegboard has two major purposes. First, the pegboard provides a solid writing base for writing on the forms by hand. Second, data are recorded on several forms with one writing.

ACCOUNTING TERMS

What is the meaning of each of the following?

1. pay period
2. payroll
3. payroll taxes
4. income taxes
5. exemption
6. unemployment insurance
7. Canada Pension Plan
8. total earnings
9. payroll register
10. employee's earnings record
11. pegboard
12. write-it-once principle

1. How frequently do businesses pay employee salaries?
2. What determines the method used for recording payroll?
3. What determines the amount of payroll taxes a business must pay?
4. How does an employer know how many exemptions each employee is entitled to?
5. Do any provinces have provincial income taxes? If so, how are these taxes collected?
6. How long must records pertaining to tax payments and deductions be retained?
7. How may a person obtain a social insurance card?
8. How is the amount of income tax withheld from an employee's salary determined?
9. Which column of the payroll register shows the amount of money due each employee?
10. Where is the information obtained to prepare a payroll cheque?
11. What is the major purpose of the Accumulated Earnings column on an employee's earnings record?
12. What are the purposes for using a pegboard device for preparing a payroll?

CASES FOR MANAGEMENT DECISION

CASE 1 Murchinson Home Supplies has 9 employees. A hand written time card currently is being used to record arrival and departure times for each employee. The accounting clerk suggests that a time clock be installed to record the arrival and departure times. The manager believes that the present system is satisfactory. Do you agree with the accounting clerk or the manager? Give your reasons.

CASE 2 Porter's Auto Repair prepares as part of its payroll procedure, a payroll register for each payroll and an earnings record for each employee. After reviewing both forms, the manager suggests that since both forms contain the same information, the company prepare only the payroll register. The manager states that omitting the earnings record will save considerable time and cost without affecting the payroll preparation. The accountant recommends that the present payroll procedure be retained. Do you agree with the accountant or the manager? Give your reasons.

DRILLS FOR UNDERSTANDING

DRILL 22-D 1 Figuring employees' earnings

The information below is taken from the time cards for each employee.

Employee Number	Hours Worked		Pay Rate	Amount of Pay		Total Earnings
	Regular	Overtime		Regular	Overtime	
1	40	1	$4.20	$168.00	$6.30	$174.30
2	40	5	6.00			
3	30	0	4.00			
4	40	4	5.50			
5	40	3	6.20			
6	40	2	5.80			

Instructions: For each employee, figure the amount of regular pay, overtime pay, and total earnings. The amounts for Employee No. 1 are given as an example. Overtime hours are paid at one and one-half times the regular pay rate.

DRILL 22-D 2   Determining payroll income tax withholdings

The information below is from a semimonthly payroll register.

1	2	3	4
Employee's Name	Marital Status	Net Claim Code	Total Earnings
1. Byers, Virgil	S	1	$425.00
2. Dario, Carmen	S	1	510.00
3. Espino, Luis	M	2	490.00
4. Frese, Margaret	S	1	575.00
5. Groom, Harold	M	3	590.00
6. Kouri, Margaret	M	4	675.00

Instructions: Determine the income tax that must be deducted for each of the six employees. Use the tax deduction table on page 450.

APPLICATION PROBLEMS

PROBLEM 22-1   Applying for a social insurance number

Instructions: Complete an application for a social insurance number. Use your own personal data. Compare your application with the illustration, page 446.

PROBLEM 22-2   Completing payroll time cards

Employees' time cards are given in the working papers accompanying this textbook.

Instructions: 1. Figure the regular, overtime, and total hours worked by each of the employees. Any hours over the regular 8-hour day are considered overtime.
   2. Determine each employee's regular, overtime, and total earnings.

PROBLEM 22-3   Preparing a semimonthly payroll

Information from employee time cards for the semimonthly pay period April 1–15 of the current year is on the next page.

Instructions: 1. Prepare a payroll register similar to the illustration on page 449. The date of payment is April 16. Use the income tax deduction table, page 450, to find the income tax deduction for each employee. Use Canada Pension Plan contribution and Unemployment Insurance premium tables to find CPP and UI deductions for each employee.
   2. Prepare a cheque for the total amount of the net pay. Make the cheque payable to *Payroll Account* and sign your name as treasurer of the company. The beginning cheque stub balance is $12 089.26.
   3. Prepare payroll cheques for Theresa Norwood, Cheque No. 411, and Sherri Rowe, Cheque No. 415. Sign your name as treasurer of the company. Record the payroll cheque numbers in the payroll register.

Quitman Equipment Company

Employee		Marital Status	Net Claim Code	Time card amounts for period April 1–15		Deductions	
No.	Name			Regular	Overtime	Hospital Insurance	Canada Savings Bonds
3	Alpine, Mark	M	1	$472.00	$ 6.75		
2	Clark, Karl	M	4	585.20		$28.00	
9	Kelley, Garrett	M	4	652.00	26.25	28.00	$20.00
10	Kirby, Kay	M	1	550.00	28.14		
5	Norwood, Theresa	M	1	564.00			15.00
4	Oatman, Sara	S	1	431.50	15.30	12.00	
1	Parker, Ralph	M	3	526.50	48.75	28.00	15.00
6	Randolph, Gary	M	2	506.00	12.95	20.00	
7	Rowe, Sherri	S	1	479.60	18.36		6.00
8	Thatcher, Grace	M	4	662.40	20.70	28.00	
12	Warren, Lila	M	2	421.95	7.28	20.00	
11	Webb, Lester	S	1	435.75			

PROBLEM 22-4   Preparing an employee's earnings record

Jim Perry's earnings for six semimonthly pay periods for April through June of the current year are below.

Pay Period Ended	Earnings		
	Regular	Overtime	Total
04/15	$572.00	$19.50	$591.50
04/30	520.00	9.75	529.75
05/15	572.00	29.25	601.25
05/31	572.00	48.75	620.75
06/15	572.00	——	572.00
06/30	572.00	39.00	611.00

Other data about Jim Perry needed to complete the record are below.

(1) Employee number: 22
(2) Marital status: married
(3) Rate of pay: regular, $6.50; overtime, $9.75
(4) Social insurance number: 444 034 236
(5) Position: nurse
(6) Accumulated earnings for first quarter: $3 640.00
(7) Deductions from total earnings are below.
    Hospitalization insurance: $11.75 each semimonthly pay period
    Canada Savings Bonds: $10.00 each semimonthly pay period
    Income tax: appropriate amount withheld each pay period; deduction table, page 450.
    CPP: use Canada Pension Plan tables
    UI: use Unemployment Insurance tables

Instructions: 1. Prepare an employee's earnings record for Jim Perry similar to the one on page 454. Prepare the earnings record for the second quarter of the current year.

2. Verify the accuracy of the completed employee's earnings record. The Quarter Total for Regular and Overtime Earnings should equal the Quarter Total for Total Earnings. The Quarter Total for Total Earnings should equal the Quarter Total for Net Pay plus Total Deductions. The Quarter Total for Total Earnings should equal the end-of-quarter Accumulated Earnings minus beginning-of-quarter Accumulated Earnings.

ENRICHMENT PROBLEMS

MASTERY PROBLEM 22-M Preparing a semimonthly payroll

Information from employee time cards for the semimonthly pay period May 16–31 of the current year is below.

				Time card amounts for period May 16–31		Deductions	
Employee		Marital Status	Net Claim Code				
No.	Names			Regular	Overtime	Hospital Insurance	Canada Savings Bonds
5	Bryant, Michael	M	1	$600.00	$18.76		
8	Chapman, Avis	M	1	624.00	24.38	$16.00	
7	Gordon, Clay	S	1	437.00			
1	Horton, Joe	M	3	540.50	25.89	25.00	$20.00
2	Humes, Jerry	M	2	657.60			20.00
9	Jones, Diane	M	1	514.15	42.40		
10	Keystone, Alberta	M	3	644.00		25.00	10.00
3	Marriott, Barbara	M	4	662.00	21.00	28.50	
4	Sanders, Roberta	M	2	601.60	19.20		10.00
6	Sutton, Victor	S	1	432.00		16.00	

Gowans Company

Instructions: 1. Prepare a payroll register similar to the illustration on page 449. The date of payment is June 1. Use the income tax table, page 450. For CPP and UI deductions use tables.

2. Prepare a cheque for the total amount of the net pay. Make the cheque payable to *Payroll Account* and sign your name as treasurer of the company. The beginning cheque stub balance is $10 629.23.

3. Prepare payroll cheques for Jerry Humes, Cheque No. 345, and Alberta Keystone, Cheque No. 347. Sign your name as treasurer of the company. Record the payroll cheque numbers in the payroll register.

CHALLENGE PROBLEM 22-C Figuring piecework wages

Introductory remarks. Production workers in factories are frequently paid on the basis of the number of units they produce. This is known as the piecework incentive wage plan. Most piecework wage plans include a guaranteed hourly rate to employees regardless of the number of units they produce. This guaranteed hourly rate is known as the base rate.

Time and motion study engineers usually determine the standard time required for producing a single unit. Assume, for example, time studies determine that one-fourth hour is the standard time required to produce a unit. Then the standard rate for an 8-hour day would be 32 units (8 hours ÷ ¼ hour = 32 units per day). If a worker's daily base pay is $44.80, the incentive rate per unit is $1.40 ($44.80 ÷ 32 units = $1.40 per unit). Therefore, the worker who produces 32 or fewer units per day is paid the base pay, $44.80 per day. However, each worker is paid an additional $1.40 for each unit over 32 produced each day.

Rivera Cabinet Company has nine employees. The employees work in three departments: Cutting, Assembly, and Finishing. Standard rates and incentive rates are as follows.

Department	Standard Rate Per Employee	Incentive Rate Per Unit
Cutting	32 units per day	$1.40
Assembly	24 units per day	2.10
Finishing	16 units per day	4.50

Each employee worked eight hours a day during the semimonthly pay period, May 1–15. Payroll records for May 1–15 show the data below.

Rivera Cabinet Company

No.	Name	Marital Status	Net Claim Code	Guaranteed Daily Rate	2	3	4	5	6	9	10	11	12	13
	Employee				units									

No.	Name	Marital Status	Net Claim Code	Guaranteed Daily Rate	2	3	4	5	6	9	10	11	12	13
	Cutting Department													
C6	Baker, Deanna	S	1	$44.80	29	30	30	32	30	31	32	30	33	29
C2	Chiang, Lu	M	2	44.80	33	34	33	36	32	34	38	33	31	35
	Assembly Department													
A3	Coker, Harvey	M	3	50.40	24	24	25	23	23	26	25	24	24	23
A5	Fouracre, Louis	S	1	50.40	22	23	24	24	22	23	25	23	22	23
A1	Valdez, Maria	M	2	50.40	25	26	27	25	24	26	28	26	26	25
	Finishing Department													
F5	Hayes, Michael	M	4	72.00	16	16	15	18	16	17	15	16	17	16
F1	Lewis, Roy	M	2	72.00	17	18	17	20	16	16	17	17	18	16
F4	Rehl, Barbara	M	3	72.00	15	17	16	18	15	16	16	17	15	16
F7	Young, Steven	M	2	72.00	14	15	15	16	14	15	16	15	16	15

The "Units Produced Per Day / Pay Period May 1–15" spans columns 2 through 13.

Instructions: Prepare a payroll register similar to the illustration, page 449. The Earnings column heading Incentive is used instead of Overtime. The date of payment is May 15. Use the income tax deduction table, page 450. Use CPP and UI tables for employee deductions. None of the employees had Hospital Insurance or Other deductions.

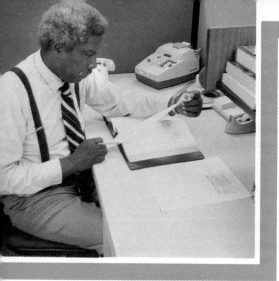

23

Payroll Accounts, Taxes, and Reports

ENABLING PERFORMANCE TASKS

After studying Chapter 23, you will be able to:

a. Explain accounting principles and practices related to payroll accounts, tax reports, and payments.
b. Analyse payroll transactions.
c. Journalize a payroll in a cash payments journal.
d. Post a payroll entry from a cash payments journal.
e. Figure an employer's payroll taxes.
f. Journalize an employer's payroll taxes in a general journal.
g. Post an employer's payroll taxes entry from a general journal.
h. Prepare an employer's Remittance Return Form PD7 AR.
i. Journalize payment of liabities for withholding and payroll taxes in a cash payments journal.

Payroll information for each employee is recorded in a payroll register at the end of each pay period. A separate employee's earnings record is kept for each employee to record payroll information for all pay periods. These two business forms provide all the payroll information needed about individual employees. Therefore, separate payroll accounts for each employee are not kept in the general ledger. Accounts are kept in the general ledger to summarize total earnings and deductions for all employees. A summary of this payroll information is recorded in the accounting records by a journal entry.

RECORDING A PAYROLL IN A JOURNAL

A portion of the payroll register for Lin's Music Centre for the semimonthly period ended February 15, is on the next page. The complete payroll register is in Chapter 22, page 449.

		PAYROLL REGISTER											

SEMIMONTHLY PERIOD ENDED *February 15, 1989*   DATE OF PAYMENT *February 15, 1989*

EMPL. NO.	EMPLOYEE'S NAME	MARITAL STATUS	NET CLAIM CODE	TOTAL EARNINGS	DEDUCTIONS							NET PAY	CH NO
					INCOME TAX	CPP	UI	MEDICAL	HOSPITAL	OTHER	TOTAL		
6	Allen, Don J.	m	3	484 00	34 30	6 90	11 37	28 00	8 78 uw	3 00	92 44	391 56	323
11	Wong, Peter C.	S	1	218 50	—	2 21	5 13	14 00	2 61	20 00	23 95	194 55	333
	Totals			4814 38	388 40	67 69	113 15	210 00	56 95 uw 8 00		864 19	3950 19	

Payroll register

Analysing payroll debits and credits

Column totals of a payroll register provide the debit and credit amounts needed to journalize a payroll. Lin's February 15 payroll is summarized in the T accounts below.

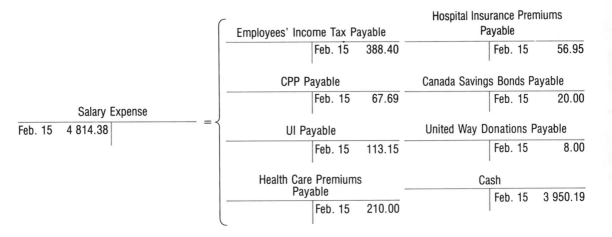

The total of the Total Earnings column, *$4 814.38*, is the salary expense for the period. Salary Expense is debited for this amount.

The total of the Income Tax column, *$388.40*, is the amount withheld from employees' salaries for income tax. The amount withheld is a liability of the business until the tax is paid to the government. Employees' Income Tax Payable is credited for $388.40 to record this liability.

The total of the CPP column, *$67.69*, is the amount withheld from salaries for Canada Pension Plan contributions. The amount withheld is a liability of the business until it is paid to the federal government. To record this liability, CPP Payable is credited for $67.69.

The total of the UI column, *$113.15*, is the amount withheld from salaries for unemployment insurance premiums. The amount withheld is a liability of the business until the premium is paid to the federal government. UI Payable is credited for $113.15 to record this liability.

The total of the Medical column, *$210.00*, is the amount withheld from salaries for health care coverage. The amount withheld is a liability of the business until it is paid to the provincial health care authority. Health Care Premiums Payable is credited for $210.00 to record this liability.

The total of the Hospital column, *$56.95*, is the amount withheld from salaries for hospital insurance. This amount is a liability of the business until it is paid to the insurance company or provincial treasurer, depending upon the province. Hospital Insurance Premiums Payable is credited for $56.95 to record this liability.

The Other column of the deductions section may contain more than one total. In the payroll register, page 463, there are two types of other deductions. The $20.00 Other column total identified with the letter *B* is withheld to buy savings bonds for employees. The $8.00 total identified with the letters *UW* is withheld for employees' United Way pledges. Until these amounts have been paid by the employer, they are liabilities of the business. Canada Savings Bonds Payable is credited for $20.00. United Way Donations Payable is credited for $8.00.

The total of the Net Pay column, *$3 950.19*, the net amount paid to employees, is credited to Cash.

Journalizing a payroll entry

A cheque for the amount of the total net pay is written on Lin's regular current account. This amount is deposited in a special bank account for employee payroll cheques. Only the cheque written for the total payroll is recorded in the cash payments journal. The entry made in the cash payments journal to record Lin's February 15 payroll is below.

	DATE	ACCOUNT TITLE	CHECK No.	POST. REF.	GENERAL DEBIT	GENERAL CREDIT	ACCOUNTS PAYABLE DEBIT	PURCHASES DISCOUNT CREDIT	CASH CREDIT	
					1	2	3	4	5	
1	1989 Feb. 15	Salary Expense	123	6113	481438				395019	1
2		Employees' Income Tax Pay.		2103		38840				2
3		CPP Payable		2105		6769				3
4		UI Payable		2107		11315				4
5		Health Care Prem. Payable		2108		21000				5
6		Hospital Ins. Prem. Payable		2109		5695				6
7		Canada Savings Bonds Pay.		2110		2000				7
8		United Way Donations Pay.		2111		800				8
9										9
10										10

CASH PAYMENTS JOURNAL — PAGE *5*

Entry to record a payroll

The source document for a payroll journal entry is the cheque stub. *(CONCEPT: Objective Evidence)* Salary Expense is debited for the total amount of the payroll, *$4 814.38*. *(CONCEPT: Historical Cost)* Cash is credited for the net amount paid to employees, *$3 950.19*. Seven liability accounts are credited for the amounts deducted from employees' salaries.

Posting a payroll entry

Amounts recorded in the General columns of a cash payments journal are posted individually to general ledger accounts. After the February 15 payroll entry is posted, the liability accounts and salary expense account appear as shown below and on the next page.

General ledger accounts after payroll entry is posted

ACCOUNT Employees' Income Tax Payable   ACCOUNT NO. 2103

DATE	ITEM	POST. REF.	DEBIT	CREDIT	BALANCE DEBIT	BALANCE CREDIT
31						80263
15		CP5		38840		119103

ACCOUNT CPP Payable   ACCOUNT NO. 2105

DATE	ITEM	POST. REF.	DEBIT	CREDIT	BALANCE DEBIT	BALANCE CREDIT
31						28092
15		CP5		6769		34861

ACCOUNT U I Payable   ACCOUNT NO. 2107

DATE	ITEM	POST. REF.	DEBIT	CREDIT	BALANCE DEBIT	BALANCE CREDIT
31						57219
15		CP5		57219		68534

ACCOUN Health Care Premiums Payable   ACCOUNT NO. 2108

DATE	ITEM	POST. REF.	DEBIT	CREDIT	BALANCE DEBIT	BALANCE CREDIT
31						42000
15		CP5		21000		63000

ACCOUNT Hospital Insurance Premiums Payable   ACCOUNT NO. 2109

DATE	ITEM	POST. REF.	DEBIT	CREDIT	BALANCE DEBIT	BALANCE CREDIT
31						11500
15		CP5		5695		17195

ACCOUNT Canada Savings Bonds Payable   ACCOUNT NO. 2110

DATE	ITEM	POST. REF.	DEBIT	CREDIT	BALANCE DEBIT	BALANCE CREDIT
31						4000
15		CP5		2000		6000

ACCOUNT *United Way Donations Payable*					ACCOUNT NO. *2111*		
DATE	ITEM	POST. REF.	DEBIT	CREDIT	BALANCE		
					DEBIT	CREDIT	
31						*800*	
15		*CP5*		*800*		*1600*	

ACCOUNT *Salary Expense*					ACCOUNT NO. *6113*		
DATE	ITEM	POST. REF.	DEBIT	CREDIT	BALANCE		
					DEBIT	CREDIT	
1989 *Feb 15*		*CP5*	*481438*		*481438*		

The credit to Cash, *$3 950.19*, is not posted separately to the cash account. The amount is included in the journal's Cash Credit column total that is posted at the end of the month.

RECORDING AN EMPLOYER'S PAYROLL TAXES

Employers must pay to the government the taxes withheld from employees' wages. In addition, employers must pay several payroll taxes of their own. An employer's payroll taxes are expenses of the business.

Figuring an employer's payroll taxes

All employers are required by law to deduct income tax, Canada Pension Plan, and Unemployment Insurance premiums from the earnings of their employees. In addition, all employers are required to contribute to the Canada Pension Plan and to the Unemployment Insurance fund on behalf of their employees. They must pay the amounts withheld plus the amount of their own contributions to Revenue Canada, Taxation, no later than the fifteenth day of the month following the month in which the remuneration is paid to the employees.

The employer contribution is equal to the employees' contributions for the Canada Pension Plan, and is 1.4 times the employees' contributions for Unemployment Insurance. For example, on Lin's February 15 payroll, the total amount deducted from all employees for Canada Pension Plan is $67.69. Therefore, Lin's has to pay an equal amount of $67.69 for Canada Pension Plan. The total deducted for Unemployment Insurance premiums is $113.15. Therefore, the premium that Lin's has to pay for Unemployment Insurance is $158.41 (1.4 × $113.15).

Employers do not make contributions for the income taxes deducted from employees. However, employers do sometimes make contributions for other employee benefits such as health care, hospitalization, dental care, group insurance, etc. Deductions such as these are determined by the employment agreement between the employer and its employees.

Journalizing an employer's payroll taxes entry

Payroll taxes expense for each payroll is recorded when the payroll is recorded. Since the payroll taxes expense is recorded but not paid until later, the expenses are recorded in a general journal.

Lin's recorded the following payroll taxes expense on February 15, 1989.

> February 15, 1989. Recorded payroll taxes expense for the semimonthly period ended February 15, 1989, $226.10. Memorandum No. 35.

GENERAL LEDGER

Payroll Taxes Expense
| 226.10 | |

CPP Payable
| | 67.69 |

UI Payable
| | 158.41 |

The source document for an employer's payroll taxes journal entry is a memorandum. (CONCEPT: Objective Evidence) The entry to record employer's payroll taxes is analysed in the T accounts at the right.

Payroll Taxes Expense is debited for $226.10 to show the increase in the balance of this expense account. Two liability accounts are credited to show the increase in these liability accounts. CPP Payable is credited for $67.69. Unemployment Insurance Payable is credited for $158.41.

Lin's two payroll tax expenses are recorded in the entry below.

	DATE	ACCOUNT TITLE	POST. REF.	DEBIT	CREDIT	
1	19-- Feb. 15	CPP Expense	6110	6769		1
2		CPP Payable	2105		6769	2
3		UI Expense	6111	15841		3
4		UI Payable	2107		15841	4
5						5
6						6
7						7

GENERAL JOURNAL   PAGE *3*

Entry for employer's payroll taxes

If a detailed breakdown of payroll expenses is not required, the expenses for Canada Pension Plan and Unemployment Insurance may be combined and recorded as payroll taxes as shown in the above T accounts. However, if details are required, these expenses may be shown separately as indicated in the entry in the journal. CPP Expense is debited and CPP Payable is credited for $67.69. UI Expense is debited and UI Payable is credited for $158.41.

Posting an employer's payroll taxes entry

After the entry for the employer's payroll taxes is posted, the four accounts involved appear as shown below.

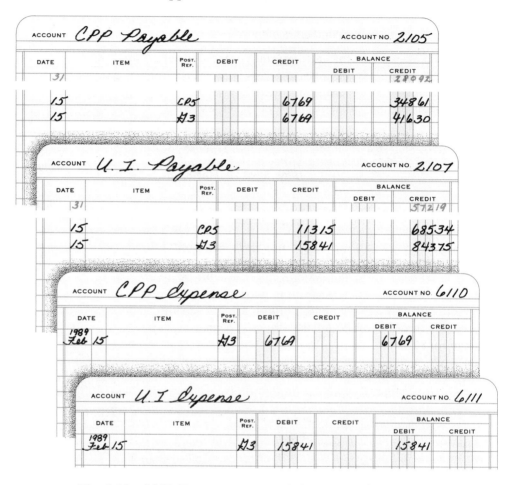

The debit of $67.69 to CPP Expense and the debit of $158.41 to UI Expense are the expenses to the employer for contributions made to Canada Pension Plan and to the Unemployment Insurance fund.

The CPP Payable account has two credits. The first credit of $67.69 is the amount withheld from the employees' earnings for the pay period ended February 15. This was posted from the entry recording the payroll, page 464. The second credit of $67.69 is the employer's liability for Canada Pension Plan.

The UI Payable account has two credits. The first credit of $113.15 is the amount withheld from the employee's earnings. This was posted from the entry recording the payroll, page 464. The second credit of $158.41 is the employer's liability for Unemployment Insurance.

CANADA PENSION PLAN CONTRIBUTIONS **COTISATIONS AU RÉGIME DE PENSIONS DU CANADA**

SEMI-MONTHLY PAY PERIOD — *PÉRIODE BI-MENSUELLE DE PAIE*

415.56 — 575.55

Rémunération From-de	To-à	C.P.P. R.P.C.	Rémunération From-de	To-à	C.P.P. R.P.C.	Rémunération From-de	To-à	C.P.P. R.P.C.	Rémunération From-de	To-à	C.P.P. R.P.C.
415.56 -	416.10	5.76	455.56 -	456.10	6.48	495.56 -	496.10	7.20	535.56 -	536.10	7.92
416.11 -	416.66	5.77	456.11 -	456.66	6.49	496.11 -	496.66	7.21	536.11 -	536.66	7.93
416.67 -	417.21	5.78	456.67 -	457.21	6.50	496.67 -	497.21	7.22	536.67 -	537.21	7.94
417.22 -	417.77	5.79	457.22 -	457.77	6.51	497.22 -	497.77	7.23	537.22 -	537.77	7.95
417.78 -	418.32	5.80	457.78 -	458.32	6.52	497.78 -	498.32	7.24	537.78 -	538.32	7.96
418.33 -	418.88	5.81	458.33 -	458.88	6.53	498.33 -	498.88	7.25	538.33 -	538.88	7.97
418.89 -	419.44	5.82	458.89 -	459.44	6.54	498.89 -	499.44	7.26	538.89 -	539.44	7.98
419.45 -	419.99	5.83	459.45 -	459.99	6.55	499.45 -	499.99	7.27	539.45 -	539.99	7.99
420.00 -	420.55	5.84	460.00 -	460.55	6.56	500.00 -	500.55	7.28	540.00 -	540.55	8.00
420.56 -	421.10	5.85	460.56 -	461.10	6.57	500.56 -	501.10	7.29	540.56 -	541.10	8.01
421.11 -	421.66	5.86	461.11 -	461.66	6.58	501.11 -	501.66	7.30	541.11 -	541.66	8.02
421.67 -	422.21	5.87	461.67 -	462.21	6.59	501.67 -	502.21	7.31	541.67 -	542.21	8.03
422.22 -	422.77	5.88	462.22 -	462.77	6.60	502.22 -	502.77	7.32	542.22 -	542.77	8.04
422.78 -	423.32	5.89	462.78 -	463.32	6.61	502.78 -	503.32	7.33	542.78 -	543.32	8.05
423.33 -	423.88	5.90	463.33 -	463.88	6.62	503.33 -	503.88	7.34	543.33 -	543.88	8.06
423.89 -	424.44	5.91	463.89 -	464.44	6.63	503.89 -	504.44	7.35	543.89 -	544.44	8.07
424.45 -	424.99	5.92	464.45 -	464.99	6.64	504.45 -	504.99	7.36	544.45 -	544.99	8.08
425.00 -	425.55	5.93	465.00 -	465.55	6.65	505.00 -	505.55	7.37	545.00 -	545.55	8.09
425.56 -	426.10	5.94	465.56 -	466.10	6.66	505.56 -	506.10	7.38	545.56 -	546.10	8.10
426.11 -	426.66	5.95	466.11 -	466.66	6.67	506.11 -	506.66	7.39	546.11 -	546.66	8.11
426.67 -	427.21	5.96	466.67 -	467.21	6.68	506.67 -	507.21	7.40	546.67 -	547.21	8.12
427.22 -	427.77	5.97	467.22 -	467.77	6.69	507.22 -	507.77	7.41	547.22 -	547.77	8.13
427.78 -	428.32	5.98	467.78 -	468.32	6.70	507.78 -	508.32	7.42	547.78 -	548.32	8.14
428.33 -	428.88	5.99	468.33 -	468.88	6.71	508.33 -	508.88	7.43	548.33 -	548.88	8.15
428.89 -	429.44	6.00	468.89 -	469.44	6.72	508.89 -	509.44	7.44	548.89 -	549.44	8.16
429.45 -	429.99	6.01	469.45 -	469.99	6.73	509.45 -	509.99	7.45	549.45 -	549.99	8.17
430.00 -	430.55	6.02	470.00 -	470.55	6.74	510.00 -	510.55	7.46	550.00 -	550.55	8.18
430.56 -	431.10	6.03	470.56 -	471.10	6.75	510.56 -	511.10	7.47	550.56 -	551.10	8.19
431.11 -	431.66	6.04	471.11 -	471.66	6.76	511.11 -	511.66	7.48	551.11 -	551.66	8.20
431.67 -	432.21	6.05	471.67 -	472.21	6.77	511.67 -	512.21	7.49	551.67 -	552.21	8.21
432.22 -	432.77	6.06	472.22 -	472.77	6.78	512.22 -	512.77	7.50	552.22 -	552.77	8.22
432.78 -	433.32	6.07	472.78 -	473.32	6.79	512.78 -	513.32	7.51	552.78 -	553.32	8.23
433.33 -	433.88	6.08	473.33 -	473.88	6.80	513.33 -	513.88	7.52	553.33 -	553.88	8.24
433.89 -	434.44	6.09	473.89 -	474.44	6.81	513.89 -	514.44	7.53	553.89 -	554.44	8.25
434.45 -	434.99	6.10	474.45 -	474.99	6.82	514.45 -	514.99	7.54	554.45 -	554.99	8.26
435.00 -	435.55	6.11	475.00 -	475.55	6.83	515.00 -	515.55	7.55	555.00 -	555.55	8.27
435.56 -	436.10	6.12	475.56 -	476.10	6.84	515.56 -	516.10	7.56	555.56 -	556.10	8.28
436.11 -	436.66	6.13	476.11 -	476.66	6.85	516.11 -	516.66	7.57	556.11 -	556.66	8.29
436.67 -	437.21	6.14	476.67 -	477.21	6.86	516.67 -	517.21	7.58	556.67 -	557.21	8.30
437.22 -	437.77	6.15	477.22 -	477.77	6.87	517.22 -	517.77	7.59	557.22 -	557.77	8.31
437.78 -	438.32	6.16	477.78 -	478.32	6.88	517.78 -	518.32	7.60	557.78 -	558.32	8.32
438.33 -	438.88	6.17	478.33 -	478.88	6.89	518.33 -	518.88	7.61	558.33 -	558.88	8.33
438.89 -	439.44	6.18	478.89 -	479.44	6.90	518.89 -	519.44	7.62	558.89 -	559.44	8.34
439.45 -	439.99	6.19	479.45 -	479.99	6.91	519.45 -	519.99	7.63	559.45 -	559.99	8.35
440.00 -	440.55	6.20	480.00 -	480.55	6.92	520.00 -	520.55	7.64	560.00 -	560.55	8.36
440.56 -	441.10	6.21	480.56 -	481.10	6.93	520.56 -	521.10	7.65	560.56 -	561.10	8.37
441.11 -	441.66	6.22	481.11 -	481.66	6.94	521.11 -	521.66	7.66	561.11 -	561.66	8.38
441.67 -	442.21	6.23	481.67 -	482.21	6.95	521.67 -	522.21	7.67	561.67 -	562.21	8.39
442.22 -	442.77	6.24	482.22 -	482.77	6.96	522.22 -	522.77	7.68	562.22 -	562.77	8.40
442.78 -	443.32	6.25	482.78 -	483.32	6.97	522.78 -	523.32	7.69	562.78 -	563.32	8.41
443.33 -	443.88	6.26	483.33 -	483.88	6.98	523.33 -	523.88	7.70	563.33 -	563.88	8.42
443.89 -	444.44	6.27	483.89 -	484.44	6.99	523.89 -	524.44	7.71	563.89 -	564.44	8.43
444.45 -	444.99	6.28	484.45 -	484.99	7.00	524.45 -	524.99	7.72	564.45 -	564.99	8.44
445.00 -	445.55	6.29	485.00 -	485.55	7.01	525.00 -	525.55	7.73	565.00 -	565.55	8.45
445.56 -	446.10	6.30	485.56 -	486.10	7.02	525.56 -	526.10	7.74	565.56 -	566.10	8.46
446.11 -	446.66	6.31	486.11 -	486.66	7.03	526.11 -	526.66	7.75	566.11 -	566.66	8.47
446.67 -	447.21	6.32	486.67 -	487.21	7.04	526.67 -	527.21	7.76	566.67 -	567.21	8.48
447.22 -	447.77	6.33	487.22 -	487.77	7.05	527.22 -	527.77	7.77	567.22 -	567.77	8.49
447.78 -	448.32	6.34	487.78 -	488.32	7.06	527.78 -	528.32	7.78	567.78 -	568.32	8.50
448.33 -	448.88	6.35	488.33 -	488.88	7.07	528.33 -	528.88	7.79	568.33 -	568.88	8.51
448.89 -	449.44	6.36	488.89 -	489.44	7.08	528.89 -	529.44	7.80	568.89 -	569.44	8.52
449.45 -	449.99	6.37	489.45 -	489.99	7.09	529.45 -	529.99	7.81	569.45 -	569.99	8.53
450.00 -	450.55	6.38	490.00 -	490.55	7.10	530.00 -	530.55	7.82	570.00 -	570.55	8.54
450.56 -	451.10	6.39	490.56 -	491.10	7.11	530.56 -	531.10	7.83	570.56 -	571.10	8.55
451.11 -	451.66	6.40	491.11 -	491.66	7.12	531.11 -	531.66	7.84	571.11 -	571.66	8.55
451.67 -	452.21	6.41	491.67 -	492.21	7.13	531.67 -	532.21	7.85	571.67 -	572.21	8.57
452.22 -	452.77	6.42	492.22 -	492.77	7.14	532.22 -	532.77	7.86	572.22 -	572.77	8.58
452.78 -	453.32	6.43	492.78 -	493.32	7.15	532.78 -	533.32	7.87	572.78 -	573.32	8.59
453.33 -	453.88	6.44	493.33 -	493.88	7.16	533.33 -	533.88	7.88	573.33 -	573.88	8.60
453.89 -	454.44	6.45	493.89 -	494.44	7.17	533.89 -	534.44	7.89	573.89 -	574.44	8.61
454.45 -	454.99	6.46	494.45 -	494.99	7.18	534.45 -	534.99	7.90	574.45 -	574.99	8.62
455.00 -	455.55	6.47	495.00 -	495.55	7.19	535.00 -	535.55	7.91	575.00 -	575.55	8.63

CPP Contributions Table

UNEMPLOYMENT INSURANCE PREMIUMS

PRIMES D'ASSURANCE-CHÔMAGE

For minimum and maximum insurable earnings amounts for various pay periods see Schedule II. For the maximimum premium deduction for various pay periods see bottom of this page.

Les montants minimum et maximum des gains assurables pour diverses périodes de paie figurent en annexe II. La déduction maximale de primes pour diverses périodes de paie figure au bas de la présente page.

Remuneration From-de – To-à	U.I. Premium d'a.-c.	Remuneration From-de – To-à	U.I. Premium d'a.-c.	Remuneration From-de – To-à	U.I. Premium d'a.-c.	Remuneration From-de – To-à	U.I. Premium d'a.-c.	Remuneration From-de – To-à	U.I. Premium d'a.-c.
459.79 – 460.21	10.81	490.43 – 490.85	11.53	521.07 – 521.48	12.25	551.71 – 552.12	12.97	582.35 – 582.76	13.69
460.22 – 460.63	10.82	490.86 – 491.27	11.54	521.49 – 521.91	12.26	552.13 – 552.55	12.98	582.77 – 583.19	13.70
460.64 – 461.06	10.83	491.28 – 491.70	11.55	521.92 – 522.34	12.27	552.56 – 552.97	12.99	583.20 – 583.61	13.71
461.07 – 461.48	10.84	491.71 – 492.12	11.56	522.35 – 522.76	12.28	552.98 – 553.40	13.00	583.62 – 584.04	13.72
461.49 – 461.91	10.85	492.13 – 492.55	11.57	522.77 – 523.19	12.29	553.41 – 553.82	13.01	584.05 – 584.46	13.73
461.92 – 462.34	10.86	492.56 – 492.97	11.58	523.20 – 523.61	12.30	553.83 – 554.25	13.02	584.47 – 584.89	13.74
462.35 – 462.76	10.87	492.98 – 493.40	11.59	523.62 – 524.04	12.31	554.26 – 554.68	13.03	584.90 – 585.31	13.75
462.77 – 463.19	10.88	493.41 – 493.82	11.60	524.05 – 524.46	12.32	554.69 – 555.10	13.04	585.32 – 585.74	13.76
463.20 – 463.61	10.89	493.83 – 494.25	11.61	524.47 – 524.89	12.33	555.11 – 555.53	13.05	585.75 – 586.17	13.77
463.62 – 464.04	10.90	494.26 – 494.68	11.62	524.90 – 525.31	12.34	555.54 – 555.95	13.06	586.18 – 586.59	13.78
464.05 – 464.46	10.91	494.69 – 495.10	11.63	525.32 – 525.74	12.35	555.96 – 556.38	13.07	586.60 – 587.02	13.79
464.47 – 464.89	10.92	495.11 – 495.53	11.64	525.75 – 526.17	12.36	556.39 – 556.80	13.08	587.03 – 587.44	13.80
464.90 – 465.31	10.93	495.54 – 495.95	11.65	526.18 – 526.59	12.37	556.81 – 557.23	13.09	587.45 – 587.87	13.81
465.32 – 465.74	10.94	495.96 – 496.38	11.66	526.60 – 527.02	12.38	557.24 – 557.65	13.10	587.88 – 588.29	13.82
465.75 – 466.17	10.95	496.39 – 496.80	11.67	527.03 – 527.44	12.39	557.66 – 558.08	13.11	588.30 – 588.72	13.83
466.18 – 466.59	10.96	496.81 – 497.23	11.68	527.45 – 527.87	12.40	558.09 – 558.51	13.12	588.73 – 589.14	13.84
466.60 – 467.02	10.97	497.24 – 497.65	11.69	527.88 – 528.29	12.41	558.52 – 558.93	13.13	589.15 – 589.57	13.85
467.03 – 467.44	10.98	497.66 – 498.08	11.70	528.30 – 528.72	12.42	558.94 – 559.36	13.14	589.58 – 589.99	13.86
467.45 – 467.87	10.99	498.09 – 498.51	11.71	528.73 – 529.14	12.43	559.37 – 559.78	13.15	590.00 – 590.42	13.87
467.88 – 468.29	11.00	498.52 – 498.93	11.72	529.15 – 529.57	12.44	559.79 – 560.21	13.16	590.43 – 590.85	13.88
468.30 – 468.72	11.01	498.94 – 499.36	11.73	529.58 – 529.99	12.45	560.22 – 560.63	13.17	590.86 – 591.27	13.89
468.73 – 469.14	11.02	499.37 – 499.78	11.74	530.00 – 530.42	12.46	560.64 – 561.06	13.18	591.28 – 591.70	13.90
469.15 – 469.57	11.03	499.79 – 500.21	11.75	530.43 – 530.85	12.47	561.07 – 561.48	13.19	591.71 – 592.12	13.91
469.58 – 469.99	11.04	500.22 – 500.63	11.76	530.86 – 531.27	12.48	561.49 – 561.91	13.20	592.13 – 592.55	13.92
470.00 – 470.42	11.05	500.64 – 501.06	11.77	531.28 – 531.70	12.49	561.92 – 562.34	13.21	592.56 – 592.97	13.93
470.43 – 470.85	11.06	501.07 – 501.48	11.78	531.71 – 532.12	12.50	562.35 – 562.76	13.22	592.98 – 593.40	13.94
470.86 – 471.27	11.07	501.49 – 501.91	11.79	532.13 – 532.55	12.51	562.77 – 563.19	13.23	593.41 – 593.82	13.95
471.28 – 471.70	11.08	501.92 – 502.34	11.80	532.56 – 532.97	12.52	563.20 – 563.61	13.24	593.83 – 594.25	13.96
471.71 – 472.12	11.09	502.35 – 502.76	11.81	532.98 – 533.40	12.53	563.62 – 564.04	13.25	594.26 – 594.68	13.97
472.13 – 472.55	11.10	502.77 – 503.19	11.82	533.41 – 533.82	12.54	564.05 – 564.46	13.26	594.69 – 595.10	13.98
472.56 – 472.97	11.11	503.20 – 503.61	11.83	533.83 – 534.25	12.55	564.47 – 564.89	13.27	595.11 – 595.53	13.99
472.98 – 473.40	11.12	503.62 – 504.04	11.84	534.26 – 534.68	12.56	564.90 – 565.31	13.28	595.54 – 595.95	14.00
473.41 – 473.82	11.13	504.05 – 504.46	11.85	534.69 – 535.10	12.57	565.32 – 565.74	13.29	595.96 – 596.38	14.01
473.83 – 474.25	11.14	504.47 – 504.89	11.86	535.11 – 535.53	12.58	565.75 – 566.17	13.30	596.39 – 596.80	14.02
474.26 – 474.68	11.15	504.90 – 505.31	11.87	535.54 – 535.95	12.59	566.18 – 566.59	13.31	596.81 – 597.23	14.03
474.69 – 475.10	11.16	505.32 – 505.74	11.88	535.96 – 536.38	12.60	566.60 – 567.02	13.32	597.24 – 597.65	14.04
475.11 – 475.53	11.17	505.75 – 506.17	11.89	536.39 – 536.80	12.61	567.03 – 567.44	13.33	597.66 – 598.08	14.05
475.54 – 475.95	11.18	506.18 – 506.59	11.90	536.81 – 537.23	12.62	567.45 – 567.87	13.34	598.09 – 598.51	14.06
475.96 – 476.38	11.19	506.60 – 507.02	11.91	537.24 – 537.65	12.63	567.88 – 568.29	13.35	598.52 – 598.93	14.07
476.39 – 476.80	11.20	507.03 – 507.44	11.92	537.66 – 538.08	12.64	568.30 – 568.72	13.36	598.94 – 599.36	14.08
476.81 – 477.23	11.21	507.45 – 507.87	11.93	538.09 – 538.51	12.65	568.73 – 569.14	13.37	599.37 – 599.78	14.09
477.24 – 477.65	11.22	507.88 – 508.29	11.94	538.52 – 538.93	12.66	569.15 – 569.57	13.38	599.79 – 600.21	14.10
477.66 – 478.08	11.23	508.30 – 508.72	11.95	538.94 – 539.36	12.67	569.58 – 569.99	13.39	600.22 – 600.63	14.11
478.09 – 478.51	11.24	508.73 – 509.14	11.96	539.37 – 539.78	12.68	570.00 – 570.42	13.40	600.64 – 601.06	14.12
478.52 – 478.93	11.25	509.15 – 509.57	11.97	539.79 – 540.21	12.69	570.43 – 570.85	13.41	601.07 – 601.48	14.13
478.94 – 479.36	11.26	509.58 – 509.99	11.98	540.22 – 540.63	12.70	570.86 – 571.27	13.42	601.49 – 601.91	14.14
479.37 – 479.78	11.27	510.00 – 510.42	11.99	540.64 – 541.06	12.71	571.28 – 571.70	13.43	601.92 – 602.34	14.15
479.79 – 480.21	11.28	510.43 – 510.85	12.00	541.07 – 541.48	12.72	571.71 – 572.12	13.44	602.35 – 602.76	14.16
480.22 – 480.63	11.29	510.86 – 511.27	12.01	541.49 – 541.91	12.73	572.13 – 572.55	13.45	602.77 – 603.19	14.17
480.64 – 481.06	11.30	511.28 – 511.70	12.02	541.92 – 542.34	12.74	572.56 – 572.97	13.46	603.20 – 603.61	14.18
481.07 – 481.48	11.31	511.71 – 512.12	12.03	542.35 – 542.76	12.75	572.98 – 573.40	13.47	603.62 – 604.04	14.19
481.49 – 481.91	11.32	512.13 – 512.55	12.04	542.77 – 543.19	12.76	573.41 – 573.82	13.48	604.05 – 604.46	14.20
481.92 – 482.34	11.33	512.56 – 512.97	12.05	543.20 – 543.61	12.77	573.83 – 574.25	13.49	604.47 – 604.89	14.21
482.35 – 482.76	11.34	512.98 – 513.40	12.06	543.62 – 544.04	12.78	574.26 – 574.68	13.50	604.90 – 605.31	14.22
482.77 – 483.19	11.35	513.41 – 513.82	12.07	544.05 – 544.46	12.79	574.69 – 575.10	13.51	605.32 – 605.74	14.23
483.20 – 483.61	11.36	513.83 – 514.25	12.08	544.47 – 544.89	12.80	575.11 – 575.53	13.52	605.75 – 606.17	14.24
483.62 – 484.04	11.37	514.26 – 514.68	12.09	544.90 – 545.31	12.81	575.54 – 575.95	13.53	606.18 – 606.59	14.25
484.05 – 484.46	11.38	514.69 – 515.10	12.10	545.32 – 545.74	12.82	575.96 – 576.38	13.54	606.60 – 607.02	14.26
484.47 – 484.89	11.39	515.11 – 515.53	12.11	545.75 – 546.17	12.83	576.39 – 576.80	13.55	607.03 – 607.44	14.27
484.90 – 485.31	11.40	515.54 – 515.95	12.12	546.18 – 546.59	12.84	576.81 – 577.23	13.56	607.45 – 607.87	14.28
485.32 – 485.74	11.41	515.96 – 516.38	12.13	546.60 – 547.02	12.85	577.24 – 577.65	13.57	607.88 – 608.29	14.29
485.75 – 486.17	11.42	516.39 – 516.80	12.14	547.03 – 547.44	12.86	577.66 – 578.08	13.58	608.30 – 608.72	14.30
486.18 – 486.59	11.43	516.81 – 517.23	12.15	547.45 – 547.87	12.87	578.09 – 578.51	13.59	608.73 – 609.14	14.31
486.60 – 487.02	11.44	517.24 – 517.65	12.16	547.88 – 548.29	12.88	578.52 – 578.93	13.60	609.15 – 609.57	14.32
487.03 – 487.44	11.45	517.66 – 518.08	12.17	548.30 – 548.72	12.89	578.94 – 579.36	13.61	609.58 – 609.99	14.33
487.45 – 487.87	11.46	518.09 – 518.51	12.18	548.73 – 549.14	12.90	579.37 – 579.78	13.62	610.00 – 610.42	14.34
487.88 – 488.29	11.47	518.52 – 518.93	12.19	549.15 – 549.57	12.91	579.79 – 580.21	13.63	610.43 – 610.85	14.35
488.30 – 488.72	11.48	518.94 – 519.36	12.20	549.58 – 549.99	12.92	580.22 – 580.63	13.64	610.86 – 611.27	14.36
488.73 – 489.14	11.49	519.37 – 519.78	12.21	550.00 – 550.42	12.93	580.64 – 581.06	13.65	611.28 – 611.70	14.37
489.15 – 489.57	11.50	519.79 – 520.21	12.22	550.43 – 550.85	12.94	581.07 – 581.48	13.66	611.71 – 612.12	14.38
489.58 – 489.99	11.51	520.22 – 520.63	12.23	550.86 – 551.27	12.95	581.49 – 581.91	13.67	612.13 – 612.55	14.39
490.00 – 490.42	11.52	520.64 – 521.06	12.24	551.28 – 551.70	12.96	581.92 – 582.34	13.68	612.56 – 612.97	14.40

Maximum Premium Deduction for a Pay Period of the stated frequency.
Déduction maximale de prime pour une période de paie d'une durée donnée.

Weekly — Hebdomadaire	10.81		10 pp per year — 10 pp par année	56.21
Bi-Weekly — Deux semaines	21.62		13 pp per year — 13 pp par année	43.24
Semi-Monthly — Bi-mensuel	23.42		22 pp per year — 22 pp par année	25.55
Monthly — Mensuellement	46.84			

UI Premiums Table

PAYING WITHHOLDING AND PAYROLL TAXES

All employers must remit to the federal government the total amount withheld each month from employees' earnings for income tax, Canada Pension Plan, and Unemployment Insurance premiums, together with the employer's contributions to the Canada Pension Plan and the Unemployment Insurance fund, by the fifteenth of the following month. The penalty for remitting late or failing to remit is 10% of the amount deducted (minimum $10), or the amount that should have been deducted, plus interest at a prescribed rate.

Upon checking the payroll liability accounts of Lin's Music Centre, it is determined that $1 655.74 is due for the month of January. Therefore, on or before February 15, a cheque payable to the Receiver General of Canada is issued and remitted to the local bank, along with Form PD7AR, Tax Deduction-Canada Pension Plan-Unemployment Insurance Remittance Return, which is illustrated on page 473. If an employer cannot remit through the bank, then the upper part only of Form PD7AR is completed and mailed with a certified cheque or money order to the appropriate Taxation Data Centre, which then processes the remittance and returns a receipt for the payment, along with a blank Form PD7AR to be used for the next month's remittance.

Entry to record payment of liability for employees' deductions

The payment of federal payroll liabilities is recorded in the cash payments journal and posted to the ledger accounts as shown below and on page 472.

					CASH PAYMENTS JOURNAL					PAGE 6	
					1	2	3	4	5		
	DATE	ACCOUNT TITLE	CH. NO.	POST. REF.	GENERAL DEBIT	GENERAL CREDIT	ACCOUNTS PAY. DEBIT	PURCHASES DISC. CREDIT	CASH CREDIT		
1	1989 Feb. 15	Employees' Inc. Tax Pay.	223	2103	80263				165574		1
2		CPP Payable		2105	28092						2
3		UI Payable		2107	57219						3
4											4
5											5
6											6
7											7
8											8
9											9
10											10

The total amount of employees' income tax withheld for the month of January is indicated by the January 31 balance or $802.63. This amount is paid on February 15, leaving a balance of $388.40, which is the amount that was withheld from the February 15 payroll.

ACCOUNT *Employees' Income Tax Payable*   ACCOUNT NO. **2103**

DATE		ITEM	POST. REF.	DEBIT	CREDIT	BALANCE	
						DEBIT	CREDIT
	31		J1		40263		80263
Feb.	15		CP5		38840		119103
	15		CP6	80263			38840

The total liability to the Canada Pension Plan for the month of January is the January 31 balance of $280.92. This is the amount to be paid by February 15, leaving a balance of $135.38, which is made up of the employee and employer contributions from the February 15 payroll.

ACCOUNT *CPP Payable*   ACCOUNT NO. **2105**

DATE		ITEM	POST. REF.	DEBIT	CREDIT	BALANCE	
						DEBIT	CREDIT
	31		J1		7164		28092
Feb.	15		CP5		6769		34861
	15		J3		6769		41630
	15		CP6	28092			13538

The total liability for Unemployment Insurance premiums for the month of January is the January 31 balance of $572.19. This is the amount to be paid by February 15, leaving a balance of $271.56, which is made up of the employee and employer contributions from the February 15 payroll.

ACCOUNT *UI Payable*   ACCOUNT NO. **2107**

DATE		ITEM	POST. REF.	DEBIT	CREDIT	BALANCE	
						DEBIT	CREDIT
	31		J1		16407		57219
Feb.	15		CP5		11315		68534
	15		J3		15841		84375
	15		CP6	57219			27156

PD7AR
REV. 85

Revenue Canada Revenu Canada
Taxation Impôt

REMITTANCE FORM - *FORMULE DE VERSEMENT*

COMPLETE THE UNSHADED BOXES ONLY
NE REMPLIR QUE LES CASES NON OMBRAGÉES

NAME, ADDRESS AND OWNERSHIP CHANGES
Please enter any changes not reported previously
CHANGEMENTS DE NOM D'ADRESSE ET DE PROPRIÉTAIRE
Prière d'indiquer le détail des changements non signalés antérieurement

New name
Nouveau nom

Care of Address
Adresse aux soins de

New address
Nouvelle adresse

City, Province, Postal Code
Ville, province, code postal

If ownership of business has changed enter effective date (Day, Month, Year)
Si la propriété de l'entreprise a changé en indiquer la date de prise d'effet (Jour, Mois, Année)

DEDUCTIONS WITHHELD
DURING THE MONTH OF
RETENUES DU MOIS DE   19

C.P.P. CONTRIBUTIONS
COTISATIONS AU RPC

U.I. PREMIUMS
PRIMES D.A.-C.

TAX DEDUCTIONS
RETENUES D'IMPÔT

1.

CURRENT PAYMENT
PAIEMENT COURANT   6

ARREARS PAYMENT
PAIEMENT D'ARRIÈRES   4

TOTAL PAYMENT
PAIEMENT TOTAL

Sub-Code *Sous-code*	LP CODE *CODE P.P.T*	NO. OF PAY'TS *NBRE VERS*	MONTH *MOIS*	YEAR *ANNÉE*
	1			

Revenue Canada Revenu Canada
Taxation Impôt

PD7A REV 85

2.

EMPLOYER NUMBER
N° DE L'EMPLOYEUR

EMPLOYER NAME
NOM DE L'EMPLOYÉ

Your payment may be made where you bank or to
Vous pouvez faire le paiement à votre institution financière ou à:

Taxation Centre - *Centre fiscal*

See
reverse
*Voir
au verso*

* If payment is made where you bank, detach and
present parts 1 and 2 to the teller. Retain part
2 for your record of payment after it is receipted
by the teller. See reverse.

* Si le paiement est fait à votre institution financière, détachez les parties 1 et 2 et présentez-les
au caissier. Gardez la partie 2 comme preuve de
votre paiement, après qu'elle a été quittancée
par le caissier. Voir au verso.

C.P.P. CONTRIBUTIONS
COTISATIONS AU RPC

U.I. PREMIUMS
PRIMES D.A.-C.

TAX DEDUCTIONS
RETENUES D'IMPÔT

CURRENT PAYMENT
PAIEMENT COURANT

ARREARS PAYMENT
PAIEMENT D'ARRIÈRES

TOTAL PAYMENT
PAIEMENT TOTAL

3.

EMPLOYER NUMBER
N° DE L'EMPLOYEUR

PD7A REV 85

	AMOUNT PAID *MONTANT PAYÉ*	AMOUNT OWING *MONTANT DÛ*
STATEMENT OF ACCOUNT AS OF *ÉTAT DE COMPTE TEL QUE*		

DATE   EXPLANATION OF CHANGES - *EXPLICATION DES CHANGEMENTS*

4.

EMPLOYER NUMBER
N° DE L'EMPLOYEUR

PD7A REV 85

IMPORTANT - SEE REVERSE

H.G. ROGERS
DEPUTY MINISTER, DEPARTMENT OF NATIONAL REVENUE, TAXATION
SOUS-MINISTRE, MINISTÈRE DU REVENU NATIONAL, IMPÔT

IMPORTANT - *VOIR AU VERSO*

Form PD7AR — Tax
Deduction–Canada
Pension Plan–
Unemployment
Insurance
Remittance
Return

Paying other deductions

In addition to paying the federal government for payroll deductions of employees' income tax, Canada Pension Plan, and Unemployment Insurance, the employer is obliged to pay other required or voluntary deductions as authorized by the employees. Each month Lin's Music Centre receives a billing from the health care commission and from the hospital insurance plan. At the end of each month premiums are paid to these insurance groups. Payments for Canada Savings Bonds are made semi-monthly. These payments eliminate the accumulated monthly liabilities in the ledger accounts. Payment of these liabilities is journalized in the cash payments journal below.

The amount owed to the United Way is not paid monthly, but is held until the end of October when the total accumulated liability is paid to the United Way organization. Any other deductions that an employer may make are treated in a similar way. The amounts deducted from employees' earnings are liabilities of the employer until they are paid at a specified time.

CASH PAYMENTS JOURNAL PAGE 6

	DATE	ACCOUNT TITLE	CH. NO.	POST. REF.	GENERAL DEBIT	GENERAL CREDIT	ACCOUNTS PAY. DEBIT	PURCHASES DISC. CREDIT	CASH CREDIT	
5	30	Hospital Ins. Prem. Pay.	284		56 95				56 95	5
6	30	Health Care Prem. Pay.	285		210 00				210 00	6
7	30	Canada Savings Bonds Pay.	286		20 00				20 00	7
8										8
9										9
10										10
11										11
12										12

Entry to record payment of liabilities for required or voluntary deductions.

Statement of remuneration paid

Every employer is required to file with the District Taxation Office a T4 Return, Statement of Remuneration Paid, by the last day of February immediately following the taxation year. This statement indicates the employee's total earnings for the year and any deductions pertaining to taxable income. Copy 1 of this form is sent to the District Taxation Office, copies 2 and 3 are sent to the employee, and copy 4 is kept by the employer. As well as sending a T4 Return to each employee, the employer is also required to summarize all T4 Returns on a T4-T4A Summary. Information for completion of T4 Return forms is obtained from the Employees' Earnings Record form discussed in the previous chapter. An example of a T4 Return form is shown on the next page.

1985 T4 Return

QUESTIONS FOR INDIVIDUAL STUDY

1. Total earnings of Lin's employees, as illustrated in the payroll register on page 461, amounted to $4 814.38. However, the total amount actually paid to the employees was 3 950.19. Why is there a difference between these two amounts?

2. What is the source document for journalizing a payroll entry?

3. What accounts does Lin's debit and credit to record a payroll?

4. What are the payroll taxes paid by most employers?

5. How does the employer's UI premium compare in amount with the employees' UI premium?

6. What accounts are debited and credited to record an employer's payroll taxes?

7. Where are the data obtained that are needed to prepare a T4 Return?

8. By what date must employers file T4 Returns?

9. How often must employers pay their withholding and payroll taxes?

10. What information is reported on a PD7AR form?

11. What should an employee do with copies 2 and 3 of the T4 Return received from an employer?

12. An employer has the following income tax withholdings and tax liabilities: January, $1 389.00; February, $1 234.00; and March, $1 478.00. When must these tax liabilities be paid?

13. To whom does an employer pay health care premiums?

14. What accounts are debited and credited to record payment of an employer's liability for employees' income tax?

15. To what employee benefits, other than CPP and UI do employers sometimes contribute?

16. What accounts are debited and credited to record payment of an employer's liability for unemployment insurance?

17. What accounts are debited and credited to record payment of an employer's liability for Canada Pension Plan?

CASES FOR MANAGEMENT DECISION

CASE 1 Carsberg Corporation had a total payroll expense for the year of $240 000. You are the payroll clerk and you have been asked by the general manager for the following information: What will be the approximate amount that the company will be required to pay for (a) Canada Pension Plan contributions and (b) Unemployment Insurance premiums?

CASE 2 The Blackstone Company has a weekly payroll of $8 000.00 with the following deductions: Employees' Income Tax, $1 760.00; CPP, $138.60; UI, $66.00; Union Dues, $160.00. The company's liabilities for payroll taxes are as follows: CPP, $138.60; UI, $92.40. What entry should the payroll clerk make in the cash payments journal to record (a) the payroll and (b) the liability of the company for payroll taxes? Explain the difference between the Unemployment Insurance paid by employees and the company.

DRILL FOR UNDERSTANDING

DRILL 23-D 1   Analysing payroll transactions

Instructions: 1. Open the following T accounts for each business. Cash, Employees' Income Tax Payable, CPP Payable, UI Payable, CPP Expense, UI Expense.

Business	Total Earnings	Income Tax	Pension Plan	Unemployment Insurance
A	$4 000.00	$320.00	$ 72.00	$ 94.00
B	2 860.00	229.00	51.48	67.21
C	7 400.00	592.00	132.20	173.90
D	8 600.00	1688.00	154.80	202.10

2. Use T accounts to analyse the payroll entries for each business.
   (a) Entry to record payroll.
   (b) Entry to record employer's payroll taxes.

APPLICATION PROBLEMS

PROBLEM 23-1   Journalizing and posting semimonthly payrolls

McKnight's payroll register totals for two semimonthly pay periods, April 1–15 and April 16–30, are below.

Pay period April 1–15

EMPL. NO	EMPLOYEE'S NAME	MARI-TAL STATUS	NET CLAIM CODE	TOTAL EARNINGS	INCOME TAX	CPP	UI	OTHER	TOTAL	NET PAY	CH. NO.
						DEDUCTIONS					
1											1
2	_Totals_			522500	41800	9405	122798	8600	72084	450416	2
3											3
4											4

OTHER DEDUCTIONS: B—CANADA SAVINGS BONDS

Pay period April 16–30

EMPL. NO.	EMPLOYEE'S NAME	MARI- TAL STATUS	NET CLAIM CODE	TOTAL EARNINGS	DEDUCTIONS					NET PAY	CH NO
					INCOME TAX	CPP	UI	OTHER	TOTAL		
1	*Totals*			467900	37432	8422	109968	6900	63750	404150	1
2											2
3											3
4											4

OTHER DEDUCTIONS: B—CANADA SAVINGS BONDS

Instructions: 1. Record the two payrolls and withholdings on page 7 of a cash payments journal. The first payroll was paid by Cheque No. 536 on April 16 of the current year. The second payroll was paid by Cheque No. 583 on May 1 of the current year.

2. Post the individual items recorded in the cash payments journal's General Debit and Credit columns. The general ledger accounts are given in the working papers. On April 15, all account balances are zero.

Account Title	Acct. No.	Account Title	Acct. No.
Employees' Income Tax Payable	2103	Canada Savings Bonds Payable	2110
UI Payable	2104	Salary Expense	6111
CPP Payable	2105		

The general ledger accounts prepared in Problem 23-1 are needed to complete Problem 23-2.

PROBLEM 23-2 Figuring, recording, and posting employer's payroll taxes

The general ledger accounts prepared in Problem 23-1 are needed to complete Problem 23-2.

McKnight's semimonthly payroll register totals are shown in Problem 23-1, pages 476 and 475.

Instructions: 1. Figure the employer's tax amounts for each pay period.

2. Record the employer's payroll taxes on page 3 of a general journal. Use the dates April 16 and May 1 of the current year. The source documents are Memorandum No. 83 and Memorandum No. 89.

3. Post the items recorded in the general journal. Use the accounts prepared in Problem 23-1 and the additional accounts given in the working papers. The additional accounts have zero balances on April 15.

Account Title	Acct. No.
CPP Expense	6103
UI Expense	6114

PROBLEM 23-3 Remitting employer's monthly withholding and payroll taxes

Payroll data for Diaz Pipe Supply are shown on the next page for March of the current year.

Month	Total Earnings	Income Tax	Canada Pension Plan	Unemployment Insurance
March	$7 356.00	$588.48	$264.82	$414.89

Additional data are below.
   a. Company address: 587 Queensdale Avenue E., Hamilton, ON   L8V 1L4
   b. Employer identification number: 38-0568292
   c. Number of employees: 8

Instructions: Prepare a PD7AR Form, Tax Deduction–Canada Pension Plan–Unemployment Insurance Remittance Return, for Diaz Pipe Supply. The return is for March of the current year. Use the date April 15. sign your name as manager of the company.

PROBLEM 23-4   Figuring and recording withholding and payroll taxes

Payroll data for Wig Imports for March and April of the current year are below.

Period	Total Wages	Income Tax Withheld
March	$7 052.00	$564.16
April	8 368.00	669.44

In addition to income tax withholdings, total wages are subject to 1.8% employees; and 1.8% employer's Canada Pension Plan contributions. Unemployment Insurance premiums for employees are calculated at 2.35% of wages, and for employers at 1.4 times the employee premiums.

The appropriate withholding and payroll tax liabilities and expenses are to be recorded in the accounts below.

Account Title	Acct. No.	Account Title	Acct. No.
Employees' Income Tax Payable	2103	CPP Expense	6107
CPP Payable	2105	UI Expense	6108
UI Payable	2106		

Instructions: 1. Figure and record the employee liabilities for Canada Pension Plan and Unemployment Insurance for March and April.
   2. Figure and record the total employer payroll liabilities for March and April.
   3. Record the payments of all payroll liabilities for both March and April. Use Cheque No. 459 for the May 15 payment.

ENRICHMENT PROBLEMS

MASTERY PROBLEM 23-M   Recording and posting payroll transactions

A-1 Garden Supply completed the payroll transactions given below during the period January 1 to February 15 of the current year. Payroll tax rates are: Canada Pension Plan, 1.8%; Unemployment Insurance, 2.35%. The company buys Canada Savings Bonds for employees as accumulated withholdings reach the necessary amount for each employee.

The ledger accounts are given in the working papers. The balances are recorded as of January 1 of the current year.

Account Title	Acct. No.	January 1 Balance
Employees' Income Tax Payable	2103	$779.00
CPP Payable	2105	350.56
UI Payable	2107	549.22
Canada Savings Bonds Payable	2110	280.00
CPP Expense	6109	——
UI Expense	6114	——
Salary Expense	6111	——

Instructions: 1. Record the selected transactions given below. Use page 3 of a cash payments journal and page 2 of a general journal. Source documents are abbreviated as cheque, C, and memorandum, M.

Jan. 15. Paid semimonthly payroll, $3 120.00 (less deductions: employees' income tax, $624.00; CPP, $56.16; UI, $73.32; Canada Savings Bonds, $84.00). C52.
  15. Recorded the employer's payroll tax liabilities. M11.
  15. Paid December payroll liabilities. C53.
  15. Bought 10 Canada Savings Bonds at $25.00 each for employees, $250.00. C54.
  31. Paid semimonthly payroll, $3 100.00 (less deductions: employees' income tax, $620.00; CPP, $55.80; UI, $72.85; Canada Savings Bonds, $96.00). C73.
  31. Recorded the employer's payroll tax liabilities. M14.
      Posting. Post the items that are to be posted individually.
Feb. 15. Paid semimonthly payroll, $3 160.00 (less deductions: employees' income tax, $632.00; CPP, $56.88; UI, $74.26; Canada Savings Bonds, $96.00). C96.
  15. Recorded the employer's payroll tax liabilities. M17.
  15. Bought 8 Canada Savings Bonds at $25.00 each for employees, $200.00. C97.
  15. Paid January payroll liabilities. C98.

Instructions: 2. Prove the cash payments journal.

3. Post the general journal entries. Post the individual items recorded in the General Debit and Credit columns of the cash payments journal.

CHALLENGE PROBLEM 23-C Recording and posting payroll transactions

Valley Sporting Goods completed the payroll transactions given below during the period January 1 to April 15. Payroll tax rates are: Canada Pension Plan, 1.8%; Unemployment Insurance, 2.35%. The company buys Canada Savings Bonds for employees as accumulated withholdings for each employee reach the necessary amounts.

The ledger accounts are given in the working papers. The balances are recorded as of January 1 of the current year.

Account Title	Acct. No.	January 1 Balance
Employees' Income Tax Payable	2103	$702.90
CPP Payable	2105	230.04
UI Payable	2107	360.39
Canada Savings Bonds Payable	2110	375.00
Payroll Taxes Expense	6109	——
Salary Expense	6111	——

Instructions: 1. Record the selected transactions shown on the next page. Use pages 4 and 5 of a cash payments journal and page 2 of a general journal. Source documents are abbreviated as cheque, C, and memorandum, M.

Jan. 2. Bought Canada Savings Bonds for employees (15 bonds at $25.00 each), $375.00. C58.

15. Paid December payroll liabilities. C68.

31. Paid monthly payroll, $7 180.00 (less deductions: employees' income tax, $1 436.00; CPP, $129.24; UI, $168.73; Canada Savings Bonds, $375.00). C83.

31. Recorded the employer's payroll tax liabilities. M31.

Posting. Post the items that are to be posted individually.

Feb. 1. Bought Canada Savings Bonds for employees, $375.00. C86.

15. Paid January payroll liabilities C93.

28. Paid monthly payroll, $7 120.00 (less deductions: employees' income tax, $1 424.00; CPP, $128.16; UI, $167.32; Canada Savings Bonds, $375.00). C113.

28. Recorded the employer's payroll tax liabilities. M34.

Posting. Post the items that are to be posted individually.

Mar. 1. Bought Canada Savings Bonds for employees, $375.00. C122.

15. Paid February payroll liabilities. C132.

31. Paid monthly payroll, $7 280.00 (less deductions: employees' income tax, $1 456.00; CPP, $131.04; UI, $171.08; Canada Savings Bonds, $375.00). C159.

31. Recorded the employer's payroll tax liabilities. M39.

Posting. Post the items that are to be posted individually.

Apr. 1. Bought Canada Savings Bonds for employees, $375.00. C163.

15. Paid March payroll liabilities. C178.

Instructions: 2. Prove the cash payments journal.

3. Post the general journal items. Post the individual items recorded in the General Debit and Credit columns of the cash payments journal.

An Accounting Cycle for a
Corporation Using Special Journals

This activity is planned to reinforce learnings from Part 5, Chapters 20 to 27. A complete accounting cycle is covered for a business organized as a corporation. The general ledger account balances of Electronic Emporium now include transactions from the first eleven months of the fiscal year ended December 31. Reinforcement Activity 4 is organized in two parts. Part A includes learnings from Chapters 20 to 23. Part B, page 564, includes learnings from Chapters 24 to 27.

ELECTRONIC EMPORIUM

Electronic Emporium is a corporation that sells stereophonic and high fidelity equipment and supplies. The business is located in a shopping centre and is open Monday through Saturday. Space for the business is rented. However, the corporation owns the office and sales equipment in the store.

Chart of accounts

Electronic Emporium uses the chart of accounts on the next page.

Journals and ledgers

Electronic Emporium uses the journals and ledgers listed below. The journals and ledgers are similar to those illustrated on the textbook pages given.

ELECTRONIC EMPORIUM
Chart of Accounts

Balance Sheet Accounts

(1) ASSETS	Account Number
11 Current Assets	
Cash	1101
Notes Receivable	1102
Accounts Receivable	1103
Allowance for Uncollectible Accounts	1103.1
Merchandise Inventory	1104
Supplies	1105
Prepaid Insurance	1106
12 Fixed Assets	
Office Equipment	1201
Accumulated Depreciation — Office Equipment	1201.1
Store Equipment	1202
Accumulated Depreciation — Store Equipment	1202.1

(2) LIABILITIES	
21 Current Liabilities	
Notes Payable	2101
Accounts Payable	2102
Employees' Income Tax Payable	2103
Federal Income Tax Payable	2104
CPP Payable	2105
Sales Tax Payable	2106
UI Payable	2107
Dividends Payable	2108

(3) SHAREHOLDERS' EQUITY	
Capital Stock	3101
Retained Earnings	3201
Income Summary	3301

Income Statement Accounts

(4) OPERATING REVENUE	Account Number
Sales	4101
Sales Returns and Allowances	4101.1

(5) COST OF MERCHANDISE	
Purchases	5101
Purchases Returns and Allowances	5101.1
Purchases Discount	5101.2

(6) OPERATING EXPENSES	
Advertising Expense	6101
Bad Debts Expense	6102
Credit Card Fee Expense	6103
Depreciation Expense — Office Equipment	6104
Depreciation Expense — Store Equipment	6105
Insurance Expense	6106
Miscellaneous Expense	6107
Payroll Taxes Expense	6108
Rent Expense	6109
Salary Expense	6110
Supplies Expense	6111

(7) OTHER REVENUE	
Interest Income	7101

(8) OTHER EXPENSES	
Interest Expense	8101

(9) INCOME TAX	
Federal Income Tax	9101

Opening a corporation's set of books

The required journal and ledger forms are given in the working papers. If you are using the working papers, omit Instructions 1 to 6. These instructions have been completed for you. Turn to page 484 and begin with Instruction 7.

Instructions: 1. Begin numbering the journals as listed. Sales journal, page 13; purchases journal, page 12; general journal, page 8; cash receipts journal, page 15; and cash payments journal, page 16.

2. Open all general ledger accounts as shown in Electronic Emporium's chart of accounts above.

3. Record the general ledger account balances given on the next page as of December 1 of the current year.

Account Title	Account Balance	
	Debit	Credit
Cash	$ 25 649.80	
Notes Receivable	3 300.00	
Accounts Receivable	15 053.10	
Allowance for Uncollectible Accounts		$ 25.50
Merchandise Inventory	83 370.20	
Supplies	1 417.90	
Prepaid Insurance	5 040.00	
Office Equipment	4 340.00	
Accumulated Depreciation — Office Equipment		1 520.00
Store Equipment	7 775.00	
Accumulated Depreciation — Store Equipment		2 955.00
Notes Payable		8 000.00
Accounts Payable		7 338.90
Employees' Income Tax Payable		992.00
Federal Income Tax Payable	—	
CPP Payable		116.60
Sales Tax Payable		2 200.90
UI Payable		923.20
Dividends Payable	—	
Capital Stock		60 000.00
Retained Earnings	—	15 622.00
Income Summary	—	
Sales		475 238.40
Sales Returns and Allowances	3 577.60	
Purchases	321 312.20	
Purchases Returns and Allowances		1 164.50
Purchases Discount		2 341.60
Advertising Expense	6 115.00	
Bad Debts Expense	—	
Credit Card Fee Expense	4 752.30	
Depreciation Expense — Office Equipment	—	—
Depreciation Expense — Store Equipment	—	—
Insurance Expense	—	—
Miscellaneous Expense	3 749.50	
Payroll Taxes Expense	4 768.90	
Rent Expense	13 750.00	
Salary Expense	68 127.10	
Supplies Expense	—	
Interest Income		1 240.00
Interest Expense	1 580.00	
Federal Income Tax	6 000.00	

Instructions: 4. Open an account in the accounts receivable ledger for each customer listed below. Record the balances as of December 1 of the current year.

Customers	Account Balance
Arlinghouse, Ltd., 830 Broadway Avenue, Saskatoon, SK S7N 1B6	$2 408.50
Hampton's, Inc., 2202 Cairns Avenue, Saskatoon, SK S7J 1T6	2 709.60
Kaleidoscape Construction, 1403 4 Street, Estevan, SK S4A 0X3	3 311.70
Owatonna's, 704 9th Avenue N.W., Moose Jaw, SK S6H 4J1	1 806.30
Strickland Systems, 6th Avenue E., Prince Albert, SK S6V 2K8	3 913.80
E.J. Traver, 405 Souris Avenue N.E., Weyburn, SK S4H 0C9	903.20

Instructions: 5. Open an account in the accounts payable ledger for each creditor listed on the next page. Record the balances as of December 1 of the current year.

Creditors	Account Balance
De Chaines Electronics, 4001 Argyle Street, Regina, SK S4S 3L5..............................	$1 761.00
Fidelity Sound Systems, 1635 Broad Street, Regina, SK S4P 1X3..............................	1 468.00
Gulf Sound, Ltd., 1672 Cameron Street, Regina, SK S4T 2T8.................................	1 687.90
Stereo Systems, Inc., 902 Princess Street, Saskatoon , SK S7K 0P3..........................	1 321.00
Westside Communications, 1119 Chaplin Street E., Swift Current, SK S9H 1J9........	1 101.00

Instructions: 6. Record the cash on hand, *$25 649.80*, on line 1 of the cash receipts journal.

Journalizing a corporation's transactions

Instructions: 7. Record the following transactions for December of the current year. Electronic Emporium must collect a 5% sales tax on all sales. Source documents are abbreviated as: cheque, C; sales invoice, S; receipt, R; cash register tape, T; credit card sales calculator tape, CT; credit memorandum, CM; memorandum, M; purchase invoice, P; debit memorandum, DM.

Dec. 1. Paid December rent, $1 250.00. C302.
  1. Received cash on account from Arlinghouse, Ltd., $2 408.50. R61.
  1. Purchased merchandise on account from Gulf Sound, Ltd., $8 425.30. P89.
  2. Credited Hampton's, Inc.'s account for merchandise returned, $378.00, plus sales tax, $18.90. CM15.
  2. Received cash on account from Hampton's, Inc., $2 312.70. R62.
  3. Sold merchandise on account to Strickland Systems, $1 478.40, plus sales tax, $73.92. S182.
  3. Paid on account to DeChaines Electronics, $1 725.78, covering P82 for $1 761.00 less a 2 percent cash discount of $35.22. C303.
  3. Recorded cash sales for the week, $3 770.20, plus sales tax, $188.51. T3.
  3. Recorded credit card sales for the week, $1 615.80, plus sales tax, $80.79. CT3.
      Posting. Post the items that are to be posted individually. Post the journals in the following order: Sales journal, purchases journal, general journal, cash receipts journal, and cash payments journal.
  5. Returned merchandise to Gulf Sound, Ltd., $1 164.50. DM17.
  6. Paid on account to Stereo Systems, Inc., $1 294.58, covering P83 for $1 321.00 less a 2 percent cash discount of $26.42. C304.
  7. Received cash on account from Strickland Systems, $3 913.80. R63.
  7. Purchased merchandise on account from Westside Communications, $4 116.00. P90.
  8. Sold merchandise on account to Kaleidoscape Construction, $1 723.10, plus sales tax, $86.16. S183.
  8. Paid on account to Westside Communications, $1 089.99, covering P84 for $1 101.00 less a 1 percent discount of $11.01. C305.
  9. Received cash on account from Kaleidoscape Construction, $3 311.70. R64.
 10. Recorded cash sales for the week, $8 361.80, plus sales tax, $418.09. T10.
 10. Recorded credit card sales for the week, $3 756.70, plus sales tax, $187.84, CT10.
      Posting. Post the items that are to be posted individually.
 12. Purchased merchandise on account from Stereo Systems, Inc., $8 370.50. P91.
 13. Paid miscellaneous expense, $163.40. C306.
 13. Bought supplies for cash, $126.50. C307.
 13. Received cash on account from Strickland Systems, $1 552.32. R65.

Dec. 14. Sold merchandise on account to Owatonna's, $518.00, plus sales tax, $25.90. S184.

14. Paid advertising expense, $416.30. C308.

15. Paid semimonthly payroll, $4 536.90 (less deductions: employees' income tax, $907.38; CPP, $81.66; UI, $106.62. C309.

15. Recorded the employer's payroll tax liabilities, $230.93 (CPP, $81.66; UI, $149.27). M23.

15. Paid November liabilities, $2 031.80 (employees' income tax, $992.00; CPP, $116.60; UI, $923.20. C310.

15. Paid quarterly estimated federal income tax, $2 000.00 (debit Federal Income Tax; credit Cash). C311.

16. Paid on account to Westside Communications, $4 074.84, covering P90 for $4 116.00 less a 1 percent discount of $41.16. C312.

16. Received cash on account from Owatonna's, $1 806.30. R66.

17. Received cash on account from Kaleidoscape Construction, $1 809.26. R67.

17. Purchased merchandise for cash, $338.20. C313.

17. Recorded cash sales for the week, $8 545.80, plus sales tax, $427.29. T17.

17. Recorded credit card sales for the week, $4 021.50, plus sales tax, $201.08. CT17.

Posting. Post the items that are to be posted individually.

19. Paid miscellaneous expense, $89.50. C314.

19. Sold merchandise on account to Hampton's, Inc., $1 856.50, plus sales tax, $92.83. S185.

20. Paid on account to Gulf Sound, Ltd., $523.40, covering P85 for $1 687.90 less DM 17 for $1 164.50; no discount. C315.

21. Paid on account to Fidelity Sound Systems, $1 468.00, covering P86; no discount. C316.

21. Paid miscellaneous expense, $207.10. C317.

22. Purchased merchandise on account from DeChaines Electronics, $5 146.50. P92.

22. Paid on account to Stereo Systems, Inc., $8 203.09, covering P91 for $8 370.50 less a 2 percent cash discount of $167.41. C318.

23. Purchased merchandise for cash, $443.60. C319.

24. Sold merchandise on account to Kaleidoscape Construction, $449.20, plus sales tax, $22.46. S186.

24. Recorded cash sales for the week, $7 818.60, plus sales tax, $390.93. T24.

24. Recorded credit card sales for the week, $3 851.10, plus sales tax, $192.56. CT24.

Posting. Post the items that are to be posted individually.

26. Bought supplies on account from Fidelity Sound Systems, $243.40. M24.

27. Sold merchandise on account to Arlinghouse, Ltd., $1 287.20, plus sales tax, $64.36. S187.

27. Paid advertising expense, $262.70. C320.

28. Purchased merchandise on account from Westside Communications, $8 243.00. P93.

29. Received on account from Hampton's, Inc., $1 949.33. R68.

29. Paid on account to Gulf Sound, Ltd., $8 425.30, covering P89; no discount. C321.

30. Sold merchandise on account to Strickland Systems, $608.20, plus sales tax, $30.41. S188.

30. Paid sales tax liability for November, $2 182.00. C322. (Debit Sales Tax Payable; credit Cash).

31. Paid semimonthly payroll, $3 024.60 (less deductions: employees' income tax, $604.92; CPP, $54.44; UI, $71.08. C323.

Dec. 31. Recorded the employer's payroll tax liabilities, $153.95 (CPP, $54.44; UI, $99.51). M25.
   31. Recorded cash sales for the week, $2 073.60, plus sales tax, $103.68. T31.
   31. Recorded credit card sales for the week, $1 068.30, plus sales tax, $53.42. CT31.
   31. Recorded the credit card fee for December, $528.00. M26.
       Posting. Post the items that are to be posted individually.

Proving and posting a corporation's special journals

Instructions: 8. Total, prove, and rule the sales journal. Post the totals of the special columns.

9. Total and rule the purchases journal. Post the total.

10. Prove the equality of debits and credits for the cash receipts and cash payments journals.

11. Prove cash. The balance on the last cheque stub on December 31 is $49 261.82.

12. Rule the cash receipts journal. Post the special column totals to the appropriate general ledger accounts.

13. Rule the cash payments journal. Post the totals of the special columns.

14. Prepare a schedule of accounts receivable and a schedule of accounts payable. Compare the schedules' totals with the balances of the accounts in the general ledger.

The general ledger used in Reinforcement Activity 4, Part A, is needed to complete Part B. The general journal used in Part A is needed to complete Part B.

A Business Simulation

VILLAGE GARDEN CENTRE Pegboard Payroll System
provides experience in preparing records using a pegboard
and no-carbon-required forms. When data are entered on
the statement of earnings and deductions stub on the
cheque, the employee's earnings record and the payroll
register are simultaneously prepared. Posting is eliminated.
A pictorial flowchart of this write-it-once system is
on the next page. This business simulation is available
from the publisher.

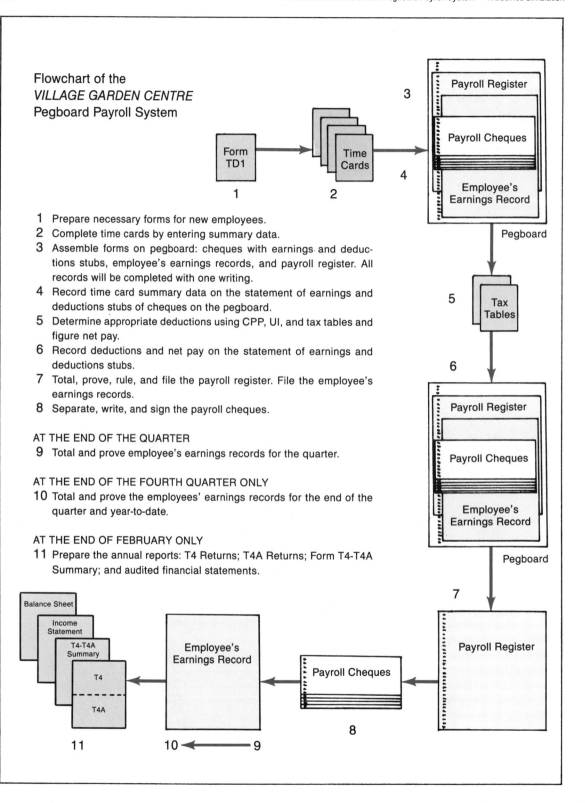

Flowchart of the
VILLAGE GARDEN CENTRE
Pegboard Payroll System

1 Prepare necessary forms for new employees.
2 Complete time cards by entering summary data.
3 Assemble forms on pegboard: cheques with earnings and deductions stubs, employee's earnings records, and payroll register. All records will be completed with one writing.
4 Record time card summary data on the statement of earnings and deductions stubs of cheques on the pegboard.
5 Determine appropriate deductions using CPP, UI, and tax tables and figure net pay.
6 Record deductions and net pay on the statement of earnings and deductions stubs.
7 Total, prove, rule, and file the payroll register. File the employee's earnings records.
8 Separate, write, and sign the payroll cheques.

AT THE END OF THE QUARTER
9 Total and prove employee's earnings records for the quarter.

AT THE END OF THE FOURTH QUARTER ONLY
10 Total and prove the employees' earnings records for the end of the quarter and year-to-date.

AT THE END OF FEBRUARY ONLY
11 Prepare the annual reports: T4 Returns; T4A Returns; Form T4-T4A Summary; and audited financial statements.

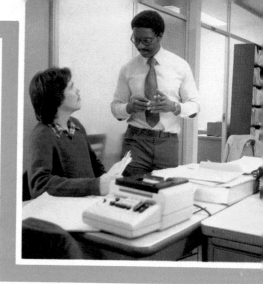

24

Accounting for Uncollectible Accounts

ENABLING PERFORMANCE TASKS

After studying Chapter 24, you will be able to:

a. Define accounting terms related to accounting for uncollectible accounts.
b. Explain accounting principles and practices related to accounting for uncollectible accounts.
c. Figure bad debts expense.
d. Journalize an entry to write off an uncollectible account.
e. Journalize an adjustment for bad debts expense.

Many businesses sell merchandise or service on account to customers. Selling on account frequently is more convenient to the business and the customer. Merchandise may be sold on one date but payment not received until a later date. Regardless of when payment is received, revenue should be recorded at the time of sale. (CONCEPT: *Realization of Revenue*)

Businesses try to insure that all of their accounts receivable will be collected. Before a business sells on account to a customer, the customer's credit rating is determined. A business may request a prospective charge customer's financial statement to evaluate the customer's ability to pay for merchandise. Also credit ratings may be obtained from local credit bureaus or national credit agencies.

> Dun & Bradstreet Canada Limited publishes a credit-rating book containing data about the financial condition of businesses throughout Canada.

DETERMINING UNCOLLECTIBLE ACCOUNTS RECEIVABLE

Even though a business is careful in selling on account, some accounts receivable cannot be collected. Accounts receivable that cannot be collected are called uncollectible accounts. Uncollectible accounts are sometimes known as bad debts. If a business fails to collect from a charge customer, the business loses part of the asset Accounts Receivable. To properly record this loss in the asset, two accounts must be adjusted. The uncollectible amount must be deducted from Accounts Receivable. The same amount must be added to an operating expense account. The expense caused by uncollectible accounts is called bad debts expense. Therefore, Lin's Music Centre uses the expense account Bad Debts Expense.

> An uncollectible amount does not decrease the amount from revenue. The loss is considered a regular expense of doing business. Therefore, the amount of the uncollectible account is recorded as an expense.

DIRECT WRITE-OFF OF AN UNCOLLECTIBLE ACCOUNT

Terms of sale for many charge sales is n/30 or n/EOM. The term *n/30* means the net invoice amount is due in 30 days. The term *n/EOM* means the net invoice amount is due by the end of the current month. Most businesses make a special effort to collect accounts not paid within the terms of sale. However, if special efforts fail and chances for collection are slight, the credit manager should declare the account uncollectible.

Some businesses assume that an account receivable is good until the account is proven uncollectible. When the account proves to be uncollectible, the amount becomes an expense. Recording bad debts expense only when a customer's account is known to be uncollectible is called the direct write-off of uncollectible accounts. The direct write-off method is used for two reasons. (a) Bad Debts Expense is increased only when an account is proven to be uncollectible. (b) The method is simple and convenient to use.

Analysing an entry for direct write-off of an uncollectible account

Galinn Company uses the direct write-off of uncollectible accounts. After several months of collection effort, the company declared the account of J. B. Boles uncollectible.

March 15, 1989. Wrote off past-due account of J. B. Boles as uncollectible, $176.00. Memorandum No. 63.

The entry to write off this uncollectible account is analysed in the T accounts at the left.

Bad Debts Expense is debited for $176.00 to show the increase in the balance of this expense account. Accounts Receivable is credited for $176.00 to reduce the amount due from charge customers. The new balance of the accounts receivable account is $9 084.00 ($9 260.00 − $176.00). J. B.

GENERAL LEDGER

Bad Debts Expense

176.00	

Accounts Receivable

Bal.	9 260.00	176.00

ACCOUNTS RECEIVABLE LEDGER

J. B. Boles

Bal.	176.00	176.00

Boles' account in the accounts receivable ledger is also credited for $176.00. This entry brings the balance of Boles' account to zero. Boles' account is written off. Cancelling the balance of a customer's account because the customer does not pay is called writing off an account.

Journalizing an entry for direct write-off of an uncollectible account

The entry to write off the account of J. B. Boles is below.

	DATE	ACCOUNT TITLE	POST. REF.	DEBIT	CREDIT	
		GENERAL JOURNAL			PAGE *5*	
1	1989 Mar. 15	Bad Debts Expense		176 00		1
2		Accounts Rec./ J. B. Boles	✓		176 00	2
3		Memorandum No. 63.				3
4						4
5						5
6						6

Entry to write off an uncollectible account when direct write-off method is used

Bad Debts Expense is debited for $176.00 in the Debit column. Accounts Receivable and J. B. Boles are both credited for $176.00.

Posting an entry for direct write-off of an uncollectible account

After the journal entry above is posted, the general ledger account Bad Debts Expense appears as shown below.

ACCOUNT *Bad Debts Expense*   ACCOUNT NO. *6102*

DATE	ITEM	POST. REF.	DEBIT	CREDIT	BALANCE DEBIT	BALANCE CREDIT
1989 Mar. 15		J5	176 00		176 00	

Bad Debts Expense after entry writing off an uncollectible account is posted

After the credit entry is posted, Accounts Receivable in the general ledger appears as shown below.

ACCOUNT *Accounts Receivable*   ACCOUNT NO. *1103*

DATE	ITEM	POST. REF.	DEBIT	CREDIT	BALANCE DEBIT	BALANCE CREDIT
Feb. 28		CR9		5350 00	9260 00	
Mar. 15		J5		176 00	9084 00	

Accounts Receivable after entry writing off an uncollectible account is posted

After the credit to J. B. Boles' account is posted, the account appears as shown below.

NAME	*J. B. Boles*					
ADDRESS	*1765 Saint-Joseph Boulevard, Drummondville, P.Q. J2C 2G6*					
DATE	ITEM	POST. REF.	DEBIT	CREDIT	DEBIT BALANCE	
1988 Sept. 10		*828*	*17600*		*17600*	
1989 Mar. 15	*Written off*	*95*		*17600*	—	

Customer's account after entry writing off the account as uncollectible is posted

ESTIMATING BAD DEBTS EXPENSE

Risk of loss occurs when a business makes a sale on account. This possible loss is present even though several months may pass before the actual loss is determined. Accurate financial reporting requires that expenses be recorded in the accounting period in which the expenses contribute to earning revenue. *(CONCEPT: Matching Expenses with Revenue)*

A business does not know which charge sales will become bad debts at the time charge sales are made. Therefore, a business should estimate the amount of its bad debts expense. This estimate normally is made at the end of each fiscal period. The estimated amount of bad debts expense is recorded for two reasons. Recording the estimated bad debts expense prevents the overstatement of the value of accounts receivable on the balance sheet. Also bad debts expense is included on the income statement for the fiscal period in which the charge sale is made.

The net value of accounts receivable is reported on a balance sheet. This is shown by subtracting the estimated value of uncollectible accounts from the balance of accounts receivable. The difference between the balance of Accounts Receivable and the estimated uncollectible accounts is called the book value of accounts receivable.

Using a contra account

A business has no way of knowing for sure now which charge customers will fail to pay in the future. Since the company does not know which customers will not pay, specific customers' accounts cannot be credited as uncollectible. Neither can the accounts receivable account in the general ledger be credited. The balance of Accounts Receivable, a controlling account, must equal the sum of the customers' accounts in the subsidiary ledger. However, the company can record an *estimated* bad debts expense.

Lin's Music Centre records estimated bad debts expense by making an adjusting entry. The estimated value of uncollectible accounts is credited to an account titled Allowance for Uncollectible Accounts. The same amount is debited to an expense account titled Bad Debts Expense.

> Allowance for Bad Debts and Allowance for Doubtful Accounts are account titles sometimes used instead of Allowance for Uncollectible Accounts.

As discussed previously, an account that reduces a related account on the financial statements is known as a contra account. Allowance for Uncollectible Accounts is a contra account to its related account Accounts Receivable. The difference between these two accounts is the book value of accounts receivable. A contra asset account has a credit balance because it reduces the balance of an asset account.

A contra account is numbered the same as its related account, followed by a decimal point and a number. Lin's accounts receivable account is numbered 1103. Allowance for Uncollectible Accounts is numbered 1103.1. Crediting the estimated value of uncollectible accounts to a contra account is called the allowance method of recording losses from uncollectible accounts.

Estimating bad debts expense based on charge sales

Lin's has found it can best estimate bad debts expense by figuring a percentage of charge sales. A review of Lin's previous financial statements shows that actual bad debts expense has been about 1% (.01) of total charge sales. The company's total charge sales for the fiscal year is $474 000.00. Lin's *estimates* that $4 740.00 ($474 000.00 × .01) of its accounts receivable may be bad debts expense.

Analysing an adjustment for bad debts expense

An adjusting entry is made to record estimated bad debts expense for a fiscal year. The T accounts at the right show the accounts Bad Debts Expense and Allowance for Uncollectible Accounts. The accounts are shown before the adjustment for bad debts expense is made.

Four questions are asked in analysing the adjustment for estimated bad debts expense.

BEFORE ADJUSTMENT

Bad Debts Expense

Allowance for
Uncollectible Accounts

Prev. Bal.   280.00

1. What is the balance of the bad debts expense account? ..... zero
2. What should the balance be for this account? $4 740.00
3. What must be done to correct the account balance? ....Add $4 740.00
4. What adjusting entry is made? ......Debit Bad Debts Expense $4 740.00
   Credit Allowance for Uncollectible Accounts $4 740.00

The T accounts are shown on the next page after the adjustment for bad debts expense is made.

AFTER ADJUSTMENT

Bad Debts Expense

Dec. 31 Adj. 4 740.00	

Allowance for
Uncollectible Accounts

	Prev. Bal. 280.00
	Dec. 31 Adj. 4 740.00
	Dec. 31 Bal. 5 020.00

Bad Debts Expense is debited for $4 740.00 to show the increase in the balance of this expense account. The balance of this account, *$4 740.00*, is the bad debts expense for the fiscal period.

Allowance for Uncollectible Accounts is credited for $4 740.00 to show the increase in the balance of this contra account. The previous balance, *$280.00*, plus the fiscal year increase, *$4 740.00*, equals the December 31 balance, *$5 020.00*.

Planning an adjustment on a work sheet for bad debts expense

At the end of the fiscal period, an adjustment for bad debts expense is planned on a work sheet. This adjustment for Lin's is shown in the Adjustments columns, lines 4 and 35, of the partial work sheet below.

Lin's Music Centre
Work Sheet
For Year Ended December 31, 1989

	ACCOUNT TITLE	TRIAL BALANCE		ADJUSTMENTS	
		DEBIT	CREDIT	DEBIT	CREDIT
4	Allow. for Uncoll. Accts.		28000		(a)474000
35	Bad Debts Expense			(a)474000	
36					
37					
38					

Partial work sheet showing adjustment for bad debts expense

On line 35 above, Bad Debts Expense is debited for $4 740.00 in the Adjustments Debit column. On line 4, Allowance for Uncollectible Accounts is credited for $4 740.00 in the Adjustments Credit column.

The percent of charge sales method of estimating assumes a portion of every charge-sale dollar will become a bad debt. An Allowance for Uncollectible Accounts balance in the Trial Balance Credit column means previous period estimates are not yet identified as uncollectible. When the allowance account has a previous balance, the amount of the adjustment is added to the previous balance. The new balance is then extended to the Balance Sheet Credit column. This new balance of the allowance account is the estimated amount of accounts receivable that will be uncollectible.

Journalizing an adjustment for bad debts expense

Information used to journalize an adjustment for bad debts expense is obtained from the Adjustments columns of a work sheet. The adjusting entry is shown in the general journal on the next page.

		GENERAL JOURNAL			PAGE 27	
	DATE	ACCOUNT TITLE	POST. REF.	DEBIT	CREDIT	
1		*Adjusting Entries*				1
2	1989 Dec. 31	*Bad Debts Expense*		474000		2
3		*Allow. for Uncoll. Accts.*			474000	3
4						4

Adjusting entry for
estimated bad debts
expense

Posting an adjustment for bad debts expense

After the adjustment is posted, Accounts Receivable, Allowance for Uncollectible
Accounts, and Bad Debts Expense appear as shown below.

General ledger accounts
after adjustment for
estimated bad debts
expense is posted

ACCOUNT *Accounts Receivable*					ACCOUNT NO. *1103*		
DATE	ITEM	POST. REF.	DEBIT	CREDIT	BALANCE DEBIT		CREDIT
Dec. 31		J48	4378000		6741500		
31		CR37		2528000	4213500		

ACCOUNT *Allowance for Uncollectible Accounts*					ACCOUNT NO. *1103.1*		
DATE	ITEM	POST. REF.	DEBIT	CREDIT	BALANCE DEBIT		CREDIT
Dec. 16		J26		17500			28000
31		J27		474000			502000

ACCOUNT *Bad Debts Expense*					ACCOUNT NO. *6102*		
DATE	ITEM	POST. REF.	DEBIT	CREDIT	BALANCE DEBIT		CREDIT
1989 Dec. 31		J27	474000		474000		

Accounts Receivable has a debit balance of $42 135.00, the total amount due
from charge customers on December 31. Allowance for Uncollectible Accounts has
a credit balance of $5 020.00 on December 31. The account number 1103.1
shows that this is a contra account. The balance of this contra account is
to be subtracted from the balance of its related account, No. 1103, on the
balance sheet. The balance of the bad debts expense account is $4 740.00.
This is the estimated bad debts expense for the fiscal period ended December 31, 1989.

Lin's figures the book value of its accounts receivable on December 31, 1989, as shown below.

Balance of accounts receivable account..............................	$42 135.00
Less allowance for uncollectible accounts	5 020.00
Equals book value of accounts receivable	$37 115.00

WRITING OFF ACTUAL UNCOLLECTIBLE ACCOUNTS THAT HAVE BEEN ESTIMATED

Lin's uses a planned collection procedure to collect customers' accounts. Most accounts are paid within the terms of sale. A few accounts, regardless of collection efforts, prove to be uncollectible. When a customer's account is determined to be uncollectible, a journal entry is made to write off the account.

Analysing an entry to write off an uncollectible account using an estimated method

Lin's decides that the past-due account of David Ott is uncollectible.

January 3, 1990. Wrote off past-due account of David Ott as uncollectible, $123.00. Memorandum No. 11.

GENERAL LEDGER

Allowance for
Uncollectible Accounts

123.00	Bal.	5 020.00

Accounts Receivable

Bal.	42 135.00		123.00

ACCOUNTS RECEIVABLE LEDGER

David Ott

Bal.	123.00		123.00

The entry to write off this uncollectible account is analysed in the T accounts at the left.

Allowance for Uncollectible Accounts is debited for $123.00 to reduce the balance of this account. This specific amount of the allowance is no longer an *estimate*; it is an actual amount. Therefore, the amount of the uncollectible account is deducted from the allowance account.

Accounts Receivable is credited for $123.00 to reduce the balance due from charge customers. The new balance of the accounts receivable account is $42 012.00 ($42 135.00 less $123.00).

David Ott's account in the accounts receivable ledger is also credited for $123.00. This entry cancels the debit balance of his account. His account is written off.

The book value of accounts receivable is the same before and after writing off an uncollectible account. The book value of accounts receivable at Lin's before writing off David Ott's account is below.

Balance of accounts receivable	$42 135.00
Less allowance for uncollectible accounts	5 020.00
Book value of accounts receivable....................................	$37 115.00

The book value of accounts receivable after writing off David Ott's account is below.

Balance of accounts receivable $42 012.00
Less allowance for uncollectible accounts 4 897.00
Book value of accounts receivable..................................... $37 115.00

The book value remains the same because the same amount is deducted from both the accounts receivable and the allowance account.

Journalizing an entry to write off an uncollectible account using an estimated method

The entry to write off the account of David Ott is shown in the general journal below.

	GENERAL JOURNAL				PAGE *1*
DATE	ACCOUNT TITLE	POST. REF.	DEBIT	CREDIT	
16	3 *Allow. for Uncollectible Accts.*		12300		16
17	*Accts. Rec. / David Ott*	/		12300	17
18	*Memorandum No. 11.*				18
19					19

Entry to write off an uncollectible account when estimated method is used

Allowance for Uncollectible Accounts is debited for $123.00 in the Debit column. Accounts Receivable and David Ott are both credited for $123.00 in the Credit column.

Posting an entry to write off an uncollectible account using an estimated method

The journal entry to write off an uncollectible account is above. After this entry is posted, Allowance for Uncollectible Accounts in the general ledger appears as shown below.

ACCOUNT *Allowance for Uncollectible Accounts*					ACCOUNT NO. *1103.1*	
DATE	ITEM	POST. REF.	DEBIT	CREDIT	BALANCE DEBIT	BALANCE CREDIT
31		*G27*		474000		502000
1990 Jan. 3		*G1*	12300			489700

Allowance for Uncollectible Accounts after entry writing off an uncollectible account is posted

After the credit entry is posted, Accounts Receivable in the general ledger appears as shown on the next page.

ACCOUNT Accounts Receivable					BALANCE		ACCOUNT NO. 1103
DATE	ITEM	POST. REF.	DEBIT	CREDIT	DEBIT	CREDIT	
	31		CR37		25 28 00	42 135 00	
1990 Jan. 3			G1		1 23 00	42 012 00	

Accounts Receivable after entry writing off an uncollectible account is posted

After the credit to David Ott's account is posted, his account appears as shown below.

NAME David Ott					
ADDRESS 3960 Lakeshore Road, Kelowna, B.C. V1W 1V5					
DATE	ITEM	POST. REF.	DEBIT	CREDIT	DEBIT BALANCE
1989 Apr. 12		S14	1 23 00		1 23 00
1990 Jan. 3	Written off	G1		1 23 00	—

Customer's account after entry writing off the account as uncollectible is posted

USING AUTOMATED DATA PROCESSING FOR VALUATION OF ACCOUNTS RECEIVABLE

The best method of estimating bad debts expense often depends on the size and type of business. Lin's estimates its bad debts expense based on charge sales. This method is simple and permits Lin's to match revenue of a period with its related bad debts expense. *(CONCEPT: Matching Expenses with Revenue)*

Credit experiences show that the longer a customer's account is overdue, the more likely the account will be uncollectible. Some businesses prefer to estimate the amount of uncollectible accounts by analysing the age of their past-due accounts. Analysing accounts receivable according to when they are due is called aging accounts receivable. Aging accounts generally gives a less accurate estimate of uncollectible accounts for a period than using a percent of charge sales. However, many businesses find that aging accounts provides a more accurate estimate of the value of accounts that will be collected.

The calculations necessary to age accounts receivable usually make this method impractical for businesses using manual data processing systems. For businesses using automated data processing systems however aging accounts receivable is a commonly used method.

When an automated data processing system is used, a report is printed that shows the status of each customer's account. A list of charge customers that shows the balances due by age of account is called a schedule of accounts receivable by age. A computer printout of a schedule of accounts receivable by age for Sound City is below.

```
●   SOUND CITY                                                  ●
    SCHEDULE OF ACCOUNTS RECEIVABLE BY AGE
●   MARCH 31, 1989                                              ●

●  CUSTOMER   CUSTOMER    DATE OF    BALANCE   DUE FOR      ACCOUNTS PAST DUE    ●
   NUMBER     NAME        LAST       DUE       LESS THAN  30-59   60-89   90 DAYS
●                        PAYMENT              30 DAYS     DAYS    DAYS    AND OVER ●

●  10040   S.R. ABALOS   89-03-03   433.80   168.00     265.80                   ●
   10085   MARIE ARDIS   89-02-12   163.20              84.00   79.20

●  10235   KATHY ZORN    89-03-15   344.78    92.40    252.38                    ●

●        TOTALS                  63 445.85* 49 677.24* 7 724.23* 4 406.04* 1 638.34* ●
```

Sound City has learned from past experience the percent of past due accounts that will be uncollectible. (a) 30–59 days, 0.5%, (b) 60–89 days, 3%, (c) 90 days and over, 10%. The schedule above, can be used to estimate the amount of uncollectible accounts Sound City has on March 31, 1989. The amount Sound City should have as the balance of Allowance for Uncollectible Accounts is figured below.

Computer printout of a schedule of accounts receivable by age

Number of Days Past Due	Amount Past Due	Percentage	Estimated Uncollectible Amounts
30–59 days	$7 724.23	0.5%	$ 38.62
60–89 days	4 406.04	3.0%	132.18
90 + days	1 638.34	10.0%	163.83
Total			$334.63

When the percent of charge sales is used, the amount of bad debts expense is estimated. When the aging method is used, the amount of uncollectible accounts is estimated. As figured above, Sound City's estimated uncollectible amount on March 31 is $334.63. Therefore, Allowance for Uncollectible Accounts should have a credit balance of $334.63. Before adjustment, the balance of the allowance account is $48.50. To bring the allowance account balance to $334.63, the estimated bad debts expense is $286.13 ($334.63 − $48.50). The following adjustment is recorded on a journal entry transmittal. (a) Debit Bad Debts Expense for $286.13. (b) Credit Allowance for Uncollectible Accounts for $286.13. After the adjustment is journalized and posted, the balance of Allowance for Uncollectible Accounts is $334.63 ($48.50 + $286.13).

ACCOUNTING TERMS

What is the meaning of each of the following?

1. uncollectible accounts
2. bad debts expense
3. direct write-off of uncollectible accounts
4. writing off an account
5. book value of accounts receivable
6. allowance method of recording losses from uncollectible accounts
7. aging accounts receivable
8. schedule of accounts receivable by age

QUESTIONS FOR INDIVIDUAL STUDY

1. When should revenue from sales be recorded?
2. If a business fails to collect from a charge customer, how should this loss be properly recorded in the accounts?
3. What does "terms of sale" mean that is stated n/EOM?
4. What are two reasons why a company may use the direct method to write off uncollectible accounts?
5. When the direct write off of uncollectible accounts method is used, what entry is made to record bad debts expense?
6. Why is recording estimated bad debts generally considered better than recording bad debts expense only when specific accounts are proven uncollectible?
7. How is the book value of accounts receivable figured?
8. Why is Allowance for Uncollectible Accounts called a contra account?
9. What is the procedure for estimating bad debts based on charge sales?
10. What journal entry is made to record bad debts expense?
11. What kind of situation would cause the account Allowance for Uncollectible Accounts to have a credit balance in the trial balance?
12. Why is the Allowance for Uncollectible Accounts debited when a customer's account is written off?
13. How does the book value of accounts receivable differ before and after writing off an account? Why?
14. Why do some businesses prefer to estimate the amount of uncollectible accounts by analysing the age of past-due accounts?

CASES FOR MANAGEMENT DECISION

CASE 1 McKenzie Corporation has always assumed an account receivable is good until the account is proven bad. When an account proves to be uncollectible, the credit manager notifies the general accounting clerk to write off the account. The accounting clerk then debits Bad Debts Expense and credits Accounts Receivable. Recently the company's auditor, Nita Barnes, suggested the method be changed for recording bad debts expense. Ms. Barnes recommended the company change to the estimating method, percent of charge sales. Ms. Barnes stated the change would provide more accurate information in the income statement and balance sheet. Which method provides the most accurate financial statements? Why?

CASE 2 Plastics Unlimited credits Accounts Receivable for the amount of estimated bad debts expense at the end of each fiscal period. Ivory Imports credits Allowance for Uncollectible Accounts for the amount of estimated bad debts expense at the end of each fiscal period. Is Plastics Unlimited or Ivory Imports using the better method? Why?

DRILLS FOR UNDERSTANDING

DRILL 24-D 1 Journalizing uncollectible accounts

Instructions: Use a form similar to the one below. For each transaction, place a check mark for each general ledger account that is either debited or credited. Place a check mark in the Accounts Not Affected column if no journal entry should be made.

Transaction	General Ledger Accounts			Accounts Not Affected
	Accounts Receivable	Allowance for Uncollectible Accounts	Bad Debts Expense	
Direct Write-Off Method Used:				
a. Estimated amount of uncollectible accounts				
b. Wrote off an uncollectible account..........................				
Estimated Method Used:				
c. Estimated amount of uncollectible accounts at end of fiscal period				
d. Wrote off an uncollectible account..........................				

DRILL 24-D 2 Figuring bad debts expense

Accounting records of three stores show the following summary information for the fiscal period ending December 31 of the current year.

Store	Total Charge Sales	Balance in Accounts Receivable Account				Actual Accounts Written off
		Current	Past Due			
			30–59 days	60–89 days	90 days & over	
1	$47 560	$ 7 168	$1 103	$ 643	$276	$415
2	98 300	19 169	2 949	1 720	737	620
3	84 550	14 509	2 232	1 302	558	425

Instructions: Figure the *bad debts expense* for each of these stores using the methods on the next page.

a. Direct write-off method.
b. Percent of charge sales method. Percent of accounts uncollectible is estimated at .005 of charge sales.
c. Aging method. Percent of accounts uncollectible is estimated as follows:

Past Due Accounts	Percent Uncollectible
30–59 days	5%
60–89 days	15%
90 days and over	30%

End-of-fiscal-period balances in the account Allowance for Uncollectible Accounts are below.

Store 1	$ 36.00 Credit Balance
Store 2	$ 89.00 Debit Balance
Store 3	$104.00 Credit Balance

APPLICATION PROBLEMS

PROBLEM 24-1 Recording entries for bad debts expense

Keltner Corporation used the direct write-off method to record uncollectible accounts and bad debts expense. Selected entries affecting uncollectible accounts are given below.

Instructions: Record all the necessary entries for the following. Use page 15 of a general journal similar to the one on page 491.

Jan. 25. Wrote off past-due account of Joyce Maloney as uncollectible, $86.00. M138.
Mar. 10. Wrote off past-due account of J. E. Prafka as uncollectible, $43.50. M161.
Apr. 27. Wrote off past-due account of Albert Chisum as uncollectible, $72.60. M183.
July 7. Wrote off past-due account of Paul Gastineau as uncollectible, $21.75. M227.
Sept. 12. Wrote off past-due account of Celia Masters as uncollectible, $37.65. M249.
Dec. 8. Wrote off past-due account of Royal Walenta as uncollectible, $97.50. M301.

PROBLEM 24-2 Recording entries for bad debts expense

Syntron Company has general ledger accounts for Allowance for Uncollectible Accounts and Bad Debts Expense. At the beginning of the current year, the credit balance of Allowance for Uncollectible Accounts was $1 023.20.

Selected entries affecting bad debts are given below.

Instructions: Record the following selected entries on page 24 of a general journal like the one on page 495.

Mar. 8. Wrote off past-due account of Joseph Merz as uncollectible, $185.40. M117.
Mar. 31. *End of first quarterly fiscal period.* Make adjusting entry for estimated bad debts expense. Bad debts expense is estimated as 0.5% of total charge sales. Total charge sales for the first quarterly fiscal period were $52 118.00.
Apr. 10. Wrote off past-due account of Ruth Hatch as uncollectible, $356.40. M152.
June 14. Wrote off past-due account of Roy Pilant, $417.30. M216.
June 30. *End of second quarterly fiscal period.* Make adjusting entry for estimated bad debts expense. Total charge sales for the second quarterly fiscal period were $45 282.10.
Aug. 24. Wrote off past-due account of Ruby Olendorff as uncollectible, $255.02. M283.

Sept. 30. *End of third quarterly fiscal period.* Make adjusting entry for estimated bad debts expense. Total charge sales for the third quarterly fiscal period were $49 690.30.

Nov. 30. Wrote off past-due account of E. L. Semones as uncollectible, $269.91. M326.

Dec. 31. *End of fourth quarterly fiscal period.* Make adjusting entry for estimated bad debts expense. Total charge sales for the fourth quarterly fiscal period were $51 269.90.

ENRICHMENT PROBLEMS

MASTERY PROBLEM 24-M Recording entries for bad debts expense

Gardiner Appliances has general ledger accounts for Allowance for Uncollectible Accounts and Bad Debts Expense. At the beginning of the current year, the credit balance of Allowance for Uncollectible Accounts was $854.19. Selected entries affecting uncollectible accounts are given below.

Instructions: Record all the necessary entries for the following on page 16 of a general journal like the one on page 495.

Jan. 17. Wrote off past-due account of Kay Taylor as uncollectible, $537.84. M26.

Mar. 31. *End of first quarterly fiscal period.* Make adjusting entry for estimated bad debts expense. Bad debts expense is estimated as 1% of the total charge sales. Total charge sales for the first quarterly fiscal period were $59 174.40.

Apr. 14. Wrote off past-due account of Margaret Ryan as uncollectible, $378.00. M48.

June 30. *End of second quarterly fiscal period.* Make adjusting entry for estimated bad debts expense. Total charge sales for the second quarterly fiscal period were $49 572.90.

July 13. Wrote off past-due account of Billy Franks as uncollectible, $398.70. M78.

Sept. 30. *End of third quarterly fiscal period.* Make adjusting entry for estimated bad debts expense. Total charge sales for the third quarterly fiscal period were $50 581.20.

Dec. 30. Wrote off past-due account of J. E. Byrd as uncollectible, $789.00. M129.

Dec. 31. *End of fourth quarterly fiscal period.* Make adjusting entry for estimated bad debts expense. Total charge sales for the fourth quarterly fiscal period were $65 895.00.

CHALLENGE PROBLEM 24-C Recording entries for bad debts expense

LaFiesta Corporation has general ledger accounts for Allowance for Uncollectible Accounts and Bad Debts Expense. The corporation ages its accounts to estimate uncollectible accounts. At the beginning of the current year, the credit balance of Allowance for Uncollectible Accounts was $1 470.00.

Selected entries affecting bad debts are given below.

Instructions: 1. Record the following selected entries on page 12 of a general journal like the one on page 497.

Mar. 18. Wrote off past-due account of Virda McGhee as uncollectible, $223.50. M38.

May 11. Wrote off past-due account of Jake Browning as uncollectible, $194.60. M69.

Aug. 22. Wrote off past-due account of Robert Palmer as uncollectible, $224.20. M116.

Dec. 20. Wrote off past-due account of Dean Molitar as uncollectible, $150.30. M158.

Instructions: 2. The totals from the Schedule of Accounts Receivable by Age for La-Fiesta Corporation on December 31 are below.

	Balance Due	Due for Less than 30 days	Accounts Past Due		
			30–59 Days	60–89 Days	90 Days And Over
Totals	$28 250.00	$22 035.00	$3 390.00	$1 978.00	$847.00

The percent of past due accounts are estimated uncollectible as shown below.

Number Days Past Due	Percentage Uncollectible
30–59 days	5%
60–89 days	10%
90 + days	50%

Figure and record the adjusting journal entry for Bad Debts Expense for the fiscal period ended December 31.

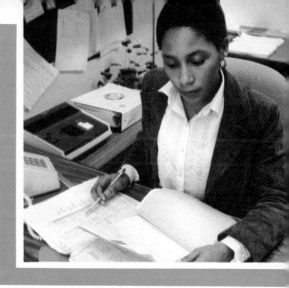

25

Accounting for Fixed Assets and Depreciation

ENABLING PERFORMANCE TASKS

After studying Chapter 25, you will be able to:

a. Define accounting terms related to accounting for fixed assets and depreciation.
b. Explain accounting principles and practices related to accounting for fixed assets and depreciation.
c. Figure depreciation expense.
d. Figure book value of a fixed asset.
e. Journalize the buying of a fixed asset in a cash payments journal.
f. Prepare a fixed asset record.
g. Journalize work sheet adjustments for depreciation expense in a general journal.
h. Journalize the sale of a fixed asset in a cash receipts journal.

Some business assets such as cash, accounts receivable, and merchandise inventory usually are turned into cash within a year. Another group of assets are used for a long period to operate a business. Assets that will be used for a number of years in the operation of a business are called fixed assets. Some examples of fixed assets are delivery equipment, store equipment, office equipment, buildings, and land. Fixed assets can be used repeatedly and are expected to last more than a year. Also, fixed assets are not bought for purposes of resale to customers in the normal course of business. Thus, land on which a business is located is classified as a fixed asset. However, land bought with the intention of renting or reselling at a profit is not classified as a fixed asset.

Some businesses use the term "plant assets." However, at the present time, the term "fixed assets" rather than "plant assets" is preferred in Canadian accounting practice.

Fixed assets such as delivery trucks, machinery, display cases, tables, word processors, and desks are called equipment. Some businesses record the cost of all equipment in one asset account titled Equipment. Other businesses record various kinds of equipment in separate fixed asset accounts such as Delivery Equipment, and Office Equipment. Lin's Music Centre uses three fixed asset accounts: Delivery Equipment, Store Equipment, and Office Equipment.

BUYING AND RECORDING FIXED ASSETS

A fixed asset is recorded at its cost. *(CONCEPT: Historical Cost)* On April 1, 1989, Lin's Music Centre bought a delivery truck for $7 000.00 cash. The entry to record this transaction is shown in the cash payments journal below.

		CASH PAYMENTS JOURNAL				PAGE 10

DATE	ACCOUNT TITLE	CHEQUE No.	POST. REF.	GENERAL DEBIT	GENERAL CREDIT	ACCOUNTS PAYABLE DEBIT	PURCHASES DISCOUNT CREDIT	CASH CREDIT
1	Delivery Equipment	248		700000				700000

Entry to record the buying of a fixed asset

Lins has a separate fixed asset account for delivery equipment. Delivery Equipment is debited for the cost of the delivery truck, *$7 000.00*, and Cash is credited for the same amount. After the entry is posted, Delivery Equipment in the general ledger appears as shown below.

ACCOUNT Delivery Equipment					ACCOUNT NO. 1201	
DATE	ITEM	POST. REF.	DEBIT	CREDIT	BALANCE DEBIT	BALANCE CREDIT
1989 Jan. 1	Balance	✓			1088000	
Apr. 1		CP10	700000		1788000	

A fixed asset account in the general ledger

The $10 880.00 balance of Delivery Equipment is the original cost of equipment owned on January 1, 1989. The $17 880.00 balance of Delivery Equipment is the original cost of equipment owned on April 1. The debit balance of Delivery Equipment always shows the original cost of all delivery equipment owned. *(CONCEPT: Historical Cost)*

DESCRIBING THE EFFECT OF DEPRECIATION ON FIXED ASSETS

A machine bought for $800.00 in January is not worth $800.00 twelve months later. Similarly, a fixed asset of any kind bought in July for $1 000.00 is not worth $1 000.00 in December. Fixed assets such as store equipment decrease in value because of use. Fixed assets also decrease in value with passage of time as they become older and new models become available. A decrease in value of a fixed asset because of use and passage of time is called depreciation. Land, because of its permanent nature, generally is not subject to depreciation.

An amount by which a fixed asset depreciates is an expense of a business. A fixed asset is used to operate a business and earn revenue. Therefore, depreciation expense should be recorded in each fiscal period that a fixed asset is used to earn revenue. *(CONCEPT: Matching Expenses with Revenue)* If depreciation expense is not recorded, an income statement will not report all expenses of a business. Therefore, net income will be overstated.

Federal income tax laws allow a business to deduct depreciation expense in figuring net income. If depreciation expenses are not included on income tax reports, a business will pay more income tax than required.

FIGURING DEPRECIATION EXPENSE

A business normally expects to use a fixed asset for several years. Depreciation expense is recorded for each fiscal period a fixed asset is used.

Factors affecting depreciation expense

Three factors affect the amount of fixed asset depreciation expense for a fiscal period.

1. The original cost of a fixed asset.
2. The amount a business estimates will be received when disposing of a fixed asset.
3. The estimated useful life of a fixed asset.

Original cost. The original cost of a fixed asset is obtained from the seller's invoice. The cost of the delivery truck bought by Lin's is $7 000.00.

Estimated salvage value. The amount an owner expects to receive when a fixed asset is removed from use is called estimated salvage value. Estimated salvage value also is known as scrap value.

Lin's estimates a salvage value of $1 000.00 for the delivery truck at the end of its useful life.

Estimated useful life. The total amount of depreciation expense is distributed over the estimated useful life of a fixed asset. When a fixed asset is bought, the exact length of useful life is impossible to predict. Therefore, the number of years of useful life must be estimated.

Lin's estimates that the useful life of a delivery truck is 5 years. An estimate of useful life should be based on prior experience with similar assets and available guidelines. Revenue Canada, Taxation issues guidelines for the estimated life of many common fixed assets. Trade associations also may publish similar guidelines for specialized fixed assets.

Figuring depreciation expense for a fiscal period

Lin's figures the total amount of estimated depreciation for the delivery truck as shown below.

Original cost	minus	Estimated salvage value	equals	Amount of estimated depreciation
$7 000.00	−	$1 000.00	=	$6 000.00

The annual depreciation expense for the delivery truck is figured as shown below.

Total amount of estimated depreciation	divided by	Years of estimated useful life	equals	Estimated amount of annual depreciation expense
$6 000.00	÷	5	=	$1 200.00

Monthly depreciation is figured by dividing annual depreciation by twelve ($1 200.00 ÷ 12 = $100.00). Lin's bought the delivery truck on April 1, 1989. Nine months passed from April 1, 1989, to the end of the fiscal year, December 31, 1989. Therefore, nine months depreciation, *$900.00*, is charged as an expense for the year 1989 ($100.00 × 9 = $900.00).

Charging an *equal* amount of annual depreciation expense for a fixed asset is called the straight-line method of depreciation. Lin's uses the straight-line method to figure depreciation.

> There are other methods of figuring depreciation expense. Canadian companies are required by income tax regulations to use the declining-balance method. This method is briefly explained in Challenge Problem 25-C.

PREPARING FIXED ASSET RECORDS

A separate record for each fixed asset is kept. An accounting form on which a business records data about each fixed asset is called a fixed asset record.

When Lin's bought a delivery truck on April 1, 1989, a fixed asset record was prepared. The fixed asset record for the delivery truck is on page 509.

A fixed asset record includes a complete description of an asset, including the serial number. A record also includes the date the asset was bought, the cost, and the estimated useful life. Other items of information on the record are the estimated salvage value and the annual amount of depreciation expense.

FIXED ASSET RECORD

Lin's Music Centre

Account No. ⟦1201⟧

Item ___ Delivery Truck ___ General Ledger Account ___ Delivery Equipment ___
Serial No. _8735M96025_ Description _____ Model C20 _____
From Whom Purchased ___ Star Motors, Vancouver, BC ___ Cost _$7 000.00_

Estimated
Life ___5 years___   Estimated Salvage or
Trade-in Value ____ $1 000.00 ____   Depreciation
per year ___ $1 200.00 ___

Disposal date _____ Disposal amount _____

Date Yr. Mo. Day	Annual Depreciation Expense	Accumulated Depreciation	Book Value
1989 04 01			7 000.00
1989 12 31	900.00	900.00	6 100.00

Fixed asset record showing first-year depreciation

On December 31, 1989, Lin's has owned the delivery truck for three fourths of a year. Therefore, the depreciation expense for 1989, *$900.00*, is recorded in the Accumulated Depreciation column. The original cost of a fixed asset minus the accumulated depreciation is called the book value of a fixed asset. Since the delivery truck had no previous depreciation, the amount, *$900.00*, is deducted from the original cost, *$7 000.00*. The new book value at the end of the fiscal period, *$6 100.00*, is recorded in the Book Value column.

At the close of each fiscal period, each fixed asset record is brought up to date. The depreciation expense for that period is recorded and the new book value of the asset is figured. The book value of Lin's delivery truck at the end of 1994, shown below, is $1 000.00. This amount, *$1 000.00*, is

FIXED ASSET RECORD

Lin's Music Centre

Account No. ⟦1201⟧

Item ___ Delivery Truck ___ General Ledger Account ___ Delivery Equipment ___
Serial No. _8735M96025_ Description _____ Model C20 _____
From Whom Purchased ___ Star Motors, Vancouver, BC ___ Cost _$7 000.00_

Estimated
Life ___5 years___   Estimated Salvage or
Trade-in Value ____ $1 000.00 ____   Depreciation
per year ___ $1 200.00 ___

Disposal date _____ Disposal amount _____

Date Yr. Mo. Day	Annual Depreciation Expense	Accumulated Depreciation	Book Value
1989 04 01			7 000.00
1989 12 31	900.00	900.00	6 100.00
1993 12 31	1 200.00	5 700.00	1 300.00
1994 12 31	300.00	6 000.00	1 000.00

Fixed asset record brought up to date the last fiscal period of a fixed asset's life the salvage value Lin's estimates the truck is worth after 5 years. When a fixed asset's book value equals its estimated salvage value, no further depreciation expense is recorded. Therefore, on December 31, 1994, only $300.00 depreciation expense is recorded on the fixed asset record.

ACCOUNTS AFFECTING THE VALUATION OF FIXED ASSETS

Three general ledger accounts are used to record data about each kind of fixed asset. (1) An asset account, such as Delivery Equipment, is used to record the original cost of the asset. (2) A contra asset account, such as Accumulated Depreciation — Delivery Equipment, is used to record the total amount of depreciation to date. (3) An expense account, such as Depreciation Expense — Delivery Equipment, is used to record the annual amount of depreciation expense.

Fixed asset accounts

Lin's uses three fixed asset accounts: Delivery Equipment, Office Equipment, and Store Equipment. The appropriate fixed asset account is debited for the cost when equipment is bought. The account is credited for the cost when equipment is disposed of. Therefore, the balance of a fixed asset account always shows the cost of all equipment in current use.

Accumulated depreciation accounts

Depreciation is credited to a contra asset account titled Accumulated Depreciation. The name of the related equipment account is added to the title, such as Accumulated Depreciation — Delivery Equipment. Lin's uses three accumulated depreciation accounts. The three accounts are Accumulated Depreciation — Delivery Equipment, Accumulated Depreciation — Office Equipment, and Accumulated Depreciation — Store Equipment.

> The location of these contra accounts in the general ledger is shown in the chart of accounts, page 394.
> The account title Allowance for Depreciation sometimes is used instead of Accumulated Depreciation.

The debit balance of each fixed asset account shows the original cost of the assets in use. The credit balance of the accumulated depreciation account shows the estimated decrease in value of the assets because of depreciation. The difference between the balances of the two accounts is the book value of the fixed assets.

Depreciation expense accounts

Depreciation expense is an expense of a business. Lin's uses three depreciation expense accounts. The three depreciation accounts are, Depreciation Expense — Delivery Equipment, Depreciation Expense — Office Equipment, and Depreciation Expense — Store Equipment.

DETERMINING ADJUSTMENTS FOR DEPRECIATION

At the end of the fiscal period, December 31, 1989, Lin's figures the depreciation expense for each asset. Next, the total depreciation expense is figured for all fixed assets of the same kind. For example, in 1983 the depreciation expense for the delivery truck is $900.00. The depreciation expense for other delivery equipment is $1 000.00. Thus, the total delivery equipment depreciation expense for 1989 is $1 900.00. Lin's total depreciation expense for each kind of fixed asset on December 31, 1989, is below.

Kind of equipment	Estimated depreciation expense this year	Previous balance of accumulated depreciation	New balance of accumulated depreciation
Delivery equipment	$1 900.00	$5 250.00	$7 150.00
Office equipment	950.00	1 950.00	2 900.00
Store equipment	2 840.00	5 400.00	8 240.00

Analysing an adjustment for estimated depreciation

An adjusting entry is made to record estimated depreciation expense for a fiscal year. The T accounts at the right show the delivery equipment account, accumulated depreciation account, and depreciation expense account. The accounts are shown before the adjustment for depreciation expense is made.

Four questions are asked in analysing the adjustment for estimated depreciation.

1. What is the balance of the depreciation expense — delivery equipment account?.. zero
2. What should the balance be for this account? $1 900.00
3. What must be done to correct the account balance? ....Add $1 900.00
4. What adjusting entry is made?.....................................
             Debit Depreciation Expense — Delivery Equipment $1 900.00
             Credit Accumulated Depreciation — Delivery Equipment $1 900.00

BEFORE ADJUSTMENT

Delivery Equipment

Jan. 1 Bal. 10 880.00
Apr. 1   7 000.00
Dec. 31 Bal. 17 880.00

Depreciation Expense —
Delivery Equipment

Accumulated Depreciation —
Delivery Equipment

          Jan. 1 Bal.   5 250.00

The T accounts are shown on the next page after the adjustment for depreciation expense is made.

Depreciation Expense — Delivery Equipment is debited for $1 900.00 to show the increase in the balance of this expense account. The balance of this account, *$1 900.00*, is the estimated depreciation expense for the fiscal period.

AFTER ADJUSTMENT

Delivery Equipment

Jan. 1 Bal. 10 880.00	
Apr. 1 7 000.00	
Dec. 31 Bal. 17 880.00	

Depreciation Expense —
Delivery Equipment

Dec. 31 Adj. 1 900.00	

Accumulated Depreciation —
Delivery Equipment

	Jan. 1 Bal. 5 250.00
	Dec. 31 Adj. 1 900.00
	Dec. 31 Bal. 7 150.00

Accumulated Depreciation — Delivery Equipment is credited for $1 900.00 to show the increase in the balance of this contra account. The January 1 balance, $5 250.00, plus the fiscal year increase, $1 900.00, equals the December 31 balance, $7 150.00. The delivery equipment account balance, $17 880.00, minus the accumulated depreciation account balance, $7 150.00, equals the delivery equipment book value, $10 730.00.

The same kind of adjusting entry is made to record estimated depreciation expense for store equipment and office equipment. The book value of each kind of fixed asset after the adjustments of December 31, 1989, is below.

Kind of equipment	Balance of asset account	less	Total accumulated depreciation	equals	Book value 1989 12 31
Delivery equipment	$17 880.00	–	$7 150.00	=	$10 730.00
Office equipment	9 710.00	–	2 900.00	=	6 810.00
Store equipment	41 175.00	–	8 240.00	=	32 935.00

Recording depreciation expense on a work sheet

Lin's plans the adjustments for depreciation expense in the Adjustments columns of a work sheet. The December 31, 1989, adjustments for depreciation of fixed assets are on the partial work sheet below.

Lin's Music Centre
Work Sheet
For Year Ended December 31, 1989

	ACCOUNT TITLE	TRIAL BALANCE DEBIT	TRIAL BALANCE CREDIT	ADJUSTMENTS DEBIT	ADJUSTMENTS CREDIT
8	Delivery Equipment	17 880 00			
9	Accum. Depr.-Delivery Equip.		5 250 00		(4) 1 900 00
10	Office Equipment	9 710 00			
11	Accum. Depr.-Office Equip.		1 950 00		(4) 950 00
12	Store Equipment	41 175 00			
13	Accum. Depr.-Store Equip.		5 400 00		(k) 2 840 00
38	Depr. Exp.-Delivery Equip.			(4) 1 900 00	
39	Depr. Exp.-Office Equip.			(4) 950 00	
40	Depr. Exp.-Store Equip.			(k) 2 840 00	

Partial work sheet with adjustments for depreciation

Adjustment for depreciation of delivery equipment. On line 38, the increase in Depreciation Expense — Delivery Equipment, $1 900.00, is listed in the Adjustments Debit column. On line 9, the increase in Accumulated Depreciation — Delivery Equipment, $1 900.00, is listed in the Adjustments Credit column.

Adjustment for depreciation of office equipment. On line 39, the increase in Depreciation Expense — Office Equipment, *$950.00*, is listed in the Adjustments Debit column. On line 11, the increase in Accumulated Depreciation — Office Equipment, *$950.00*, is listed in the Adjustments Credit column.

Adjustment for depreciation of store equipment. On line 40, the increase in Depreciation Expense — Store Equipment, *$2 840.00*, is listed in the Adjustments Debit column. On line 13, the increase in Accumulated Depreciation — Store Equipment, *$2 840.00*, is listed in the Adjustments Credit column.

Journalizing adjustments for depreciation expense

Data needed to journalize adjustments for depreciation expense are obtained from the Adjustments columns of a work sheet. Lin's three adjusting entries are shown in the general journal below.

		GENERAL JOURNAL			PAGE 27		
	DATE	ACCOUNT TITLE	POST. REF.	DEBIT	CREDIT		
1		*Adjusting Entries*					1
12	31	Depreciation Exp. - Delivery Equip.		1 90000			12
13		Accum. Depr. - Delivery Equip.			1 90000		13
14	31	Depreciation Exp. - Office Equip.		95000			14
15		Accum. Depr. - Office Equip.			95000		15
16	31	Depreciation Exp. - Store Equip.		2 84000			16
17		Accum. Depr. - Store Equip.			2 84000		17

Adjusting entries to record depreciation

Posting adjustments for estimated depreciation

After adjusting entries for depreciation expense are posted, the accounts appear as shown below and on page 514.

ACCOUNT *Delivery Equipment* ACCOUNT NO. *1201*

DATE	ITEM	POST. REF.	DEBIT	CREDIT	BALANCE DEBIT	BALANCE CREDIT
1989 Jan. 1	Balance	✓			10 88000	
Apr. 1		CP10	7 00000		17 88000	

ACCOUNT *Accumulated Depreciation - Delivery Equip.* ACCOUNT NO. *1201.1*

DATE	ITEM	POST. REF.	DEBIT	CREDIT	BALANCE DEBIT	BALANCE CREDIT
1989 Jan. 1	Balance	✓				5 25000
Dec. 31		G27		1 90000		7 15000

General ledger accounts after posting adjusting entries for depreciation

ACCOUNT *Office Equipment*   ACCOUNT NO. *1202*

DATE	ITEM	POST. REF.	DEBIT	CREDIT	BALANCE DEBIT	BALANCE CREDIT
1989 Jan. 1	Balance	✓			971000	

ACCOUNT *Accumulated Depreciation – Office Equip.*   ACCOUNT NO. *1202.1*

DATE	ITEM	POST. REF.	DEBIT	CREDIT	BALANCE DEBIT	BALANCE CREDIT
1989 Jan. 1	Balance	✓				195000
Dec. 31		G27		95000		290000

ACCOUNT *Store Equipment*   ACCOUNT NO. *1203*

DATE	ITEM	POST. REF.	DEBIT	CREDIT	BALANCE DEBIT	BALANCE CREDIT
1989 Jan. 1	Balance	✓			3840000	
July 1		CP19	335000		4175000	

ACCOUNT *Accumulated Depreciation – Store Equip.*   ACCOUNT NO. *1203.1*

DATE	ITEM	POST. REF.	DEBIT	CREDIT	BALANCE DEBIT	BALANCE CREDIT
1989 Jan. 1		✓				540000
Dec. 31		G27		284000		824000

ACCOUNT *Depreciation Expense – Delivery Equipment*   ACCOUNT NO. *6105*

DATE	ITEM	POST. REF.	DEBIT	CREDIT	BALANCE DEBIT	BALANCE CREDIT
1989 Dec. 31		G27	190000		190000	

ACCOUNT *Depreciation Expense – Office Equipment*   ACCOUNT NO. *6106*

DATE	ITEM	POST. REF.	DEBIT	CREDIT	BALANCE DEBIT	BALANCE CREDIT
1989 Dec. 31		G27	95000		95000	

ACCOUNT *Depreciation Expense – Store Equipment*   ACCOUNT NO. *6107*

DATE	ITEM	POST. REF.	DEBIT	CREDIT	BALANCE DEBIT	BALANCE CREDIT
1989 Dec. 31		G27	284000		284000	

General ledger accounts
after posting adjusting
entries for depreciation

Delivery Equipment, Office Equipment, and Store Equipment have debit balances
showing the original cost of equipment. The three contra accounts for the

equipment accounts have credit balances showing the accumulated depreciation recorded to date. The three depreciation expense accounts have debit balances showing depreciation expense for the current fiscal period.

DISPOSAL OF A FIXED ASSET

When no longer used, a fixed asset may be sold or discarded. After over five years of use, Lin's sold a delivery truck.

> *January 5, 1995. Received cash, $1 000.00, from the sale of a delivery truck bought on April 1, 1989, for $7 000.00. Receipt No. 106.*

The fixed asset record for the delivery truck is below.

FIXED ASSET RECORD

Lin's Music Centre

Account No. 1201

Item __Delivery Truck__   General Ledger Account __Delivery Equipment__
Serial No. __8735M96025__   Description __Model C20__
From Whom Purchased __Star Motors, Vancouver, BC__   Cost $7 000.00

Estimated Life __5 years__   Estimated Salvage or Trade-In Value __$1 000.00__   Depreciation per year __$1 200.00__

Disposal date _____   Disposal amount __$1 000.00__

Date Yr. Mo. Day	Annual Depreciation Expense	Accumulated Depreciation	Book Value
1989 04 01			7 000.00
1989 12 31	900.00	900.00	6 100.00
1990 12 31	1 200.00	2 100.00	4 900.00
1991 12 31	1 200.00	3 300.00	3 700.00
1992 12 31	1 200.00	4 500.00	2 500.00
1993 12 31	1 200.00	5 700.00	1 300.00
1994 12 31	300.00	6 000.00	1 000.00

Fixed asset record showing disposal of a fixed asset

When a fixed asset is disposed of, a notation is made on the fixed asset record. The date of disposal, *January 5, 1995*, is written on the *Disposal date* line. The amount received, *$1 000.00*, is written on the *Disposal amount* line.

Analysing the sale of a fixed asset

The delivery truck was sold for $1 000.00. The book value of the delivery truck on January 5, 1995, is $1 000.00. (Cost, $7 000.00, less accumu-

```
           Cash
  1 000.00 |
```

```
  Accumulated Depreciation —
      Delivery Equipment
  6 000.00 |
```

```
       Delivery Equipment
           |  7 000.00
```

lated depreciation, $6 000.00, equals book value, $1 000.00). The analysis of this transaction is shown in the T accounts at the left.

Cash is debited for $1 000.00 to show the increase in the balance of this asset.

Accumulated Depreciation — Delivery Equipment is debited for $6 000.00 to show the decrease in this contra account's balance. The amount, *$6 000.00*, is the total depreciation recorded during the entire life of the delivery truck.

Delivery Equipment is credited for $7 000.00 to show the decrease in the balance of this fixed asset account. This entry cancels the original cost, $7 000.00, debited to the delivery equipment account when the truck was bought.

Journalizing the sale of a fixed asset

The entry to record the sale of the delivery truck is shown in the cash receipts journal below.

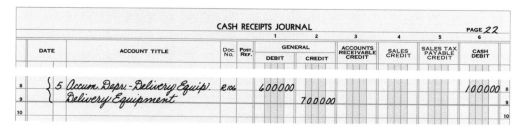

Entry to record the sale of a fixed asset   Cash is debited for $1 000.00 in the Cash Debit column. Accumulated Depreciation — Delivery Equipment is debited for $6 000.00 in the General Debit column. Delivery Equipment is credited for $7 000.00 in the General Credit column.

ACCOUNTING TERMS

What is the meaning of each of the following?

1. fixed assets
2. equipment
3. depreciation
4. estimated salvage value
5. straight-line method of depreciation
6. fixed asset record
7. book value of a fixed asset

QUESTIONS FOR INDIVIDUAL STUDY

1. What accounts are debited and credited when a fixed asset is bought for cash?
2. Why are most fixed assets worth less than their original cost after being used for a period of time?

3. If the expense of using a fixed asset is not recorded, how will this omission affect total business expenses? How will this omission affect the net income for the period?
4. What three factors affect the amount of

depreciation of a fixed asset?

5. How is the annual depreciation expense figured for a fixed asset using the straight-line method of depreciation?

6. How is the book value of a fixed asset figured?

7. What amount is always shown as the balance of a fixed asset account?

8. What accounts are debited and credited on a work sheet in planning adjustments for depreciation of a fixed asset?

9. What accounts are debited and credited to record the sale of a fixed asset for its salvage value?

CASES FOR MANAGEMENT DECISION

CASE 1 Josephine Alvarez, owner of a small business, does not record depreciation expense for the business' fixed assets. Ms. Alvarez says that she does not make actual cash payments for depreciation. Therefore, she records an expense for the use of fixed assets only when cash is paid for a fixed asset. Do you agree with Ms. Alvarez's method? Explain.

CASE 2 Kwik Delivery Service has more business than can be handled with the present number of trucks it owns. The company is investigating the cost of buying an additional delivery truck. One dealer recommends a small truck costing $8 500.00. The useful life of the truck is estimated to be 5 years with an estimated salvage value of $1 000.00. Another dealer recommends a larger truck with 50% more capacity than the smaller truck. The cost price is $12 000.00, with a useful life of 7 years, and estimated salvage value of $1 500.00. Which truck would you recommend Kwik Delivery Service buy? Why?

DRILLS FOR UNDERSTANDING

DRILL 25-D 1 Figuring depreciation expense

Instructions: Use the straight-line method of figuring depreciation described on page 504. Figure the amount of annual depreciation for each of the following fixed assets.

Fixed Asset	Original Cost	Estimated Salvage Value	Estimated Life
1	$ 2 850.00	$ 450.00	4 years
2	1 700.00	200.00	5 years
3	900.00	none	3 years
4	36 600.00	1 600.00	20 years
5	17 000.00	2 400.00	8 years
6	12 160.00	800.00	16 years
7	2 280.00	300.00	3 years
8	2 210.00	240.00	5 years
9	29 280.00	1 280.00	10 years
10	14 500.00	2 800.00	20 years

DRILL 25-D 2 Figuring book value of a fixed asset

Instructions: Figure two amounts for each of the fixed assets on page 518. (a) Figure the total amount of estimated depreciation as of December 31, 1989. (b) Figure the book value as of December 31, 1989. Figure the time of depreciation to the nearest number of months.

Fixed Asset	Date Bought	Original Cost	Estimated Salvage Value	Estimated Life
1	Jan. 1, 1985	$ 2 400.00	$150.00	5 years
2	July 1, 1985	7 150.00	550.00	10 years
3	Dec. 31, 1985	10 725.00	825.00	15 years
4	Jan. 1, 1986	1 865.00	245.00	20 years
5	July 1, 1986	3 360.00	210.00	5 years
6	Nov. 1, 1986	240.00	24.00	4 years
7	Jan. 1, 1987	1 320.00	none	10 years
8	April 1, 1988	2 770.00	500.00	5 years
9	Jan. 1, 1989	2 900.00	300.00	10 years
10	Dec. 1, 1989	428.00	50.00	7 years

APPLICATION PROBLEMS

PROBLEM 25-1   Recording the buying of fixed assets

Superior Company bought for cash the fixed assets listed below.

Fixed Asset	Date Bought	Original Cost	Asset Account Recorded In
1	Feb 1, 1989	$1 950.00	Store Equipment
2	April 1, 1989	8 200.00	Delivery Equipment
3	May 1, 1989	975.00	Office Equipment
4	July 1, 1989	2 850.00	Store Equipment
5	Sept. 1, 1989	150.00	Office Equipment
6	Dec. 1, 1989	750.00	Store Equipment

Instructions: Record on page 5 of a cash payments journal the buying of the fixed assets listed above.

PROBLEM 25-2   Figuring depreciation expense

Expressway Auto Repair owns the fixed assets listed below.

Fixed Asset	Date Bought	Original Cost	Estimated Salvage Value	Estimated Life
1	Jan. 1, 1982	$5 200.00	$400.00	10 years
2	July 1, 1984	1 372.00	300.00	8 years
3	July 1, 1984	1 650.00	150.00	6 years
4	Oct. 1, 1985	2 700.00	300.00	5 years
5	April 1, 1989	4 000.00	400.00	5 years
6	July 1, 1989	1 734.00	150.00	6 years

Instructions: For each fixed asset above, figure the depreciation expense to be recorded for the year ended December 31, 1989. Use the straight-line method of figuring depreciation described on page 508. Figure the time of depreciation to the nearest number of months.

PROBLEM 25-3   Preparing a fixed asset record

Wood Creations bought a new bench saw July 1, 1989. Other information pertaining to the bench saw is listed below and on page 519.

General ledger account: Shop Equipment
Account number: 1303

Serial number of saw: 68358M
Model number of saw: H900
From whom purchased: T & M Equipment Company, Brantford, ON
Original cost: $2 750.00
Estimated life: 4 years
Estimated salvage value: $350.00

Instructions: Prepare a fixed asset record for the bench saw similar to the record described on page 509. For each year of the fixed asset's life, record year-end date, annual depreciation expense, accumulated depreciation, and book value.

PROBLEM 25-4 Recording work sheet adjustments and journal entries for depreciation expense

A partial trial balance of Edgewood Appliances is below. The accounts for depreciation of fixed assets are illustrated on this partial trial balance.

Instructions: 1. Record the information in a work sheet's Trial Balance columns for the year ended December 31, 1989.

Edgewood Appliances
Trial Balance
December 31, 1989

Delivery Equipment	27 810 00	
Accumulated Depreciation — Delivery Equipment		15 490 00
Store Equipment	17 160 00	
Accumulated Depreciation — Store Equipment		4 934 00
Depreciation Expense — Delivery Equipment		
Depreciation Expense — Store Equipment		

Instructions: 2. Record on the work sheet the adjustments for estimated depreciation for the year. Depreciation expenses are below.

Annual depreciation of delivery equipment, $6 330.00
Annual depreciation of store equipment, $1 020.00

3. Journalize the adjusting entries on page 24 of a general journal.

ENRICHMENT PROBLEMS

MASTERY PROBLEM 25-M Figuring depreciation expense and book value of fixed assets; journalizing depreciation expense and disposal of a fixed asset

Air Systems owns the fixed assets listed below.

Fixed Asset	Asset Account	Date Bought	Original Cost	Estimated Salvage Value	Estimated Life
1	Delivery Equip.	Oct. 1, 1982	$8 000.00	$440.00	7 years
2	Delivery Equip.	July 1, 1989	7 400.00	500.00	5 years
3	Shop Equipment	Oct. 1, 1985	1 638.00	150.00	8 years
4	Shop Equipment	Feb. 1, 1986	2 820.00	none	10 years
5	Shop Equipment	April 1, 1989	1 060.00	100.00	4 years
6	Shop Equipment	July 1, 1989	1 150.00	70.00	3 years

Instructions: 1. Figure each fixed asset's depreciation expense for the year ended December 31, 1989. Use the straight-line method of figuring depreciation. Figure the time of depreciation to the nearest number of months.

2. Figure each fixed asset's book value as of December 31, 1989.

3. Record on page 15 of a general journal the two adjusting entries for depreciation expense for the year ended December 31, 1989. Record delivery equipment depreciation in Depreciation Expense — Delivery Equipment. Record shop equipment depreciation in Depreciation Expense — Shop Equipment.

4. On January 25, 1990, received cash, $440.00, from the sale of delivery equipment, Fixed Asset No. 1, bought October 1, 1982, for $8 000.00. Receipt No. 324. Record the sale of this asset on page 18 of a cash receipts journal.

CHALLENGE PROBLEM 25-C   Figuring depreciation expense using a declining-balance method

Introductory remarks. Canadian income tax regulations require that businesses use the declining-balance method of calculating depreciation when reporting income, rather than the straight-line method used in this chapter. The declining-balance method is also referred to as the capital cost allowance method.

Revenue Canada, Taxation divides fixed assets into classes, each class being allowed a maximum percentage rate of depreciation. For example, a brick building is Class 3 with a maximum depreciation rate of 5%, whereas manufacturing machinery may be depreciated at a rate of 50% per year as it is in Class 29. However, if no rate is available the depreciation rate may be taken as being twice the straight-line rate as an approximation.

A delivery truck was bought on January 2, 1988 and estimated to have a 10-year life. The straight-line depreciation rate would be 10% per year. However, a delivery truck is in the Revenue Canada Class 10 category with a maximum depreciation rate of 30%. Using the declining-balance method, the book value at the end of the tenth year will be approximately the estimated salvage value of the truck.

Instructions: Using a chart similar to the one given below, calculate the book value at the beginning of each of the ten years of useful life of the truck; the amount of annual depreciation; the accumulated depreciation at the end of each year; and the book value at the end of each year. (The book value at the end of one year is the book value at the beginning of the next year.) Figures for the first two years are given as examples.

Year	Book value at beginning of year	Rate of depreciation	Annual depreciation this year	Accumulated depreciation at end of year	Book value at end of year
1988		30%	$2 100.00	$2 100.00	4 900.00
1989		30%	1 470.00	3 570.00	3 430.00

26

Accounting for Notes and Interest

ENABLING PERFORMANCE TASKS

After studying Chapter 26, you will be able to:

a. Define accounting terms related to accounting for notes and interest.
b. Explain accounting principles and practices related to accounting for notes and interest.
c. Journalize notes payable transactions.
d. Journalize notes receivable transactions.

Most businesses receive cash from sales of merchandise or services. They pay out cash to purchase merchandise, pay operating expenses, and buy new equipment. Merchandise purchased may not be sold for several months. Equipment bought may be used for several years. For these and other reasons, a business may pay out more cash some months than it receives. Therefore, many businesses borrow cash from a bank or other business when cash payments are greater than cash receipts. Then the business repays the cash in later periods when cash receipts are greater than cash payments.

A written and signed promise to pay a sum of money is called a promissory note. A promissory note is frequently referred to simply as a note.

Promissory notes are used to borrow money or to obtain an extension of time on an account. Sometimes a business requests a note from a customer who wants credit beyond the usual time given for sales on account. Notes have an advantage over oral promises and accounts receivable or payable. A note, like a cheque, can be endorsed and transferred to a bank. The bank then gives the business cash for the note. Thus, the business can get its money before the note is due. Notes can also be useful in a court of law as evidence of a debt.

One form of a promissory note is on the next page.

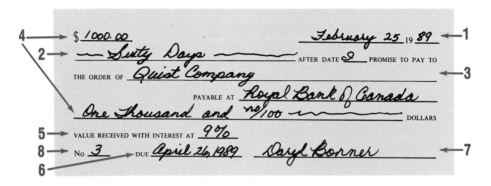

A promissory note

The terms defined below are used in analysing the above note.

Term	Definition	Illustration
1 Date of a note	The day a note is issued.	February 25, 1989
2 Time of a note	The days, months, or years from the date of issue until a note is to be paid.	Sixty days
3 Payee of a note	The person to whom a note is payable.	Quist Company
4 Principal of a note	The amount a borrower promises to pay — the face of a note.	$1 000.00
5 Interest rate of a note	The percentage of the principal that is paid for use of the money.	9%
6 Maturity date of a note	The date a note is due.	April 26, 1989
7 Maker of a note	The person who signs a note and thus promises to make payment.	Daryl Bonner
8 Number of a note	The number assigned by the maker to identify a specific note.	3

INTEREST ON NOTES

An amount paid for the use of the principal of a note for a period of time is called interest. Most promissory notes require the payment of interest. Promissory notes that require interest payments are called interest-bearing notes. Promissory notes that do not contain a provision for the payment of interest are called non-interest-bearing notes.

The interest rate is stated as a percentage of the principal. Interest at 9% means that 9 cents will be paid for the use of each dollar borrowed for a full year. The interest on $100.00 for a full year at 9% is $9.00.

The principal plus the interest on a note is called the maturity value. A one-year note for $100.00 with a 9% interest rate will have a maturity value of $109.00 ($100.00 principal plus $9.00 interest).

Sometimes partial payments are made on a note each month. This is particularly true when an individual buys a car and signs a note for the amount owed. The monthly payment includes part of the money owed and part of the interest to be paid.

NOTES PAYABLE

Promissory notes that a business gives creditors are called notes payable. Notes payable within one year are classified as current liabilities of a business.

Issuing a note payable to borrow money from a bank

On February 1, 1989, Lin's Music Centre arranges to borrow money from its bank. A note payable is issued to the bank as evidence of indebtedness. The bank credits Lin's current account for the principal amount of the note.

> February 1, 1989. Issued a 6-month, 9% note to the Royal Bank of Canada, $4 000.00. Note Payable No. 4.

Analysing the issuance of a note payable for cash. A copy of the note payable is the source document used by Lin's for recording the transaction. (CONCEPT: Objective Evidence) In this transaction the balance of the asset account Cash is increased. The balance of the liability account Notes Payable is also increased. Therefore, Cash is debited for $4 000.00 and Notes Payable is credited for $4 000.00. No entry is made for the interest until a later date when the interest is paid.

Cash	
4 000.00	

Notes Payable	
	4 000.00

Recording the issuance of a note payable and the receipt of cash. This transaction is recorded in a cash receipts journal as shown below.

	DATE	ACCOUNT TITLE	Doc. No.	Post. Ref.	GENERAL DEBIT	GENERAL CREDIT	ACCOUNTS RECEIVABLE CREDIT	SALES CREDIT	SALES TAX PAYABLE CREDIT	CASH DEBIT	
6	1	Notes Payable	NP4			4 000 00				4 000 00	6

CASH RECEIPTS JOURNAL   PAGE 6

The abbreviation *NP* in the Doc. No. column stands for *Note Payable*.

Entry to record cash received for a note payable

Paying principal and interest on a note payable at maturity

When cash is paid for interest, the amount paid is debited to another expense account titled Interest Expense.

> August 1, 1989. Paid the Royal Bank of Canada in full for Note Payable No. 4 (principal, $4 000.00; interest, $180.00), $4 180.00. Cheque No. 724.

Notes Payable	
4 000.00	

Interest Expense	
180.00	

Cash	
	4 180.00

Analysing the payment of principal and interest. The cheque stub is the source document for recording the transaction. *(CONCEPT: Objective Evidence)* In this transaction the balance of the liability account Notes Payable is decreased. The balance of the other expense account Interest Expense is increased. The balance of the asset account Cash is decreased. Therefore, Notes Payable is debited for $4 000.00; Interest Expense is debited for $180.00; and Cash is credited for $4 180.00.

Recording the payment of principal and interest. This transaction is recorded in a cash payments journal as shown below.

					GENERAL		ACCOUNTS PAYABLE DEBIT	PURCHASES DISCOUNT CREDIT	CASH CREDIT	
		DATE	ACCOUNT TITLE	CHEQUE NO.	POST. REF.	DEBIT	CREDIT			
3	{		*Notes Payable*	724		4 000 00				4 180 00	3
4	{		*Interest Expense*			180 00					4

CASH PAYMENTS JOURNAL — PAGE 22

Entry to record paying principal and interest on a note payable at maturity

Issuing a note payable for an extension of time

If a business is unable to pay an account when due, the business may ask for an extension of time. Sometimes, when a request for more time is made, the business is asked to issue a note payable. The note payable does not pay the amount owed to the creditor. However, the form of the liability is changed from an account payable to a note payable.

> *February 25, 1989. Issued a 60-day, 8% note to Sykes Lumber Company for an extension of time on this account payable, $3 000.00. Note Payable No. 5.*

Analysing the issuance of a note payable for an extension of time. A copy of the note is the source document for recording the transaction. *(CONCEPT: Objective Evidence)* In this transaction the balance of the liability account Accounts Payable is decreased. The balance of the liability account Notes Payable is increased. The balance of the creditor's account, Sykes Lumber Company, in the accounts payable ledger, is also decreased. Therefore, Accounts Payable is debited for $3 000.00. Notes Payable is credited for $3 000.00. The creditor's account, Sykes Lumber Company, is debited for $3 000.00.

Whenever Accounts Payable is decreased, the creditor's account in the accounts payable ledger also is decreased by the same amount.

GENERAL LEDGER

Accounts Payable	
3 000.00	

Notes Payable	
	3 000.00

ACCOUNTS PAYABLE LEDGER

Sykes Lumber Company	
3 000.00	

Recording the issuance of a note payable. This transaction is recorded in a general journal as shown below.

	DATE	ACCOUNT TITLE	POST. REF.	DEBIT	CREDIT	
17	25	Accts. Pay./Sykes Lumber Co.	/	300000		17
18		Notes Payable			300000	18
19		Note Payable No. 5.				19
20						20
21						21

GENERAL JOURNAL — PAGE 3

Entry to record issuance of a note payable for an extension of time on an account payable

When this entry is posted, the accounts payable account for Sykes Lumber Company will be closed. The account payable is replaced by the note payable.

Paying a note payable. Note Payable No. 5 is due on April 26. On that date, Lin's issues a cheque for $3 039.45 to Sykes Lumber Company. This cheque is in payment of the principal, $3 000.00, and interest, $39.45. The cheque is recorded in the cash payments journal as the payment of Note Payable No. 5. Notes Payable is debited for $3 000.00. Interest Expense is debited for $39.45. Cash is credited for $3 039.45. The journal entry for Note Payable No. 5 is similar to the one for Note Payable No. 4, page 524.

Bank discount

Some banks require that the interest be paid in advance of the time a borrower signs a note. Interest on a note collected in advance by a bank is called bank discount. The amount received for a note after the bank has deducted the bank discount is called proceeds. A note on which interest is paid in advance is called a discounted note.

> *March 25, 1989. Discounted at 10% at the Royal Bank of Canada Lin's 6-month non-interest-bearing note, $2 500.00. Note Payable No. 6. The bank credited Lin's current account for the proceeds, $2 375.00.*

Analysing the issuance of a discounted note payable. A copy of the note payable is the source document for recording the transaction. *(CONCEPT: Objective Evidence)* In this transaction the balances of the asset account Cash and the other expense account Interest Expense are increased. Therefore, Cash is debited for $2 375.00. Interest Expense is debited for $125.00. Notes Payable is credited for $2 500.00. The amount of interest is figured on the next page.

Cash	
2 375.00	

Interest Expense	
125.00	

Notes Payable	
	2 500.00

$$\begin{array}{ccccccc} \text{Maturity} & & \text{Interest} & & & & \text{Bank} \\ \text{Value} & \times & \text{Rate} & \times & \text{Time} & = & \text{Discount} \end{array}$$

$$\$2\,500.00 \times 10\% \times \frac{6}{12}\,\text{Year} = \$125.00$$

The proceeds are figured below.

$$\begin{array}{ccccc} \text{Maturity} & & \text{Bank} & & \\ \text{Value} & - & \text{Discount} & = & \text{Proceeds} \end{array}$$

$$\$2\,500.00 - \$125.00 = \$2\,375.00$$

Entry to record cash received for a discounted note payable

Recording the issuance of a discounted note payable and the receipt of cash. This transaction is recorded in a cash receipts journal as shown below.

Recording the payment of a discounted note payable. When Note Payable No. 6 is paid on September 25, Cheque No. 956 is issued to the Royal Bank of Canada. This cheque is in payment of the principal. No payment of interest is necessary at this time because the bank collected the interest in advance. This transaction is recorded in a cash payments journal as shown below.

Entry to record payment of a discounted note payable

NOTES RECEIVABLE

Promissory notes that a business accepts from customers are called notes receivable. Notes receivable within one year are classified as current assets of a business.

Accepting a note receivable from a customer

A charge customer who is unable to pay an account on the due date may request additional time. When a request for more time is made, a business may agree to accept a note receivable. A note receivable does not pay the amount the customer owes. However, the form of the asset is changed from an account receivable to a note receivable.

> February 15, 1989. Received a 2-month, 9% note from Dona Konich for an extension of time on her account, $500.00. Note Receivable No. 8.

Analysing the acceptance of a note receivable. The original copy of a note receivable is the source document for recording the transaction. *(CONCEPT: Objective Evidence)* In this transaction the balance of the asset account Notes Receivable is increased. The balance of the asset account Accounts Receivable is decreased. The balance of the customer's account, Dona Konich, in the accounts receivable ledger is also decreased. Therefore, Notes Receivable is debited for $500.00. Accounts Receivable is credited for $500.00. The customer's account, Dona Konich, is credited for $500.00.

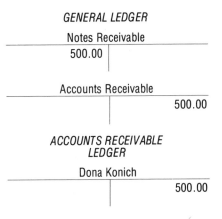

GENERAL LEDGER

Notes Receivable

| 500.00 | |

Accounts Receivable

| | 500.00 |

ACCOUNTS RECEIVABLE LEDGER

Dona Konich

| | 500.00 |

> Whenever Accounts Receivable is decreased, the named customer's account in the accounts receivable ledger must also be decreased the same amount.

Recording the acceptance of a note receivable. This transaction is recorded in a general journal as shown below.

	DATE	ACCOUNT TITLE	POST. REF.	DEBIT	CREDIT	
		GENERAL JOURNAL			PAGE 3	
6	15	Notes Receivable		50000		6
7		Accts. Rec. / Dona Konich	✓		50000	7
8		Note Rec. No. 8.				8
9						9

Entry to record a note received for an extension of time on an account

When this entry is posted, the account receivable account for Dona Konich will be closed. This account receivable is replaced by the note receivable.

Collecting principal and interest on a note receivable at maturity

The amount of interest received is credited to a revenue account titled Interest Income.

> April 15, 1989. Received cash from Dona Konich in settlement of Note Receivable No. 8 (principal, $500.00; interest, $7.50), $507.50. Receipt No. 238.

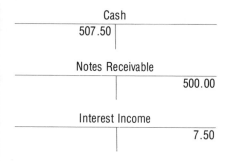

Cash	
507.50	

Notes Receivable	
	500.00

Interest Income	
	7.50

Analysing the receipt of principal and interest. The receipt issued for the cash received from Dona Konich is the source document for recording the transaction. *(CONCEPT: Objective Evidence)* In this transaction the balance of the asset account Cash is increased. The balance of the asset account Notes Receivable is decreased. The balance of the other revenue account Interest Income is increased. Therefore, Cash is debited for $507.50. Notes Receivable is credited for $500.00. Interest Income is credited for $7.50.

Recording the receipt of principal and interest. This transaction is recorded in a cash receipts journal as shown below.

				CASH RECEIPTS JOURNAL						PAGE *18*
				1	2	3	4	5	6	
				GENERAL		ACCOUNTS RECEIVABLE CREDIT	SALES CREDIT	SALES TAX PAYABLE CREDIT	CASH DEBIT	
	DATE	ACCOUNT TITLE	DOC. NO.	POST. REF.	DEBIT	CREDIT				
18	*15*	*Notes Receivable*	*R238*			*500 00*				*507 50*	18
19		*Interest Income*				*7 50*					19
20											20
21											21

Entry to record collection of principal and interest on a note receivable at maturity

After the entry is recorded, Note Receivable No. 8 is marked *Paid* and is returned to Dona Konich, the maker.

Dishonored note receivable

A note that is not paid when due is called a dishonored note. The balance of the notes receivable account should show only the amount of those notes that probably will be collected. The amount of a dishonored note receivable should therefore be removed from the notes receivable account. The amount of the note plus interest income earned on the note is still owed by the customer. Therefore, the amount owed should be debited to the accounts receivable account in the general ledger. The amount owed also should be debited to the customer's account in the accounts receivable ledger. The customer's account will then show the total amount owed by the customer including the amount of the dishonored note. This information may be important if the customer requests credit in the future.

> *February 20, 1989. John Vargo dishonored Note Receivable No. 3, a 1 month, 9% note for $400.00 plus interest due today (principal, $400.00; interest, $3.00), $403.00. Memorandum No. 36.*

Analysing a dishonored note receivable. A memorandum is the source document for recording the transaction. *(CONCEPT: Objective Evidence)*

In this transaction the balance of the asset account Accounts Receivable is increased. The balance of the asset account Notes Receivable is decreased. The balance of the other revenue account Interest Income is increased. The balance of the customer's account, John Vargo, in the accounts receivable ledger also is increased. Therefore, Accounts Receivable and John Vargo are each debited for $403.00 ($400.00 principal plus $3.00 interest). Notes Receivable is credited for $400.00, the amount of the note. Interest Income is credited for $3.00, the amount of interest earned ($400.00 × .09 × 1/12 yr. = $3.00). The interest income has been earned even though it is not paid. John Vargo owes the principal amount of the note plus the interest earned. Therefore, both principal and interest are debited to Accounts Receivable and the customer's account.

GENERAL LEDGER

Accounts Receivable

| 403.00 | |

Notes Receivable

| | 400.00 |

Interest Income

| | 3.00 |

ACCOUNTS RECEIVABLE LEDGER

John Vargo

| 403.00 | |

Recording a dishonored note receivable. This transaction is recorded in a general journal as shown below.

	DATE	ACCOUNT TITLE	POST. REF.	DEBIT	CREDIT	
		GENERAL JOURNAL			PAGE *3*	
9	20	Accts. Rec. / John Vargo		40300		9
10		Notes Receivable			40000	10
11		Interest Income			300	11
12		Memorandum No. 36.				12
13						13
14						14

Entry to record a dishonored note receivable

Later Lin's may decide that the account cannot be collected from Mr. Vargo. If so, the balance of the account will be written off as a bad debt. At that time Allowance for Uncollectible Accounts will be debited, and Accounts Receivable and John Vargo's account will be credited.

ACCOUNTING TERMS

What is the meaning of each of the following?

1. promissory note
2. date of a note
3. time of a note
4. payee of a note
5. principal of a note
6. interest rate of a note
7. maturity date of a note
8. maker of a note
9. number of a note
10. interest
11. interest-bearing notes
12. non-interest-bearing notes
13. maturity value
14. notes payable
15. bank discount
16. proceeds
17. discounted note
18. notes receivable
19. dishonored note

QUESTIONS FOR INDIVIDUAL STUDY

1. Why do many businesses periodically borrow cash for short periods of time?
2. Why do many businesses prefer to have a note receivable from a customer than an account receivable?
3. What is the difference between the payee and the maker of a note?
4. What does "interest at 8%" mean?
5. What is the source document for recording the issuance of a note payable?
6. When an interest-bearing note is paid, why is Cash credited for a greater amount than Notes Payable is debited?
7. What accounts are debited and credited when a business issues an interest-bearing note payable as an extension of time on its account payable?
8. How much will the maker receive for a one-year non-interest-bearing note of $2 000.00, discounted at 10%?

9. What accounts are debited and credited when a non-interest-bearing note payable is discounted at a bank?
10. What accounts are debited and credited when a discounted note payable is paid at maturity?
11. A business may accept a note receivable from a charge customer for an extension of time on the customer's account receivable. Does this acceptance change the total amount of the assets of the business?
12. What accounts are debited and credited when a business receives the principal and interest on a note receivable at maturity?
13. Why is interest income recorded at the time a note is dishonored even though cash has not been received?
14. What accounts are debited and credited when a customer dishonors an interest-bearing note receivable?

CASES FOR MANAGEMENT DECISION

CASE 1 Bonita Booker purchased $4 000.00 worth of merchandise on account from Duncan Appliances on February 1. Duncan Appliances' terms of sale require payment on accounts within 30 days. However, Mrs. Booker purchased the merchandise with the understanding that she could issue a 9% note payable with payment due no later than July 1. On February 1 Mrs. Booker instructed her accountant to issue the note payable to Duncan Appliances. As payments on account are due in 30 days, the accountant suggested that the note be issued on March 2. On what date would you suggest that the note be issued? Why?

CASE 2 Byers Corporation has a $3 000.00, 4-month, 9% note receivable which has been dishonored. Two company accounting clerks cannot agree on the best way to record the dishonored note. Karl Hodovan recommends Notes Receivable be credited $3 000.00 and Allowance for Uncollectible Accounts be debited for $3 000.00. Nancy Soltis recommends Accounts Receivable and the customer's account be debited for $3 090.00. Then Notes Receivable be credited for $3 000.00 and Interest Income be credited for $90.00. Which recommendation is the more desirable entry? Why?

DRILLS FOR UNDERSTANDING

DRILL 26-D 1   Recording principal, interest, and bank discount for notes payable

Instructions: Use a form such as the one on the next page. Based on the transactions given, indicate by a check mark which account(s) should be debited and which account(s) credited. Transaction 1 is shown as an example. Note payable is abbreviated NP.

Trans. No.	Cash		Notes Payable		Accounts Payable		Interest Expense	
	Debit	Credit	Debit	Credit	Debit	Credit	Debit	Credit
1.	✓			✓				

Transactions

1. Issued a 3-month, 9% note, $2 000.00, for cash. NP216.
2. Issued a 60-day, 9½% note, $600.00, for an extension of time on an account payable. NP217.
3. Issued a 1-year, 10% note, $3 000.00, for cash. NP218.
4. Discounted at 8% a 6-month non-interest-bearing note, $2 500.00. NP219.
5. Discounted at 9% a 90-day non-interest-bearing note, $4 000.00. NP220.
6. Discounted at 10% a 1-year non-interest-bearing note, $5 000.00. NP221.
7. Paid in full NP216.
8. Paid in full NP217.
9. Paid in full NP218.
10. Paid in full NP219.
11. Paid in full NP220.
12. Paid in full NP221.

DRILL 26-D 2 Recording principal and interest for notes receivable

Instructions: Use a form such as the one below. Based on the transactions given, indicate by a check mark which account(s) should be debited and which account(s) credited. Transaction 1 is shown as an example. Note receivable is abbreviated NR.

Trans. No.	Cash		Notes Receivable		Accounts Receivable		Interest Income	
	Debit	Credit	Debit	Credit	Debit	Credit	Debit	Credit
1.			✓			✓		

Transactions

1. Received a 3-month, 9% note for an extension of time on account, $800.00. NR15.
2. Received a 60-day, 8% note for an extension of time on account, $3 000.00. NR16.
3. Received a 6-month, 10% note for an extension of time on account, $4 000.00. NR17.
4. Received a 1-year, 9% note for an extension of time on account, $5 000.00. NR18.
5. Received cash in settlement of NR15.
6. Received cash in settlement of NR16.
7. Received notice that maker of NR17 has dishonored the note on this date.
8. Received cash in settlement of NR18.

APPLICATION PROBLEMS

PROBLEM 26-1 Recording notes payable, interest, and bank discount

The transactions on the next page were completed by Kresky Furniture during part of the current fiscal year.

instructions: 1. Record the following transactions. Use a cash receipts journal (page 15), a cash payments journal (page 12), and a general journal (page 5) similar to those illustrated in this chapter. Source documents are abbreviated as: cheque, C; note payable, NP.

Jan. 3. Issued a 30-day, 9% note payable to Havericak Company for an extension of time on account, $1 500.00. NP111.
   4. Paid Cedar River Marina for NP71 (90–day, 8½% note due today; principal, $8 000.00; interest, $167.67), $8 167.67. C62.
   10. Paid Canadian Imperial Bank of Commerce for NP83 (60-day, 9% note due today; principal, $2 500.00; interest, $36.99), $2 536.99. C122.
   17. Discounted at 10% at Bank of Nova Scotia a 45-day, non-interest-bearing note payable, $4 000.00 (bank discount, $49.32; proceeds, $3 950.68). NP112. The bank credited our current account for the proceeds.
Feb. 2. Paid Havericak Company for NP111 (principal, $1 500.00; interest, $11.10), $1 511.10. C198.
   20. Issued a 90-day, 10% note payable to Toronto-Dominion Bank, $2 500.00. The bank credited our current account for the principal. NP113.
Mar. 1. Paid Bank of Nova Scotia for NP112, $4 000.00. C267.
   10. Issued a 30-day, 9½% note payable to Southwest Supplies for an extension of time on account, $500.00. NP114.
Apr. 9. Paid Southwest Supplies for NP114 (principal, $500.00; interest, $3.90), $503.90. C341.
May 21. Paid Bank of Nova Scotia for NP113 (principal, $2 500.00; interest, $61.64), $2 561.64. C401.

Instructions: 2. Prove the cash receipts and cash payments journals.

PROBLEM 26-2 Recording notes receivable and interest

The transactions below were completed by Bertram Boat Supplies during part of the current fiscal year.

Instructions: 1. Record the following transactions. Use a cash receipts journal (page 11) and a general journal (page 3) similar to those illustrated in this chapter. Source documents are abbreviated as: memorandum, M; note receivable, NR; receipt, R.

Jan. 10. Received a 60-day, 9½% note receivable from Karl Grimes for an extension of time on account, $1 000.00. NR32.
   12. Received a cheque from Carlota Campillo in settlement of NR28 (20-day, 9% note receivable due today; principal, $300.00; interest, $1.48), $301.48. R28.
   22. Received a 3-month, 9% note receivable from Fred Chaney for an extension of time on account, $750.00. NR33.
Feb. 17. Received a cheque from Cynthia Hill in settlement of NR21 (6-month, 8½% note receivable due today; principal, $800.00; interest, $34.00), $834.00. R31.
Mar. 11. Received a cheque from Karl Grimes in settlement of NR32 (principal, $1 000.00; interest, $15.62), $1 015.62. R78.
Apr. 22. Fred Chaney dishonored NR33 due today. Charged the amount of the note receivable and the interest to his account (principal, $750.00; interest, $16.88), $766.88. M145.

Instructions: 2. Prove the cash receipts journal.

ENRICHMENT PROBLEMS

MASTERY PROBLEM 26-M Recording notes, interest, and bank discount

The transactions below were completed by Mayport Corporation during part of the current fiscal year.

Instructions: 1. Record the following transactions. Use a cash receipts journal (page 15), a cash payments journal (page 9), and a general journal (page 6) like those illustrated in this chapter. Source documents are abbreviated as: cheque, C; memorandum, M; note payable, NP; note receivable, NR; receipt, R.

Jan. 2. Received a 2-month, non-interest-bearing note receivable from Jack Romain for an extension of time on account, $400.00. NR132.
   5. Issued a 60-day, 9% note payable to Soforenko Development Company for an extension of time on account, $2 500.00. NP115.
   7. Discounted at 9½% at Continental Bank of Canada our 60-day, non-interest-bearing note payable, $8 000.00 (bank discount, $124.93; proceeds, $7 875.07). NP116. The bank credited our current account for the proceeds.
   10. Received a 45-day, 10% note receivable from Judy Elsmore for an extension of time on account, $750.00. NR133.
   17. Issued a 30-day, 9% note payable to McDaniel's for an extension of time on account, $2 400.00. NP117.
   27. Issued a 2-month, 9½% note payable to Bank of Montreal, $3 000.00. NP118. The bank credited our current account for the principal.
Feb. 14. Received a 1-month, 9% note receivable from Don Walters for an extension of time on account, $900.00. NR134.
   16. Paid McDaniel's for NP117 (principal $2 400.00; interest, $17.75), $2 417.75. C318.
   24. Received a cheque from Judy Elsmore in settlement of NR133 (principal, $750.00; interest, $9.25), $759.25. R212.
Mar. 2. Jack Romain dishonored NR132 due today, $400.00. Charged the amount of the note receivable to his account. M85.
   6. Paid Soforenko Development Company for NP115 (principal, $2 500.00; interest, $36.99), $2 536.99. C329.
   8. Paid Continental Bank of Canada for NP116. C333.
   14. Received a cheque from Don Walters in settlement of NR134 (principal, $900.00; interest, $6.75), $906.75. R296.
   20. Received a 2-month, non-interest-bearing note receivable from Katharine McNeil for an extension of time on account, $450.00. NR135.
   27. Paid Bank of Montreal for NP118 (principal, $3 000.00; interest, $47.50), $3 047.50. C346.

Instructions: 2. Prove the cash receipts and cash payments journals.

CHALLENGE PROBLEM 26-C Recording notes, interest, and bank discount

Introductory remarks. Interest may be figured for a period of less than one year. To do this the principal is multiplied by the interest rate and by the fraction of the year. The interest on a 9% interest-bearing note for $600.00 for 4 months is figured on the next page.

$$\begin{array}{ccccccc} & & \text{Interest} & & \text{Fraction} & & \text{Interest for} \\ \text{Principal} & \times & \text{Rate} & \times & \text{of Year} & = & \text{Fraction of Year} \\ \$600.00 & \times & .09 & \times & \dfrac{4}{12} & = & \dfrac{\$216.00}{12} = \$18.00 \end{array}$$

The time of a note is stated often as a number of days, such as 30 days or 60 days. Interest on a 9% interest-bearing note for $900.00 for 60 days is figured below. Interest is normally rounded to the nearest cent.

$$\begin{array}{ccccccc} & & \text{Interest} & & \text{Fraction} & & \text{Interest for} \\ \text{Principal} & \times & \text{Rate} & \times & \text{of Year} & = & \text{Fraction of Year} \\ \$900.00 & \times & .09 & \times & \dfrac{60}{365} & = & \dfrac{\$4\,860.00}{365} = \$13.32 \end{array}$$

The transactions below were completed by Helco Equipment Company during the current year.

Instructions: 1. Record the following transactions. Use a cash receipts journal (page 40), a cash payments journal (page 26), and a general journal (page 12) similar to those illustrated in this chapter. Source documents are abbreviated as: cheque, C; memorandum, M; note payable, NP; note receivable, NR; receipt, R.

Jan. 3. Received a 3-month, 9½% note receivable dated December 29 from Paula Ferrell for an extension of time on account, $800.00. NR62.

6. Received a 30-day, 10% note receivable dated January 5 from Daryl Seaver for an extension of time on account, $350.00. NR63.

24. Issued a 1-month, 9% note payable to Holman Distributors for an extension of time on account, $1 500.00. NP21.

Feb. 4. Received a cheque from Daryl Seaver in settlement of NR63. R260.

24. Paid Holman Distributors for NP21. C105.

Mar. 4. Issued a 90-day, 8½% note payable to Lee & Gates Company for an extension of time on account, $4 000.00. NP22.

11. Purchased sales display equipment from Merita Company, $2 500.00. Paid cash, $1 000.00, and issued a 60-day, 9% note payable for the balance, $1 500.00. C130; NP23.

Record the transaction in the cash payments journal in one combined entry.

29. Received notice from the bank that Paula Ferrell dishonored NR62. Charged principal and interest to her account. M72.

May 3. Discounted at 9½% at Bank of Nova Scotia our 30-day, non-interest-bearing note, $1 800.00. NP24. The bank credited our current account for the proceeds.

10. Paid Merita Company for NP23. C148.

June 2. Paid Bank of Nova Scotia for NP24. C191.

2. Paid Lee & Gates Company for NP22. C198.

Oct. 15. Received a cheque from Paula Ferrell for half of the $819.00 balance charged to her account on March 29. R279. Wrote off the remainder of this account receivable as uncollectible. M124.

Record the cheque in the cash receipts journal. Record the write-off of the customer's account in the general journal.

Instructions: 2. Prove the cash receipts and cash payments journals.

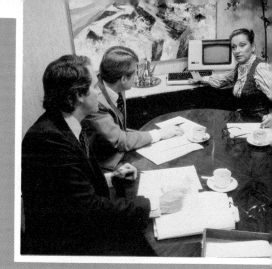

End-of-Fiscal-Period Work for a Corporation

ENABLING PERFORMANCE TASKS

After studying Chapter 27, you will be able to:

a. Define accounting terms related to end-of-fiscal-period work for a corporation.
b. Explain accounting principles and practices related to end-of-fiscal-period work for a corporation.
c. Record a trial balance on a work sheet for a corporation.
d. Plan adjustments on a work sheet for a corporation.
e. Complete a work sheet for a corporation.
f. Prepare financial statements for a corporation.
g. Journalize adjusting and closing entries for a corporation.
h. Journalize the declaration and payment of a dividend.

Financial information about a corporation is needed by a number of people. *(CONCEPT: Adequate Disclosure)* Managers need information to help make sound management decisions. Owners need to know how well their investment is doing. Creditors need to know how well the corporation is meeting its credit obligations.

PREPARING A WORK SHEET FOR A CORPORATION

Work sheets for sole proprietorships, partnerships, and corporations are similar. All businesses use a work sheet to plan adjustments and provide information for financial statements. Lin's Music Centre prepares a work sheet and financial statements at the end of each year. *(CONCEPT: Accounting Period Cycle)* Lin's eight-column work sheet is similar to the one used by Denim Threads in Part 3.

Recording a trial balance on a work sheet

To prepare a work sheet, a trial balance is first entered in the Trial Balance columns. General ledger accounts are listed in the same order as they appear in a general ledger. Trial Balance columns are totalled to prove equality of debits and credits.

Lin's trial balance on December 31, 1989, is shown on the work sheet, pages 538 and 539. Accounts are similar to a sole proprietorship or partnership except for a corporation's capital, federal income tax, and dividends.

Separate general ledger capital accounts are kept for each owner of a sole proprietorship or a partnership. However, for a corporation a separate capital account is not kept for each owner. Instead, a single capital account is kept for the investment of all owners. A corporation's ownership is divided into units. Each unit of ownership in a corporation is called a share of stock. An owner of one or more shares of a corporation is called a shareholder. Total shares of ownership in a corporation are called capital stock. A second capital account is used to record a corporation's earnings. An amount earned by a corporation and not yet distributed to shareholders is called retained earnings.

Preparing adjustments on a work sheet

Some general ledger accounts need to be brought up to date before end-of-fiscal-period reports are prepared. Accounts are brought up to date by planning adjustments on a work sheet as described in Chapter 14. Most corporation adjustments on a work sheet are similar to those for sole proprietorships and partnerships.

Seven expense accounts and Merchandise Inventory of Lin's need adjustments at the end of a fiscal period. Three adjustments are similar to those made by Denim Threads in Chapter 14. (1) Merchandise Inventory. (2) Supplies Expense. (3) Insurance Expense. Lin's makes adjusting entries for four other expense accounts that are also similar for corporations, sole proprietorships, and partnerships. (1) Bad Debts Expense. (2) Depreciation Expense — Delivery Equipment. (3) Depreciation Expense — Office Equipment. (4) Depreciation Expense — Store Equipment.One additional adjustment for federal income tax owed is necessary for a corporation. This adjustment is not made for sole proprietorships and partnerships because taxes are paid by the owners, not the business. Adjustments for related asset or liability accounts generally are made in the order listed on a work sheet.

Adjustment for bad debts expense. Estimated bad debts expense for a fiscal period needs to be brought up to date. Two accounts are used for a bad debts adjustment — Bad Debts Expense and Allowance for Uncollectible Accounts. An analysis of Lin's bad debts expense adjustment is described in

Chapter 24, page 489. Lin's bad debts expense adjustment is shown in the work sheet Adjustments columns, pages 538 and 539.

Steps for recording the adjustment for bad debts expense on a work sheet are described below.

1 Write the amount, $4 740.00, in the Adjustments Debit column on line with the title Bad Debts Expense. (Line 35)

2 Write the amount, $4 740.00, in the Adjustments Credit column on line with the title Allowance for Uncollectible Accounts. (Line 4)

3 Label the two parts of this adjustment with the small letter "a" in parentheses, (a).

Adjustments for merchandise inventory. The merchandise inventory balance shown in a trial balance is the beginning inventory for a fiscal period. Two adjusting entries are made to bring the merchandise inventory account up to date. These adjustments are the same as described in Chapter 14.

The beginning merchandise inventory, $182 224.00, is credited to Merchandise Inventory and debited to Income Summary. This adjustment is shown on lines 5 and 28 of the work sheet, pages 538 and 539. After the beginning merchandise inventory adjustment is journalized and posted, Merchandise Inventory has a zero balance. The amount of the beginning merchandise inventory is a debit in the income summary account.

The merchandise inventory account is debited, $187 462.00, the value of the ending merchandise inventory. *(CONCEPT: Historical Cost)* The same amount is credited to the income summary account. The balance of Merchandise Inventory, after the second adjustment, is $187 462.00. The amount of the ending merchandise inventory is a credit to Income Summary. The adjustment for ending merchandise inventory is on lines 5 and 28 of the work sheet.

Adjustment for supplies. Two accounts are used in adjusting supplies: Supplies and Supplies Expense. Lin's supplies adjustment is the same as the one described in Chapter 14.

The value of supplies used, $4 284.00, is a credit to Supplies. Supplies Expense is debited for the same amount. The supplies adjustment is on lines 6 and 46 of the work sheet, pages 538 and 539.

Adjustment for prepaid insurance. Insurance premiums are debited to a prepaid insurance account when paid. Insurance expenses however must be recorded for the fiscal period in which they are used. *(CONCEPT: Matching Expenses with Revenue)* Therefore, Prepaid Insurance and Insurance Expense are adjusted at the end of a fiscal period.

Lin's Music Centre
Work Sheet
For Year Ended December 31, 1989

#	ACCOUNT TITLE	TRIAL BALANCE Debit	TRIAL BALANCE Credit	ADJUSTMENTS Debit	ADJUSTMENTS Credit	INCOME STATEMENT Debit	INCOME STATEMENT Credit	BALANCE SHEET Debit	BALANCE SHEET Credit
1	Cash	65 903 00						65 903 00	
2	Notes Receivable	2 649 00						2 649 00	
3	Accounts Receivable	42 135 00						42 135 00	
4	Allow. for Uncoll. Accts.		280 00		(a) 474 00				502 00
5	Merchandise Inventory	182 224 00		(c) 187 462 00	(b) 182 224 00			187 462 00	
6	Supplies	6 691 00			(d) 4 284 00			2 407 00	
7	Prepaid Insurance	12 662 00			(e) 7 884 00			4 778 00	
8	Delivery Equipment	17 880 00						17 880 00	
9	Accum. Depn.-Delivery Equip.		5 250 00		(f) 1 900 00				7 150 00
10	Office Equipment	9 710 00						9 710 00	
11	Accum. Depn.-Office Equip.		1 950 00		(g) 950 00				2 900 00
12	Store Equipment	41 175 00						41 175 00	
13	Accum. Depn.-Store Equip.		5 400 00		(h) 2 840 00				8 240 00
14	Notes Payable								
15	Accounts Payable		16 805 00						16 805 00
16	Employees' Income Tax Pay.		1 816 00						1 816 00
17	Federal Income Tax Pay.				(i) 970 00				970 00
18	CPP Payable		327 00						327 00
19	Sales Tax Payable		4 740 00						4 740 00
20	UI Payable		506 00						506 00
21	Hosp. Ins. Premiums Pay.		398 00						398 00
22	Canada Savings Bonds Pay.		400 00						400 00
23	United Way Donations Pay.		16 00						16 00
24	Donations Payable								

Account Title	Trial Balance Debit	Trial Balance Credit	Adjustments Debit	Adjustments Credit	Income Statement Debit	Income Statement Credit	Balance Sheet Debit	Balance Sheet Credit
25 Capital Stock		200 000 00						200 000 00
26 Retained Earnings		87 929 00						87 929 00
27 Income Summary			(b) 182 224 00	(c) 187 462 00	182 224 00	187 462 00		
28 Sales		959 376 00				959 376 00		
29 Sales Returns & Allow.	11 376 00				11 376 00			
30 Purchases	685 902 00				685 902 00			
31 Purchases Returns & Allow.		2 503 00				2 503 00		
32 Purchases Discount		5 081 00				5 081 00		
33 Advertising Expense	15 166 00				15 166 00			
34 Bad Debt Expense			(a) 4 740 00		4 740 00			
35 Credit Card Fee Expense	9 594 00				9 594 00			
36 Delivery Expense	5 040 00				5 040 00			
37 Depr. Exp.—Delivery Equip.			(f) 1 900 00		1 900 00			
38 Depr. Exp.—Office Equip.			(g) 950 00		950 00			
39 Depr. Exp.—Store Equip.			(h) 2 840 00		2 840 00			
40 Insurance Expense			(e) 7 884 00		7 884 00			
41 Miscellaneous Expense	10 417 00				10 417 00			
42 Payroll Taxes Expense	8 869 00				8 869 00			
43 Rent Expense	26 544 00				26 544 00			
44 Salary Expense	117 552 00				117 552 00			
45 Supplies Expense			(d) 4 284 00		4 284 00			
46 Interest Income		3 782 00				3 782 00		
47 Interest Expense	4 730 00				4 730 00			
48 Federal Income Tax	19 980 00		(i) 970 00		20 950 00			
49	1296 199 00	1296 199 00	393 254 00	393 254 00	1120 962 00	1158 204 00	374 099 00	336 857 00
50 Net Inc. after Fed. Inc. Tax					37 242 00			37 242 00
51					1158 204 00	1158 204 00	374 099 00	374 099 00

Completed work sheet for a corporation

Lin's prepaid insurance adjustment is the same as the one described in Chapter 14. The value of insurance used, *$7 884.00*, is credited to Prepaid Insurance. The same amount is debited to Insurance Expense. The prepaid insurance adjustment is on lines 7 and 41 of the work sheet, pages 538 and 539.

Adjustments for depreciation expense. Lin's depreciation expense adjustments are described in Chapter 25, pages 511–515.

Depreciation Expense — Delivery Equipment is debited for *$1 900.00*. Accumulated Depreciation — Delivery Equipment is credited for the same amount. This adjustment is on lines 9 and 38 of the work sheet, pages 538 and 539.

Depreciation Expense — Office Equipment is debited for *$950.00*. Accumulated Depreciation — Office Equipment is credited for the same amount. This adjustment is on lines 11 and 39 of the work sheet.

Depreciation Expense — Store Equipment is debited for *$2 840.00*. Accumulated Depreciation — Store Equipment is credited for the same amount. This adjustment is on lines 13 and 40 of the work sheet.

Preparing an adjustment for federal income tax and extending amounts on a work sheet

Corporations anticipating annual federal income taxes are required to estimate their current taxes based on the previous year's actual taxes. The estimated income tax is paid in monthly instalments. However, the actual income tax owed is computed at the end of the fiscal year. Based on the actual tax owed for a year, a corporation must file an annual tax return. Income tax owing but not paid in monthly instalments, must be paid within three months of the end of the fiscal year.

Lin's estimated $20 000.00 for income tax for 1989. They paid $1 665.00 in twelve monthly instalments for a total of $19 980.00. Each tax payment was recorded as a debit to Federal Income Tax and a credit to Cash.

Federal income tax is an expense of a corporation. However, the amount of tax depends on net income before the tax is recorded. Before federal income tax is figured, all adjustments on the work sheet are completed except the federal income tax adjustment. All amounts except the federal income tax account balance are extended to the appropriate Income Statement or Balance Sheet columns. Procedures for extending amounts are similar to those described in Chapter 14.

Two steps are followed to figure the amount of federal income tax owed.

1 Total on a separate sheet of paper the Income Statement columns of a work sheet. Figure the difference between the two totals. This difference is the net income before federal income tax. Lin's net income

before federal income tax is figured from the Income Statement columns of the work sheet, pages 538 and 539.

Total of Income Statement Credit column..................	$1 158 204.00
Less Total of Income Statement Debit column before federal income tax..	1 100 012.00
Equals Net Income before federal income tax	$ 58 192.00

2 Figure the amount of federal income tax using the tax rates provided by Revenue Canada, Taxation. Lin's federal income tax for 1989 is $20 950.00.

> Tax rates are obtainable from Revenue Canada, Taxation, indicating income tax rates for corporations. Each corporation should obtain the current applicable rates. The corporation rates current at the time of writing were used to compute Lin's federal income taxes.

Lin's federal income tax adjustment is shown in the T accounts at the right. Accounts are shown before and after the adjustment for federal income tax. Lin's paid monthly federal income tax instalments of $1 665.00 each. Federal Income Tax has a debit balance of $19 980.00 at the end of the fiscal period before adjustments are made.

Four questions are asked in analysing the adjustment for federal income tax.

1. What is the balance of the federal income tax account?.............................. $19 980.00
2. What should the balance be for this account?... $20 950.00
3. What must be done to correct the account balance? ....Add $ 970.00
4. What adjusting entry is made?..............
   Debit Federal Income Tax $ 970.00
   Credit Federal Income Tax Payable $ 970.00

BEFORE ADJUSTMENT

Federal Income Tax

Bal.	14 985.00
Oct. 15	1 665.00
Nov. 15	1 665.00
Dec. 15	1 665.00
Dec. 15 Bal. 19 980.00	

Federal Income Tax Payable

AFTER ADJUSTMENT

Federal Income Tax

Bal.	14 985.00
Oct. 15	1 665.00
Nov. 15	1 665.00
Dec. 15	1 665.00
Dec. 15 Bal. 19 980.00	
Dec. 31 (i)	970.00
Dec. 31 Bal. 20 950.00	

Federal Income Tax Payable

Dec. 31	(i)	970.00

Federal Income Tax is debited for $970.00 to show the increase in the balance of this expense account. The new balance of this account, *$20 950.00*, is the total federal income tax expense for the fiscal period. Federal Income Tax Payable is credited for $970.00 to show the increase in this liability account's balance. Lin's federal income tax payable account balance, *$970.00*, is the amount of income tax expense not paid at year end. Lin's federal income tax adjustment is on lines 17 and 49 of the work sheet, pages 538 and 539.

Steps in recording Lin's federal income tax adjustment on a work sheet are on the next page.

1 Write the amount, $970.00, in the Adjustments Debit column on line with Federal Income Tax. (Line 49)

2 Write the amount, $970.00, in the Adjustments Credit column on line with Federal Income Tax Payable. (Line 17)

>Federal Income Tax is an expense account. The account appears under a special heading "Income Tax" as the last item in the chart of accounts, page 394. Federal Income Tax Payable, a liability account, appears under the heading "Current Liabilities."

3 Label the two parts of this adjustment with the small letter "i" in parentheses, *(i)*.

After the federal income tax adjustment is recorded, the income tax accounts are extended to the appropriate work sheet columns. The federal income tax account balance is extended to the Income Statement Debit column. The federal income tax payable account balance is extended to the Balance Sheet Credit column.

Completing a corporate work sheet

Income Statement and Balance Sheet columns are totalled. Totals are written as shown on line 50 of the work sheet, page 539. The Income Statement Credit column total for Lin's is $37 242.00 more than the Income Statement Debit column total. (Credit column total, *$1 158 204.00,* less Debit column total, *$1 120 962.00,* equals difference, *$37 242.00.*) This amount, *$37 242.00,* is written in the Income Statement Debit column, line 51 of the work sheet. *Net Income After Federal Income Tax* is written in the Account Title column on the same line as the amount. Income Statement columns are then totalled as shown on line 52, page 539.

The net income amount after federal income tax, *$37 242.00,* is written in the Balance Sheet Credit column, line 51. Balance Sheet columns are totalled as shown on line 52, page 539. Double lines are ruled across all Income Statement and Balance Sheet columns as shown on line 52. The double lines show that the columns are in balance and assumed to be correct.

PREPARING FINANCIAL STATEMENTS FOR A CORPORATION

Financial statements are used to report financial progress and condition of a business. Corporation financial statements are similar to those prepared by sole proprietorships and partnerships. Lin's prepares three important financial statements. (1) Income statement. (2) Statement of shareholders' equity. (3) Balance sheet.

Income statement

An income statement reports financial progress of a business during a fiscal period. *(CONCEPT: Accounting Period Cycle)* Revenue, cost of merchandise sold, gross profit, operating expenses, and net income or loss are generally reported on income statements. *(CONCEPT: Adequate Disclosure)*

Lin's income statement is prepared from information on the work sheet, page 539. Procedures for preparing Lin's income statement are similar to those described in Chapter 15. Lin's income statement for the year ended December 31, 1989, is on page 544.

Lin's income statement differs from Denim Threads' income statement in four ways.

1. Income from operations is reported separately from net income. Income from operations is the income earned only from normal business activities. Lin's normal business activities are selling musical instruments and stereo equipment. Other revenue and expenses, such as interest income and interest expense, are not normal business activities. Other revenue and expenses are not used to figure income from operations.

2. Net sales is listed in the Operating Revenue section. Total sales less sales returns and allowances is called net sales . Net sales is reported in the Operating Revenue section of Lin's income statement as shown below.

```
Operating Revenue:
    Sales . . . . . . . . . . . . . . . . . . .   $959 376.00
    Less Sales Returns & Allowances . . . .        11 376.00
    Net Sales . . . . . . . . . . . . . . .                      $948 000.00
```

3. Net purchases is reported in the Cost of Merchandise Sold section. Total purchases less purchases returns and allowances and purchases discount is called net purchases. Net purchases is reported in the Cost of Merchandise Sold section of Lin's income statement as shown below.

```
    Purchases  . . . . . . . . .   . . . .   $685 902.00
    Less: Purch. Ret. & Allow.    $2 503.00
          Purchases Discount . .   5 081.00      7 584.00
    Net Purchases . . . . . . . . . . . .                 678 318.00
```

4. Net income before and net income after federal income tax are reported separately. Reporting net income before and after federal income tax is unique to corporation income statements. Corporations

pay federal income tax on their net income. However, federal income taxes are not paid by sole proprietorships and partnerships but are paid by the owners. Thus, sole proprietorships and partnerships do not report federal income tax on their income statements.

Lin's income statement for the year ended December 31, 1989, is below.

```
                     Lin's Music Centre
                     Income Statement
                For Year Ended December 31, 1989
Operating Revenue:
  Sales ....................................        $959 376.00
  Less Sales Returns & Allowances ...........         11 376.00
  Net Sales ................................                        $948 000.00
Cost of Merchandise Sold:
  Merchandise Inventory, January 1, 1989 .....        $182 224.00
  Purchases ....................  $685 902.00
  Less: Purch. Ret. & Allow.   $2 503.00
        Purchases Discount       5 081.00      7 584.00
  Net Purchases ...........................           678 318.00
  Total Cost of Mdse. Avail. for Sale .......        $860 542.00
  Less Mdse. Inventory, Dec. 31, 1989 ........        187 462.00
  Cost of Merchandise Sold ..................                       673 080.00
Gross Profit on Operations ...................                     $274 920.00
Operating Expenses:
  Advertising Expense .......................        $ 15 166.00
  Bad Debts Expense .........................           4 740.00
  Credit Card Fee Expense ...................           9 594.00
  Delivery Expense ..........................           5 040.00
  Depreciation Exp.--Delivery Equip. ........           1 900.00
  Depreciation Exp.--Office Equip. ..........             950.00
  Depreciation Exp.--Store Equip. ...........           2 840.00
  Insurance Expense .........................           7 884.00
  Miscellaneous Expense .....................          10 417.00
  Payroll Taxes Expense .....................           8 869.00
  Rent Expense ..............................          26 544.00
  Salary Expense ............................         117 552.00
  Supplies Expense ..........................           4 284.00
  Total Operating Expenses ..................                      215 780.00
Income from Operations ......................                     $ 59 140.00
Other Revenue:
  Interest Income ...........................        $  3 782.00
Other Expenses:
  Interest Expense ..........................           4 730.00
  Net Deduction .............................                          948.00
Net Income Before Federal Income Tax ..........                   $ 58 192.00
  Less Federal Income Tax ...................                       20 950.00
Net Income After Federal Income Tax ..........                    $ 37 242.00
```

Income statement for a corporation

Statement of shareholders' equity

A financial statement showing changes in a corporation's ownership for a fiscal period is called a statement of shareholders' equity. A shareholders' equity statement is similar to a capital statement for a sole proprietorship or a partnership.

A shareholders' equity statement contains two major sections. These sections relate to (a) capital stock and (b) earnings retained in a corporation. Lin's statement of shareholders' equity for the year ended December 31, 1989, is below.

```
                           Lin's Music Centre
                    Statement of Shareholders' Equity
                    For Year Ended December 31, 1989

Capital Stock:
    $100.00 Per Share ...........................
    Jan. 1, 1989, 2 000 Shares Issued ...........    $200 000.00
    Issued during 1989, None ...................        -0-
    Balance, Dec. 31, 1989, 2 000 Shares
      Issued ...................................                    $200 000.00
Retained Earnings:
    Jan. 1, 1989 ...............................    $117 929.00
    Plus Net Income After Taxes for 1989 ........  $ 37 242.00
    Less Dividends Declared and Paid
      during 1989 ..............................    30 000.00
    Net Increase during 1989 ...................                     7 242.00
    Balance, Dec. 31, 1989 .....................                    125 171.00
Total Shareholders' Equity, Dec. 31, 1989 .......                  $325 171.00
```

The first section of this statement shows that Lin's started the fiscal year, January 1, 1989, with $200 000.00 capital stock. This capital stock consisted of 2 000 shares of stock issued before January 1, 1989, for $100.00 per share. During 1989, Lin's did not issue any more capital stock. Thus, at the end of the fiscal year, Lin's still had $200 000.00 capital stock outstanding. This information is obtained from the previous year's statement and the capital stock account.

Statement of shareholders' equity for a corporation

The second section of Lin's equity statement shows that Lin's started on January 1, 1989, with $117 929.00 retained earnings. This amount represents previous years' earnings that have been kept in the business. For the fiscal year ended December 31, 1989, Lin's earned net income after federal income tax of $37 242.00. This amount is obtained from line 51 on the work sheet, page 539. During the year, dividends of $30 000.00 were paid. Earnings distributed to shareholders are called dividends. The amount of dividends paid is obtained from the general ledger account Retained Earnings. Changes in Lin's retained earnings during the fiscal year, 1989, are below.

Retained earnings balance, January 1, 1989		$117 929.00
Plus net income after taxes for 1989	$37 242.00	
Less dividends paid during 1989........................	30 000.00	
Net increase in retained earnings during 1989		7 242.00
Retained earnings balance, December 31, 1989		$125 171.00

Lin's capital stock, *$200 000.00,* plus retained earnings, *$125 171.00,* equals total shareholders' equity on December 31, 1989, *$325 171.00.* (CONCEPT: *Adequate Disclosure*)

Balance Sheet

A corporation balance sheet reports assets, liabilities, and shareholders' equity on a specific date. *(CONCEPT: Accounting Period Cycle)*

Lin's balance sheet is prepared from information on the work sheet, pages 538 and 539, and shareholders' equity statement, page 545.

```
                        Lin's Music Centre
                          Balance Sheet
                        December 31, 1989

                      ASSETS
Current Assets:
  Cash ........................................           $ 65 903.00
  Notes Receivable ...........................             2 649.00
  Accounts Receivable .....................   $42 135.00
    Less Allow. for Uncoll. Accounts .........  5 020.00    37 115.00
  Merchandise Inventory .....................            187 462.00
  Supplies ..................................              2 407.00
  Prepaid Insurance .........................             4 778.00
  Total Current Assets .....................                          $300 314.00
Fixed Assets:
  Delivery Equipment ........................  $ 17 880.00
    Less Accum. Depr.--Delivery Equip.........   7 150.00  $ 10 730.00
  Office Equipment ..........................  $  9 710.00
    Less Accum. Depr.--Office Equip ..........   2 900.00     6 810.00
  Store Equipment ...........................  $ 41 175.00
    Less Accum. Depr.--Store Equip ..........    8 240.00    32 935.00
  Total Fixed Assets .......................                            50 475.00
Total Assets ...............................                          $350 789.00
                     LIABILITIES
Current Liabilities:
  Accounts Payable ..........................            $ 16 805.00
  Employees' Income Tax Payable .............             1 816.00
  Federal Income Tax Payable ................              970.00
  CPP Payable ...............................              327.00
  Sales Tax Payable .........................             4 740.00
  UI Payable ................................              506.00
  Hospital Insurance Premiums Payable ........            398.00
  Canada Savings Bonds Payable ..............              40.00
  United Way Donations Payable ..............              16.00
Total Liabilities ..........................                          $ 25 618.00
               SHAREHOLDERS' EQUITY
Capital Stock ..............................            $200 000.00
Retained Earnings ..........................            125 171.00
Total Shareholders' Equity .................                          325 171.00
Total Liabilities and Shareholders' Equity.....                      $350 789.00
```

Balance sheet for a corporation

Procedures for preparing Lin's balance sheet are similar to those described in Chapter 15. Differences between Lin's balance sheet and the one prepared for Denim Threads are described below.

Classifying assets on a balance sheet. Lin's classifies its assets in two categories: Current Assets and Fixed Assets. These categories are based on the length of time the assets will be in use. A business owning both current assets and fixed assets usually lists them under separate headings on a balance sheet.

Cash and assets readily exchanged for cash or consumed within a year are called current assets. Current assets include such things as cash, accounts receivable, merchandise inventory, supplies, and prepaid insurance. Current asset accounts are listed on a balance sheet under the heading *Current Assets*. Current asset accounts usually are listed with Cash first followed by the other current assets. The other current assets often are listed in the order that they can be exchanged most readily for cash.

Assets to be used for a number of years are listed on a balance sheet under the heading *Fixed Assets*. Fixed assets include such things as delivery equipment, office equipment, and store equipment.

Classifying liabilities on a balance sheet

Lin's classifies both liabilities and assets on a balance sheet. Liabilities are classified according to the length of time until they are due. Liabilities due within a short time, usually within a year, are called current liabilities. Examples of current liabilities are Accounts Payable, Employees' Income Tax Payable, Federal Income Tax Payable, and CPP Payable. All of Lin's liabilities are listed on a balance sheet as current liabilities because they become due within a year.

Liabilities owed for more than a year are called long-term liabilities. An example of a long-term liability is Mortgage Payable. On December 31, 1989, Lin's does not have any long-term liabilities.

Sav-Energy Company has both current liabilities and long-term liabilities. A portion of Sav-Energy's balance sheet is below.

Total Assets		$172 862.69
Liabilities		
Current Liabilities:		
Accounts Payable	$6 699.00	
Sales Tax Payable	1 295.27	
Total Current Liabilities		$ 25 795.00
Long-term Liabilities:		
Mortgage Payable		46 000.00
Total Liabilities		$ 71 795.00

Reporting book value of asset accounts on a balance sheet. An asset's book value is reported on a balance sheet by listing three amounts. The amounts are (1) balance of the asset account, (2) balance of the asset's contra account, and (3) book value. Book value of Lin's accounts receivable and fixed asset accounts are on the partial balance sheet on the next page.

Liabilities section of a balance sheet showing current and long-term liabilities

```
                    Lin's Music Centre
                     Balance Sheet
                   December 31, 1989

          ASSETS

   Accounts Receivable ........................  $ 42 135.00
      Less Allow. for Uncoll. Accounts ..........    5 020.00      37 115.00

Fixed Assets:
   Delivery Equipment ........................  $ 17 880.00
      Less Accum. Depr.--Delivery Equip .........    7 150.00   $ 10 730.00
   Office Equipment ..........................  $  9 710.00
      Less Accum. Depr.--Office Equip ..........     2 900.00      6 810.00
   Store Equipment ...........................  $ 41 175.00
      Less Accum. Depr.--Store Equip ...........     8 240.00     32 935.00
   Total Fixed Assets ........................                                50 475.00
```

Book value of accounts receivable and fixed assets on a partial balance sheet

The book value of accounts receivable is reported on Lin's balance sheet as follows. The total amount of accounts receivable, $42 135.00, is written in the first column of the balance sheet. *Less Allowance for Uncollectible Accounts* is written on the next line, indented about 1 cm. The amount, $5 020.00, is written below the $42 135.00. The difference between the two amounts, $37 115.00, is written in the second amount column on the same line. The amount of the difference, $37 115.00, is the book value of accounts receivable on December 31, 1989. Similar procedures are followed to report book values of fixed asset accounts.

Reporting shareholders' equity on a balance sheet. A major difference between corporation balance sheets and sole proprietorship or partnership balance sheets is in the capital section. The capital section of Lin's balance sheet, page 546, is labelled *Shareholders' Equity*. Some corporations use the same label as sole proprietorships and partnerships: *Capital*. Either label is acceptable.

The shareholders' equity section contains accounts relating to capital stock and earnings kept in the business. For Lin's these accounts are Capital Stock and Retained Earnings. Total shareholders' equity on Lin's balance sheet, $325 171.00, is the same as on Lin's statement of shareholders' equity, page 545.

PREPARING ADJUSTING AND CLOSING ENTRIES

Corporations' end-of-period work is the same as for sole proprietorships and partnerships except for differences in equity accounts. After corporate financial statements are prepared, adjusting and closing entries are recorded and posted. A post-closing trial balance is then prepared.

Adjusting entries

A corporation's adjusting entries are made from the Adjustments columns of a work sheet. Each adjustment is journalized and posted to general ledger accounts. With the exception of federal income tax, adjustments are similar to those for sole proprietorships and partnerships. Lin's adjusting entries for December 31, 1989, taken from the work sheet, pages 538 and 539, are below.

	DATE	ACCOUNT TITLE	POST. REF.	DEBIT	CREDIT	
1	1989	*Adjusting Entries*				1
2	Dec. 31	Bad Debts Expense		4 740 00		2
3		Allow. for Uncoll. Accts.			4 740 00	3
4	31	Income Summary		182 224 00		4
5		Merchandise Inventory			182 224 00	5
6	31	Merchandise Inventory		187 462 00		6
7		Income Summary			187 462 00	7
8	31	Supplies Expense		4 284 00		8
9		Supplies			4 284 00	9
10	31	Insurance Expense		7 884 00		10
11		Prepaid Insurance			7 884 00	11
12	31	Depreciation Exp. - Delivery Equip.		1 900 00		12
13		Accum. Depr. - Delivery Equip.			1 900 00	13
14	31	Depreciation Exp. - Office Equip.		950 00		14
15		Accum. Depr. - Office Equip.			950 00	15
16	31	Depreciation Exp. - Store Equip.		2 840 00		16
17		Accum. Depr. - Store Equip.			2 840 00	17
18	31	Federal Income Tax		970 00		18
19		Federal Income Tax Payable			970 00	19
20						20
21						21
22						22

GENERAL JOURNAL — PAGE 27

Procedures for journalizing Lin's adjusting entries are similar to those described in Chapter 16. However, since Lin's uses special journals, adjusting entries are recorded in a general journal.

Adjusting entries for a corporation

Closing entries

Closing entries for a corporation are made from a work sheet's Income Statement columns. Closing entries for revenue and expense accounts are similar to those for sole proprietorships or partnerships. However, a corporation's final closing entry differs from those previously studied. After all revenue and expense balances are closed to Income Summary, the income summary balance is closed to Retained Earnings.

Closing entry for credit balance accounts. The closing entry for Lin's credit balance accounts on December 31, 1989, is below. Credit balance accounts are revenue (*Sales* and *Interest Income*) and reduction in cost accounts (*Purchases Returns and Allowances* and *Purchases Discount*). Information needed for closing credit balance accounts is on lines 29, 32, 33, and 47 of Lin's work sheet, page 539.

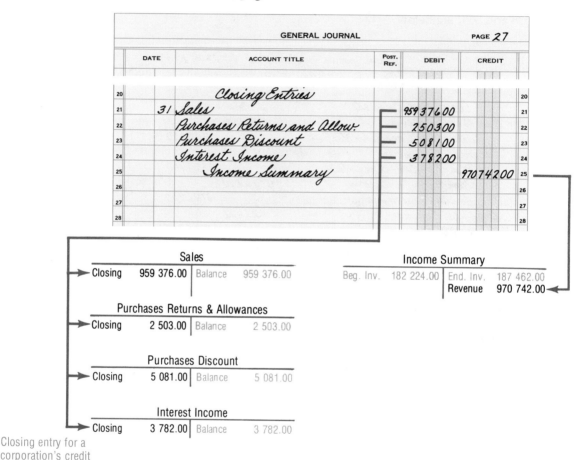

Closing entry for a corporation's credit balance accounts

Closing entry for debit balance accounts. The closing entry for Lin's debit balance accounts on December 31, 1989, is on page 551. Debit balance accounts are the cost and expense accounts and the reduction in revenue account (*Sales Returns and Allowances*). Information needed for closing the debit balance accounts is from lines 30–31, 34–46, and 48–49 of Lin's work sheet, page 539.

When closing entries for the income statement accounts are posted, Income Summary has a credit balance of $37 242.00. This credit balance, $37 242.00, is the amount of net income. This amount is the same as on line 51 of the work sheet, page 539 and on the income statement, page 544.

	DATE	ACCOUNT TITLE	POST. REF.	DEBIT	CREDIT	
		GENERAL JOURNAL			PAGE 28	
1		*Closing Entries*				1
2	1989 Dec. 31	Income Summary		938 738.00		2
3		Sales Returns and Allow.			11 376.00	3
4		Purchases			685 902.00	4
5		Advertising Expense			15 166.00	5
6		Bad Debts Expense			4 740.00	6
7		Credit Card Fee Expense			9 594.00	7
8		Delivery Expense			5 040.00	8
9		Depr. Exp. - Delivery Equip.			1 900.00	9
10		Depr. Exp. - Office Equip.			950.00	10
11		Depr. Exp. - Store Equip.			2 840.00	11
12		Insurance Expense			7 884.00	12
13		Misc. Expense			10 417.00	13
14		Payroll Taxes Expense			8 869.00	14
15		Rent Expense			26 544.00	15
16		Salary Expense			117 552.00	16
17		Supplies Expense			4 284.00	17
18		Interest Expense			4 730.00	18
19		Federal Income Tax			20 950.00	19

Income Summary

Beg. Inv.	182 224.00	End. Inv.	187 462.00
Cost & Exp.	938 738.00	Revenue	970 742.00

Sales Returns & Allowances

Balance	11 376.00	Closing	11 376.00

Purchases

Balance	685 902.00	Closing	685 902.00

Advertising Expense

Balance	15 166.00	Closing	15 166.00

Bad Debts Expense

Balance	4 740.00	Closing	4 740.00

Credit Card Fee Expense

Balance	9 594.00	Closing	9 594.00

Delivery Expense

Balance	5 040.00	Closing	5 040.00

Depreciation Expense — Delivery Equipment

Balance	1 900.00	Closing	1 900.00

Depreciation Expense — Office Equipment

Balance	950.00	Closing	950.00

Depreciation Expense — Store Equipment

Balance	2 840.00	Closing	2 840.00

Insurance Expense

Balance	7 884.00	Closing	7 884.00

Miscellaneous Expense

Balance	10 417.00	Closing	10 417.00

Payroll Taxes Expense

Balance	8 869.00	Closing	8 869.00

Rent Expense

Balance	26 544.00	Closing	26 544.00

Salary Expense

Balance	117 552.00	Closing	117 552.00

Supplies Expense

Balance	4 284.00	Closing	4 284.00

Interest Expense

Balance	4 730.00	Closing	4 730.00

Federal Income Tax

Balance	20 950.00	Closing	20 950.00

Closing entry for a corporation's debit balance accounts

Closing entry for recording net income in a retained earnings account. A corporation's net income is recorded in a retained earnings account. The closing entry to record Lin's income on December 31, 1989, is below. Information needed for this entry is taken from line 51 of Lin's work sheet, page 539.

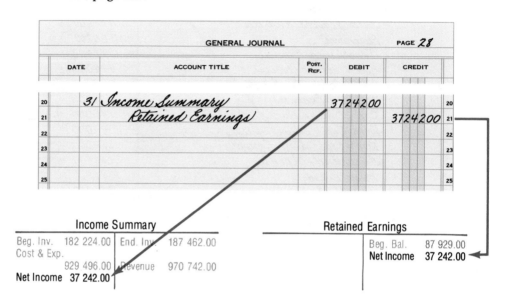

Closing entry to record a corporation's net income in a retained earnings account

When the entry to record net income is posted, Income Summary has a zero balance. The net income, *$37 242.00*, has been recorded as a credit in Retained Earnings.

If a corporation has a net loss, Income Summary has a debit balance. Retained Earnings would then be debited and Income Summary credited for the net loss amount.

After adjusting and closing entries are journalized, the entries are posted to the general ledger accounts. Lin's uses four-column general ledger account forms with separate debit balance and credit balance columns. Each time an entry is posted, the account balance is figured.

After adjusting and closing entries are posted, balance sheet accounts all have up-to-date balances. Assets, liabilities, and shareholders' equity account balances agree with amounts on the balance sheet, page 546. Revenue, cost, and expense accounts all begin the new fiscal period with zero balances.

Post-closing trial balance

A post-closing trial balance is prepared after adjusting and closing entries have been posted. Lin's post-closing trial balance, December 31, 1989, is on the next page.

```
                         Lin's Music Centre
                      Post-Closing Trial Balance
                        December 31, 1989

              Account Title                    Debit            Credit
Cash ...............................................  $65 903.00
Notes Receivable ..................................    2 649.00
Accounts Receivable ...............................   42 135.00
Allowance for Uncoll. Accts .......................                   $  5 020.00
Merchandise Inventory .............................  187 462.00
Supplies ..........................................    2 407.00
Prepaid Insurance .................................    4 778.00
Delivery Equipment ................................   17 880.00
Accum. Depr.--Delivery Equip. .....................                      7 150.00
Office Equipment ..................................    9 710.00
Accum. Depr.--Office Equip. .......................                      2 900.00
Store Equipment ...................................   41 175.00
Accum. Depr.--Store Equip. ........................                      8 240.00
Accounts Payable ..................................                     16 805.00
Employees' Income Tax Payable .....................                      1 816.00
Federal Income Tax Payable ........................                        970.00
CPP Payable .......................................                        327.00
Sales Tax Payable .................................                      4 740.00
UI Payable ........................................                        506.00
Hospital Insurance Premiums Payable ...............                        398.00
Canada Savings Bonds Payable ......................                         40.00
United Way Donations Payable ......................                         16.00
Capital Stock .....................................                    200 000.00
Retained Earnings .................................                    125 171.00
                                                     374 099.00       374 099.00
```

The equality of debits and credits is proved. Lin's general ledger is Post-closing trial balance
ready for the next fiscal period. *(CONCEPT: Accounting Period Cycle)*   for a corporation

DISTRIBUTING INCOME TO SHAREHOLDERS

Net income earned by a corporation belongs to the shareholders. Some income may be retained by a corporation for business expansion and increased needs. Some income may be given to shareholders as a return on their investments. No income can be distributed to shareholders except by formal action of a corporation's board of directors. *(CONCEPT: Business Entity)* A group of persons elected by the shareholders to manage a corporation is called a board of directors.

Declaring a dividend

Action by a board of directors to distribute corporate earnings to shareholders is called declaring a dividend. When a corporation's board of directors declares a dividend, the corporation is obligated to pay the dividend. The declared dividend is a liability. This liability must be recorded in the corporation's accounts. A memorandum is used as a source document for recording declaration of a dividend. *(CONCEPT: Objective Evidence)*

June 15, 1990. Lin's board of directors declared a dividend of $20.00 a share. Date of payment is July 15, 1990. Capital stock issued is 2 000 shares. Memorandum No. 108.

The journal entry to record Lin's declaration of a dividend is below. The amount declared is $40 000.00 ($20.00 a share for 2 000 shares).

<table>
<tr><td colspan="6">GENERAL JOURNAL</td><td>PAGE 13</td></tr>
<tr><td colspan="2">DATE</td><td>ACCOUNT TITLE</td><td>POST. REF.</td><td>DEBIT</td><td>CREDIT</td></tr>
<tr><td>1990
June</td><td>15</td><td>Retained Earnings</td><td></td><td>40 000 00</td><td></td></tr>
<tr><td></td><td></td><td>Dividends Payable</td><td></td><td></td><td>40 000 00</td></tr>
<tr><td></td><td></td><td>Memorandum No. 108.</td><td></td><td></td><td></td></tr>
</table>

Entry to record the declaration of a dividend by a corporation

Retained Earnings is debited for $40 000.00 to record the reduction in retained earnings. Dividends Payable is credited for $40 000.00 to record the liability the corporation now has for the dividend declared.

Paying a dividend

On July 15, 1990, Lin's issues one cheque for the amount of the total dividend.

July 15, 1990. Paid $40 000.00 cash for dividend declared July 15, 1990. Cheque No. 739.

This cheque is deposited in a special dividend current account. A separate cheque for each shareholder is drawn on this special account. The special account avoids a large number of cash payments journal entries. The special dividend current account also reserves cash specifically for paying dividends.

> A cheque is often made payable to an agent, such as a bank. The agent then handles the details of sending dividend cheques to individual shareholders.

The journal entry to record Lin's dividend payment of $40 000.00 is below.

<table>
<tr><td colspan="10">CASH PAYMENTS JOURNAL</td><td>PAGE 26</td></tr>
<tr><td></td><td></td><td></td><td></td><td></td><td>1</td><td>2</td><td>3</td><td>4</td><td>5</td></tr>
<tr><td colspan="2">DATE</td><td>ACCOUNT TITLE</td><td>CHEQUE No.</td><td>POST. REF.</td><td colspan="2">GENERAL</td><td>ACCOUNTS PAYABLE DEBIT</td><td>PURCHASES DISCOUNT CREDIT</td><td>CASH CREDIT</td></tr>
<tr><td></td><td></td><td></td><td></td><td></td><td>DEBIT</td><td>CREDIT</td><td></td><td></td><td></td></tr>
<tr><td>19</td><td>15</td><td>Dividends Payable</td><td>739</td><td></td><td>40 000 00</td><td></td><td></td><td></td><td>40 000 00</td></tr>
</table>

Entry to record the payment of a dividend

Dividends Payable is debited for the amount of dividends paid, *$40 000.00*. Cash is credited for the total amount of cash paid, *$40 000.00*. When this entry is posted, the dividends payable account is closed.

ACCOUNTING TERMS

What is the meaning of each of the following?

1. share of stock
2. shareholder
3. capital stock
4. retained earnings
5. net sales
6. net purchases
7. statement of shareholders' equity
8. dividends
9. current assets
10. current liabilities
11. long-term liabilities
12. board of directors
13. declaring a dividend

QUESTIONS FOR INDIVIDUAL STUDY

1. Why do managers, owners, and creditors need financial information about how well a corporation is doing?
2. How does a work sheet for a corporation differ from a work sheet for a proprietorship?
3. In what order are general ledger accounts listed on a corporation work sheet?
4. How many capital accounts are kept for the investment of owners of Lin's Music Centre?
5. Which of Lin's general ledger accounts need to be adjusted?
6. What two accounts are used in the adjustment for bad debts?
7. What are the purposes of the two adjustments for Merchandise Inventory?
8. What adjusting entry is made for the supplies account?
9. What adjusting entry is made for the prepaid insurance account?
10. What adjusting entry is made for the estimated depreciation for a fixed asset?
11. Why is federal income tax not figured until all other adjustments have been planned on Lin's work sheet?
12. What entry is made to update the federal income tax expense for a fiscal period?
13. What three corporation financial statements does Lin's prepare?
14. What financial information does an income statement report?
15. Where is the information found to prepare a corporation income statement?
16. How does Lin's income statement differ from Denim Threads' income statement?
17. What financial information does a statement of shareholders' equity report?
18. What are the two main sections of a statement of shareholders' equity?
19. Where is the information found to prepare a statement of shareholders' equity?
20. What financial information does a corporation balance sheet report?
21. Where is the information found to prepare a balance sheet?
22. What three amounts are listed when the book value of an asset is reported on a balance sheet?
23. Where is the information obtained for journalizing a corporation's adjusting entries?
24. Where is the information found for journalizing a corporation's closing entries?
25. What kind of balances do income statement accounts have immediately after adjusting and closing entries are posted?
26. Why is a post-closing trial balance prepared?
27. When is a dividend recorded as a liability in a corporation's general ledger accounts?
28. What entry is made to record the declaration of a dividend?
29. What entry is made to record paying a dividend?

CASES FOR MANAGEMENT DECISION

CASE 1 Financial information for B & J Corporation for the current year is listed below.

Total revenue............................ $428 000.00
Total expenses 396 000.00
Net income before federal income tax.............................   32 000.00
Federal income tax 6 400.00

The company prepared an income statement reporting $32 000.00 as net income for the year. A closing entry was prepared debiting Income Summary for $32 000.00 and crediting Retained Earnings for $32 000.00. Are the income statement and closing entry correct? If not, what should they be? Explain.

CASE 2 Graphics Company recently formed into a corporation with five shareholders. Carla Okano, the bookkeeper, is developing the accounting system. She suggested that, since there are only five shareholders, only one equity account be used. The account would be Corporation Capital. The president of Graphics questions the bookkeeper's recommendation. Is the bookkeeper's recommendation acceptable? If not, how should capital be recorded and reported? Explain your answer.

DRILLS FOR UNDERSTANDING

DRILL 27-D 1   Analysing adjustments on a work sheet

Use a form similar to the one below.

Adjustment No.	Work Sheet Adjustment	
	(a) Account Debited	(b) Account Credited
1.	*Income Summary*	*Merchandise Inventory*

Instructions: For each adjustment below: (a) Write the name of the account debited. (b) Write the name of the account credited. Adjustment No. 1 is given as an example in the form above.

1. Adjustment for beginning merchandise inventory.
2. Adjustment for ending merchandise inventory.
3. Adjustment for bad debts expense.
4. Adjustment for supplies.
5. Adjustment for delivery equipment depreciation expense.
6. Adjustment for prepaid insurance.
7. Adjustment for office equipment depreciation expense.
8. Adjustment for additional federal income tax owed.
9. Adjustment for store equipment depreciation expense.

DRILL 27-D 2   Classifying assets, liabilities, and shareholders' equity accounts on a balance sheet

Use a form similar to the one on the next page.

Account No.	Current Assets	Contra Acct. of a Current Asset	Fixed Assets	Contra Acct. of a Fixed Asset	Current Liability	Long-Term Liability	Shareholders' Equity
1.	√						

Instructions: For each account below, place a check mark in the column that correctly classifies the account on a balance sheet. Account No. 1 is given as an example in the form above.

1. Cash
2. Accounts Payable
3. Supplies
4. Office Equipment
5. CPP Payable
6. Merchandise Inventory
7. Allowance for Uncollectible Accounts
8. Notes Receivable
9. Accumulated Depreciation — Office Equipment
10. Retained Earnings
11. Accounts Receivable
12. Accumulated Depreciation — Delivery Equipment
13. Federal Income Tax Payable
14. Prepaid Insurance
15. Delivery Equipment
16. Capital Stock
17. UI Payable
18. Supplies
19. Mortgage Payable
20. Employees' Income Tax Payable

DRILL 27-D 3 Analysing closing entries

Use a form similar to the one below.

Closing Entry No.	Closing Entry	
	(a) Account Debited	(b) Account Credited
1.	*Income Summary*	*Delivery Expense*

Instructions: For each closing entry below and on page 558: (a) Write the name of the account debited. (b) Write the name of the account credited. Closing Entry No. 1 is given as an example in the form above.

1. Close Delivery Expense
2. Close Federal Income Tax
3. Close Purchases Returns and Allowances

    4. Close Payroll Taxes Expense
    5. Close Interest Income
    6. Close Depreciation Expense — Office Equipment
    7. Close Net Income
    8. Close Sales
    9. Close Sales Returns and Allowances
  10. Close Insurance Expense
  11. Close Purchases Discount
  12. Close Bad Debts Expense

APPLICATION PROBLEMS

PROBLEM 27-1   Preparing a work sheet

The accounts and their balances in Melody Shop's general ledger appear as below on December 31 of the current year. The trial balance is recorded on the work sheet in the working papers.

Account Title	Account Balance	
	Debits	Credits
Cash	$ 51 906.00	
Notes Receivable	2 120.00	
Accounts Receivable	33 708.00	
Allow. for Uncoll. Accounts		$ 220.00
Merchandise Inventory	145 780.00	
Supplies	4 682.00	
Prepaid Insurance	8 880.00	
Delivery Equipment	14 300.00	
Accum. Depr. — Delivery Equip.		4 200.00
Office Equipment	7 770.00	
Accum. Depr. — Office Equip.		1 560.00
Store Equipment	32 900.00	
Accum. Depr. — Store Equip.		4 860.00
Notes Payable		1 000.00
Accounts Payable		15 120.00
Employees' Income Tax Pay.		1 452.00
Federal Income Tax Pay.		—
CPP Payable		261.00
Sales Tax Payable		3 792.00
UI Payable		406.00
Hosp. Insurance Premium Pay.		318.00
Canada Savings Bonds Payable		50.00
United Way Donations Pay.		20.00
Dividends Payable		—
Capital Stock		150 000.00
Retained Earnings		67 134.00
Income Summary	—	—
Sales		767 500.00
Sales Returns and Allow.	9 100.00	
Purchases	548 722.00	
Purch. Returns and Allow.		2 000.00
Purchases Discount		4 065.00
Advertising Expense	12 133.00	
Bad Debts Expense	—	

	Account Balance	
Account Title	Debits	Credits
Delivery Expense	$ 4 032.00	
Depr. Exp. — Delivery Equip.	——	
Depr. Exp. — Office Equip.	——	
Depr. Exp. — Store Equip.	——	
Insurance Expense	——	
Miscellaneous Expense	14 408.00	
Payroll Taxes Expense	7 095.00	
Rent Expense	24 000.00	
Salary Expense	94 042.00	
Supplies Expense	——	
Interest Income		3 404.00
Interest Expense	3 784.00	
Federal Income Tax	8 000.00	
	$1 027 362.00	$1 027 362.00

Instructions: Complete the eight-column work sheet for the fiscal year ended December 31 of the current year. Use as a guide the work sheet, pages 538 and 539. Information needed for the adjustments is below.

Bad debts expense is estimated as 1.0% of charge sales. Charge sales were $307 000.00.

Merchandise inventory, December 31	$149 970.00
Supplies inventory, December 31	1 872.00
Value of insurance policies, December 31	2 960.00
Annual depreciation expense on delivery equipment	1 716.00
Annual depreciation expense on office equipment	777.00
Annual depreciation expense on store equipment	2 632.00
Federal income tax for the year	8 634.00

The solution to Problem 27-1 is needed to complete Problem 27-2 and Problem 27-3.

PROBLEM 27-2   Preparing financial statements

The work sheet prepared in Problem 27-1 is needed to complete Problem 27-2.

Instructions: 1. From the work sheet, prepare an income statement for the fiscal year ended December 31 of the current year.

2. Prepare a statement of shareholders' equity. Additional information needed is below.

January 1 balance of capital stock account	$150 000.00
(1 500 shares issued for $100.00 per share.)	
January 1 balance of retained earnings account	97 134.00
Dividends declared and paid during the current year	30 000.00

3. Prepare a balance sheet for December 31 of the current year.

PROBLEM 27-3   Recording adjusting and closing entries

The work sheet prepared in Problem 27-1 is needed to complete Problem 27-3.

Instructions: 1. From the work sheet prepared in Problem 27-1, record the adjusting entries on page 18 of a general journal.

2. Record the closing entries on page 19 of a general journal.

PROBLEM 27-4 Distributing income to shareholders

On January 10 following the current year, the board of directors of Melody Shop declared a dividend of $24.00 a share to shareholders. Date of payment is January 31. Capital stock issue is 1 500 shares.

Instructions: 1. Record the dividend declared on January 10 on page 20 of a general journal. Source document is Memorandum No. 126.

2. Record payment of the dividend on page 36 of a cash payments journal. Source document is Cheque No. 486.

ENRICHMENT PROBLEMS

MASTERY PROBLEM 27-M Preparing end-of-fiscal-period work for a corporation

The accounts and their balances in RSD Corporation's general ledger appear as below on December 31 of the current year. The trial balance is recorded on the work sheet in the working papers.

Account Title	Account Balance
Cash	$ 44 120.10
Notes Receivable	1 800.00
Accounts Receivable	28 653.80
Allow. for Uncoll. Accounts	187.00
Merchandise Inventory	123 913.00
Supplies	3 991.70
Prepaid Insurance	7 560.00
Delivery Equipment	12 155.00
Accum. Depr. — Delivery Equip.	3 570.00
Office Equipment	6 604.50
Accum. Depr. — Office Equip.	1 326.00
Store Equipment	27 965.00
Accum. Depr. — Store Equip.	4 131.00
Accounts Payable	13 702.00
Employees' Income Tax Payable	1 250.00
Federal Income Tax Payable	——
CPP Payable	220.50
Sales Tax Payable	3 223.20
UI Payable	330.65
Hosp. Insurance Premium Pay.	270.30
Canada Savings Bonds Payable	44.50
United Way Donations Payable	15.00
Dividends Payable	——
Capital Stock	150 000.00
Retained Earnings	34 587.85
Income Summary	——
Sales	652 375.00
Sales Returns and Allow.	7 735.00
Purchases	466 413.70
Purch. Returns and Allow.	1 700.00
Purchases Discount	3 455.20
Advertising Expense	10 313.00
Bad Debts Expense	——
Delivery Expense	3 427.20
Depr. Exp. — Delivery Equip.	——
Depr. Exp. — Office Equip.	——
Depr. Exp. — Store Equip.	——

Account Title	Account Balance
Insurance Expense	——
Miscellaneous Expense...	$ 12 246.80
Payroll Taxes Expense	6 030.70
Rent Expense	20 400.00
Salary Expense...	79 935.70
Supplies Expense	——
Interest Income	2 893.40
Interest Expense	3 216.40
Federal Income Tax	6 800.00

Instructions: 1. Prepare an eight-column work sheet for the fiscal year ended December 31 of the current year. Use as a guide the work sheet, pages 538 and 539. Information needed for the adjustments is below.

Bad debts expense is estimated as 1.5% of charge sales. Charge sales were $163 100.00.	
Merchandise inventory, December 31	$130 108.60
Supplies inventory, December 31	849.40
Value of insurance policies, December 31	3 150.00
Annual depreciation expense on delivery equipment	2 431.00
Annual depreciation expense on office equipment.............................	660.45
Annual depreciation expense on store equipment..............................	2 796.50
Federal income tax for the year...	7 452.79

2. Prepare an income statement similar to the one on page 540.

3. Prepare a statement of shareholders' equity similar to the one on page 545. Additional information needed is below.

January 1 balance of capital stock account	$150 000.00
(15 000 shares issued for $10.00 per share.)	
January 1 balance of retained earnings account.................................	64 587.85
Dividends declared and paid during the current year	30 000.00

4. Prepare a balance sheet for December 31 of the current year.

5. Record the adjusting entries on page 15 of a general journal.

6. Record the closing entries on page 16 of a general journal.

7. On January 20 following the current year, the board of directors declared a dividend of $2.00 a share to shareholders. Record the dividend declared on page 18 of a general journal. Source document is Memorandum No. 98.

8. The dividend declared in Instruction 7 was paid on February 10. Record payment of the dividend on page 32 of a cash payments journal. Source document is Cheque No. 339.

CHALLENGE PROBLEM 27-C   Preparing end-of-fiscal-period work for a corporation

The accounts and their balances in Aquarian Electronics' general ledger appear as below and on the next page on December 31 of the current year. The trial balance is recorded on the work sheet in the working papers.

Account Title	Account Balance
Cash	$ 28 937.20
Notes Receivable	4 134.00
Accounts Receivable	31 316.36
Allow. for Uncoll. Accounts...	31.00
Merchandise Inventory	86 331.00
Supplies	1 772.40

Account Title	Account Balance
Prepaid Insurance..	$ 6 300.00
Delivery Equipment..	8 240.00
Accum. Depr. — Delivery Equip..	2 472.00
Office Equipment...	4 820.00
Accum. Depr. — Office Equip.	1 205.00
Store Equipment...	6 480.00
Accum. Depr. — Store Equip.	1 944.00
Notes Payable...	10 000.00
Accounts Payable...	9 173.70
Employees' Income Tax Payable	1 131.00
Federal Income Tax Payable	————
CPP Payable	203.00
Sales Tax Payable	2 751.16
UI Payable	306.00
Hosp. Insurance Premium Pay..	222.50
Dividends Payable...	7 500.00
Capital Stock	75 000.00
Retained Earnings	4 638.69
Income Summary	————
Sales..	660 053.40
Sales Returns and Allow.	4 968.90
Purchases	438 978.50
Purch. Returns and Allow.	1 617.40
Purchases Discount...	3 252.56
Advertising Expense..	9 493.00
Bad Debts Expense..	————
Delivery Expense...	3 225.60
Depr. Exp. — Delivery Equip...	————
Depr. Exp. — Office Equip.	————
Depr. Exp. — Store Equip.	————
Insurance Expense	————
Miscellaneous Expense...	5 763.20
Payroll Taxes Expense	6 615.00
Rent Expense	19 200.00
Salary Expense..	94 622.00
Supplies Expense	————
Interest Income	1 723.20
Interest Expense	3 027.45
Federal Income Tax	19 000.00

Instructions: 1. Prepare an eight-column work sheet for the fiscal year ended December 31 of the current year. Use as a guide the work sheet, pages 538 and 539.

Bad debts expense is estimated as 1.5% of charge sales. Charge sales were $660 053.40.	
Merchandise inventory, December 31	$104 212.80
Supplies inventory, December 31...	227.80
Value of insurance policies, December 31	2 100.00
Annual depreciation expense on delivery equipment	1 030.00
Annual depreciation expense on office equipment..............................	482.00
Annual depreciation expense on store equipment...............................	518.40

Federal income tax for the year is figured at the following rates:
   17% of the first $25 000.00 net income before taxes.
   20% of the next $25 000.00 net income before taxes.
   30% of the next $25 000.00 net income before taxes.
   40% of the next $25 000.00 net income before taxes or amount above
      $75 000.00.

2. Prepare an income statement similar to the one on page 544.

3. Prepare a statement of shareholders' equity similar to the one on page 545. Additional information needed is below.

January 1 balance of capital stock account	$75 000.00
(750 shares issued for $100.00 per share.)	
January 1 balance of retained earnings account	12 138.69
Dividend declared December 31 of the current year	7 500.00

4. Prepare a balance sheet for December 31 of the current year.

5. Record the adjusting entries on page 20 of a general journal.

6. Record the closing entries on page 21 of a general journal.

7. The dividend declared on December 31 was paid on January 10 following the current year. Record payment of the dividend on page 40 of a cash payments journal. Source document is Cheque No. 667.

Reinforcement Activity 4

PART B

An Accounting Cycle for a Corporation Using Special Journals

The general ledger and general journal prepared in Part A are needed to complete Part B.

Reinforcement Activity 4, Part B, includes the accounting activities needed to complete an accounting cycle for a corporation. In Part A, Electronic Emporium's transactions were recorded for the month of December. The general ledger account balances of Electronic Emporium now include transactions for the fiscal year ended December 31. (Beginning account balances given in Part A included transactions from the first eleven months of the fiscal year.)

In Part B, end-of-fiscal-period work will be completed for Electronic Emporium.

Preparing end-of-fiscal-period work for a corporation

Instructions: 1. Prepare an eight-column work sheet for the fiscal year ended December 31 of the current year. Information needed for the adjustments is below. Bad debts expense is estimated as 2.0% of charge sales. Charge sales were $79 206.50 for the fiscal year.

Merchandise inventory, December 31	$75 033.20
Supplies inventory, December 31	182.20
Value of insurance policies, December 31	1 680.00
Annual depreciation expense on office equipment...................................	434.00
Annual depreciation expense on store equipment...................................	622.00
Federal income tax for the year	8 075.56

2. Prepare an income statement for the year ended December 31.

3. Prepare a statement of shareholders' equity. Additional information needed is below.

January 1 balance of capital stock account...	$60 000.00
(6 000 shares issued for $10.00 per share.)	
January 1 balance of retained earnings account......................................	45 622.00
Dividends declared and paid during the current year...............................	30 000.00

4. Prepare a balance sheet for December 31 of the current year.

5. Record the adjusting entries on pages 8 and 9 of the general journal. Post to the general ledger accounts.

6. Record the closing entries on page 9 of the general journal. Post to the general ledger accounts.

7. Prepare a post-closing trial balance.

CORPORATION, LTD.

A Business Simulation

Environmental
Residential Apparatus

ENVIROTROL CORPORATION, LTD. is a distributor of
residential environmental control products. This business
simulation covers the realistic transactions completed by a
corporation. Transactions are recorded in special journals
from source documents. In addition, a payroll register,
employees' earnings records, a general journal, a general
ledger, an accounts receivable ledger, and an accounts
payable ledger are used. A pictorial flowchart of the
accounting cycle of ENVIROTROL is shown on the next two
pages. This business simulation is available from the
publisher.

Flowchart of the
Accounting Cycle of

ENVIROTROL CORPORATION, LTD.

Source Documents

General File

1a

1 Record transactions in the appropriate special journals from
   source documents.
1a File source documents.
2 Post items to be posted individually to the general ledger and
   subsidiary ledgers.
3 Prepare the payroll and record the entries. Update the employees'
   earnings records.
4 Post column totals to the general ledger.
5 Prepare schedules of accounts receivable and accounts payable from
   subsidiary ledgers.
6 Prepare the trial balance on the work sheet.
7 Plan adjustments and complete the work sheet.
8 Prepare financial statements.
9 Record adjusting and closing entries from the work sheet.
10 Post adjusting and closing entries to the general ledger.
11 Prepare a post-closing trial balance from the general ledger.
12 Journalize the reversing entries.
13 Post the reversing entries to the general ledger.

6 ACCOUNTING CONTROL SYSTEMS

GENERAL BEHAVIORAL GOALS

1. Know accounting terminology related to accounting control systems for a merchandising business organized as a corporation.
2. Understand accounting principles and practices for accounting control systems of a merchandising business organized as a corporation.
3. Demonstrate accounting procedures for control systems of a merchandising business organized as a corporation.

Solar Power, the business for Part 6, sells solar equipment.

SOLAR POWER
Chart of Accounts

| Balance Sheet Accounts | Income Statement Accounts |

Balance Sheet Accounts

(1) ASSETS — Account Number

11 Current Assets

Cash.. 1101
Petty Cash.................................. 1102
Notes Receivable....................... 1103
Accounts Receivable................ 1104
Allowance for Uncollectible
    Accounts............................. 1104.1
Merchandise Inventory 1105
Supplies 1106
Prepaid Insurance..................... 1107

12 Fixed Assets

Delivery Equipment................... 1201
Accumulated Depreciation —
    Delivery Equipment 1201.1
Office Equipment 1202
Accumulated Depreciation —
    Office Equipment................... 1202.1
Store Equipment 1203
Accumulated Depreciation —
    Store Equipment................... 1203.1

(2) LIABILITIES

21 Current Liabilities

Notes Payable........................... 2101
Vouchers Payable..................... 2102
Employees' Income Tax
    Payable................................. 2103
CPP Payable.............................. 2104
UI Payable.................................. 2105
Income Tax Payable.................. 2106
Sales Tax Payable..................... 2107
Hospital Insurance Premiums
    Payable................................. 2108
Dividends Payable..................... 2109

(3) SHAREHOLDERS' EQUITY

Capital Stock 3101
Retained Earnings..................... 3201
Income Summary 3301

Income Statement Accounts

(4) OPERATING REVENUE — Account Number

Sales.. 4101
Sales Returns and Allowances. 4101.1

(5) COST OF MERCHANDISE

Purchases.................................. 5101
Purchases Returns and
    Allowances............................ 5101.1
Purchases Discount................... 5101.2
Discounts Lost 5101.3

(6) OPERATING EXPENSES

Advertising Expense................. 6101
Bad Debts Expense 6102
Delivery Expense 6103
Depreciation Expense —
    Delivery Equipment............... 6104
Depreciation Expense —
    Office Equipment................... 6105
Depreciation Expense — Store
    Equipment............................. 6106
Insurance Expense.................... 6107
Miscellaneous Expense 6108
Payroll Taxes Expense............. 6109
Rent Expense............................ 6110
Salary Expense 6111
Supplies Expense 6112

(7) OTHER REVENUE

Interest Income.......................... 7101

(8) OTHER EXPENSES

Interest Expense....................... 8101
Cash Short and Over................. 8102

(9) INCOME TAX

Federal Income Tax.................. 9101

The chart of accounts for Solar Power is illustrated above for ready
reference as you study Part 6 of this textbook.

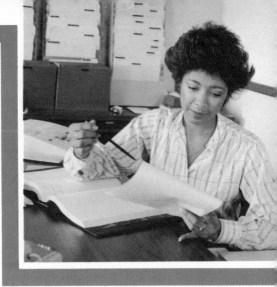

28

A Voucher System

ENABLING PERFORMANCE TASKS

After studying Chapter 28, you will be able to:

a. Define accounting terms related to a voucher system.
b. Explain accounting principles and practices related to a voucher system.
c. Prepare a voucher.
d. Record vouchers in a voucher register.
e. Record cash transactions in a cheque register.
f. Record purchases returns and allowances and payroll transactions in a voucher system.

Business transactions affect the cash account more often than any other general ledger account. Cash also is more often subject to misuse because ownership is so easy to transfer. Thus, a procedure is needed that places accounting controls on the asset cash.

Many businesses use a control procedure that requires all cash payments to be approved by someone in authority. In small businesses, usually the owner or manager approves cash payments. In large businesses, more than one person may have authority to approve cash payments. A voucher system is frequently used for controlling cash payments when several persons are authorized to approve cash payments. Controlling cash payments by preparing and approving vouchers before payments are made is called a voucher system.

USING A VOUCHER SYSTEM

A business form showing approval by an authorized person for a cash payment is called a voucher. A business paper used to authorize an accounting entry often is referred to as a voucher. When a voucher system is used however *voucher* refers only to the cash payment approval form.

A journal in which vouchers are recorded is called a voucher register. A journal used in a voucher system to record cash payments is called a cheque register.

Major steps in using a voucher system are listed below.

1 Verify amounts and data on invoice.

2 Prepare voucher. Determine accounts and amounts to be debited and credited.

3 Obtain approval of voucher.

4 Record voucher in voucher register and make notation on voucher.

5 File unpaid voucher in "unpaid vouchers file."

6 Obtain approval for payment of voucher. Issue cheque. Make notation on voucher.

7 File voucher in "paid vouchers file."

8 Record cheque in cheque register. Make notation in voucher register.

PREPARING VOUCHERS

Solar Power, a solar equipment business, uses a voucher system to control all cash payments. A voucher is prepared for each cash payment to be made.

Verifying an invoice

When Solar Power receives an invoice, a verification form is stamped on the invoice as shown on the next page.

The invoice is verified for such details as quantities received, terms, prices, and amounts. Account or accounts to be debited and credited are also shown. The person doing each part of this work initials the verification form to show the responsibility for that part.

Preparing a voucher

A verified invoice is used to prepare a voucher. The voucher prepared for the verified invoice, page 573, is on the next page.

Four kinds of information are listed in Section 1 of Solar Power's voucher. (1) Voucher number. (2) Date on which the voucher is being prepared. (3) Date on which payment is to be made. (4) Name and address of the person or business to which money is to be paid.

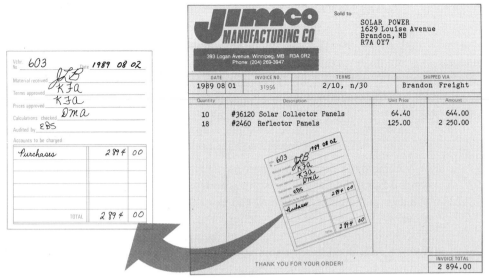

Verification of invoice

Outside of voucher for an invoice

Vouchers are numbered consecutively to identify and account for all vouchers.

Accounts and amounts to be debited and credited, total debits, and total credits are listed in Section 2. Account titles not printed on a voucher form are written on blank lines in Section 2.

August 2, 1989. Purchased merchandise on account from Jimco Manufacturing Company, $2 894.00. Voucher No. 603.

The cost account Purchases is debited, $2 894.00. The liability account Vouchers Payable is credited, $2 894.00.

Purchases	
2 894.00	

Vouchers Payable	
	2 894.00

In a voucher system, Vouchers Payable is used as the liability account rather than Accounts Payable. Also, no accounts payable ledger is kept. An unpaid vouchers file shows amounts owed. A paid vouchers file shows amounts that have been paid.

A voucher is folded and becomes a folder in which related documents can be placed. For this reason, a voucher is sometimes referred to as a voucher jacket. The inside of the voucher, page 573, contains space for other details about the transaction. For Voucher No. 603, all details are contained on the invoice used to prepare the voucher. Therefore, the invoice is placed inside the voucher. No further information need be recorded on the inside of the voucher.

A separate voucher is usually prepared for each invoice received. However, several invoices received at the same time from the same creditor may be combined into one voucher.

After a voucher is completed, the voucher is sent to a person authorized to approve it. Louis Zink, manager, is the person who approves vouchers for Solar Power. He checks the voucher and indicates approval by signing the voucher in Section 3 as on page 573. The approved voucher is then recorded.

PAGE *24*   **VOUCHER REGISTER**

	DATE	PAYEE	VCHR. NO.	PAID DATE	CH. NO.	VOUCHERS PAYABLE CREDIT	
	1989						
1	Aug. 2	Jimco Manufacturing Company	603	Aug. 10	741	2 894 00	1
2	3	Trinity Motors	604			7 950 00	2
3	4	Energy Electronics	605	Aug. 11	742	826 50	3
4	5	Solano Company	606			372 00	4
5	8	Colonial Service Centre	607			47 50	5
6	8	Moreno's, Inc.	608	See Vchr. No. 611		136 00	6
7	10	Central Supply	609			73 25	7
8	11	Mandarin, Inc.	610	Aug. 21	748	248 40	8
9	12	Moreno's, Inc.	611			90 00	9
10							10
30	31	Payroll	628	Aug. 31	755	4 126 73	30
31							31
32							32
33							33
34	31	Totals				91 865 10	34
35						(2 102)	35

Voucher register (left page)

RECORDING VOUCHERS IN A VOUCHER REGISTER

A voucher register is similar to and replaces a purchases journal described in Chapter 20. The source document for an entry in a voucher register is a voucher. *(CONCEPT: Objective Evidence)* Vouchers are recorded in numerical order. A missing number shows that a voucher has not been recorded.

Solar Power's voucher register is below and on page 574. Special columns are used for Purchases Debit, Delivery Expense Debit, Supplies Debit, and Vouchers Payable Credit. For accounts with no special amount columns, amounts are recorded in the General columns.

Recording a voucher in special amount columns of a voucher register

The entry on line 1 of the voucher register, page 574, is for Voucher No. 603, page 573. The date of the voucher, *1989, Aug. 2*, is written in the Date column. The name of the creditor, *Jimco Manufacturing Company*, is written in the Payee column. The number of the voucher, *603*, is written in the Vchr. No. column. The total amount to be paid for this voucher, *$2 894.00*, is written in the Vouchers Payable Credit column. As the total amount of the voucher is debited to Purchases, $2 894.00 is also written in the Purchases Debit column. This information is obtained from Sections 1 and 2 of the voucher.

After Voucher No. 603 is recorded in the voucher register, a notation is made on the voucher jacket, Section 4. The illustration on the next page

FOR MONTH OF *August* 19 *89*   PAGE *24*

	PURCHASES DEBIT	DELIVERY EXPENSE DEBIT	SUPPLIES DEBIT	ACCOUNT	POST REF.	DEBIT	CREDIT	
1	2894 00							1
2				Delivery Equipment	1201	7950 00		2
3	826 50							3
4	372 00							4
5		47 50						5
6	136 00							6
7			73 25					7
8	248 40							8
9				Vouchers Payable	2102	136 00		9
10				Purchases Returns + Allow.	5101.1		46 00	10
30				Salary Expense	6111	5072 80		30
31				Employees' Inc. Tax Pay.	2103		735 55	31
32				CPP Payable	2104		91 31	32
33				U I Payable	2105		119 21	33
34	6783000	50400	42840			2564480	254210	34
35	(5101)	(6103)	(1106)			(✓)	(✓)	35

Voucher register (right page)

shows that Voucher No. 603 was recorded on page 24 of the voucher register. The voucher is initialed in this section to show who recorded the entry. The voucher is then filed in an unpaid vouchers file. The voucher is filed by the date payment should be made, August 10, 1989.

Voucher clerk's notation
on the voucher to show
that the voucher has been
recorded

Recording a voucher in the General columns of a voucher register

*August 3, 1989. Bought delivery truck on account from Trinity Motors,
$7 950.00. Voucher No. 604.*

Delivery Equipment
7 950.00

Vouchers Payable
7 950.00

The fixed asset account Delivery Equipment is debited and the liability account Vouchers Payable is credited, $7 950.00.

The entry on line 2 of the voucher register, pages 574 and 575, is made from information on Voucher No. 604. *(CONCEPT: Objective Evidence)* The total voucher amount, *$7 950.00*, is written in the Vouchers Payable Credit column. No special amount column is provided to record a debit to the delivery equipment account. Delivery Equipment is written in the General Account column. The amount, *$7 950.00*, is written in the General Debit column.

Posting from a voucher register

Only items recorded in the General Debit or General Credit columns are posted individually from a voucher register. As each amount is posted, an account number is written in the voucher register's Post. Ref. column.

At the end of each month, a voucher register is totalled, proved, and ruled as on pages 574 and 575.

Totals of special amount columns are posted to general ledger accounts named in the column headings. The number of the account to which each special amount column total is posted is written in parentheses below the total. Check marks are placed below the General Debit and General Credit columns to show that these totals are not posted.

PAYING VOUCHERS

When a voucher system is used, each voucher is paid by a cheque. Each day all vouchers to be paid that day are removed from the unpaid vouchers file. A cheque is prepared for the amount of each voucher less any deductions for cash discounts. Cheques are issued only for approved vouchers.

Preparing a voucher cheque

A cheque with space for writing the purpose of the payment is called a voucher cheque. A voucher cheque is below.

Voucher cheques can be used when a voucher system is not used. For example, the cheque on page 453, Chapter 22, is a voucher cheque.

Voucher check

The cheque above is issued by Solar Power in payment of Voucher No. 603. The items listed below are recorded in the space provided for voucher data.

1. Voucher number.
2. Invoice number.
3. Amount of the invoice.
4. Amount of the discount, if any.
5. Net amount for which the cheque is written.

The main portion of the cheque is prepared in the usual manner.

Recording a payment on a voucher

After a voucher cheque is written, a notation is made in Section 5 of the voucher. The notation on Voucher No. 603, below, shows that Cheque No. 741 was issued on August 10, 1989. The payment is approved and the cheque is signed by Lorene Vaden.

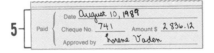

Notation on a voucher to show that a voucher has been paid

When a voucher is paid, the date and cheque number are written in a voucher register's Paid columns. This gives a cross-reference from a voucher register to a cheque register.

After payment is noted on a voucher, the voucher is filed in numerical order in a paid vouchers file. The voucher is then available for future reference.

RECORDING CASH TRANSACTIONS IN A CHEQUE REGISTER

Solar Power's cheque register is below. The cheque register is similar to and replaces the cash payments journal described in Chapter 20.

	DATE	PAYEE	CH. No.	VCHR. No.	VOUCHERS PAYABLE DEBIT (1)	PURCHASES DISCOUNT CREDIT (2)	CASH CREDIT (3)	BANK DEPOSITS (4)	BANK BALANCE (5)	
1	1989 Aug. 10	Brought Forward		✓	1788210	17780	1770430		8940260	1
2	10	Jimco Manufacturing Co.	741	603	289400	5788	283612		8656648	2
3	11	Energy Electronics	742	605	82650	1653	80997		8575651	3
4	15	Payroll	743	612	378284		378284		8197367	4
5	15	Ebensberger Supply	744	582	14625		14625		8182742	5
6	15	Deposit		✓				1632140	9814882	6
18	31	Payroll	755	628	412673		412673		8358480	18
19	31	Deposit		✓				1527480	9885960	19
20	31	Totals			8941020	50810	8890210			20
21					(2102)	(5102)	(1101)			21
22										22

CHEQUE REGISTER   PAGE 28

Cheque register

A cheque is written each time a voucher is paid. Solar Power prepares each voucher cheque in duplicate. The duplicate copy is the source document for the entry in the cheque register. (CONCEPT: *Objective Evidence*) Source document for cash payments transactions, described in Chapter 20, is a cheque stub. Each cheque is recorded in a cheque register in numerical order.

Each cheque is recorded in a cheque register as a debit to Vouchers Payable and a credit to Cash. If a discount is earned for prompt payment, the amount is recorded in the Purchases Discount Credit column. In a voucher system, these general ledger accounts are the only ones affected by cash payments transactions. All other accounts are debited or credited when a voucher is recorded in a voucher register. Special amount columns are used in a cheque register only for Vouchers Payable Debit, Purchases Discount Credit, and Cash Credit.

Maintaining bank balance columns in a cheque register

The cheque register above has two columns headed *Bank*. These two columns are used to keep an up-to-date record of cash in the bank account. The Bank Deposit column is used to record the amounts deposited in the bank account. The Bank Balance column shows the bank account balance after each cheque is issued and after each deposit is made. Solar Power uses these columns instead of cheque stubs to maintain a record of deposits and bank balance. Solar Power's cheque register combines a cash payments journal and cheque stub information.

Recording cheques in a cheque register

On August 10, 1989, Solar Power's cheque register column totals are forwarded from page 27 to page 28. Amounts brought forward are shown on line 1 of the cheque register, page 578.

August 10, 1989. Paid Voucher No. 603, $2 894.00, less Purchases Discount of $57.88. Cheque No. 741.

The liability account Vouchers Payable is debited for $2 894.00. The contra account, Purchases Discount, is credited for $57.88. Cash is credited for $2 836.12.

The entry to record this cheque is on line 2 of the cheque register, page 578. The date, *10*, is entered in the Date column. The payee's name, *Jimco Manufacturing Company*, is written in the Payee column. The cheque number, 741, is written in the Ch. No. column, and the voucher number, *603*, is written in the Vchr. No. column. The total voucher amount, *$2 894.00*, is written in the Vouchers Payable Debit column. The discount amount, *$57.88*, is written in the Purchases Discount Credit column. The cheque amount, *$2 836.12*, is written in the Cash Credit column. The cheque amount is subtracted from the balance in the Bank Balance column on line 1. The amount of the new balance, *$86 566.48*, is written in the Bank Balance column on line 2.

On August 15, 1989, Solar Power made a bank deposit of $16 321.40. The entry to record this deposit is on line 6 of the cheque register, page 578. The date, *15*, is written in the Date column. The word, *Deposit*, is written in the Payee column. A check mark is placed in the Vchr. No. column to show that no voucher is used for this entry. The amount of the deposit, *$16 321.40*, is written in the Bank Deposits column. The deposit amount is then added to the previous bank balance shown in the Bank Balance column on line 5. The new bank balance, *$98 148.82*, is written in the Bank Balance column. Information to record this entry is taken from the bank deposit slip.

Posting from a cheque register

Solar Power's cheque register has only special amount columns. Individual items in the cheque register are not posted. At the end of each month, the cheque register's debit and credit columns are totalled, proved, and ruled as on page 578.

Totals of special amount columns are posted to the accounts named in the column headings. The account number to which each amount column total is posted is written in parentheses below the total.

Bank Deposits and Bank Balance columns show only the current balance of the bank account. These columns are neither totalled, ruled, nor posted.

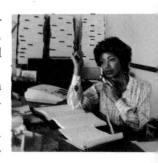

USING A VOUCHER SYSTEM FOR SELECTED BUSINESS TRANSACTIONS

For transactions described previously, a voucher was prepared from each invoice and each voucher was paid in full when due. Some transactions however require different procedures. Examples are purchases returns and allowances and payroll payments.

Recording purchases returns and allowances

A purchases returns and allowances transaction reduces the total invoice amount owed. A voucher for an original invoice must be changed to show reduction in the amount owed.

August 12, 1989. Issued Debit Memorandum No. 64 to Moreno's, Inc., for the return of merchandise purchased, $46.00. Cancelled Voucher No. 608 and issued Voucher No. 611.

Vouchers Payable		
Vchr. 611 136.00	Vchr. 608	136.00
	Vchr. 611	90.00

Purchases Returns and Allowances	
	Vchr. 611 46.00

The liability account Vouchers Payable is debited for the amount of Voucher No. 608, *$136.00*. Vouchers Payable is credited for the amount of the new Voucher No. 611, *$90.00*. The contra account, Purchases Returns and Allowances, is credited for $46.00. The following procedure is used to change the amount owed on Voucher No. 608.

1 Remove Voucher No. 608 from the unpaid vouchers file. Write *Cancelled* across the outside of the voucher.

2 Prepare a new voucher and have it approved. Voucher No. 611 is prepared for the new amount, $90.00. (Original voucher amount, $136.00, less amount of purchases return, $46.00.) The cancelled copy of Voucher No. 608, original invoice, and debit memorandum are placed inside Voucher No. 611.

3 Write *See Vchr. No. 611* in the voucher register's Paid columns on the line for Voucher No. 608. This notation is on line 6 of the voucher register, page 574.

4 Record the new voucher in the voucher register. This entry is on the voucher register, lines 9–10, pages 574 and 575. The date, *12*, is entered in the Date column. The payee's name, *Moreno's, Inc.,* is written in the Payee column. The voucher number, *611*, is written in the Vchr. No. column. The account debited, *Vouchers Payable*, is written in the General Account column. The cancelled voucher's amount, *$136.00*, is written in the General Debit column. The amount of the

new voucher, *$90.00*, is written in the Vouchers Payable Credit column. This is the amount of the original voucher less the purchases return. ($136.00 − 46.00 = $90.00) On the next voucher register line, the account credited, *Purchases Returns and Allowances*, is written in the General Account column. The amount of purchases return, *$46.00*, is written in the General Credit column.

5 File Voucher No. 611 in the unpaid vouchers file by the due date.

Paying a payroll

Solar Power pays its employees semimonthly. A payroll register is prepared to show the details of each payroll. Information from a payroll register is used in preparing a payroll voucher.

> *August 31, 1989. Recorded semimonthly payroll for period ending August 31, 1989, $5 072.80. Voucher No. 628.*

Data from a payroll register are recorded in summary form on the inside of a voucher. Solar Power's August 31, 1989, payroll summary is recorded on the inside of the voucher below. The outside of the voucher is completed as shown below at the right.

VOUCHER

Vchr. No. 628 Date August 31, 19 89 Terms _____ Due August 31, 19 89

To Payroll

Address

For the following: Attach all invoices or other papers permanently to voucher.

DATE	VOUCHER DETAILS		AMOUNT
Aug. 31	Payroll for period ended 1989 08 31		
	Salary Expense		$5 072.80
	Deductions:		
	Employees' Inc. Tax Pay.	$735.55	
	CPP Payable	91.31	
	UI Payable	119.21	946.07
	Net cash payment		$4 126.73

Inside of voucher for a payroll

Vchr. No. 628 Date 1989 08 31 Due Date 1989 08 31

To Payroll

Address

ACCOUNTS DEBITED	AMOUNT
PURCHASES	
SUPPLIES	
ADVERTISING EXPENSE	
DELIVERY EXPENSE	
INSURANCE EXPENSE	
MISCELLANEOUS EXPENSE	
PAYROLL TAXES EXPENSE	
RENT EXPENSE	
SALARY EXPENSE	5 072 80
TOTAL DEBITS	5 072 80

ACCOUNTS CREDITED	AMOUNT
VOUCHERS PAYABLE	4 126 73
EMPLOYEES' INC. TAX PAY.	735 55
CPP PAYABLE	91 31
UI PAYABLE	119 21
TOTAL CREDITS	5 072 80

Voucher Approved by *Louis Zink*

Recorded in Voucher Register Page 24 by BRB

Paid { Date August 31, 1989
Cheque No. 755 Amount $4 126.73
Approved by *Lorene Vader*

Outside of voucher for a payroll

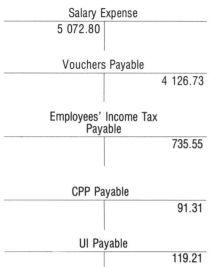

The amounts for each of Solar Power's payroll accounts are shown on the outside of Voucher No. 628. Salary Expense is debited for $5 072.80. The total of the debits, *$5 072.80*, is entered on the Total Debits line. Vouchers Payable is credited for $4 126.73, the net payroll amount to be paid to the employees. Employees' Income Tax Payable is credited for $735.55. CPP Payable is credited for $91.31. UI Payable is credited for $119.21. These amounts are the withholding taxes for the employees' salaries. The four credits are added and the total, *$5 072.80*, is entered on the Total Credits line. The voucher's total debits must equal the total credits.

The voucher is approved by Louis Zink. Mr. Zink signs the outside of Section 3. The approved voucher is then recorded in the voucher register. The entry to record Voucher No. 628 is in the voucher register, lines 30–33, pages 574 and 575. After this entry is recorded, a notation is made in Section 4 on the outside of Voucher No. 628. The voucher register page number and the recording clerk's initials are recorded.

Since Voucher No. 628 is to be paid immediately, the voucher is not placed in the unpaid vouchers file. Rather, Cheque No. 755 is issued for the payroll voucher. The paid section of Voucher No. 628 is completed. The payment is approved and the cheque is signed by Lorene Vaden. The paid voucher is then filed in the paid vouchers file.

August 31, 1989. Paid Voucher No. 628, $4 126.73. Cheque No. 755.

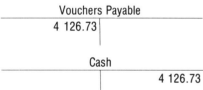

The entry to record Cheque No. 755 is in the cheque register, line 18, page 578. Vouchers Payable is debited and Cash is credited for $4 126.73. The date and cheque number are written in the voucher register's Paid columns, line 30, page 574.

A journal entry to record an employer's payroll taxes is described in Chapter 23. When payroll taxes are due to a government, a voucher is prepared and approved. The approved voucher is recorded in the voucher register. A cheque is then issued for the voucher.

SUMMARIZING THE ADVANTAGES OF A VOUCHER SYSTEM

A voucher system has advantages for businesses that make many cash payments. Some of these advantages are listed below and on the next page.

1. Responsibility for authorizing and approving all expenditures is limited to a few persons.

2. A voucher jacket provides a convenient method of filing invoices for reference. This is especially true when invoices received from creditors may be of different sizes.
3. Filing vouchers according to their due dates helps assure invoice payments within discount periods.
4. A paid vouchers file and an unpaid vouchers file replace the accounts payable ledger.
5. The voucher system eliminates all posting to creditors' accounts.

ACCOUNTING TERMS

What is the meaning of each of the following?

1. voucher system
2. voucher

3. voucher register
4. cheque register

5. voucher cheque

QUESTIONS FOR INDIVIDUAL STUDY

1. Why is a procedure needed that places accounting controls on the asset Cash?
2. What are the major steps in using a voucher system?
3. Why are vouchers numbered consecutively?
4. In a voucher system what liability account is used in place of accounts payable?
5. What ledger is usually not kept when a voucher system is used?
6. When an invoice is received for merchandise purchased on account, which accounts are debited and credited in a voucher system?
7. What journal does the voucher register replace when a voucher system is used?
8. In the voucher register, pages 574–575, which amount columns are posted individually?

9. In the voucher register, page 574, why is there no entry in the Paid columns on line 2?
10. What five items does Solar Power include in the voucher space on its voucher cheques?
11. What journal does the cheque register replace in Solar Power's voucher system?
12. Why does Solar Power's cheque register have Bank Deposits and Bank Balance columns?
13. Why are no amounts posted individually from any of the columns in the cheque register used by Solar Power?
14. How is a purchases return recorded on a voucher?
15. What is the source of data for a payroll voucher?
16. What are five advantages of a voucher system?

CASES FOR MANAGEMENT DECISION

CASE 1 Barbara Vornberg owns and operates two sportswear stores. Mrs. Vornberg keeps most of the accounting records herself. She employs a public accountant part time to assist her. Mrs. Vornberg is considering using a voucher system for her business. What questions should she answer before deciding whether to install a voucher system?

CASE 2 Alan Rodgers owns a hardware store. He uses a voucher system involving four steps. (1) An invoice is received and verified and a voucher is prepared. (2) The voucher is filed in an unpaid vouchers file by the due date. (3) When the voucher is due, a cheque is issued. A notation of the payment is made on the voucher and it is filed in the paid vouchers file. (4) The cheque issued is recorded in a cash payments journal. Mr. Rodgers does not record a voucher in any journal. The cheque is recorded as the only entry. For example, payment for purchases with a discount is entered in a cash payments journal. This transaction debits Purchases and credits Purchases Discount and Cash. What are the advantages and disadvantages of this procedure?

DRILLS FOR UNDERSTANDING

DRILL 28-D 1 Analysing transactions using a voucher register

Use a form similar to the one below.

Trans. No.	Name of Amount Column Used in Voucher Register	
	(a) For Amount Debited	(b) For Amount Credited
1.	Supplies Debit	Vouchers Payable Credit

Instructions: Complete the following steps for each transaction given below. (a) Write the name(s) of the voucher register amount column(s) in which the debit amount(s) will be recorded. (b) Write the name(s) of the voucher register amount column(s) in which the credit amount(s) will be recorded. Amount columns are like those on voucher register, pages 574 and 575. Transaction 1 is given as an example in the form above.

1. Bought supplies on account.
2. Purchased merchandise on account.
3. Received a statement for delivery expenses for the month.
4. Bought a desk (office equipment).
5. Purchased merchandise on account.
6. Received monthly bill from telephone company (miscellaneous expense).
7. Issued debit memorandum for the return of merchandise purchased earlier. Cancelled original voucher and issued new voucher.
8. Payroll register showed entries in the following accounts: Salary Expense, Employees' Income Tax Payable, CPP Payable, and Vouchers Payable.
9. Bought supplies on account.
10. Bought new delivery truck.

DRILL 28-D 2 Analysing transactions using a cheque register

Use a form similar to the one below.

Trans. or Activity No.	Vouchers Payable Debit	Purchases Discount Credit	Cash Credit	Bank	
				Deposits	Balance
1.	√		√		√

Instructions: For each transaction or activity given below, place a check mark in each column that should have an amount recorded. Transaction 1 is given as an example in the form, page 584.

1. Paid a voucher; no discount.
2. Made a deposit in the bank.
3. Paid a voucher less discount.
4. Recorded the cash balance on the first day of the month.
5. Paid a voucher; no discount.
6. Paid a voucher less discount.
7. Brought forward account balances from previous page of cheque register.
8. Paid voucher less discount.
9. Totalled, proved, and ruled the cheque register.

APPLICATION PROBLEMS

PROBLEM 28-1   Preparing a voucher

Capri Building Supplies uses a voucher form similar to the one on pages 574 and 575.

Instructions: 1. Record in Sections 1 and 2 of the outside of a voucher the following selected transactions. Use July of the current year. Voucher is abbreviated as V.

July 6. Purchased merchandise on account from Four Seasons Inc., 1366 Prince Street, Truro, NS B2N 1J7, $1 890.00. V123. Due date is July 14.

  8. Bought supplies on account from Elder Supplies, 1208 Robie Street, Halifax, NS B3H 3C9, $258.25. V124. Due date is July 18.

  11. Received a statement from Custom Delivery Service, 148 Church Street, Amherst, NS B4H 3C4, $127.50. Statement is for delivery expenses. V125. Due date is July 12.

Instructions: 2. Check the accuracy of each completed voucher. Then sign your name on the "Voucher Approved by" line.

PROBLEM 28-2   Recording vouchers in a voucher register

Airco Energy uses a voucher register similar to the one on pages 574 and 575.

Instructions: 1. Record on page 7 of a voucher register the following selected transactions completed during March of the current year. Voucher is abbreviated as V.

Mar. 1. Received bill for March rent owed to Katz Real Estate, $1 000.00. V63.
  4. Purchased merchandise on account from Kohler Company, $2 338.40. V64.
  7. Purchased merchandise on account from Fox Corporation, $2 987.25. V65.
  7. Bought supplies on account from Office Centre, $296.50. V66.
  8. Received monthly bill from Bell Canada, $136.80. V67.
  11. Received monthly statement from *The Star* for newspaper advertising, $78.30. V68.
  14. Purchased merchandise on account from DiLeo Equipment, $4 577.40. V69.
  18. Bought supplies on account from Office Centre, $137.60. V70.
  21. Bought a desk from Herkes Office Equipment, $600.00. V71.
  26. Purchased merchandise on account from Energy Search, $2 445.00. V72.
  28. Bought supplies on account from Ryan Supplies, $325.50. V73.
  30. Purchased merchandise on account from Zeff Enterprises, $1 890.30. V74.

Instructions: 2. Total, prove, and rule the voucher register.

The voucher register prepared in Problem 28-2 is needed to complete Problem 28-3.

PROBLEM 28-3 Recording cash transactions in a cheque register

The voucher register prepared in Problem 28-2 is needed to complete Problem 28-3.

Airco Energy uses a cheque register similar to the one on page 578 to record all cash payments.

Instructions: 1. Record on page 5 of a cheque register the following cash payments made during March of the current year. Source documents are abbreviated as: cheque, C; voucher, V.

2. Vouchers paid are for transactions in Problem 28-2. Record the date and cheque number for each transaction in the Paid columns of the voucher register completed in Problem 28-2.

Mar. 1. Recorded cash balance on March 1, $15 532.90.
      1. Paid V63, $1 000.00. C56.
      8. Paid V67, $136.80. C57.
     11. Paid V68, $78.30. C58.
     14. Paid V65, $2 987.25, less purchases discount, $59.75. C59.
     14. Paid V64, $2 338.40, less purchases discount, $23.38. C60.
     14. Made a deposit in the bank, $5 979.60.
     15. Paid V66, $296.50; no discount. C61.
     21. Paid V69, $4 577.40, less purchases discount, $45.77. C62.
     26. Paid V70, $137.60; no discount. C63.
     28. Paid V71, $600.00; no discount. C64.
     30. Made a deposit in the bank, $9 130.25.

Instructions: 3. Total, prove, and rule the cheque register.

PROBLEM 28-4 Preparing payroll vouchers

Airco Energy's payroll register shows the following information. Voucher is abbreviated as V.

May 15. The payroll register shows the following: Salary Expense, $2 588.60; Employees' Income Tax Payable, $483.78; CPP Payable, $51.78; UI Payable, $77.66. V120.
    31. The payroll register shows the following: Salary Expense, $2 735.70; Employees' Income Tax Payable, $518.86; CPP Payable, $54.71; UI Payable, $82.07. V139.

Instructions: Prepare a voucher for each of the payroll entries above.

PROBLEM 28-5 Recording purchases returns and allowances and payroll transactions in a voucher system

Airco Energy uses a voucher register similar to the one on pages 574 and 575. The company uses a cheque register similar to the one on page 578.

Instructions: 1. Record the following selected transactions completed during May of the current year. Use page 9 of a voucher register and page 7 of a cheque register. Source documents are abbreviated as: cheque, C; debit memorandum, DM; voucher, V.

May 1. Recorded cash balance on May 1, $14 235.50.
     5. Purchased merchandise on account from Yetka Corporation, $2 565.00. V104.
     9. Issued DM48 to Yetka Corporation for the return of merchandise purchased, $125.00. Cancelled V104 and issued V107.
   15. The payroll register for the semimonthly payroll showed the following information. Salary Expense, $2 588.60; Employees' Income Tax Payable, $483.78; Canada Pension Plan Payable, $51.78; Unemployment Insurance Payable, $77.66. V120.
   15. Paid V120, $1 975.38. C94.
   18. Paid V107, $2 440.00; no discount. C98.
   24. Purchased merchandise on account from LiteRite Company, $1 315.00. V130.
   28. Issued DM49 to LiteRite Company for the return of merchandise purchased, $165.00. Cancelled V130 and issued V136.
   31. The payroll register for the semimonthly payroll showed the following information. Salary Expense, $2 735.70; Employees' Income Tax Payable, $518.86; Canada Pension Plan Payable, $54.71; Unemployment Insurance Payable, $82.07. V139.
   31. Paid V139, $2 080.06. C124.

Instructions: 2. Total, prove, and rule the voucher register and cheque register.

ENRICHMENT PROBLEMS

MASTERY PROBLEM 28-M   Recording transactions in a voucher system

Carson Company uses a voucher system. A voucher register and a cheque register similar to those on pages 574–575 and 578 are used.

Instructions: 1. Record the following transactions completed during June of the current year. Use page 15 of a voucher register and page 12 of a cheque register. Source documents are abbreviated as: cheque, C; debit memorandum, DM; voucher, V.

All purchases of merchandise on account are subject to a 2% purchases discount if paid within 10 days. No discounts are allowed on other payments.

June 1. Recorded the cash balance on June 1, $10 636.44.
     2. Purchased merchandise on account from Merriam Supplies, $400.40. V223.
     9. Purchased merchandise on account from Western Enterprises, $1 797.04. V224.
     9. Made a deposit in the bank, $3 763.66.
   12. Paid V223 less discount. C176.
   20. Purchased merchandise on account from Gonzalez Wholesale Company, $610.66. V225.
   21. Made a deposit in the bank, $3 178.22.
   22. Bought supplies from Jericho Supplies, $373.24. V226.
   22. Paid V226; no discount. C177.
   24. Issued DM39 to Western Enterprises for the return of merchandise purchased, $324.04. Cancelled V224 and issued V227.

June 27. Paid V227. Since this voucher was not paid within the discount period, no discount is to be taken. C178.
28. Received a statement from Northpark Delivery Service for delivery expenses for the month, $402.50. V228.
28. Paid V228; no discount. C179.
28. Paid V225 less discount. C180.
29. Purchased merchandise on account from Western Enterprises, $921.48. V229.
29. Paid V229 less discount. C181.
30. The payroll register for the monthly payroll showed the following information. Salary Expense, $6 918.24; Employees' Income Tax Payable, $1 122.23; Canada Pension Plan Payable, $138.36; Unemployment Insurance Payable, $207.55. V230.
30. Paid V230. C182.
30. Made a deposit in the bank, $3 174.47.

Instructions: 2. Total, prove, and rule the voucher register and cheque register.

CHALLENGE PROBLEM 28-C Recording purchase invoices at the net amount in a voucher system

Introductory remarks. Some businesses make a practice of paying all invoices within the discount period. These businesses can record invoices at the net amount to be paid at the time the invoice is received. For example, a $1 000.00 invoice with a 2% discount allowed if paid within 10 days would be recorded at $980.00. At the time the voucher is prepared and recorded in the voucher register, Purchases is debited for $980.00. Vouchers Payable is credited for the same amount. The purchases discount amount is not recorded.

If an invoice is not paid within the discount period, Discounts Lost is debited for the amount of discount lost. For example, if the invoice described above were not paid within the discount period, $1 000.00 would have to be paid. The entry would be debits to Vouchers Payable, $980.00, and Discounts Lost, $20.00. Cash would be credited for the amount paid, $1 000.00.

If the invoice above is recorded at the net amount, a purchases return also is recorded at the net amount. If a debit memorandum is issued for $100.00, the purchases return is recorded at $98.00. (Purchases return, $100.00, less 2% discount.) The entry is a debit to Vouchers Payable, $980.00, to cancel the original voucher. Vouchers Payable is credited for the amount of the new voucher, $882.00. (Original voucher amount, $980.00, less amount of purchases return, $98.00.) Purchases Returns and Allowances is credited for $98.00. If the invoice is not paid within the discount period, $900.00 would have to be paid. The entry would be debits to Vouchers Payable, $882.00, and Discounts Lost, $18.00. Cash would be credited for the amount paid, $900.00.

This system uses a cheque register with special amount columns for Vouchers Payable Debit, Discounts Lost Debit, and Cash Credit.

Instructions: 1. Use the transactions and information given in Mastery Problem 28-M. In the cheque register, record the beginning cash balance, $10 636.44.

2. Record the transactions for June on page 17 of a voucher register and on page 14 of a cheque register. Record all vouchers at the net amount to be paid. If the discount is lost, record this in the cheque register at the time the voucher is paid.

3. Total, prove, and rule the voucher register and the cheque register.

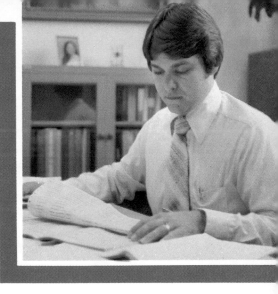

29

A Petty Cash System

ENABLING PERFORMANCE TASKS

After studying Chapter 29, you will be able to:

a. Define accounting terms related to a petty cash system.
b. Explain accounting principles and practices related to a petty cash system.
c. Establish a petty cash fund using a voucher system.
d. Record payments from a petty cash fund in a petty cash record.
e. Prepare a voucher to replenish a petty cash fund.
f. Determine if a petty cash fund is short or over.
g. Establish and replenish a petty cash fund using a cash payments journal.

Good cash control requires that businesses deposit all cash receipts in a bank account. Good control also requires that cheques be written for all major cash payments. Most businesses however make small cash payments for items such as postage, delivery charges, collect telegrams, and some supplies.

Writing a separate cheque for each small purchase becomes a time-consuming and expensive process. To avoid writing many cheques for small amounts, some businesses establish a special cash fund. These small payments are then made from this fund. An amount of cash kept on hand and used for making small payments is called petty cash. Making such payments from petty cash avoids issuing cheques for small amounts.

Using a petty cash fund enables a business to practice good cash control. A business can then deposit all receipts and write cheques for all payments except petty cash payments. When this practice is followed, most small payments made by a business are from petty cash. Special procedures may then be used to control the petty cash fund. These cash control procedures permit a business to use monthly bank statements to prove its cash records. A specific employee should be assigned responsibility for safekeeping and maintaining the fund. This person generally is referred to as petty cash custodian or petty cash cashier.

ESTABLISHING A PETTY CASH FUND

In establishing a petty cash fund, an estimate is made of an amount of cash needed for small payments. An amount should be sufficient to last for a period of time, usually a month. Solar Power establishes a petty cash fund on September 1, 1989. Based on past experience, the company determines that $250.00 will be an adequate petty cash fund.

If a voucher system is used, a voucher is prepared for the amount of the petty cash fund to be established. A memorandum is used as authorization to prepare a voucher to establish Solar Power's petty cash fund. (*CONCEPT: Objective Evidence*)

September 1, 1989. Established a petty cash fund, $250.00. Voucher No. 629.

Petty Cash	
250.00	

Vouchers Payable	
	250.00

The asset account Petty Cash is debited, *$250.00*. The liability account Vouchers Payable is credited, *$250.00*.

The voucher prepared to establish Solar Power's petty cash fund is on the next page.

The voucher register below and on page 591 shows the entry to record the establishment of a petty cash fund for Solar Power. The voucher register payee is Petty Cash Custodian, Solar Power. The debit is to Petty Cash, *$250.00*. The credit is to Vouchers Payable, *$250.00*.

Voucher register entry establishing a petty cash fund (left page)

				PAID		VOUCHERS
	DATE	PAYEE	VCHR. NO.	DATE	CH. NO.	PAYABLE CREDIT
1	*1989 Sept. 1*	*Petty Cash Custodian, Solar Power*	*629*	*Sept. 1*	*756*	*250 00*

PAGE **25**   **VOUCHER REGISTER**

The cheque for establishing Solar Power's petty cash fund is made payable to Petty Cash Custodian, Solar Power. The cheque is recorded in a cheque register below as a debit to Vouchers Payable and a credit to Cash, $250.00.

Solar Power now has two general ledger accounts for cash. The account Cash includes all cash in Solar Power's bank account. The new account Petty Cash includes cash kept in the business to pay small amounts. Petty Cash is placed immediately after Cash in the general ledger as on the chart of accounts, page 570.

Cheque register entry establishing a petty cash fund

CHEQUE REGISTER   PAGE **29**

	DATE	PAYEE	CH. NO.	VCHR. NO.	VOUCHERS PAYABLE DEBIT	PURCHASES DISCOUNT CREDIT	CASH CREDIT	DEPOSITS	BALANCE
1	*1989 Sept. 1*	*Balance on hand*		✓					*98 859 60*
2	*1*	*Petty Cash Custodian, Solar Power*	*756*	*629*	*250 00*		*250 00*		*98 609 60*

Vchr. No. _629_	Date 1989 09 01	Due Date 1989 09 01

To _Petty Cash Custodian, Solar Power_

Address _1629 Louise Avenue_

Brandon, MB R7A 0Y7

ACCOUNTS DEBITED	AMOUNT
PURCHASES	
SUPPLIES	
ADVERTISING EXPENSE	
DELIVERY EXPENSE	
INSURANCE EXPENSE	
MISCELLANEOUS EXPENSE	
PAYROLL TAXES EXPENSE	
RENT EXPENSE	
SALARY EXPENSE	
Petty Cash	250 00
TOTAL DEBITS	250 00
ACCOUNTS CREDITED	AMOUNT
VOUCHERS PAYABLE	250 00
EMPLOYEES' INC. TAX PAY.	
CPP PAYABLE	
UI PAYABLE	
TOTAL CREDITS	250 00

Voucher Approved by _Louis Zink_

Recorded in Voucher Register Page _25_   by _DRD_

Paid { Date _Sept. 1, 1989_
Cheque No. _756_____ Amount $ _250.00_
Approved by _Lorena Vader_

Voucher to establish a petty cash fund

FOR MONTH OF _September_ 19 **89**				PAGE _25_	
2	3	4		5	6
DISTRIBUTION			GENERAL		
PURCHASES DEBIT	DELIVERY EXPENSE DEBIT	SUPPLIES DEBIT	ACCOUNT	POST REF.	DEBIT	CREDIT	
			Petty Cash	1102	250 00		1

Voucher register entry establishing a petty cash fund (right page)

Solar Power appointed its cashier, George Hernandez, Petty Cash Custodian. Mr. Hernandez cashed the cheque payable to Petty Cash Custodian. He placed the $250.00 in a petty cash box in the office safe. Mr. Hernandez is responsible for keeping the petty cash secure and separate from all other cash.

MAKING PAYMENTS FROM A PETTY CASH FUND

Before the business opens each day, Solar Power's petty cash custodian removes the petty cash box from the office safe. The petty cash box is placed in a separate compartment of the cash register. Petty cash payments are made from the cash box. The custodian is authorized to make petty cash payments up to $30.00 for a single payment. Petty cash payments more than $30.00 must have the manager's approval.

Each time a petty cash payment is made, a petty cash voucher is prepared. A form showing proof of petty cash payments is called a petty cash voucher. A petty cash voucher shows the following information. (a) Voucher number. (b) Date. (c) To whom paid. (d) Reason for payment. (e) Amount paid. (f) Account charged. (g) Signature of person to whom payment is made. (h) Signature of person approving payment, normally the petty cash custodian. A petty cash voucher for cash paid to buy stamps on September 2 is below.

Petty cash voucher

After each petty cash payment, the voucher is recorded in a petty cash record and placed in the petty cash box. A form on which petty cash receipts and payments are recorded is called a petty cash record. Solar Power's petty cash record showing a payment, line 2, for postage stamps is on the next page.

A petty cash record usually is a supplementary record, not a journal from which accounts are posted. Solar Power uses its petty cash record to summarize petty cash receipts and payments for a month. The record is totalled monthly to summarize the amounts for an entry in a voucher register.

At the end of each day *all* vouchers in the petty cash box are added and all money is counted. The vouchers plus cash in the petty cash box should always equal the original amount of the petty cash fund. The total of all vouchers plus cash in the petty cash box must equal $250.00. For example, on September 8, four vouchers totalling $54.95 and the remaining cash, *$195.05*, are in the petty cash box. The vouchers total, *$54.95*, plus cash, *$195.05*, equals $250.00. This total amount, *$250.00*, is the amount placed in the petty cash fund originally.

REPLENISHING A PETTY CASH FUND

As money is paid out of petty cash, the vouchers amount increases and the cash amount decreases. Therefore, petty cash is replenished periodically.

A petty cash fund should be replenished at two different times. (1) Petty cash is replenished when only a small amount of cash remains in the petty cash box. (2) Petty cash is always replenished at the end of each fiscal period. Vouchers in a petty cash box represent transactions that must be journalized and posted. If accounting records are to be accurate, a petty cash fund must be replenished at the end of fiscal periods. If a fund is not replenished at the end of each fiscal period, the following inaccuracies occur. The balance of Petty Cash in the general ledger is not an accurate statement of cash on hand. The balance sheet is not an accurate statement of assets. The income statement expenses are not an accurate statement of expenses.

Solar Power replenishes its petty cash fund when cash in the cash box is reduced not lower than $50.00. This practice assures cash available for unexpected cash payments. Solar Power also replenishes its fund at the end of each fiscal period. This practice assures that all petty cash payments will be posted before financial statements are prepared.

Solar Power's procedures for replenishing its petty cash fund are described below.

1 The custodian totals, proves, and rules the petty cash record amount columns as shown on line 13 of the record below.

Petty cash record at the end of a fiscal period

PETTY CASH RECORD

MONTH OF *September 1989*   PAGE *1*

	DATE	EXPLANATION	PETTY CASH VCHR. NO.	RECEIPTS	PAYMENTS	SUPPLIES	DELIVERY EXPENSE	MISC. EXPENSE	OTHER PAYMENTS ACCOUNT	AMOUNT	
1	1989 Sept. 1 Established fund			250 00							1
2	2 Postage stamps	1		30 00	30 00					2
3	5 Collect telegram	2		3 50			3 50			3
4	7 Postage on a sale	3		6 85		6 85				4
5	8 Printer ribbons	4		14 60	14 60					5
6	12 Repair of calculator	5		22 50			22 50			6
7	14 Ad in school yearbook	6		25 00				Advertising Expense	25 00	7
8	15 Postage on a sale	7		6 25		6 25				8
9	19 Postage stamps	8		30 00	30 00					9
10	20 Special envelopes	9		16 50	16 50					10
11	26 Award certificates	10		10 80			10 80			11
12	30 Coffee for conference	11		8 50			8 50			12
13	Totals		250 00	174 50	91 10	13 10	45 30		25 00	13
14	Cash balance			75 50						14
15	Totals		250 00	250 00						15
16	Sept. 30 Cash balance		75 50							16
17	30 Replenished fund		174 50							17

The sum of Distribution of Payments column totals, $174.50, must be equal to Payments column total, $174.50. Payments column total, $174.50, is subtracted from Receipts column total, $250.00. The difference, $75.50, is recorded as shown on line 14 of the petty cash record. *Cash balance* is written in the Explanation column. The cash balance, $75.50, should be the same as the amount in the petty cash box, $75.50. The Receipts and Payments columns are then ruled as shown on line 15 of the petty cash record.

2 A voucher is prepared to replenish the petty cash fund for the amount paid out, $174.50. This amount will restore the cash balance of the fund to its original amount, $250.00. Voucher debit entry accounts and amounts are from the Distribution of Payments column totals, line 13 of the record, page 591. The supporting petty cash vouchers are enclosed in the voucher. (CONCEPT: *Objective Evidence*)

Supplies	
91.10	

Delivery Expense	
13.10	

Miscellaneous Expense	
45.30	

Advertising Expense	
25.00	

Vouchers Payable	
	174.50

September 30, 1989. Replenished petty cash fund. Debit the following accounts: Supplies, $91.10; Delivery Expense, $13.10; Miscellaneous Expense, $45.30; Advertising Expense, $25.00; total, $174.50. Voucher No. 665.

The debit entries are Supplies, $91.10, Delivery Expense, $13.10, Miscellaneous Expense, $45.30, Advertising Expense, $25.00. The liability account Vouchers Payable is credited, $174.50.

The voucher prepared to replenish Solar Power's petty cash fund is on the next page.

3 The voucher to replenish the petty cash fund is recorded in a voucher register as shown below and on page 595. The voucher register payee is Petty Cash Custodian, Solar Power. The following accounts are debited. Supplies, $91.10. Delivery Expense, $13.10. Miscellaneous Expense, $45.30. Advertising Expense, $25.00. Vouchers Payable is credited for $174.50.

					PAID			
	DATE		PAYEE	VCHR. NO.	DATE	CH. NO.	VOUCHERS PAYABLE CREDIT	
10	30		Petty Cash Custodian, Solar Power	665	Sept. 30	790	17450	10
11								11
12								12
13								13
14								14

PAGE 26   **VOUCHER REGISTER**

Voucher register entry replenishing a petty cash fund (left page)

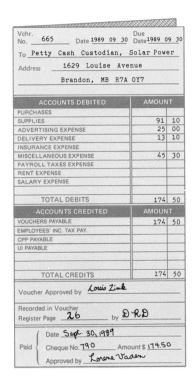

Voucher to replenish a
petty cash fund

4 The cheque for replenishing Solar Power's petty cash fund is made
payable to Petty Cash Custodian, Solar Power. The cheque is recorded
in Solar Power's cheque register. The custodian cashes the cheque and
places the cash in the petty cash box.

5 The custodian records the cash balance, *$75.50*, and replenished
fund, *$174.50*, in the Receipts column of the petty cash record. This
entry for Solar Power is on lines 16 and 17 of a petty cash record,
page 593. The cash balance plus replenished fund equals the original
fund balance ($75.50 plus $174.50 equals $250.00). This amount,
$250.00, is the beginning balance for the next fiscal period.

				FOR MONTH OF *September* 19 *89*		PAGE *26*			
	2	3	4			5	6		
		DISTRIBUTION			GENERAL				
	PURCHASES DEBIT	DELIVERY EXPENSE DEBIT	SUPPLIES DEBIT	ACCOUNT	POST REF.	DEBIT	CREDIT		
10		*13 10*	*91 10*	*Advertising Expense*		*25 00*			10
11				*Miscellaneous Expense*		*45 30*			11
12									12
13									13
14									14

Voucher register entry
replenishing a petty cash
fund (right page)

RECORDING PETTY CASH THAT IS SHORT OR OVER

Errors may be made when making payments from a petty cash fund. These errors cause a difference between actual cash on hand and the cash balance in the petty cash record. Differences are discovered at the end of each day when petty cash vouchers and cash are totalled. To keep the petty cash fund at a constant amount, differences are recorded at the end of a fiscal period. Differences for a fiscal period are determined by comparing the payments record with the cash box amount before replenishment.

Petty cash short

Cash in the petty cash box may be less than the cash balance shown in the petty cash record. A petty cash on hand amount less than a recorded amount is called cash short. Column totals for Solar Power's petty cash record prior to replenishment on October 31 are below, line 10. Receipts total, *$250.00*, less Payments total, *$156.40*, equals the balance, *$93.60*. The balance, *$93.60*, should equal the amount in the petty cash box. A count shows *$89.85* in the petty cash box. Cash on hand, *$89.85*, is $3.75 less than the record shows, *$93.60* ($250.00 − $156.40). Therefore, the petty cash fund is short.

Petty cash record with a cash short entry

Cash short, *$3.75*, is recorded on line 11 of the record above. *Cash short* is written in the Explanation column. The cash shortage, *$3.75*, is entered in the Payments column and Other Payments Amount column. The account *Cash Short and Over* is written in the Other Payments Account column. Actual cash on hand, *$89.85*, is then recorded in the Payments column, on line 12. The Receipts and Payments columns are totalled and ruled as shown on the record, line 13.

A voucher is prepared when the fund is replenished for the amount paid out, *$156.40*, plus cash short, *$3.75*. This amount, *$160.15*, will restore the fund's cash balance to its original amount, *$250.00* ($156.40 + $3.75 + $89.85 cash on hand).

October 31, 1989. Replenished petty cash fund. Debit the following accounts: Supplies, $78.75; Delivery Expense, $28.50; Miscellaneous Expense, $38.10; Advertising Expense, $11.05; Cash Short and Over, $3.75; total, $160.15. Voucher No. 705.

Supplies	
78.75	

Delivery Expense	
28.50	

Miscellaneous Expense	
38.10	

Advertising Expense	
11.05	

Cash Short and Over	
3.75	

Vouchers Payable	
	160.15

A voucher is prepared with entries shown at the right to replenish Solar Power's petty cash fund. Debit entries include each account in the petty cash record's Distribution of Payments columns plus Cash Short and Over. The credit entry, Vouchers Payable, is the sum of the debit entries. Procedures for preparing the voucher and completing the replenishment process are the same as steps 2–5, pages 594 and 595.

Petty cash over

Cash in the petty cash box may be more than the cash balance shown in the petty cash record. An error in making change generally causes this difference. A petty cash on hand amount more than a recorded amount is called cash over.

Column totals for Solar Power's petty cash record on January 31, 1990, are below, line 12.

PETTY CASH RECORD

MONTH OF *January 1990*   PAGE *5*

	DATE	EXPLANATION	PETTY CASH VCHR. NO.	RECEIPTS	PAYMENTS	DISTRIBUTION OF PAYMENTS					
						SUPPLIES	DELIVERY EXPENSE	MISC. EXPENSE	OTHER PAYMENTS ACCOUNT	AMOUNT	
1	1990 Jan. 1	Beginning balance		25000							1
12		Totals		25000	16625	8850	3640	4135		000	12
13		Cash over			(100)				Cash Short and Over	(100)	13
14		Cash balance			8475						14
15		Totals		25000	25000						15
16	Jan. 31	Cash balance		8475							16
17	31	Replenished fund		16525							17

Receipts column total, *$250.00*, less Payments column total, *$166.25*, equals $83.75, the amount of cash that should be on hand. However, a cash count shows $84.75 in the cash box. Cash on hand, *$84.75*, is $1.00 more than the record shows, $83.75 ($250.00 − $166.25). Therefore, the petty cash fund is over.

Petty cash record with a cash over entry

Cash over is recorded as shown on line 13 of the record above. *Cash over* is written in the Explanation column. Cash over amount, *$1.00*, is written within parentheses in the Payments column and Other Payments Amount column to indicate subtraction from other amounts. The account *Cash Short and Over* is written in the Other Payments Account column. Actual cash on hand, *$84.75*, is entered in the Payments column, on line 14. The Receipts and Payments columns are totalled and ruled as shown on line 15 of the record, page 597.

A voucher is prepared replenishing the petty cash fund to its original amount, *$250.00*. The vouchers payable amount, $165.25, is the amount paid out, $166.25, less cash over, *$1.00*.

January 31, 1990. Replenished petty cash fund. Debit the following accounts: Supplies, $88.50; Delivery Expense, $36.40; Miscellaneous Expense, $41.35. Credit Vouchers Payable, $165.25; Cash Short and Over, $1.00. Voucher No. 832.

Supplies	
88.50	

Delivery Expense	
36.40	

Miscellaneous Expense	
41.35	

Vouchers Payable	
	165.25

Cash Short and Over	
	1.00

A voucher is prepared with entries shown at the left. Debit entries are the accounts in the petty cash record's Distribution of Payments columns. Credit entries are Vouchers Payable and Cash Short and Over. Procedures for preparing the voucher and completing the replenishment process are the same as steps 2–5, pages 594 and 595.

Any balance in a cash short and over account is closed to Income Summary at the end of a fiscal period. A Cash Short and Over debit balance is reported on an income statement as other expenses. A credit balance is reported as other revenue.

USING A PETTY CASH FUND WITH A CASH PAYMENTS JOURNAL

Businesses using a cash payments journal follow similar petty cash fund procedures as businesses using a voucher system. In a voucher system, a voucher and voucher register are used to establish and replenish a petty cash fund. Other businesses may use a cash payments journal to establish and replenish a petty cash fund.

Way Station Appliances, using a cash payments journal, maintains and replenishes its petty cash fund as described below.

1 Petty cash vouchers are recorded in a petty cash record for each payment similar to Solar Power, page 593.

2 Before replenishing the fund, the petty cash record is totalled, proved, and ruled similar to Solar Power's step 1, page 593.

3 From the petty cash record's column totals, a request to replenish petty cash fund is prepared. On October 31, 1989, the following column totals were listed on Way Station's petty cash record. Receipts, $150.00. Payments, $113.05. Supplies, $64.20. Delivery Expense, $32.75.

Miscellaneous Expense, $16.10. A cash count shows $36.95 in the petty cash box. Receipts, *$150.00*, less payments, *$113.05*, equals cash balance, *$36.95*. Equality of the fund is proven. Way Station's October 31 request form to replenish petty cash is below.

REQUEST TO REPLENISH PETTY CASH FUND	
PAYMENTS	
Account	Amount
Supplies	64.20
Delivery Expense	32.75
Miscellaneous Expense	16.10
Total needed to replenish	113.05

Requested by:
Jan Rogue   Custodian

October 31, 19 89

Approved by:
Paul Whitaker

October 31, 19 89

Issued Cheque No. _____ 316

Request form for replenishing a petty cash fund

October 31, 1989. Issued a cheque to replenish the petty cash fund. Debit the following accounts: Supplies, $64.20; Delivery Expense, $32.75; Miscellaneous Expense, $16.10; total, $113.05. Cheque No. 316.

A cheque for $113.05 is approved and issued to the petty cash custodian. The petty cash fund is restored to $150.00, the original amount.

4 Information for a cash payments journal entry is from the completed form Request to Replenish Petty Cash Fund. The cheque stub is the source document for the entry. (*CONCEPT: Objective Evidence*) Each account listed on the form is debited for the amount shown. Cash is credited for the total amount. The entry for petty cash fund replenishment is recorded in a cash payments journal as shown below.

Cash payments journal entry to replenish a petty cash fund

CASH PAYMENTS JOURNAL PAGE 19

	DATE	ACCOUNT TITLE	CH. No.	POST. REF.	GENERAL DEBIT	GENERAL CREDIT	ACCOUNTS PAYABLE DEBIT	PURCHASES DISCOUNT CREDIT	CASH CREDIT	
12	31	Supplies	316		6420				11305	12
13		Delivery Expense			3275					13
14		Miscellaneous Expense			1610					14

ACCOUNTING TERMS

What is the meaning of each of the following?

1. petty cash
2. petty cash voucher
3. petty cash record
4. cash short
5. cash over

QUESTIONS FOR INDIVIDUAL STUDY

1. What practices are a required part of a business' good cash control?
2. How can a business avoid writing cheques for very small purchases and still practice good cash control?
3. What amount of cash should be placed in a petty cash fund?
4. What accounts did Solar Power debit and credit in the voucher register to establish a petty cash fund?
5. To whom is a cheque for establishing a petty cash fund made payable?
6. Where is a petty cash account located in a general ledger?
7. What are the principal responsibilities of a petty cash custodian?
8. What form does Solar Power prepare each time a payment is made from petty cash?
9. Why does Solar Power use a petty cash record?
10. How can a custodian determine if, at the end of any day, the cash in the petty cash box is the correct amount?
11. When should a petty cash fund be replenished?
12. Why must the petty cash fund be replenished at the end of each fiscal period?
13. What accounts are debited and credited to replenish a petty cash fund?
14. What is the amount for which a fund is replenished?
15. If cash is short when a fund is replenished, what account is used to record the shortage?
16. If cash is over when a fund is replenished, what account is used to record the overage?
17. How is a balance in the cash short and over account treated at the end of a fiscal period?
18. How is a Cash Short and Over debit balance reported on the financial statements?
19. How is a Cash Short and Over credit balance reported on the financial statements?
20. What is the difference between a petty cash fund using a voucher system and one using a cash payments journal?

CASES FOR MANAGEMENT DECISION

CASE 1 Fairmont Company has decided to establish a petty cash fund. Estimated weekly expenditures from the fund are $50.00. Roy Dorries, the accountant, recommends the fund amount be established at $50.00. Mr. Dorries states that this amount will permit frequent review of the expenditures and better cash control.

Mary Yarbro, the manager, prefers the fund be established for $2 500.00 to "avoid writing so many cheques." Is Mr. Dorries' or Ms. Yarbro's recommendation better? Or do you recommend an amount not suggested by either Dorries or Yarbro? Give the reason for your recommendation.

CASE 2 Delta Company has established a $200.00 petty cash fund. During a routine review of the petty cash records, you discover small shortages totalling $15.00 have occurred over the past four months. The fund custodian, Deb Hopkins, has not listed Cash Short and Over on any of the vouchers prepared for replenishment.

When asked about this practice, Miss Hopkins said she always waited until the amount of shortage was significant, approximately $50.00. Then she requested replenishment for the amount of shortage. What is your opinion of this practice? What action do you recommend?

DRILL 29-D 1   Replenishing a petty cash fund

Petty cash is replenished for the amounts and on the dates shown in the table below.

Date on which Replenished	Totals of Petty Cash Record Amount Columns			
	Supplies	Delivery Expense	Miscellaneous Expense	Advertising Expense
March 31	$47.25	$23.60	$32.15	$15.25
April 30	$68.40	$41.90	$24.25	$20.00
May 31	$36.95	$28.20	$20.25	$32.50
June 30	$73.16	$51.22	$36.93	$28.75

Instructions: For each date, prepare T accounts for the accounts affected by the voucher register entry to replenish petty cash. Record the amounts on the debit or credit side of each T account to show how accounts are affected.

APPLICATION PROBLEMS

PROBLEM 29-1   Establishing and making payments from a petty cash fund

Metro Company decided to establish a petty cash fund on June 1 of the current year. The amount of the fund is to be $200.00.

Instructions: 1. Record on a voucher register like the one on pages 590 and 591 the establishment of the petty cash fund. Voucher number is 336. Voucher register page is 12. Payee is Petty Cash Custodian.

2. Record on a cheque register like the one on page 590 the cheque to establish the petty cash fund. June 1 cash balance on hand is $84 623.50. Cheque number is 381. Cheque register page is 10.

3. Record the beginning balance and the following payments from Metro's petty cash fund during June of the current year. Record the transactions on page 1 of a petty cash record like the one on page 593. Source document petty cash voucher is abbreviated PV.

June   2. Paid for note paper, $10.50. PV1 (Supplies)
  6. Paid collect telegram, $5.40. PV2. (Miscellaneous Expense)
  7. Paid repair of word processor, $26.50. PV3. (Miscellaneous Expense)
  9. Paid postage on a sale, $7.35. PV4. (Delivery Expense)
  13. Paid for postage stamps, $15.00. PV5. (Supplies)
  15. Paid for ad in school paper, $20.00. PV6. (Advertising Expense)
  17. Paid postage on a sale, $8.90. PV7. (Delivery Expense)
  20. Paid for telegram, $7.25. PV8. (Miscellaneous Expense)
  21. Paid for carbon paper, $10.60. PV9. (Supplies)
  23. Paid postage on a sale, $12.75. PV10. (Delivery Expense)
  27. Paid for postage stamps, $30.00. PV11. (Supplies)
  30. Paid for postage on a sale, $7.75. PV12. (Delivery Expense)

The petty cash record prepared in Problem 29-1 is needed to complete Problem 29-2.

PROBLEM 29-2   Replenishing a petty cash fund

The petty cash record prepared in Problem 29-1 is needed to complete Problem 29-2.

Instructions: 1. Total and rule the Distribution of Payments columns in the petty cash record prepared in Problem 29-1.

2. The petty cash box has $38.00 at the end of the day, June 30. Compare for equality the sum of cash and payments with the petty cash beginning balance.

3. Record the cash balance. Total and rule the Receipts and Payments columns.

4. Prepare a voucher like the one on page 595 to replenish Metro's petty cash fund on June 30. Additional information on the voucher is listed below.

Voucher No.: 392
Metro's address: 154 Alsek Road, Whitehorse, YT   Y1A 3V6
Voucher approved by: Mari Tanaka
Voucher register page: 14
Recorded by: LBK
Cheque No.: 423
Payment approved by: Michael MacIver

5. Record Voucher No. 392 on page 14 of a voucher register like the one on pages 594 and 595.

6. Record Cheque No. 423 on page 12 of a cheque register like the one on page 590. June 30 cash balance brought forward is $87 019.27.

7. Record the June 30 cash balance and amount of replenished fund in the petty cash record. Use lines 16 and 17 of petty cash record, page 593, as a model.

PROBLEM 29-3   Establishing and replenishing a petty cash fund using a cash payments journal

On May 1 of the current year, Datascribe issued Cheque No. 49 for $200.00 to establish a petty cash fund. During May the custodian made payments from the petty cash fund. On May 31, the custodian submitted the request form below.

REQUEST TO REPLENISH PETTY CASH FUND	
PAYMENTS	
Account	Amount
Supplies	73.25
Delivery Expense	42.30
Miscellaneous Expense	27.60
Total needed to replenish	143.15

Requested by:
Joe Mendel
                     Custodian
May 31, 19**89**

Approved by:

_____ 19 ___

Issued Cheque No. _____

Instructions: 1. Record Cheque No. 49 on page 8 of a cash payments journal to establish Datascribe's petty cash fund. Record the transaction in a journal like the one on page 599.

2. The petty cash box has $56.85 at the end of the day, May 31. Compare for equality the sum of cash and payments with the petty cash beginning balance.

3. Record Cheque No. 84 in the cash payments journal to replenish the petty cash fund May 31.

ENRICHMENT PROBLEMS

MASTERY PROBLEM 29-M   Establishing and replenishing a petty cash fund

Audio Alert Company established a $250.00 petty cash fund on July 1 of the current year.

Instructions: 1. Record on page 20 of a voucher register establishment of a petty cash fund. Voucher number is 479. Payee is Petty Cash Custodian.

2. Record on page 14 of a cheque register Cheque No. 469 to establish the petty cash fund. July 1 cash balance on hand is $96 739.40.

Totals of the petty cash record's amount columns on July 31 are listed below.

			Distribution of Payments			
	Receipts	Payments	Supplies	Delivery Expense	Misc. Expense	Other Payments Amount
Totals	250.00	202.15	86.45	38.50	42.20	35.00

Instructions: 3. Record the totals above on line 11 of a petty cash record. Petty cash record page is 16.

4. The petty cash box has $46.35 at the end of the day July 31. Compare for equality the sum of cash and payments with the petty cash beginning balance (Receipts column total).

5. Record any cash short or cash over and the cash balance, then total and rule the Receipts and Payments columns. Make entries like those in petty cash record, page 596 or 597.

6. From information in petty cash record, record voucher register entry to replenish petty cash fund on July 31. Amount in the Other Payments column is Advertising Expense. Voucher number is 544.

7. Record Cheque No. 530 in the cheque register to replenish the fund.

8. Record the July 31 cash balance and amount of replenished fund on the petty cash record. Use lines 16 and 17 of petty cash record, page 597, as a model.

CHALLENGE PROBLEM 29-C   Establishing, making payments from, and replenishing a petty cash fund

Continental Company established a $200.00 petty cash fund on August 1 of the current year.

Instructions: 1. Record on page 24 of a voucher register establishment of a petty cash fund. Voucher number is 579. Payee is Petty Cash Custodian.

2. Record on page 17 of a cheque register Cheque No. 563 to establish the petty cash fund. August 1 cash balance on hand is $86 598.25.

3. Record the beginning balance and the payments below from Continental's petty cash fund during August of the current year. Record the transactions on page 1 of a petty cash record like the one on page 593. Source document petty cash voucher is abbreviated PV.

Aug. 2. Paid postage on a sale, $8.50. PV1
      4. Paid for pencils, $21.40. PV2
      8. Paid for telegram, $6.90. PV3
    10. Paid for ad in community newspaper, $20.00. PV4 (Advertising Expense)
    11. Paid for postage stamps, $30.00. PV5
    15. Paid for calculator repair, $22.50. PV6
    18. Paid postage on a sale, $9.45. PV7
    22. Paid for calculator paper tape, $12.75. PV8
    25. Paid a collect telegram, $5.70. PV9
    29. Paid for ad in local high school paper, $15.00. PV10 (Advertising Expense)
    31. Paid postage on a sale, $9.60. PV11

Instructions: 4. Total and rule the Distribution of Payments columns in the petty cash record.

5. The petty cash box has $40.00 at the end of the day August 31. Compare for equality the sum of cash and payments with the petty cash beginning balance.

6. Record any cash short or cash over and the cash balance, then total and rule the Receipts and Payments columns. Make entries like those in petty cash record, page 596 or 597.

7. Prepare a voucher like the one on page 595 to replenish Continental's petty cash fund on August 31. Additional information on the voucher is listed below.

Voucher No.: 661
Continental's address: 101 Elizabeth Drive, Gander, NF A1V 1G8
Voucher Approved by: Jean Lebel
Voucher register page: 24
Recorded by: AML
Cheque No.: 641
Payment approved by: Patrick Yeager

8. Record Voucher No. 661 in the voucher register.
9. Record Cheque No. 641 in the cheque register.
10. Record the August 31 cash balance and amount of replenished fund on the petty cash record. Use lines 16 and 17 of petty cash record, page 597, as a model.

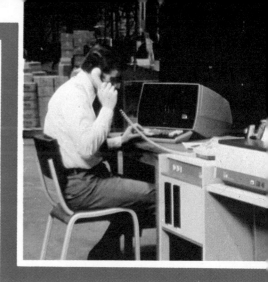

An Inventory System

ENABLING PERFORMANCE TASKS

After studying Chapter 30, you will be able to:

a. Define accounting terms related to an inventory system.
b. Explain accounting principles and practices related to an inventory system.
c. Determine the cost of merchandise inventory using the fifo and lifo methods.
d. Determine the valuation of merchandise inventory using the lower of cost or market method.
e. Estimate the value of merchandise inventory using the gross profit method.

Merchandise purchases are a large part of total costs of a merchandising business. Therefore, an effective inventory system is needed to control merchandise inventory.

Sale of merchandise provides a major source of revenue for a merchandising business. To encourage sales, a business must have merchandise available for sale that customers want. A business therefore needs controls that help maintain a merchandise inventory of sufficient quantity, variety, and price.

The value of merchandise on hand is reported on both the balance sheet and the income statement. If merchandise inventory is recorded incorrectly, current assets and retained earnings will be misstated on the balance sheet. The inventory error also will cause a misstatement of gross profit and net income reported on the income statement. (CONCEPT: Adequate Disclosure)

CONTROLLING THE QUANTITY OF MERCHANDISE INVENTORY

Knowing the size of inventory to maintain requires frequent analyses of purchases, sales, and inventory records. Many businesses fail because too much or too little merchandise inventory is kept on hand. Sometimes the wrong merchandise is kept on hand. If the merchandise is not sold, the result is less revenue. In addition, greater expense results from storing merchandise that sells slowly.

Merchandise inventory larger than needed

Merchandise inventory that is larger than needed may decrease net income of a business for several reasons.

1. Storage and warehouse space used by the unneeded part of inventory is expensive.
2. Part of the capital invested in excess inventory could be invested to better advantage in other assets.
3. Taxes and insurance premiums must be paid on excess merchandise inventory.
4. Excess merchandise may become obsolete and unsalable.

Merchandise inventory smaller than needed

Merchandise inventory that is smaller than needed may decrease net income of a business for several reasons.

1. Sales will be lost to competitors if items wanted by customers are not on hand.
2. Sales will be lost if there is insufficient variety of merchandise that customers want.
3. Merchandise reordered often and in small quantities costs more than if ordered in larger quantities.

DETERMINING THE QUANTITIES OF MERCHANDISE INVENTORY

A merchandising business needs to know the quantity of merchandise on hand. Two principal methods are used to determine the quantity of each type of merchandise on hand.

1. Quantities may be determined by counting, weighing, or measuring each kind of merchandise on hand.
2. A continuous record may be kept of increases, decreases, and the current balance of each kind of merchandise on hand.

Merchandise inventory determined by counting, weighing, or measuring items of merchandise on hand is called a periodic inventory. A periodic inventory is sometimes known as a physical inventory. Merchandise inventory determined by keeping a continuous record of increases, decreases, and balance on hand is called a perpetual inventory. A perpetual inventory is sometimes known as a book inventory.

Periodic inventory

Counting, weighing, or measuring a periodic inventory is commonly known as "taking an inventory." Inventories on hand at the end of a fiscal period must be known to figure the cost of merchandise sold. However, taking a periodic inventory is usually a large task. Therefore, periodic inventories normally are taken only at the end of a fiscal year.

Businesses frequently set their end of fiscal period when inventory is at a low point. A lower inventory thus takes less time to count. For example, a department store may take a periodic inventory at the end of January. The amount of merchandise on hand is low because of Christmas sales. January clearance sales have been held and few purchases of additional merchandise are made in January. All of these activities make the merchandise inventory low at the end of January.

Solar Power takes its periodic inventory during the last week of December. Solar Power has found from past experience that relatively few sales are made during that week. Few customers start energy improvement or new construction projects during the holiday season. Also, the stock of merchandise is relatively low at that time.

Solar Power uses a form to record important information about each major item of merchandise. The form has space to record stock number, unit of count, number of units, unit cost, and total value. The form used by Solar Power is below.

Information is typed in the Stock No. column and Unit of Count column before the count is begun. Employees taking the periodic inventory write the actual count in the No. of Units on Hand column. Inventory forms are then sent to the accounting department where the Unit Cost and Total Value columns are completed.

			Form No. __2__	
	POWER	Merchandise Inventory		

Date __December 31, 1989__   Item __Solar Collector Panels__

Stock No.	Unit of Count	No. of Units on Hand	Unit Cost Price	Total Value
6212	.5 x 1.5m panels	20	8.00	160.00
6213	1.0 x 1.5m panels	50	15.50	775.00
6215	1.5 x 1.5m panels	30	23.00	690.00
6216	.5 x 2.0m panels	100	60 @ 10.00 ⎱ 40 @ 11.25 ⎰	1 050.00
6640	1.0 x 2.0m panels	60	21.00	1 260.00
6696	2.0 x 4.0m panels	120	68.50	8 220.00
				23 155.00

Inventory record form

Perpetual inventory

Some businesses keep inventory records that show continuously the quantity on hand for each kind of merchandise. A form used to show kind of merchandise, quantity received, quantity sold, and balance on hand is called a stock record. The form also may be known as an inventory card. A file of stock records for all merchandise on hand is called a stock ledger.

A perpetual inventory system provides day-to-day information about the quantity of merchandise on hand. On each stock record is shown the minimum balance allowed before a reorder must be placed. When the minimum balance is reached, additional merchandise should be ordered. The minimum balance is the amount of merchandise that will last until additional merchandise can be received from the suppliers. For example, daily reports of merchandise on hand may be necessary to determine when to reorder specific items that are selling rapidly. These daily reports may be prepared from information on perpetual inventory records.

When a perpetual inventory of merchandise is kept, entries are made on stock records to show the following information.

1. Increases in the quantity on hand when additional merchandise is received.
2. Decreases in the quantity on hand when merchandise is sold.
3. The balance on hand after each increase or decrease is recorded.

A stock record in card form is below.

Description _Solenoid Solar Switch_				Stock No. _C 460_		
Maximum _20_		Minimum _4_			Location _Aisle 2_	
INCREASES			DECREASES			BALANCE
DATE	PURCHASE NO.	QUANTITY	DATE	SALES INVOICE NO.	QUANTITY	QUANTITY
1989 Jan. 1						6
			1989 Jan. 18	4387	2	4
Jan. 19	633	16				20
			Feb. 3	4705	2	18.

Stock record card

Usually a stock record shows quantity but not value of merchandise.

A separate stock record card is prepared for each kind of merchandise carried in stock. Each time additional merchandise is purchased, an entry is recorded in the Increases columns. Then the balance on hand is updated in the Balance column. Each time merchandise is sold, an entry is recorded in the Decreases columns and the balance is updated. The quantity of merchandise on hand is the last amount in the Balance column of a stock record card.

When a perpetual inventory is kept manually, errors may be made in recording or figuring amounts. Also, some records may be incorrect because merchandise is taken from stock and not recorded on stock record cards. A customary practice is to take a periodic inventory at least once a year. The periodic inventory is then compared with the perpetual inventory records. If errors are discovered, they are corrected on the stock record cards.

Perpetual inventory with a cash register and automated equipment

Businesses keeping a computerized perpetual inventory may use a special cash register as part of the system. Each item of merchandise has a code number on the price tag. The code number is recorded on the cash register when the sale is recorded. As a result, a punched paper tape is prepared inside the cash register with a coded record of items sold. Each day the punched paper tape is used to bring the perpetual inventory in a computer up to date.

Special cash registers may also be connected directly to a computer. As a sale is recorded on a cash register, information is fed directly to a computer. Thus, inventory records are brought up to date immediately.

DETERMINING THE COST OF MERCHANDISE INVENTORY

Costs often are not recorded on inventory forms at the time a periodic inventory is taken. After the quantities of merchandise on hand are counted, purchase invoices or catalogues are used to find merchandise costs. Costs are recorded on the inventory forms and necessary extensions made. Total cost value of the inventory is then figured.

First-in, first-out method

Solar Power takes a periodic inventory at the end of each fiscal period. The company assumes that the merchandise purchased first is also the merchandise sold first. Solar Power also assumes that the ending inventory consists of the most recently purchased merchandise. Only the most recent invoices for purchases are used in recording costs for each item on the inventory forms. For example, the most recently received filters are placed on the shelves behind older filters. Therefore, the merchandise purchased first is also the merchandise sold first.

The first-in, first-out method is frequently abbreviated as *fifo* (the first letter of each of the four words). On December 31, a periodic count of solar collector panels, Stock No. 6650, showed 80 panels on hand. Cost information for this item is on the next page.

	Units	Unit Cost
January 1, beginning inventory......................	20 panels	$20.00
March 10, purchases....................................	30 panels	20.00
May 18, purchases	30 panels	21.00
July 7, purchases	50 panels	22.00
November 18, purchases...............................	50 panels	24.00

Under the fifo method, the 80 units are priced at the most recent costs. The most recent costs are $24.00 and $22.00. Computations are summarized below.

Most recent costs, November 18, 50 units @ $24.00...............	$1 200.00
Next most recent costs, July 7, 30 units @ $22.00	660.00
Total value of 80 units..	$1 860.00

On the inventory forms the 80 panels would be shown as having a total value of $1 860.00.

Last-in, first-out method

The last-in, first-out method is frequently abbreviated as *lifo*. In the lifo method, an inventory is recorded at the amount paid for the merchandise purchased first. This method is based on the idea that the most recent costs of merchandise should be charged against current revenue. (*CONCEPT: Matching Expenses with Revenue*)

Under the lifo method, each item on the inventory forms is recorded at the earliest costs paid for the merchandise. Inventory value for the 80 panels described above is figured below using the lifo method.

Earliest costs, January 1, 20 units @ $20.00..........................	$ 400.00
Next earliest costs, March 10, 30 units @ $20.00	600.00
Next earliest costs, May 18, 30 units @ $21.00......................	630.00
Total value of 80 units..	$1 630.00

On the inventory forms, the 80 units of this kind of merchandise would therefore show a total value of $1 630.00.

A comparison of fifo and lifo pricing methods

The figures above show inventory cost for 80 solar collector panels using both fifo and lifo methods during rising prices. To show the effect of falling prices, the cost figures for the items are reversed as shown below.

	Units	Unit Cost
January 1, beginning inventory......................	20 panels	$24.00
March 10, purchases....................................	30 panels	22.00
May 18, purchases	30 panels	21.00
July 7, purchases	50 panels	20.00
November 18, purchases...............................	50 panels	20.00

Under the fifo method, the 80 units are priced at the most recent costs. The most recent costs are $20.00 and $20.00. The figures are summarized below.

Most recent costs, November 18, 50 units @ $20.00...............	$1 000.00
Next most recent costs, July 7, 30 units @ $20.00..................	600.00
Total value of 80 units...	$1 600.00

Under the lifo method, the 80 units are priced at the earliest costs. The earliest costs are $24.00, $22.00, and $21.00. The figures are summarized below.

Earliest costs, January 1, 20 units @ $24.00..........................	$ 480.00
Next earliest costs, March 10, 30 units @ $22.00	660.00
Next earliest costs, May 18, 30 units @ $21.00......................	630.00
Total value of 80 units..	$1 770.00

A comparison of the fifo and lifo methods in determining gross profit with net sales of $4 000.00 is below.

	RISING PRICES				FALLING PRICES			
	FIFO		LIFO		FIFO		LIFO	
Revenue:								
Net Sales		$4 000.00		$4 000.00		$4 000.00		$4 000.00
Cost of Merchandise Sold:								
Merchandise Inventory, Jan. 1 .	$ 400.00		$ 400.00		$ 480.00		$ 480.00	
Net Purchases	3 530.00		3 530.00		3 290.00		3 290.00	
Merchandise Available for Sale .	3 930.00		3 930.00		3 770.00		3 770.00	
Less Ending Inventory, Dec. 31	1 860.00		1 630.00		1 600.00		1 770.00	
Cost of Merchandise Sold		2 070.00		2 300.00		2 170.00		2 000.00
Gross Profit on Operations		$1 930.00		$1 700.00		$1 830.00		$2 000.00

In a year of rising prices, the fifo method gives the highest possible valuation of ending inventory. The lifo method gives the lowest possible valuation during rising prices. Therefore, the fifo method gives the highest and lifo method the lowest net income during a year of rising prices.

In a year of falling prices, the fifo method gives the lowest possible valuation of ending inventory. The lifo method gives the highest possible valuation during falling prices. Therefore, the fifo method gives the lowest and lifo method the highest net income during a year of falling prices.

DETERMINING THE VALUATION OF MERCHANDISE INVENTORY AT LOWER OF COST OR MARKET

Another inventory valuation method uses both the cost and market price of each item of merchandise. This method is referred to as the *lower of cost or market.* "Market" as used in this phrase means the cost to re-place the merchandise on the date of inventory. This method applies a conservative approach to valuing merchandise inventory. If the market value of an inventory declines, the loss is recognized even though the merchandise has not been sold. *(CONCEPT: Conservatism)*

When this inventory valuation method is applied to the pricing of each inventory item, the rules below are followed.

1. When the cost is lower than the current market price, use the cost.
2. When the market price is lower than the cost, use the market price.

When the lower of cost or market method is used, the inventory form has four amount columns.

1. The cost of each item is recorded in one column.
2. The market price of each item is recorded in one column.
3. The unit price to be used is recorded in one column.
4. The total value of all identical items using the lower of cost or market price is recorded in one column.

One form of inventory record form using this inventory pricing method is below.

KOOL AIR CO.

MERCHANDISE INVENTORY   ITEM __Filters__

DATE __December 31, 1989__   SHEET NO. ___3___

Item No.	No. of Units on Hand	Unit Price Cost	Unit Price Current Market	Unit Price to be Used	Value at Lower of Cost or Market
G1010	24	$ 6.00	$ 4.00	$ 4.00	$ 96.00
H1221	32	9.60	11.50	9.60	307.20
I2342	70	9.50	12.00	9.50	665.00
J3425	12	2.25	2.25	2.25	27.00
K5748	18	21.80	13.90	13.90	250.20
V9053	120	7.15	6.90	6.90	828.00
W7532	40	3.60	3.70	3.60	144.00
X5937	8	131.95	139.80	131.95	1 055.00
Y4908	9	35.90	33.30	33.30	299.70
					$10 326.30

Inventory record form for pricing at lower of cost or market

The first item on the inventory form above, *G1010*, has a lower market price, *$4.00*, than the cost price, *$6.00*. Therefore, the market price is used for this item on the inventory form. The number of items on hand, *24*, times the price to be used, *$4.00*, equals the value, *$96.00*. The value, *$96.00*, is recorded in the column headed "Value at Lower of Cost or Market."

Each business decides which method to use in pricing merchandise inventory. However, the method selected (fifo, lifo, lower of cost or market) is used consistently from year to year. *(CONCEPT: Consistent Reporting)* Revenue Canada, Taxation requires that a business use the same method from year to year. If a business wishes to change inventory pricing methods, permission of Revenue Canada must be obtained.

ESTIMATING THE VALUE OF MERCHANDISE INVENTORY

Estimating inventory by using previous years' percent of gross profit on operations is called gross profit method of estimating inventory. Solar Power prepares an income statement at the end of each month. *(CONCEPT: Accounting Period Cycle)* The gross profit method of estimating the ending merchandise inventory is used. To estimate the ending merchandise inventory on September 30, 1989, the following information is obtained.

Beginning inventory, January 1, 1989.............................. $ 58 140.00
Net purchases for the period, January 1 to September 30..... 434 112.40
Net sales for the period, January 1 to September 30........... 657 378.50
Gross profit on operations (percentage based on records of
previous years' operations) .... 30% of sales

Three steps are followed to estimate the ending merchandise inventory for Solar Power on September 30, 1989.

1 Determine the value of the cost of merchandise available for sale.

Beginning inventory, January 1................................ $ 58 140.00
Plus net purchases, January 1 to September 30 .... <u>434 112.40</u>
Equals value of merchandise available for sale............. $492 252.40

2 Determine the estimated value of the cost of merchandise sold.

Net sales for January 1 to September 30 .... $657 378.50
Less estimated gross profit on operations ($657 378.50
× 30%).. <u>197 213.55</u>
Equals estimated cost of merchandise sold.................. $460 164.95

3 Subtract the estimated cost of merchandise sold from the value of the merchandise available for sale. This step determines the estimated ending merchandise inventory.

Merchandise available for sale (from step 1) $492 252.40
Less estimated cost of merchandise sold (from step 2)... <u>460 164.95</u>
Equals estimated ending merchandise inventory .... $ 32 087.45

The estimated merchandise inventory for Solar Power on September 30, 1989, is $32 087.45. This value is used on the monthly income statement.

An estimated inventory is not completely accurate. The rate of gross profit on operations may not be exactly the percentage used in the estimate. Also, some merchandise may have been stolen or damaged. However, estimated ending inventory is accurate enough for a monthly income statement without taking the time to count the inventory.

Solar Power's income statement prepared on September 30, 1989, is below. The beginning inventory recorded is the estimated ending inventory from the income statement for August 31, 1989.

Income statement with
estimated ending
inventory

The estimated ending inventory is used on Solar Power's monthly income statements. However, a periodic inventory is used for the end-of-fiscal-period income statement for greater accuracy.

```
                        Solar Power
                     Income Statement
              For Month Ended September 30, 1989

Revenue:
  Net Sales................................          $73 045.00
Cost of Merchandise Sold:
  Estimated Merchandise Inventory, Sept. 1..  $34 957.25
  Net Purchases...........................     48 265.70
  Merchandise Available for Sale...........   $83 222.95
  Less Estimated Ending Inventory, Sept. 30.  32 087.45
  Cost of Merchandise Sold.................                51 135.50
Gross Profit on Operations.................               $21 909.50
Operating Expenses.........................               13 245.70
Net Income.................................               $ 8 663.80
```

ACCOUNTING TERMS

What is the meaning of each of the following?

1. periodic inventory
2. perpetual inventory
3. stock record
4. stock ledger
5. gross profit method of estimating inventory

QUESTIONS FOR INDIVIDUAL STUDY

1. What item is a large part of total costs of a merchandising business?
2. Why does a business need controls for its merchandise inventory?
3. What effect does an error in determining the value of the merchandise inventory have on the balance sheet and income statement?
4. If the merchandise inventory is larger than needed, what effect may this value have on the net income of a business? Why?
5. If the inventory is smaller than needed, what effect may this have on the net income of a business? Why?
6. What two methods can be used to determine the quantity of each item of merchandise on hand?
7. How often are periodic inventories taken?
8. When should a business use a perpetual inventory system?
9. How may the balance on hand of an item of merchandise be determined when a manual perpetual inventory is used?

10. How is the accuracy of a perpetual inventory checked?
11. When the fifo method is used, how is the value of each kind of merchandise determined?
12. When the lifo method is used, how is the value of each kind of merchandise determined?
13. In a year of rising prices, which inventory method, fifo or lifo, gives the highest net income?

14. In a year of falling prices, which inventory method, fifo or lifo, gives the highest net income?
15. Why is the lower of cost or market method considered a conservative approach to valuing inventory?
16. When neither a perpetual nor a periodic inventory is taken, how can an ending merchandise inventory be determined that is accurate enough for a monthly income statement?

CASES FOR MANAGEMENT DECISION

CASE 1 Thermtron Company recently started a perpetual inventory system. Mr. Nadolski, the manager, asks you if there is any reason for the company to continue with periodic inventories now that a perpetual inventory system is used. How would you answer Mr. Nadolski?

CASE 2 Valentino's uses the lifo method of valuing its merchandise inventory. The manager is considering a change to the fifo method. Prices have increased steadily over the past three years. What effect will the change have on the following items? (1) The amount of net income as shown by the income statement. (2) The amount of income taxes to be paid. (3) The quantity of each item of merchandise that must be kept in stock? Why?

CASE 3 Garratt Hardware has many small and large items of merchandise. The store has always taken a periodic inventory at the end of a fiscal year. The store has not kept a perpetual inventory because of the cost. However, the manager wants a reasonably accurate inventory at the end of each month. The manager needs the inventory to prepare monthly income statements and to help in making decisions about the business. What would you recommend?

DRILL FOR UNDERSTANDING

DRILL 30-D 1 Determining the quantities of merchandise on hand using perpetual inventory

Accounting records at Garland Supply showed inventory increases and decreases for Item 16-Z as listed below. Beginning inventory on May 1 was 136 units.

Increases		Decreases	
Date	Quantity	Date	Quantity
		May 5	52
		May 9	45
May 10	125		
		May 16	62
		May 23	75
May 25	150		
		May 31	65

Use a stock record with the column headings below.

Increases		Decreases		Balance
Date	Quantity	Date	Quantity	Quantity
May 1				136

Instructions: 1. Record the increases and decreases.
2. Figure the balance of units on hand for each date a transaction occurred.
3. Record the balance of units on hand in the Balance Quantity column.

APPLICATION PROBLEMS

PROBLEM 30-1 Determining cost of inventory using the fifo and lifo methods

Accounting records at Energy-Wise showed the purchases and periodic inventory counts listed below.

Model	Beginning Inventory January 1	First Purchase	Second Purchase	Third Purchase	Periodic Inventory Count December 31
A 36	16 @ $ 38	25 @ $ 39	10 @ $ 40	20 @ $ 41	24
A 49	7 @ $ 85	12 @ $ 87	10 @ $ 88	24 @ $ 89	22
C 17	22 @ $ 21	25 @ $ 24	30 @ $ 25	30 @ $ 20	28
C 72	10 @ $ 41	12 @ $ 42	15 @ $ 38	10 @ $ 44	15
F 96	5 @ $140	5 @ $142	6 @ $148	8 @ $150	18
G 12	85 @ $ 16	20 @ $ 18	25 @ $ 19	40 @ $ 20	35
J 78	36 @ $ 50	40 @ $ 54	44 @ $ 55	50 @ $ 58	32
M 61	72 @ $ 60	48 @ $ 58	50 @ $ 54	60 @ $ 50	75

Use a form with the column headings below.

Model	No. of Units on Hand	Unit Cost	Inventory Value December 31
A 36	24	20 @ $41⎫ 4 @ 40⎭	$980

Instructions: 1. Figure the total amount of the inventory on December 31 according to the *fifo* method. Determining the inventory value for Model A36 is given as an example. Use the following procedure.
  (a) Record the model number and the number of units of each model on hand December 31.
  (b) Record the unit cost of each model. When more than one unit cost is used, list the units and unit costs on separate lines.
  (c) Figure the total inventory value of each model and write the amount in the Value column.
  (d) Add the Value column to determine the total amount of inventory.

2. On another form, figure the total amount of inventory using the *lifo* method. Follow the steps given in Instruction 1.

3. Compare the total amount of the inventory obtained in Instructions 1 and 2. Which method, *fifo* or *lifo*, resulted in the lower total amount for the inventory?

PROBLEM 30-2 Determining valuation of inventory at lower of cost or market

Part of the inventory form of Stonegate Company on December 31 of the current year is below.

1	2	3	4
Item	No. of Units on Hand	Unit Cost	Current Unit Market Price
14 C	48	$ 16.50	$ 17.25
28 L	125	11.20	11.25
11 M	72	36.60	34.40
96 N	90	25.00	26.36
42 Q	12	322.50	296.40
56 R	256	26.75	24.70
38 S	60	43.40	48.60
73 T	85	18.20	19.20
21 U	30	51.50	49.35
99 W	105	12.50	12.60

Instructions: 1. Record the inventory information from Columns 1–4 on an inventory form with the column headings below.

1	2	3	4	5	6
Item	No. of Units on Hand	Unit Cost	Current Unit Market Price	Unit Price to be Used	Value at Lower of Cost or Market

Instructions: 2. Record the unit price to be used in Column 5.

3. Figure the value of each kind of merchandise at lower of cost or market. Record the value in Column 6.

4. Total Column 6 to determine the value of the ending merchandise inventory.

PROBLEM 30-3 Estimating the value of inventory using the gross profit method

The following information is available from the accounting records of Sundrops Corporation for January of the current year.

Beginning inventory, January 1	$ 69 900.00
Net purchases for January	76 400.00
Net sales for January	121 700.00
Gross profit on operations	30% of sales
Operating expenses for January	30 870.00

Instructions: 1. Estimate the value of the ending inventory for January of the current year. Use the gross profit method of estimating an inventory.

2. Prepare an income statement similar to the one on page 614 for the month ended January 31 of the current year.

ENRICHMENT PROBLEMS

MASTERY PROBLEM 30-M   Determining cost of inventory using the fifo and lifo methods

Accounting records at Manatee Company showed the purchases and periodic inventory counts listed below.

Model	Beginning Inventory January 1	First Purchase	Second Purchase	Third Purchase	Periodic Inventory Count December 31
250	40 @ $10.50	50 @ $10.00	90 @ $ 8.50	40 @ $ 8.10	60
251	10 @ $32.50	30 @ $32.50	60 @ $33.30	50 @ $31.80	60
252	20 @ $10.00	40 @ $10.00	60 @ $10.50	60 @ $10.80	20
360	60 @ $12.00	30 @ $12.50	20 @ $13.00	40 @ $13.50	70
361	80 @ $15.50	30 @ $14.50	120 @ $15.00	60 @ $15.50	80
362	20 @ $17.50	40 @ $18.00	20 @ $19.50	70 @ $20.00	100
470	25 @ $46.00	30 @ $48.50	40 @ $50.00	50 @ $45.00	35
471	10 @ $82.00	40 @ $85.00	60 @ $81.00	70 @ $79.00	40

Use a form with the column headings below.

Model	No. of Units on Hand	Unit Cost	Inventory Value December 31

Instructions: 1. Figure the total amount of the inventory on December 31 according to the *fifo* method. Use the following procedure.

(a) Record the model number and number of units of each model on hand on December 31.

(b) Record the unit cost of each model. When more than one unit cost is used, list the units and unit costs on separate lines.

(c) Figure the total inventory value of each model and write the amount in the Value column.

(d) Add the Value column to determine the total amount of the inventory.

2. On another form, figure the total amount of inventory using the *lifo* method. Follow the steps given in Instruction 1.

3. Compare the total amount of the inventory obtained in Instructions 1 and 2. Which method, *fifo* or *lifo*, resulted in the lower total amount for the inventory?

CHALLENGE PROBLEM 30-C   Determining cost of inventory using the lifo method with perpetual inventory

Accounting records at Orbit Company showed inventory increases (purchases) and decreases (sales) for Product 32-X as listed on page 619. Beginning inventory on June 1 was $1 000.00 (50 units at $20.00 each).

Date	Increases		Decreases
	No. of Units	Unit Cost	Units
June 2	20	$22.00	
6			25
9			15
13	50	23.00	
16			25
20			20
24	50	24.00	
28			30

Use a form with the column headings below. *Beginning inventory and the first two transactions are given as examples.*

Date	Increases			Decreases			Balance		
	No. of Units	Unit Cost	Total Cost	No. of Units	Unit Cost	Total Cost	No. of Units	Unit Cost	Total Cost
June 1							50	$20.00	$1 000.00
2	20	$22.00	$440.00				50 20	20.00 } 22.00 }	1 440.00
6				20 5	$22.00 } 20.00 }	$540.00	45	20.00	900.00

Instructions: Figure the amount of increase or decrease and the inventory balance for each transaction. Orbit keeps a perpetual cost inventory. Therefore, the amount of inventory is figured after each transaction. Orbit uses the *lifo* method. Therefore, purchases (increases) that are added most recently (last in) are removed first (first out) when a sale occurs.

Use the following procedures.

(a) Record the beginning inventory date, number of units, unit cost, and total cost.

(b) Record each transaction in the order it occurs.

(c) For each increase, record the number of units, unit cost, and total cost. Record the inventory balance (previous balance plus this transaction increase), number of units, unit cost, and total cost. When inventory has more than one unit cost, list the units and unit costs on separate lines. Bracket the unit cost lines and record a combined total inventory cost.

(d) For each decrease, record the number of units, unit cost, and total cost. Decreases are taken from the "last-in" units. When the decrease includes more than one unit cost, list the units and unit costs on separate lines. Bracket the unit cost lines and record a combined total decrease cost. Record the balance number of units, unit cost, and total cost after subtracting the "decrease" units and costs. Remember the decrease is subtracted from the "last-in" units and costs in the balance.

New Horizons

Select Camping Gear
A Business Simulation

NEW HORIZONS is a small retail store that sells select camping gear. This business simulation provides additional practice in some of the basic transactions completed throughout this text. The business uses a special journal, a general ledger, accounts receivable and accounts payable ledgers, and a chequebook. A pictorial flowchart of the accounting cycle for NEW HORIZONS is shown on the next two pages. This business simulation is available from the publisher.

Flowchart of the
Accounting Cycle of

NEW HORIZONS

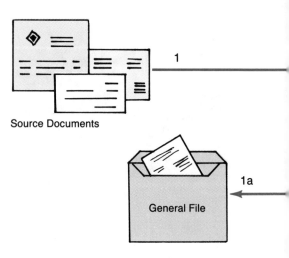

Source Documents

General File

1 Record transactions in the appropriate special journals from
source documents.

1a File source documents.

2 Post items to be posted individually to the general ledger and
subsidiary ledgers.

3 Post column totals to the general ledger.

4 Prepare schedules of accounts receivable and accounts payable from
subsidiary ledgers.

5 Prepare the trial balance on the work sheet.

6 Plan adjustments and complete the work sheet.

7 Prepare financial statements.

8 Record adjusting and closing entries from the work sheet.

9 Post adjusting and closing entries to the general ledger.

10 Prepare a post-closing trial balance from the general ledger.

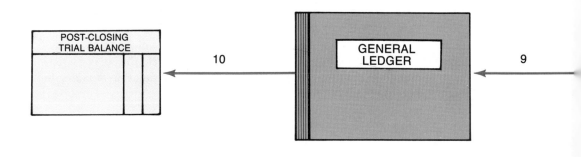

POST-CLOSING
TRIAL BALANCE

GENERAL
LEDGER

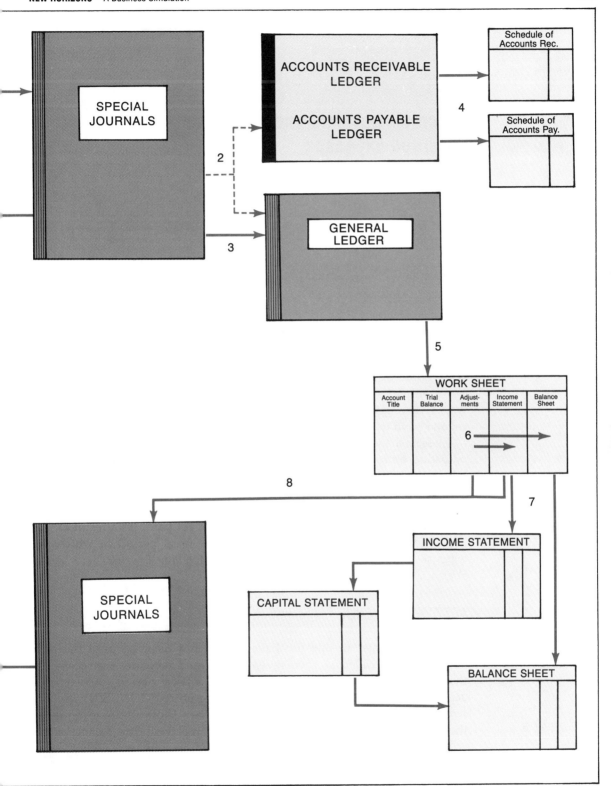

Accrued Revenue and Accrued Expenses

Most journal entries that record revenue are made when the revenue is received. However, some revenue may be earned before it is actually received. For example, interest is earned for each day an interest-bearing note receivable is held. The interest is not received however until the maturity date of the note.

Most entries recording expenses are also made when the expense is paid. Some expenses though are incurred before they are actually paid. For example, salary expense is incurred for each day that an employee works. The payment for salary expense is not made however until the regular payday.

To record the revenue that has been earned but not yet received, an adjusting entry is made at the end of the fiscal period. Because of this adjustment, the revenue is reported for the fiscal period in which the revenue is actually earned. *(CONCEPT: Realization of Revenue)* An adjusting entry also is made at the end of a fiscal period to record the amount of an expense that has been incurred but not yet paid. As a result of this adjustment, the expense is reported for the fiscal period in which the expense is actually incurred. *(CONCEPT: Matching Expenses with Revenue)*

ACCRUED REVENUE

Revenue earned in one fiscal period but not received until the next fiscal period is called accrued revenue. Accrued revenue is a receivable that is classified as an asset. At the end of a fiscal period, each type of accrued revenue is recorded by an adjusting entry. *(CONCEPT: Realization of Revenue)* The income statement will then show all the revenue for the period even though some has not been received. The balance sheet will show all the assets, including the accrued revenue receivable. *(CONCEPT: Adequate Disclosure)*

Adjusting entry for accrued interest income

At the end of each fiscal period, Furniture Mart examines the notes receivable on hand. The amount of interest income earned but not collected is determined. Interest earned on notes receivable but not yet collected is called accrued interest income. On December 31, 1988, there is only one note receivable on hand. This is Note Receivable No. 41, a 60-day, 9% note for $1 000.00 from Susan Price, dated December 1, 1988. The accounting records should show all the interest income for the fiscal period. Therefore, an adjusting entry must be made to record the amount of interest earned to date on this note.

Analysing the adjusting entry for accrued interest income. Interest on $1 000.00 at 9% for 30 days (December 1 to 31) is $7.40. The adjustment for accrued interest income is analysed in the T accounts at the right.

Interest Receivable is debited for $7.40. The balance of the interest receivable account is the amount of interest income that has accrued at the end of the fiscal period. However, this revenue is not received until the next fiscal period.

Interest Receivable	
7.40	

Interest Income	
	7.40

Interest Income is credited for $7.40 to show the increase in the balance of this account. The new balance of the interest income account is the amount of interest income earned during the fiscal period.

Adjustment for accrued interest income on a work sheet. The adjusting entry for accrued interest income is planned on a work sheet. The adjustment is below.

		1	2	3	4	5	6	7	8
	ACCOUNT TITLE	TRIAL BALANCE		ADJUSTMENTS		INCOME STATEMENT		BALANCE SHEET	
		DEBIT	CREDIT	DEBIT	CREDIT	DEBIT	CREDIT	DEBIT	CREDIT
4	Interest Receivable			(a) 7 40				7 40		4
42	Interest Income		78 60		(a) 7 40		86 00			42

Interest Receivable is debited for $7.40. This amount is extended to the Balance Sheet Debit column. Interest Income is credited for $7.40. This amount, $7.40, is added to the amount in the Trial Balance Credit column, $78.60. The new balance, $86.00, is extended to the Income Statement Credit column.

Accrued interest income on a work sheet

Recording and posting the adjustment for accrued interest income. Data needed to journalize the adjustment for accrued interest income are obtained from the Adjustments columns of the work sheet. The adjusting entry in the general journal is on the next page.

Adjusting entry for accrued interest income

After the adjusting entry is posted, the interest receivable and interest income accounts appear as shown below.

Accounts after posting the adjusting entry for accrued interest income

The interest receivable account has a debit balance of $7.40. This is the accrued interest income earned but not collected at the end of the fiscal period. The interest income account has a credit balance of $86.00. This is the total interest income for the fiscal period.

Reporting accrued interest income on financial statements

The asset account Interest Receivable is listed on a balance sheet in the Current Assets section. The account Interest Income is listed on an income statement in the Other Revenue section.

Closing entry for the interest income account

One closing entry is recorded for accounts listed in the Income Statement Credit column of a work sheet. Interest Income is closed into the income summary account. The closing entry in the general journal on December 31, 1988, is below. After the closing entry is posted, the interest income account is closed.

Closing entry including the interest income account

1988				
Dec. 31	Closing Entries			
	Sales	8561600		
	Purchases Returns & Allow.	129100		
	Purchases Discount	297600		
	Interest Income	8600		
	Income Summary		8996900	

Need for readjusting the interest receivable and interest income accounts

When cash is received for Note Receivable No. 41 on January 30, 1989, the cash will include principal, $1 000.00, plus interest, $14.79. To record the cash receipt, Cash will be debited for the amount received, $1 014.79. Notes Receivable will be credited for the principal, $1 000.00. Interest Income will be credited for the interest received, $14.79. But $7.40 of this interest was credited to Interest Income as accrued revenue at the end of the 1988 fiscal period. Only $7.39 applies to the 1989 fiscal period.

Accrued interest income recorded in one fiscal period should not be credited to Interest Income a second time when actually received in the following fiscal period. To avoid this double credit, the interest receivable and interest income accounts are readjusted at the beginning of the new fiscal period. An entry made at the beginning of one fiscal period to reverse an adjusting entry made in a previous fiscal period is called a re-versing entry.

After the reversing entry has been recorded and posted, all interest income transactions during the new fiscal period are recorded in the usual way. That is, the full amount of interest is credited to Interest Income. Using reversing entries makes it unnecesary to analyse each receipt of interest to determine how much was earned during a previous fiscal period.

Reversing entry for accrued interest income

A reversing entry is exactly the opposite of the original adjusting entry. Furniture Mart's adjusting entry for accrued interest income on December 31, 1988, debited Interest Receivable for $7.40 and credited Interest Income for $7.40. The reversing entry on January 1, 1989, reverses this adjusting entry.

Analysing the reversing entry for accrued interest income. The reversing entry for accrued interest income is analysed in the T accounts at the right.

Interest Income is debited for $7.40 and Interest Receivable is credited for $7.40. This reversing entry closes the interest receivable account and transfers the original debit balance to the debit side of the interest income account. The debit to Interest Income is a temporary balance that represents uncollected interest income earned and recorded during the previous fiscal period.

Interest Income			
Closing	86.00	Balance	78.50
Reversing	7.40	Adjusting	7.40

Interest Receivable			
Adjusting	7.40	Reversing	7.40

During the new fiscal period, receipts of interest income are credited to Interest Income. The portion of each receipt of interest that applies to the previous fiscal period will automatically be deducted because of the debit balance.

Recording and posting the reversing entry for accrued interest income. The reversing entry is recorded in the general journal as of January 1, 1989, under the centred heading *Reversing Entries* as shown below.

Reversing entry for
accrued interest income

	1989					
1	Jan. 1	Reversing Entries				1
2		Interest Income		7 40		2
3		Interest Receivable			7 40	3

After the reversing entry is posted, the interest receivable and interest income accounts appear as shown below.

Accounts after posting the
reversing entry for
accrued interest income

ACCOUNT *Interest Receivable*   ACCOUNT NO. *1103*

DATE	ITEM	POST. REF.	DEBIT	CREDIT	BALANCE DEBIT	BALANCE CREDIT
1988 Dec. 31		G42	7 40		7 40	
1989 Jan. 1		G44		7 40	—	—

ACCOUNT *Interest Income*   ACCOUNT NO. *7101*

DATE	ITEM	POST. REF.	DEBIT	CREDIT	BALANCE DEBIT	BALANCE CREDIT
31		G43		86 00		
1989 Jan. 1		G44	7 40		7 40	

Interest Receivable has a zero balance at the beginning of the new 1989 fiscal period. Interest Receivable will not be used again until it is needed for an adjusting entry at the end of the 1989 fiscal period. Interest Receivable is needed for only one day each period to prepare complete financial reports. (*CONCEPT: Adequate Disclosure*)

Interest Income has a debit balance of $7.40 on January 1, 1989. This balance on the first day of the new fiscal year is the result of posting the reversing entry for accrued interest income. During 1989 Interest Income will be credited each time cash is received for interest income. At the end of the 1989 fiscal period, the credit balance will show the amount of interest income that belongs to the 1989 fiscal period. (*CONCEPT: Realization of Revenue*) At the end of the 1989 fiscal period there will be new accrued interest income, earned in 1989 but not collected in 1989. The accrued interest income on December 31, 1989, will be recorded in the same manner as the accrued interest income on December 31, 1988.

ACCRUED EXPENSES

Expenses incurred in one fiscal period but not paid until the next fiscal period are called accrued expenses. An example of an accrued expense is interest expense incurred during one fiscal period but not paid until the next fiscal period. Another example is salaries earned by employees in one fiscal period but not paid until the next fiscal period. At the end of a fiscal period, each type of accrued expense is recorded by an adjusting entry. *(CONCEPT: Matching Expenses with Revenue)* The income statement will show all expenses for the period even though some have not been paid. The balance sheet will show all liabilities, including amounts owed for accrued expenses. *(CONCEPT: Adequate Disclosure)*

Adjusting entry for accrued interest expense

At the end of each fiscal period, Furniture Mart examines the notes payable on hand to determine the amount of interest expense incurred but not paid. Interest incurred on notes payable but not yet paid is called accrued interest expense. On December 31, 1988, there is only one note payable on hand. This is Note Payable No. 11, a 90-day, 8% note for $3 000.00 issued to the Davis Company on November 1, 1988. An adjusting entry is made to record the amount of interest expense incurred to date on this note.

Analysing the adjusting entry for accrued interest expense. The interest on $3 000.00 at 8% for 60 days (November 1 to December 31) is $39.45. The adjustment for accrued interest expense is analysed in the T accounts at the right.

Interest Expense is debited for $39.45 to show the increase in the balance of this account. The new balance of Interest Expense is the total amount of interest expense incurred during the fiscal period. Interest Payable is credited for $39.45. The balance of Interest Payable is interest expense that has accrued at the end of the fiscal period but that is not paid until the next fiscal period.

Interest Expense	
39.45	

Interest Payable	
	39.45

Adjustment for accrued interest expense on a work sheet. The adjusting entry for accrued interest expense is planned on a work sheet. The adjustment is below.

	1 TRIAL BALANCE DEBIT	2 TRIAL BALANCE CREDIT	3 ADJUSTMENTS DEBIT	4 ADJUSTMENTS CREDIT	5 INCOME STATEMENT DEBIT	6 INCOME STATEMENT CREDIT	7 BALANCE SHEET DEBIT	8 BALANCE SHEET CREDIT	
15 *Interest Payable*				(i) 3945				3945	15
44 *Interest Expense*	19055		(i) 3945		23000				44

Interest Expense is debited for $39.45. This amount, $39.45, is added to the amount in the Trial Balance Debit column, $190.55. The new balance, $230.00, is extended to the Income Statement Debit column.

Accrued interest expense on a work sheet

Interest Payable is credited for $39.45. This amount is extended to the Balance Sheet Credit column.

Recording and posting the adjustment for accrued interest expense. Data needed to journalize the adjustment for accrued interest expense are obtained from the Adjustments columns of the work sheet. The adjusting entry in the general journal is below.

Adjusting entry for accrued interest expense

17		31	Interest Expense		3945		17
18			Interest Payable			3945	18

After the adjusting entry is posted, the interest payable and interest expense accounts appear as shown below.

ACCOUNT *Interest Payable*   ACCOUNT NO. *2102*

DATE	ITEM	POST. REF.	DEBIT	CREDIT	BALANCE DEBIT	BALANCE CREDIT
1988 Dec. 31		G42		3945		3945

ACCOUNT *Interest Expense*   ACCOUNT NO. *8101*

DATE	ITEM	POST. REF.	DEBIT	CREDIT	BALANCE DEBIT	BALANCE CREDIT
Dec. 15		CP37	2000		19055	
31		G42	3945		23000	

Accounts after posting the adjusting entry for accrued interest expense

Interest Payable has a credit balance of $39.45. This balance is the accrued interest expense incurred in the current fiscal period but to be paid in the next fiscal period. Interest Expense has a debit balance of $230.00, which is the total interest expense for the fiscal period.

Reporting accrued interest expense on financial statements

The liability account Interest Payable is listed on the balance sheet in the Current Liabilities section. The expense account Interest Expense is listed on the income statement in the Other Expenses section.

Closing entry for the interest expense account

One closing entry is recorded for accounts listed in the Income Statement Debit column of the work sheet. Interest Expense is closed into the income summary account. The closing entry in Furniture Mart's general journal on December 31, 1988, is on the next page. After the closing entry is posted, the interest expense account is closed.

Need for readjusting interest payable and interest expense accounts

When Furniture Mart pays Note Payable No. 11 on January 30, 1989, it will pay the principal, $3 000.00, plus the interest, $59.18. To record the

7		31	*Income Summary*		75 89 20 0				7
8			*Sales Returns + Allow.*			2 1 07 10		8
9			*Purchases*			227 1 6 00		9
10			*Bad Debts Expense*			4 28 40		10
11			*Delivery Expense*			1 87 3 00		11
12			*Depr. Expense-Office Equip.*			2 24 6 00		12
13			*Depr. Expense-Store Equip.*			4 1 1 6 50		13
14			*Insurance Expense*			1 80 00		14
15			*Miscellaneous Expense*			6 47 15		15
16			*Payroll Taxes Expense*			2 96 8 60		16
17			*Rent Expense*			60 0 00		17
18			*Salary Expense*			37 1 08 00		18
19			*Supplies Expense*			6 7 2 25		19
20			*Interest Expense*			2 30 00		20
21								21

Closing entry including the interest expense account

payment Notes Payable will be debited for the principal of the note, $3 000.00. Interest Expense will be debited for the interest paid, $59.18. Cash will be credited for the total amount paid, $3 059.18. But $39.45 of the interest paid has been debited to Interest Expense as accrued expense at the end of the 1988 fiscal period. Only $19.73 applies to the 1989 fiscal period.

Accrued interest expense recorded in one fiscal period should not be debited to Interest Expense a second time when actually paid in the following fiscal period. To avoid this double debit, Interest Payable and Interest Expense are readjusted at the beginning of the new fiscal period by a reversing entry. After the reversing entry has been recorded and posted, all interest expense transactions during the new fiscal period are recorded in the usual way.

Reversing entry for accrued interest expense

Furniture Mart's adjusting entry for accrued interest expense on December 31, 1988, debited Interest Expense for $39.45 and credited Interest Payable for $39.45. The reversing entry on January 1, 1989, reverses this adjusting entry.

Analysing the reversing entry for accrued interest expense. The reversing entry for accrued interest expense is analysed in the T accounts at the right.

Interest Payable is debited for $39.45 and Interest Expense is credited for $39.45. This reversing entry closes the interest payable account and transfers the original credit balance to the credit side of the interest expense account. The credit to Interest Expense is a temporary balance that represents unpaid interest expense incurred and recorded during the previous fiscal period.

Interest Payable		
Reversing	39.45	Adjusting 39.45

Interest Expense		
Balance	190.55	Closing 230.00
Adjusting	39.45	Reversing 39.45

During the new fiscal period, payments of interest expense are debited to Interest Expense. The portion of each interest payment that applies to the previous fiscal period will automatically be deducted because of the credit balance. *(CONCEPT: Matching Expenses with Revenue)*

Recording and posting the reversing entry for accrued interest expense. The reversing entry is recorded in the general journal as of January 1, 1989, as shown below.

Reversing entry for accrued interest expense

After the reversing entry is posted, the interest payable and interest expense accounts appear as shown below.

Accounts after posting the reversing entry for accrued interest expense

Interest Payable has a zero balance at the beginning of the new 1989 fiscal period. Interest Payable will not receive any entries until the end of the 1989 fiscal period. Interest Payable is needed for only one day each period to prepare complete financial reports.

Interest Expense has a credit balance of $39.45 on January 1, 1989. This balance on the first day of the new fiscal year is the result of posting the reversing entry for accrued interest expense. During 1989 Interest Expense will be debited each time cash is paid for interest expense. At the end of the 1989 fiscal period, the debit balance will show the amount of interest expense that belongs to the 1989 fiscal period. Then, at the end of the 1989 fiscal period there will be new accrued interest expense, incurred in 1989 but not paid in 1989. The new accrued interest expense on December 31, 1989, will be handled in the same manner as the accrued interest expense on December 31, 1988.

Adjusting entry for accrued salary expense

Furniture Mart pays its employees weekly on Friday. At the end of the fiscal period on Saturday, December 31, 1988, one day's salary amounting to $120.00 is owed to employees for work performed on Saturday. This salary expense will not be paid until the next regular payday on Friday, January 6, 1989. The $120.00 owed is a salary expense of the 1988 fiscal period. The accounting records must show all the salary expense for the 1988 fiscal period. *(CONCEPT: Matching Expenses with Revenue)* An adjusting entry is made to record the amount of salary owed at the end of December, 1988, but to be paid in January, 1989. Salary owed but not yet paid is called accrued salary expense.

Analysing the adjusting entry for accrued salary expense. The amount of salary owed but not paid on December 31, 1988, is $120.00. The adjustment for accrued salary expense is analysed in the T accounts at the right.

Salary Expense is debited for $120.00 to show the increase in the balance of this account. The new balance of Salary Expense is the total amount of salary expense incurred during the fiscal period.

Salaries Payable is credited for $120.00. The balance of Salaries Payable is the amount of accrued salary expense at the end of the fiscal period.

Salary Expense	
120.00	

Salaries Payable	
	120.00

Adjustment for accrued salary expense on a work sheet. The adjusting entry for accrued salary expense is planned on a work sheet. The adjustment is below.

	ACCOUNT TITLE	TRIAL BALANCE		ADJUSTMENTS		INCOME STATEMENT		BALANCE SHEET		
		DEBIT	CREDIT	DEBIT	CREDIT	DEBIT	CREDIT	DEBIT	CREDIT	
16	Salaries Payable				(4) 12000				12000	16
39	Salary Expense	36988 00		(4) 12000		37 108 00				39

Salary Expense is debited for $120.00. This amount, $120.00, is added to the amount in the Trial Balance Debit column, $36 988.00. The new balance, $37 108.00, is extended to the Income Statement Debit column. Accrued salary expense on a work sheet

Salaries Payable is credited for $120.00. This amount is extended to the Balance Sheet Credit column.

Recording and posting the adjustment for accrued salary expense. Data needed to journalize the adjustment for accrued salary expense are obtained from the Adjustments columns of the work sheet. The adjusting entry in the general journal is on the next page.

		31	*Salary Expense*							120 00				
			Salaries Payable									120 00		

Adjusting entry for accrued salary expense

After the adjusting entry is posted, the salaries payable and salary expense accounts appear as shown below.

ACCOUNT *Salaries Payable*						ACCOUNT NO. *2103*	
DATE	ITEM	POST. REF.	DEBIT	CREDIT	BALANCE	
					DEBIT	CREDIT
1988 *Dec. 31*		*G42*		120 00		120 00

ACCOUNT *Salary Expense*						ACCOUNT NO. *6112*	
DATE	ITEM	POST. REF.	DEBIT	CREDIT	BALANCE	
					DEBIT	CREDIT
	30	*CP37*	720 00		36 988 00	
	31	*G42*	120 00		37 108 00	

Accounts after posting the adjusting entry for accrued salary expense

Salaries Payable has a credit balance of $120.00. This is the accrued salary expense incurred in the current fiscal period but to be paid in the next fiscal period. Salary Expense has a debit balance of $37 108.00, which is the total salary expense for the fiscal period. (CONCEPT: *Matching Expenses with Revenue*)

Reporting accrued salary expense on financial statements

The liability account Salaries Payable is listed on the balance sheet in the Current Liabilities section. The expense account Salary Expense is listed on the income statement in the Operating Expenses section.

Closing entry for the salary expense account

Salary expense is included in the closing entry made for the accounts listed in the Income Statement Debit column of the work sheet. Furniture Mart's closing entry on December 31, 1988, for the salary expense account is on page 631. After this closing entry is posted, the salary expense account is closed.

Need for readjusting the salaries payable and salary expense accounts

Furniture Mart's next weekly payroll is January 6, 1989. The entire amount of salaries for the week, $720.00, is debited to Salary Expense. This entry is the same as that for each weekly payroll in 1988. But $120.00 of these salaries has already been debited to Salary Expense as accrued expense at the end of the 1988 fiscal period. Therefore, only $600.00 applies to the 1989 fiscal period.

Accrued salary expense recorded in one fiscal period should not be debited to Salary Expense a second time when actually paid in the following fiscal period. To avoid this double debit, the salaries payable and salary expense accounts are readjusted at the beginning of the new fiscal period by a reversing entry.

Reversing entry for accrued salary expense

Furniture Mart's adjusting entry for accrued salary expense on December 31, 1988, debited Salary Expense for $120.00 and credited Salaries Payable for $120.00. The reversing entry on January 1, 1989, reverses this adjusting entry.

Analysing the reversing entry for accrued salary expense. The reversing entry for accrued salary expense is analysed at the right.

Salaries Payable is debited for $120.00 and Salary Expense is credited for $120.00. This reversing entry closes the salaries payable account and transfers the original credit balance to the credit side of the salary expense account. The credit to Salary Expense is a temporary balance that represents unpaid salary expense incurred and recorded during the previous fiscal period.

Salaries Payable			
Reversing	120.00	Adjusting	120.00

Salary Expense			
Balance	36 988.00	Closing	37 108.00
Adjusting	120.00	Reversing	120.00

Recording and posting the reversing entry for accrued salary expense. The reversing entry is recorded in the general journal as of January 1, 1989, as shown below.

Reversing entry for accrued salary expense

After the reversing entry is posted, the salaries payable and salary expense accounts appear as shown below.

Accounts after posting the reversing entry for accrued salary expense

Salaries Payable has a zero balance at the beginning of the new 1989 fiscal period. Like Interest Payable, Salaries Payable will not receive any entries until the end of the 1989 fiscal period.

Salary Expense is credited at the beginning of the new 1989 fiscal period for the amount of salary expense that belongs to the 1988 fiscal period. This amount will be paid in 1989. During 1988 Salary Expense will be debited each time the weekly payroll is paid.

ACCOUNTING TERMS

What is the meaning of each of the following?

1. accrued revenue
2. accrued interest income
3. reversing entry
4. accrued expenses
5. accrued interest expense
6. accrued salary expense

QUESTIONS FOR INDIVIDUAL STUDY

1. When are most journal entries made that record revenue?
2. Why should revenue that has been earned but not received be recorded before financial statements are prepared at the end of a fiscal period?
3. What accounts are debited and credited to record the adjusting entry for accrued interest income?
4. Under what heading on the balance sheet is the balance of the interest receivable account listed?
5. Why are the interest receivable and interest income accounts readjusted at the beginning of a new fiscal period?
6. What accounts are debited and credited to record the reversing entry for accrued interest income?
7. Why should expenses that have been incurred but not paid be recorded before financial statements are prepared at the end of a fiscal period?
8. What accounts are debited and credited to record the adjusting entry for accrued interest expense?
9. Under what heading on the income statement is the balance of the interest expense account listed?
10. Why are the interest payable and interest expense accounts readjusted at the beginning of a new fiscal period?
11. What accounts are debited and credited to record the reversing entry for accrued interest expense?
12. Why are the salaries payable and salary expense accounts readjusted at the beginning of a new fiscal period?

CASES FOR MANAGEMENT DECISION

CASE 1 At the end of the fiscal period, Lawson Company failed to record accrued interest income amounting to $300.00 on notes receivable. What effect does this omission have on (a) the income statement and (b) the balance sheet?

CASE 2 At the end of the fiscal period, Scott Company failed to record accrued interest expense amounting to $100.00 on notes payable. They also failed to record accrued salary expense amounting to $200.00. What effect do these omissions have on (a) the income statement and (b) the balance sheet?

DRILL FOR UNDERSTANDING

DRILL   Recording adjusting and reversing entries for accrued revenue and accrued expenses

Instructions: 1. Prepare a form similar to the one below. Enter each number and item on the form.

No.	Item	Account Titles Affected By			
		Adjusting Entry		Reversing Entry	
		Account Debited	Account Credited	Account Debited	Account Credited
1.	Accrued interest income				
2.	Accrued interest expense				
3.	Accrued salary expense				

Instructions: 2. For each item, indicate the titles of the accounts debited and credited to record the adjusting entry on December 31 of the current year.

3. For each item, indicate the titles of the accounts debited and credited to record the reversing entry on January 1 of the following year.

APPLICATION PROBLEM

APPLICATION PROBLEM   Recording and posting adjusting, closing, and reversing entries for accrued revenue and accrued expenses

Selected accounts from Brook's ledger are below. The balances are for December 31 of the current fiscal year before adjusting entries.

Account Title	Acct. No.	Balance	Account Title	Acct. No.	Balance
Interest Receivable	1103	——	Salary Expense	6112	$8 918.00
Interest Payable	2102	——	Interest Income	7101	296.80
Salaries Payable	2103	——	Interest Expense	8101	122.50
Income Summary	3301	——			

On December 31, accrued interest income on notes receivable is $27.30. Accrued salaries are $169.40. Accrued interest expense on notes payable is $61.00.

Instructions: 1. Open the general ledger accounts and record the balances.

2. Use page 14 of a general journal. Record the adjusting entries for accrued revenue and accrued expenses on December 31 of the current year.

3. Post the adjusting entries.

4. Record the entries to close (a) the interest income account and (b) the salary expense and interest expense accounts.

5. Post the closing entries.

6. Record the reversing entries on January 1 of the next year.

7. Post the reversing entries.

ENRICHMENT PROBLEMS

MASTERY PROBLEM   Recording and posting adjusting, closing, and reversing entries for accrued revenue and accrued expenses

Selected accounts from Hoffman's ledger are below. The balances are for December 31 of the current fiscal year before adjusting entries.

Account Title	Acct. No.	Balance	Account Title	Acct. No.	Balance
Interest Receivable	1103	——	Salary Expense	6112	$18 952.50
Interest Payable	2102	——	Interest Income	7101	72.00
Salaries Payable	2103	——	Interest Expense	8101	165.00
Income Summary	3301	——			

Adjustment data at the end of the fiscal period on December 31:

Accrued interest income on notes receivable, $33.75.

Accrued salaries payable, $372.00.

Accrued interest expense on notes payable, $60.00.

Instructions: 1. Open the general ledger accounts and record the balances.

2. Use page 8 of a general journal. Record the adjusting entries for accrued revenue and accrued expenses on December 31 of the current year. Post the adjusting entries.

3. Record the entries to close the revenue and expense accounts. Post the closing entries.

4. Record the reversing entries for the accruals as of January 1 of the next year. Post the reversing entries.

CHALLENGE PROBLEM   Recording and posting adjusting, closing, and reversing entries for accrued revenue and accrued expenses

Selected accounts from Jackson's ledger are below. The balances are for December 31 of the current fiscal year before adjusting entries.

Account Title	Acct. No.	Balance	Account Title	Acct. No.	Balance
Interest Receivable	1103	——	Salary Expense	6112	$36 468.00
Rent Receivable	1104	——	Interest Income	7101	225.00
Interest Payable	2102	——	Rent Income	7102	1 500.00
Salaries Payable	2103	——	Interest Expense	8101	90.00
Income Summary	3301	——			

Adjustment data at the end of the fiscal period on December 31:

Accrued interest income has been earned on a 60-day, 9% note for $6 000.00 dated November 21.

Accrued interest expense has been incurred on a 120-day, 8% note for $4 000.00 dated December 16.

Accrued rent receivable, $300.00.

Accrued salaries payable, $280.00.

Instructions: 1. Open the general ledger accounts and record the balances.

2. Use page 23 of a general journal. Record the adjusting entries for accrued revenue and accrued expenses on December 31 of the current year. Post the adjusting entries.

3. Record the entries to close the revenue and expense accounts. Post the closing entries.

4. Record the reversing entries on January 1 of the new year. Post the reversing entries.

Recycling Problems

NOTE: No recycling problems are provided for Chapter 1.

RECYCLING PROBLEM 2-R 1 Preparing a beginning balance sheet; recording and posting an opening entry

The following financial information is listed by Lucia Sanchez for a new business, Sanchez Company.

Assets: Cash, $2 430.00; Supplies, $570.00; Equipment, $4 770.00.
Liabilities: Menington Supply Company, $800.00; Ramon's Equipment Company, $2 880.00.

Instructions: 1. Prepare a beginning balance sheet using the date October 1 of the current year.
2. Record the opening entry for Sanchez Company using page 1 of a general journal.
3. Open the following ledger accounts for the partial chart of accounts below.

Account Title	Account Number	Account Title	Account Number
Cash	11	Menington Supply Company	21
Supplies	12	Ramon's Equipment Company	22
Equipment	13	Lucia Sanchez, Capital	31

Instructions: 4. Post the opening entry recorded in Instruction 2 above.

RECYCLING PROBLEM 3-R 1 Determining how transactions change the expanded accounting equation

The transactions below were completed for Kawoski Cleaning Service, operated by Josef Kawoski. Use a form similar to the one below.

Trans. No.	Assets			=	Liabilities	+	Capital
	Cash	Supplies	Equipment		Showse Supply & Service Co.		
Bal. 1.	9 000 −500	600	6 600	=	1 550	+	14 650 −500
Bal. 2.	8 500	600	6 600	=	1 550	+	14 150

640

Transactions

1. Paid cash for gasoline bill, $500.00.
2. Paid cash for supplies, $150.00.
3. Paid cash for a new piece of equipment, $450.00.
4. Received cash from day's sales, $600.00.
5. Paid cash for part of amount owed Showse Supply & Service Company, $450.00.
6. Paid cash for the telephone bill, $130.00.
7. Received cash from day's sales, $375.00.
8. Paid cash for repairs to station wagon used by the business, $155.00.
9. Paid cash for a new piece of cleaning equipment, $600.00.
10. Paid cash to the owner for personal use, $300.00.
11. Received cash from the sale of an old piece of equipment, $75.00.
12. Received cash from day's sales, $450.00.
13. Paid cash for the electric bill, $100.00.
14. Paid cash for next month's rent, $400.00.
15. Received cash from day's sales, $325.00.

Instructions: 1. Complete steps a, b, and c for each transaction. (a) Analyse the transaction and show the amount increased (+) and decreased (−) for the items affected on the equation. Transaction 1 is shown as an example. (b) Figure the new balance for each item and write it on the next line. (c) Check that *Assets = Liabilities + Capital* for each new balance line.

2. Prepare a balance sheet using the information on the last balance line of the solution to Instruction 1. Use the date October 15 of the current year.

RECYCLING PROBLEM 4-R 1   Analysing transactions into debit and credit parts

Mrs. Rosa Benitez operates a private swimming club. She pays a monthly rent for the use of the swimming pool and facilities. Revenue for the business comes from two sources. (a) Annual membership dues. (b) Daily swim fees paid by non-members. The ledger of the club includes the accounts below on October 1 of the current year.

Cash, $2 360.00	Admissions Revenue
Supplies, $600.00.	Membership Revenue
Pool Equipment, $965.00	Electricity Expense
Swim-set Equipment Company (liability), $675.00	Maintenance Expense
Rosa Benitez, Capital, $3 250.00	Miscellaneous Expense
Rosa Benitez, Drawing	Rent Expense
	Water Expense

Instructions: 1. Prepare T accounts for the accounts listed above. Record the account balance for those accounts that have a balance.

2. Analyse each of the following transactions into debit and credit parts. Record the amounts in the correct T accounts for each transaction. The T accounts at the right show the accounts affected by Transaction 1 as an example.

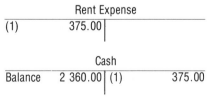

Transactions

1. Paid cash for month's rent, $375.00.
2. Paid cash for the water bill, $85.00.
3. Received cash from membership dues, $860.00.

4. Paid cash for maintaining the pool, $52.00.
5. Received cash from daily pool admissions, $45.00.
6. Paid cash to Swim-set Equipment Company for part payment of amount owed, $150.00.
7. Received cash from membership dues, $520.00.
8. Received cash from the sale of a used pool pump and filter, $390.00.
9. Paid cash for a new pool pump and filter, $1 500.00.
10. Paid cash for the electric bill, $85.00.
11. Received cash from daily pool admissions, $120.00.
12. Paid cash for a new diving board, $130.00.
13. Received cash from daily pool admissions, $135.00.
14. Paid cash for general supplies, $25.00.
15. Paid cash for folding chairs to be used around the poolside, $100.00.
16. Paid cash to Swim-set Equipment Company for part payment of amount owed, $200.00.
17. Paid cash to the owner for personal use, $200.00.
18. Received cash from daily pool admissions, $165.00.
19. Paid cash for minor repair to a leak in pool filtering equipment, $25.00.

RECYCLING PROBLEM 5-R 1 Recording transactions in a cash journal

Carl Johnson operates a hunting lodge. The lodge is open only during the hunting season. The lodge opened on October 1 of the current year. The business' cash journal is similar to the one described on page 71.

The following are some of the accounts in the business' ledger. *Assets*: Cash, Supplies, Equipment. *Liabilities*: Ackerman Plumbing Company, Commercial Furniture Company. *Capital*: Carl Johnson, Capital; Carl Johnson, Drawing. *Revenue*: Room Sales. *Expenses*: Advertising Expense, Laundry Expense, Miscellaneous Expense, Rent Expense, Utilities Expense.

Instructions: 1. Record the cash balance on hand, $819.00, on page 1 of a cash journal.

2. Record the following transactions. All payments are made by cheque beginning with Cheque No. 1. All cash received is recorded on a cash register. Number all cash register tapes with the letter T plus the date.

Oct. 1. Paid cash for having the lodge cleaned, $85.00.
 1. Paid cash for month's rent of lodge, $300.00.
 2. Received cash from sale of old furniture, $45.00.
 3. Received cash from room sales, $145.00.
 6. Paid cash to Ackerman Plumbing Company for amount owed, $58.00.
 9. Received cash from room sales, $147.00.
 13. Paid cash for laundry, $44.10.
 15. Received cash from sale of old piece of equipment, $32.00.
 16. Received cash from room sales, $270.00.
 19. Paid cash for installing road signs advertising the lodge, $115.00.
 23. Received cash from room sales, $230.00.
 27. Paid cash for telephone bill, $78.50.
 28. Paid cash for laundry, $25.00.
 29. Paid cash for electric bill, $45.00.
 30. Received cash from room sales, $294.00.
 30. Paid cash for advertisement in local newspaper, $75.00.

Instructions: 3. Prove cash. The ending balance on Cheque Stub No. 9 is $1 156.40.

4. Prove the cash journal.

5. Rule the cash journal.

RECYCLING PROBLEM 6-R 1 Journalizing and posting using a cash journal

Rachael Moser, an attorney, uses the ledger accounts below.

Account Title	Acct. No.	Account Balance	Account Title	Acct. No.	Account Balance
Cash	11	$8 587.00	Professional Fees	41	——
Supplies	12	125.00	Miscellaneous Expense	51	——
Office Furniture	13	870.00	Rent Expense	52	——
Law Library	14	645.00	Utilities Expense	53	——
Castle Garage (liability)	21	685.00			
Huffer Company (liability)	22	110.00			
Rachael Moser, Capital	31	9 432.00			
Rachael Moser, Drawing	32	——			

Instructions: 1. Open a ledger account for each account listed above. Write the account title and number at the top of the form. Record the balance for each account that has a balance. Write the word *Balance* in the Item column and place a check mark in the Post. Ref. column. Use October 1 of the current year.

2. Record the following transactions on page 10 of a cash journal similar to the one on page 96. Use the revenue column heading *Professional Fees Credit* instead of Sales Credit. Source documents are abbreviated as: cheque, C; receipts, R.

Oct. 1. Record cash balance on hand, $8 587.00.
   1. Paid cash for October rent, $350.00. C150.
   4. Received cash for legal services, $50.00. R45.
   6. Paid cash for new office furniture, $145.00. C151.
   8. Received cash for sale of old office furniture, $12.00. R46.
   8. Received cash for legal services, $100.00. R47.
   11. Paid cash to Huffer Company, $50.00. C152.
   12. Paid cash for supplies, $240.00. C153.
   15. Paid cash for miscellaneous expense, $6.00. C154.
   18. Paid cash for the miscellaneous expense of taking a client to dinner, $28.50. C155.
   19. Paid cash for telephone bill, $25.80. C156.
   21. Received cash for legal services, $360.00. R48.
   22. Paid cash to Castle Garage, $300.00. C157.
   25. Received cash from sale of old office furniture, $20.00. R49.
   26. Received cash for legal services, $150.00. R50.
   27. Received cash for legal services, $95.00. R51.
   29. Paid cash for gas bill, $32.00. C158.
   31. Paid cash for electric bill, $38.00. C159.
   31. Paid cash for supplies, $200.00. C160.
   31. Paid cash to Miss Moser for personal use, $500.00. C161.

Instructions: 3. Prove cash. The balance on Cheque Stub No. 161 is $7 458.70.

4. Total, prove, and rule the cash journal.

5. Post from the cash journal to the ledger.

RECYCLING PROBLEM 7-R 1   Completing a work sheet

Lanahan Insurance Agency's ledger accounts and balances on July 31 of the current year are below.

Account Title	Account Balance	Account Title	Account Balance
Cash	$2 860.00	Premiums Revenue	$2 600.00
Automobiles	9 000.00	Advertising Expense	182.00
Office Furniture	1 440.00	Automobile Expense	250.00
Office Equipment	1 321.00	Miscellaneous Expense	72.00
Nichols Company (liability)	753.00	Rent Expense	450.00
Poldark Motors (liability)	2 800.00	Utilities Expense	302.00
Richards Products Co. (liability)	1 481.00		
Teresa Lanahan, Capital	8 443.00		
Teresa Lanahan, Drawing	200.00		
Income Summary	——		

Instructions: 1. Complete the heading on a work sheet. The Agency uses a one-month fiscal period. Prepare a trial balance on the work sheet.

2. Extend the asset, liability, and capital account balances to the Balance Sheet columns.

3. Extend the revenue and expense account balances to the Income Statement columns.

4. Figure the net income or net loss and complete the Income Statement columns.

5. Complete the Balance Sheet columns.

RECYCLING PROBLEM 8-R 1   Preparing a work sheet and financial statements

The ledger accounts and balances for Midtown Cinema are below.

Account Title	Account Balance	Account Title	Account Balance
Cash	$ 3 994.71	Admissions Revenue	$ 4 701.76
Air Conditioning Equipment	4 080.00	Advertising Expense	262.40
Projection Equipment	10 560.00	Film Rental Expense	1 624.00
Sound Equipment	5 207.99	Maintenance Expense	132.80
Allied Studios (liability)	171.68	Miscellaneous Expense	42.10
Bader Films Company (liability)	52.96	Projection Expense	367.68
Gibson Sound Service (liability)	212.80	Rent Expense	600.00
Elisa Downs, Capital	23 065.60	Utilities Expense	333.12
Elisa Downs, Drawing	1 000.00		
Income Summary	——		

Instructions: 1. Prepare a work sheet for the month ending October 31 of the current year.

2. Prepare an income statement.

3. Prepare a balance sheet.

RECYCLING PROBLEM 9-R 1   Recording closing entries

Parts of Manor Car Wash's work sheet are given on the next page. The balance of the account David Filipe, Drawing on December 31 is $150.00.

Instructions: Record the closing entries. Use page 1 of a general journal.

Manor Car Wash
Work Sheet
For Month Ended December 31, 19--

Account Title	Income Statement	
	Debit	Credit
Sales		1 366 00
Advertising Expense..	112 84	
Miscellaneous Expense.......................................	98 80	
Rent Expense	650 00	
Repairs Expense	48 10	
Utilities Expense	239 36	
	1 149 10	1 366 00
Net Income...	216 90	
	1 366 00	1 366 00

RECYCLING PROBLEM 10-R 1   Reconciling a bank statement; recording a bank service charge and dishonored cheque

On November 1 of the current year, Mason's Miniature Golf receives a bank statement dated October 29. A comparison of the bank statement and the chequebook shows the information below.

> The outstanding cheques are: No. 251, $25.52; No. 252, $11.40; No. 257, $29.28.
> An outstanding deposit was made on October 31, $66.88.
> The bank service charge is $1.10.
> The bank statement balance is $256.67.
> The chequebook balance on Cheque Stub No. 258 is $258.45.

Instructions: 1. Prepare a bank reconciliation. Use November 1 of the current year.
2. Record the bank service charge on page 6 of a cash journal. Memorandum No. 12.
3. Record a dishonored cheque on page 6 of a cash journal. Use November 2 of the current year. Amount of cheque, $15.00; bank fee, $1.00. Memorandum No. 13.

RECYCLING PROBLEM 11-R 1   Journalizing transactions in a synoptic journal

Raymond Anthony and Jack Almond, partners in a sporting goods store, completed the transactions below for November of the current year. The cash balance on November 1 was $5 200.00.

Instructions: 1. Record the cash balance on hand on page 8 of a synoptic journal like the one on pages 192 and 193.
2. Record the following transactions. Source documents are abbreviated as: cheque, *C*; purchase invoice, *P*; memorandum, *M*.

Nov. 1. Paid November rent, $650.00. C260.
     1. Paid salaries, $1 250.00. C261.
     1. Purchased merchandise on account from Kramer Sporting Goods, $725.00. P72.
     2. Paid on account to Greenville Supply, $82.00. C262.
     3. Raymond Anthony, partner, withdrew cash, $450.00. C263.

Nov. 3. Jack Almond, partner, withdrew cash, $450.00. C264.
    5. Purchased merchandise on account from Schultz Co., $525.00. P73.
    6. Jack Almond, partner, withdrew merchandise, $33.00. M22.
    8. Paid advertising bill, $26.00. C265. (Miscellaneous Expense)
    9. Bought supplies on account from Hillsdale Supply, $43.00. M23.
   11. Purchased merchandise for cash, $175.00. C266.
   12. Paid on account to Kramer Sporting Goods, $460.00. C267.
   15. Purchased merchandise on account from Stevens Sportswear, $280.00. P74.
   15. Purchased merchandise for cash, $185.00. C268.
   16. Bought supplies for cash, $26.00. C269.
   16. Paid on account to Schultz Co., $410.00. C270.
   17. Raymond Anthony, partner, withdrew merchandise, $26.00. M24.
   19. Purchased merchandise for cash, $115.00. C271.
   20. Bought supplies on account from Eastside Supply, $44.00. M25.
   22. Purchased merchandise on account from Berry, Inc., $235.00. P75.
   23. Bought supplies for cash, $74.00. C272.
   25. Discovered that supplies bought last month had been recorded in error as a debit to Purchases instead of Supplies, $64.00. M26.
   27. Bought supplies on account from Janer Supply, $29.00. M27.
   29. Paid on account to Kramer Sporting Goods, $725.00. C273.
   30. Purchased merchandise for cash, $135.00. C274.
   30. Paid on account to Schultz Co., $525.00. C275.

RECYCLING PROBLEM 12-R 1   Journalizing sales and cash receipts in a synoptic journal

David Franklin and Lu Chi, partners in a retail shoe store, completed the transactions below for December of the current year. The cash balance on December 1 was $3 750.00.

Instructions: 1. Record the cash balance on page 12 of a synoptic journal like the one on pages 218 and 219.

2. Record the following transactions. Credit card sales are recorded as cash sales. Source documents are abbreviated as: sales invoice, *S*; receipt, *R*; cash register tape, *T*; calculator tape, *CT*.

Dec. 1. Sold merchandise on account to Martha Howard, $35.00, plus sales tax, $1.75. Total, $36.75. S53.
    1. Received on account from Mary Hopkins, $42.00. R72.
    2. Received on account from Jerry Shields, $63.00. R73.
    4. Cash sales for the week, $1 460.00, plus sales tax, $73.00. Total, $1 533.00. T4.
    4. Credit card sales for the week, $540.00, plus sales tax, $27.00. Total, $567.00. CT4.
    6. Sold merchandise on account to Phillip Kane, $45.00, plus sales tax, $2.25. Total, $47.25. S54.
    7. Sold merchandise on account to Sandra King, $72.00, plus sales tax, $3.60. Total, $75.60. S55.
    9. Received on account from Robert Davis, $68.25. R74.
   11. Cash sales for the week, $1 830.00, plus sales tax, $91.50. Total, $1 921.50. T11.
   11. Credit card sales for the week, $715.00, plus sales tax, $35.75. Total, $750.75. CT11.
   14. Sold merchandise on account to James Barrett, $45.00, plus sales tax, $2.25. Total, $47.25. S56.
   17. Received on account from Martha Howard, $36.75. R75.

Dec. 18. Sold merchandise on account to Phillip Kane, $30.00, plus sales tax, $1.50. Total, $31.50. S57.

20. Cash sales for the week, $1 920.00, plus sales tax, $96.00. Total, $2 016.00. T20.

20. Credit card sales for the week, $760.00, plus sales tax, $38.00. Total, $798.00. CT20.

21. Sold merchandise on account to Charlotte Reynolds, $92.00, plus sales tax, $4.60. Total, $96.60. S58.

22. Received on account from Phillip Kane, $47.25. R76.

24. Sold merchandise on account to Mary Hopkins, $42.00, plus sales tax, $2.10. Total, $44.10. S59.

24. Cash sales for the week, $2 160.00, plus sales tax, $108.00. Total, $2 268.00. T24.

24. Credit card sales for the week, $830.00, plus sales tax, $41.50. Total, $871.50. CT24.

27. Received on account from Sandra King, $75.60. R77.

31. Cash sales for the week, $1 340.00, plus sales tax, $67.00. Total, $1 407.00. T31.

31. Credit card sales for the week, $240.00, plus sales tax, $12.00. Total, $252.00. CT31.

Instructions: 3. Total the amount columns on the synoptic journal. Prove the equality of debits and credits.

4. Rule the synoptic journal. Use the illustration on pages 220 and 221 as a guide.

RECYCLING PROBLEM 13-R 1 Posting to ledgers from a synoptic journal

Instructions: 1. Open the following creditors' accounts in the accounts payable ledger. Record the balances as of November 1 of the current year.

Creditor	Address	Account Balance
Eastern Distributors	2200 McDonald Street, Regina, SK S4N 2Y9	——
Grayling Building Supply	1303 Queen Street, Regina, SK S4T 4B7	$1 780.00
R & J Manufacturing	619 Wascana Street, Regina, SK S4T 4H4	——

2. Open the following customers' accounts in the accounts receivable ledger. Record the balances as of November 1 of the current year.

Customer	Address	Account Balance
Theresa Harris	1310 Arlington Avenue, Saskatoon, SK S7H 2X9	$1 250.00
Louise Hamagami	2601 Taylor Street E., Saskatoon, SK S7H 1X1	——
Rodney Paxton	190 Sangster Boulevard, Regina, SK S4R 7G9	1 500.00
Julio Ruiz	1352 11 Avenue N. W., Moose Jaw, SK S6H 4M3	——

3. Open the following accounts in the general ledger of James Home Improvement Centre. Record the balances as of November 1 of the current year.

Account Title	Acct. No.	Account Balance
Cash	11	$ 5 400.00
Accounts Receivable	12	2 750.00
Merchandise Inventory	13	84 000.00
Supplies	14	800.00
Prepaid Insurance	15	300.00
Accounts Payable	21	1 780.00
Sales Tax Payable	22	364.00

Account Title	Acct. No.	Account Balance
Marcus Fields, Capital.................	31	$45 553.00
Marcus Fields, Drawing..............	32	——
Randolph Pearson, Capital........	33	45 553.00
Randolph Pearson, Drawing.......	34	——
Income Summary........................	35	——
Sales	41	——
Purchases...................................	51	——
Credit Card Fee Expense	61	——
Delivery Expense	62	——
Insurance Expense	63	——
Miscellaneous Expense..............	64	——
Rent Expense..............................	65	——
Salary Expense	66	——
Supplies Expense	67	——

Instructions: 4. Record the following transactions on page 17 of a synoptic journal similar to the one on pages 242 and 243. The beginning cash balance is $5 400.00. Add a 5% sales tax to all sales transactions. Credit card sales are recorded as cash sales. Source documents are abbreviated as: cheque, C; memorandum, M; purchase invoice, P; receipt, R; sales invoice, S; cash register tape, T; calculator tape, CT.

Nov. 1. Paid delivery expense, $83.00. C121.
    1. Paid rent expense, $950.00. C122.
    1. Paid salaries, $1 830.00. C123.
    3. Purchased merchandise on account from R & J Manufacturing, $1 380.00. P64.
    4. Purchased merchandise for cash, $750.00. C124.
    6. Sold merchandise on account to Julio Ruiz, $260.00. S48.
    6. Cash sales for the week, $2 360.00. T6.
    6. Credit card sales for the week, $506.00. CT6.
    8. Paid for advertising, $36.00. C125. (Miscellaneous Expense)
    8. Purchased merchandise on account from Eastern Distributors, $1 480.00. P65.
    9. Received on account from Theresa Harris, $1 250.00. R32.
   13. Cash sales for the week, $2 050.00. T13.
   13. Credit card sales for the week, $580.00. CT13.
   15. Received on account from Rodney Paxton, $1 500.00. R33.
   16. Sold merchandise on account to Louise Hamagami, $1 100.00. S49.
   17. Marcus Fields, partner, withdrew cash, $700.00. C126.
   17. Randolph Pearson, partner, withdrew cash, $700.00. C127.
   18. Bought supplies for cash, $200.00. C128.
   20. Paid on account to Grayling Building Supply, $1 780.00. C129.
   20. Cash sales for the week, $2 240.00. T20.
   20. Credit card sales for the week, $615.00. CT20.
   21. Discovered that supplies bought on account had been recorded as a debit to Purchases instead of Supplies, $345.00. M23.
   23. Marcus Fields, partner, withdrew merchandise, $40.00. M24.
   25. Sold merchandise on account to Theresa Harris, $880.00. S50.
   27. Cash sales for the week, $2 550.00. T27.
   27. Credit card sales for the week, $740.00. CT27.
   29. Sold merchandise on account to Julio Ruiz, $1 250.00. S51.
   30. Cash sales for the week, $925.00. T30.
   30. Credit card sales for the week, $180.00. CT30.

Instructions: 5. Total the columns of the synoptic journal on a calculator or on paper. Prove that the sum of the debit totals equals the sum of the credit totals.

6. Prove cash. The balance on Cheque Stub No. 130 is $14 504.30.

7. Write the column totals in the synoptic journal.

8. Rule the synoptic journal.

9. Post the individual items recorded in the following columns of the synoptic journal. (a) General Debit and Credit. (b) Accounts Receivable Debit and Credit. (c) Accounts Payable Debit and Credit.

10. Post the totals of the special columns of the synoptic journal.

11. Prepare a schedule of accounts payable and a schedule of accounts receivable. Prove the accuracy of the subsidiary ledgers. Compare the schedule totals with the balances of the controlling accounts in the general ledger. If the totals are not the same, find and correct the errors.

12. Prove the equality of debits and credits in the general ledger. On a calculator or on paper, add the balances of all accounts with debit balances. Then add the balances of all accounts with credit balances. If the two totals are not the same, find and correct the errors.

RECYCLING PROBLEM 14-R 1 Preparing a work sheet

The accounts and their balances in Teen Fashions' general ledger appear below. Ending inventories and the value of insurance policies are also given.

Instructions: Prepare Teen Fashions' eight-column work sheet for the monthly fiscal period ending December 31 of the current year. Use as a guide the eight-column work sheet, page 274.

Account Title	Account Balance	Account Title	Account Balance
Cash	$ 9 350.00	Todd Drake, Drawing	$ 830.00
Accounts Receivable	620.00	Income Summary	—
Merchandise Inventory	83 700.00	Sales	14 800.00
Supplies	460.00	Purchases	4 400.00
Prepaid Insurance	340.00	Credit Card Fee Expense	230.00
Accounts Payable	3 610.00	Insurance Expense	—
Sales Tax Payable	592.00	Miscellaneous Expense	92.00
Susan Casper, Capital	42 300.00	Rent Expense	750.00
Susan Casper, Drawing	750.00	Salary Expense	1 300.00
Todd Drake, Capital	41 520.00	Supplies Expense	—

Adjustment Information, December 31

Merchandise inventory	$80 600.00
Supplies inventory	330.00
Value of insurance policies	258.00

RECYCLING PROBLEM 15-R 1 Preparing financial statements

The work sheet for Gift Gallery for the month ended November 30 of the current year is on the next page.

Instructions: 1. Prepare an income statement similar to one on page 285.

2. Prepare a distribution of net income statement similar to one on page 287. The net income is to be shared equally.

3. Prepare a capital statement similar to one on page 290. No additional investments were made during November.

4. Prepare a balance sheet in report form similar to the one on page 294.

Gift Gallery
Work Sheet
For Month Ended November 30, 19--

	1	2	3	4	5	6	7	8
	Trial Balance		Adjustments		Income Statement		Balance Sheet	
Account Title	Debit	Credit	Debit	Credit	Debit	Credit	Debit	Credit
1 Cash	6 400 00						6 400 00	
2 Accounts Receivable	280 00						280 00	
3 Merchandise Inventory..	56 000 00		(b)54 500 00	(a)56 000 00			54 500 00	
4 Supplies..................	260 00			(c) 140 00			120 00	
5 Prepaid Insurance	320 00			(d) 60 00			260 00	
6 Accounts Payable........		2 580 00						2 580 00
7 Sales Tax Payable		626 00						626 00
8 Stella Sanders, Capital..		27 811 50						27 811 50
9 Stella Sanders, Drawing	650 00						650 00	
10 Silvia Wicks, Capital.....		27 811 50						27 811 50
11 Silvia Wicks, Drawing...	600 00						600 00	
12 Income Summary........			(a)56 000 00	(b)54 500 00	56 000 00	54 500 00		
13 Sales		12 520 00				12 520 00		
14 Purchases	4 600 00				4 600 00			
15 Credit Card Fee Expense	275 00				275 00			
16 Insurance Expense			(d) 60 00		60 00			
17 Miscellaneous Expense .	74 00				74 00			
18 Rent Expense.............	750 00				750 00			
19 Salary Expense...........	1 140 00				1 140 00			
20 Supplies Expense........			(c) 140 00		140 00			
21	71 349 00	71 349 00	110 700 00	110 700 00	63 039 00	67 020 00	62 810 00	58 829 00
22 Net Income					3 981 00			3 981 00
23					67 020 00	67 020 00	62 810 00	62 810 00

RECYCLING PROBLEM 16-R 1   Completing the work at the end of a fiscal period

Recycling Problem 15-R 1 above shows the completed work sheet for Gift Gallery. Use this completed work sheet to complete this problem.

Instructions: 1. On page 3 of a synoptic journal record the adjusting entries shown in the Adjustments columns of the work sheet.

2. Record in the synoptic journal the closing entries from the information on the work sheet. The distribution of net income statement showed equal distribution of earnings.

RECYCLING PROBLEM 17-R 1   Preparing a general ledger chart of accounts and financial statement setup forms

The general ledger chart of accounts for Kimura Furniture is on the next page.

Instructions: 1. Prepare a general ledger chart of accounts setup form dated February 23 of the current year for the accounts given on page 651. Kimura Furniture's client number is 262. Use chart of accounts setup form, page 337, as a guide.

2. Prepare the following financial statement setup forms for Kimura Furniture dated February 24 of the current year. (1) Income statement. (2) Distribution of net income statement. Net income is to be shared equally. (3) Capital statement. (4) Balance sheet. Use fionancial statement setup forms, pages 339–341, as a guide.

Account Number	ASSETS	Account Number	REVENUE
11000	Cash	41000	Sales
11500	Accounts Receivable		
12000	Merchandise Inventory		COST OF MERCHANDISE SOLD
12500	Supplies	51000	Purchases
13000	Prepaid Insurance		
13500	Office Equipment		EXPENSES
14000	Store Equipment		
		61000	Advertising Expense
	LIABILITIES	61500	Credit Card Fee Expense
		62000	Insurance Expense
21000	Accounts Payable	62500	Miscellaneous Expense
		63000	Rent Expense
	CAPITAL	63500	Salary Expense
31000	Emi Kimura, Capital	64000	Supplies Expense
31500	Emi Kimura, Drawing		
32000	Saburo Kimura, Capital		
32500	Saburo Kimura, Drawing		
33000	Income Summary		

RECYCLING PROBLEM 18-R 1 Recording an opening entry in an EDP general ledger accounting system

The chart of accounts given in Recycling Problem 17-R 1, Chapter 17, is needed to complete Recycling Problem 18-R 1.

Kimura Furniture's balance sheet for February 28 of the current year is below.

Kimura Furniture Balance Sheet February 28, 19--		
Assets		
Cash	9 460 00	
Accounts Receivable	780 00	
Merchandise Inventory	265 650 00	
Supplies	730 00	
Prepaid Insurance	880 00	
Office Equipment	1 340 00	
Store Equipment	950 00	
Total Assets		279 790 00
Liabilities		
Accounts Payable		4 830 00
Capital		
Emi Kimura, Capital	140 160 00	
Saburo Kimura, Capital	134 800 00	
Total Capital		274 960 00
Total Liabilities and Capital		279 790 00

Instructions: Record the opening entry for Kimura Furniture, Client No. 262, on a journal entry transmittal. Use March 1 of the current year as the date of the opening entry. Use account numbers from the chart of accounts shown in Recycling Problem 17-R 1.

RECYCLING PROBLEM 19-R 1   Recording weekly batched transactions for EDP using a journal entry transmittal

The chart of accounts given in Recycling Problem 17-R 1, Chapter 17, is needed to complete Recycling Problem 19-R 1.

Kimura Furniture arranges source documents into five batches. (1) Accounts payable. (2) Cash payments. (3) Accounts receivable. (4) Cash receipts. (5) General. Reference numbers are assigned to transaction source documents within each batch. The batched transactions are recorded as combined entries weekly. Batched transactions for week ended March 6 of the current year are below.

Accounts payable

Bought supplies on account	$ 200.00.	Ref. No. 1000.
Purchased merchandise on account	$ 450.00.	Ref. No. 1001.
Total accounts payable	$ 650.00.	

Cash payments

Bought supplies for cash	$ 50.00.	Ref. No. 2000.
Paid on account	$ 180.00.	Ref. No. 2001.
Emi Kimura, partner, withdrew cash	$ 600.00.	Ref. No. 2002.
Saburo Kimura, partner, withdrew cash	$ 600.00.	Ref. No. 2003.
Paid March rent	$ 750.00.	Ref. No. 2004.
Paid salaries	$1 000.00.	Ref. No. 2005.
Total cash payments	$3 180.00.	

Accounts receivable

Sold merchandise on account	$ 140.00.	Ref. No. 3000.
Total accounts receivable	$ 140.00.	

Cash receipts

Cash received on account	$ 250.00.	Ref. No. 4000.
Cash received from sales	$2 830.00.	Ref. No. 4001.
Total cash receipts	$3 080.00.	

General

Emi Kimura, partner, withdrew merchandise	$ 75.00.	Ref. No. 5000.
Total withdrawals of merchandise by partners	$ 75.00.	

Instructions: Record the batched transactions for Kimura Furniture, Client No. 262, on a journal entry transmittal. Use March 6 of the current year as the date of the last business day for the week's transactions. Use account numbers from the chart of accounts shown in Recycling Problem 17-R 1, page 651. Use the journal entry transmittal, page 367, as your model.

RECYCLING PROBLEM 19-R 2   Recording adjusting and closing entries for EDP using a journal entry transmittal

The chart of accounts given in Recycling Problem 17-R 1, Chapter 17, is needed to complete Recycling Problem 19-R 2.

Kimura Furniture's trial balance is shown in the partial work sheet printout on the next page. Ending inventories and the value of insurance policies are also given.

	TRIAL BALANCE	
	DEBIT	CREDIT
CASH....................	$ 15 500.00	
ACCOUNTS RECEIVABLE......	380.00	
MERCHANDISE INVENTORY....	265 650.00	
SUPPLIES................	930.00	
PREPAID INSURANCE........	880.00	
OFFICE EQUIPMENT........	1 340.00	
STORE EQUIPMENT.........	950.00	
ACCOUNTS PAYABLE........		$ 2 290.00
EMI KIMURA, CAPITAL......		140 160.00
EMI KIMURA, DRAWING......	675.00	
SABURO KIMURA, CAPITAL...		134 800.00
SABURO KIMURA, DRAWING...	600.00	
INCOME SUMMARY..........		
SALES...................		15 830.00
PURCHASES...............	3 540.00	
ADVERTISING EXPENSE......	60.00	
CREDIT CARD FEE EXPENSE..	233.00	
INSURANCE EXPENSE........		
MISCELLANEOUS EXPENSE....	92.00	
RENT EXPENSE............	950.00	
SALARY EXPENSE..........	1 300.00	
SUPPLIES EXPENSE........		
	$293 080.00	$293 080.00

Adjustment Information, March 31

Merchandise inventory...	$262 140.00
Supplies inventory..	700.00
Value of insurance policies..	800.00

Instructions: 1. Enter adjustments and complete work sheet printout for month ended March 31 of the current year. Use as a guide the work sheet printout, page 373.

2. Record adjusting entries for Kimura Furniture, Client No. 262, on a journal entry transmittal. Use account numbers from the chart of accounts shown in Recycling Problem 17-R 1, page 651. Use the journal entry transmittal, page 367, as your model.

3. Record closing entries for Kimura Furniture on a journal entry transmittal. Distribution of net income statement printout shows net income shared equally: Emi Kimura, $2 917.50; Saburo Kimura, $2 917.50.

RECYCLING PROBLEM 20-R 1 Journalizing and posting transactions affecting purchases and cash payments

Instructions: 1. Open the creditors' accounts, page 654, in the accounts payable ledger of Cantrell Company. Record the balances as of July 1 of the current year.

Creditor	Account Balance
Conley Supply Company, 2327 Macleod Trail S.E., Calgary, AB T2G 2P1	——
Gaither Company, 1092 Acadia Drive S.E., Calgary, AB T2J 0E3	——
Iverson Exports, 3601 14 Street N.W., Calgary, AB T2K 1J3	——
Ivory Company, 939 17 Avenue S.W., Calgary, AB T2T 0A4	$1 440.00
Perlich Company, 4430 Blackfoot Trail S.E., Calgary, AB T2G 4G1	675.00
Zeigler Company, 2020 32 Avenue N.E., Calgary, AB T2E 6T4	——

Instructions: 2. Open the following partial list of accounts in the general ledger of Cantrell Company. Record the balances as of July 1 of the current year.

Account Title	Account No.	Account Balance
Cash	1101	$17 400.00
Supplies	1105	778.70
Accounts Payable..............................	2102	2 115.00
Purchases	5101	——
Purchases Returns and Allowances	5101.1	——
Purchases Discount	5101.2	——
Delivery Expense...............................	6103	——
Miscellaneous Expense	6108	——
Rent Expense	6110	——

Instructions: 3. The following transactions affecting purchases and cash payments were completed by Cantrell Company during July of the current year. Record these transactions in a purchases journal, general journal, and cash payments journal similar to those in Chapter 20. Use page 12 for each journal. Source documents are abbreviated as: cheque, C; memorandum, M; purchase invoice, P; debit memorandum, DM.

July 1. Paid July rent, $1 500.00. C240.
    2. Purchased merchandise on account from Gaither Company, $900.00. P122.
    2. Returned merchandise to Perlich Company, $42.00. DM37.
    5. Purchased merchandise on account from Iverson Exports, $270.00. P123.
    6. Paid on account to Perlich Company, $633.00, covering P118 for $675.00 less DM37 for $42.00; no discount. C241.
        Posting. Post the items that are to be posted individually. Post from the journals in this order: Purchases journal, general journal, and cash payments journal.
    8. Paid on account to Ivory Company, $1 425.60, covering P104 for $1 440.00 less a 1% discount of $14.40. C242.
   11. Purchased merchandise for cash, $396.00. C243.
   13. Paid on account to Iverson Exports, $267.30, covering P123 for $270.00 less a 1% discount of $2.70. C244.
   13. Bought supplies on account from Conley Supply Company, $216.00. M76.
        Posting. Post the items that are to be posted individually.
   15. Purchased merchandise on account from Zeigler Company, $684.00. P124.
   15. Purchased merchandise on account from Iverson Exports, $360.00. P125.
   18. Paid miscellaneous expense, $36.00. C245.
   20. Returned merchandise to Gaither Company, $108.00. DM38.
        Posting. Post the items that are to be posted individually.
   22. Purchased merchandise on account from Zeigler Company, $720.00. P126.
   22. Paid on account to Gaither Company, $792.00, covering P122 for $900.00 less DM38 for $108.00; no discount. C246.
   22. Paid delivery expense, $54.00. C247.
   22. Paid on account to Zeigler Company, $670.32, covering P124 for $684.00 less a 2% discount of $13.68. C248.

July 25. Paid miscellaneous expense, $60.00. C249.
   27. Paid on account to Conley Supply Company, $216.00; no discount. C250.
   28. Returned merchandise to Zeigler Company, $30.00. DM39.
   29. Purchased merchandise on account from Perlich Company, $528.00. P127.
      Posting. Post the items that are to be posted individually.

Instructions: 4. Total and rule the purchases journal. Post the total.

5. Total, prove, and rule the cash payments journal. Post the totals of the special columns.

6. Prepare a schedule of accounts payable similar to the one on page 250. Compare the schedule total with the balance of the accounts payable account in the general ledger. The total and the balance should be the same.

RECYCLING PROBLEM 21-R 1   Journalizing and posting sales and cash receipts transactions

Instructions: 1. Open the charge customers' accounts given below in the accounts receivable ledger of Johnston Company. Record the balance as of March 1 of the current year.

Charge Customer	Account Balance
Stephanie Cook, 735 15 Street W., Prince Albert, SK S6V 3R7	$325.00
Ron Kennedy, 11102 Railway AVenue E., North Battleford, SK S9A 2R7	235.00
Luis Livermore, 1132 Central Avenue, Prince Albert, SK S6V 4V6	489.00
Pam Pembrook, 228 13 Street W., Prince Albert, SK S6V 3G2	284.00
Steven Phillips, 2120 1 Avenue E., Prince Albert, SK S6V 2B8	390.00

Instructions: 2. Open the following partial list of accounts in the general ledger of Johnston Company. Record the balances as of March 1 of the current year.

Account Title	Acct. No.	Account Balance
Cash..............................	1101	$4 800.00
Accounts Receivable......................	1103	1 723.00
Sales Tax Payable	2106	——
Sales..............................	4101	——
Sales Returns and Allowances.......	4101.1	——

Instructions: 3. The following transactions affecting sales and cash receipts were completed by Johnston Company during March of the current year. Record these transactions in a sales journal, general journal, and cash receipts journal similar to those illustrated in Chapter 21. Use page 12 of each journal. Source documents are abbreviated: sales invoice, S; receipt, R; cash register tape, T; credit card sales calculator tape, CT; credit memorandum, CM.

Mar. 1. Recorded the cash balance on hand in the cash receipts journal, $4 800.00.
   2. Received cash on account from Ron Kennedy, $235.00. R41.
   4. Sold merchandise on account to Pam Pembrook, $531.00, plus sales tax, $26.55. S73.
   4. Credited Luis Livermore's account for merchandise returned, $80.00, plus sales tax, $4.00. CM18.
   5. Recorded cash sales for the week, $653.00, plus sales tax, $32.65. T5.
   5. Recorded credit card sales for the week, $535.00, plus sales tax, $26.75. CT5.
      Posting. Post the items that are to be posted individually. Post from the journals in this order: sales journal, general journal, and cash receipts journal.

Mar. 7. Received cash on account from Luis Livermore, $405.00. R42.
  8. Received cash on account from Pam Pembrook, $284.00. R43.
  10. Received cash on account from Steven Phillips, $390.00. R44.
  12. Recorded cash sales for the week, $701.00, plus sales tax, $35.05. T12.
  12. Recorded credit card sales for the week, $589.00, plus sales tax, $29.45. CT12.
  Posting. Post the items that are to be posted individually.
  14. Sold merchandise on account to Luis Livermore, $250.00, plus sales tax, $12.50. S74.
  15. Credited Pam Pembrook's account for merchandise returned, $25.00, plus sales tax, $1.25. CM19.
  15. Received cash on account from Stephanie Cook, $325.00. R45.
  17. Sold merchandise on account to Ron Kennedy, $750.00, plus sales tax, $37.50. S75.
  19. Recorded cash sales for the week, $654.00, plus sales tax, $32.70. T19.
  19. Recorded credit card sales for the week, $592.00, plus sales tax, $29.60. CT19.
  Posting. Post the items that are to be posted individually.
  21. Sold merchandise on account to Steven Phillips, $340.00, plus sales tax, $17.00. S76.
  22. Sold merchandise on account to Stephanie Cook, $376.00, plus sales tax, $18.80. S77.
  24. Received cash on account from Pam Pembrook, $504.75. R46.
  26. Recorded cash sales for the week, $690.00, plus sales tax, $34.50. T26.
  26. Recorded credit card sales for the week, $605.00, plus sales tax, $30.25. CT26.
  Posting. Post the items that are to be posted individually.
  28. Received cash on account from Luis Livermore, $262.50. R47.
  28. Received cash on account from Ron Kennedy, $750.00. R48.
  31. Recorded cash sales for the week, $590.00, plus sales tax, $29.50. T31.
  31. Recorded credit card sales for the week, $435.00, plus sales tax, $21.75. CT31.
  Posting. Post the items that are to be posted individually.

Instructions: 4. Total, prove, and rule the sales journal. Post the totals of the special columns.

5. Prove the equality of debits and credits for the cash receipts journal.

6. Prove cash. The total of the Cash Credit column of the cash payments journal for Johnston Company is $10 345.25. The balance on the last cheque stub on March 31 is $3 957.20.

7. Rule the cash receipts journal. Post the special column totals to the appropriate general ledger accounts.

8. Prepare a schedule of accounts receivable similar to the one on page 250. Compare the schedule total with the balance of the accounts receivable account in the general ledger. The total and the balance should be the same.

RECYCLING PROBLEM 22-R 1 Preparing a semimonthly payroll

Information from employee time cards for the semimonthly pay period March 16–31 of the current year is on the next page.

Instructions: 1. Prepare for the semimonthly pay period March 16–31 a payroll register similar to the illustration, page 449. The date of payment is April 1. Use the income tax deductions table on page 450 and the CPP and UI tables on pages 469 and 470.

2. Prepare Cheque No. 904 for the total net pay. Make the cheque payable to *Payroll Account* and sign your name. The beginning cheque stub balance is $9 545.00.

3. Prepare payroll cheques for Gary Jackson, Cheque No. 104, and Diane Simpson, Cheque No. 105. Sign your name as treasurer of the company. Record the payroll cheque numbers in the payroll register.

Ling Company

				Time card amounts for period March 16–31		Deductions
Employee		Marital Status	Net Claim Code			
No.	Name			Regular	Overtime	Hospital Insurance
1	Banks, Harvey	M	2	$544.00	$20.25	$25.00
2	Barton, Melvin	M	1	516.00	13.50	
3	Cox, Mark	S	1	560.00		
4	Jackson, Gary	S	1	496.00	13.50	
5	Simpson, Diane	M	4	532.00	28.14	28.00
6	Van Norren, Agnes	M	3	570.00		14.00
7	Webber, Vickie	S	1	480.00		

RECYCLING PROBLEM 23-R 1   Recording payroll transactions

Jackson Stationers completed the payroll transactions given below.

Feb. 28. Paid monthly payroll, $3 792.00 (less deductions: employees' income tax, $758.40; CPP, $68.26; UI, $89.11). C88.
   28. Recorded the employer's payroll tax liabilities. M22.
Mar. 15. Paid February payroll liabilities. C103.
   31. Paid monthly payroll, $3 806.00 (less deductions: employees' income tax, $761.20; CPP, $68.51; UI, $89.44. C145.
   31. Recorded the employer's payroll tax liabilities. M25.
Apr. 15. Paid March payroll liabilities. C178.
   30. Paid monthly payroll, $3 850.00 (less deductions: employees' income tax, $770.00; CPP, $69.30; UI, $90.48). C190.
   30. Recorded the employer's payroll tax liabilities. M28.

Instructions: 1. Record the selected transactions on page 5 of a cash payments journal and page 2 of a general journal. Use the current year in the date.

2. Prove the cash payments journal.

RECYCLING PROBLEM 24-R 1   Recording entries for bad debts expense

Brett Associates has general ledger accounts for Allowance for Uncollectible Accounts and Bad Debts Expense. On January 1 of the current year, the credit balance of Allowance for Uncollectible Accounts was $220.50. Selected entries affecting uncollectible accounts are given on page 658.

Instructions: Record all the necessary entries for the transactions, page 658, on page 24 of a general journal like the one on page 497.

Feb. 18. Wrote off past-due account of Willie Iverson as uncollectible, $167.64. M17.

Mar. 31. *End of the first quarterly fiscal period.* Make adjusting entry for estimated bad debts expense. Bad debts expense is estimated as ½% (.005) of the total charge sales. Total charge sales for the first quarterly fiscal period were $40 833.15.

Apr. 11. Wrote off past-due account of W. C. Causey as uncollectible, $220.95. M88.

June 30. *End of the second quarterly fiscal period.* Make adjusting entry for estimated bad debts expense. Total charge sales for the second quarterly fiscal period were $45 856.23.

July 20. Wrote off past-due account of Ray Hammond as uncollectible, $243.15. M125.

Sept. 30. *End of third quarterly fiscal period.* Make adjusting entry for estimated bad debts expense. Total charge sales for the third quarterly fiscal period were $42 212.20.

Dec. 31. Wrote off past-due account of Frank Ikard as uncollectible, $232.20. M340.

Dec. 31. *End of the fourth quarterly fiscal period.* Make adjusting entry for estimated bad debts expense. Total charge sales for the fourth quarterly fiscal period were $54 048.36.

RECYCLING PROBLEM 25-R 1 Figuring depreciation expense and book value of fixed assets; journalizing depreciation expense and disposal of a fixed asset

Discount Music owns the fixed assets listed below.

Plant Asset	Asset Account	Date Bought	Original Cost	Estimated Salvage Value	Estimated Life
1	Delivery Equipment	July 1, 1983	$7 500.00	$300.00	6 years
2	Delivery Equipment	June 1, 1989	8 600.00	500.00	5 years
3	Store Equipment	April 1, 1982	2 840.00	200.00	10 years
4	Store Equipment	Jan. 1, 1986	3 000.00	300.00	15 years
5	Store Equipment	Oct. 1, 1989	1 000.00	100.00	3 years

Instructions: 1. Figure each fixed asset's depreciation expense for the year ended December 31, 1989. Use the straight-line method of figuring depreciation. Figure the time of depreciation to the nearest number of months.

2. Figure each fixed asset's book value as of December 31, 1989.

3. Record on page 12 of a general journal the two adjusting entries for depreciation expense for the year ended December 31, 1989. Record delivery equipment depreciation in Depreciation Expense — Delivery Equipment. Record store equipment depreciation in Depreciation Expense — Store Equipment.

4. On February 2, 1990, received cash, $300.00, from the sale of delivery equipment, Fixed Asset No. 1, bought July 1, 1983, for $7 500.00. Receipt No. 189. Record the sale of this fixed asset on page 15 of a cash receipts journal.

RECYCLING PROBLEM 26-R 1 Recording notes, interest, and bank discount

The transactions below were completed by Brockway Corporation during March of the current year.

Instructions: 1. Record the transactions on page 659. Use a cash receipts journal (page 15) and a cash payments journal (page 7) similar to those illustrated in Chapter 26. Source documents are abbreviated as: cheque, C; note payable, NP; note receivable, NR; receipt, R.

Mar. 3. Paid Liehr Supply Company for NP71 (60-day, 8% note payable due today; principal, $1 200.00; interest, $15.78), $1 215.78. C122.
   7. Discounted at 9½% at the Bank of Nova Scotia our 30-day, non-interest-bearing note payable, $4 000.00 (bank discount, $31.23; proceeds, $3 968.77). NP75. The Bank of Nova Scotia credited our current account for the proceeds.
   8. Received a cheque from Doris Ellefson in settlement of NR98 (20-day, 9% note receivable due today; principal, $650.00; interest, $3.21), $653.21. R88.
   10. Paid Bank of Montreal for NP66 (90-day, 8½% note payable due today; principal, $4 200.00; interest, $88.03), $4 288.03. C128.
   16. Issued a 30-day, 9% note payable to Bank of Montreal, $2 500.00. NP76. The bank credited our current account for the principal.
   17. Received a cheque from Marilyn McClure in settlement of NR81 (6-month, 9% note receivable due today; principal, $1 100.00; interest, $49.50), $1 149.50. R91.
   18. Paid Equipment Sales Company for NP52 (60-day, 9½% note payable due today; principal, $1 800.00; interest, $28.11), $1 828.11. C136.
   24. Discounted at 10% at Bank of Nova Scotia, our 20-day non-interest-bearing note payable, $1 500.00 (bank discount, $8.22; proceeds, $1 491.78). NP77. The Bank of Nova Scotia credited our current account for the proceeds.
   25. Received a cheque from Larry Rothermel in settlement of NR99 (30-day, 9% note receivable due today; principal, $850.00; interest, $6.29), $856.29. R93.
   28. Paid Hailey Corporation for NP68 (90-day, 9½% note payable due today; principal, $3 000.00; interest, $70.27), $3 070.27. C145.

Instructions: 2. Prove the cash receipts and cash payments journals.

RECYCLING PROBLEM 27-R 1 Preparing end-of-fiscal-period work for a corporation

The accounts and their balances in Bike Mart's general ledger appear as below and on page 662 on December 31 of the current year.

Account Title	Account Balance
Cash	$ 41 339.00
Accounts Receivable	39 145.00
Allow. for Uncoll. Accounts	22.00
Merchandise Inventory	107 914.00
Supplies	2 212.00
Prepaid Insurance	7 875.00
Delivery Equipment	7 350.00
Accum. Depr. — Delivery Equip.	1 470.00
Office Equipment	6 020.00
Accum. Depr. — Office Equip.	626.00
Store Equipment	8 100.00
Accum. Depr. — Store Equip.	2 167.00
Accounts Payable	23 966.00
Employees' Income Tax Payable	1 890.00
Federal Income Tax Payable	—
CPP Payable	394.00
Sales Tax Payable	3 984.00
UI Payable	537.00
Hosp. Insurance Premium Pay	980.00
Dividends Payable	—
Capital Stock	150 000.00
Retained Earnings	29 995.00
Income Summary	—

Account Title	Account Balance
Sales..	$796 800.00
Sales Returns and Allow.	2 023.00
Purchases...	633 127.00
Purch. Returns and Allow.	2 180.00
Purchases Discount......................................	2 849.00
Advertising Expense.....................................	2 394.00
Bad Debts Expense.......................................	———
Delivery Expense..	11 352.00
Depr. Exp. — Delivery Equip..........................	———
Depr. Exp. — Office Equip.	———
Depr. Exp. — Store Equip.	———
Insurance Expense	———
Miscellaneous Expense..................................	1 318.00
Payroll Taxes Expense	9 449.00
Rent Expense	25 200.00
Salary Expense...	106 604.00
Supplies Expense	———
Interest Income	1 082.00
Interest Expense	2 520.00
Federal Income Tax	5 000.00

Instructions: 1. Prepare an eight-column work sheet for the fiscal year ended December 31 of the current year. Use as a guide the work sheet, pages 538 and 539. Information needed for the adjustments is below.

Bad debts expense is estimated as 1.5% of charge sales. Charge sales were $199 200.00.	
Merchandise inventory, December 31	$144 740.00
Supplies inventory, December 31..	288.00
Value of insurance policies, December 31	2 835.00
Annual depreciation expense on delivery equipment	1 470.00
Annual depreciation expense on office equipment.............................	602.00
Annual depreciation expense on store equipment.............................	810.00
Federal income tax for the year...	5 833.00

2. Prepare an income statement similar to the one on page 544.

3. Prepare a statement of shareholders' equity similar to the one on page 545. Additional information needed is below.

January 1 balance of capital stock account	$150 000.00
(1 500 shares issued for $100.00 per share.)	
January 1 balance of retained earnings account..................................	52 495.00
Dividend declared and paid during the current year............................	22 500.00

4. Prepare a balance sheet for December 31 of the current year.

5. Record the adjusting entries on page 12 of a general journal.

6. Record the closing entries on page 13 of a general journal.

7. On January 10 following the current year, the board of directors declared a dividend of $15.00 a share to shareholders. Record the dividend declared on page 14 of a general journal. Source document is Memorandum No. 189.

8. The dividend declared in Instruction 7 was paid on January 31. Record payment of the dividend on page 28 of a cash payments journal. Source document is Cheque No. 246.

RECYCLING PROBLEM 28-R 1 Recording transactions in a voucher system

Innovation Products uses a voucher system. A voucher register and a cheque register similar to those on pages 574–575 and 578 are used.

Instructions: 1. Record the following transactions completed during May of the current year. Use page 14 of a voucher register and page 11 of a cheque register. Source documents are abbreviated as: cheque, C; debit memorandum, DM; voucher, V.

May 1. Recorded cash balance on May 1, $15 940.80.
 2. Purchased merchandise on account from Kalman Exchange, $551.30. V216.
 4. Purchased merchandise on account from Homestead Corporation, $2 348.20. V217.
 5. Bought supplies from Kwik Supplies, $107.30. V218.
 5. Paid V218, $107.30; no discount. C183.
 8. Issued DM62 to Kalman Exchange for the return of merchandise purchased, $43.00. Cancelled V216 and issued V219.
 10. Paid V219, $508.30, less purchases discount, $5.08. C184.
 11. Bought supplies from Camacho Supplies, $206.60. V220.
 12. Paid V217, $2 348.20; no discount. C185.
 16. Made a deposit in the bank, $7 516.40.
 16. Purchased merchandise on account from Constellation, $2 103.10. V221.
 19. Paid V221, $2 103.10, less purchases discount, $42.06. C186.
 26. Paid V220, $206.60; no discount. C187.
 29. Bought gasoline for delivery truck from Mohawk Service Station, $186.00. V222. (Delivery Expense)
 29. Paid V222, $186.00; no discount. C188.
 30. Made a deposit in the bank, $7 012.70.
 31. The payroll register for the monthly payroll showed the following information. Salary Expense, $4 207.90; Employees' Income Tax Payable, $841.60; Canada Pension Plan Payable, $75.74; Unemployment Insurance Payable, $98.88. V223.
 31. Paid V223, $3 198.68. C189.

Instructions: 2. Total, prove, and rule the voucher register and cheque register.

RECYCLING PROBLEM 29-R 1 Establishing and replenishing a petty cash fund

LaRoche, Inc., established a $150.00 petty cash fund on April 1 of the current year.

Instructions: 1. Record on page 12 of a voucher register establishment of a petty cash fund. Voucher number is 289. Payee is Petty Cash Custodian.
2. Record on page 8 of a cheque register Cheque No. 281 to establish the petty cash fund. April 1 cash balance on hand is $65 482.50.
Totals of the petty cash record's amount columns on April 30 are listed below.

			Distribution of Payments			
	Receipts	Payments	Supplies	Delivery Expense	Misc. Expense	Other Payments Amount
Totals	$150.00	121.30	51.90	23.10	25.30	21.00

Instructions: 3. Record the totals above on line 10 of a petty cash record. Petty cash record page is 14.
4. The petty cash box has $27.70 at the end of the day April 30. Compare for equality the sum of cash and payments with the petty cash beginning balance.

5. Record any cash short or cash over and the cash balance, then total and rule the Receipts and Payments columns. Make entries like those in petty cash record, pages 596 and 597.

6. From information in petty cash record, record voucher register entry to replenish petty cash fund on April 30. Amount in the Other Payments column is Advertising Expense. Voucher number is 326.

7. Record Cheque No. 318 in the cheque register to replenish the fund.

8. Record the April 30 cash balance and amount of replenished fund on the petty cash record. Use lines 16 and 17 of the petty cash record, page 597, as a model.

RECYCLING PROBLEM 30-R 1   Determining cost of inventory using the fifo and lifo methods

Accounting records at Chaparral Company showed the purchases and periodic inventory counts listed below.

Model	Beginning Inventory January 1	First Purchase	Second Purchase	Third Purchase	Periodic Inventory Count December 31
S 32	320 @ $ 8.40	150 @ $8.75	200 @ $9.00	150 @ $9.20	280
S 34	210 @ $ 7.60	200 @ $8.00	200 @ $8.20	200 @ $7.80	250
M 36	300 @ $ 9.00	250 @ $9.20	200 @ $9.20	250 @ $9.20	180
M 38	250 @ $10.00	225 @ $9.80	225 @ $9.50	200 @ $9.40	200
L 42	160 @ $ 5.60	150 @ $5.20	180 @ $5.75	120 @ $6.00	160
L 44	800 @ $ 4.80	100 @ $5.00	100 @ $5.25	100 @ $5.50	400
XL 48	50 @ $ 6.00	300 @ $6.20	300 @ $6.40	400 @ $6.50	200
XL 50	120 @ $ 8.50	250 @ $8.60	500 @ $8.00	250 @ $8.90	260

Use a form with the column headings below.

Model	Number of Units on Hand	Unit Cost	Inventory Value December 31
S 32	280	150 @ $9.20 ⎫ 130 @ $9.00 ⎭	$2 550.00

Instructions: 1. Figure the total amount of the inventory on December 31 according to the *fifo* method. Determining the inventory value for model S32 is given as an example. Use the following procedure.

  (a) Record the model number and number of units of each model on hand on December 31.

  (b) Record the unit cost of each model. When more than one unit cost is used, list the units and unit costs on separate lines.

  (c) Figure the total inventory value of each model and write the amount in the Value column.

  (d) Add the value column to determine the total amount of the inventory.

2. On another form, figure the total amount of inventory using the *lifo* method. Follow the steps given in Instruction 1.

3. Compare the total amount of the inventory obtained in Instructions 1 and 2. Which method, *fifo* or *lifo*, resulted in the lower total amount for the inventory?

Index